Film Review

2000-2001

James Cameron-Wilson became a committed film buff when he moved to London at the age of 17. After a stint at the Webber Douglas Academy of Dramatic Art he joined *What's On In London* and took over from F. Maurice Speed as cinema editor. Later, he edited the trade newspaper *Showbiz*, was commissioning editor for *Film Review*, was consultant for *The Movie Show* on BSkyB and a frequent presenter of Radio 2's *Arts Programme*.

He is also author of the books *Hollywood: The New Generation*, *Young Hollywood*, *The Cinema of Robert De Niro* and *The Moviegoer's Quiz Book*. His film reviews are currently syndicated in the *What's On* magazines distributed in Birmingham, Manchester and Liverpool, and he has a regular column in *Film Review*, Britain's longest-running film magazine.

He is currently radio critic for the BBC and has written frequently for *The Times*, as well as contributing to *The Sunday Times*, *The Guardian*, *Flicks*, *Film Monthly*, *Xposé*, *Shivers*, etc, etc. On television he made over 100 appearances on *The Movie Show* both as critic and quiz master. He has also regularly popped up on CNN, Channel One and BBC Worldwide Television and was Britain's resident 'dial-a-film critic' for two years.

Besides the cinema, James Cameron-Wilson's academic interests include bookbinding, the brain and Buddhism, while his personal interests include his wife, nine-year-old daughter, cats and fish.

Includes video releases and websites

Film Review 2000-2001

JAMES CAMERON-WILSON

Founding father: F. Maurice Speed
1911-1998

Reynolds & Hearn Ltd
London

TO PETER JAQUES, FOR HIS LOYALTY,
STABILITY AND UNSTINTING SUPPORT

Acknowledgements

The author would like to declare his eternal apprecia-
tion to the following, without whom this book would
not have been possible: David Aldridge, Charles Bacon,
Jeff Bench, Josephine Botting, Ewen Brownrigg,
Christopher Cameron, Juliet Cameron-Wilson, The
Joel Finler Collection, Marcus Hearn, Peter Jaques,
Karen Krizanovich, Wendy Lloyd, Howard Maxford,
Nigel Mulock, my mother, Frances Palmer, Virginia
Palmer, Richard Reynolds, Simon Rose, Peter Scott,
Mansel Stimpson, Hilary Swank, Debbie Turner, Barbie
Wilde and David Nicholas Wilkinson.
Till next year...

Founding father:
F. Maurice Speed, 1911-1998

First published in 2000 by
Reynolds & Hearn Ltd
61a Priory Road
Kew Gardens
Richmond
Surrey TW9 3DH

A CIP catalogue record for this book is available from the
British Library.

ISBN 1-903111-12-9

Designed by Paul Chamberlain

Printed and bound in Great Britain by MPG Books Ltd,
Bodmin, Cornwall.

Contents

Introduction   6

Top 20 UK Box-Office Hits   8

Top 10 Box-Office Stars   9

Releases of the Year   10

Video Releases   149

Faces of the Year   156

Film World Diary   159

Movie Quotations of the Year   164

Film Soundtracks   166

Bookshelf   169

Internet   172

Awards and Festivals   174

In Memoriam   179

Index   187

Right: Tom Hanks
in The Green Mile,
*taken from the story
by Stephen King*

Opposite: Oliver
Reed and Russell
Crowe in Ridley
Scott's Gladiator
(see page 62)

Introduction

As the impact of the Internet continues apace, the world is becoming a very different place. With the democratic click of a mouse, the whole infrastructure of finance, travel and shopping is changing on an almost daily basis. Indeed, the smug concept of 'the world at your fingertips' has never seemed more tenable. And, for all its benefits, the Net, the World Wide Web, the Information Superhighway – call it what you will – is yet another reflection of the era we live in: the age of fast food, instant information, disposable incomes, built-in obsolescence, the quick buck. Why slog off to the local library when what you're looking for might not even be there? At the flick of your wrist you can have a whole world of possibilities fly up on your computer screen.

Of course, by the time you read this there will have been so many advances in computer technology that most of what I'm saying will not only be old hat but irrelevant – as will the arguments against the intransigence of the phenomenon. But let me have my say. As a dedicated bibliophile, I find it is the experience of curling up with a book that is so rewarding. I am an inveterate annotator, underlining in pencil certain passages that I wish to return to later. Also, there is something ineffably reassuring about tucking a book into one's briefcase and being able to pluck

it out at will. Likewise, the experience of sitting in a dark auditorium with one's fellow species and subjecting oneself to a shared adventure is all part of the appeal of going to the cinema. Thus, I find, the activities of reading and cinemagoing are a perfect complement to one another. You can lend a book to a friend. You can discuss the merits of a movie with a stranger. But when it comes to the Internet, a favourite site can vanish overnight.

Now, I don't deny that for educational purposes the Web is an invaluable resource. But its impermanence is frightening. The rules keep on changing; the technology is forever being outmoded. No sooner have you downloaded Flash Plugin than you need to upgrade to QuickTime Plugin. Computers themselves are also time-consuming, expensive and often unbearably frustrating. Who cannot share the communal angst of one's keyboard jamming or – Heaven forbid – one's hard drive crashing. It's like sitting in a train, buried in the final chapter of a Stephen King novel and having someone rip the book out of your hands and throw it out the window. Except, of course, you can always buy another copy. But if your hard disc dies, a large part of your life dies with it.

Talking of Stephen King, the best-selling novelist has thrust another nail into the

publishing coffin. On 24 July 2000 he unveiled the first chapter of his new novel, *The Plant*, on the Internet. And this from the man who claimed that 'I love my editors and I also like books. I'm a conservative on this particular subject, and I love the smell of glue.' Yet, King, who has reputedly sold more than 300 million books, is wresting the glue from his own industry. By cutting out the middlemen – the editors, publishers and shopkeepers – he is denying his readers the giddy joy of giving logic to the term 'page-turner.' Will the loyal subjects of the King dynasty really choose to read the writer's stories off a computer screen? I would like to think not.

Likewise, will film buffs really gain greater satisfaction from seeing a film on a monitor than on a movie screen? While the interactive site itsyourmovie.com is fun for the sheer thrill of participating in the storytelling process (you vote on the next scene, they film it) it cannot replace the sheer excitement of being engulfed by a damned good story projected onto a giant screen in front of you (ideally accompanied by a THX sound system).

Of course, as you're probably reading this on the printed page (in hardback, no less), I may be preaching to the converted.

James Cameron-Wilson
July 2000

Right: Liam Neeson as Qui-Gon Jinn in Star Wars: Episode I *The Phantom Menace*

Below, clockwise from top left:
Toy Story 2, The World is Not Enough, The Sixth Sense *and* Austin Powers: The Spy Who Shagged Me

Top 20 UK Box-Office Hits
July 1999 – June 2000

1. Star Wars: Episode I The Phantom Menace
2. Toy Story 2
3. Notting Hill
4. The World is Not Enough
5. Austin Powers: The Spy Who Shagged Me
6. The Sixth Sense
7. Gladiator
8. American Beauty
9. The Mummy
10. The Matrix
11. Tarzan
12. The Blair Witch Project
13. American Pie
14. The Beach
15. Pokémon – The First Movie
16. Sleepy Hollow
17. Kevin & Perry Go Large
18. East is East
19. Mulan
20. Deep Blue Sea

2. Bruce Willis
3. Mike Myers
4. Hugh Grant
5. Pierce Brosnan
6. Brendan Fraser
7. Keanu Reeves
8. Leonardo DiCaprio
9. Tom Hanks
10. Kevin Spacey

Top 10 Box-Office Stars
Star of the Year: Julia Roberts

Last year the combined success of *Shakespeare in Love* and *Sliding Doors* put Gwyneth Paltrow into the top slot. However, her supporting role in the commercially middling *The Talented Mr Ripley* could not return her to this year's chart. Instead, Julia Roberts has moved up to first place on the coattails of *Notting Hill*, *Erin Brockovich* and *Runaway Bride*, a hat trick that has beaten out all comers. Meanwhile, after *Armageddon* and now *The Sixth Sense*, Bruce Willis qualifies easily for pole position, while Mike Myers definitely had something to do with the extraordinary success of the *Austin Powers* sequel. Hugh Grant also retained his commercial clout with *Notting Hill* and, perhaps surprisingly, *Mickey Blue Eyes*, the latter out-performing such American stalwarts as *Double Jeopardy* and *End of Days* (sorry Arnold, you've had your day). The rest of the chart more or less speaks for itself, while the runners-up this year include, in order of box-office zap, Johnny Depp, Will Smith, Harry Enfield, Liam Neeson, George Clooney, Robert Carlyle, Sean Connery, Brad Pitt and Tom Cruise.

Releases of the Year

This section contains details of all the films released in Great Britain from 1 July 1999 to the end of June 2000 – the period covered by all the reference features in this book.

Leading actors are generally credited with the roles they played, followed by a summary of supporting players. Where an actor further down a cast list is of special interest then his/her role is generally credited as well.

For technical credits the normal abbreviations operate, and are as follows: Dir – for Director; Pro – for Producer; Ex Pro – for Executive Producer; Co-Pro – for Co-Producer; Assoc Pro – for Associate Producer; Line Pro – for Line Producer; Ph – for Cinematographer; Ed – for Editor; Pro Des – for Production Designer; and M – for composer.

Abbreviations for the names of film companies are obvious when used, such as Fox for Twentieth Century Fox, and UIP for United International Pictures. The production company (or companies) is given first, the distribution company last.

Information at the foot of each entry is presented in the following order: running time/country of origin/year of production/date of British release/British certification.

Contributors: James Cameron-Wilson, with Charles Bacon, Jeff Bench, Ewen Brownrigg, Marianne Gray, Peter Jaques, Karen Krizanovich, Barbra Michaels, Simon Rose, Mansel Stimpson and Barbie Wilde.

Star ratings
★★★★★ **Wonderful**
★★★★ **Very good**
★★★ **Good**
★★ **Mediocre**
★ **Insulting**

Left: *The Dubliners – Marion O'Dwyer and Anjelica Huston in the latter's perky if predictable* Agnes Browne *(from UIP)*

The Adventures of Elmo in Grouchland ★★★

Sesame Street/Grouchland. When Elmo attempts to retrieve his beloved Blanket from the trash can that Oscar calls home, he finds himself sucked into a tunnel leading to Grouchland. Here, not only is everybody as grumpy as Oscar, but a greedy character called Huxley has snatched up Elmo's blanket and is determined to keep it. So, marshalling all his reserves of courage, Elmo treks off to Huxley's mountain lair – Mount Pickanose – to retrieve what is rightfully his … Aimed squarely at the pre-school crowd, this second feature from the Children's Television Workshop (who previously brought us *Sesame Street Presents Follow That Bird*) is good innocent fun with a strong moral fibre (the benefits of friendship and sharing are duly headlined). Unencumbered by cynicism or tweeness, this certainly has its place and adults may even find moments of enlightenment. [*Charles Bacon*]

● *Huxley* Mandy Patinkin, *Queen of Trash* Vanessa Williams, *Maria* Sonia Manzano, *Gordon* Roscoe Orman, *Gina* Alison Bartlett-O'Reilly, *Ruthie* Ruth Buzzi, *Luis* Emilio Delgado, *Bob* Bob McGath; Voices: *Elmo, Pestie, Grouch jailer, Grouch cab driver* Kevin Clash, *Zoe, Pestie, Prairie Dawn* Fran Brill, *Grizzie, Pestie* Stephanie D'Abruzzo, *Humongous*

Chicken Dave Goetz, *Bug* Joseph Mazzarino, *Count, Pestie, Grouch Mayor* Jerry Nelson, *Rosita* Carmen Osbahr, *Telly, Pestie* Martin P. Robinson, *Big Bird, Oscar* Caroll Spinney, *Ernie, Stuckweed* Steve Whitmire, *Bert, Grover, Cookie Monster* Frank Oz.
● *Dir* Gary Halvorson, *Pro* Alex Rockwell and Marjorie Kalins, *Ex Pro* Brian Henson, Stephanie Allain and Martin G. Baker, *Co-Pro* Kevin Clash and Timothy M. Bourne, *Screenplay* Mitchell Kriegman and Joseph Mazzarino, *Ph* Alan Caso, *Pro Des* Alan Cassie, *Ed* Alan Baumgarten, *M* John Debney, *Costumes* Polly Smith.

Jim Henson Pictures/Children's Television Workshop-Columbia TriStar.
73 mins. USA/Germany. 1999. Rel: 19 May 2000. Cert U.

After Life ★★★½

This highly original film from the Japanese writer-director Kore-eda is subdued, penetrating and as memorable as its intriguing concept. Set somewhere between Heaven and earth, it finds the newly dead being guided in the need to choose a single memory from their lives which will be re-created on film to accompany them into eternity – but, ironically, their guides in this are those who have themselves failed to make the choice. In the later stages a romantic triangle is revealed, and on that level this film is eclipsed by *A Matter of Life and Death*. But more importantly it makes the audience share its concerns with life's disappointments and its treasures, however small. Combining fact with its fiction (some of the memories recalled here were the real thing), *After Life* is quintessentially Japanese and universally meaningful. [*Mansel Stimpson*]

● *Takashi Mohizuki* Arata, *Shiori Satonaka* Erika Oda, *Sator Kawashim* Susumu Terajima, *Ichiro Watanabe* Takashi Naito, *Ken-nosuke Nakamura* Kei Tani, Toru Yuri, Hisako Hara, Akio Yokohama, Kazuko Shirakawa.
● *Dir, Screenplay* and *Ed* Kore-eda Hirokazu, *Pro* Shiho Sato and Masayuki Akieda, *Ex Pro* Yutaka Shigenobu and Masahiro Yasuda, *Ph* Yutaka Yamazaki, *Pro Des* Toshihiro Isomi and Hideo Gunji, *M* Yasuhiro Kasamatsu.

TV Man Union/Engine Film-ICA Projects.
118 mins. Japan. 1998. Rel: 1 October 1999. No cert.

Agnes Browne ★★★

Dublin; 1967. Agnes Browne is a hard-smoking, tough-cussing mother of seven who ekes out a living selling fruit and veg in the local market. Then, when her husband dies, she borrows £40 from a loan shark to pay for the funeral, an occasion that turns into a shambles. And now she's saddled with the £2-a-week interest. However, with the help of her best friend Marion and the attentions of a French baker, she finds the strength to struggle on ... Brimming with picturesque

detail and enlivened by some ripe dialogue (Agnes, to herself: 'Fuck that, Mrs Browne – seven children and not one organism to show for it'), Anjelica Huston's second directorial outing largely fends off the spectre of Blarney. It's only the predictable and somewhat contrived arc of the story itself that sounds a false note. But if *Angela's Ashes* gave the miserable Irish childhood a poetic perspective, *Agnes Browne* gives it the kiss of life. FYI: The character of Agnes Browne originated in the radio serial *Mrs Browne's Boys*, itself the basis for Brendan O'Carroll's 1994 novel *The Mammy*.

● *Agnes Browne* Anjelica Huston, *Marion Monks* Marion O'Dwyer, *Mr Billy* Ray Winstone, *Pierre* Arno Chevrier, *Mr Aherne* Gerard McSorley, *Mark Browne* Niall O'Shea, *Frankie Browne* Ciaran Owens, *Cathy Browne* Roxanna Williams, *Simon Browne* Carl Power, *Dermot Browne* Mark Power, *Rory Browne* Gareth O'Connor, *Trevor Browne* James Lappin, *Tom Jones* Tom Jones, *Tommo Monks* Steve Blount, *Tom O'Toole* Frank McCusker, June Rodgers, Jennifer Gibney, Gavin Kelty, Arthur Lappin, Doreen Keogh.
● *Dir* Anjelica Huston, *Pro* Huston, Jim Sheridan, Arthur Lappin and Greg Smith, *Ex Pro* Morgan O'Sullivan, Tom Palmieri, Laurie Mansfield and Gerry Browne, *Line Pro* Paul Myler, *Screenplay* John Goldsmith and Brendan O'Carroll, *Ph* Anthony B. Richmond, *Pro Des* David Brockhurst, *Ed* Eva Gardos, *M* Paddy Moloney; songs performed by Tom Jones, *Costumes* Joan Bergin.

October Films/Hell's Kitchen/Bord Scannán na hÉireann/Irish Film Board-UIP.
92 mins. Ireland. 1999. Rel: 3 March 2000. Cert 15.

À la Place du Coeur ★★★

Robert Guédiguian follows the entertaining *Marius et Jeannette* with a successful transposition of James Baldwin's novel *If Beale Street Could Talk* to his home town of Marseilles. It's the interracial love story of two teenagers whose happiness is threatened when the boy, who is black, is falsely accused of rape. The film has its less convincing moments, including a sudden volte face for its resolution, and it could be tauter. But there are good performances (not least from Laure Raoust and Alexandre Ogou as the youngsters, and from Ariane Ascaride as the girl's mother who leads the determined efforts for justice). Combining warmth and a forthright approach to the theme of racism, the film is commendable if not wholly satisfactory. [*Mansel Stimpson*]

● *Marianne Patché* Ariane Ascaride, *Joël Patché* Jean-Pierre Darroussin, *Franck Lopez* Gérard Meylan, *Monsieur Lévy* Jacques Boudet, *Francine Lopez* Christine Brücher, *Clémentine 'Clim' Patché* Laure Raoust, *François 'Bébé' Lopez* Alexandre Ogou, Veronique Balme, Pierre Banderet, Hélène Surgère.
● *Dir* Robert Guédiguian, *Pro* Gilles Sandoz,

Michel Saint-Jean and Guédiguian, *Line Pro* Malek Hamzaoui, *Screenplay* Guédiguian and Jean Louis Milesi, *Ph* Bernard Cavalié, *Pro Des* Michel Vandestien, *Ed* Bernard Sasia, *M* Liszt/various.

Agat Film and Cie/Canal Plus/France 2 Cinema/LA7 Cinema/Diaphana-Artificial Eye.
112 mins. France. 1998. Rel: 17 September 1999. Cert 15.

The Alarmist ★★

Los Angeles; today. Heinrich Grigoris has a neat way to turn a profit: he sells security systems to the rich and then burgles their homes. But matters come to a head when new employee Tommy Hudler falls for a sexy client, who is subsequently bumped off during what appears to be a raid on her house ... Part satire, part slapstick free-for-all, *The Alarmist* was slipped into British cinemas without any press screenings. It's safe to say that this first feature from writer-director Evan Dunsky (based on Keith Reddin's play) would not have received much critical support, but it's head and shoulders above a lot of 1999 releases. As usual, Stanley Tucci is a joy to watch as the slippery Heinrich, while young Ryan Reynolds is a genuine discovery as Capshaw's sexually confused son. Previously known as *Life During Wartime.* [*Ewen Brownrigg*]

● *Tommy Hudler* David Arquette, *Heinrich Grigoris* Stanley Tucci, *Gale Ancona* Kate Capshaw, *Sally Brown* Mary McCormack, *Howard Ancona* Ryan Reynolds, *April* Tricia Vessey, *Beth Hudler* Michael Learned, *Bruce Hudler* Lewis Arquette, Eric Zivot, Hoke Howell, David Brisbin, Ruth Miller, Richmond Arquette, Valerie Long, Kim Tobin, Clea DuVall, Matt Malloy, Alex Nepomniaschy.
● *Dir and Screenplay* Evan Dunsky, *Pro* Dan Stone and Lisa Zimble, *Ex Pro* Beau Flynn, Stefan Simchowitz, Matthias Emcke and Thomas Augberger, *Co-Pro* Jonathan King, *Ph* Alex Nepomniaschy, *Pro Des* Amy B. Ancona, *Ed* Norman Buckley, *M* Christopher Beck, *Costumes* Denise Wingate.

Key Entertainment/Bandeira Entertainment-Columbia TriStar.
91 mins. USA. 1997. Rel: 10 September 1999. Cert 15.

Alice et Martin ★★¹/₂

Following the accidental death of his autocratic father, the 20-year-old Martin runs away and lives off the land. Rounded up by police, he moves to Paris where he stays with his half-brother Benjamin, a homosexual actor, and the latter's flatmate, a violinist called Alice. At first intimidated by the older woman, Martin gradually finds himself drawn to her. Soon, his interest turns to passion and, for the first time in his life, he finds a reason to live ... There are certainly intriguing depths to Andre Téchiné's study of romantic obsession, but the journey there is heavy-going and somewhat artless.

Favouring short, sharp scenes and little exposition, Téchiné has an almost random approach to his narrative, so that one stumbles across the story almost by accident. Had the filmmaker allowed us a little time to get to know his protagonists, then we might have cared more for them. As it is, they dart about with their own obscure agendas doing rather daft things. By turns frustrating, fascinating, cold and deeply unsatisfactory.

● *Alice* Juliette Binoche, *Martin Sauvagnac* Alexis Loret, *Jeanine Sauvagnac* Carmen Maura, *Benjamin Sauvagnac* Mathieu Amalric, *Frédéric* Jean-Pierre Lorit, *Lucie* Marthe Villalonga, *Victor Sauvagnac* Pierre Lacroix, *François Sauvagnac* Laurent Cirade, Jeremy Kreikenmayer, Kevin Goffette, Christiane Ludot, Roschdy Zem.
● *Dir* André Téchiné, *Ex Pro* Alain Sarde, *Line Pro* Jean-Jacques Albert, *Screenplay* Téchiné, Gilles Taurand and Olivier Assayas, *Ph* Caroline Champetier, *Pro Des* Ze Branco, *Ed* Martine Giordano, *M* Philippe Sarde; songs performed by Quintette Tres & Dos, The Beach Boys, Craig Armstrong, Divine Comedy, Wasis Diop, Pulp, etc, *Costumes* Elisabeth Tavernier, *Choreography* Jorge Rodriguez.

A Les Films Alain Sarde/France 2 Cinema/France 3 Cinema/Vertigo Films/Canal Plus-Artificial Eye.
124 mins. France. 1998. Rel: 3 December 1999. Cert 15.

All About My Mother – Todo sobre mi madre ★★★¹/₂

Madrid/Barcelona, Spain; the present. For 17 years Manuela, a hospital transplant coordinator, has refused to tell her son who his father was. But now that he intends to write a story dedicated to her – *All About My Mother* – she agrees to reveal all. However, before this happens, he is run down by a car and killed. Now she is resolved to track down the boy's father herself ... A thematic off-shoot of *All About Eve*, Almodovar's thirteenth film is an intricately structured celebration of womanhood in all its many guises. While not ignoring the more sexually bizarre aspects of his earlier work (transvestism abounds), the film finds Almodovar maturing nicely as a director of women and as an observer of human character. Peppering his narrative with cultural allusions (Capote, Tennessee Williams), he is not beneath plundering his own oeuvre, as the nurse at the beginning of his *The Flower of My Secret* (1995) takes on her own story. Women should especially warm to this quirky, compassionate piece, although it doesn't quite have the narrative hold of his last picture, *Live Flesh*. FYI: *All About My Mother* is dedicated to Gena Rowlands, Bette Davis and Romy Schneider, actresses who have played actresses on screen.

● *Manuela* Cecilia Roth, *Huma Rojo* Marisa Paredes, *Sister Rosa* Penelope Cruz, *Nina* Candela Pena, *Agrado* Antonia San Juan, *Rosa's mother* Rosa Maria Sarda, *Lola* Toni Canto, *Esteban* Eloy Azorin, Fernando

Fernan-Gomez, Fernando Guillen, Michel Ruben.
● *Dir and Screenplay* Pedro Almodovar, *Ex Pro* Agustín Almodóvar, *Assoc Pro* Michel Ruben, *Ph* Affonso Beato, *Pro Des* Antxon Gomez, *Ed* Pepe Salcedo, *M* Alberto Iglesias, *Costumes* Jose Maria de Cossio and Sabine Daigeler.

El Deseo S.A./Renn Prods/France 2 Cinema-Pathe. 101 mins. Spain/France. 1999. Rel: 27 August 1999. Cert 15.

All the Little Animals ★★★

London/Cornwall, England; today. Since his childhood accident, Bobby has never been quite right in the head and he has a nasty scar to prove it. Then, when his mother dies, he finds himself at the mercy of his domineering stepfather, a cruel man obsessed by material gain. So Bobby runs away and is befriended by a strange old loner whose life work is to provide dead animals with the dignified burial they deserve ... Marking the directorial debut of veteran film producer Jeremy Thomas (*The Last Emperor, Crash*), *All the Little Animals* is a confident and competent adaptation of Walker Hamilton's 1968 novel. An intriguing cross between bucolic fable and conventional thriller, the film holds the interest due to its unusual subject matter and unpredictable path. John Hurt, characteristically cast as an eccentric recluse, is predictably wonderful, while Daniel Benzali delivers another exemplary display of controlled evil (and an uncanny impersonation of Rod Steiger).

● *Mr Summers* John Hurt, *Bobby Platt* Christian Bale, *De Winer* Daniel Benzali, *Mr Whiteside* James Faulkner, *dean* John Higgins, John O'Toole, Amanda Boyle, Amy Robbins, Kaye Griffiths.
● *Dir* and *Pro* Jeremy Thomas, *Ex Pro* Chris Auty, *Co-Pro* Denise O'Dell, *Assoc Pro* Hercules Bellville,

Screenplay *Easki Thomas,* Ph Mike Molloy, *Pro Des* Andrew Sanders, *Ed* John Victor Smith, *M* Richard Hartley; Puccini; songs performed by The Screaming Orphans, *Costumes* Louise Stjernsward.

Recorded Picture Company/British Screen/J&M Entertainment/Isle of Man Commission/BBC Films/ Entertainment/European Script Fund/Indigo-Entertainment. 112 mins. UK. 1998. Rel: 9 July 1999. Cert 15.

American Beauty ★★★★

A victim of the suburban American nightmare – stultifying routine, numbed aspirations, middle-age flab, Stepford wife – advertising salesman Lester Burnham announces that he will be dead before the year is out. And he's right, but before he takes his last disappointed breath he gets to say exactly what he thinks to his phoney, unfulfilled wife and then falls for his 16-year-old daughter's sexy best friend ... Acclaimed as 'a millennial classic' (*Boston Globe*) and as 'a flat-out masterpiece' (*New York Post*), *American Beauty* is a beautifully measured satire with wit and teeth to spare. It is also a remarkable cinematic debut for the 33-year-old theatre director Sam Mendes – best known for his work at London's Donmar Warehouse – who has conjured entertaining performances from a magnificent cast. Yet Kevin Spacey is too steely an actor to perfectly convey the wretchedness of his loser and Annette Bening's performance is too shrill and overstated for credibility. Much more convincing – and touching – are Birch and Suvari as the Yin and Yang of American teenage youth and Bentley as their classmate who sees and understands everything. So, *American Beauty* is no masterpiece, but its dark edge is honed to a fine polish.

● *Lester Burnham* Kevin Spacey, *Carolyn Burnham* Annette Bening, *Jane Burnham* Thora Birch, *Ricky*

Fitts Wes Bentley, *Angela Hayes* Mena Suvari, *Buddy Kane* Peter Gallagher, *Barbara Fitts* Allison Janney, *Jim #1* Scott Bakukla, *Jim #2* Sam Robards, *Colonel Fits* Chris Cooper, *Brad* Barry Del Sherman, Amber Smith, Marissa Jaret Winokur, Matthew Kimbrough.
● *Dir* Sam Mendes, *Pro* Bruce Cohen and Dan Jinks, *Screenplay and Co-Pro* Alan Ball, *Ph* Conrad L. Hall, *Pro Des* Naomi Shohan, *Ed* Tariq Anwar and Chris Greenbury, *M* Thomas Newman; songs performed by Elliott Smith, Peggy Lee, Bill Withers, Betty Carter, Zen Radio, Gomez, Eels, The Guess Who, Bob Dylan, Bobby Darin, The Who, Free, and Annie Lennox, *Costumes* Julie Weiss.

DreamWorks-UIP.
122 mins. USA. 1999. Rel: 28 January 2000. Cert 18.

American Pie ★'/2

Four best friends on the verge of graduating from high school make a pact to lose their virginity by the night of their prom ... *American Pie* is not offensive because it makes fun of diarrhoea, premature ejaculation and bizarre forms of masturbation (apple pie anyone?). It is offensive because it delights in the humiliation of its protagonists, everyday misfits at the mercy of their own human limitations. In real life, if somebody was seen suffering from premature ejaculation live on the Internet or caught wetting themselves in front of the entire school, the repercussions could be anything from severe psychological trauma to suicide. Here, such shame is played for laughs, as if the very act of filming one's most private moments is, in itself, funny. Moreover, much of the film is downright plagiaristic (the diarrhoea sequence in *Dumb & Dumb* was done much better), not to mention formulaic, although there is the occasional good joke. For the most part, however, *American Pie* is not so much black as smugly sadistic.

● *Jim* Jason Biggs, *Chris 'Oz' Ostreicher* Chris Klein, *Jessica* Natasha Lyonne, *Kevin* Thomas Ian Nicholas, *Vicky* Tara Reid, *Heather* Mena Suvari, *Jim's dad* Eugene Levy, *Nadia* Shannon Elizabeth, *Michelle* Alysson Hannigan, *Sherman* Chris Owen, *Stifler* Seann W. Scott, *Finch* Eddie Kay Thomas, Jennifer Coolidge, Clyde Kusatsu, Lawrence Pressman, Molly Cheek, Akuyoe Graham, and *uncredited* Casey Affleck.
● *Dir* Paul Weitz, *Pro* Warren Zide, Craig Perry, Chris Moore and Chris Weitz, *Co-Pro* Louis G. Friedman and Chris Bender, *Screenplay* Adam Herz, *Ph* Richard Crudo, *Pro Des* Paul Peters, *Ed* Priscilla Nedd-Friendly, *M* David Lawrence; songs performed by Libra Presents Taylor, Etta James, Hole, Everclear, Dishwalla, The Brian Jonestown Massacre, Sugar Ray, Oleander, Simon and Garfunkel, Blink 182, Third Eye Blind, Barenaked Ladies, Five Easy Pieces, Goldfinger, Tonic, etc, *Costumes* Leesa Evans.

Universal-UIP.
95 mins. USA. 1999. Rel: 8 October 1999. Cert 15.

American Psycho ★★★'/2

New York City; 1988. Patrick Bateman, a ruthless and highly successful inside trader, has reached a level of physical and material perfection that he is determined to maintain. It is not so much Gekko's greed that motivates him as an overwhelming need for one-upmanship. The sex and cocaine merely dull the pain, the real rush arrives with the ability to trump his peers. So, when Paul Allen shows off a more elegant business card than his own, Bateman splits his face open with an axe ... On a simplistic level, *American Psycho* is three consecutive movies, each less immediately satisfying than the last. The first chapter is a dark, incisive satire on the materialistic Eighties, beautifully evoked in broad, straight strokes. The second is an uncomfortable thriller in which the sickness of the first part is made flesh. And the last act is a surreal, disturbing dream in which the physical sickness takes on a psychological dementia. An entertaining treatise on the evil of misogyny, this slick adaptation of Brett Easton Ellis's controversial 1991 novel is all the more anomalous in that it is adapted and directed by two women. Ultimately, then, it is an unsettling, provocative work that addresses a serious malaise in our society and, by soliciting our laughter, indicts us all. FYI: Christian Bale was Harron's original choice to play Bateman but he temporarily lost the role when Lions Gate offered Leonardo DiCaprio $21 million to take over. Thankfully, DiCaprio got cold feet.

● *Patrick Bateman* Christian Bale, *Donald Kimball* Willem Dafoe, *Paul Allen* Jared Leto, *Courtney Rawlinson* Samantha Mathis, *Jean* Chloë Sevigny, *Evelyn Williams* Reese Witherspoon, *Timothy Bryce* Justin Theroux, *Craig McDermott* Josh Lucas, *Elizabeth* Guinevere Turner, *Luis Carruthers* Matt Ross, *David Van Patten* Bill Sage, *Christie* Cara Seymour, Park Bench, Catherine Black, Stephen Bogaert, Monika Meier, Marie Dame, Kelley Harron, Patricia Gage, Krista Sutton, Connie Chen.
● *Dir* Mary Harron, *Pro* Edward R. Pressman, Chris Hanley and Christian Halsey Solomon, *Ex Pro* Michael Paseornek, Jeff Sackman and Joseph Drake, *Co-Pro* Ernie Barbaresh, Clifford Streit, Rob Weiss and Alessandro Camon, *Line Pro* Victoria Hirst, *Screenplay* Harron and Guinevere Turner, *Ph* Andrzej Sekula, *Pro Des* Gideon Ponte, *Ed* Andrew Marcus, *M* John Cale; songs performed by New Order, Katrina and The Waves, Robert Allen Palmer, Book of Love, Huey Lewis & The News, John Cale, Chris De Burgh, Simply Red, Genesis, Phil Collins, M/A/R/R/S, Curiosity Killed the Cat, David Bowie, The Cure, Daniel Ash, etc, *Costumes* Isis Mussenden, *Sound* Ben Cheah and Paul Urmson.

Lions Gate Films/MUSE Prods-Entertainment.
101 mins. USA/Canada. 2000. Rel: 21 April 2000. Cert 18.

Analyze This ★★'/2

New York/Florida; the present. Ben Sobel is a successful psychiatrist specialising in family problems. However, that's family with a small 'f', so when he's strong-armed

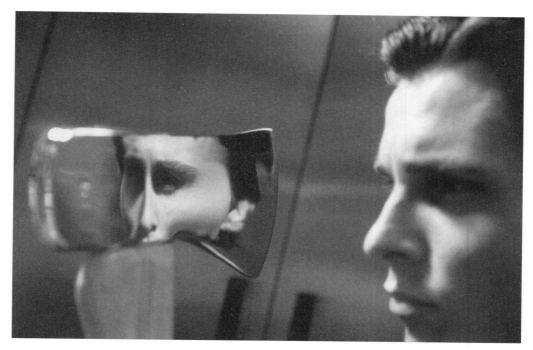

Right: The axeman cometh – Christian Bale reflects his edge in Mary Harron's unsettling and provocative American Psycho (from Entertainment)

into treating a notorious gangster suffering from panic attacks, there's a serious 'transfer of neurosis' between patient and doctor. The dreaded Paul Vitti just wants to get his will to kill back, but Sobel wants a new kind of family life ... The Mob is always good for a laugh and this farcical addition to the genre (cf. *Married to the Mob, Honeymoon in Vegas, Mickey Blue Eyes*) milks its subject with few clichés to spare. Still, it's always good to watch Billy Crystal play the urbanite out of his depth (à la *City Slickers*) and he underplays his role perfectly – which is more than can be said for Robert De Niro. De Niro can do many things, but comedy is not one of them (remember *We're No Angels*?). Here, he's simply OTT and embarrassing (and who told him he could sob convincingly?). Incidentally, Lisa Kudrow is totally wasted.

● *Paul Vitti* Robert De Niro, *Ben Sobol* Billy Crystal, *Laura MacNamara* Lisa Kudrow, *Jelly* Joe Viterelli, *Primo Sindone* Chazz Palminteri, *Jimmy* Richard Castellano, *Caroline* Molly Shannon, *Michael Sobel* Kyle Sabihy, *Isaac Sobel* Bill Macy, *Dorothy Sobel* Rebecca Schull, *Marie Vitti* Elizabeth Bracco, Max Casella, Frank Pietrangolare, Pat Cooper, Leo Rossi, Tony Darrow, Donnamarie Recco, Jimmy Ray Weeks, Ira Wheeler, Luce Ennis, Michael Harkins, Tony Bennett.
● *Dir* Harold Ramis, *Pro* Paula Weinstein and Jane Rosenthal, *Ex Pro* Billy Crystal, Chris Brigham and Bruce Berman, *Co-Pro* Len Amato, *Screenplay* Peter Tolan and Harold Ramis and Kenneth Lonergan, *Ph* Stuart Dryburgh, *Pro Des* Wynn Thomas, *Ed* Christopher Tellefsen, *M* Howard Shore; Prokofiev, Verdi; songs performed by Louis Prima, Luciano Pavarotti, Gloria Estefan and Miami Sound Machine, Marky Mark and The Funky Bunch, Tony Bennett, etc, *Costumes* Aude Bronson-Howard, *Sound* Sandy Berman.

Warner Bros/Village Roadshow Pictures/NPV Entertainment/ Baltimore/Spring Creek Pictures/Face/Tribeca-Warner. 103 mins. USA. 1999. Rel: 24 September 1999. Cert 15.

Angela's Ashes ★★¹/₂

Limerick, Ireland; 1935-1949. Following the death of the beautiful baby Margaret Mary in Brooklyn, the McCourts – Malachy and Angela and their four children – travel back to Ireland where, apparently, there is no work and people are dying of disease. And, sure enough, the conditions there are appalling. Ostracised by her family for having married a northerner, Angela finds accommodation in a flooded slum opposite a communal latrine and attempts to pull her life together. But her husband's drinking gets worse and what meagre money he does make, he spends in the pub ... Like any Alan Parker production, *Angela's Ashes* – based on the Pulitzer Prize-winning 'memoir' by Frank McCourt – is a meticulously crafted work shot through with shards of dark humour. But the sheer misery of the subject – unimaginable squalor, alcoholism, starvation, infant mortality – gets the last moan, creating an experience of unremitting gloom. Neil Jordan's *The Butcher's Boy*, also detailing a miserable Irish childhood exacerbated by a father's drinking, was a much sharper and more imaginative film. FYI: Ciaran Owens, who plays Frank McCourt as a boy, is the brother of Eamonn Owens, who had the title role in *The Butcher's Boy*.

● *Angela McCourt* Emily Watson, *Malachy McCourt* Robert Carlyle, *young Frank McCourt* Joe Breen, *middle Frank McCourt* Ciaran Owens, *older Frank McCourt* Michael Legge, *Grandma Sheehan* Ronnie Masterson, *Aunt Aggie* Pauline McLynn, *Uncle Pa Keating* Liam

Right: *Getting To Know Her – Jodie Foster in Andy Tennant's sumptuous if prolonged* Anna and the King *(from Fox)*

Carney, *Uncle Pat* Eanna MacLiam, *Narrator* Andrew Bennett, *Mr O'Halloran* Brendan Cauldwell, *Laman Griffin* Alvaro Lucchesi, *Theresa Carmody* Kerry Condon, *Quasimodo* Eamonn Owens, *Dr Campbell* Alan Parker, Lucas Neville, Walter Mansfield, Les Doherty, Shay Gorman, Eileen Pollock, Gerard McSorley, Maggie McCarthy, Bairbre Ni Chaoimh, David Ahern, Sarah Pilkington, Frankie McCafferty, Birdy Sweeney.
● *Dir* Alan Parker, *Pro* Scott Rudin, David Brown and Alan Parker, *Ex Pro* Adam Schroeder and Eric Steel, *Line Pro* David Wimbury, *Screenplay* Laura Jones and Alan Parker, *Ph* Michael Seresin, *Pro Des* Geoffrey Kirkland, *Ed* Gerry Hambling, *M* John Williams; Verdi, Max Steiner; songs performed by Billie Holiday, Al Bowlly, Matthias Seuffert, etc, *Costumes* Consolata Boyle.

Universal/Paramount/Dirty Hands/Irish Film Industry-UIP. 146 mins. USA/UK. 1999. Rel: 14 January 2000. Cert 15.

Anna and the King ★★★¹/₂

Bangkok; 1862. Still struggling to come to terms with the death of her husband 23 months ago, English school-teacher Anna Leonowens accepts an invitation to tutor the king of Siam's oldest son. However, when she arrives in Bangkok, Anna not only finds that the king is preoccupied with matters of state, but that he has reneged on some of her conditions of employment. Disregarding the strict rules of sovereign protocol, Anna forces the monarch to meet her demands and to accept her on her own terms ... The fourth cinematic interpretation of Anna Leonowens' diaries (whose authenticity have come under some question), Andy Tennant's film is sumptuous and enthralling if a tad over-long. The clash of Western and Eastern cultures always makes for good drama and is intelligently developed here by scenarists Meerson and Krikes (who previously collaborated on the Jean-Claude

Van Damme vehicle *Double Impact*). And thanks to charismatic turns from Foster and Chow, the human drama is not overwhelmed by the magnificent sets and locations. Filmed in Malaysia. FYI: Apparently, the seven acre set of the king's palace – erected by a construction crew of close to 1,300 – is the biggest built from scratch since *The Fall of the Roman Empire* (in 1964).

● *Anna Leonowens* Jodie Foster, *King Mongkut* Chow Yun-Fat, *Tuptim* Bai Ling, *Louis Leonowens* Tom Felton, *The Kralahome* Syed Alwi, *General Alak* Randall Duk Kim, *Prince Chowfa* Lim Kay Siu, *Princess Fa-Ying* Melissa Campbell, *Prince Chulalongkorn* Keith Chin, *Lady Thiang* Deanna Yusoff, *Lord John Bradley* Geoffrey Palmer, *Lady Bradley* Ann Firbank, *Mycroft Kincaid* Bill Stewart, Mano Maniam, Shanthini Venugopal, Sean Ghazi, Robert Hands.
● *Dir* Andy Tennant, *Pro* Lawrence Bender and Ed Elbert, *Ex Pro* Terence Chang, *Co-Pro* Jon Jashni and G. Mac Brown, *Screenplay* Steve Meerson and Peter Krikes, *Ph* Caleb Deschanel, *Pro Des* Luciana Arrighi, *Ed* Roger Bondelli, *M* George Fenton, *Costumes* Jenny Beavan, *Sound* Craig Berkey.

Fox 2000-Fox. 148 mins. USA. 1999. Rel: 17 December 1999. Cert 12.

Another Day in Paradise ★★★¹/₂

Oklahoma; the 1970s. There's little nirvana in the lives of Mel, Sid, Bobbie and Rosie, other than the high they get off heroin. But when professional thief and drug dealer Mel takes the teenage Bobbie and Rosie under his wing – after saving Bobbie's life after a savage encounter with a security guard – a sense of family emerges. However, Mel's constant quest for a bigger `job' leads his new kin down a decidedly treacherous path ... Having chronicled the sexual exploits of the dermally challenged in *Kids*, photographer Larry Clark turns his camera on crime, heroin and more carnal grappling in this, his second outing as director. Cultivating improvisation and personality conflicts on set, Clark has hewn some edgy, adrenaline-rushing cinema from a frequently visited milieu. As the paternalistic, impulsive Mel, James Woods is on even more intense and scuzzier form than usual, while Melanie Griffith injects a new honesty into her ageing bimbo act. This is tough, honest drama with a look of uncomfortable authenticity.

● *Mel* James Woods, *Sid* Melanie Griffith, *Bobby* Vincent Kartheiser, *Rosie* Natasha Gregson Wagner, *Reverend* James Otis, *Danny* Branden Williams, *Clem* Brent Briscoe, Peter Sarsgaard, Paul Hipp, Kim Flowers, Christopher Doyle, Jay Leggett, Clarence Carter, and *Jewels* Lou Diamond Phillips (*uncredited*).
● *Dir* Larry Clark, *Pro* Clark, Stephen Chin and James Woods, *Co-Pro* Scott Shiffman, *Screenplay* Christopher Landon and Stephen Chin, from the book by Eddie Little, *Ph* Eric Edwards, *Pro Des* Aaron Osborne, *Ed* Luis Colina, *M:* songs performed by Fantastic Johnny, Polyester Players, Otis Redding, Clarence Carter, Percy Sledge, The Tornadoes, Chocolate Genius, Willie Dixon, Sam Moore, Bob Dylan, etc, *Costumes* Kathryn Morris (ex-wife of James Woods).

Chinese Bookies Pictures-Metrodome.
101 mins. USA. 1998. Rel: 13 August 1999. Cert 18.

Any Given Sunday ★★★

'You can win or lose – but can you win or lose like a man?' Thus sermonises Tony D'Amato, the tough but caring coach for the Miami Sharks football team. With the Sharks losing their third consecutive game, D'Amato is facing a battle of wills with the team's ruthless president, Christina Pagniacci, while fielding the ego of his star player, the volatile and self-centred Willie Beamen. So, is D'Amato himself ready to lose like a man? Having explored – and exploded – the myths surrounding politics, economics, war and music, Oliver Stone turns his attention to professional football, a sport that he describes as being 'both a religion practised on a Sunday' and 'our version of the gladiator games of the Roman empire.' Following the self-indulgent experimentation of *Natural Born Killers*, *Nixon* and *U Turn*, Stone is back on terrific form, reminding us that, with a bit of self discipline, he is still one of America's most dynamic filmmakers. Here, he has ripped tremendous performances out of a crackerjack cast, supplied some terrific dialogue and provided a hard-hitting, eclectic soundtrack that drives, rather than distracts from, the action. But once one pares away the music, sound effects and ratatat-tat editing, what is left is a mediocre plot and a stadium full of sports movies clichés. Just don't look too closely. FYI: When Pacino backed out of Oliver Stone's production of *Born of the Fourth of July*, the director publicly denounced the actor.

● *Tony D'Amato* Al Pacino, *Christina Pagniacci* Cameron Diaz, *Jack 'Cap' Rooney* Dennis Quaid, *Dr Harvey Mandrake* James Woods, *'Steamin' Willie Beamen* Jamie Foxx, *Julian Washington* LL Cool J, *Dr Ollie Powers* Matthew Modine, *AFFA Football Commissioner* Charlton Heston, *Margaret Pagniacci* Ann-Margret, *Nick Crozier* Aaron Eckhart, *Jack Rose* John C. McGinley, *Montezuma Monroe* Jim Brown, *Luther 'Shark' Lavay* Lawrence Taylor, *Vanessa Struthers* Lela Rochon, *Cindy Rooney* Lauren Holly, *Mandy Murphy* Elizabeth Berkley, Bill Bellamy, Andrew Bryniarski, James Karen, Gianni Russo, Duane Martin, Clifton Davis, Oliver Stone, Phil Latzman, Sean C. Stone, Michael Stone, Tara Stone.
● *Dir* Oliver Stone, *Pro* Lauren Shuler Donner, Clayton Townsend and Dan Halsted, *Ex Pro* Richard Donner and Oliver Stone, *Co-Pro* Eric Hamburg and Jonathan Krauss, *Screenplay* John Logan and Oliver Stone, from a story by Logan and Daniel Pyne, *Ph* Salvatore Totino, *Pro Des* Victor Kempster, *Ed* Tom Nordberg, Keith Salmon and Stuart Waks, *M* Robbie Robertson, Paul Kelly and Richard Horowitz; songs performed by Robbie Robertson, The Horse Flies, Michael Brook and Nusrat Fateh Ali Khan, Gary Glitter, FatBoy Slim, Godsmack, Moby, P.O.D., Smokey Robinson, 4AD, Bill Brown, OVERSEER, DMX, Roger, !Cubanismo!, KC & The Sunshine Band, Ella Fitzgerald, Trick Daddy, Propellerheads, LL Cool J, Black Sabbath, Metallica, Missy 'Misdemeanor' Elliott, Hole, Havoc, Jamie Foxx, Thelonious Monk, Kid Rock, Ben Webster and Oscar Peterson, Billie Holiday, Hawkwind, Nina Simone, Bill Withers, Queen, The Chemical Brothers, Labradford, etc, etc, *Costumes* Mary Zophres.

Ixtlan/The Donners' Company- Warner.
151 mins. USA. 1999. Rel: 31 March 2000. Cert 15.

Anywhere But Here ★★¹/₂

When Adele August eats, observes her 14-year-old daughter Ann, it's as if she's tasting the whole world. Ann, who would rather nibble at life's edges, is not wild at the idea of moving from Wisconsin to Beverly Hills with her mother. Bored of her second husband, Adele has elected to start a new life in California and rather fancies the idea of Ann being an actress. Obviously, it's not going to be an easy ride ... The trouble with the ditsy, impulsive, streetwise yet emotionally naive Adele August is that she's not only a caricature but is too good to be true. While at one moment childishly perverse and at the next compassionately insightful, Adele never sacrifices the integrity of her maternal instincts. And she is a gift to an actress, an opportunity Ms Sarandon makes the most of. Yet it is Natalie Portman as Adele's grounded, sensible daughter who supplies the ballast of credibility and reason, even when her character appears to be acting against it. So, there are some interesting levels here, but the film desperately lacks edge and is victim to one too many longueurs.

● *Adele August* Susan Sarandon, *Ann August* Natalie Portman, *Carol* Bonnie Bedelia, *Benny* Shawn Hatosy, *Josh Spritzer* Hart Bochner, *Lillian* Eileen Ryan, *Ted* Ray Baker, *Gail Letterfine* Caroline Aaron, *George Franklin* Paul Guilfoyle, *Peter* Corbin Allred, *Jack Irwin* John Carroll Lynch, John Diehl, Faran Tahir, Shishir Kurup, Sharona Alperin, Mary Ellen Trainor, Elisabeth Moss, Ashley Johnson, Heather DeLoach, Heather McComb, Michael Milhoan, Megan Mullally, and (uncredited) *Mary* Thora Birch.
● *Dir* Wayne Wang, *Pro* Laurence Mark, *Ex Pro* Ginny Nugent, *Screenplay* Alvin Sargent, from the book by Mona Simpson, *Ph* Roger Deakins, *Pro Des* Donald Graham Burt, *Ed* Nicholas C. Smith, *M* Danny Elfman; Johann Strauss; songs performed by k.d. lang, The Beach Boys, Poe, LeAnn Rimes, Sarah McLachlan, BB Swing, Carly Simon and Sally Taylor, Lisa Loeb, 21st Century Girls, Bif Naked, Patty Griffin, Marie Wilson, etc, *Costumes* Betsy Heimann.

Fox 2000-Fox.
114 mins. USA. 1999. Rel: 3 December 1999. Cert 12.

L'Arche du desert ★★★

An insider's view of life among the tribes who inhabit the deserts of Algeria, this is a visually striking and deeply heartfelt plea for tolerance and understanding in a war-like world. It's done through the story of lovers from two different tribes who, in the manner of Romeo and Juliet, meet opposition which here leads to wide-scale slaughter. Unfortunately, the sincerity of filmmaker Mohammed Chouikh is not matched by the skill needed to tell his story clearly, and his attempt to offer hope at the end for the next generation is naively expressed. There are also times when the movie's blend of the naturalistic and the mythic proves uneasy. Nevertheless, despite its faults, this film is patently the work of an artist who cares. [Mansel Stimpson]

● *Myriam* Myriam Aouffen, *Houiria du Ksar* Messaouda Adami, *Amin* Hacen Abdou, *the cousin* Shyraz Aliane, *the child* Amin Chouikh, Abdelkader Belmokadem, Fatyha Nesserine, Lynda Fares.
● *Dir and Screenplay* Mohammed Chouikh, *Pro* Nadjet Taibouni and Sandrine Vernet, *Assoc Pro* Klaus Gerke and Thomas Kroh, *Ph* Mustapha Belmilhoub, *Ed* Yamina Chouikh, *M* Philippe Arthuys, *Camels* Laid Benchekchek.

Atlas Films/K-Films/ENPA/Vulkan Kultur GmbH, etc-Downtown.
90 mins. Algeria/France/Germany/Switzerland. 1997. Rel: 16 July 1999. Cert 12.

Asterix & Obelix Take On Caesar – Asterix & Obelix Contre Cesar ★★

Brittany, France; 50 B.C. Caesar is bad enough, but when his treacherous aide Lucius Detritus decides to take on the impregnable Gaul village protected by a magic potion, Asterix and Obelix find themselves in real trouble ... Humour is a funny business and French humour even more so. An earthy, rambunctious phenomenon rooted in ancient Gaul history, the Asterix comics have sold 280 million copies worldwide and produced seven full-length animated features. Now comes the live-action version which, at a cost of $48 million, is the most expensive French film ever made. Leaning on digital technology and lavish production values, the enterprise has lost much of the original's charm (and humour), while the comic's more violent episodes now make a nightmarish impact (particularly the sequence in which Asterix is subjected to poisonous snakes and a pit of tarantulas). At its best it resembles a Pythonesque history lesson for irreverent schoolchildren, which is probably why Python's very own Terry Jones was recruited to supervise this English-language version.

● *Asterix* Christian Clavier, *Obelix* Gerard Depardieu, *Lucius Detritus* Roberto Benigni, *Tunnabrix* aka *Abraracourcix* Michel Galabru, *Panoramix* Claude Pieplu, *Prolix* Daniel Prevost, *Cacofonix* aka *Assuranceetourix* Pierre Palmade, *Paraphanalia* aka *Falbala* Lætitia Casta, *Mrs Jerry Atrix* aka *Mme Agecanonix* Arielle Dombasle, *Jerry Atrix* aka *Agecanonix* Sim, *Caesar* Gottfried John, *Tragicomix* Hardy Krüger Jr., Marianne Sägebrecht, Jean-Pierre Castaldi, Jean-Roger Milo, Jean-Jacques Devaux, Michel Muller.
● *Dir* and *Screenplay* Claude Zidi, based on characters created by Albert Uderzo and René Goscinny, *English adaptation* Terry Jones, *Pro* Claude Berri, *Ex Pro* Pierre Grunstein, *Line Pro* Patrick Bordier, *Ph* Tony Pierce-Roberts, *Pro Des* Jean Rabasse, *Ed* Nicole Saunier and Hervé de Luze, *M* Jean-Jacques Goldman and Roland Romanelli, *Costumes* Sylvie Gautrelet.

Katharina/Renn Prods/TF1 Films/Bavaria Film/Melampo Cinematografica/Canal Plus, etc-Pathé.
110 mins. France/Germany/Italy. 1999. Rel: 14 April 2000. Cert PG.

The Astronaut's Wife ★★★

Florida/New York; the present. For just two minutes NASA loses contact with a couple of astronauts making routine repairs to their space shuttle. But in those two minutes something very strange has happened, something that slips through the exhaustive tests carried out after the astronauts' return. But gradually Jillian Armacost is not so sure her husband is who he used to be ... Inviting obvious comparisons to *Rosemary's Baby* (reinforced by Charlize Theron's short blonde hair à la Mia Farrow), *The Astronaut's Wife* is an excessively stylish, frequently suspenseful thriller promising great things for its director. However, the film is *so* glossy that it's hard to get under the fingernails of its beautiful protagonists, their spotless apartment (without a maid or hoover in sight) and their immaculate lives. A little work on the script would have helped (at one point Johnny Depp asks his wife is she

Right: 'Yeah, baby!' Mike Myers and Heather Graham in Jay Roach's over-the-top and derivative Austin Powers: The Spy Who Shagged Me *(from Entertainment)*

likes fruit – I mean, really), but top honours go to Ms Theron and some skilful editing and sound design.

● *Spencer Armacost* Johnny Depp, *Jillian Armacost* Charlize Theron, *Sherman Reese* Joe Morton, *Nan* Clea DuVall, *doctor* Samantha Eggar, *Natalie Streck* Donna Murphy, *Alex Streck* Nick Cassavetes, *Shelly McLaren* Blair Brown, *Jackson McLaren* Tom Noonan, Gary Grubbs, Tom O'Brien, Lucy Lin, Michael Crider, Jacob Stein, Julian Barnes.
● *Dir and Screenplay* Rand Ravich, *Pro* Andrew Lazar, *Ex Pro* Mark Johnson, Brian Witten and Donna Langley, *Co-Pro* Diana Pokorny, *Ph* Allen Daviau, *Pro Des* Jan Roelfs, *Ed* Steve Mirkovich and Tim Alverson, *M* George S. Clinton; 'My Way' 'sung' by The Sex Pistols, *Costumes* Isis Mussenden.

New Line/Mad Chance-Entertainment.
109 mins. USA. 1999. Rel: 26 November 1999. Cert 18.

Austin Powers: The Spy Who Shagged Me ★★¹/₂

When Dr Evil escapes from his cryogenic prison, he nips back to 1969 to steal Austin Powers' 'mojo' – i.e. the secret agent's very lifeforce and libido. So Austin pursues him to the Swinging Sixties and stumbles across Evil's dastardly plan to subjugate the world ... Mike Myers tries so hard to cram his James Bond spoof with gags, that he begs, steals and borrows them from any source he can think of, from the Marx Brothers and the Carry On series to the *Airplane!* films. However, when he does introduce a joke all his own – like Dr Evil's phallic rocket soliciting various reactions from onlookers ('it looks just like a...' cut to a musician calling out 'Willie!' to Willie Nelson) – he milks it to death. But his own

performances – as Austin, Dr Evil and the grotesque 'Fat Bastard' – are so self-effacing and energised that he eventually kicks the laughter out of you (unless, that is, you are a dwarf, lesbian or lard-ass). Any film that boasts such a large quota of guffaws has to be forgiven its worst moments, however reluctantly. It's just a shame that the best jokes are pushed well beyond their shelf-life.

● *Austin Powers/Dr Evil/Fat Bastard* Mike Myers, *Felicity Shagwell* Heather Graham, *Basil Exposition* Michael York, *Number Two* Robert Wagner, *Scott Evil* Seth Green, *Vanessa Kensington* Elizabeth Hurley, *Young Number Two* Rob Lowe, *Frau Farbissina* Mindy Sterling, *Ivana Humpalot* Kristen Johnston, *Mustafa* Will Ferrell, *Mini-Me* Verne J. Troyer, *Robin Swallows nee Spitz* Gia Caredes, Oliver Muirhead, Muse Watson, Clint Howard, Jane Carr, Jennifer Coolidge, *The President* Tim Robbins, *and as themslves:* Woody Harrelson, Willie Nelson, Jerry Springer.
● *Dir* Jay Roach, *Pro* John Lyons, Mike Myers and Suzanne Todd, Jennifer Todd, Demi Moore and Eric McLeod, *Ex Pro* Erwin Stoff, Michael De Luca and Donna Langley, *Assoc Pro* Emma Chasin, *Screenplay* Myers and Michael McCullers, *Ph* Ueli Steiger, *Pro Des* Rusty Smith, *Ed* John Poll and Debra Neil-Fisher, *M* George S. Clinton; songs performed by They Might Be Giants, Quincy Jones, REM, Lords of Acid, Fantastic Plastic Machine, The Who, Steppenwolf, The Guess Who, Green Day, Marvin Gaye, The Monkees, Burt Bacharach and Elvis Costello, Madonna, Dr Evil, Propellerheads, Bangles, Lenny Kravitz, Melanie G (aka Scary Spice), etc, *Costumes* Deena Appel.

New Line Cinema/Eric's Boy/Moving Pictures/Team Todd-Entertainment.
95 mins. USA. 1999. Rel: 30 July 1999. Cert 12.

Left: Life's a Beach – Leonardo DiCaprio splashes out in Danny Boyle's vivid and seductive drama (from Fox)

The Bachelor ★

Less than 24 hours from his birthday, Jimmie Shannon, 29, discovers that he is to inherit $100 million – but only if he is married by 30. It's a shame, then, that he's just botched a proposal to the one woman he loves … If one good thing can come out of this woefully mechanical, deadly unfunny comedy is that it might, just might, turn contemporary filmgoers onto the original. A miserably misconceived update of the 1925 Buster Keaton classic *Seven Chances*, *The Bachelor* is a slur against the memory of the silent cinema's funniest ambassador. If imitation is the sincerest form of flattery, then pray for criticism. *[Charles Bacon]*

● *Jimmie Shannon* Chris O'Donnell, *Anne* Renée Zellweger, *O'Dell* Hal Holbrook, *priest* James Cromwell, *Marco* Artie Lange, *Gluckman* Edward Asner, *Natalie* Marley Shelton, *Grandad* Peter Ustinov, *Ilana* Mariah Carey, *Buckley* Brooke Shields, Sarah Silverman, Stacy Edwards, Rebecca Cross, Jennifer Esposito, Katharine Towne, Nicholas Pryor.
● *Dir* Gary Sinyor, *Pro* Lloyd Segan and Bing Howenstein, *Ex Pro* Michael De Luca, Chris O'Donnell and Donna Langley, *Co-Pro* Leon Dudevoir and Stephen Hollocker, *Line Pro* Gene Levy, *Screenplay* Steve Cohen, *Ph* Simon Archer, *Pro Des* Craig Stearns, *Ed* Robert Reitano, *M* David A. Hughes and John Murphy; Carl Orff; songs performed by David Byrne, Leapy Lee, Barry White, Louis Prima, Madness, Buster Pointdexter, Hughes & Murphy, Pat Reader, Bob Marley, Jackie Wilson, etc, *Costumes* Terry Dresbach.

New Line Cinema/Lloyd Segan/George Street Pictures-Entertainment.
102 mins. USA. 1999. Rel: 18 February 2000. Cert 12.

The Barber of Siberia ★★¹/₂

If looks were all, Nikita Mikhalkov's latest film photographed by Pavel Lebeshev would be great. But, sadly, this technically adroit epic – nearly three hours in length – fails drastically with its blend of clod-hopping comedy and manipulative drama. The main narrative, set in Russia in 1885, concerns Jane from Chicago and the men in her life. Her real love is a military cadet who sings Mozart but, other rivals apart, she is pursued by General Radlov. She has set out to flatter the general in order to gain support for the inventor McCracken, who is supposedly her father. The mood switches reflect both Russian tragi-comedy and the mix found in many Mozart operas, but the comparison only underlines the lack of subtlety and finesse here. The director himself takes the role of the Czar. *[Mansel Stimpson]*

● *Jane Callahan* Julia Ormond, *Douglas McCracken* Richard Harris, *Andrey Tolstoy* Oleg Menshikov, *General Radlov* Alexey Petrenko, *Captain Mokin* Vladimir Ilyin, *Maximich* Alexander Yakovlev, *Polievsky* Marat Basharov, *Kopnovsky* Daniel Olbrychski, Nikita Tatarenkov, Georgy Dronov, Artyom Mikhalkov, Robert Hardy, Elizabeth Spriggs, Nikita Mikhalkov, Isabelle Renauld, Alexander Sannikov.
● *Dir* and *Co-Pro* Nikita Mikhalkov, *Pro* Michel Seydoux, *Ex Pro* Leonid Vereschagin, *Screenplay* Mikhalkov, Rustam Ibragimbekov and Rospo Pallenberg, *Ph* Pavel Lebeshev, *Pro Des* Vladimir Aronin, *Ed* Enzo Meniconi, *M* Edward Nicolay Artemyev, *Costumes* Natacha Ivanova and Sergey Struchev.

Camera One/Three T Prods/France 2 Cinema/Medusa-Pathé.
179 mins. France/Russia/Italy/Czech Republic. 1999.
Rel: 9 June 2000. Cert 12.

Bats ★★★

Gallup, Texas; the present. As part of a top-secret military research programme, a batch of Indonesian flying foxes are infected with a virus that boosts both their intelligence and their aggression. Then the blighters escape the lab and infect the local bat population … This was all but thrown away by its distributor in June, which is a shame considering the film's credentials. Resisting the built-in campiness of recent horror flicks, *Bats* dares to play it absolutely straight and consequently cranks up the thrills. The animatronic effects are extremely effective, the pacing lively, the actors well chosen (Lou Diamond Phillips cast against type, Bob Gunton predictably compelling) and there are several neat, unexpected touches – even the soundtrack is above-average. [*Charles Bacon*]

● *Sheriff Emmett Kimsey* Lou Diamond Phillips, *Dr Sheila Casper* Dina Meyer, *Jimmy* Leon, *Dr Alexander McCabe* Bob Gunton, *Dr Tobe Hodge* Carlos Jacott, *Deputy Munn David* Shawn McConnell, *Mayor Branson* Marcia Dangerfield, *Dr Swanbeck* Oscar Rowland.
● *Dir* Louis Morneau, *Pro* Brad Jenkel and Louise Rosner, *Ex Pro* Steve Stabler, Brent Baum, John Logan and Dale Pollock, *Screenplay* John Logan, *Ph* George Mooradian, *Pro Des* Phillip J.C. Duffin, *Ed* Glenn Garland, *M* Graeme Revell, *Costumes* Alexis Scott, *Special effects* Eric J. Allard.

Destination Films-Columbia TriStar.
91 mins. USA. 1999. Rel: 23 June 2000. Cert 15.

Battlefield Earth ★★

3000 AD; Earth. Following the colonisation of Earth by a breed of ten-foot-tall aliens, mankind has been reduced to a depleted race of outcasts and slaves. Only the resilient and spunky Jonnie Goodboy Tyler seems to have the wherewithal to stand up to the unscrupulous aggressors ... Impaired by cluttered narrative, duff dialogue, over-active sound effects and Barry Pepper's tendency to flare his nostrils, *Battlefield Earth* is a mess from the word go. What few good ideas the original premise had – man as an endangered species, the ill-formed presumption of a supposedly superior race – are engulfed by an unwieldy framework that sacrifices story and sympathetic characters for more noise, explosions and a shot of Barry Pepper running (in slow motion). On the plus side, John Travolta enjoys himself enormously as the villain (complete with cod English accent) and the digitally produced backdrops are suitably awe-inspiring. P.S. For such a violent film it is extraordinary that most of the killing is kept off-camera. FYI: So keen was Travolta to make the movie that he took a $10m cut in his upfront salary.

● *Terl* John Travolta, *Jonnie Goodboy Tyler* Barry Pepper, *Ker* Forest Whitaker, *Carlo* Kim Coates, *Robert the Fox* Richard Tyson, *Chrissy* Sabine Karsenti, *Parson Staffer* Michael Byrne, *Mickey* Christian Tessier, *Chirk* Kelly Preston, Sylvain Landry, Earl Pastko,

Michel Perron, Shaun Austin-Olsen, Jason Cavalier, Sean Hewitt, Alan LeGros, Andy Bradshaw.
● *Dir* Roger Christian, *Pro* Elie Samaha, Jonathan D. Krane and John Travolta, *Ex Pro* Andrew Stevens, Ashok Amritraj and Don Carmody, *Co-Pro* Tracee Stanley and James Holt, *Screenplay* Corey Mandell and J.D. Shapiro, from the novel by L. Ron Hubbard, *Ph* Giles Nuttgens, *Pro Des* and *Costumes* Patrick Tatopoulos, *Ed* Robin Russell, *M* Elia Cmiral, *Sound* John Fasal, John Nutt and James LeBrecht, *Visual effects* Erik Henry, *Stunt double for Travolta* Mark Riccardi, *Costumer for Travolta* Jimmy Cullen, *Hairdresser for Travolta* Susan Kalinowski, *Make-up for Travolta* Michelle Buhler, *Special effects make-up for Travolta* Mike Smithson, *Executive assistant for Travolta* Susan Such, *Stand-in for Travolta* Tony Brazas, *Security for Travolta* Miguel Sanchez, `Craft service' for Travolta* Peter Evangelatos, *Organic entity* Brett Paton and Steve Arguello.

Morgan Creek/Franchise Pictures/JTP Films-Warner.
112 mins. USA. 2000. Rel: 2 June 2000. Cert 12.

The Beach ★★★¹/₂

Thailand; the present. Imagine a secret lagoon bordered by white sands and a barrier of tall, protective cliffs. Imagine that this lagoon, set in a tropical paradise, backs on to acres of free-growing marijuana. And imagine that this sanctuary is unknown to the outside world. For Richard, a young American backpacker, the beach is the realisation of his wildest dreams. Supported by a commune of like-minded idealists, he settles down to a life of idyllic bliss. But how much nirvana can one individual take? Echoing Mark Renton's voice-over on the soundtrack of Danny Boyle's *Trainspotting*, Richard draws the viewer into his own personal agenda. 'Never resist the unfamiliar,' he instructs us, knocking back a tipple of fresh snake blood, 'just keep your mind and suck in the experience.' Instead of heroin, Richard settles for fields of locoweed, with the white sands of his illicit beach embodying a lifetime supply of cocaine. Of course, it all goes sour, but there's plenty of food for thought in this vivid adaptation of Alex Garland's novel, while the seductive photography and throbbing score attend to the senses.

● *Richard* Leonardo DiCaprio, *Sal* Tilda Swinton, *Françoise* Virginie Ledoyen, *Etienne* Guillaume Canet, *Daffy Duck* Robert Carlyle, *Keaty* Paterson Joseph, *Bugs* Lars Arentz Hansen, *Unhygenix* Daniel Caltagirone, *Christo* Staffan Kihlbom, Daniel York, Somboon Phutaroth, Peter Youngblood Hills, Jerry Swindall, Abhijati (Muek) Jusakul, Zelda Tinska, Victoria Smurfit, Samuel Gough, Saskia Mulder, Simone Huber.
● *Dir* Danny Boyle, *Pro* Andrew Macdonald, *Co-Pro* Callum McDougall, *Screenplay* John Hodge, *Ph* Darius Khondji, *Pro Des* Andrew McAlpine, *Ed* Masahiro Hirakubo, *M* Angelo Badalamenti; songs performed by Leftfield, Faithless, Rollo & New Order, Orbital, Moby,

Sugar Ray, All Saints, Asian Dub Foundation, The Chemical Brothers, Blur, Lunatic Calm, Barry Adamson, etc, *Costumes* Rachael Fleming, *Sound* Glenn Freemantle.

Fox/Figment-Fox.
118 mins. USA/UK. 2000. Rel: 11 February 2000. Cert 15.

Beautiful People ★★★★

War is seldom contained within the borders of its own conflict. And so the Yugoslav debacle spills over into London via a series of tragic, touching, funny and always surprising ways. A wide cross-section of English society – a nurse, back-bench Tory MP, overworked obstetrician, football hooligan and TV news reporter – all find themselves inadvertently touched by a situation they cannot begin to understand ... Written and directed by the 28-year-old Bosnian emigrant Jasmin Dizdar (now a naturalised Englishman), *Beautiful People* is as much a scabrous commentary on Britain today as it is an ingenious examination of the futility of the Balkan conflict. Recalling the work of Robert Altman in its ambitious narrative sweep and dark undercurrents of humour, the film is an engrossing stew of human tragedy, broad farce and social caricature. A quirky, disturbing and enterprising work, it contains enough material to sustain several future projects.

● *Portia Thornton* Charlotte Coleman, *Pero Guzina* Edin Dzandzanovic, *George Thornton* Charles Kay, *Nora Thornton* Rosalind Ayres, *Roger Midge* Roger Sloman, *Felicity Midge* Heather Tobias, *Griffin Midge* Danny Nussbaum, *Kate Higgins* Siobhan Redmond, *Jerry Higgins* Gilbert Martin, *Dr Mouldy* Nicholas Farrell, *Edward Thornton* Julian Firth, *sister* Linda Bassett, *Glyn* Nicholas McGaughey, Faruk Pruti, Dado Jehan, Edward Jewesbury, Bobby Williams, Joseph Williams, Steve Sweeney, Jay Simpson, Elizabeth Isiorho, Melee Hutton, Sharon D. Clarke, Walentine Giorgiewa, Radoslav Youroukov, Jonny Phillips, Annette Badland, Andrew Logan, Anthony Carrick.
● *Dir and Screenplay* Jasmin Dizdar, *Pro* Ben Woolford, *Ex Pro* Roger Shannon and Ben Gibson, *Line Pro* Christopher Collins, *Ph* Barry Ackroyd, *Pro Des* Jon Henson, *Ed* Justin Krish, *M* Garry Bell; Elgar; songs performed by Paradise Lost, Elizabeth Isiorho, Emma Jane Fox, Ghostland, Kirsty MacColl, The Wedding Present, *Costumes* Louise Page.

BFI/Channel Four/Tall Stories/Arts Council of England/ Merseyside Film Production/BskyB/British Screen/ National Lottery-Alliance Atlantis.
107 mins. UK. 1999. Rel: 17 September 1999. Cert 15.

Being John Malkovich ★★★★¹/₂

New York City; today. Craig Schwartz is an extremely talented, uncompromising puppeteer whose work is largely unappreciated by the great American public. Lotte Schwartz, his wife, is a workaholic pet shop employee who brings home her more vulnerable animals, including a chimpanzee with emotional trauma. Desperate for work, Craig takes a job as a filing clerk at a company whose ceilings are only 5'3" high and wherein lies a portal that runs directly into the head of John Malkovich ... It takes a film like *Being John Malkovich* to remind one of the limitless bounds of what is possible in the cinema. Like a modern day *Alice in Wonderland* with celebrity credentials, the film is not only a total original but is very, very funny and about as unpredictable as the cinema can get. Incidentally, the real John Malkovich lives with his two children in Provence, France.

● *Craig Schwartz* John Cusack, *Lotte Schwartz* Cameron Diaz, *Maxine* Catherine Keener, *John Malkovich* John Malkovich, *Dr Lester* Orson Bean, *Floris* Mary Kay Place, *Charlie* Charlie Sheen, W. Earl Brown, Carlos Jacott, Willie Garson, Bryne Piven, Gregory Sporleder, Ned Bellamy, K.K. Dodds, Richard Fancy, Kelly Teacher, *as themselves* Christopher Bing, Sean Penn, Brad Pitt, Winona Ryder.
● *Dir* Spike Jonze, *Pro* Michael Stipe and Sandy Stern, Steve Golin and Vincent Landay, *Ex Pro* Charlie Kaufman and Michael Kuhn, *Screenplay* Kaufman, *Ph* Lance Acord, *Pro Des* K.K. Barrett, *Ed* Eric Zumbrunnen, *M* Carter Burwell, Bartok, Verdi, Vivaldi, Tchaikovsky; songs performed by Ruperto, Bjork, Madsaaki Kono, Nick Peck, and Fibre HevyBrain, *Costumes* Casey Storm.

Gramercy Pictures/Propaganda Films/Single Cell Pictures-UIP.
112 mins. USA. 1999. Rel: 17 March 2000. Cert 15.

Belly ★

New York; 1999. Tommy Brown and Sincere are childhood friends who've made a comfortable living dealing drugs. But now Sincere, egged on by his wife, wants a more stable lifestyle. Tommy, however, is having none of it ... A Kane and Abel fable for the crime-infested 1990s, *Belly* is an attempt to marry the flash style of rap video director Hype Williams with some homespun philosophy on good versus evil. Unfortunately, some incomprehensible plotting, facile moralising and one too many unpleasant characters make this virtually unwatchable. [*Charles Bacon*]

● *Sincere* Nas, *Tommy Brown* DMX, *Kisha* Taral Hicks, *Tionne* Tionne 'T-Boz' Watkins, *Shameek* Method Man, Hassan Johnson, Oliver 'Power' Grant, Louie Rankin, Tyrin Turner, Kurt Loder, Frank Vincent.
● *Dir* Hype Williams, *Pro* Larry Meistrich, Ron Rotholz, Robert Salerno and Williams, *Ex Pro* James Bigwood, *Screenplay* Williams, Anthony Bodden and Nas, *Ph* Malik Hassan Sayeed, *Pro Des* Regan Jackson, *Ed* David Leonard II, *M* Stephen Cullo; songs performed by Soul II Soul, Wu-Tang Clan, Braveheart,

Above: *Me, Myself & John Malkovich* – Malkovich checks his nappy supply in Spike Jonze's original and hilarious existential comedy (from UIP)

Lady, Hot Totti, Ja Rule, DMX, Mr Vegas, Sparkle, Frisco Kid, Taral Hicks, etc, *Costumes* June Ambrose.

Artisan Entertainment/Big Dog Films-Alliance Atlantis. 95 mins. USA. 1998. Rel: 2 July 1999. Cert 18.

Best ★

George Best joined Manchester United at 15 and just six years later was named European Footballer of the Year. A national hero and *bona fide* sex symbol, he quickly succumbed to the temptations of money and fame, eventually drinking himself from grace. This is his pathetic story ... A film about a football icon that fails to capture any excitement of the game, *Best* is astonishing in the amount of talent it has squandered (even Stephen Fry's cameo is a non-starter). Contaminated with hackneyed dialogue, flat direction, sub-standard acting, pointless musical cues and poor sound, the film suffers most of all at the hands of co-writer and executive producer John Lynch who has taken it on himself to play Best without an ounce of energy or a shred of charisma. A sad spectacle, then, of both a fallen idol and the amateurish film that chronicles his degeneration.

● *George Best* John Lynch, *Sir Matt Busby* Ian Bannen, *Bobby Charlton* Jerome Flynn, *Nobby Stiles* Ian Hart, *Anna* Patsy Kensit, *Denis Law* Linus Roache, *Rodney Marsh* Roger Daltrey, *Fraser Crane* Stephen Fry, *Rocky* Adrian Lester, *interviewer* Clive Anderson, *Bob Bishop* Jim Sheridan, *Dickie Best* James Ellis, *Paddy Crerand* Cal MacAninch, *Norma Charlton*

Mary McGuckian, *Tommy Docherty/barman* David Hayman, *Eva Haraldsted* Sophie Dahl, Pauline Lynch, Jacqueline Lynch, Owen O'Neill, Philip Madoc, Marie Jones, Ray Wilkins, Amanda Ryan, Sara Stockbridge, and, *as themselves*, Alex and George Best.
● *Dir* Mary McGuckian, *Pro* McGuckian, Elvira Bolz and Chris Roff, *Ex Pro* Steve Christian, Guy Collins, Michael Ryan and John Lynch, *Line Pro* Carol Rodger, *Screenplay* Lynch and McGuckian, *Ph* Witold Stok, *Pro Des* Max Gottlieb, *Ed* Kant Pan, *M* Mark Stevens; songs performed by Blues & Grooves, Sugarfree, The Beach Boys, Roger Daltrey, Fontella Bass, The Pretty Things, Python Lee Jackson and Rod Stewart, Steve Harley, etc, *Costumes* Anushia Nieradzik, *Football choreography* Ray Wilkins, *Script consultant* George Best.

IAC Film/Sky Pictures/Isle of Man Film Commission/ Smoke & Mirrors Film/Pembridge Pictures/Bord Scannán Na hÉireann-Optimum Releasing. 106 mins. UK/Ireland. 1999. Rel: 12 May 2000. Cert 15.

The Best Man ★★¹/₂

First-time novelist Harper Stewart is the best man at Lance and Mia's upcoming nuptials. However, having written a thinly veiled exposé of all his old friends' lives, Harper is nervous about showing his face. Of course, the book hasn't hit the shops quite yet, but then TV producer and bridesmaid Jordan Armstrong obtains an advance copy... While it's reassuring to encounter a film that portrays its cast of Afro-Americans as such likeable and vaguely responsible grown-ups, it's a shame that the plot is not more inventive or novel. Still, the dialogue is punchy and amusing and there are wonderful turns from Morris Chestnut as the emotionally volatile groom and Harold Perrineau as the terminally agreeable and gentle Murch. Incidentally, first-time director Malcolm D. Lee is the cousin of the film's producer Spike. [*Ewen Brownrigg*]

● *Harper Stewart* Taye Diggs, *Jordan Armstrong* Nia Long, *Lance Sullivan* Morris Chestnut, *Murch* Harold Perrineau, *Quentin* Terrence Howard, *Robin* Sanaa Lathan, *Mia* Monica Calhoun, *Shelby* Melissa De Sousa, *Anita* Victoria Dillard, *Candy* Regina Hall, *Uncle Skeeter* Jim Moody, Jarrod Bunch, Stu 'Large' Riley, Liris Crosse, Lady Madonna, Willie Carpenter, Malcolm D.Lee, Doug Banks, DeDe McGuire.
● *Dir* and *Screenplay* Malcolm D.Lee, *Pro* Spike Lee, Sam Kitt and Bill Carraro, *Ph* Frank Prinzi, *Pro Des* Kalina Ivanov, *Ed* Cara Silverman, *M* Stanley Clarke; songs performed by The Roots and Jaguar, Lauryn Hill and Bob Marley, Stevie Wonder, Terrence Howard, Me'Shell Ndegéocello, Chubb Rock, Maxwell, Heavy D & The Boyz, Faith Evans, Destiny's Child, Ruff Life, Cameo, Sean Lee, D'Angelo, Allure, Mint Condition, Case, Tyrese, Ginuwine, RL, etc, *Costumes* Danielle Hollowell.

Universal Pictures/40 Acres and a Mule Filmworks-UIP.
121 mins. USA. 1999. Rel: 30 June 2000. Cert 15.

Beyond the Mat ★★★¹/₂

Lifting the lid on the public bravura of professional wrestling in America and probing its humanity, comedy writer and first-time director Barry W. Blaustein has fashioned a funny, gruesome and compelling documentary. Whisking his camera into the fighters' homes, the promoters' offices and even the hospital, Blaustein gets a headlock on a sport commonly ridiculed by those who know nuttin'. The truth is that these professionals are actually a fraternity of losers, crack addicts and sadomasochists who rigorously promote the science of violence. Yet there's still plenty of humour here (as one might expect from Eddie Murphy's gag writer), albeit of a grisly nature. Fascinating. [*Ewen Brownrigg*]

● With Mick 'Mankind' Foley, Terry Funk, Jake 'The Snake' Roberts, The Rock, Chyna, Vince McMahon, Darren Drozdov, Roland Alexander, Tony Jones, Mike Modest, Vicki Funk, Stacey Funk, Brandee Funk, Jesse Ventura, etc
● *Dir and narrative written by* Barry W. Blaustein, *Pro* Blaustein, Brian Grazer, Ron Howard, Michael Rosenberg and Barry Bloom, *Co-Pro* Debra Marie Simon, *Ph* Michael Grady, *Ed* Jeff Werner, *M* Nathan Barr.

Universal-UIP.
103 mins. USA. 1999. Rel: 30 June 2000. Cert 15.

Bicentennial Man ★★★¹/₂

California; 2005-2205. Robot number NDR-114 – aka 'Andrew' – was engineered to do the cooking, washing-up and any number of menial household chores. However, due to a blip in his neural pathways, Andrew has started to undergo extracurricular changes, enabling him to acquire such advanced complexities as curiosity, pleasure and even humiliation. Soon, the machine is being treated like a member of the family, a situation that merely feeds the robot's need to be human ... There are few things more touching than seeing a robot get in touch with its feelings. And to prove it the cinema has exploited the theme regularly over the decades (most recently in The Iron Giant). However, this is the first time that Robin Williams has played an android, so one can anticipate a sentimental twist. Reining in his more manic tendencies, Williams invests his machine with an affecting gentleness, contrasting effectively with the elaborate visuals (Oliver Platt's organic concoctions are particularly impressive). However, the story's ambitious structure – stretching over 200 years – works against the film, while the more interesting permutations of Isaac Asimov's original concept are mired in viewer-friendly bathos.

● *Andrew* Robin Williams, *Sir* Sam Neill, *Little Miss/Portia* Embeth Davidtz, *Rupert Burns* Oliver Platt, *Ma'am* Wendy Crewson, *Little Miss (as seven)* Hallie Kate Eisenberg, *Dennis Mansky* Stephen Root, *female president* Lynne Thigpen, *Lloyd* Bradley Whitford, *Galatea* Kiersten Warren, *Bill Feingold* John Michael Higgins, George D. Wallace, Quinn Smith, Kristy Connelly, Jay Johnston, Marcia Pizzo, Paula West.
● *Dir* Chris Columbus, *Pro* Wolfgang Petersen, Gail Katz, Laurence Mark, Neal Miller, Chris Columbus, Mark Radcliffe and Michael Barnathan, *Ex Pro* Dan Kolsrud, *Assoc Pro* Paula Dupre' Pesmen, *Screenplay* Nicholas Kazan, based on the short story by Isaac Asimov and the novel *The Positronic Man* by Asimov and Robert Silverberg, *Ph* Phil Meheux, *Pro Des* Norman Reynolds, *Ed* Neil Travis, *M* James Horner; Dvorak, Faure, Debussy, Haydn; 'Then You Look At Me' sung by Celine Dion, other songs performed by Bing Crosby and Aretha Franklin; *Costumes* Joseph G. Aulisi, *Sound* Randy Thom, *Visual effects* James E. Price, *Make-up effects* Greg Cannom.

Columbia Pictures/Touchstone Pictures/1492/Radiant Prods-Columbia TriStar.
128 mins. USA. 1999. Rel: 21 January 2000. Cert PG.

Big Daddy ★★★

New York City; today. The film's original title was better: *Guy Gets Kid*. Anyway, the guy is Sonny Koufax, a failed lawyer who has turned irresponsibility into an art form. Then a five-year-old boy is dumped on his doorstep and Sonny adopts him to impress his vacillating girlfriend. So Guy Loses Girl and has to learn that bed-wetting, projectile vomiting and sleep deprivation are not as fun as

Right: Like father, like son – Cole Sprouse and Adam Sandler face some bracing life lessons in Dennis Dugan's grotesque and drippy Big Daddy (from Columbia TriStar)

they may sound ... Much like child rearing itself, this extraordinarily popular film is at times grotesque and at others overwhelmingly drippy. On the one hand we have Sonny teaching his ward to trip up rollerbladers and play yo-yo with his phlegm and on the other he sacrifices everything for fatherhood. But there is something about Adam Sandler, a sort of slobbish Everyman with a rebellious lethargy, that lets him get away with such emotional trickery. The antithesis of Jim Carrey's hyped-up Crazy Guy, he is a sweet-toothed Bill Murray for the slacker generation, a goofball with ingrowing attitude. The worrying thing is that the more time you spend with him, the more you get to warm to the guy. Thankfully, the distinguished supporting cast plays it mercifully straight.

● *Sonny Koufax* Adam Sandler, *Layla Maloney* Joey Lauren Adams, *Kevin Gerrity* Jon Stewart, *Phil* Allen Covert, *delivery guy* Rob Schneider, *Arthur Brooks* Josh Mostel, *Julian* Cole Sprouse and Dylan Sprouse, *Corinne* Leslie Mann, *Vanessa* Kristy Swanson, *Mr Koufax* Joe Bologna, *singing kangaroo* Tim Herlihy, Peter Dante, Jonathan Loughran, Steve Buscemi, Edmund Lyndeck, Geoffrey Horn, Jacqueline Titone, Kelly Dugan, Jared Sandler, Jillian Sandler, Helen Lloyd Breed, Carmen deLavallade, Steve Brill, Jorge Buccio, Cole Hawkins, Michael Giarraputo.
● *Dir* Dennis Dugan, *Pro* Sid Ganis and Jack Giarraputo, *Ex Pro* Adam Sandler, Robert Simonds and Joseph M. Caracciolo, *Co-Pro* Alex Siskin, *Screenplay* Sandler, Tim Herlihy & Steve Franks, *Ph* Theo Van de Sande, *Pro Des* Perry Andelin Blake, *Ed* Jeff Gourson, *M* Teddy Castellucci; songs performed by The Pharcyde, Melanie C, Rufus Wainright, Eurythmics, Garbage, Everlast & The White Folx, Styx, Limp Bizkit, Tim Herlihy, Yvonne Elliman, Van Halen, Jorge Buccio, Big Audio Dynamite, Bruce Springsteen, Sheryl Crow, Shawn Mullins, Guns N' Roses, etc, *Costumes* Ellen Lutter.

Columbia/Out of the Blue Entertainment-Columbia TriStar. 93 mins. USA. 1999. Rel: 1 October 1999. Cert 12.

Big Momma's House ★★

Big Momma's house is currently under surveillance by FBI agents awaiting the arrival of her granddaughter, the ex-flame of a recently escaped convict. The cops believe that the girl, Sherry, is still in contact with the brutal bank robber and could lead the Feds to their man. Just then Big Momma leaves town, forcing Malcolm Turner, a master of disguise, to fill her considerable shoes (and brassiere) so as not to blow the plan… Playing on the lightweight appeal of Martin Lawrence and the memory of Eddie Murphy in *The Nutty Professor*, this scatological farce just doesn't get by. The miraculous prosthetic effects aside, the film has little to distinguish itself, while the plot is shamefully derivative (think *Stakeout* meets *Mrs Doubtfire*). Far-fetched, obvious and sketchily constructed, this Big Momma has its moments but you can see them coming a mile off. [*Ewen Brownrigg*]

● *Malcolm Turner* Martin Lawrence, *Sherry* Nia Long, *John* Paul Giamatti, *Trent* Jascha Washington, *Lester* Terrence Howard, *Nolan* Anthony Anderson, *Big Momma* Ella Mitchell, Carl Wright, Phyllis Applegate, Starletta DuPois, Jessie Mae Holmes, Nicole Prescott, Philip Tan, Ellis Hall.
● *Dir* Raja Gosnell, *Pro* David T. Friendly and Michael Green, *Ex Pro* Martin Lawrence, Jeffrey Kwatinetz, Rodney Liber and Arnon Milchan, *Co-Pro*

Peaches Davis, David W. Higgins and Aaron Ray, *Screenplay* Darryl Quarles and Don Rhymer, *Ph* Michael D. O'Shea, *Pro Des* Craig Stearns, *Ed* Bruce Green and Kent Beyda, *M* Richard Gibbs; songs performed by Da Brat & Vita and Destiny's Child, JD & Nas, Jagged Edge and Blaque, Dirty, Lil Jon & The Eastside Boyz, Kandi, Marc Nelson, Jessica, Otis Redding, Taj Mahal, The Pointer Sisters, B. Bumble & The Stingers, Willie Dixon, etc, *Costumes* Francine Jamison-Tanchuck, *Make-up effects* Greg Cannom.

Twentieth Century Fox/Regency Enterprises/David T. Friendly/Runteldat Entertainment-Fox.
98 mins. USA. 2000. Rel: 23 June 2000. Cert 12.

The Big Tease ★★★

Invited to participate in The World Freestyle Hairdressing Championship – the 'Platinum Scissors' – in Los Angeles, Glaswegian hairdresser Crawford Mackenzie aims to cut a swathe through the competition. Followed by a British TV crew, the stylist soaks up the glamorous lifestyle of Hollywood only to find out later that he has only been selected to attend the show, not to compete in it ... While employing a somewhat overworked format (most recently exploited by *Drop Dead Gorgeous, The Disappearance of Kevin Johnson* and *Man of the Year*), this Anglo-American mockumentary does have the advantage of an engagingly offbeat protagonist (a gay Scottish hairdresser for chrissakes) and a subject matter virtually ignored since *The Hairdresser's Husband* nine years ago. And while little advantage is taken of the fly-on-the-wall approach, Chris Langham is a joy as the lugubrious, disconcerted director/interviewer, a perfect foil for the outrageous antics of his subject. There are also some delightful cameos, especially from Larry Miller as the smarmy manager of the Century Plaza Hotel and Isabella Aitken as Crawford's doting mother. Previously known as *Je M'Appelle Crawford*.

● *Crawford Mackenzie* Craig Ferguson, *Candy Harper* Frances Fisher, *Martin Samuels* Chris Langham, *Stig Ludwiggssen* David Rasche, *Monique* Mary McCormack, *Eamonn* Donal Logue, *Mrs Beasie Mackenzie* Isabella Aitken, *Gareth Trundle* Kevin Allen, *Senator Warren Crockett* Charles Napier, *Dave London* Lawrence Young, *Dunston Cactus* Larry Miller, Francine York, Nina Seimaszko, Ted McGinley, Sara Gilbert, Emily Proctor, *and as themselves*: David Hasselhoff, Drew Carey, Cathy Lee Crosby, Bruce Jenner, Veronica Webb, Jose Eber.
● *Dir* Kevin Allen, *Pro* Philip Rose, *Ex Pro* Sacha Gervasi, Craig Ferguson and Kevin Allen, *Assoc Pro* M. Mark McNair and Cathy Schwartz, *Screenplay* Gervasi and Ferguson, *Ph* Seamus McGarvey, *Pro Des* Joseph Hodges, *Ed* Chris Peppe, *M* Mark Thomas; songs performed by Millie Small, High Jinx, Blondie, Loose Joints, Day One, Roy Budd, Queen, etc, *Costumes* Beth Rogers.

Crawford P. Inc./I Should Coco Films-Warner.
86 mins. UK/USA. 1999. Rel: 4 February 2000. Cert 15.

Billy's Hollywood Screen Kiss ★★★¹/₂

Billy is a photographer, film buff, all-round nice guy and, on the Kinsey homosexual scale, a perfect six. He is also unemployed and out-of-love and thus at the peak of his creative powers. His dream of producing a series of polaroids recreating famous Hollywood clinches is then financed by an old friend and the perfect male model materialises at the local coffee bar. All Billy needs now is a boyfriend ... Seasoning his romantic fable with polaroid stills, Hollywood-inspired fantasies and show-stopping musical numbers, first-time writer-director Tommy O'Haver has fashioned a fresh, original and sweet entertainment that is both irresistibly funny and touching. The filmmaker has also secured a winning performance from Sean P. Hayes as his alter ego, an engaging presence interesting enough not to be chicken fodder yet too handsome to be an auntie.

● *Billy* Sean P. Hayes, *Gabriel* Brad Rowe, *Perry* Richard Ganoung, *Georgiana* Meredith Scott Lynn, *Rex Webster* Paul Bartel, *Whitey* Matthew Ashford, *Holly* Holly Woodlawn, *Fernando* Armando Valdes-Kennedy, *Donna* Kimiko Gelman, *Gundy* Carmine D. Giovinazzo, *Mr Dan*, Chad Boardman, Rodney Chester, Eric Davenport, Les Borsay, Niles Jenson, Christopher Bradley, Mark Anderson, Annabelle Gurwitch, Bonnie Biehl, Jason-Shane Scott, Mark Conley.
● *Dir* and *Screenplay* Tommy O'Haver, *Pro* David Mosley, *Line Pro* Irene Turner, *Co-Pro* Meredith Scott Lynn and Irene Turner, *Assoc Pro* Marcus Hu, *Ph* Mark Mervis, *Pro Des* Franco-Giacomo Carbone, *Ed* Jeff Betancourt, *M* Alan Ari Lazar; songs performed by Parafin Jack Flash Ltd., Nina Simone, Xavier Cugat, Medeski Martin and Wood, Petula Clark, Ramsey Lewis, Tonya Kelly, etc, *Costumes* Julia Bartholomew, *Billy's artwork* Garen Hagobian.

Revolutionary Eye-Metro Tartan.
93 mins. USA. 1998. Rel: 9 July 1999. Cert 15.

The Blair Witch Project ★★

In October 1994 three student filmmakers – Heather, Mike and Joshua – disappeared in the woods near Burkittsville, Maryland, while shooting a documentary about the 200-year-old curse of the so-called Blair Witch. A year later, their footage was found, although there remained no trace of the students. The resultant video package reveals all – at least, it gives some pretty jolting affirmation to what might have happened ... As soon as cinemagoers caught on that this wasn't a real documentary (as if), the chill went out of the gimmick. Still, co-writer/directors Myrick and Sanchez get an A for effort for successfully putting the heebie-jeebies into their actors (aided by military techniques, sleep depri-

Right: Video camera obscura – Joshua Leonard in Daniel Myrick and Eduardo Sanchez's artless, gimmicky The Blair Witch Project *(from Pathé)*

vation and starvation) and for turning a $22,000 exercise into a $220+ million hit – that is, the most profitable film of all time. Yet, while the artlessness of the project is to be admired, such one-note jiggery-pokery cannot substitute the power of a skilful story, subtly spooky music and atmospheric photography.

● *Heather* Heather Donahue, *Michael* Michael Williams, *Joshua* Joshua Leonard, Bob Griffith, Jim King, Sandra Sanchez, Ed Swanson, Patricia Decou.
● *Dir, Screenplay and Ed* Daniel Myrick and Eduardo Sanchez, *Pro* Gregg Hale and Robin Cowie, *Ex Pro* Bob Eick and Kevin J. Foxe, *Co-Pro* Michael Monello, *Ph* Neal Fredericks, *Pro Des* Ben Rock, *M* Tony Cora.

Artisan Entertainment/Haxan Films-Pathe.
87 mins. USA. 1999. Rel: 22 October 1999. Cert 15.

Bleeder ★★★★

The cinema eye of Denmark's Nicolas Winding Refn is something special. His previous film, *Pusher*, gave an unflinching view of low-life Copenhagen, and that's equally true here, especially when *Bleeder* reaches a denouement as dramatic and bloody as the title might lead one to expect. But this new tale, that of a man anguished by his girlfriend's pregnancy because ours is no world into which to bring children, has substantially more to offer. As writer, Refn creates a touching and even tender relationship between the couple which makes it all the more harrowing when the man's violence erupts. Snatches of choral music carry a hint of religious drama in Bresson mode. That may not be intended, but *Bleeder* certainly marks out Refn as a director of note. [*Mansel Stimpson*]

● *Leo* Kim Bodnia, *Lenny* Mads Mikkelsen, *Louise* Rikke Louise Andersson, *Lea* Liv Corfixen, *Louis* Levino Jensen, *Kitjo* Zlatko Buric, *Joe* Claus Flüggare.
● *Dir* and *Screenplay* Nicolas Winding Refn, *Pro* Winding Refn, Henrik Danstrup and Thomas Falck, *Line Pro* Christel C.D. Hansen, *Ph* Morten Syborg, *Pro Des* Peter de Neergaard, *Ed* Anne Østerud, *M* Peter Peter, *Costumes* Loa Miller, *Sound* Svenn Jakobsen.

Akamikaze/Scanbox Denmark/TV2 Denmark/Zentropa Entertainment/TempoMedia-Metrodome.
97 mins. Denmark. 1999. Rel: 24 March 2000. Cert 18.

Blue Streak ★★★

A master safecracker, Miles Logan engineers an ingenious theft of a $17 million diamond when he is double-crossed by his partner. However, before he is rounded up by police, Miles hides the precious stone in an air vent. Then, following two years behind bars, Miles discovers that his secret hiding place is now slap bang in the middle of the robbery and homicide division of the LAPD. So, with the aid of a fake badge, forged papers and a whole lotta chutzpah, Miles passes himself off as a cop ... Much of one's enjoyment – or lack thereof – of this star vehicle depends on whether or not one finds Martin Lawrence funny. As it is, Lawrence provides his usual wide-eyed routines, silly walks and so on, while being served by some extremely slick production values and a clever premise. Otherwise this is pretty routine stuff – albeit executed with some brio.

● *Miles Logan* Martin Lawrence, *Det. Carlson* Luke Wilson, *Deacon* Peter Greene, *Tulley* Dave Chappelle,

Melissa Green Nicole Ari Parker, *Captain Rizzo* Graham Beckel, *Glenfiddish* Robert Miranda, *Det. Hardcastle* William Forsythe, Olek Krupa, Saverio Guerra, Richard C. Sarafian, Tamala Jones, Julio Oscar Mechoso, Steve Rankin, Carmen Argenziano, Frank Medrano, Googy Gress, Jane Carr, J. Kenneth Campbell.
● *Dir* Les Mayfield, *Pro* Toby Jaffe and Neal H. Moritz, *Ex Pro* Daniel Melnick and Allen Shapiro, *Co-Pro* Michael Fottrell and Peaches Davis, *Screenplay* Michael Berry & John Blumenthal and Steve Carpenter, *Ph* David Egby, *Pro Des* Bill Brzeski, *Ed* Michael Tronick, *M* Edward Shearmur; songs performed by Jay-Z, Tyrese and Heavy D, Rehab, Plush, Jungle Brothers, TQ and Krayzie Bone, etc, *Costumes* Denise Wingate.

Global Entertainment/Columbia/IndieProd-Columbia TriStar. 94 mins. USA. 1999. Rel: 26 December 1999. Cert 12.

Body Shots ★¹/₂

Los Angeles; the present. A group of eight twentysomething men and women converge for an evening of clubbing, drinking and loving, when an act of sexual indiscretion threatens to transform their lives forever… The trouble with *Body Shots* is that it wants to have its cocktail and drink it. At once a serious contemplation on the pitfalls of heavy drinking and promiscuity, it also attempts to be a glossy Brat Package with actors too attractive to be true. Of course, it succeeds as neither. Borrowing its multi-perspective viewpoint from *Rashomon* and any number of movies since, it ends up being both derivative and shallow. It's also narcissistic to the point of being offensive. [*Charles Bacon*]

● *Rick Hamilton* Sean Patrick Flanery, *Michael Penorisi* Jerry O'Connell, *Jane Bannister* Amanda Peet, *Sara Olswang* Tara Reid, *Trent* Ron Livingston, *Whitney Bryant* Emily Procter, *Shawn Denigan* Brad Rowe, *Emma Cooper* Sybil Temchen, Edmond Genest, Larry Joshua, Elizabeth Liebel, Adina Porter, Wendy Schenker, Nick Spano.
● *Dir* Michael Cristofer, *Pro* Jennifer Keohane and Harry Colomby, *Ex Pro* Michael Keaton, and Guy Riedel, Michael De Luca and Lynn Harris, *Screenplay* David McKenna, *Ph* Rodrigo Garcia, *Pro Des* David J. Bomba, *Ed* Eric Sears, *M* Mark Isham; songs performed by Mike Figgis, Jon B, Buddy Guy, Courtney Pine, Mark Isham, Apollo Four Forty, Moby, DJ Rap, Propellerheads, The Cardigans, Morcheeba, Me'Shell Ndegéocello, Joe 90, etc, *Costumes* Carolyn Leigh Greco.

New Line Cinema/Colomby/Keaton-Entertainment. 105 mins. USA. 1999. Rel: 18 February 2000. Cert 18.

Boiler Room ★★★★

Long Island/Queens, New York; the recent past. Noting that Microsoft secretaries have stock options worth millions, 19-year-old college drop-out Seth Davis has

resolved to nail his own personal fortune. Tipped off about a small brokerage firm that guarantees to make its stock-jocks millionaires within their first three years, Davis quickly adapts to the high-pressured life of flogging dubious shares to unsuspecting buyers. But, surrounded by sharp suits, yellow Ferraris and useless luxury toys, Davis makes the fatal mistake of questioning the morality of his new trade ... Marking a dynamic feature debut for writer-director Ben Younger (a former corporate video cameraman and 'boiler room' recruit), this is one slick, adrenaline-pumping morality tale. Displaying a keen satirical edge and a canny ear for its subject's jargon (an education in itself), the film never strays far from the reality behind its own hyped-up prospectus. Both seductive and disturbing, it spotlights a world that is altogether too familiar from the sensation of recent headlines.

● *Seth Davis* Giovanni Ribisi, *Chris* Vin Diesel, *Abby Halperin* Nia Long, *Greg* Nicky Katt, *Richie* Scott Caan, *Jim Young* Ben Affleck, *Marty Davis, Seth's father* Ron Rifkin, *Adam* Jamie Kennedy, *Harry Reynard* Taylor Nichols, *Agent Drew* Bill Sage, *Michael* Tom Everett Scott, *Seth's mother* Donna Mitchell, David Younger, André Vippolis, Jon Abrahams, Peter Maloney, Alex Webb, Taylor Patterson, Michael McCarthy, Marsha Dietlein, Siobhan Fallon.
● *Dir* and *Screenplay* Ben Younger, *Pro* Suzanne Todd and Jennifer Todd, *Ex Pro* Claire Rudnick Polstein and Richard Brener, *Co-Pro* E. Bennett Walsh, *Ph* Enrique Chediak, *Pro Des* Anne Stuhler, *Ed* Chris Peppe, *M*

Above: Cop 'n' robber – Martin Lawrence as reluctant hero in Les Mayfield's slick but routine Blue Streak *(from Columbia TriStar)*

Above: *Hollywood shuffle – Steve Martin and Eddie Murphy bend the rules in Frank Oz's rather obvious* Bowfinger *(from UIP)*

● *Lincoln Rhyme* Denzel Washington, *Amelia Donaghy* Angelina Jolie, *Thelma* Queen Latifah, *Captain Howard Cheney* Michael Rooker, *Det. Kenny Solomon* Mike McGlone, *Eddie Ortiz* Luis Guzman, *Richard Thompson* Leland Orser, *Dr Barry Lehman* John Benjamin Hickey, *Det. Paulie Sellitto* Ed O'Neill, Bobby Cannavale, Olivia Birkeland, Gary Swanson, Zena Grey, Yashmin Daviault.
● *Dir* Phillip Noyce, *Pro* Martin Bregman, Louis A. Stroller and Michael Bregman, *Ex Pro* Michael Klawitter and Dan Jinks, *Assoc Pro* Bo Dietl, *Screenplay* Jeremy Iacone, *Ph* Dean Semler, *Pro Des* Nigel Phelps, *Ed* William Hoy, *M* Craig Armstrong; songs performed by Gaïnde, Mitsou, Craig Armstrong, Joseph Arthur, and Peter Gabriel and Kate Bush, *Costumes* Odette Gadoury.

Columbia Pictures/Universal.
118 mins. USA. 1999. Rel: 14 January 2000. Cert 15.

Bowfinger ★★

Los Angeles; today. Bobby Bowfinger may be a lousy movie director, but he has tenacity. When Kit Ramsey, the ideal star of his next project, *Chubby Rain*, chucks the screenplay out of his limo window, Bowfinger has an idea. He'll go ahead and use Ramsey anyway, but without his knowledge ... This is a great idea for a movie (to add to the stream of movies about movies) but is undone by lousy direction. There is also some terrific dialogue here ('we're going to make a movie here, not a film!', 'I may be from Ohio, but I'm not from Ohio'), but this, too, is undone by lousy direction. Wouldn't it have been a wonderful gag if Steve Martin, while playing a lousy director, directed himself in his wonderful script? As it is, Frank Oz goes for the obvious laughs and bleeds Martin's premise dry. So, it's time to watch *Living in Oblivion* again.

The Angel; songs performed by Rakim, James Brown, Chief Rocker Busy Bee, De la Soul, Lords of the Underground, The Angel, Tricky, Brand Nubian, Pharoahe Monch, 50 Cents, etc, *Costumes* Julia Caston.

New Line Cinema/Team Todd-Entertainment.
119 mins. USA. 2000. Rel: 5 May 2000. Cert 15.

The Bone Collector ★★★★

New York; the present. Even though he has only the use of his head, one shoulder and two fingers, forensic mastermind Lincoln Rhyme is an invaluable asset to the NYPD. When a ballsy rookie cop – Amelia Donaghy – shows some initiative at the scene of a horrific murder, Lincoln insists that she collaborate with him on the case. It's an odd partnership, but great minds can even circumvent the drawbacks of physical paralysis ... As serial killer thrillers go, this is one of the most suspenseful, visceral and inventive you are likely to find. As an update of the *Rear Window* scenario (in which a paraplegic tracks the killer with just the powers of his observation and intuition), it is both ingenious and inspired. With the added bonus of some terrific location work (deserted pockets of ancient New York) and above-average performances, the film engages on a number of levels. Some may find the murders themselves too sick to stomach, and the ending is a little nonsensical (how does a train's serial number and Lincoln's badge number lead Amelia to her conclusions?), but these are minor quibbles. Be afraid.

● *Bobby Bowfinger* Steve Martin, *Kit Ramsey/Jiff Ramsey* Eddie Murphy, *Daisy* Heather Graham, *Carol* Christine Baranski, *Dave* Jamie Kennedy, *Kit's agent* Barry Newman, *Afrim* Adam Alexi-Malle, *Slater* Kohl Sudduth, *Terry Stricter* Terence Stamp, *Jerry Renfro* Robert Downey Jr., Alejandro Patino, Alfred De Contreras, Ramiro Fabian, Claude Brooks, Nevin Scannell, John Prosky.
● *Dir* Frank Oz, *Pro* Brian Grazer, *Ex Pro* Karen Kehela and Bernie Williams, *Screenplay* Steve Martin, *Ph* Ueli Steiger, *Pro Des* Jackson Degovia, *Ed* Richard Pearson, *M* David Newman; songs performed by Johnny Adams, Marvin Gaye, Daniel May, Quincy Jones, Perry Como, James Brown, Michael McGregor, Average White Band, Johnny Rivers, Bus Stop and Carl Douglas, etc, *Costumes* Joseph G. Aulisi.

Universal/Imagine Entertainment-UIP.
97 mins. USA. 1999. Rel: 22 October 1999. Cert 12.

Boys Don't Cry ★★★★½

Lincoln/Falls City; Nebraska; 1993. Brandon Teena may have small hands and an ingenuous manner, but he's determined to prove himself as one of the boys. On the run from the law for petty larceny, he stands up for himself with his fists, knocks back his share of beer and has a winning way with the girls. But Brandon has a terrible secret – he is actually a girl ... An articulate cry against myopic bigotry, *Boys Don't Cry* succeeds on so many levels that it's close to a cinematic miracle. At once tender and brutal, stylish and credible, the film – which is based on a true story – heralds a major new talent in first-time director Kimberly Peirce, a former photographer and journalist who wrote this script for her graduate thesis. The power of the piece is that it presents Brandon's ruthless detractors as real people. John Lotter, although prone to irrational impulses and a fondness for beer, is a devoted father with beautiful eyes, while Lana's mother is a fun-loving woman with a strong hospitable streak. But it's the performance of Hilary Swank – until now best known as the high-kicking star of *The Next Karate Kid* – that really distinguishes this extraordinary film. The actress immerses herself so deeply in the part of Brandon that it's a recurring shock whenever she discloses her true biology.

● *Brandon Teena/Teena Brandon* Hilary Swank, *Lana Tisdel* Chloë Sevigny, *John Lotter* Peter Sarsgaard, *Thomas Nissen* Brendan Sexton III, *Kate* Alison Folland, *Candace* Alicia Goranson, *Lonny* Matt McGrath, *Brian* Rob Campbell, *Lana's mom* Jeannetta Arnette, *Nicole* Cheyenne Rushing, Robert Prentiss, Stephanie Sechrist, Lisa Wilson.
● *Dir* Kimberly Peirce, *Pro* Jeffrey Sharp, John Hart, Eva Kolodner and Christine Vachon, *Ex Pro* Pamela Koffler, Jonathan Sehring, Caroline Kaplan and John Sloss, *Co-Pro* Morton Swinsky, *Assoc Pro* Bradford Simpson, *Line Pro* Jill Footlick, *Screenplay* Peirce and Andy Bienen, *Ph* Jim Denault, *Pro Des* Michael Shaw, *Ed* Lee Percy and Tracy Granger, *M* Nathan Larsen; songs performed by The Cars, The Dictators, Butthole Surfers, Nathan Larsen and Nina Persson, Chloë Sevigny, Bobby Fuller, The Isley Brothers, Quicksilver Messenger Service, Roky Erickson, Ed Hall, X, The Charlatans, Opal, Lynyrd Skynyrd, George McCrae, and Timmy Thomas, *Costumes* Victoria Farrell.

Fox Searchlight/The Independent Film Channel/Killer Films/Hart-Sharp Entertainment/Sundance Institute-Fox. 118 mins. USA. 1999. Rel: 7 April 2000. Cert 18.

Boys On the Beach – Le ciel, les oiseaux...et ta mere! ★

Paris/Biarritz; today. With the winnings from their prize-winning but phony student movie, the ethnically diverse quartet of Christophe, Stephane, Yucef and Mike head to the coastal resort of Biarritz. There, after quickly running out of funds, they attempt to score with the local babes ... Smugly doffing his baseball cap to the guerrilla filmmaking style of Mathieu Kassovitz, 21-year-old director Djamel Bensalah has dashed off a film that's virtually unwatchable in its amateurishness. Over-written and poorly made, the film presupposes that an audience could endure 90 minutes with such unpleasant, unrefined and witless losers. Lacking both the canny observation of Eric Rohmer and the hard-hitting authenticity of Kassovitz himself, *Boys On the Beach* is crude, cacophonous and bereft of any shred of credibility. US title: *Homeboys On the Beach*. Translation of French title: *The Sky, the Birds and...Yo' Mamma!*

● *Youssef* Jamel Debbouze, *Stéphane* Stéphane Soo Mongo, *Christophe* Lorant Deutsch, *Mike* Julien Courbey, *Lydie* Olivia Bonamy, *Christelle* Mariù Roversi, *Dora* Jessica Beudaert, *Lea* Julia Vaidis-Bogard, *headmaster* Jean-Louis Livi.
● *Dir* Djamel Bensalah, *Pro* Didier Creste, Yann Gilbert, Joel Leydendecker and Nicolas Vannier, *Ex Pro* Yann Gilbert and Pierre-Francois Racine, *Line Pro* Patrice Arrat, *Screenplay* Bensalah and Gilles Laurent, *Ph* Martin Legrand, *Pro Des* Gerard Marcireau, *Ed* Fabrice Rouaud, *M* Enfaz; Tchaikovsky, Beethoven; songs performed by Luis Mariano, Shazz, Rachid Taha, Enfaz, etc, *Costumes* Thierry Delettre.

Extravaganza & Orly Films/Sédif/France 2 Cinéma/sofica Sofinergie 4/Canal Plus, etc-Gala. 90 mins. France. 1998. Rel: 22 October 1999. Cert 15.

Bringing Out the Dead ★★★

New York City; the graveyard shift, the early 1990s. For over-worked paramedic Frank Pierce things ain't what they used to be. 'Why is everything a cardiac arrest?' he asks. 'What happened to chest pains, trouble with breathing?' For Frank, saving somebody's life is the best drug in the world – like falling in love. Yet lately his job has become less about saving lives than just showing up at the scene; in short, he has become a 'grief mop'. But who will grieve for his soul? Returning to the gritty, dirty, violent streets of his beloved New York, Martin Scorsese eases back into the type of film he does so well. Here, he mainlines into the ghosts of paramedic Nicolas Cage and shows what a haunting, nasty world the Emergency Medical Service is. Suffusing Manhattan with an otherworldly pallor, Scorsese gradually transfers Frank's paranoia onto the viewer as the sheer hopelessness of the death count takes its spiritual toll. Performances, photography, writing are all top notch, but do we really want to whiff these distempered streets again? FYI: Technical advisor Joe Connelly, on whose novel this is based, spent ten years in the EMS.

● *Frank Pierce* Nicolas Cage, *Mary Burke* Patricia Arquette, *Larry* John Goodman, *Marcus* Ving Rhames, *Tom Walls* Tom Sizemore, *Noel* Marc Anthony, *Nurse Constance* Mary Kay Place, *Cy Coates* Cliff Curtis, *Dr Hazmat* Nestor Serrano, *Nurse Crupp*

Above: *Medic care – Nicolas Cage bares his heart in Martin Scorsese's gritty, atmospheric* Bringing Out the Dead *(from Buena Vista)*

Aida Turturro, *Kanita* Sonja Sohn, *Rosa* Cynthia Roman, *Captain Barney* Arthur Nascarella, Afemo Omilami, Cullen Oliver Johnson, Julyana Soelistyo, and the voices of Martin Scorsese and Queen Latifah.
● *Dir* Martin Scorsese, *Pro* Scott Rudin and Barbara De Fina, *Ex Pro* Adam Schroeder and Bruce S. Pustin, *Screenplay* Paul Schrader, *Ph* Robert Richardson, *Pro Des* Dante Ferretti, *Ed* Thelma Schoonmaker, *M* Elmer Bernstein; Stravinsky; songs performed by Van Morrison, Johnny Thunders, Frank Sinatra, The Who, REM, Marc Anthony, The Marvelettes, Jane's Addiction, 10,000 Maniacs, Martha Reeves & The Vandellas, Burning Spear, The Melodians, The Cellos, Big Brother & The Holding Company, UB40, and The Clash, *Costumes* Rita Ryack.

Touchstone Pictures/Paramount-Buena Vista.
121 mins. USA. 1999. Rel: 7 January 2000. Cert 18.

Brokedown Palace ★¹/₂

Ohio/Thailand; the present. Alice and Darlene, who have been best friends all their lives, decide to take a ten-day trip to Bangkok before settling down to further education and adult responsibility. There, they befriend a hunky Australian who invites them to Hong Kong for a couple of days and even pays their air fare. But at the airport they are stopped by police and two kilos of heroin is discovered in Alice's backpack ... There's nothing like having a young, good-looking American thrown into a Third World jail to get the ire pumping (see *Midnight Express*, *Red Corner*, *Return to Paradise*, etc). Now it's the turn of babes behind bars, complete with music video clips of Thailand, gushing female vocals on the soundtrack and lots of giggling and winning looks to show how happy and innocent these gels really are. As an examination of the appalling injustice of the Thai legal system and the unconscionable living conditions of its victims, this soft-focus melodrama should really grip the core readership of *Just Seventeen*. The sad thing is that both Claire Danes and Kate Beckinsale are deserving of so much better material.

● *Alice Marano* Claire Danes, *Darlene Davis* Kate Beckinsale, *Hank Greene* Bill Pullman, *Yon Greene* Jacqueline Kim, *Roy Knox* Lou Diamond Phillips, *Nick Parks* Daniel Lapaine, *Doug Davis* Tom Amandes, *Chief Detective Jagkrit* Kay Tong Lim, *Jamaican prisoner* Bahni Turpin, Aimee Graham, John Doe, Beulah Quo, Henry O, Amanda De Cadenet, Indhira Charoenpura, Somsuda Chotikasupa, Maya Elise Goodwin, Chad Todhunter, M. Tom Visvachat, Harry E. Northup.
● *Dir* Jonathan Kaplan, *Pro* Adam Fields, *Ex Pro* A. Kitman Ho, *Screenplay* David Arata, from a story by Fields and Arata, *Ph* Newton Thomas Sigel, *Pro Des* James Newport, *Ed* Curtiss Clayton, *M* David Newman; Chopin; songs performed by Delerium, Audioweb, Joi, Solar Twins, Moist, Tricky, Hummie Mann, Asian Dub Foundation, Sarah Brightman, Brother Sun Sister Moon, P.J. Harvey, etc, *Costumes* April Ferry.

Fox 2000 Pictures-Fox.
100 mins. USA. 1999. Rel: 19 November 1999. Cert 12.

Broken Vessels ★★★

It was a cruel twist of fate when this 1998 drama about the seamy side of life in LA as experienced by two paramedics reached London after having been overtaken by Martin Scorsese's superior portrayal of comparable conditions in New York (*Bringing Out the Dead*). But, although it centres on a new recruit, Tom, and on another ambulance driver who influences him dangerously, Jimmy, their story is mainly concerned with a dark descent into drug-taking and crime. It's well played and often able, but *Broken Vessels* has nothing new to say, and it quite lacks the freshness that *Trainspotting* had in its day. An elderly victim of drugs played by Patrick Cranshaw provides the most memorable moments, but we have been here before, and more than once. [*Mansel Stimpson*]

● *Jimmy Warzniak* Todd Field, *Tom Meyer* Jason London, *Elizabeth Capalino* Roxana Zal, *Susy* Susan Traylor, *Mr Chen* James Hong, *Gramps* Patrick Cranshaw, Brent Fraser, Stephanie Feury, David Nelson, William Smith, David Baer, Al Israel, John McMahon, Ron Jeremy, Marcia Gray.
● *Dir* Scott Ziehl, *Pro* Roxana Zal and Scott Ziehl, *Co-Pro* David Baer, Robyn Knoll and Todd Field, *Assoc Pro* Vidette Schine and John Sjogren, *Screenplay* David Baer and John McMahon, *Ph* Antonio Calvache, *Pro Des* Rodrigo Castillo, *Ed* David Moritz and Chris Figler, *M* Bill Laswell, Martin Blasick and Brent David Fraser, *Costumes* Roseanne Fiedler, *Sound* Clive Taylor.

Unapix and Zeitgeist Films/Ziehl and Zal-Feature Film Co. 91 mins. USA. 1999. Rel: 2 June 2000. Cert 18.

Brother – Brat ★★★¹⁄₂

Russia's Alexei Balabanov, born in 1959, has had two features released in Britain this year. This one, made in 1997, tells of a youth arriving in St Petersburg and being sucked into the world of his criminal brother, an assassin for hire. A cult hit with young Russians, the appeal may be the contemporary view of themselves as obsessed with sex, drugs and trendy music, for the action, ably handled, dominates less than in most thrillers. For others, the film's indirect social comment (the city is seen as a source of corruption) is more memorable. Interesting though this is, it's the stylistically extraordinary *Of Freaks and Men* (qv) which for this reviewer proves Balabanov's quality. The seemingly iconic lead role is played by Sergei Bodrov, previously seen here in *Prisoner of the Mountains*. [*Mansel Stimpson*]

● *Danila Bagrov* Sergei Bodrov, *Vitia Bagrov, Danila's brother* Viktor Sukhorukov, *Sveta* Svetlana Pismichenko, *Ket* Maria Zhukova, *German* Yuri Kuznetsov, Vyacheslav Butusov, Irina Rakshina, Sergei Murzin, Igor Shibanov.
● *Dir* and *Screenplay* Alexei Balabanov, *Pro* Sergei Selyanov, *Ph* Sergei Astakhov, *Pro Des* Vladimir Kartashov, *Ed* Marina Lipartia, *M* Vyacheslav Butusov, *Costumes* Nadya Vasilyeva.

STV Film Company/State Cinema Committee of the Russian Federation-Kino Kino. 99 mins. Russia. 1997. Rel: 7 April 2000. Cert 15.

Brothers ★★★

This aims low and hits its target. The assumption behind Martin Dunkerton's first feature is related to the number of young British males who take Mediterranean holidays in quest of sun, booze and sex (but not necessarily in that order). By offering a fictional equivalent (Greece being his country of choice), he hopes to attract those who will compare their own experiences with those portrayed, and those who dream of such a holiday but have yet to go. It's not a notion to draw audiences into a cinema, but on video for a home night with the boys, and with beer to hand, it should be just the thing. Given the intention, the treatment is efficient and, if the film is as unsophisticated as they come, that's in keeping. The curious may like to know that Dunkerton's cast listing as 'nude director' is justified by what you see after the end credits. [*Mansel Stimpson*]

● *Matt Davidson aka 'Mystic Matey'* Justin Brett, *Chris Sullivan aka 'Beercan'* Daren Jacobs, *Julian Davidson aka 'The King'* Daniel Fredenburgh, *Anna Stefanos* Rebecca Cardinale, *Alex Webb aka 'Driftwood'* Nick Valentine, *Victor Newson aka 'Tarzan'* Fin Wild, *Joseph Richards aka 'Fats Joey'* Leigh Tapper, *Ben Urquhart aka 'Wildman'* Stephen Maggio, Ralph Saint-Rose, Jane Kemlo, Suzy Kewer, *naked film director* Martin Dunkerton.
● *Dir* Martin Dunkerton, *Pro* Martin Dunkerton and Joanna Garvin, *Ex Pro* Julian Dunkerton, *Screenplay* Martin Dunkerton and Nick Valentine, *Ph* Richard Terry, *Pro Des* Conrad Butlin, *Ed* John Grover, *M* Julian Stewart Lindsey; songs performed by Blur, Freeloader, Fatboy Slim, Pizzaman, N-Trance, Chumbawamba, Soundstation, The Harbingers, Moke, Gomera, Blue Adonis, Sash!, Sons of Shaft, etc.

Brothers Films-Paradise Films. 98 mins. UK. 1999. Rel: 23 June 2000. Cert 18.

Buena Vista Social Club ★★★★

Must-see documentary by Wim Wenders (and the most accessible work he has done in years) about a group of legendary Cuban musicians recording an album produced by Ry Cooder. Havana is at its disreputable best and the music gets in your blood and does a salsa. We hear the stories of the old times and see just how tough life can be in Cuba, but as long as they can play and sing, these wonderfully dignified guys are still living 'la vida loca'. It just goes to show that true musical ability doesn't fade in your golden years. *Buena Vista Social Club* is a celebration of musical maturity that culminates in a triumphant performance at Carnegie Hall. [*Barbie Wilde*]

● With Joachim Cooder, Ry Cooder, Ibrahim Ferrer, Juan de Marcos González, Rubén González, Pío Leyva, Manuel 'Puntillita' Licea, Orlando 'Cachaito' López, Manuel 'Guajiro' Mirabel, Eliades Ochoa, Omara Portuondo, Company Segundo, Barbarito Torres, Amadito Valdés.
● *Dir* Wim Wenders, *Pro* Ulrich Felsberg and Deepak Nayar, *Ex Pro* Felsberg, *Assoc Pro* Rosa Bosch, *Ph* Robby Müller, Lisa Rinzler and Jörg Widmer, *Ed* Brian Johnson.

Road Movies/Kintop Pictures/ARTE-Film Four. 104 mins. Germany. 1998. Rel: 17 September 1999. Cert U.

Right: Truth and consequences – the lovely Alessandra Martines in her husband Claude Lelouch's seductive Chance or Coincidence (from Gala)

The Carriers Are Waiting – Les Convoyeurs Attendent ★★★¹/₂

Benoît Mariage's idiosyncratic tragi-comedy features a family living in a town in rural Belgium. The father, a journalist, forces his 15-year-old son into a money-raising contest in which he is to challenge the world record for opening doors (40,000 times in 24 hours). If the father's obsession is comic, his manipulation of his son regardless of the stress caused makes the film increasingly dark-toned. Distantly echoing the early work of Mike Leigh, this is atmospheric, individual and well acted. But Mariage lets off the father too easily when providing an up-beat ending, and the tone of the film, photographed in black-and-white, will not appeal to all equally. However, you can't deny that the blend is quirkily different, even if sometimes uneasy. [*Mansel Stimpson*]

● *Roger Closset, the father* Benoît Poelvoorde, *Luise Closset* Morgane Simon, *Richard* Bouli Lanners, *Madeleine Closset, mother* Dominique Baeyens, *Felix* Philippe Grand'henry, *Michel* Jean-François Devigne, Lisa Lacroix, Edith Le Merdy, Patrick Audin.
● *Dir* and *Screenplay* Benoît Mariage, *Pro* Dominique Janne, *Ex Pro* K2, *Assoc Pro* Arlette Zylberberg, *Ph* Philippe Guilbert, *Pro Des* Chris Cornil, *Ed* Philippe Bourgueil, *M* Stéphane Huguenin and Yves Sanna, *Costumes* Anne Fournier.

K-Star/Canal Plus/K2/RTBF, etc-Artificial Eye. 94 mins. France/Belgium/Switzerland. 1999. Rel: 31 March 2000. Cert 15.

Chance or Coincidence – Hasards ou coincidences ★★★★¹/₂

Bruised by love, divorcee and former ballerina Myriam Lini is on holiday in Venice with her eight-year-old son, Serge. There she meets a charming art forger, Pierre, who has just painted her and Serge in a fake Soutine he is selling to a wealthy club owner in New York. Pierre is instantly convinced that he and Myriam are destined to become man and wife. Meanwhile, on a parallel path of coincidence, a futurologist and performance artist continues his quest for the ultimate truth ... Any film that starts with a documentary about polar bears, switches to a fascinating stage show that blurs the line between theatre and film, jumps to a mesmerising dance sequence that turns out to be a scene from an old movie and then segues to a domestic sequence in contemporary Venice can't be all bad. Fans of Claude Lelouch, a filmmaker who manipulates the possibilities of cinema to the full, will adore this playful, beautiful, profound, teasing, epic and ultimately poignant exercise in imagery and emotion. Add to this the sensual presence of Lelouch's beautiful and elegant dancer/actress wife (Martines) and you have an irresistible and seductive cinematic experience.

● *Myriam Lini* Alessandra Martines, *Pierre Turi* Pierre Arditi, *Marc Deschamps* Marc Hollogne, *Laurent* Laurent Hilaire, *Catherine Desvilles* Veronique Moreau, *Michel Bonhomme* Patrick Labbe, *Gerry* Geoffrey Holder, *Mauro Lini* Luigi Bonino, France Castel, Arthur Cheysson, Sophie Clement, Charles Gerard, Gaston Lepage, Vincenzo Martines.
● *Dir, Pro and Screenplay* Claude Lelouch, *Assoc Pro* Tania Zazulinsky, *Ph* Pierre-William Glenn, *Pro Des* Jacques Bufnoir, *Ed* Helene de Luze, *M* Francis Lai and Claude Bolling, *Costumes* Dominique Borg, *Choreography* Richard Wherlock.

Les Films 13/TF1 Films/UGC Images/Canal Plus, etc-Gala. 121 mins. France/Canada. 1998. Rel: 6 August 1999. Cert PG.

The Cherry Orchard ★

Russia; 1900. Representing different nostalgic ideals for those who have grown up with it, the cherry orchard of the Ranevsky estate is one of the finest in all of Russia. However, if the Ranevskys cannot meet their mounting debts, the orchard will have to be cut down to make way for holiday villas ... Pretty pictures, even of glorious cherry orchards in bloom, do not turn a stage play into a cinematic event. A Greek-French-Cypriot co-production of Anton Chekhov's Russian play featuring a cast of English, Welsh, Scottish, American and New Zealand performers, this *Cherry Orchard* is ripe for picking apart. Slow, ponderous and leaden, it misses all the comedy, farce and sly satire of the original by a mile (as Chekhov intended), leaving a work of thundering stasis that is as much a burden on the eyelids as it is on the buttocks. The omnipresent drone of Tchaikovsky – played by the celebrated pianist Vladimir Ashkenazy – only drags the film deeper into the mire.

● *Lyubov Andreyevna* Charlotte Rampling, *Gaev* Alan Bates, *Varya* Katrin Cartlidge, *Lopahin* Owen Teale, *Charlotta* Frances De La Tour, *Feers* Michael Gough, *Anya* Tushka Bergen, *Epihodov* Xander Berkeley, *Yasha* Gerard Butler, *Trofimov* Andrew Howard, *Dunyasha* Melanie Lynskey, *Pishchik* Ian McNeice, *Doridanov* Simeon Victorov.
● *Dir, Pro and Screenplay* Michael Cacoyannis, *Ex Pro* Yannoulla Wakefield and Alexander Metodiev, *Ph* Aris Stavrou, *Pro Des* Dionysis Fotopoulos, *Ed* Cacoyannis and Takis Hadzis, *M* Tchaikovsky.

Melanda Films/The Greek Film Centre/Amanda Prods/Films de l'Astre/Canal Plus/Eurimages-Melanda Film Prods.
141 mins. Greece/Cyprus/France. 1998. Rel: 11 February 2000. Cert PG.

Chicken Run ★★★¹/₂

Incarcerated in a high security chicken run, the poultry are getting restless. Yet, after repeated fowl-ups of their ingenious escape attempts, the chickens are becoming resolved to their fate. Until, that is, an American rooster flies into their midst ... Arguably one of the year's most unconventional movies, this extraordinary combination of claymation and high-octane thrills should delight children and adults alike. Brimful of the off-centre detail that made Nick Park's shorts *Creature Comforts* and *The Wrong Trousers* so endearing, *Chicken Run* manages to retain the individuality of its makers' personality while deferring to the demands of a Hollywood studio. Thus, there are plenty of visual references to such genre staples as *Raiders of the Lost Ark* and *The Colditz Story*, yet still enough eccentric charm to secure the loyalty of the Wallace and Gromit brigade. A splendid cast of British actors do comic wonders with Karey Kirkpatrick's witty script ('I've met some hard-boiled eggs in my time – but you're 20 minutes'), matched beak and claw by John Powell and Harry Gregson-William's affectionately allusive score. FYI: Due to the constraints of time, Mel Gibson literally 'phoned in' much of his performance from America.

● Voices: *Fletcher* Phil Daniels, *Mac* Lynn Ferguson, *Rocky* Mel Gibson, *Mr Tweedy* Tony Haygarth, *Babs* Jane Horrocks, *Mrs Tweedy* Miranda Richardson, *Ginger* Julia Sawalha, *Nick* Timothy Spall, *Bunty* Imelda Staunton, *Fowler* Benjamin Whitrow.
● *Dir* Peter Lord and Nick Park, *Pro* Lord, Park and David Sproxton, *Ex Pro* Jake Eberts, Jeffrey Katzenberg and Michael Rose, *Line Pro* Carla Shelley, *Screenplay* Karey Kirkpatrick, based on an original story by Lord and Park, *Ph* Dave Alex Riddett, *Pro Des* Phil Lewis, *Ed* Mark Solomon, *M* John Powell and Harry Gregson-Williams, *Animation* Loyd Price, *Model design* Jan Sanger.

DreamWorks/Aardman-Pathé.
80 mins. UK/USA. 2000. Rel: 30 June 2000. Cert U.

The Children of the Marshland – Les Enfants du Marais ★★★★¹/₂

The 1930s; France. In the marshlands of the Loire Valley, two men live off the spoils of the land, picking flowers, catching frogs and selecting Burgundy snails to sell off in the nearby town. For the most part it's an idyllic existence, even if Riton cannot afford to buy his crabby wife a hat and Garris constantly dreams of leaving. But do they know how good they have it? In the tradition of Bertrand Tavernier's *Sunday in the Country* and Yves Robert's *La Glorie de mon pere* and *Le Chateaude ma mere*, this celebration of the French countryside is an exquisite and reflective look at simpler times. Adapted from the novel by Georges Montforez, the film gleans its poetic power as much from the glorious widescreen photography as it does from the coexistent chorus of birdsong, insect hum and frog baritone. And there are some wonderful performances here, too, particularly from the incomparable Michel Serrault as a local self-made millionaire and André Dussollier as a hopelessly romantic, eager-to-please dandy. A genuine, nostalgic rhapsody.

● *Riton Pignolle* Jacques Villeret, *Garris* Jacques Gamblin, *Amedée* André Dussollier, *Hyacinth Pépé* Michel Serrault, *Marie* Isabelle Carré, *Jo Sardi* Eric Cantona, *old Cri-Cri* Suzanne Flon, *old man* Jacques Dufilho, *Mrs Mercier* Gisèle Casadesus, *Cri-Cri* Marlène Baffier, *Pierrot of the City* Romain Dreyfus, Philippe Magnan, Elisabeth Commelin, Jacques Boudet, Jenny Cleve, Julie Marboeuf, Jacques Challier.
● *Dir* Jean Becker, *Pro* Christian Fechner, *Ex Pro* Hervé Truffaut, *Ph* Jean-Marie Dreujou, *Pro Des* Thérèse Ripaud, *Ed* Jacques Witta, *M* Pierre Bachelet; 'West End Blues' performed by Louis Armstrong, *Costumes* Sylvie de Segonzac.

Films Christian Fechner/UGCF/France 2 Cinema/UGC Images/Canal Plus, etc-Gala.
115 mins. France. 1998. Rel: 26 November 1999. Cert PG.

Right: Apple squash – Charlize Theron in Lasse Hallström's reverential, misty-eyed The Cider House Rules (from Buena Vista)

Chill Factor ★★

Montana; the present. A lowly ice cream vendor and a diner employee are thrown together when they are forced to carry a deadly defoliant – dubbed 'Elvis' – 90 miles in an ice cream truck. Should Elvis thaw in the interim, it could wipe out everything within hundreds of miles. So it's particularly annoying that the reluctant couriers are being pursued by a gang of ruthless mercenaries... Capitalising on the streamlined concept of *Speed* and its pretenders, this buddy action-comedy lacks the style and oomph of the former and frequently loses its way. It's lucky then that Gooding Jr and Ulrich make such a palatable team, although they are introduced far too late in the action. Which leaves Peter Firth as the fanatical villain to dominate the proceedings, as only an English actor can. FYI: Gooding Jr and Ulrich previously appeared together in *As Good As It Gets*, although their scenes together ended up on the cutting room floor. [*Ewen Brownrigg*]

● *Arlo* Cuba Gooding Jr, *Tim Mason* Skeet Ulrich, *Captain Andrew Brynner* Peter Firth, *Dr Richard Long* David Paymer, *Vaughn* Hudson Leick, *Telstar* Kevin J. O'Connor, *Colonel Leo Vitelli* Daniel Hugh Kelly, *Dennis* Judson Mills, Jordan Mott, Dwayne Macopson, Jim Grimshaw, Suzi Bass.
● *Dir* Hugh Johnson, *Pro* James G. Robinson, *Ex Pro* Jonathan A. Zimbert and Bill Bannerman, *Co-Pro* Jeff Neuman and Martin Wiley, *Screenplay* Drew Gitlin and Mike Cheda, *Ph* David Gribble, *Pro Des* Jeremy Conway, *Ed* Pamela Power, *M* Hans Zimmer and John Powell, *Costumes* Deborah Everton.

Morgan Creek-Warner.
102 mins. USA. 1999. Rel: 23 June 2000. Cert 15.

The Cider House Rules ★★

Maine, New England; 1943. Brought up in an orphanage that performs humane but illegal abortions, Homer Wells has grown into an expert obstetrician. However, he seeks a world that plays by the rules and so turns his back on his own very real talent. Strangely, he finds greater comfort on a farm picking apples and pressing cider ... The trouble with writers adapting their own work to the screen is that they can bestow it with a reverence that suffocates the material. John Irving, whose eccentric novels *The World According to Garp* and *The Hotel New Hampshire* were adapted by others, succumbs to the curse here with his first screenplay. However, director Hallström does him no favours by embalming the whole thing in a quasi-sepia patina that gives the film all the excitement of looking at yellowed photographs of people you don't know. In addition, Rachel Portman's score (which sounds like half the theme of *Emma*), wraps it all up in a comfort blanket that promises profound and wonderful sleep. It's a miracle that such fine actors as Delroy Lindo and Michael Caine register at all.

● *Homer Wells* Tobey Maguire, *Candy Kendall* Charlize Theron, *Mr Rose* Delroy Lindo, *Wally Worthington* Paul Rudd, *Dr Wilbur Larch* Michael Caine, *Nurse Edna* Jane Alexander, *Nurse Angela* Kathy Baker, *Rose Rose* Erykah Badu *Buster* Kieran Culkin, *Olive Worthington* Kate Nelligan, *Jack* Evan Dexter Parke, *Fuzzy* Erik Per Sullivan, Heavy D, K. Todd Freeman, Paz De La Huerta, J.K. Simmons, Jimmy Flynn, Sky McCole-Bartusiak, Annie Corley, *stationmaster* John Irving.
● *Dir* Lasse Hallström, *Pro* Richard N. Gladstein, *Ex Pro* Bob Weinstein, Harvey Weinstein, Bobby Cohen and Meryl Poster, *Co-Pro* Alan C. Blomquist and Leslie Holleran, *Screenplay* John Irving, *Ph* Oliver Stapleton, *Pro Des* David Gropman, *Ed* Lisa Zeno Churgin, *M*

Rachel Portman; songs performed by Vaughn DeLeath, George Gershwin, Louis Armstrong, Tommy Dorsey, George Olsen, etc, *Costumes* Reneé Ehlrich Lalfus.

Miramax/FilmColony-Buena Vista.
125 mins. 1999. USA. Rel: 17 March 2000. Cert 12.

Circus ★★½

Brighton, England; the present. Leo Garfield is a happily married conman who decides to quit his life of crime after one last job. He has been hired to kill a rich man's wife for a tidy sum but after the act is double-crossed, framed and blackmailed by his client. Worse still, the dead woman turns out to be the girlfriend of a vicious gangster's most lethal henchman ... Oh, if only the Coen brothers had got hold of this script. Because what is the makings of a terrific plot is nudged, stretched and pummelled into the realms of cartoon lunacy. Part of the problem is the tone of the film. While the central characters are played relatively straight and sympathetically by John Hannah and Famke Janssen, everybody else turns up to deliver a stand-up routine of comic menace before something really nasty happens (like Christopher Biggins having his ear bitten off). The production values are slick, the locations fresh and the throwaway gags very funny (like the bleating of a sheep on an off-screen porn video), but the film's heights of caricature and log-jam of twists sour the brew.

● *Leo Garfield* John Hannah, *Lily Garfield* Famke Janssen, *Julius Harvey* Peter Stormare, *Bruno Maitland* Brian Conley, *George 'Moose' Marley* Tiny Lister, *Gloria* Amanda Donohoe, *Elmo Somerset* Fred Ward, *Troy Cabrara* Eddie Izzard, *Caspar Glit* Ian Burfield, *Roscoe* Neil Stuke, *Magnus* Michael Attwell, *Dom* Jason Watkins, Christopher Biggins, Lucy Akhurst, Louise Rolfe, Marcus Heath, Steve Toussaint.
● *Dir* Rob Walker, *Pro* Alan Latham and James Gibb, *Ex Pro* Alberto Ardissone, *Screenplay* David Logan, *Ph* Ben Seresin, *Pro Des* James Merifield, *Ed* Oral Norrie Ottey, *M* Simon Boswell, *Costumes* Anna Sheppard.

Columbia/Film Development Corp-Columbia TriStar.
96 mins. UK/USA. 2000. Rel: 5 May 2000. Cert 18.

The Clandestine Marriage ★

When the money ran out during the filming of this 18th century Hogarthian comedy, Nigel Hawthorne stepped in with his own cash. He could have spent his money more wisely. He stars in this tale of two families on the point of a merger by marriage, one with money but no class and the other with class but no money, along with Timothy Spall, Tom Hollander and Joan Collins, although debate continues as to whether it is her voice we hear. Romantic lead Paul Nicholls is too insipid to make us care and the disjointed direction by Christopher Miles (Sarah Miles' older brother) is infuriating, particularly during the woefully unfunny slapstick moments. [*Simon Rose*]

● *Lord Ogelby* Nigel Hawthorne, *Mrs Heidelberg* Joan Collins, *Sterling* Timothy Spall, *Sir John Ogelby* Tom Hollander, *Richard Lovewell* Paul Nicholls, *Fanny* Natasha Little, *Betsy* Emma Chambers, *Canton* Cyril Shaps, *Capstick* Mark Burns, *Brush* Ray Fearon, Timothy Bateson, Craster Pringle, Hugh Lloyd, Lara Harvey, Jenny Galloway, Philippa Stanton, Roger Hammond.
● *Dir* Christopher Miles, *Pro* Rod Gunner and Johnathan B. Stables, and Steve Clark Hall, *Ex Pro* Alan Howden and Tim Buxton, *Co-Pro* Andrew Warren, *Assoc Pro* Nigel Hawthorne and Joan Collins, *Screenplay* Trevor Bentham, *Ph* Denis Crossan, *Pro Des* Martin Childs, *Ed* George Akers, *M* Stanislas Syrewicz, *Costumes* Deirdre Clancy.

Portman Entertainment/BBC Films/British Screen-Universal.
91 mins. UK. 1999. Rel: 3 December 1999. Cert 15.

Les Convoyeurs Attendent
See The Carriers Are Waiting.

Cookie's Fortune ★★★★

Holly Springs, Mississippi; the present. They don't come much more eccentric than Jewel Mae 'Cookie' Orcutt. Sharing her ramshackle antebellum home with a hard-drinking black man, she puffs on a corncob pipe, refuses to answer the phone and talks incessantly about her late husband. Meanwhile, across town, her nieces Camille and Cora plot to win back the family fortune ... A return to form for Robert Altman (following the critically dismissed *Pret-a-Porter*, *Kansas City* and *The Gingerbread Man*), this is a gentle, affectionate and quirky Southern Gothic farce that is as beguiling in its charm as it is entertaining in its narrative. A wonderful cast of characters are played like movements in a symphony, with their respective motifs and melodic threads, with particularly attractive turns from Charles S. Dutton (as the good-natured, bourbon-swigging suspect), Liv Tyler (a no-nonsense waif), Chris O'Donnell (the latter's boyfriend, a gung-ho cop) and Patricia Neal (Cookie Orcutt) – but, hell, they're all good. Full marks, too, to Anne Rapp's richly human and witty script (which bears all the hallmarks of a well plotted play) and Kurita's atmospheric photography.

● *Camille Dixon* Glenn Close, *Cora Duvall* Julianne Moore, *Emma Duvall* Liv Tyler, *Jason Brown* Chris O'Donnell, *Willis Richland* Charles S. Dutton, *Jewel Mae 'Cookie' Orcutt* Patricia Neal, *Lester Boyle* Ned Beatty, *Otis Tucker* Courtney B. Vance, *Jack Palmer* Donald Moffatt, *Manny Hood* Lyle Lovett, Danny Darst, Matt Malloy, Randle Mell, Ruby Wilson.
● *Dir* Robert Altman, *Pro* Robert Altman and Etchie Stroh, *Ex Pro* Willi Baer, *Co-Pro* David Levy and James McLindon, *Screenplay* Anne Rapp, *Ph* Toyomichi Kurita, *Pro Des* Stephen Altman, *Ed* Abraham Lim, *M* David A. Stewart, *Costumes* Dona Granata.

Right: Misfortune cooking – Chris O'Donnell quizzes Julianne Moore in Robert Altman's gentle, affectionate and quirky Cookie's Fortune (from Alliance Atlantis)

October Films/Sandcastle 5/Elysian Dreams-Alliance Atlantis. 118 mins. USA. 1998. Rel: 20 August 1999. Cert 12.

Merchant Ivory-UIP. 123 mins. UK. 1999. Rel: 17 December 1999. Cert 15.

Cotton Mary ★★★¹/₂

Kerala, The Malabar Coast, India; 1954. The daughter of an English soldier and an Indian mother, Cotton Mary is proud of her British heritage. Working as a nurse at an English army hospital, she is delighted to help out when a *memsahib* is unable to breast-feed her premature baby. Taking matters into her own hands, Mary nurses the child back to health and is only too delighted when she is invited to the woman's home as a live-in nanny ... Following the disappointment of Ismail Merchant's last two forays into directing (*In Custody* and *The Proprietor*), *Cotton Mary* is a delightful surprise. Dominated by a spirited performance from Madhur Jaffrey (the actress-chef who originally introduced Merchant to his filmmaking partner James Ivory), the film is a rich, humorous and poignant look at the dilemma of Anglo-Indians trapped in a cultural vacuum in post-colonial India. FYI: Sakina Jaffrey, who plays Cotton Mary's hot-blooded, rebellious friend Rosie, is the daughter of Madhur Jaffrey.

● *Lily Macintosh* Greta Scacchi, *Cotton Mary* Madhur Jaffrey, *John Macintosh* James Wilby, *Rosie* Sakina Jaffrey, *Abraham* Prayag Raaj, *Theresa Macintosh* Laura Lumley, *Blossom* Neena Gupta, *Mrs Davids* Gemma Jones, *Mrs Smythe* Joanna David, *Mrs Evans* Sarah Badel, Riju Bajaj, Gerson Da Cunha, Mahabanoo Mody-Kotwal, Surekha Sikri, Nadira, Harshiya Rafiq, Ashok Koshy, Susan Malick.
● *Dir* Ismail Merchant, *Co-Dir* Madhur Jaffrey, *Pro* Nayeem Hafizka and Richard Hawley, *Ex Pro* Paul Bradley, *Screenplay* Alexandra Viets, *Ph* Pierre Lhomme, *Pro Des* Alison Riva, *Ed* John David Allen, *M* Richard Robbins and L. Subramaniam, *Costumes* Sheena Napier.

Cradle Will Rock ★★★

New York City; 1936-37. During the Great Depression, the Works Progress Administration was established to help combat America's terrible unemployment. Out of this evolved the Federal Theatre Project which, in turn, commissioned the production of an ambitious musical called *The Cradle Will Rock*, to be directed by Orson Welles. However, the show's extreme left-wing politics ruffled a number of governmental feathers and so a battle of bureaucratic red-tape and the freedom of artistic expression ensued ... Tim Robbins, who starred in Robert Altman's *The Player* and *Short Cuts*, made the most of his experience working with the master. His opening scene in this, his third movie as a director, recalls the magnificent curtain-raiser of *The Player* in which, in one continuous take, the camera swept across a parking lot, prowled down corridors and eavesdropped through windows. Indeed, *Cradle Will Rock*, like Paul Thomas Anderson's similarly mosaic *Magnolia*, is a giddy display of its director's skill. But for all its merits – elegant camerawork, fluid editing, vivid performances – the film fails to come together as a dramatic piece. This is partly due to the lack of a central sympathetic character and partly to a period of social upheaval that holds little resonance today. Furthermore, the central musical just isn't that good. FYI: A British production of the show was performed in 1997 at London's Battersea Arts Centre.

● *Marc Blitzein* Hank Azaria, *Diego Rivera* Ruben Blades, *Hazel Huffman* Joan Cusack, *Nelson Rockefeller* John Cusack, *John Houseman* Cary Elwes, *Gray Mathers* Philip Baker Hall, *Hallie Flanagan* Cherry Jones, *Orson Welles* Angus Macfadyen, *Tommy Crickshaw* Bill Murray, *Countess La Grange* Vanessa Redgrave, *Margherita Sarfatti* Susan Sarandon, *John Adair* Jamey Sheridan, *Aldo Silvano* John Turturro,

Left: *Travailing players – Barbara Sukowa and John Turturro in Tim Robbins' over-ambitious* Cradle Will Rock *(from Buena Vista)*

Olive Stanton Emily Watson, *Harry Hopkins* Bob Balaban, *Sid* Jack Black, *Carlo* Paul Giamatti, *Sophie Silvano* Barbara Sukowa, *Will Geer* Daniel Jenkins, *Canada Lee* Chris McKinney, *Donald O'Hara* Stephen Spinella, *William Randolph Hearst* John Carpenter, *Marion Davies* Gretchen Mol, *Chairman Martin Dies* Harris Yulin, *Bertold Brecht* Steven Skybell, *Frida Kahlo* Corina Katt, Kyle Gass, Barnard Hughes, Victoria Clark, Erin Hill, Timothy Jerome, Henry Stram, Adele Robbins, Brenda Pressley, David Costabile, Gil Robbins, Ned Bellamy, William Duell, Lynn Cohen, Dominic Chianese, Evan Katz, Spanky McHugh, Susan Heimbinder, Audra McDonald, Gilbert Cruz, Josie Whittlesey, Sandra Lindquist, Tamika Lamison, Leonardo Cimino, Tony Amendola.
● *Dir and Screenplay* Tim Robbins, *Pro* Robbins, Jon Kilik and Lydia Dean Pilcher, *Ex Pro* Louise Krakower, Frank Beacham and Allan Nicholls, *Ph* Jean Yves Escoffier, *Pro Des* Richard Hoover, *Ed* Geraldine Peroni, *M* David Robbins; Mozart, songs by Marc Blitzein, sung by Charles Carlisle, Billie Holiday, Eddie Vedder and Susan Sarandon, Polly Jean Harvey, Emily Watson, Audra McDonald, Erin Hill and Daniel Jenkins, Victoria Clark and Chris McKinney, Henry Stram and Timothy Jerome, etc, *Costumes* Ruth Myers.

Touchstone Pictures/Havoc-Buena Vista.
134 mins. USA. 1999. Rel: 21 April 2000. Cert 15.

The Cup – Phörpa ★★★¹/₂

India; 1998. In the foothills of the Himalayas, life goes on much as normal in a Tibetan monastery-in-exile. There, the monks attend their prayer meetings, tend their gardens and tend to concentrate on matters spiritual. However, the 14-year-old Orygen is more wrapped up in the final stages of the World Cup and has taken to sneak- ing out at night to watch the game on television. Finding the sport an inexplicable pastime (in which two nations fight over a ball), the monastery's tutor threatens Orgyen with expulsion should he wander off again. So Orgyen suggests screening the Final in the monastery itself ... Few films can boast as much authenticity as this unique pro- ject which was filmed in a real monastery with the com- plete co-operation of the residents. Not only that, but all monastic activity was suspended in order to facilitate the production, with members of the Chokling Monastery playing the characters in the film and learning their scenes on the spot. Furthermore, the film's star – Orgyen Tobgyal – is none other than an incarnate lama (who also acted as technical consultant), while his son, Jamyang Lodro, more or less plays himself. It is remarkable then that such an unlikely cinematic outfit has created such a funny, charming and beautifully under-stated film. Based on a true story, *The Cup* sheds a fascinating light on monastic life, dispelling many Western misconceptions of what goes on in such an establishment. FYI: The director is himself the revered reincarnation of a major Buddhist lama and the film the first feature-length production made in the Tibetan language.

● *Geko* Orgyen Tobgyal, *Orgyen* Jamyang Lodro, *Lodo* Neten Chokling, *Palden* Kunzang Nyima, *The Abbot* Lama Chonjor, *Old Lama* Godu Lama, *Tibetan layman* Thinley Nudi, Kunsang, Kunsang Nyima, Pema Tshundup.
● *Dir and Screenplay* Khyentse Norbu, *Pro* Malcolm Watson and Raymond Steiner, *Ex Pro* Hooman Majd and Jeremy Thomas, *Ph* Paul Warren, *Pro Des* Raymond Steiner, *Ed* John Scott, *M* Douglas Mills and Phillip Beazley, *Sound* Mark Blackwell.

Palm Pictures/Coffee Stain Prods-Alliance Releasing.
94 mins. Australia. 1999. Rel: 19 November 1999. Cert PG.

The Darkest Light ★★★¹/₂

The 'darkest light' – an incomprehensible explosion of light on the Yorkshire Dales – means different things to different people. To 11-year-old Catherine it promises the recovery of her leukaemia-stricken younger brother. To Uma, it is a Hindu goddess warning of a terrible plight. And to Uma's mother it could even signal a time of re-birth. Taking a raft of ideas and issues – race, faith, religion, culture, death, rural malaise, terminal illness – and setting them in the deceptively simple locale of a Yorkshire farm, scenarist and co-director Simon Beaufoy has created a fascinating commentary on contemporary Britain. While at times the film may seem out of date, such old concerns as the foot-and-mouth epidemic nestle neatly beside the current crisis facing farmers (BSB, declining food prices, escalating costs). But even without its metaphorical overtures and inconclusive philosophising, *The Darkest Light* is a handsome, touching and powerful film that is both strikingly unusual and superbly played.

● *Tom* Stephen Dillane, *Sue* Kerry Fox, *Catherine* Keri Arnold, *Uma* Kavita Sungha, *Matthew* Jason Walton, *Nisha* Nisha K. Nayar, *Father Mark* Nicholas Hope, *Dick* Rob Jarvis, Alvin Blossom, Kathryn Hunt, Isobel Raine, Emma Palmer, Romy Baskerville, Joanna Swain, Imran Ali, Clive Mantle.
● *Dirs* Bille Eltringham and Simon Beaufoy, *Pro* Mark Blaney, *Ex Pro* Andrea Calderwood, Alexis Lloyd and Barbara McKissack, *Screenplay* Beaufoy, *Ph* Mary Farbrother, *Pro Des* Chris Townsend, *Ed* Ewa J. Lind, *M* Adrian Johnston, *Costumes* Ffion Elinor.

Arts Council of England/Canal Plus/BBC Films/Yorkshire Media Production Agency/Footprint Films-Pathé.
94 mins. UK/France. 1999. Rel: 14 January 2000. Cert 12.

Darkness Falls ★¹/₂

The Isle of Man; the present. Having staked out the mansion of the attractive and wealthy Mark and Sally Driscoll, a shifty, anonymous figure makes his presence known. It transpires that the Driscolls have already met this man, John Barrat, and made more of an impression on him than he did on them. But tonight Barrat is determined that they will never forget him again ... For a stage play to take off on film requires a director of spectacular cinematic skill and Gerry Lively doesn't live up to his name. This static piece, liberally punctuated with cliché and unintentional laughs, is so boring that this reviewer fell asleep – only to be woken by other critics giggling uncontrollably. Poor Ray Winstone (so good in *Nil by Mouth*), who comes so close to giving an interesting performance but is defeated by a ludicrous and stodgy script. And two pointers, Gerry: *never* start a film with a pan over water (it's been done to death and invites drowsiness) and if you're going to get your leading lady to take her clothes off, why just show her feet?

● *Sally Driscoll* Sherilyn Fenn, *John Barret* Ray Winstone, *Mark Driscoll,* Tim Dutton, *Jane Barret* Robin McCaffrey, *Simpson* Oliver Tobias, *'Blue Eyes'* Michael Praed, *Mr Hayter* Brian Pringle, *Mrs Hayter* Anita Dobson.
● *Dir* Gerry Lively, *Pro* Alan Latham and Clifford Haydn Tovey, *Ex Pro* Alberto Ardissone and Kari Ardissone, *Line Pro* James Gibb, *Screenplay* John Howlett, from the play *Dangerous Obsession* by N.J. Crisp, *Ph* Adam Santelli, *Pro Des* Edward Thomas, *Ed* David Spiers, *M* Guy Farley, *Costumes* Ffion Elinor.

Film Development Corporation/The Isle of Man Film Commission/Vine International/Bloomsbury Films-Downtown.
91 mins. UK. 1998. Rel: 27 August 1999. Cert 15.

Deception ★★

Northern Michigan; mid-winter, the present. What if your prison cellmate talked non-stop for six months about the beautiful pen-pal he was going to bed? And what if, two days before his release, he is stabbed to death in a prison riot? Starved for affection, car thief Rudy Duncan takes on the identity of his dead friend, only to find that his new sweetheart's homicidal brother has some rather unsavoury plans for him ... This is the sort of idea that looks irresistible scribbled on the back of an envelope. But it's an impossible one to pull off and, here, with the standard quota of genre stereotypes, it just gets more ludicrous and improbable as the plot thickens. Still, director Frankenheimer makes the most of the film's picturesque locations (the snowy wastes of British Columbia) and moves the action along at an agreeable clip. US title: *Reindeer Games*.

● *Rudy Duncan* Ben Affleck, *Gabriel* Gary Sinise, *Ashley Mercer* Charlize Theron, *Jack Bangs* Dennis Farina, *Nick* James Frain, *Pug* Donal Logue, *Merlin* Clarence Williams III, *The Alamo* Dana Stubblefield, *Jumpy* Danny Trejo, Isaac Hayes, Gordon Tootoosis, Enuka Okuma, Robyn Driscoll, Lonny Chapman.
● *Dir* John Frankenheimer, *Pro* Marty Katz, Bob Weinstein and Chris Moore, *Ex Pro* Harvey Weinstein, Cary Granat and Andrew Rona, *Co-Pro* B. Casey Grant and Mark Indig, *Ph* Alan Caso, *Pro Des* Barbara Dunphy, *Ed* Tony Gibbs and Michael Kahn, *M* Alan Silvestri; songs performed by Dean Martin, Percy Faith, Ohio Players, Etta James, Brenda Lee, Stevie Wonder, etc, *Costumes* May Routh.

Miramax/Dimension Films-Buena Vista.
104 mins. USA. 2000. Rel: 23 June 2000. Cert 15.

Deep Blue Sea ★★★

Aquatica, a marine facility off the Mexican coast; today. Since its debut 400 million years ago, the shark has

evolved into the most efficient killing machine in nature's spectrum. When marine biologist Susan McAlester upgrades three makos' brain capacity in order to produce a protein that will inhibit degenerative brain disorders in humans, the creatures become a cataclysm waiting to happen ... Like a calculated blend of *The Poseidon Adventure*, *Jaws* and *Alien*, *Deep Blue Sea* sticks way too closely to its genre's formula which no amount of impressive digital effects can disguise. Unfortunately, the CGI visuals aren't even that convincing, while the size of the sharks varies wildly depending on which situation they are in. These carps aside, the film does have a ferocious intensity that clamps the heart muscles and features a number of genuine grisly surprises. It helps, too, that the mix of familiar faces and up-and-coming stars gives little clue as to who will end up as fish food next.

● *Dr Susan McAlester* Saffron Burrows, *Carter Blake* Thomas Jane, *Sherman 'Preacher' Dudley* LL Cool J, *Janice Higgins* Jacqueline McKenzie, *Tom Scoggins* Michael Rapaport, *Jim Whitlock* Stellan Skarsgard, *Russell Franklin* Samuel L. Jackson, *Brenda Kerns* Aida Turturro, and (*uncredited*) Ronny Cox.
● *Dir* Renny Harlin, *Pro* Akiva Goldsman, Tony Ludwig and Alan Riche, *Ex Pro* Duncan Henderson and Bruce Berman, *Co-Pro* Rebecca Spikings, *Screenplay* Duncan Kennedy and Donna Powers & Wayne Powers, *Ph* Stephen Windon, *Pro Des* William Sandell, *Ed* Frank

J. Urioste, Derek G. Brechin and Dallas S. Puett, *M* Trevor Rabin, *Costumes* Mark Bridges, *Visual effects* Jeffrey A. Okun, *Shark action* Walt Conti, *Special effects* John Richardson, *Underwater ph* Pete Romano.

Warner/Village Roadshow/Groucho III-Warner. 105 mins. USA. 1999. Rel: 15 October 1999. Cert 15.

Detroit Rock City ★★¹/₂

Cleveland/Detroit; 1978. In an era that fostered Sonny & Cher, The Carpenters and the Fonz, high school rebels Hawk, Lex, Jam and Trip worship the ground that KISS spit on. In fact, the glitter rock group (whose name some thought was an acronym for Knights In Satan's Service) exert such a hold on the unruly quartet, that they risk the wrath of both parents and teachers to see their idols in concert in Detroit. Then they lose their tickets ... Packing the same flashy energy of its subjects' idolatry, *Detroit Rock City* is raucous, irreverent and high-spirited good fun. While much of the humour is broader than Lake Huron, the general tone is so unpretentious that it's hard to knock it. P.S. The film features the most spectacular vomiting sequence committed to celluloid since *The Exorcist*.

● *Hawk* Edward Furlong, *Lex* Giuseppe Andrews, *Trip* James DeBello, *Jeremiah 'Jam' Bruce* Sam

Above: The Fin Man – Thomas Jane inspects his co-star in Renny Harlin's intense but formulaic Deep Blue Sea (from Warner)

Right: A scene from Adam Rifkin's irreverent and high-spirited Detroit Rock City *(from Entertainment)*

Huntington, KISS (Gene Simmons, Paul Stanley, Ace Frehley and Peter Criss), *Christine* Natasha Lyonne, *Mrs Bruce* Lin Shaye, *Beth Bumsteen* Melanie Lynskey, *MC* Ron Jeremy Hyatt, Miles Dougal, Nick Scotti, Emmanuelle Chriqui, David Gardner, Shannon Tweed, Joe Flaherty, Cody Jones, Matt Taylor, Chris Benson, Kevin Corrigan, Steve Schirripa.
● *Dir* Adam Rifkin, *Pro* Gene Simmons, Barry Levine and Kathleen Haase, *Ex Pro* Michael De Luca and Brian Witten, *Co-Pro* Art Schaefer, *Ph* John R. Leonetti, *Pro Des* Steve Hardie, *Ed* Mark Goldblatt and Peter Schink, *M* J. Peter Robinson; Tchaikovsky, Grieg, Carl Orff; songs performed by Marilyn Manson, KISS, Giuseppe Andrews, James DeBello, Edward Furlong and Sam Huntington, Ted Nugent, T-Rex, The James Gang, The Sweet, The Runaways, Thin Lizzy, Edgar Winter, Angel, Golden Earring, Black Sabbath, AC/DC, Electric Light Orchestra, Cheap Trick, Ramones, Santana, Hot Chocolate, David Bowie, Blue Oyster Cult, KC & The Sunshine Band, Ohio Players, Captain & Tenille, Styx, George McCrae, Nazareth, Van Halen, UFO, Everclear, etc, *Costumes* Rosanna Norton.

New Line Cinema/Takoma Entertainment/Base-12 Prods/Kissnation-Entertainment.
94 mins. USA. 1999. Rel: 22 October 1999. Cert 15.

Deuce Bigalow: Male Gigolo ★★★★

Deuce Bigelow is a poor'n'stupid'n'randy pool cleaner who house-sits for a wealthy gigolo (*The Mummy*'s Oded Fehr). When he breaks his host's exotic fish tank, there's only one way out: being a man whore pimped by T.J. who proclaims Deuce to be 'da best he-bitch in my man-stable' because he takes the women other escorts won't

touch: narcoleptics, Tourette's Syndromes, etc. The whole thing is crammed with lines like, 'don't make me he-bitch man-slap you,' but it works. The first project from Adam Sandler's production company knows how to get stupidity just right. A comedy which will make you laugh and question your IQ. *[Karen Krizanovich]*

● *Deuce Bigalow* Rob Schneider, *Det. Chuck Fowler* William Forsythe, *T.J. Hicks* Eddie Griffin, *Kate* Arija Bareikis, *Antoine Laconte* Oded Fehr, *Claire* Gail O'Grady, *Bob Bigalow* Richard Riehle, Jacqueline Obradors, Big Boy, Amy Poehler, Dina Platias, Allen Covert, Pilar Schneider.
● *Dir* Mike Mitchell, *Pro* Sid Ganis and Barry Bernardi, *Ex Pro* Adam Sandler and Jack Giarraputo, *Co-Pro* Alex Siskin and Harris Goldberg, *Screenplay* Harris Goldberg, Rob Schneider and Sid Ganis, *Ph* Peter Lyons Collister, *Pro Des* Alan Au, *Ed* George Bowers and Lawrence Jordan, *M* Teddy Castellucci; songs performed by Hepcat, Blondie, Wyclef Jean and The Refugee All-Stars, Bee Gees, Stereo MC's, Propellerheads, Hot Chocolate, Marvin Gaye, Smash Mouth, Sean Beal, 10CC, Jeff Lynne, etc, *Costumes* Molly Maginnis.

Touchstone Pictures/Happy Madison/Out of the Blue Entertainment-Buena Vista.
88 mins. USA. 1999. Rel: 26 May 2000. Cert 15.

Le Diner de Cons ★★★★

Every Wednesday evening a group of affluent friends hold a dinner party to which they each invite a new companion. And the more stupid the companion, the more fun they have at his or her

Left: Idiot's delight – Thierry Lhermitte rues the day he invited Jacques Villeret into his home, in Francis Veber's hilarious Le Diner de Cons (from Pathé)

expense. Alerted to a prize idiot by an accomplice, successful publisher Pierre Brochant invites the hapless victim to his apartment – for a pre-dinner drink – on the premise that he will issue a book of the latter's matchstick constructions. But when Pierre strains his back and his wife walks out on him, his guest unintentionally turns a critical turn of events into escalating catastrophe ... Unashamedly refusing to veer away from its theatrical origins, this dark, extremely well-constructed farce is a triumph of plot over logic. Thanks to a peerless turn from Thierry Lhermitte as the straight man and a hilarious exhibition from Jacques Villeret as the ingenuous, all too-human fool, this is the funniest film to cross the channel in aeons. Both absurd and ingenious, it gains a rare comic momentum that is all the more effective for its naturalistic mise en scene. Expect an American remake at the earliest possible opportunity. US title: *The Dinner Game.*

● *Pierre Brochant* Thierry Lhermitte, *Francois Pignon* Jacques Villeret, *LeBlanc* Francis Huster, *Christine* Alexandra Vandernoot, *Cheval* Daniel Prevost, *Marlene* Catherine Frot, *Dr Sorbier* Christian Pereira, Edgar Givry, Petronille Moss, Daniel Martin, Elvire Melliere.
● *Dir and Screenplay* Francis Veber, *Pro* Alain Poire, *Ph* Luciano Tovoli, *Pro Des* Philippe Desmoulins and Henri Brichetti, *Ed* Georges Klotz, *M* Vladimir Cosma, *Costumes* Jacqueline Bouchard.

Gaumont/Efve/TF1 Films/TPS Cinema-Pathe. 80 mins. France. 1998. Rel: 2 July 1999. Cert 15.

The Dinner Game
See Le Diner de Cons.

Disturbing Behavior ★¹/₂

Following the suicide of his brother in Chicago, Steve Clark moves with his family to the picturesque community of Cradle Bay. Here, far away from the urban chaos of his former home, Steve finds his new classmates devoted to their studies, cardigans and Barry Manilow. In fact, there is something almost unnatural about their good behaviour, a prognosis ignored by parents, professors and police ... Redolent of the 1975 classic *The Stepford Wives*, this derivative, hackneyed thriller misses a ballpark of satirical opportunities. And while attempting to cash in on the hip horror oeuvre kick-started by *Scream*, it lacks the former's knowing stance and dark wit. Bereft of subtlety, humour or logic, it merely underscores the disturbing behaviour of filmmakers in the market for a quick buck. [*Ewen Brownrigg*]

● *Steve Clark* James Marsden, *Rachel Wagner* Katie Holmes, *Gavin Strick* Nick Stahl, *Officer Cox* Steve Railsback, *Dr Caldicott* Bruce Greenwood, *Dorian Newberry* William Sadler, *U.V.* Chad E. Donella, *Allen Clark* Ethan Embry, Katherine Isabelle, Chris Owens, Terry David Mulligan, Susan Hogan, Stephen James Lang.
● *Dir* David Nutter, *Pro* Armyan Bernstein and Jon Shestack, *Ex Pro* C.O. Erickson and Phillip B. Goldfine, *Co-Pro* Scott Rosenberg and Elisabeth Seldes, *Screenplay* Rosenberg, *Ph* John S. Bartley, *Pro Des* Nelson Coates, *Ed* Randy Jon Morgan, *M* Mark Snow; songs performed by The Flys, Janus Stark, Addict, Skold, Hutt, Olivia Newton-John, Wayne Newton, Driver, Barry Manilow, Scarface and Rag Tag, etc, *Costumes* Trish Keating, *Sound* Stephen Hunter Flick.

MGM/Village Roadshow/Hoyts Film Partnership/Beacon Communications-Columbia TriStar. 83 mins. USA. 1998. Rel: 13 August 1999. Cert 15.

Dogma ★★★¹/₂

Having spent an eternity in Wisconsin, fallen angels Bartleby and Loki stumble across a loophole in God's plan allowing them re-entry into Heaven. All they have to do is walk into a certain church in New Jersey and – bingo! – they will be through the Pearly Gates. The only drawback is that their act – which would prove God to be fallible – would automatically obliterate all corporeal existence. Thus the destiny of mankind falls on the shoulders of a single mortal woman who, as it happens, is undergoing a crisis of faith ... Dismantling theological preconceptions with the irreverence they deserve, writer-director Kevin Smith has produced a comedy that is as provocative and funny as it is articulate and surprising. The power of the piece is that its drama (and humour) evolves out of very real questions that have dogged the director and have now been put in a comic perspective. As ever, Smith's writing is startlingly inventive and informed, creating a world where anything could happen, yet never beyond the realms of a credible context. And it's priceless to see Jay and Silent Bob – the moronic duo from Smith's previous films *Clerks*, *Mallrats* and *Chasing Amy* – reappear alongside an excremental demon, a Heavenly muse and the Voice of God herself!

● *Bartleby* Ben Affleck, *Loki* Matt Damon, *Bethany Sloane* Linda Fiorentino, *Serendipity* Salma Hayek, *Azrael* Jason Lee, *Jay* Jason Mewes, *Metatron* Alan Rickman, *Rufus* Chris Rock, *God* Alanis Morissette, *Cardinal Glick* George Carlin, *Silent Bob* Kevin Smith, *married man* Scott Mosier, Bud Cort, Barrett Hackney, Jared Pfennigwerth, Kitao Sakurai, Brian Christopher O'Halloran, Betty Aberlin, Janeane Garofalo, Jeff Anderson, Dwight Ewell, Mark Joy, Guinevere Turner.
● *Dir and Screenplay* Kevin Smith, *Pro* Scott Mosier, *Co-Pro* Laura Greenlee, *Ph* Robert Yeoman, *Pro Des* Robert 'Ratface' Holtzman, *Ed* Kevin Smith and Scott Mosier, *M* Howard Shore, *Costumes* Abigail Murray, *Sound* Tom Myers, *Visual effects* Richard 'Dickie' Payne, *Make-up/creature effects* Vincent Guastini.

View Askew/Miramax-Film Four.
128 mins. USA. 1999. Rel: 26 December 1999. Cert 15.

Donald Cammell's Wildside

See Wild Side

Double Jeopardy ★★★

Washington/Colorado/San Francisco/New Orleans; the present. It's a fact: by American law (see the Fifth Amendment) anybody who's served time for a specific murder cannot be jailed a second time for the same offence. That is, if you go down for six years for killing your husband, you can't be jailed a second time for murdering him again. So, what happens if you're set up by your old man, serve the requisite time for his murder and then, on your release, feel a tinge of lethal resent-

ment? As high concept movies go, *Double Jeopardy* is pretty high up the conceptual ladder. Better still, the story is slickly developed by scenarists Weisberg and Cook (who collaborated on *The Rock*) and boasts two charismatic leads in Ashley Judd and Tommy Lee Jones (the latter reprising his recurrent turn as the dogged tracker, this time a bitter parole officer). Of course, you can't believe a word of it, but it certainly holds the attention and keeps the heart pounding merrily.

● *Travis Lehman* Tommy Lee Jones, *Libby Parsons* Ashley Judd, *Nick Parsons* Bruce Greenwood, *Angie* Annabeth Gish, *Matty Parsons, aged four* Benjamin Weir, *Bobby* Jay Brazeau, *Rudy* John McLaren, *Margaret Skolowski* Roma Maffia, *Evelyn Lake* Davenia McFadden, Edward Evanko, Bruce Campbell, Gillian Barber, Betsy Brantley, Woody Jeffreys, French Tickner, Ben Bodé, Joy Coghill, Bernard Cuffling, Jason Douglas, Michelle Stafford, George Montgomery II, Harold Evans.
● *Dir* Bruce Beresford, *Pro* Leonard Goldberg, *Co-Pro* Richard Luke Rothschild, *Screenplay* David Weisberg and Douglas S. Cook, *Ph* Peter James, *Pro Des* Howard Cummings, *Ed* Mark Warner, *M* Normand Corbeil; songs performed by The Jeff Hamilton Trio, Bob James, Joe Simon, Professor Longhair, Queen Ida, Irma Thomas, Marcia Ball, Spirit of New Orleans Brass Band, etc, *Costumes* Rudy Dillon and Linda Bass.

Paramount/MFP Munich Film-UIP.
105 mins. USA/Germany. 1999. Rel: 28 January 2000. Cert 15.

Doug's 1st Movie ★¹/₂

Doug Funnie, a decent if personality-challenged 12-year-old, has just befriended a mutant creature that's escaped from a nearby contaminated lake. Doug realises that the creature's disclosure could make him a celebrity, but at what risk to the poor mutant? There's nothing particularly despicable about Doug's first foray into the cinematic firmament, it just seems rather pointless – and brazenly commercial. The primitive animation suffers painfully from large-screen scrutiny and the blandness of Doug's world just isn't exciting enough to merit movie aggrandisement. And the film's credibility level – where a mutant monster can attend a school dance 'disguised' in a wig and frock – is beyond rationalisation.

● *Voices: Doug Funnie/Lincoln* Thomas McHugh, *Skeeter Valentine/Mr Dink/Porkchop/Ned* Fred Newman, *Patti Mayonnaise* Constance Shulman, *Roger Klotz/Bloomer/Larry* Chris Phillips, *Guy Graham* Guy Hadley, *Mr Funnie/Bill Bluff/Willie/Chalky/first Bluff agent* Doug Preis, *Beebe Bluff* Alice Playten, *Judy Funnie/Mrs Funnie* Becca Lish, *The Monster aka Herman Melville* Frank Welker, Doris Belack, Fran Brill, Phil Proctor.
● *Dir* Maurice Joyce, *Pro* Jim Jinkins, David Campbell, Jack Spillum and Melanie Grisanti, *Assoc Pro* Bruce Knapp, *Screenplay* Ken Scarborough,

Design Freya Tanz, Pete List and Eugene Salandra, *Ed* Alysha Nadine Cohen and Christopher K. Gee, *M* Mark Watters, *Creator* Jinkins, *Mouth direction* Simi Nallaseth.

Jumbo Pictures/Walt Disney-Buena Vista. 77 mins. USA. 1999. Rel: 6 August 1999. Cert U.

Down To You ★¹/₂

New York; the present Al Connolly is an aspiring chef at college. Imogen is a freshman art student. They meet in a bar and fall in love. It's the first major affair for both of them, but love ain't ever easy… The good news is that Imogen isn't dying of an incurable, camera-friendly disease; the bad that maybe the film would've been more interesting if she was. As simplistic as they come, *Down To You* attempts to capture the magic of first love but is so anodyne that it doesn't give us a reason to care. There is good support from Selma Blair, Zak Orth and Henry Winkler, but this merely serves to highlight the vacuity of the leads, particularly Freddie Prinze who has all the personality of a yoghurt. [*Charles Bacon*]

● *Al Connolly* Freddie Prinze Jr, *Imogen* Julia Stiles, *Cyrus* Selma Blair, *Eddie Hicks* Shawn Hatosy, *Monk Jablonski* Zak Orth, *Jim Morrison* Ashton Kutcher, *Lana* Rosario Dawson, *Judy Connolly* Lucie Arnaz, *Chef Ray Connolly* Henry Winkler, Amanda Barfield, Chloe Hunter, Granger Green, Jed Rhein, Joseff Stevenson, Mark Blum.
● *Dir and Screenplay* Kris Isacsson, *Pro* Jason Kliot and Joana Vicente, *Ex Pro* Bobby Cohen, Bob Weinstein, Harvey Weinstein and Jeremy Kramer, *Co-Pro* Trish Hofmann, *Ph* Robert Yeoman, *Pro Des* Kevin Thompson, *Ed* Stephen A. Rotter, *M* Edmund Choi; songs performed by Billie Myers, Formosa, David Bowie, Dee Lite, P.J. Olsson, Big Lazy, The Drowners, Folk Implosion, Goo Goo Dolls, Deanna Kirk, Miranda Lee Richards, Inner Circle, Ginger Mackenzie, Citizen King, Luscious Jackson, Everything But the Girl, Gus Gus, The Velvet Crush, Psychic Rain, James Darren, Sam Phillips, Barry White, Al Green, etc, *Costumes* Michael Clancy.

Miramax/Open City Films-Film Four. 92 mins. USA. 2000. Rel: 19 May 2000. Cert 12.

Dreaming of Joseph Lees ★★

Somerset, England; 1958. Growing up with her aged father and much younger sister in a rural backwater, Eva Babbins dreams of a world beyond the hedgerows and pig pens that surround her. She also dreams of her cousin, Joseph Lees, a dashing young geologist who lost his leg in a quarry explosion. But the family have lost contact with Lees, who now works in Italy, and Eva is beginning to succumb to the romantic overtures of a local farmer, Harry. Just then Joseph turns up for a fam-

ily funeral … Although written directly for the screen, this picturesque tale of doomed love feels like something stretched out of a novella. Padded with numerous establishing shots accompanied by an impassioned score, the film feels like a lot about nothing, at least, in cinematic turns. An hour's slot on television would have served the material much better. Still, Samantha Morton proves yet again what a fine actress she is (reminiscent of a young Emily Watson or Sarah Miles), making the most of very little dialogue. Even so, her scenes with Rupert Graves don't ring entirely true, but that's the fault of the screenplay, not her. Do these two lost souls share more in common than just a love for Italian art?

● *Eva Babbins* Samantha Morton, *Harry Flyte* Lee Ross, *Signora Caldoni* Miriam Margolyes, *Eva's father* Frank Finlay, *Mr Dian* Nick Woodeson, *Maria Flyte* Holly Aird, *Joseph Lees* Rupert Graves, *Janie Babbins* Lauren Richardson, Felix Billson, Vernon Dobtcheff, Freddie Douglas, Emma Cunniffe, Siân James, Margaret John.
● *Dir* Eric Styles, *Pro* Chris Milburn, *Ex Pro* Milburn and Mark Thomas, *Line Pro* Matthew Kuipers, *Screenplay* Catherine Linstrum, *Ph* Jimmy Dibling, *Pro Des* Humphrey Jaeger, *Ed* Caroline Limmer, *M* Zbigniew Preisner, *Costumes* Maggie Chappelhow.

Fox Searchlight Pictures/Isle of Man Film Commission-Fox. 92 mins. USA/UK. 1998. Rel: 26 November 1999. Cert 12.

Drive Me Crazy ★

Timothy Zonin High, Utah; the present. Hip and peppy Nicole Maris dreams of dating the school basketball jock, Brad. Her laid-back neighbour, Chase, wants to make up with his sexy girlfriend, Dulcie. So Nicole hits on the idea of 'dating' Chase so that jealousy can secure their respective romantic goals … An insipid, predictable high school romantic comedy aimed squarely at the adolescent fans of Melissa Joan Hart (of TV's *Sabrina, the*

Above: Did you eat garlic last night? Freddie Prinze Jr sniffs Selma Blair in Kris Isacsson's vacuous and anodyne *Down To You* (from Film Four)

Above: Smile, while you're dying – Kirsten Dunst gives it her all in Michael Patrick Jann's dark and outrageously funny Drop Dead Gorgeous (from Icon)

Teenage Witch), this really doesn't bear thinking about. Chock full of the clichés of the genre (rock soundtrack, the politics of dating, social stereotypes), *Drive Me Crazy* is Saturday afternoon soap without the bubbles. Not so much *Clueless* as *Clawless* – so why the 12 certificate? Still, one minor character – The De-Virginator – deserves his own movie. Formerly known as *Next To You*.

● *Nicole Maris* Melissa Joan Hart, *Chase Hammond* Adrian Grenier, *Mr Maris* Stephen Collins, *Mr Rope* Mark Metcalf, *Mr Hammond* William Converse-Roberts, *Mrs Maris* Faye Grant, *Alicia* Susan May Pratt, *Ray Neeley* Kris Park, *Dulcie* Ali Larter, *'Designated' Dave* Mark Webber, *Brad* Gabriel Carpenter, *Dee Vine* Keri Lynn Pratt, Lourdes Benedicto, Natasha Pearce, Derrick Shore, Jordan Bridges, Keram Malicki-Sanchez, Andrew Roach.
● *Dir* John Schultz, *Pro* Amy Robinson, *Co-Pro* Nancy Paloian-Breznikar, *Screenplay* Rob Thomas, from the novel *How I Created My Perfect Prom Date* by Todd Strasser, *Ph* Kees Van Oostrum, *Pro Des* Aaron Osborne, *Ed* John Pace, *M* Greg Kendall, songs per-

formed by Sugar High, Supergrass, REO Speedwagon, Far Too Jones, Barenaked Ladies, Britney Spears, Don Philip, Backstreet Boys, Phantom Planet, Steps, The Donnas, Sweet, etc, *Costumes* Genevieve Tyrrell.

Fox-Fox.
91 mins. USA. 1999. Rel: 9 June 2000. Cert 12.

Drop Dead Gorgeous ★★★

In the gut of America's God-fearing, cow-eating heartland, the small Lutheran community of Mount Rose, Minnesota, is preparing for its annual American Teen Princess Beauty Pageant. As a film crew records the final days before the event, it becomes clear just how important winning is to these ambitious, bright-eyed girls. As tragic accidents start to befall the more promising competitors, the excitement becomes unbearable ... Adopting the mockumentary format established by *This is Spinal Tap* 15 years ago, *Drop Dead Gorgeous* takes some brutal swipes at a mile-wide target and (naturally) scores a whole bunch of bullseyes. Much of the satire is very broad indeed and some of the running gags pushed way too far (such as one judge's insistence that he's not interested in young girls), but the film's laugh quotient is still very high. Making fun of everything from anorexia to mental illness, this is the year's blackest comedy endowed with the whitest smile. Previously known as *Dairy Queens*.

● *Gladys Leeman* Kirstie Alley, *Annette Atkins* Ellen Barkin, *Amber Atkins* Kirsten Dunst, *Becky Leeman* Denise Richards, *Loretta* Allison Janney, *Lester Leeman* Sam McMurray, *Iris Clark* Mindy Sterling, *Lisa Swenson* Brittany Murphy, *Leslie Miller* Amy Adams, *Michelle Johnson* Laurie Sinclair, *Tess Weinhaus* Shannon Nelson, *Molly Howard* Tara Redepenning, *Jenelle Betz* Sarah Stewart, *John Dough* Matt Malloy, *Harold Vilmes* Michael McShane, *Hank Vilmes* Will Sasso, *voice of documentarian* Thomas Lennon, Alexandra Holden, Brooke Bushman, Jon T. Olson, Casey Tyler Garven, Nora Dunn, Mo Gaffney, *himself* Adam West, Richard Narita, Patti Yasutake, Seiko Matsuda, Dale Dunham, Peter Aitchison, Jennifer Baldwin Peden, Mary Johanson, Tammy Curry, Lona Williams.
● *Dir* Michael Patrick Jann, *Pro* Gavin Polone and Judy Hofflund, *Ex Pro* Claire Rudnick Polstein, Donna Langley and Lona Williams, *Screenplay* Lona Williams, *Ph* Michael Spiller, *Pro Des* Ruth Ammon, *Ed* Janice Hampton, *M* Mark Mothersbaugh; Johann Strauss, Aaron Copland, Richard Strauss; songs performed by The Nevers, Ethel Merman, New Staple Singers, Primitive Radio Gods, Skirt, Lifeboy, Melissa Manchester, Gloria Estefan and Miami Sound Machine, Petula Clark, Elton John, Joan Jett and The Blackhearts, Sunday Suit, Everything, etc, *Costumes* Mimi Melgaard.

New Line/Capella/KC Medien-Icon.
98 mins. USA/Germany. 1999. Rel: 17 September 1999. Cert 15.

Left: *Permissive society pressures – Damien O'Donnell's vibrant and insightful* East is East *tackles sex in the suburbs (from Film Four)*

Earth ★★

Lahore, Pakistan; August 1947. Prior to Britain's withdrawal from India and the subsequent Partition of the country's Muslim, Hindu and Sikh populations, a family of Parsees lived in peaceful harmony. Effectively distanced from the warring factions of the other sects, Rustom and Bunty Sethna, their eight-year-old daughter Lenny and the latter's beautiful Hindu nanny seem blissfully untroubled by the prospect of an imminent Holocaust ... The second in Deepa Mehta's elemental trilogy (following on from the 1996 *Fire*), *Earth* is a picturesque if sluggish and uninspired adaptation of Bapsi Sidhwa's semi-autobiographical novel *Cracking India*. Sensually lit and peopled by extremely beautiful Indians, the film seems strangely removed from the gritty reality of its historical context. Consequently, it's hard to identify with the terrible plight of these designer-friendly individuals.

● *Dil Nawaz, the Ice Candy Man* Aamir Khan, *Ayah, Sharita* Nandita Das, *Hasan, the Masseur* Rahul Khanna, *Lenny* Maia Sethna, *Bunty Sethna* Kitu Gidwani, *Rustom Sethna* Arif Zakaria, *adult Lenny* Bapsi Sidhwa, Kulbushan Kharbanda, Gulshan Grover, Eric Peterson, Pavan Malhotra,
● *Dir* and *Screenplay* Deepa Mehta, *Pro* Mehta and Anne Masson, *Ex Pro* David Hamilton and Jhamm Sughand, *Ph* Giles Nuttgens, *Pro Des* Aradhana Seth, *Ed* Barry Farrell, *M* A.R. Rahman; Johann Strauss, *Costumes* Dolly Ahluwalia Tewari.

David Hamilton/ Jhamm Sughand-Pathé.
106 mins. Canada. 1998. Rel: 14 April 2000. Cert 15.

East is East ★★★★

Salford, Manchester; 1971. A proud, headstrong and arrogant man, George Khan is a Pakistani immigrant steeped in tradition, even though he has an English wife. He also has seven children – six sons and one daughter – who readily embrace the corrupt lifestyle of 1970s' Britain: saucy magazines, swinging discos and fried sausages and bacon. So when Khan sets about marrying his sons off to preordained Pakistani brides, the family braces itself for a domestic meltdown ... Adapted from the play by Ayub Khan Din, *East is East* is an entertaining look at the Anglo-Pakistani divide – and collision – given a wonderful visual flourish by first-time director Damien O'Donnell. Wearing its period on its sleeve (with omnipresent Space Hoppers in the street and Enoch Powell bellowing from a black-and-white TV), the film escapes the claustrophobia of its setting (largely one row of red brick houses in England's North West) with rich production values and a vibrant pace. Both hilarious and insightful, *East is East* recalls a Mike Leigh farce with an Asian twist.

● *George Khan* Om Puri, *Ella Khan* Linda Bassett, *Sajid Khan* Jordan Routledge, *Meenah Khan* Archie Panjabi, *Maneer 'Gandhi' Khan* Emil Marwa, *Saleem Khan* Chris Bisson, *Tariq Khan* Jimi Mistry, *Stella Moorhouse* Emma Rydal, *Peggy* Ruth Jones, *Mr Shah* Madhav Sharma, *Mrs Shah* Leena Dhingra, Raji James, Ian Aspinall, Lesley Nicol, Gary Damer, John Bardon, Kriss Dosanjh, Albert Moses, Rosalind March, Thierry Harcourt, Gary Lewis.
● *Dir* Damien O'Donnell, *Pro* Leslee Udwin, *Ex Pro* Alan J. Wands, *Assoc Pro* Stephanie Guerrasio,

Right: Candid camera – Matthew McConaughey and Elizabeth Hurley in Ron Howard's predictable and heavy-handed EDtv (from UIP)

Line Pro Shellie Smith, *Screenplay* Ayub Khan-Din, *Ph* Brian Tufano, *Pro Des* Tom Conroy, *Ed* Michael Parker, *M* Deborah Mollison; songs performed by Blue Mink, Deep Purple, Jimmy Cliff, Ansell Collins, Georgie Fame, The Hollies, and McGuinnes Flint, *Costumes* Lorna Marie Mugan.

FilmFour/Assassin Films/BBC-Film Four.
96 mins. UK. 1999. Rel: 5 November 1999. Cert 15.

EDtv ★★

Buffeted by the ratings of the gardening channel, the executives at True TV decide to try something really novel: to record the life of a real Joe Blow, 24 hours a day *live*. Video clerk Ed Pekurny volunteers for the post and quickly finds his life transformed for the better. But celebrity has its price ... Even if *EDtv* didn't have so much in common with *The Truman Show* it would still be a simplistic, hackneyed and ludicrous exercise. And, where Truman Burbank was an Everyman plagued by a very real solipsistic nightmare, Ed Pekurny is a narcissistic dupe selling his soul to the devil. Heavy-handed moralising, broad caricatures and a predictable narrative arc further blunt the blade of satire in an already overcrowded genre. Other films that got there first: Albert Brooks' *Real Life* (1979) and Michael Lindsay-Hogg's *Guy* (1996).

● *Ed Pekurny* Matthew McConaughey, *Shari* Jenna Elfman, *Ray Pekurny* Woody Harrelson, *Cynthia Topping* Ellen DeGeneres, *Jeanette* Sally Kirkland, *Al* Martin Landau, *Whitaker* Rob Reiner, *Hank Pekurny* Dennis Hopper, *Jill* Elizabeth Hurley, *Ken,*

the director Clint Howard, *John* Adam Goldberg, *himself* Jay Leno, Geoffrey Blake, Gavin Grazer, Don Most, Rick Overton, RuPaul, Rusty Schwimmer, Steven Shenbaum, Gedde Watanabe, Viveka Davis, Googy Gress, Kathleen Marshall, Harry Shearer, Michael Moore, Merrill Markoe, George Plimpton, Cheryl Howard, Bill Maher, Lowell Ganz, Jordan Harrelson.
● *Dir* Ron Howard, *Pro* Brian Grazer and Ron Howard, *Ex Pro* Todd Hallowell, Michel Roy and Richard Sadler, *Screenplay* Lowell Ganz and Babaloo Mandel, based on Michel Poulette's film *Louis XIX: Roi Des Ondes*, *Ph* John Schwazrtzman, *Pro Des* Michael Corenblith, *Ed* Mike Hill and Dan Hanley, *M* Randy Edelman; Grieg; songs performed by Joe Tex, Al Green, Ted Nugent, Three Dog Night, The Staple Singers, Otis Redding, Gavin Grazer, Sly & The Family Stone, James Brown, Barenaked Ladies, UB40, Meredith Brooks, Morcheeba, The Spencer Davis Group, Jon Bon Jovi, Barry White, Bobbi Page and Jim Lang, *Costumes* Rita Ryack.

Universal/Imagine-UIP.
123 mins. USA. 1999. Rel: 19 November 1999. Cert 12.

8½ Women ★★½

Tokyo/Kyoto/Geneva; the present. When his wife of 35 years passes away, English banker Philip Emmenthal goes into a deep decline. However, through her death he comes to an unusual understanding with his 24-year-old son Storey, who gently teases him about his sexual conformity and naivete. Thus the two men embark on installing the family chateau with various women of erotic potential who represent the eight-and-a-half archetypes of male fantasy ... Even a bad Peter Greenaway film is more interesting than your average multiplex fare. And, quite frankly, *8½ Women* isn't very good. However, it still has a number of striking sequences, unforgettable images and even a few genuine chuckles. Greenaway has striven to create a black comedy – taking Fellini's *8½* as his starting point – and has gone completely mad. But then the director's sense of humour is an island unto itself. Laconic, dark and completely unpredictable, his whimsy defies categorisation. It is nonetheless refreshingly off-the-wall. Whether or not you find the sight of a geisha singing with a pig or a father and son comparing their naked bodies remotely funny is irrelevant, it is still alarmingly original.

● *Philip Emmenthal* John Standing, *Storey Emmenthal* Matthew Delamere, *Kito* Vivian Wu, *Simato* Shizuka Inoh, *Clothilde* Barbara Sarafian, *Mio* Kirina Mano, *Griselda* Toni Collette, *Beryl* Amanda Plummer, *Giaconda* Natacha Amal, *Giulietta/half woman* Manna Fujiwara, *Palmira* Polly Walker, *Simon* Don Warrington, Elizabeth Berrington, Myriam Muller, Claire Johnston, Tony Kaye, Katsuya Kobayashi.
● *Dir, Screenplay and Paintings* Peter Greenaway, *Pro*

Kees Kasander, *Ex Pro* Terry Glinwood, Bob Hubar and Denis Wigman, *Co-Pro* Jimmy De Brabant and Michael Pakleppa, *Line Pro* Kosaku Wada, *Ph* Sacha Vierny and Reinier van Brummelen, *Pro Des* Emi Wada and Wilbert Van Dorp, *Ed* Elmer Leupen, *M* Hirokazu Sugiura; Verdi, *Costumes* Emi Wada.

Woodline Prods/Movie Masters/Delux Prods/Continent Film/Eurimages/Dutch Film Fund-Pathé.
120 mins. Luxembourg/The Netherlands/Germany/UK. 1999. Rel: 10 December 1999. Cert 15.

Election ★★★¹/₂

Good intentions, they say, pave the way to hell. And in a society that promotes ambition above individual choice, the saying could never have been more apt. Jim McAllister, a conscientious history and civics teacher at Omaha's Carver High, strives to provide the best for his students. But he cannot overcome his dislike for Tracy Flick, an overachiever who is using the classroom as a springboard for her own ambition. When he opts to sabotage her unchallenged claim to the presidency of the student body, his and his school's status quo take an unexpected thrashing ... Casting a jaundiced eye on the pitfalls of personal interference with the smooth running of fate, *Election* is a sublimely witty examination of American small-mindedness. Stylishly adapted from the 1998 novel by Tom Perrotta, this is one high school comedy that is way ahead of its class, crowned by some superb playing from Matthew Broderick and Reese Witherspoon. But then the film is awash with sharply drawn caricatures, empowering a grown-up satire that draws real blood from its humour.

● *Jim McAllister* Matthew Broderick, *Tracy Flick* Reese Witherspoon, *Paul Metzler* Chris Klein, *Principal Walt Hendricks* Phil Reeves, *Dave Novotny* Mark Harelik, *Linda Novotny* Delaney Driscoll, *Diane McAllister* Molly Hagan, *Tammy Metzler* Jessica Campbell, *Lisa Flanagan* Frankie Ingrassia, Colleen Camp, Holmes Osborne, Jeanine Jackson, Matt Malloy, Loren Nelson.
● *Dir* Alexander Payne, *Pro* Albert Berger, Ron Yerxa, David Gale and Keith Samples, *Ex Pro* Van Toffler, *Co-Pro* Jacobus Rose and Jim Burke, *Screenplay* Payne and Jim Taylor, *Ph* James Glennon, *Pro Des* Jane Ann Stewart, *Ed* Kevin Tent, *M* Rolfe Kent; Ennio Morricone; songs performed by Quintetto X, The Commodores, Joey Altruda and The Cocktail Crew, Mojave 3, Spacehog, Donovan, Jolene, Mandy Barnett, Frank Morocco, etc, *Costumes* Wendy Chuck.

Paramount/MTV Films/Bona Fide Prods-UIP.
103 mins. USA. 1999. Rel: 24 September 1999. Cert 15.

End of Days ★★¹/₂

In the Book of Revelations, chapter 20, verse 7, it says that, 'and when the thousand years are expired, Satan shall be loosed out of his prison.' Well, it's Tuesday, 28 December 1999, and Old Nick has popped into New York to claim the virtue of a virgin predestined to bear him the Antichrist. He has just four days to find and woo her, a task that proves a little more difficult than planned thanks to an alcoholic ex-cop called Jericho Cane ... Ridiculous? Of course. Scary? Not quite. Arnold Schwarzenegger, two-and-a-half years since his last film (due to heart surgery), wanted to make something 'really, really, really scary' but forgot that his own pop-cultural image automatically forestalls such things. At the best, *End of Days* could have been a rip-roaring chunk of escapism in which the Austrian Oak hand-wrestles Satan into the next Millennium. As it is, Arnold plays down the laughs and accelerates some prime-time religion in a scenario that gamely resists such heavy touches. So concentrate on the effects, admire a lovely turn from Gabriel Byrne as Lucifer (complete with a delicious speech pinched straight from *Devil's Advocate*) and forget Arnie ever opened his prayer book.

● *Jericho Cane* Arnold Schwarzenegger, *The Man* Gabriel Byrne, *Chicago* Kevin Pollak, *Christine York* Robin Tunney, *Father Kovak* Rod Steiger, *Det. Margie Francis* CCH Pounder, *Thomas Aquinas* Derrick O'Connor, *Mabel* Miriam Margolyes, *head priest* Udo Kier, Victor Varnado, Michael O'Hagan, Mark Margolis, Jack Shearer, Marc Lawrence, Father Michael Rocha.
● *Dir and Ph* Peter Hyams, *Pro* Armyan Bernstein and Bill Borden, *Co-Pro* Paul Deason and Andrew W. Marlowe, *Ex Pro* Marc Abraham and Thomas A. Bliss, *Screenplay* Marlowe, *Pro Des* Richard Holland, *Ed* Steve Kemper, *M* John Debney, songs performed by Ondar, Bing Crosby, Rob Zombie, Limp Bizkit, Professional Murder Music, Korn, Nat King Cole, Guns 'n' Roses, and Everlast, *Costumes* Bobbie Mannix, *Creature effects* Stan Winston Studio.

Universal/Beacon Pictures-Buena Vista.
122 mins. USA. 1999. Rel: 10 December 1999. Cert 18.

The End of the Affair ★★★★

London; 1939-1941. Sitting at his typewriter, successful novelist Maurice Bendrix reveals that he is composing a diary of hate. But who does he hate? And who does he love? As the details of his affair with Sarah Miles, the passionate wife of a civil servant, gradually manifest themselves, so the tragic circumstances that stifled the illicit liaison come clearer ... A *Brief Encounter* with edge, Neil Jordan's adaptation of Graham Greene's 1951 novel is a powerful and intelligent love story. Anchored by superlative production values and a moving score by Michael Nyman, the film grows in emotional potency as the expertly crafted dialogue leads to a complex scenario which, layer by layer, reveals the drama within. As the novel is recognised as Greene's most autobiographical work, the part of Bendrix has been developed to encompass much of the author himself, a move that adds considerable poignancy to the story. FYI: The film that Bendrix takes Sarah to is actually *21 Days*, the story of a tragic extramarital affair which was scripted by Greene himself.

● *Maurice Bendrix* Ralph Fiennes, *Sarah Miles* Julianne Moore, *Henry Miles* Stephen Rea, *Mr Parkis* Ian Hart, *Father Smythe* Jason Isaacs, *Mr Savage* James Bolam, *Samuel Bould* Lance Parkis, Heather

Jay Jones, Cyril Shaps, Penny Morrell, Dr Simon Turner, Deborah Findlay.
● *Dir and Screenplay* Neil Jordan, *Pro* Jordan and Stephen Woolley, *Co-Pro* Kathy Sykes, *Ph* Roger Pratt, *Pro Des* Anthony Pratt, *Ed* Tony Lawson, *M* Michael Nyman; Johann Strauss, *Costumes* Sandy Powell.

Global Entertainment/Columbia-Columbia TriStar.
101 mins. USA/Germany. 1999. Rel: 11 February 2000. Cert 18.

L'Ennui ★★★

Paris; the present. A professor of philosophy, Martin has become disillusioned with teaching and intends to pour his energies into a new book. But following a chance encounter with an elderly painter, he is distracted by the old man's 17-year-old muse. The psychological and physical opposite of Martin's ex-wife, Cécilia becomes an all-consuming obsession for the professor ... Recalling Bertrand Blier's 1989 *Trop belle pour toi!* – in which Gerard Depardieu cheated on his beautiful wife with his dumpy secretary – *L'Ennui* sets up an intriguing scenario which it explores with some vigour and wit. And like Isabelle Huppert's Pomme in *The Lacemaker* and Marcélia Cartaxo's Macabéa in the Brazilian *Hour of the Star*, Sophie Guillemin's *non*-character Cécilia is a fascinating creation. The total antithesis of the traditional Parisian sexpot (à la Vanessa Paradis, Marie Gillain), Cécilia is podgy, ingenuous, unformed and disarmingly transparent – a blank canvas on which Martin can vent his intellectual frustrations. However, with little plot and a character whose dialogue consists mainly of 'I don't know' and 'I can't remember', the two-hour film does overstay its welcome. FYI: *L'Ennui* is based on the novel *La Noia* by Alberto Moravia, which was previously filmed in 1963 as *The Empty Canvas*, starring Bette Davis and Horst Buchholz.

● *Martin* Charles Berling, *Cécilia* Sophie Guillemin, *Sophie* Arielle Dombasle, *Leopold Meyers* Robert Kramer, *Cécilia's mother* Alice Grey, *Cécilia's father* Maurice Antoni, *Momo* Tom Ouedraogo.
● *Dir* Cédric Kahn, *Pro* Paulo Branco, *Screenplay* Kahn and Laurence Ferreira Barbosa, *Ph* Pascal Marti, *Pro Des* François Abelanet, *Ed* Yann Dedet, *M* various, *Costumes* Françoise Clavel.

Gemini Films/IMA Films/Madragoa Filmes/Canal Plus/CNC-Artificial Eye.
122 mins. France. 1998. Rel: 14 April 2000. Cert 18.

Entrapment ★★★

New York/London/Scotland/Kuala Lumpur; the last days of 1999. Convinced that legendary thief Robert 'Mac' MacDougal is behind the theft of a $24 million Rembrandt, insurance investigator Gin Baker gets the green light to shadow him to London. But Gin's own

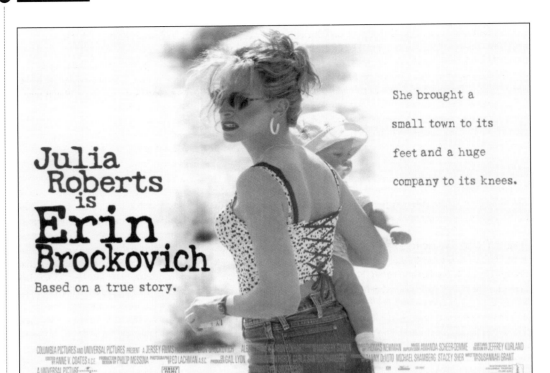

Julia
Roberts
is
**Erin
Brockovich**
Based on a true story.

She brought a
small town to its
feet and a huge
company to its knees.

agenda is far from clear and soon she is embarking on an elaborate scam to help MacDougal relieve Bedford Palace of a $40 million Chinese mask. But then who is using whom? Taken in the right spirit, *Entrapment* is slick and audacious good fun, harking back to the romantic crime capers of the 1950s and '60s. And, besides the obvious screen presence of Connery, Zeta-Jones and Ving Rhames – not to mention some exotic locations and fantastic gadgetry – the film works so well because the audience is never entirely sure who holds the upper hand. And the stunts – particularly those performed near the top of Kuala Lumpur's vertiginous Petronas Twin Towers – are simply gut-twisting. The fact that Connery is old enough to be Zeta-Jones' grandfather is another matter entirely...

● *Robert 'Mac' MacDougal* Sean Connery, *Virginia 'Gin' Baker* Catherine Zeta-Jones, *Thibadeaux* Ving Rhames, *Hector Cruz* Will Patton, *Conrad Greene* Maury Chaykin, *Haas* Kevin McNally, Terry O'Neill, Madhav Sharma, David Yip, Tim Potter, Eric Meyers, Aaron Swartz, William Marsh, Tony Xuicb, Rolf Saxon.
● *Dir* Jon Amiel, *Pro* Sean Connery, Michael Hertzberg and Rhonda Tollefson, *Ex Pro* Iain Smith, Ron Bass and Arnon Milchan, *Screenplay* Ron Bass and William Broyles, from a story by Bass and Hertzberg, *Ph* Phil Meheux, *Pro Des* Norman Garwood, *Ed* Terry Rawlings, *M* Christopher Young; songs performed by Seal, Loop Guru, Faithless, Karen Ramirez, etc, *Costumes* Penny Rose.

Fox/Monarchy Enterprises/Regency Enterprises-Fox). 113 mins. USA/UK/Germany. 1999. Rel: 2 July 1999. Cert 12.

Erin Brockovich ★★★★★

Los Angeles; 1993-1997. Erin Brockovich is a twice-divorced mother of three with $16 in the bank, a fractured neck and no hope of getting a job. Erin Brockovich is also a sassy, outspoken, driven and profane hellcat who will take no truck from anybody. Then, when she loses her case against the driver who put her neck in plaster, she manages to get a job in the office of the attorney who `failed' her. There, she discovers a taste for the legal profession and instigates the biggest lawsuit of her employer's career ... Sometimes a story comes along, true or not, that inspires a writer to produce a great script. And sometimes a script comes along that motivates a director to deliver his best work. And sometimes a director can create an environment where his actors go beyond the call of duty. In a gift of a part, Julia Roberts delivers the performance of her life, tapping into all the conviction, humour and sex appeal that her real-life character must have had to overcome such insurmountable odds. But then *Erin Brockovich* works on every level, from the economic plotting of the screenplay to the expeditious editing of veteran Oscar-winner Anne V. Coates. An inspiring, provocative, touching, funny and exhilarating entertainment that Hollywood is all too seldom heir to.

● *Erin Brockovich* Julia Roberts, *Ed Masry* Albert Finney, *George* Aaron Eckhart, *Donna Jensen* Marg Helgenberger, *Pamela Duncan* Cherry Jones, *Theresa Dallavale* Veanne Cox, *Brenda* Conchata Ferrell, *Charles Embry* Tracey Walter, *Kurt Potter* Peter Coyote, *waitress* Erin Brockovich-Ellis, David Brisbin, Dawn Didawick, Valente Rodriguez, Jack Gill, Scotty Leavenworth, Gemmenne De La Peña, Adilah Barnes, Irina V.

Passmoore, Randy Lowell, Jamie Harrold, Joe Chrest, Meredith Zinner, Michael Harney, William Lucking, Mimi Kennedy, Scott Sowers, Judge LeRoy A. Simmons. ● *Dir* Steven Soderbergh, *Pro* Danny DeVito, Michael Shamberg and Stacey Sher, *Ex Pro* John Hardy and Carla Santos Shamberg, *Co-Pro* Gail Lyon, *Screenplay* Susannah Grant, *Ph* Ed Lachman, *Pro Des* Philip Messina, *Ed* Anne V. Coates, *M* Thomas Newman; songs performed by Sheryl Crow, *Costumes* Jeffrey Kurland.

Universal Pictures/Columbia Pictures/Jersey Films-Columbia TriStar.
133 mins. USA. 2000. Rel: 7 April 2000. Cert 15.

Eye of the Beholder ★¹⁄₂

Washington DC/Philadelphia/New York/San Francisco/ Boston/Death Valley/Utah/Miami/Chicago/ Alaska; the present. A high-tech surveillance agent for British intelligence, the enigmatically dubbed 'The Eye' is asked to track down a woman suspected of blackmail. Witnessing her callous murder of a lover, The Eye becomes obsessed by this beautiful, enigmatic mistress of disguise, with whom he feels a bizarre connection. Risking both his job and his safety, he follows her across America, becoming her guardian angel and an invisible accomplice in a string of murders ... Based on the 1980 novel by Marc Behm, this visually elegant attempt to invert the *film noir*/private eye genre is continually undermined by ludicrous leaps in logic. The premise itself is not without merit – *The Conversation* meets *Black Widow* – but Ewan McGregor is as unconvincing as a government agent as his *modus operandi* (how does he *always* manage to secure an apartment next to his quarry?). A profoundly silly movie.

● *The Eye* Ewan McGregor, *Joanna Eris/Dorothy Bishop/Debra Yates/Charlotte Vincent*, etc Ashley Judd, *Alexander Leonard* Patrick Bergen, *Gary* Jason Priestley, *Hilary* k.d. lang, *Dr Brault* Geneviève Bujold, *Lucy* Anne-Marie Brown and Kaitlin Brown, David Nerman, Steven McCarthy, Vlasta Vrana, Michelle Sweeney.
● *Dir* and *Screenplay* Stephan Elliott, *Pro* Nicolas Clermont and Tony Smith, *Ex Pro* Hilary Shor and Mark Damon, *Co-Pro* Al Clark, *Ph* Guy Dufaux, *Pro Des* Jean-Baptiste Tard, *Ed* Sue Blainey, *M* Marius De Vries, *Costumes* Lizzy Gardiner, *Sound*

Right: Clinging to their marriage – Tom Cruise and Nicole Kidman in Stanley Kubrick's powerful and deeply disturbing Eyes Wide Shut (from Warner)

Martin Pinsonnault.

Behaviour Worldwide/Village Roadshow/Ambridge Film Partnership/hit & run/Filmline International-Metrodome.
109 mins. Canada/UK/USA/Australia. 1998. Rel: 9 June 2000. Cert 18.

Eyes Wide Shut ★★★★

William Harford is a successful doctor with a beautiful wife and daughter who lives on New York's exclusive Central Park West. Following a party hosted by one of his patients, William and his wife Alice discuss their behaviour during the evening, leading to an unforeseen emotional showdown. Alice confesses that she once thought of leaving William for another man and, disconsolate, William goes off a for a night on the town that leads him into extremely dangerous waters ... Drawing its raw material from the 1926 novella *Traumnovelle* by Arthur Schnitzler, *Eyes Wide Shut* is an excoriating examination of the undercurrents that conspire to waylay even the soundest marriages. Intensely acted by Tom Cruise and Nicole Kidman (who worked on the film for a staggering 15 months), there is much psychological meat here, underscored by Kubrick's meticulous attention to detail. Yet, while both powerful and deeply disturbing, the director's characteristic emotional detachment and overindulgence in specifics ultimately leaves an unsatisfactory vacuum. Still, there's plenty of food for thought and an unsettling malaise that refuses to dissipate lightly. FYI: Kubrick originally approached the novelist John Le Carré to write the script, but after numerous meetings with the director Le Carré passed.

● *Dr William Harford* Tom Cruise, *Alice Harford* Nicole Kidman, *Victor Ziegler* Sydney Pollack, *Marion Nathanson* Marie Richardson, *Helena Harford* Madison Eginton, *Nick Nightingale* Todd Field, *Sandor Szavost* Sky Dumont, *Carl* Thomas Gibson, *Domino* Vinessa Shaw, *Milich* Rade Sherbedgia, *Milich's daughter* Leelee Sobieski, *desk clerk* Alan Cumming, *Sally* Fay Masterson, Jackie Sawiris, Leslie Lowe, Louise Taylor, Stewart Thorndike, Randall Paul, Julienne Davis, Lisa Leone, Kevin Connealy, Mariana Hewett, Gary Goba, Togo Igawa, Eiji Kusuhara, Angus MacInnes, Abigail Good, Brian W. Cook, Leon Vitali, Phil Davies.
● *Dir and Pro* Stanley Kubrick, *Ex Pro* Jan Harlan, *Co-Pro* Brian W. Cook, *Screenplay* Kubrick and Frederic Raphael, *Ph* Larry Smith, *Ed* Nigel Galt, *Pro Des* Les Tomkins and Roy Walker, *M* Jocelyn Pook; Shostakovich, György Ligeti; songs performed by The Victor Silvester Orchestra, Tommy Sanderson and The Sandman, The Oscar Peterson Trio, Chris Isaak, The Del-Vets, Rais Chamber Chorus, etc, *Costumes* Marit Allen, *Original paintings* Christiane Kubrick and Katharina Hobbs, *Venetian masks* Barbara Del Greco.

Warner/Pole Star/Hobby Films-Warner.
159 mins. USA/UK. 1999. Rel: 10 September 1999. Cert 18.

Fanny & Elvis ★★

Hebden Bridge, Yorkshire; the present. Just as she has put the finishing touches to her first novel, Kate Dickson decides she is ready to have a baby. But then a perfect day is scuttled when she rams her VW banger into the nose of a brand new Jaguar and is verbally assaulted by the car's owner, Dave Parker. Worse still, her husband then announces that he is leaving her for Dave's wife ... Although Kay Mellor is known for her work as a writer (TV's *Band of Gold*, *Playing the Field*, *Jane Eyre*), her directorial debut proves she is actually better at directing than structure. A more contrived and unbelievable romance you could not find, as no sooner have Kate and Dave found true love than, for the flimsiest and unlikeliest of reasons, they split up again, creating a second movie tagged onto the first. But the performances, photography and comedy sequences are all extremely adequate, although what Kate's best friend and lodger Andrew, a jobbing actor, is doing living in rural Yorkshire is a mystery.

● *Kate Dickson* Kerry Fox, *Dave Parker* Ray Winstone, *Andrew* Ben Daniels, *Rob Dickson* David Morrissey, *Roanna* Jennifer Saunders, *Alan* Colin Salmon, *Samantha Parker* Gaynor Faye, *Rick* William Ash, Gareth Tudor Price, Bridget Forsythe, Eileen O'Brien, Nick Lane, Richard Moore, Michael Medwin, Yvonne Mellor, Joyce Kennedy.
● *Dir and Screenplay* Kay Mellor, *Pro* Laurie Borg, *Ex Pro* Nik Powell, *Co-Ex Pro* Georges Benayoun, *Co-Pro* Marina Gefter, *Line Pro* Jane Robertson, *Assoc Pro* Rachel Wood, *Ph* John Daly, *Pro Des* Maria Djurkovic, *Ed* Christopher Blunden, *M* Stephen Warbeck; songs performed by Elvis Presley, Haircut 100, Dusty Springfield, Ray Winstone, Ben Daniels, Kelly Marie, John Paul Young, Cerys Matthews, etc, *Costumes* Stewart Meachem.

Scala Prods/Film Consortium/Ima Films-UIP. 111 mins. UK/France. 1999. Rel: 19 November 1999. Cert 15.

Fantasia/2000 ★★¹/₂

Sixty-two years after Walt Disney dreamed of creating an annual celebration of animation and classical music, Walt's nephew Roy has produced a second instalment. However, at less than two thirds the running time of the first *Fantasia* (1940), this troubled production cannot help but feel like a belated dilution of the original concept. And with the best sequence – featuring Mickey Mouse as 'The Sorcerer's Apprentice' – purloined from the first film, the new material pales in comparison. That is not to say that *Fantasia/2000* doesn't have its merits – it most certainly does – but after so long a wait it is something of a disappointment. The animation itself is nowhere near as impressive as that found in *The Lion King* – or even *Tarzan* – and there is an overall lack of wit and visual ingenuity (in spite of the advances of computer animation). And the addition of celebrity padding between the seven new segments merely underlines the misguided smugness of the whole enterprise.

Above: Behind closed doors – Elaine Cassidy in Atom Egoyan's commanding and otherworldly *Felicia's Journey* (from Icon)

Still, the inventive choice of music (see credits) is to be commended, as is the variety of animation styles.

● *Hosts*: Steve Martin, Itzhak Perlman, Quincy Jones, Bette Midler, James Earl Jones, Penn & Teller, Angela Lansbury.
● *Symphony No. 5 Dir* Pixote Hunt, *M* Ludwig van Beethoven; *Pines of Rome Dir* Hendel Butoy, *M* Ottorino Respighi; *Rhapsody in Blue Dir* Eric Goldberg, *M* George Gershwin; *Piano Concerto No. 2, Allegro, Opus 102*, *Dir* Hendel Butoy, *M* Dmitri Shostakovich; *Carnival of the Animals Dir* Eric Goldberg, *M* Camille Saint-Saëns; *The Sorcerer's Apprentice Dir* James Algar, *M* Paul Dukas; *Pomp and Circumstance Dir* Francis Glebas, *M* Edward Elgar; *Firebird Suite – 1919 Version Dir* Gaëtan and Paul Brizzi, *M* Igor Stravinsky; *Host Sequences Dir* Don Hahn.
● *Pro* Donald W. Ernst, *Ex Pro* Roy Edward Disney, *Supervising animation dir* Hendel Butoy, *Conductors* James Levine, Bruce Broughton, Leopold Stokowski, *Pianists* Yefim Bronfman, Ralph Grierson.

Walt Disney-Buena Vista.
74 mins. USA. 1999. Rel: 1 January 2000. Cert U.

Fast Food ★¹/₂

After countless years abroad, telephone engineer Benny Anstruther returns to the East End of London to be reunited with his childhood mates. But Zac, Jacko, Bisto and Flea have failed to make a success of their lives and are now planning to rob the local sweet shop to make their fortune. And they want Benny to help them ... Rough-edged, nasty and derivative to the point of being plagiaristic (*Reservoir Dogs* being an oft-plundered model), *Fast Food* feels more like a calling card for its first-time writer-director than a film in its own right. And while Stewart Sugg does show some potential as a filmmaker (particularly considering the production's minuscule budget of £48,736.17p.), it's hard to warm to his debut work. Next time, such additional qualities as focus, credibility and sympathetic characters could reap dividends.

● *Benny Anstruther* Douglas Henshall, *Letitia/Claudia* Emily Woof, *Dwayne* Miles Anderson, *Flea* Stephen Lord, *Jacko* Gerard Butler, *Bisto* Danny Midwinter, *Zac* Robert Donovan, *Mr Fortune Cookie* David Yip, *Ernie* Graham Turner, *Fish* Sean Hughes, Michael Chmielwski, Lesley Duff, Gary Sefton.
● *Dir and Screenplay* Stewart Sugg, *Pro* Phil Hunt, *Ex Pro* Sugg and Tessa Gibbs, *Ph* Simon Reeves, *Pro Des* Katie Franklyn-Thompson, *Ed* Jeremy Gibbs, *M* Ben Lee-Delisle; songs performed by Brock Landers, Doris, Johnny Harris, Moo, Mint Royale and Stephen Lord, The Supernaturals, etc, *Costumes* Clara Apollo, *Sound* Mike Prestwood Smith.

Twin Pictures/Fast Food Films/Vine International-Optimum Releasing.
99 mins. UK. 1998. Rel: 28 January 2000. Cert 18.

Felicia's Journey ★★★★

Leaving her provincial roots behind her in rural Ireland, Felicia sets off to find her boyfriend in the alien, bustling world of Birmingham, England. There, Joseph Hilditch, a lonely, middle-aged catering manager, takes pity on her and offers to help track down the young man who has made her pregnant. Both firmly set in their own distinctive ways, Felicia and Joseph form a tentative bond that is to transform their lives forever, but not necessarily for the better ... Like Michael Winterbottom's *I Want You*, this deeply unsettling psychological drama offers a fresh visual perspective of a familiar British landscape. Employing the wide-screen photography of Peter Sarossy (*Affliction*, *The Sweet Hereafter*) and the obtrusive, exotic score of Mychael Danna (*The Sweet Hereafter*, *Kama Sutra*), the Canadian director Atom Egoyan (*The Sweet Hereafter*, *Exotica*) infuses William Trevor's 1994 novel with a stark otherworldliness that perfectly mirrors the book's interior displacement. And, with his deceptive bedside manner and carefully tooled Birmingham accent, Bob Hoskins delivers his best performance since *Mona Lisa*.

● *Joseph `Joey' Ambrose Hilditch* Bob Hoskins, *Felicia* Elaine Cassidy, *Miss Calligary* Claire Benedict, *Mrs Lysaght* Brid Brennan, *Johnny Lysaght* Peter McDonald, *Felicia's father* Gerard McSorley, *Gala Hilditch* Arsinée Khanjian, *Iris* Sheila Reid, *young Joey Hilditch* Danny Turner, Nizwar Karanj, Kriss Dosanjh, Susan Parry, Bob Mason, Julie Cox.
● *Dir and Screenplay* Atom Egoyan, *Pro* Bruce Davey, *Ex Pro* Paul Tucker and Ralph Kamp, *Co-Pro* Robert Lantos, *Assoc Pro* Karen Glasser, *Ph* Paul Sarossy, *Pro Des* Jim Clay, *Ed* Susan Shipton, *M* Mychael Danna; songs performed by Malcolm Vaughan, and Kate Bush, *Costumes* Sandy Powell, *Sound* Steven Munro.

Alliance Atlantis/Marquis Films/Icon Entertainment/The Movie Network/CAVCO Prods-Icon.
116 mins. UK/Canada. 1999. Rel: 8 October 1999. Cert 12.

Fight Club ★★★★¹/₂

A paid-up member of the Ikea lifestyle and a victim of insomnia, an auto-recall supervisor attends a support group for sufferers of testicular cancer to put his own pain in perspective. However, when he meets the brash and charismatic Tyler Durden, a part-time waiter and projectionist, he begins to see pain as a liberating force for the male psyche. Soon, he and Durden are setting up a series of bare-knuckle marathons in which the participants savour the life-enhancing rush of physical confrontation ... As a movie, *Fight Club* is inventive, dynamic, witty, daring and brilliant. As a social document it is amoral, gratuitously violent and extremely dangerous. Seldom has one film caused such diametric reactions in the critical fold, perhaps not since *A Clockwork Orange* 28 years ago. For, while one can applaud such a vivid and original piece of filmmaking, one also has to take in account its effects on a less accountable portion of the cinemagoing public. Because regardless of the subject's eventual moral switch – and supposed satire and reflection of contemporary society – it does glamorise and glory in violence and irresponsible behaviour. Approach with caution.

● *Tyler Durden* Brad Pitt, *Narrator* Edward Norton, *Marla Singer* Helena Bonham Carter, *Robert Paulsen* Meat Loaf Aday, *Angel Face* Jared Leto, *Richard Chesler* Zach Grenier, Richmond Arquette, David Andrews, Rachel Singer, Eion Bailey, Evan Mirand, Thom Gossom Jr., Peter Iacangelo, Joon B. Kim, Pat McNamara, Leonard Termo.
● *Dir* David Fincher, *Pro* Art Linson, Cean Chaffin and Ross Grayson Bell, *Ex Pro* Arnon Milchan, *Screenplay* Jim Uhls, from the novel by Chuck Palahniuk, *Ph* Jeff Cronenweth, *Pro Des* Alex McDowell, *Ed* James Haygood, *M* The Dust Brothers (Michael Simpson and John King); songs performed by Vas, Junk Ferry, Tom Waits, Marlene Dietrich, Black Francis, etc, *Costumes* Michael Kaplan, *Sound* Ren Klyce, *Make-up Effects* Rob Bottin.

Fox 2000 Pictures/Regency Enterprises/Linson Films-Fox. 135 mins. USA. 1999. Rel: 12 November 1999. Cert 18.

The Filth and the Fury ★★★★

It's twenty years since Julien Temple made *The Great Rock 'n' Roll Swindle*, but in returning now to the career of The Sex Pistols he has produced a decidedly lively and inventive documentary feature. It uses not only archival interview clips of the late Sid Vicious, but comments from the survivors including Johnny Rotten. The film will inevitably appeal most to those who like their music. Nevertheless, while looking back on the pop scene of 1975 to 1979 and showing it from their arguably biased viewpoint, the film also reflects fascinatingly the many changes in British society. In particular, what was once seen as anarchic nihilism and part of a wholly alternative lifestyle now seems a kind of pop culture which any rebellious kid might embrace. [*Mansel Stimpson*]

● With The Sex Pistols: Paul Cook, Steve Jones, Glen Matlock, Johnny Rotten, Sid Vicious.
● *Dir* Julien Temple, *Pro* Anita Camarata and Amanda Temple, *Ex Pro* Eric Gardner and Jonathan Weisgal, *Ed* Niven Howie, *Research* John Shearlaw.

Film Four/The Sex Pistols/Jersey Shore/Nitrate Film Prods-Film Four. 107 mins. UK/USA. 1999. Rel: 12 May 2000. Cert 15.

Final Cut ★★

A group of friends get together at the home of Jude and Sadie to mourn the recently deceased Jude, an actor who had the foresight to be a voyeur at his own wake. His legacy to his grieving widow and friends is a home video he'd been working on featuring all of them unsuspectingly at play and worse. As the footage reveals revelations of the assembled, camaraderie starts to fade as the fabric of their friendship shows its frayed ends. Nice idea but not carried out to the full. [*Marianne Gray*]

● *Ray* Ray Winstone, *Sadie* Sadie Frost, *Jude* Jude Law, *Dominic* Dominic Anciano, *Burdis* Ray Burdis, *John* John Beckett, *Tony* Perry Benson, *Mark* Mark Burdis, *Holly* Holly Davidson, *Lisa* Lisa Marsh, *Bill* William Scully, Ali Brown, Sunshine Frost.
● *Dir, Pro and Screenplay* Dominic Anciano and Ray Burdis, *Ex Pro* Jim Beach, *Line Pro* Sarah-Jane Wright, *Ph* John Ward, *Pro Des* Sabina Sattar, *Ed* Sam Sneade, *M* John Beckett; songs performed by Feelybooth, Thierry Lang and His Trio, and Wagen, *Costumes* Ali Brown.

Fugitive Features-Downtown Pictures. 93 mins. UK. 1998. Rel: 1 October 1999. Cert 18.

Final Destination ★★★ ¹/₂

New York; the present. Setting out for a school trip to Paris, Alex Browning begins to feel decidedly uneasy. Then, while waiting for his plane to take off, he falls asleep and has a horrific nightmare, dreaming that the aircraft explodes mid-air. Fighting his way off the plane, he, five fellow students and a teacher find themselves stranded at the airport. Moments later their 747 takes off, explodes and 39 of Alex's classmates die in the conflagration. However, as the lucky survivors struggle with their

Above: Brad Pitt hosts another basement punch-up in David Fincher's inventive and dynamic Fight Club (from Fox)

Above: Johnny Rotten, Steve Jones, Glen Matlock and Paul Cook – aka The Sex Pistols – cause an outrage on live television in The Filth and the Fury *(from Film Four)*

feelings of relief, grief and guilt, Alex realises that death is not going to let them off so lightly ... The joy of this stylishly conceived and sharply edited comic thriller is that the idea behind it is so blissfully simple. Here, death has no face but comes as invisibly and unexpectedly as it does in real life. But, as viewers, we are allowed a glimpse of its devious modus operandi. Thus kitchens and bathrooms, with their arsenal of sharp edges, power points and endless supply of slippery agents, become precarious chambers of destruction. Succinct, funny, suspenseful and unpredictable, *Final Destination* is a minor classic in the teen thriller genre. P.S. Older viewers should appreciate the slew of in-jokes which are discreetly buried in the text (remember, John Denver was killed in a plane crash).

● *Alex Browning* Devon Sawa, *Clear Rivers* Ali Larter, *Carter Horton* Kerr Smith, *Valerie Lewton* Kristen Cloke, *Bludworth* Tony Todd, *Billy Hitchcock* Seann William Scott, *Tod Waggner* Chad E. Donella, *Terry Chaney* Amanda Detmer, *Agent Weine* Daniel Roebuck, *Agent Schreck* Roger Guenveur Smith, Brenden Fehr, Forbes Angus, Lisa Marie Caruk, Christine Chatelain, Barbara Tyson, Robert Wisden, P. Lynn Johnson, Larry Gilman, Guy Fauchon.
● *Dir* James Wong, *Pro* Glen Morgan, Warren Zide and Craig Perry, *Ex Pro* Brian Witten and Richard Brener, *Co-Pro* Art Schaefer, *Screenplay* Morgan, Wong and Jeffrey Reddick, *Ph* Robert McLachlan, *Pro Des* John Willet, *Ed* James Coblentz, *M* Shirley Walker; songs performed by John Denver, Pete Atherton, Jane Siberry, Nine Inch Nails, Alessandro Juliani, and Joe 90, *Costumes* Jori Woodman, *Visual effects* Ariel Velasco Shaw.

New Line Cinema-Entertainment.
98 mins. USA. 2000. Rel: 19 May 2000. Cert 15.

The Five Senses ★★★

A multi-narrative, ensemble drama set in and around the same apartment building in Toronto, this marks the second film from the Canadian director Jeremy Podeswa, who made his debut with the entirely more pretentious *Eclipse* five years ago. Here, displaying a hypnotic painterly eye that one has come to associate with Canadian filmmakers, Podeswa draws the viewer into his sensual mosaic more through the power of expectation than any emotional resonance. Thus, an alienated massage therapist reaches out through her ability to touch; a professional house cleaner searches for the ideal 'smell' of love; an optician discovers that he is going deaf; a professional cake maker produces elaborate spongescapes with little flavour; and a truculent teenager learns to share her passion for voyeurism with a fellow misfit. While it's hard to perceive *The Five Senses* as anything more than an intellectual exercise, the journey is for the most part sensuous, unsettling and touching – no pun intended.

● *Rona* Mary-Louise Parker, *Gail* Pascale Bussières, *Rupert* Brendan Fletcher, *Anna Miller* Molly Parker, *Roberto* Marco Leonardi, *Rachel Seraph* Nadia Litz, *Robert* Daniel MacIvor, *Ruth Seraph* Gabrielle Rose, *Dr Richard Jacob* Philippe Volter, *Raymond* Richard Clarkin, *Amy Lee Miller* Elise Francis Stolk, *Carl* Clinton Walker, *Monica* Sonia LaPlante, Astrid Van Wieren, Paul Bettis, James Allodi, Amanda Soha, Gisele Rousseau, Clare Coulter, Tracy Wright.
● *Dir and Screenplay* Jeremy Podeswa, *Pro* Podeswa and Camelia Frieberg, *Ex Pro* Charlotte Mickie, Ted East and David R. Ginsburg, *Assoc Pro* Shimmy Brandes, *Ph* Gregory Middleton, *Pro Des* Taavo Soodor, *Ed* Wiebke Von Caroldfeld, *M* Alexina Louie and Alex Pauk, *Costumes* Gersha Phillips.

Telefilm Canada/Canadian Television Fund/TMN-The Movie Network-Alliance Releasing.
101 mins. Canada. 1999. Rel: 10 December 1999. Cert 15.

Following ★★★★

London; today. Bill is a writer who likes to follow people, people he doesn't know. The idea is to trigger an idea for his offbeat fiction. Then Bill follows Cobb, a well-heeled stranger who turns out to be a thief. But Cobb, as Bill soon finds out, doesn't just steal for material gain. He likes to uncover the secrets of strangers... A superb example of economic plotting melded to ingenious exposition, *Following* is an unexpected treasure. An assured cross between the game-playing of David Mamet and the unpredictable thrillers of early Wenders, Christopher Nolan's debut feature quickly establishes its own unique signature. What is all the more remarkable is that Nolan shot it on weekends with unknown actors and a hand-held, 16mm camera. It's a shame, then, that just because a film is 69 minutes (and 48 seconds) long – and shot in black-and-white – that it can't receive a wider cinema release. So, it's back to the TV, then. [*Ewen Brownrigg*]

● *Bill* Jeremy Theobald, *Cobb* Alex Haw, *the blonde* Lucy Russell, *the policeman* John Nolan, *the bald guy* Dick Bradsell, Gillian El-Kadi, JenniferAngel, Nicolas Carlotti, Emma Thomas.
● *Dir, Screenplay and Ph* Christopher Nolan, *Pro* Nolan, Emma Thomas and Jeremy Theobald, *Ex Pro* Peter Broderick, *Pro Des* Tristan Martin, *Ed* Nolan and Gareth Heal, *M* David Julyan.

Syncopy Films/Next Wave Films-Alliance Atlantic.
69 mins. UK. 1998. Rel: 5 November 1999. Cert 15.

Food of Love ★

Suffocated by the impersonal onslaught of modern technology, Alex Salmon – assistant manager of a prominent London bank – takes up teaching drama to students in his spare time. Thus stirred with a romantic nostalgia, Alex decides to stage a production of *Twelfth Night* at the bucolic village he left for the City so many years ago. All he has to do now is coerce the original cast to return for his whimsical revival ... Recalling Kenneth Branagh's disastrous *In the Bleak Midwinter*, this heavy-handed comedy trots out all the clichés of the `let's-put-on-a-show' scenario complete with the genre's overbearing sentimentality. Worse, the acting is startlingly bad, which hardly helps the characters' stereotyping. FYI: On screen, Richard E. Grant played Andrew Aguecheek in Trevor Nunn's *Twelfth Night*. [*Charles Bacon*]

● *Alex Salmon* Richard E. Grant, *Michèle* Nathalie Baye, *Sam* Joe McGann, *Madeleine* Juliet Aubrey, *Mary* Penny Downie, *Robin* Mark Tandy, Lorcan Cranitch, John Ramm, Holly Davidson, Sylvia Syms, Tameka Empson, Paula Bacon, Nicola Duffet,

Rupert Penry-Jones, Richard Dixon, Elizabeth Banks.
● *Dir and Screenplay* Stephen Poliakoff, *Pro* Karin Bamborough, *Ex Pro* David Rose, *Co-Pro* Michel Propper, *Line Pro* John Downes, *Ph* Wit Dabal, *Pro Des* Michael Pickwoad, *Ed* Anne Sopel, *M* Adrian Johnston; saongs performed by Orchestra JB, Art of Silence, Aswad, Crowsdell, and The Pretenders, *Costumes* Pam Tait.

Channel Four/Arts Council of England/MP Prods/Canal Plus/National Lottery-Film Four.
109 mins. UK/France. 1997. Rel: 22 October 1999. Cert 15.

For Love of the Game ★★¹/₂

The Detroit Tigers' Billy Chapel is the Ultimate Guy: rich, famous, handsome and prepared to give his all to what he believes in – baseball. Jane Aubrey, a beautiful and promising writer, just wants a Regular Guy. However, one day, five years ago, Billy and Jane meet on the side of the freeway and sort of fall for each other. Now Billy is playing what is probably his most demanding game – a do-or-die showdown against the New York Yankees. But Jane is on the way to the airport to start a new life in London ... The quintessential valentine to America's favourite sport – framed by a bittersweet love story – *For Love of the Game* parades its clichés with abandon. From the opening slo' mo' shot to the predictable finale, this bears all the hallmarks of a Kevin Costner vanity project: baseball, airbrushed romance, impeccable craftsmanship and endless close-ups of the star himself. It's hard to believe that this all-American indulgence is directed by the man who brought us the innovative *Evil Dead*.

● *Billy Chapel* Kevin Costner, *Jane Aubrey* Kelly Preston, *Gus Sinski* John C.Reilly, *Heather* Jena Malone, *Gary Wheeler* Brian Cox, *Frank Perry* J.K.Simmons, *himself* Vin Scully, *himself* Steve Lyons, *Ken Strout* Carmine D. Giovinazzo, *Davis Birch* Bill Rogers, Domenick Lombardozzi, Arnetia Walker, Larry Joshua, Jacob Reynolds, Billy V.Costner, Sharon Rae Costner, Ted Raimi.
● *Dir* Sam Raimi, *Pro* Armyan Bernstein and Amy Robinson, *Ex Pro* Ron Bozman and Marc Abraham, *Screenplay* Dana Stevens, from the novel by Michael Shaara, *Ph* John Bailey, *Pro Des* Neil Spisak, *Ed* Eric L. Beason and Arthur Coburn, *M* Basil Poledouris, *Costumes* Judianna Makovsky.

Universal/Beacon Pictures/TIG Prods/Mirage Enterprises-UIP.
138 mins. USA. 1999. Rel: 16 June 2000. Cert 12.

Frequency ★★★¹/₂

Queens, New York; October 1969/October 1999. During a freak solar storm, New York cop John Sullivan tunes into an old ham radio and is startled by who he finds on the other end. Equally dumbstruck is Frank Sullivan who, in the very same house, but 30 years ear-

Right: Kevin Costner reminisces on the success of Bull Durham in Sam Raimi's clichéd For the Love of the Game *(from UIP)*

lier, has somehow bypassed a wormhole in time to communicate with his grown-up son in the future. The possibilities are fantastic, but neither suspected that it would lead them on a hunt for a serial killer whose very bodycount rests in their hands ... With the revelation that Stephen Hawking no longer believes time travel to be impossible, temporal distortion has taken on a whole new vestment of consequence. Here, the concept is treated fairly scientifically (sound, not people, is able to circumnavigate the known boundaries of linear physics), although not without considerable humour (John Sullivan's Christmas gift to the six-year-old version of his best friend is the magic word 'Yahoo'). At times, the film tries too hard to be all things to its audience (fantasy, thriller, sci-fi conjecture, satire, domestic drama), but its entertainment quotient is high.

● *Frank Sullivan* Dennis Quaid, *John Sullivan* Jim Caviezel, *Satch DeLeon* Andre Braugher, *Julia Sullivan* Elizabeth Mitchell, *Gordo Hersch* Noah Emmerich, *Jack Shepard* Shawn Doyle, *Graham Gibson* Jordan Bridges, *Samantha Thomas* Melissa Errico, *Johnny Sullivan (at 6 years)* Daniel Henson, *Gordo Hersch (at 8 years)* Stephen Joffe, *Commander O'Connell* Jack McCormack, *Butch Foster* Peter MacNeill, Michael Cera, Marin Hinkle, Richard Sali, Dick Cavett, Brian Greene.
● *Dir* Gregory Hoblit, *Pro* Hoblit, Bill Carraro, Toby Emmerich and Hawk Koch, *Ex Pro* Robert Shaye and Richard Saperstein, *Co-Ex Pro* Janis Chaskin, *Assoc Pro* Patricia Graf, *Screenplay* Emmerich, *Ph* Alar Kivilo, *Pro Des* Paul Eads, *Ed* David Rosenbloom, *M* Michael Kamen and J. Peter Robinson; songs performed by Tommy James & the Shondells, Creedence Clearwater Revival, Martha & the Vandellas, Elvis Presley, Carly Simon, Steppenwolf, Fleetwood Mac, Dusty Springfield, Canned Heat, Philip Bastiste and the

Twilights, and Garth Brooks, *Costumes* Elisabetta Beraldo, *Sound* Steve Boeddeker.

New Line Cinema-Entertainment.
118 mins. USA. 2000. Rel: 16 June 2000. Cert 15.

From the Edge of the City – Apo Tin Akri Tis Polis ★★★

Athens; 1997. Having made films in Britain and America, Constantino Giannaris returns to his roots but chooses a low-life drama featuring young hustlers and drug dealers. His visual skills are again in evidence and, by portraying Greek Russians from the Black Sea coast not fitting readily into either location, he offers us an unfamiliar milieu. His central figure is a rent boy confronted by moral choice when implicated into a pimp's decision to sell a Russian girl already inveigled into prostitution. A non-professional actor, Stathis Papadopoulos convinces as the boy, and this is a believable view of a particular society. What seriously weakens the film, however, is its jumbled set of largely unsympathetic characters who, despite their novel setting, are now clichéd figures. [*Mansel Stimpson*]

● *Sasha* Stathis Papadopoulos, *Cotsian* Costas Cotsianidis, *Panagiotis* Panagiotis Chartomatsidis, *Anestis* Anestis Polychronidis, Dimitris Papoulidis, Nicos Camondos, Stelios Tsemboglidis.
● *Dir* and *Screenplay* Constantino Giannaris, *Pro* Dionysis Samiotis and Anastasios Vasiliou, *Ex Pro* Maria Powell, *Ph* George Argiroilipoulos, *Pro Des* Roula Nicolaou, *Ed* Ioanna Spiliopoulo, *M* Akis Daoutis, *Costumes* Sanny Alberti.

Mythos/Cultural Action/Rosebud/Hot Shot Prods/Hellenic Film Centre-Millivres Multimedia.
83 mins. Greece. 1998. Rel: 18 February 2000. Cert 18.

Galaxy Quest ★★★★

It has been 18 years since the last episode of *Galaxy Quest* was filmed, yet the five actors who played the crew of the NSEA Protector are still prisoners of the series. Desperate for work, they trudge round the circuit of *GQ* conventions, signing autographs and sporting silly costumes. The egomaniacal Jason Nesmith – aka Commander Peter Quincy Taggert – loves the attention, but his co-stars are sick of the routine. Then, the series' most devoted fans – aliens under the illusion that the show is for real – spirit Nesmith away to help them combat a deadly intergalactic enemy ... The great joy of *Galaxy Quest* is that it is much funnier than but every bit as enjoyable – and exciting – as the phenomenon it spoofs. And, if anything, the special effects are *better* than those encountered in the *Star Trek* series. And, thanks to characters loosely moulded on Captain Kirk, Spock & co., we are instantly in tune with the protagonists yet have the added thrill of getting to know their alter egos (Alan Rickman is particularly memorable as a Shakespearean actor reduced to playing the show's token alien). There is also plenty of comic book action for younger viewers while the more sophisticated can relish the in-jokes.

● *Jason Nesmith/Commander Peter Quincy Taggert* Tim Allen, *Gwen DeMarco/Lt. Tawny Madison* Sigourney Weaver, *Alexander Dane/Dr Lazarus* Alan Rickman, *Fred Kwan/Tech Sergeant Chen* Tony Shalhoub, *Guy Fleegman* Sam Rockwell, *Tommy Webber/Laredo* Daryl Mitchell, *Mathesar* Enrico Colantoni, *Sarris* Robin Sachs, *Quellek* Patrick Breen, *Laliari* Missi Pyle, *Teb* Jed Rees, *Brandon* Justin Long, Jeremy Howard, Kaitlin Cullum, Jonathan Feyer, Matt Winston, Susan Egan, Heidi Swedberg, Kevin Hamilton McDonald.
● *Dir* Dean Parisot, *Pro* Mark Johnson and Charles Newirth, *Ex Pro* Elizabeth Cantillon, *Co-Pro* Suzann Ellis & Sona Gourgouris, *Screenplay* David Howard and Robert Gordon, *Ph* Jerzy Zielinski, *Pro Des* Linda DeScenna, *Ed* Don Zimmerman, *M* David Newman, *Costumes* Albert Wolsky, *Visual Effects* Bill George, *Alien Make-up/Creature Effects* Stan Winston.

DreamWorks-UIP.
102 mins. USA. 1999. Rel: 28 April 2000. Cert PG.

Gangster No. 1 ★★★½

London; 1968-1999. 'Gangster No. 1' didn't get to where he is today without stepping on a few hoodlums on the way up. So, as his former employer is released from the nick, he reminisces about the good old bad old days ... As the spate of British gangster films continues apace, *Gangster No. 1* arrives in town to kick some serious butt. With Malcolm McDowell a canny choice to play the older Gangster (like Alex from *A Clockwork Orange* matured into a psychotic old fart) and with an electric performance from Paul Bettany as his younger incarnation (recalling a 1960s' Michael Caine), *Gangster No. 1* displays some persuasive muscle. In addition, director McGuigan (*The Acid House*) exhibits a flashy style that recalls the razzmatazz of *Lock, Stock*, while the oeuvre of Tarantino is inevitably acknowledged.

Above: Star tricks – Tim Allen, Alan Rickman and Sigourney Weaver fluff their lines in Dean Parisot's very, very funny Galaxy Quest *(from UIP)*

However, the film's most powerful moment comes with an understated yet breathless episode of anticipated violence in which Bettany 'tortures' a small-time thief with a babygro. Nonetheless, the scene that will be most fondly quoted is the one in which Bettany dispenses with Jamie Foreman with the aid of various household tools. Oh, and by the way, the moral of the story is that there is no substitute for the love of a good woman.

● *Gangster* Malcolm McDowell, *Freddie Mays* David Thewlis, *young Gangster* Paul Bettany, *Karen* Saffron Burrows, *Tommy* Kenneth Cranham, *Lennie Taylor* Jamie Foreman, *Roland* Razaaq Adoti, *Mad John* Dou Allen, *Eddie Miller* Eddie Marsan, David Kennedy, Andrew Lincoln, Cavan Clerkin, Johnny Harris, Anton Valensi, Martin Wimbush, Ralph Collis, Emma Griffiths-Malin, Sean Chapman.
● *Dir* Paul McGuigan, *Pro* Norma Heyman and Jonathan Cavendish, *Ex Pro* Peter Bowles, *Co-Pro* Nicky Kentish Barnes and Ulrich Felsberg, *Screenplay* Johnny Ferguson, *Ph* Peter Sova, *Pro Des* Richard Bridgland, *Ed* Andrew Hulme, *M* John Dankworth; songs performed by Neil Hannon, The Small Faces, Engelbert Humperdinck, Anthony Newley, Saffron Burrows, The Sweet, etc, *Costumes* Jany Temine, *Sound* Simon Fisher Turner.

Film Four/Pagoda Film/Road Movies Filmproduktion/ British Screen/BskyB/NFH/LittleBird Prods/Filmboard Berlin Brandenburg-Film Four.
102 mins. UK/Germany/Ireland. 2000. Rel: 9 June 2000. Cert 18.

The General's Daughter ★★★¹/₂

When the beautiful and popular daughter of a general is found stripped, bound, raped and strangled at Fort MacCallum in Savannah, Georgia, a top investigator from the army's Criminal Investigation Division is called in. But the latter finds that the army's unbending code of ethics constantly obstructs his enquiries ... Taking a number of weighty issues – sexism, duty, honour, loyalty and the legal immunity of high-ranking military officials – and weaving them into a complex, photogenic thriller, *The General's Daughter* is the cinematic equivalent of a gripping and stimulating airport novel. Aided by a charismatic and commanding turn from Travolta (in one his best performances) and some atmospheric, Spanish moss-enhanced locations, the film grabs the attention from the word go. Several critics found some of the story's elements a little *too* unpleasant, but to soft-pedal a subject as critical as sexual harassment in the army would be to anaesthetise the seriousness of the problem. Only a welter of last-minute revelations and suspects dilutes what is otherwise provocative and gripping cinema. FYI: The Department of Defence was so disturbed by the film's subject matter that it refused to cooperate in any way whatsoever.

● *Paul Brenner* John Travolta, *Sarah Sunhill* Madeleine Stowe, *General 'Fighting Joe' Campbell* James Cromwell, *Colonel William Kent* Timothy Hutton, *Colonel George Fowler* Clarence Williams III, *Colonel Robert Moore* James Woods, *Captain Elisabeth Campbell* Leslie Stefanson, *Chief Yardley* Daniel Von Bargen, *Captain Elby* Boyd Kestner, *General Sonnenberg* John Frankenheimer, Peter Weireter, Mark Boone Junior, John Beasley, Brad Beyer, John Benjamin Hickey, Rick Dial, Chris Snyder, Cooper Huckabee.
● *Dir* Simon West, *Pro* Mace Neufeld, *Ex Pro* Jonathan D. Krane, *Co-Pro* Stratton Leopold, *Screenplay* William Goldman and Christopher Bertolini, *Ph* Peter menzies, *Pro Des* Dennis Washington, *Ed* Glen Scantlebury, *M* Carter Burwell; Mozart, Carl Orff; songs performed by Christine and Catherine Shipp, The Rockatts, Kenny Burrell, etc, *Costumes* Erica Phillips, *Sound* Stephen Hunter Flick, *Visual effects* Glenn Neufeld, *Special effects* Paul Lombardi, *Stunts* Mark Riccardi, *Military advisor* Jared Chandler.

Paramount Pictures-UIP.
116 mins. USA/Germany. 1999. Rel: 17 September 1999. Cert 18.

Ghost Dog: The Way of the Samurai
★★★★

Jersey City; the present. Ghost Dog is a lugubrious, bear-like hitman with a penchant for Eastern philosophy who carries out his deadly business with the aid of high-tech gadgetry and a flock of carrier pigeons. However, when a girl witnesses his last 'contract' he falls foul of the Mafia and is put on its own hit list. But the Mob underestimates the unusual working methods of this modern-day Samurai ... After Jarmusch's years in the wilderness this marks a triumphant comeback for the filmmaker, being his most assured, completely satisfying feature to date. Beautifully paced and photographed, this is a subtle blend of the suspenseful, amusing and offbeat, packed with Jarmusch's trademark eccentric detail. As the eponymous Ghost Dog, Forest Whitaker lends the proceedings an enormous strength and poignancy, while Isaach de Bankole is delightful as GD's best friend, a French-speaking ice cream vendor, and Henry Silva a scream as a mobster who spends most of his time staring intently at ancient cartoons on TV.

● *Ghost Dog* Forest Whitaker, *Louie Bonacelli* John Tormey, *Sonny Valerio* Cliff Gorman, *Ray Vargo* Henry Silva, *Raymond* Isaach de Bankole, *Vinny* Victor Argo, *Louise Vargo* Tricia Vessey, *Old Consigliere* Gene Ruffini, *Handsome Frank* Richard Portnow, *Pearline* Camille Winbush, *young Ghost Dog* Damon Whitaker, *Nobody* Gary Farmer, Dennis Liu, Frank Minucci, Vince Viverito, Vinnie Vella, Jerry Sturiano, Tony Rigo, Alfred Nittoli, The RZA
● *Dir* and *Screenplay* Jim Jarmusch, *Pro* Jarmusch

Left: *Forest Whitaker gets the message in Jim Jarmusch's suspenseful, offbeat and amusing* Ghost Dog: The Way of the Samurai *(from Film Four)*

and Richard Guay, *Co-Pro* Diana Schmidt, *Ph* Robby Müller, *Pro Des* Ted Berner, *Ed* Jay Rabinowitz, *M* RZA, *Costumes* John Dunn, *Sound* Chic Ciccolini III.

JVC/Canal Plus/BAC Films/Pandora Film/ARD-Degeto Film/Plywood Prods-Film Four.
116 mins. USA/Japan/France/Germany. 1999. Rel: 28 April 2000. Cert 15.

Girl ★¹/₂

West Hills, Porter City, Washington; the present. Privileged, bright, beautiful and sexy, high school senior Andrea Marr cannot understand why she is still hymenally challenged. So she and her best friend Darcy set out to become 'real women,' buddying up to the sport-obsessed, beer-guzzling jocks of their alma mater. Then Andrea spots local music legend Todd Sparrow and sets her sights on true love ... An inexplicably vapid and unconvincing romantic drama for teenage bimbettes, *Girl* limps through the motions with the insight of a cereal packet. And so much is unexplained, like why the 17-year-old Andrea has a mother and father old enough to be her grandparents and why all men are belching, inconsiderate lovers. Still, there are a host of interesting faces here (Dominique Swain, Summer Phoenix, Selma Blair), all begging for a better director to show them the light.

● *Andrea Marr* Dominique Swain, *Rebecca Farnhurst* Summer Phoenix, *Cybil* Tara Reid, *Todd Sparrow* Sean Patrick Flanery, *Darcy* Selma Blair, *Kevin* Channon Roe, *Carla* Portia de Rossi, *Richard* Christopher Kennedy Masterson, *Greg* David Moscow, *Andrea's mother* Rosemary Forsyth, *Andrea's father* James Karen,

Christopher Wiehl, Victor Togunde, Jay R. Ferguson, Robert Bower, John Philbin, Bodhi Elfman, Chris Wiehl, Kathleen Wilhoite, Clea DuVall.
● *Dir* Jonathan Kahn, *Pro* Jeff Most, Chris Hanley and Brad Wyman, *Ex Pro* Michael Burns, Peter Locke and Donald Kushner, *Co-Pro* John Saviano, Mary Vernieu and Michael Alan Kahn, *Assoc Pro* David E. Tolchinsky, *Screenplay* Jonathan Kahn and Tolchinsky, *Ph* Tami Reiker, *Pro Des* Johnna Butler, *Ed* Gillian Hutshing, *M* Michael Tavera, songs performed by Melissa Ferrick, Brain Garden, Sixpense None the Richer, Magnet, Flo 13, The Moles, Crooked Tom, JFT, etc, *Costumes* Magda Lavandez-Berliner.

Kusner-Locke/HSX Films-Feature Film Co.
96 mins. USA. 1998. Rel: 24 September 1999. Cert 15.

Girl, Interrupted ★★¹/₂

Claymoore Psychiatric Hospital, Massachusetts; 1967-69. After chasing a bottle of aspirin with a bottle of vodka, 17-year-old Susanna Kaysen finds herself checked into a 'rest home'. She's diagnosed as suffering from Borderline Personality Disorder, but she's just feeling confused, insecure, interrupted. Gradually, however, she discovers that she has more in common with her fellow patients than she might have thought ... Regardless of the fact that *Girl, Interrupted* is 'based on a true story' (and boasts its main protagonist as associate producer) it oozes phoniness. Meticulously crafted to a fault and featuring the most beautiful retards in the history of cinema, the film adopts a solemnity of tone that is stifling and boring. *One Flew Over the Cuckoo's Nest* was tragic but it was also funny – like life – and bracingly idiosyncratic.

Here, the electric Angelina Jolie whips the movie from underneath Winona's nose and runs off with it screaming into the night. Everybody else just looks like they're acting – and looking pretty for the camera.

● *Susanna Kaysen* Winona Ryder, *Lisa* Angelina Jolie, *Georgina* Clea Duvall, *Daisy* Brittany Murphy, *Polly aka `Torch'* Elisabeth Moss, *Tobias Jacobs* Jared Leto, *Dr Potts* Jeffrey Tambor, *John* Travis Fine, *Cynthia* Jillian Armenante, *Janet* Angela Bettis, *Dr Wick* Vanessa Redgrave, *Valerie* Whoopi Goldberg, *Annette Kaysen* Joanna Kerns, *Professor Gilcrest* Bruce Altman, *Barbara Gilcrest* Mary Kay Place, *Mr Kaysen* Ray Baker, Drucie McDaniel, Alison Claire, Christina Myers, Gloria Barnhart, KaDee Strickland, Kurtwood Smith.
● *Dir* James Mangold, *Pro* Douglas Wick and Cathy Konrad, *Ex Pro* Carol Bodie and Winona Ryder, *Co-Pro* Georgia Kacandes, *Screenplay* James Mangold, Lisa Loomer and Anna Hamilton Phelan, *Ph* Jack Green, *Pro Des* Richard Hoover, *Ed* Kevin Tent, *M* Mychael Danna; songs performed by Simon and Garfunkel, Petula Clark, Them, The Mamas & The Papas, Jefferson Airplane, Doris Day, Aretha Franklin, Wilco, The Band, The Doors, The Feminine Complex, etc, *Costumes* Arianne Phillips.

Columbia Pictures/Red Wagon Prods-Columbia TriStar. 127 mins. USA. 1999. Rel: 24 March 2000. Cert 15.

The Girl On the Bridge – La fille sur le pont ★★★★¹/₂

Paris/Monaco/San Remo/Istanbul/Athens; the present. Like two halves of a bank note, Gabor and Adèle are of little value by themselves. Yet, together, they are a formidable and estimable duo, a double act capable of beating incredible odds. But Gabor being a knife-thrower by trade and Adèle a suicidal nymphomaniac, their union is fraught with unpredictable twists and turns ... Director Patrice Leconte tends to take a theme – voyeurism, touch, scent, conversation – and run with it, creating an atmospheric, stylish world emanating from a single image or idea. Here, he turns his attention to the phenomenon of luck and has fashioned an unexpected, innovative, magical and above all else a *cinematic* odyssey suffused with his characteristic romanticism – like a work by Truffaut reinvented by Fellini. As the unlikely couple, Daniel Auteuil and Vanessa Paradis are a sensational match, the former all manic charisma, the latter pouting sensuality, and both are on exceptionally good form. The scene in which the duo finally consummate their feelings for one another – in a frenzied knife-throwing escapade accompanied by the sound of Marianne Faithful – is a classic instance of implied eroticism. It's a shame the ending is so contrived, though. Filmed in black-and-white.

● *Gabor* Daniel Auteuil, *Adèle* Vanessa Paradis, *Takis* Demetre Georgalas, *Iréne* Catherine Lascault, *contortionist* Frédéric Pfluger, *bride* Isabelle Petit-Jacques.
● *Dir* Patrice Leconte, *Pro* Christian Fechner, *Ex Pro* Hervé Truffaut, *Screenplay* Serge Frydman, *Ph* Jean-Marie Dreujou, *Pro Des* Ivan Maussion, *Ed* Joëlle Hache, *M* Didier Lizé; Mozart; songs performed by Brenda Lee, Marianne Faithful, etc, *Costumes* Annie Périer.

UGC-Fechner/UGCF/France 2 Cinéma/Canal Plus, etc-Pathé. 92 mins. France. 1998. Rel: 26 May 2000. Cert 15.

Gladiator ★★★★¹/₂

Germania/Zucchabar/Rome; 180 A.D. Following his triumphant conquest of the Germanic hordes, Roman general Maximus is asked by Emperor Marcus Aurelius to take over his mantle of power. But before Aurelius can officially declare Maximus his successor, the emperor's son Commodus murders him and orders the death of the general and his wife and son. Barely escaping his own execution, Maximus swears revenge on Commodus, but is sold into slavery and becomes a gladiator ... Not since Ridley Scott himself brought a whole new dimension to sci-fi horror with *Alien*, has a genre been redefined so magnificently. With the aid of digital technology and extraordinary imagination, *Gladiator* is a breathtaking, head-spinning, adrenaline-pumping sword and sandal epic that is a dream come true for bloodthirsty teenage film buffs. With its lavish sets, ingenious weaponry, heart-arresting stunts, rousing score, the inspired casting of Joaquin Phoenix as Commodus and even the clutter of everyday Roman life (nobody does incidental clutter better than Scott), this is a film that astonishes and enthrals. And they'll be talking about that aerial shot of Rome for years to come.

Left: Roman candour – Russell Crowe speaks his mind in Ridley Scott's adrenaline-fuelled Gladiator *(from UIP)*

● *Maximus* Russell Crowe, *Commodus* Joaquin Phoenix, *Lucilla* Connie Nielsen, *Proximo* Oliver Reed, *Gracchus* Derek Jacobi, *Juba* Djimon Hounsou, *Emperor Marcus Aurelius* Richard Harris, *Falco* David Schofield, *Gaius* John Shrapnel, *Quintus* Tomas Arana, *Lucius* Spencer Treat Clark, *Cassius* David Hemmings, *Cicero* Tommy Flanagan, Ralf Moeller, Sven-Ole Thorsen, Mid Djalili, Dave Nicholls, Giannina Facio.
● *Dir* Ridley Scott, *Pro* Douglas Wick, David Franzoni and Branko Lustig, *Ex Pro* Walter F. Parkes and Laurie MacDonald, *Screenplay* David Franzoni, John Logan and William Nicholson, *Ph* John Mathieson, *Pro Des* Arthur Max, *Ed* Pietro Scalia, *M* Hans Zimmer and Lisa Gerrard, *Costumes* Janty Yates, *Visual Effects* John Nelson.

Universal/DreamWorks/Scott Free-UIP.
154 mins. USA. 2000. Rel: 12 May 2000. Cert 15.

Go ★★★¹/₂

Los Angeles/Las Vegas; Christmas Eve. Because Ronna agrees to take on a colleague's shift at the checkout counter of a 24-hour supermarket, the lives of a number of characters take a dramatic U-turn. Ronna finds herself confronted with an opportunity to make her first drugs deal; Simon gets to make out with two stoned wedding guests; and Zack and Adam, two TV actors, get embroiled in a police bust. Of course, nothing goes according to plan ... 'Borrowing' the format of *Pulp Fiction* – in which a single event acts as a catalyst for a variety of characters and narrative strands – *Go* takes some time in gathering steam. But, once the action shifts to Vegas the film's true nature emerges and the fragments of a terrific story start falling rapidly into pace. An attractive up-and-coming cast, a sly sense of humour and the edgy direction of Doug Liman (*Swingers*) reap dividends.

● *Simon Baines* Desmond Askew, *Marcus* Taye Diggs, *Burke* William Fichtner, *Victor Snr* J.E. Freeman, *Claire Montgomery* Katie Holmes, *Irene* Jane Krakowski, *Tiny* Breckin Meyer, *Zack* Jay Mohr, *Todd Gaines* Timothy Olyphant, *Ronna Martin* Sarah Polley, *Adam* Scott Wolf, *Mannie* Nathan Bexton, *Singh* James Duval, *Victor Jr* Jimmy Shubert, Suzanne Krull, Robert Peters, Jodi Bianca Wise, Rita Bland, Katharine Towne, Marisa Morell, Nikki Fritz, Tane McClure, Jay Paulson.
● *Dir and Ph* Doug Liman, *Pro* Paul Rosenberg, Mickey Liddell and Matt Freeman, *Co-Pro* Paddy Cullen, *Screenplay* John August, *Pro Des* Tom Wilkins, *Ed* Stephen Mirrione, *M* BT; songs performed by Lionrock, Starlite Pop Orchestra, No Doubt, Massive Attack, Leftfield, Goldo, BT, Dean Martin, Fatboy Slim, Bellamy Brothers, LEN, Lenny Kravitz, Eagle-Eye Cherry, Steppenwolf, Sunset Sky, Natalie Imbruglia, DJ Rap, etc, *Costumes* Genevieve Tyrrell.

Banner Entertainment/Saratoga Entertainment-Columbia TriStar.
102 mins. USA. 1999. Rel: 3 September 1999. Cert 18.

Goodbye Lover ★★

Jake Dunmore's beautiful wife Sandra is carrying on a highly-charged affair with his own brother, the successful public relations executive Ben Dunmore. Ben, meanwhile, has his roving eye fixed on his efficient new secretary Peggy, while Jake himself is deeply involved with the bottle. So who's gonna kill who? While it may be a kick to see Roland Joffé tackle something so completely different, the director of *The Killing Fields* and *The Mission* might have alighted on a better script than this. Superficially quirky and ingenious, *Goodbye Lover* bears little scrutiny and suffers from a profound surplus of plot twists. And with such one-dimensional and unsympathetic characters, the humour has little traction. Still, there's a spicy turn from Ellen DeGeneres as a deeply cynical, vaguely homophobic cop (right up Kathy Bates' street, in fact), and fans of *The Sound of Music* will be rewarded by the musical's use as a thematic yardstick.

● *Sandra Dunmore* Patricia Arquette, *Jake Dunmore* Dermot Mulroney, *Rita Pompano* Ellen DeGeneres, *Peggy Blaine* Mary-Louise Parker, *Ben Dunmore* Don Johnson, *Nathaniel Rollins* Ray McKinnon, *Detective Crowley* Alex Rocco, *Reverend Finlayson* André Gregory, *Senator Roy Lassetter* Barry Newman, John Neville, Jo Neil Kennedy, Akane Nelson, Nina Siemaszko, David Brisbin, Lisa Eichhorn, George Furth, Max Perlich, Richard T. Jones, Frances Bay, Ernie Lively, Lou Myers, Lee Weaver.
● *Dir* Roland Joffé, *Pro* Alexandra Milchan, Patrick McDarrah, Joel Roodman and Chris Daniel, *Ex Pro* Arnon Milchan and Michael G. Nathanson, *Line Pro* Gerald T. Olson, *Screenplay* Ron Peer, Joel Cohen and Alec Sokolow, *Ph* Dante Spinotti, *Pro Des* Stewart Starkin, *Ed* William Steinkamp, *M* John Ottman; songs performed by Save Ferris, Casual, James Brown, Peter Cetera, and Wessyde Goon Squad, *Costumes* Theodora Van Runkle.

Regency Enterprises/Gotham Entertainment Group/Lightmotive-Warner.
101 mins. USA/Germany. 1998. Rel: 6 August 1999. Cert 15.

The Green Mile ★★★¹/₂

Louisiana; 1935. Presiding over Death Row – 'the Green Mile' – at the Louisiana State Penitentiary, prison warder Paul Edgecombe believes in a non-violent approach in his daily dealings with the prisoners. Then a human giant is put in his custody, an apparently simple-minded man convicted of the murder of two little sisters. However, the newcomer is not all he seems and the lives of the prisoners begin to benefit substantially from his presence ... Like *The Shawshank Redemption*, this is based on a story by Stephen King, is written and directed by Frank Darabont, is set in a prison and even features two of the same actors (William Sadler and Jeffrey DeMunn). But there the comparison ends, as this sentimental, shocking yet moving and meticulously crafted drama veers into the realms of the supernatural. And here is where it is at its weakest, as the scenes of miraculous transformation lose their power through a lack of ambiguity and by tacked-on special effects. Nonetheless, the acting is of the highest order (with Sam Rockwell a standout as a repugnant psycho), bringing compassion and substance to an absorbing if predictable tale. It's unfortunate, though, that at 189 minutes, the movie's last line is '...sometimes the Green Mile seems so long.'

● *Paul Edgecombe* Tom Hanks, *Brutus 'Brutal' Howell* David Morse, *Jan Edgecombe* Bonnie Hunt, *John Coffey* Michael Clarke Duncan, *Warden Hal Moores* James Cromwell, *Eduard 'Del' Delacroix* Michael Jeter, *Arlen Bitterbuck* Graham Greene, *Percy Wetmore* Doug Hutchison, *William 'Wild Bill' Wharton* Sam Rockwell, *Dean Stanton* Barry Pepper, *Harry Terwilliger* Jeffrey DeMunn, *Melinda Moores* Patricia Clarkson, *Toot-Toot* Harry Dean Stanton, *elderly Paul Edgecombe* Dabbs Greer, *Elaine Connely* Eve Brent, *Bill Dodge* Brent Briscoe, *Burt Hammersmith* Gary Sinise, William Sadler, Mack C. Miles, Brian Libby, Bill McKinney, Rachel Singer, Scotty Leavenworth, Katelyn Leavenworth.
● *Dir* and *Screenplay* Frank Darabont, *Pro* Darabont and David Valdes, *Ph* David Tattersall, *Pro Des* Terence Marsh, *Ed* Richard Francis-Bruce, *M* Thomas Newman, *Costumes* Karyn Wagner, *Sound* Eric Lindeman, *Acting coach* Larry Moss.

Castle Rock Entertainment/Dark Woods-UIP.
189 mins. USA. 1999. Rel: 25 February 2000. Cert 18.

Greenwich Mean Time ★★¹/₂

Greenwich, South London; today. Four years after leaving school, a group of friends are on the edge of realising their dream of launching their own rock band, GMT. But then reality makes some nasty adjustments to their plans ... A cutting-edge, musically-empowered drama expressing the hopes and fears of contemporary British youth, *Greenwich Mean Time* shows as much promise as it does uneven acting and tangled exposition. But after a really cheesy start, it settles into its stride and finds its own rhythm. In fact, every half an hour or so the film kicks into an even higher gear, so that by the end you actually want it to continue. Ultimately, it's the editing and music – and some striking visuals – that get under the skin, making up for ropey dialogue and stock yoof movie clichés. FYI: The screenplay is a first effort by Helen Mirren's nephew.

● *Sam* Steve John Shepherd, *Charlie* Alec Newman, *Rix* Chiwetel Ejiofor, *Bean* Benjamin Waters, *Sherry* Anjela Lauren Smith, *Lucy* Melanie Gutteridge, *Bobby* Alicya Eyo, *Rachel* Georgia Mackenzie, *Uncle Harry* Alun Armstrong, *Elroy* Freddie Annobil-Dodoo, *Iona* Hinda Hicks, Debbi Blythe, Trevor Byfield, Karl Collins, Charles De'ath, Joe Duttine, Perry Fenwick, David Gant, Roger Griffiths, Simon Mirren, George Sweeney.
● *Dir* John Strickland, *Pro* Taylor Hackford, *Ex Pro* Ralph Kamp and Jamie Carmichael, *Line Pro* Simon Hardy and Simon Scotland, *Screenplay and Assoc Pro* Simon Mirren, *Ph* Alan Almond, *Pro Des* Luana Hanson, *Ed* Patrick Moore, *M* Guy Sigsworth; songs performed by Lester Bowie, GMT, Hinda Hicks, Imogen Heap, The Orb, Deus, Tricky, Rachel Stamp, etc , *Costumes* Stephanie Collie.

Icon Entertainment/Anvil Films-Icon.
117 mins. UK. 1998. Rel: 1 October 1999. Cert 18.

Gregory's Two Girls ★¹/₂

It's almost 20 years since *Gregory's Girl* charmed cinema audiences. Writer-director Bill Forsyth was never able to work the same magic again but, for his latest film he has gone back to Gregory's old stamping ground. Again played by John Gordon-Sinclair, Gregory is now a teacher at his old school ostensibly tutoring his pupils in English. However, he spends much of his time lecturing them on assorted agitprop ideas. And while fellow teacher Maria Doyle Kennedy fancies him, he shies away, having wild fantasies about one of his pupils, who's the same age as Dorothy, the girl he was besotted with 20 years earlier ... The sequel is at its strongest in dealing with the relationship between the central character and the two women. There is considerable charm and humour in these more human moments which recapture a little of the essence of the original. Unfortunately, a manufactured subplot involving torture weapons is ridiculous, the script is frequently unsubtle – not to say downright dull – and the jokes are few and largely feeble. [*Simon Rose*]

● *Gregory Underwood* John Gordon-Sinclair, *Fraser Rowan* Dougray Scott, *Bel* Maria Doyle Kennedy, *Jon* Kevin Anderson, *Dimitri* Martin Schwab, *Maddy Underwood* Fiona Bell, *Frances* Carly McKinnnon, *Douglas* Hugh McCue, *headmaster* John Murtagh, *Mr McCance* Gary Lewis, Alexander Morton, Dawn Steele, Matt Costello, Jane Stabler, Kirsty Anderson, Aisling Friel.
● *Dir and Screenplay* Bill Forsyth, *Pro* Christopher Young, *Line Pro* Alan J. Wands, *Ph* John de Borman, *Pro Des* Andy Harris, *Ed* John Gow, *M* Michael Gibbs, *Costumes* Kate Carin.

FilmFour/Scottish Arts Council/National Lottery/ Kinowelt/ Young Lake-Film Four.
116 mins. UK/Germany. 1999. Rel: 15 October 1999. Cert 15.

Guest House Paradiso ★

Competition for the worst film of 1999 was hot, but this crass comedy, lacking both style and timing, came in the winner. Rik Mayall and Adrian Edmondson running Britain's least efficient guest house might have seemed a promising concept, but the leaden vulgarity of the jokes makes the *Carry On*s seem sophisticated. Special effects assist in the grand climax – a tidal wave of vomit – which might well appeal greatly to the ten-year-olds kept away by the 15 certificate. It's sad to see Bill Nighy, Vincent Cassel and Fenella Fielding involved. However, appreciation of comedy is always a very personal thing so, if a room labelled 'Honeymoon Suet' instead of 'Honeymoon Suite' strikes you as hilarious, please ignore this dismissal. [*Mansel Stimpson*]

● *Richie Twist* Rik Mayall, *Eddie Elizabeth Ndinggobaba* Adrian Edmondson, *Gino Bolognese* Vincent Cassel, *Gina Carbonara* Hélène Mahieu, *Mr*

Johnson Bill Nighy, *Mr Nice* Simon Pegg, *Mrs Foxfur* Fenella Fielding, Lisa Palfrey, Kate Ashfield, Steve O'Donnell, Joseph Hughes, Richard Strange.
● *Dir* Adrian Edmondson, *Pro* Phil McIntyre, *Ex Pro* Helen Parker, Marc Samuelson and Peter Samuelson, *Line Pro* Shellie Smith, *Screenplay* Rik Mayall and Adrian Edmondson, *Ph* Alan Almond, *Pro Des* Tom Brown, *Ed* Sean Barton, *M* Colin Towns, *Costumes* Pam Downe.

Vision Video/Universal Pictures-Universal.
90 mins. UK. 1999. Rel: 3 December 1999. Cert 15.

Above: John Gordon-Sinclair in Bill Forsyth's manufactured and unsubtle Gregory's Two Girls (from Film Four)

Left: Rik Mayall hams it up in Adrian Edmondson's dreadful Guest House Paradiso (from Universal)

Hanging Up ★

Georgia is the self-obsessed editor of a women's magazine (*Georgia*), Eve a distracted 'events organiser' and Maddy a budding TV soap actress. Clinging to their hectic lifestyles by the edge of their mobile phones, the sisters are forced to reconcile their differences when their curmudgeonly, 79-year-old father suffers a stroke ... An unendurably shrill and schmaltzy 'comedy', *Hanging Up* lacks structure, credibility and focus. A series of half-formed vignettes, this tale of sibling rivalry from real-life sisters Delia and Nora Ephron slides all over the place without going anywhere. The saddest spectacle of all is watching Walter Matthau, at 79 a shadow of his former self, poking fun at senility. It's hard to believe that this slush is the creation of the writer of *When Harry Met Sally ...* and the director of the resonant *Unstrung Heroes*.

● *Eve Marks* Meg Ryan, *Georgia Mozell* Diane Keaton, *Maddy Mozell* Lisa Kudrow, *Lou Mozell* Walter Matthau, *Joe Marks* Adam Arkin, *Pat Mozell* Cloris Leachman, *Jesse Marks* Jesse James, *Esther* Edie McClurg, *Omar Kunundar* Duke Moosekian, *Ogmed Kunundar* Ann Bortolotti, *Dr Kelly* Myndy Crist, Maree Cheatham, Libby Hudson, Tracee Ellis Ross, Celia Weston, Charles Matthau.
● *Dir* Diane Keaton, *Pro* Laurence Mark and Nora Ephron, *Ex Pro* Delia Ephron and Bill Robinson, *Co-Pro* Diana Pokorny, *Screenplay* Delia Ephron and Nora Ephron, *Ph* Howard Atherton, *Pro Des* Waldemar Kalinowski, *Ed* Julie Monroe, *M* David Hirschfelder; songs performed by Jay McShann, Paul McCartney, Judy Garland, Dean Martin, Ja'net Dubois, Annie Lennox, and Steve Tyrell, *Costumes* Bobbie Read.

Columbia Pictures-Columbia TriStar.
92 mins. USA. 2000. Rel: 12 May 2000. Cert 15.

Happy, Texas ★★★¹/₂

Happy is a small town in Texas that lives up to its name. In fact, so sweet is this backwater that when two bank robbers roll into town in the guise of pageant advisors – supposedly to help out with the annual Little Miss Fresh-Squeezed Pre-Teen Talent Competition – they find themselves reluctant to take advantage of their hosts ... Any film that opens with a bully being beaten about the head by an armadillo can't be all bad. And *Happy, Texas* begins well. By turns black, wry and absurdist, yet consistently amusing, the film is unusual in that it keeps its protagonists believable and sympathetic in spite of the ludicrous plot shifts. And here are some wonderful characters: the oversensitive sheriff (surprisingly in touch with his feminine side), the aggressive and inarticulate jailbird forced to master the intricacies of stitching

and the no-nonsense female bank manager looking for true love.

● *Harry Sawyer* Jeremy Northam, *Wayne Wayne Wayne Jr* Steve Zahn, *Josephine McClintlock* Ally Walker, *Doreen Schaefer* Ileanna Douglas, *Sheriff Chappy Dent* William H. Macy, *Bob Maslow* M.C. Gainey, *Nalhober* Ron Perlman, Mo Gaffney, Paul Dooley, Jillian Berard, Scarlett Pomers, Tim Bagley, Michael Hitchcock, Rance Howard.
● *Dir* Mark Illsley, *Pro* Illsley, Rick Montgomery and Ed Stone, *Ex Pro* Jason Clark, *Co-Pro* Glenn S. Gainor, *Screenplay* Stone, Illsley and Phil Reeves, *Ph* Bruce Douglas Johnson, *Pro Des* Maurin Scarlata, *Ed* Norman Buckley, *M* Peter Harris; songs performed by Randy Scruggs, Emmylou Harris, Pam Tillis, The Road Kings, Big Sandy and His Fly-Rite Boys, Southern Culture On the Skids, Jillian Berard, etc, *Costumes* Julia Schklair.

Miramax/Marked Entertainment/Illsley/Stone-Buena Vista. 98 mins. USA. 1999. Rel: 3 December 1999. Cert 12.

The Haunting ★★★

New England; the present. To assist his research on the automatic reflexes of fear, scientist Dr David Marrow invites three guinea pigs to a Gothic mansion on the excuse that he is studying the intricacies of insomnia. But the house has its own agenda ... This $80 million remake of Robert Wise's 1963 classic was given a general trouncing by the critics. But what did they expect the director of *Speed* and *Twister* to do with a haunted house tale? As it is, Jan De Bont has created the biggest, baddest and boldest ghost story that money can buy, a full-blown *Casper* for adults – with knobs on. But then one man's fetish is another man's phobia. I, personally, found myself contemplating a month of nightmares as the nocturnal creaking, groaning and sighing pushed Lili Taylor to the point of madness. But then, as with *The Exorcist*, as soon as the visual effects rolled on, I remembered it was just a movie.

● *Dr David Marrow* Liam Neeson, *Theo* Catherine Zeta-Jones, *Luke Sanderson* Owen Wilson, *Nell* Lili Taylor, *Mr Dudley* Bruce Dern, *Mrs Dudley* Marian Seldes, Alix Koromzay, Todd Field, Virgina Madsen, Michael Cavanaugh, Tom Irwin, M.C. Gainey.
● *Dir and Ex Pro* Jan De Bont, *Pro* Susan Arnold, Donna Arkoff Roth and Colin Wilson, *Screenplay* David Self, based upon the novel *The Haunting of Hill House* by Shirley Jackson, *Ph* Karl Walter Lindenlaub, *Pro Des* Eugenio Zanetti, *Ed* Michael Kahn, *M* Jerry Goldsmith, *Costumes* Ellen

Mirojnick, *Sound* Gary Rydstrom, *Visaul effects* Phil Tippett and Craig Hayes.

DreamWorks-UIP.
113 mins. USA. 1999. Rel: 24 September 1999. Cert 12.

Head On ★★★¹/₂

Ari's parents, Greek immigrants living in Melbourne, would like their son, now 19, to get a job, find a nice Greek girl and settle down. However, Ari sees things differently: he wants to enjoy the boys he meets in back alleys, partake in a bit of gambling and pop some pills. In short, he wants to experience life head on... Powered by pounding techno music and MTV-style editing, *Head On* is a film that adopts the stylistic mindset of its compelling – if fatally flawed – hero while also addressing the issues of cultural identity with well-rounded insight. Marking the directorial debut of the Australian filmmaker Ana Kokkinos, herself of Greek extraction, the film holds together because its star, Alex Dimitriades, is such a compelling presence and because the film refuses to take sides. FYI: *Head On* is the top-grossing Australian film of 1998. [*Ewen Brownrigg*]

● *Ari* Alex Dimitriades, *Johnny aka 'Toula'* Paul Capsis, *Sean* Julian Garner, *Dimitri* Tony Nikolakopoulos, *Betty* Elena Mandalis, *Sophia* Eugenia Fragos, *Joe* Damien Fotiou, Andrea Mandalis, Maria Mercedes, Dora Kaskanis.
● *Dir* Ana Kokkinos, *Pro* Jane Scott, *Screenplay* Kokkinos, Andrew Bovell and Mira Robertson, from the novel *Loaded* by Christos Tsiolkas, *Ph* Jaems Grant, *Pro Des* Nikki Di Falco, *Ed* Jill Bilcock, *M* Ollie Olsen; songs performed by Death in Vegas, Lunatic Calm, Way Out West, Underground Lovers, Dannii, Isaac Hayes, Silverchair, Primal Scream, Hot Chocolate, haBiBis, Irine Vela, etc, *Costumes* Anna Borghesi, *Sound* Craig Carter and Livia Ruzic.

Australian Film Finance Corporation/Great Scott/Film Victoria-Millivres Multimedia.
104 mins. Australia. 1997. Rel: 15 October 1999. Cert 18.

The Hi-Lo Country ★★★

Hi-Lo, New Mexico; the 1940s. In the four years that Pete Calder and Big Boy Matson were away fighting the war, their back yard changed irrevocably. Just as they were hoping to prove themselves as masters of the cattle drive, mass transport and new ethics are transforming the very code of the old West. Then even their friendship is tested when the wife of a ranch employee starts making sexual overtures ... Thirty-five years after Sam Peckinpah failed to bring Max Evans' 1961 novel to the screen, Stephen Frears (of all people) makes a creditable stab, conjuring up a powerful sense of time and place. And he's well served by some impressive braggadocio from Woody Harrelson as the impulsive Big Boy and by the grounded broodiness

Above: *You'll just feel a little prick – Lili Taylor has trouble sleeping in Jan De Bont's spectacular The Haunting (from UIP)*

of Billy Crudup. Although, as the woman who threatens to divide them, Patricia Arquette seems a somewhat spent spark. But it's the story itself that ultimately fails the film which, near the end, seems to trail off into a haze of irony. The journey, though, is evocative and gripping.

● *Big Boy Matson* Woody Harrelson, *Pete* Billy Crudup, *Mona* Patricia Arquette, *Little Boy Matson* Cole Hauser, *Hoover Young* James Gammon, *Josepha O'Neil* Penelope Cruz, *Jim Ed Love* Sam Elliott, *Billy Harte* Darren Burrows, *Les Birk* John Diehl, *Steve Shaw* Lane Smith, *Meesa* Katy Jurado, Enrique Castillo, Jacob Vargas, Robert Knott, Rosaleen Linehan, Rose Maddox, Marty Stuart.
● *Dir* Stephen Frears, *Pro* Barbara De Fina, Martin Scorsese, Eric Fellner and Tim Bevan, *Ex Pro* Rudd Simmons, *Co-Pro* Liza Chasin, *Screenplay* Walon Green, *Ph* Oliver Stapleton, *Pro Des and Costumes* Patricia Norris, *Ed* Masahiro Hirakubo, *M* Carter Burwell; songs performed by Leon Rausch, Johnny Degollado y su Conjunto, Hank Williams, Hermanas Ayala, etc.

PolyGram/Working Title-PolyGram.
114 mins. UK/USA. 1998. Rel: 23 July 1999. Cert 15.

Hold Back the Night ★★

Discovering that her younger sister is on the pill, Charleen throws a few belongings into a knapsack and runs away from home. Meeting up with an animal-cum-environmental activist called Declan, Charleen finds herself inadvertently embroiled in a fight with police during a protest over the construction of a new bypass. Now on the run, Charleen and Declan discover that they have more in common than they might at first have thought ... Attempting to be a hard-hitting contemporary tale with a heart of gold, *Hold Back the Night* is a road movie that breaks the rules to its detriment. By its very nature, the genre has little plot to speak of and so needs strong, sympathetic characters to hold the attention. Unfortunately, Charleen is such an unattractive and strident individual (regardless of the reasons that made her

Above: 'I'm the king of the castle!' Kate Winslet steps out in Jane Campion's visually rich but ultimately ridiculous Holy Smoke (from Film Four)

that way), it's hard to spend time with her. And where the additional character of an eccentric itinerant lesbian (played a little too broadly by Sheila Hancock) is introduced as an emotional counterpoint, it merely serves to underline the schematic nature of the film. A glum tale, then, and one that fails to engage the emotions.

● *Charleen* Christine Tremarco, *Declan* Stuart Sinclair Blyth, *Vera* Sheila Hancock, *Michael* Richard Platt, *Bob* Kenneth Colley, *Jacob* Peter Anders, *Torsten* Lars Oostveen, Julie Ann Watson, Tommy Tiernan, Andrew Livingstone, Bruce Bryon.
● *Dir* Phil Davis, *Pro* Sally Hibbin, *Co-Pro* Torsten Leschly and Sarah McCarthy, *Screenplay* Steve Chambers, *Ph* Cinders Forshaw, *Pro Des* Chris Roope, *Ed* Adam Ross, *M* Peter John Vettese, songs performed by Grand Theft Auto, and Heather Small, *Costumes* Paul Farrow.

The Film Consortium/Film On Four/Arts Council of England/BIM and Wave Pictures/Parallax Pictures/National Lottery/Swingbridge Video-UIP.
104 mins. UK/Italy. 1999. Rel: 17 December 1999. Cert 15.

Holy Smoke ★★½

While backpacking in India, Ruth Barron falls in with a religious sect and finds true Nirvana. However, her family back in suburban Sydney fear the worst and usher her back to Australia under false pretences. There, they subject her to an intensive three-day de-programming session with an arrogant 'cult buster' from the US. But Ruth's will is stronger than the deprogrammer could have imagined ... Flaunting director Jane Campion's characteristically rich visual style, *Holy Smoke* is as much a display of smoke and mirrors as its subject matter. The problem is the film's plausibility – and its predictability. The psychological transition between the leading characters just doesn't ring true, in spite of the emotional investment by both Winslet and Keitel. And the film's narrative arc brings no surprise, only bewilderment.

● *Ruth Barron* Kate Winslet, *P.J. Waters* Harvey Keitel, *Carol* Pam Grier, *Miriam Barron* Julie Hamilton, *Yvonne Barron* Sophie Lee, *Robbie Barron* Daniel Wyllie, *Tim Barron* Paul Goddard, *Gilbert Barron* Tim Robertson, *Yani* George Mangos, Kerry Walker, Leslie Dayman, Samantha Murray.
● *Dir* Jane Campion, *Pro* Jan Chapman, *Ex Pro* Bob Weinstein, Harvey Weinstein and Julie Goldstein, *Assoc Pro* Mark Turnbull, *Screenplay* Anna Campion and Jane Campion, *Ph* Dion Beebe, *Pro Des and Costumes* Janet Patterson, *Ed* Veronika Jenet, *M* Angelo Badalamenti, *Sound* Lee Smith.

Miramax-Film Four.
114 mins. USA/New Zealand. 1999. Rel: 31 March 2000. Cert 18.

Honest ★ ¹/₂

Mistresses of disguise, three sisters from the East End of London carry out a series of audacious robberies out of sheer avarice. However, when they break into the offices of an 'alternative' magazine in Carnaby Street, they are disturbed by a young American journalist, who takes a liking to Gerry, the ringleader. Inviting her back to his pad, he tries to get into her pants but discovers that she is really a girl of some moral fibre ... A vehicle for three of the four-member girl band All Saints, *Honest* is an excruciating attempt to re-live the era of Swinging London, psychedelia and chemical enhancement. Marking the directorial debut of musician Dave A. Stewart (co-founder of Eurythmics), the film recalls little of the style or iconoclastic nature and much of the mediocrity of the films of that period. Illogical and risible, *Honest* is an embarrassment for all concerned.

● *Daniel Wheaton* Peter Facinelli, *Gerry Chase* Nicole Appleton, *Mandy Chase* Natalie Appleton, *Jo Chase* Melanie Blatt, *Tommy Chase* James Cosmo, *Rose* Annette Badland, *Baz* Rick Warren, *Andrew Pryce-Stevens* Jonathan Cake, *Duggie Ord* Corin Redgrave, *Matt Bardock*, Sean Giller, Heathcote Williams, Graham Fletcher Cook, Tony Maudsley, Sam Kelly, Lynn Ferguson, Rolf Saxon, Susannah Fellows, Chrissie Cotterill.
● *Dir* David A. Stewart, *Pro* Eileen Gregory and Michael Peyser, *Ex Pro* Keith Northrop, *Line Pro* Paul Sarony, *Screenplay* Stewart, Dick Clement and Ian La Fresnais, *Ph* David Johnson, *Pro Des* Michael Pickwood, *Ed* David Martin, *M* David A. Stewart; Faure; songs performed by Bob Dylan, Marvin Gaye, Al Stewart, Smokey Robinson & The Miracles, The Sires, The Temptations, Small Faces, Jacques Dutronc, Natalie Appleton and Bootsy Collins, etc, *Costumes* Mary-Jane Reyner.

Pathé/Seven Dials Films/Pandora/European Script Fund-Pathé.
105 mins. UK/France. 2000. Rel: 26 May 2000. Cert 18.

House On Haunted Hill ★★ ¹/₂

Stephen Price is one sick thoroughbred. The mastermind behind a series of state-of-the-fear amusement parks, the self-made billionaire plans the ultimate birthday party for his equally sick wife. He hires the abandoned Vannacutt Psychiatric Institute for the Criminally Insane and invites five guests to spend the night there. Anybody who stays the course – and remains alive – will receive a cheque for $1 million. But whose party is this anyway? Stephen's? His wife's? Or something else entirely more sinister? A remake of William Castle's 1958 film of the same name, this cheerfully gruesome horror film suffers from comparisons with Jan De Bont's *The Haunting*, itself a remake of a classic haunted house chiller.

Here, however, the humour is a little more finely tuned (and intentional), although things just get too silly in the final quarter and the visions of torture unnecessarily sadistic.

● *Stephen Price* Geoffrey Rush, *Evelyn Price* Famke Janssen, *Eddie* Taye Diggs, *Sara Wolfe* Ali Larter, *Melissa Marr* Bridgette Wilson, *Dr Blackburn* Peter Gallagher, *Watson Pritchett* Chris Kattan, *Schecter* Max Perlich, *Dr Vannacutt* Jeffrey Combs, Dick Beebe, Lisa Loeb, Jeannette Lewis, Peter Graves.
● *Dir* William Malone, *Pro* Robert Zemeckis, Joel Silver and Gilbert Adler, *Ex Pro* Dan Cracchiolo and Steve Richards, *Co-Pro* Terry Castle, *Screenplay* Dick Beebe, from a story by Robb White, *Ph* Rick Bota, *Pro Des* David F. Klassen, *Ed* Anthony Adler, *M* Don Davis; 'Sweet Dreams (Are Made Of This)' performed by Marilyn Manson, *Costumes* Ha Nguyen, *Sound* Dane A. Davis.

Dark Castle Entertainment-Warner.
93 mins. USA. 1999. Rel: 4 February 2000. Cert 18.

House! ★★★

Wales; the present. Just one year away from celebrating its centenary, the crumbling La Scala bingo hall is facing closure. A glamorous new facility – the soulless Mega Pleasure centre – has opened up the road and claims to be the biggest bingo arena in the United Kingdom. But La Scala employee Linda discovers that she has an unusual gift that might just save the day ... In the tradition of such small-scale British treasures as *The Smallest Show On Earth*, *Comfort and Joy* and *Whatever Happened to Harold Smith?*, *House!* is a feel-good entertainment with charm to spare. Directed in broad strokes by first-timer Julian Kemp (whose apprenticeship in children's TV is vividly apparent), the film is fresh, funny and generous in spirit. It's just a shame that the pay-off is a bit of a let-down. FYI: Cinematographer Kjell Vassdal, who manages to make rain-sodden Wales look pic-

Above: Gangsta pap – The Appletons, Melanie Blatt and Peter Facinelli in David A. Stewart's excruciating Honest *(from Pathé)*

turesque, previously worked on the beguiling Norwegian fable *Junk Mail*.

● *Linda* Kelly Macdonald, *Mr Anzani* Freddie Jones, *Beth* Miriam Margolyes, *Gavin* Jason Hughes, *Kay* Mossie Smith, Gwenllian Davies, Sue Hopkins, Eileen Edwards, Marlene Griffiths, Bruce Forsyth, William Thomas, Helen Griffin, Lynn Hunter, Julian Kemp, Daniel Roberts, Keith Chegwin, Sian Rivers, Ifan Huw Dafydd.
● *Dir* Julian Kemp, *Pro* Michael Kelk, *Ex Pro* Christopher Figg and Adam Sutcliffe, *Co-Pro* David Ball, *Screenplay* Jason Sutton, from an idea by Eric Styles, *Ph* Kjell Vassdal, *Pro Des* Kit Line, *Ed* Jonathan Rudd, *M* Puccini, Mozart, Richard Strauss; songs performed by Terry Snyder, Visage, Orange Juice, Ray McVay, The Amigos, etc, *Costumes* Leila Ransley.

House Film Ltd/National Lottery/Arts Council of England-Pathé.
90 mins. UK. 1999. Rel: 5 May 2000. Cert 15.

hurlyburly ★★★

The Hollywood Hills; a few years ago. Eddie, a high-powered casting director, is sharing his luxurious condo with his business partner, Mickey, and is falling apart at the seams. As Eddie snorts coke and chain-smokes, Mickey takes up with Eddie's girlfriend, while Eddie's best friend, the dangerously impulsive actor Phil, contributes his own set of unique problems ... Take a coterie of fascinating characters, give them some terrific dialogue, feed the result to a top-drawer cast and, inevitably, you will have something rather special. Add some stylish direction and superior production values and you still have what is essentially a rather talky, melodramatic movie about a lot of insensitive, self-obsessed jerks. Theatre and film have always been uneasy allies and American drama in particular is prone to narrative stasis. But at least this is sizzling theatre, with particularly memorable turns from Kevin Spacey as the amoral Mickey and Anna Paquin as a sexually available runaway.

● *Eddie* Sean Penn, *Mickey* Kevin Spacey, *Darlene* Robin Wright Penn, *Phil* Chazz Palminteri, *Artie* Garry Shandling, *Donna* Anna Paquin, *Bonnie* Meg Ryan, *Susie* Gianna Renaudo, David Fabrizio, Kenny Vance, Michaline Babich, Frank Sommerville, Laura Brownson.
● *Dir* Anthony Drazan, *Pro* Drazan, Richard N. Gladstein and David S. Hamburger, *Ex Pro* H. Michael Heuser, Frederick Zollo, Nicholas Paleologos and Carl Colpaert, *Screenplay* David Rabe, *Ph* Changwei Gu, *Pro Des* Michael Haller, *Ed* Dylan Tichenor, *M* David Baerwald and Steve Lindsey; 'There Goes the Neighbourhood' sung by Sheryl Crow, *Costumes* Mary Claire Hannan.

Storm Entertainment-Metrodome.
122 mins. USA. 1998. Rel: 7 April 2000. Cert 18.

The Hurricane ★★★

New Jersey/Toronto; 1949-1985. On 17 June 1966 two black gunmen stormed into a bar in Paterson, New Jersey, and shot dead two men and a woman. Shortly afterwards, middleweight prize-fighter Rubin 'The Hurricane' Carter and a young fan are stopped by police. Against all reasonable evidence (and with clean lie detector tests), Carter is convicted of murder and sent down for three life terms. Later, Carter writes his autobiography, a second-hand copy of which is bought by a young black boy who becomes convinced of the boxer's innocence ... There is no denying the powerful and emotional essence of this extraordinary true story. And, as the dignified and embittered Carter, Denzel Washington gives one of his finest performances (in a career of outstanding performances). But with so much material at their disposal – largely drawn from Carter's autobiography *The Sixteenth Round* and Chaiton and Swinton's first-person *Lazarus and the Hurricane* – scenarists Bernstein and Gordon have not found the simplest way of unfolding their tale. With flashbacks materialising within flash-backs and dates flicking across the screen, the film takes a long time to get into its stride. It's a shame, too, that the intriguing characters of Chaiton, Swinton and Peters – career do-gooders? *menage-a-trois*? – are so sketchily drawn.

● *Rubin Carter* Denzel Washington, *Terry Swinton* John Hannah, *Lisa Peters* Deborah Kara Unger, *Sam Chaiton* Liev Schreiber, *Lesra Martin* Vicellous Reon Shannon, *Myron Beldock* David Paymer, *Della Pesca* Dan Hedaya, *Leon Friedman* Harris Yulin, *Judge Sarokin* Rod Steiger, *Mae Thelma* Debbi Morgan, *Lt. Jimmy Williams* Clancy Brown, *Mobutu* Badja Djola, *John Artis* Garland Whitt, Vincent Pastore, Al Waxman, David Lansbury, Chuck Cooper, Brenda Thomas Denmark, Beatrice Winde, Bill Raymond, Merwin Goldsmith, Moynan King.
● *Dir* Norman Jewison, *Pro* Norman Jewison, Armyan Bernstein and John Ketcham, *Ex Pro* Rudy Langlais, Thomas A. Bliss, Marc Abraham, Irving Azoff, Tom Rosenberg and William Teitler, *Co-Pro* Suzann Ellis, Michael Jewison and Jon Jashni, *Screenplay* Armyan Bernstein and Dan Gordon, *Ph* Roger Deakins, *Pro Des* Philip Rosenberg, *Ed* Stephen Rivkin, *M* Christopher Young; songs performed by Bob Dylan, Ruth Brown, Marvin Gaye, Gil Scott-Heron, Ray Charles, Etta James, Dinah Washington, Ray Charles, Kool & The Gang, The Roots, etc, *Costumes* Aggie Guerard Rodgers.

Universal Pictures/Beacon Pictures/Azoff Films-UIP.
145 mins. USA. 1999. Rel: 24 March 2000. Cert 15.

In All Innocence – En plein coeur ★★★

Previously filmed with Bardot and Gabin, this new adaptation of Simenon's novel *En cas de malheur* updates it, thereby losing the author's tone. Gérard Lanvin plays a successful Parisian lawyer who decides to defend Cécile Maudet when she's accused of robbery. In this class-conscious drama, the lawyer's motivation may lie in the way he identifies with an accused from his own background, but Cécile's looks are not beside the point. Before long, Cécile finds herself torn sexually between her lawyer and her younger boyfriend Vincent, while the lawyer's wife (Carole Bouquet in the film's best performance) has her own decision to make on discovering what is happening. Pierre Jolivet's movie is no disaster, but it's instantly forgettable: see this after reading Simenon and it's like fast food after a gourmet's repast. [*Mansel Stimpson*]

● *Michel* Gérard Lanvin, *Cécile Maudet* Virginie Ledoyen, *Viviane* Carole Bouquet, *Vincent* Guillaume Canet, *Semira Allahoui* Aurelie Verillon, *Antoine* Jean-Pierre Lorit, Denis Podalydes, Anne Le Ny, Nadia Barentin, Mar Sodupe, Francois Berleand.
● *Dir* Pierre Jolivet, *Pro* Alain Goldman, *Screenplay* Roselyne Bosch, *Ph* Pascal Ridao, *Pro Des* Thierry Flamand, *Ed* Yves Deschamps, *M* Serge Perathoner and Jannick Top; Mozart, *Costumes* Valerie Pozzo Di Borgo.

Légendes Enterprises-France 2 Cinéma/Canal Plus/Soficas Sofygram 2/Gimages-Pathé.
101 mins. France. 1998. Rel: 28 April 2000. Cert 15.

The Insider ★★★★

New York/Iran/Kentucky/Mississippi; 1993-1996. Veteran TV producer Lowell Bergman is proud of the integrity and objectivity of his top-rated news magazine *60 Minutes*. Jeffrey Wigand was less proud of his position as a company executive of Brown and Williamson, the third largest tobacco manufacturer in the US. Lowell needs Wigand to check some facts on a routine story about fires started by smoking in bed. As it happens, Wigand would seem to have a more interesting tale to tell but is muzzled by an ironclad confidentiality contract. However, there are ways of circumventing a confidentiality agreement – although, likewise, there are ways of silencing a whistle blower ... While the corruption of tobacco companies and the pussyfooting of TV networks may not inspire the same moral indignation as a betrayal by the American presidency, *The Insider* wields a muscular stick. Thanks to a trio of outstanding performances from Pacino, Plummer and Crowe (the latter piling on 40 pounds to flesh out his role), the film displays some human traction, albeit at a self-indulgent length of 158 minutes. Intellectually visceral and handsomely crafted, this is a class act, even though some characters are given short thrift (Wigand's wife is particularly underdeveloped). Incidentally, star anchor Mike Wallace was so upset by his representation in the film that some of his scenes were soft-pedalled.

● *Lowell Bergman* Al Pacino, *Jeffrey Wigand* Russell Crowe, *Mike Wallace* Christopher Plummer, *Liane*

Above: Innocent as sin – Virginie Ledoyen in Pierre Jolivet's instantly forgettable In All Innocence *(from Pathé)*

Wigand Diane Venora, *Don Hewitt* Philip Baker Hall, *Sharon Tiller* Lindsay Crouse, *Debbie De Luca* Debi Mazar, *Thomas Sandefur* Michael Gambon, *Richard Scruggs* Colm Feore, *Ron Motley* Bruce McGill, *Helen Caperelli* Gina Gershon, *Barbara Wigand* Hallie Kate Eisenberg, *Sheikh Fadlallah* Clifford Curtis, *Michael Moore* Michael Moore, *Jack Palladino* Jack Palladino, Stephen Tobolowsky, Rip Torn, Lynne Thigpen, Michael Paul Chan, Linda Hart, Robert Harper, Nestor Serrano, Pete Hamill, Wings Hauser, Renee Olstead, Gary Sandy, Willie C. Carpenter, Roger Bart, Doug McGrath, Bill Sage, Breckin Meyer, Vyto Ruginis.
● *Dir* Michael Mann, *Pro* Mann and Pieter Jan Brugge, *Co-Pro* Michael Waxman, *Screenplay* Mann and Eric Roth, from the *Vanity Fair* article *The Man Who Knew Too Much* by Marie Brenner, *Ph* Dante Spinotti, *Pro Des* Brian Morris, *Ed* William Goldenberg, Paul Rubell and David Rosenbloom, *M* Lisa Gerrard and Pieter Bourke and Graeme Revell, *Costumes* Anna Sheppard, *Russell Crowe's make-up* Greg Cannom, *Snow* Snow Business.

Touchstone Pictures/Spyglass Entertainment/Forward Pass-Buena Vista.
158 mins. USA. 1999. Rel: 10 March 2000. Cert 15.

Inspector Gadget ★

John Brown, a friendly if somewhat inept security guard, has always dreamed of being a heroic police officer. Then, following a fateful run-in with the scheming tycoon Sanford Scolex, he becomes the unwitting recipient of 14,000 mechanised implants – as part of a unique law enforcement project. Now Brown is the best equipped law enforcer in the world, but is reduced to rescuing cats from trees and helping children cross the street. At least, for the time being ... A $75 million adaptation of the TV cartoon series, this is a genuine embarrassment. Accepting the wisdom that if you cut a film fast enough no one will notice its shortcomings, *Inspector Gadget* has been hacked down to a frenzied 78 minutes. Unfortunately, such dreadful dialogue, hackneyed film references, over-acting (Rupert, how could you?) and a meddlesome score could effortlessly destroy a 30-second commercial. Here, old jokes wrestle with archaic clichés to produce one of the most insulting children's films of the year.

● *John Brown/Inspector Gadget/RoboGadget* Matthew Broderick, *Sanford Scolex* Rupert Everett, *Brenda/RoboBrenda* Joely Fisher, *Penny* Michelle Trachtenberg, *Kramer* Andy Dick, *Mayor Wilson* Cheri Oteri, *Sikes* Michael G. Hagerty, *Chief Quimby* Dabney Coleman, *Gadgetmobile voice* D.L. Hughley, *voice of Brain* Don Adams, René Auberjonois, Frances Bay, Cliff Emmich, Richard Penn, Sam Brown, William Smith, Jacob Avnet, Richard Kiel, Mr T, Richard Lee-Sung, Hank Barrera, Keith Morrison, Aaron Meyerson.
● *Dir* David Kellogg, *Pro* Jordan Kerner, Roger Birnbaum and Andy Heyward, *Ex Pro* Jon Avnet, Barry Bernardi, Aaron Meyerson, Jonathan Glickman and Ralph Winter, *Co-Pro* Lou Arkoff and Jean Chalopin,

Screenplay Kerry Ehrin and Zak Penn, from a story by Ehrin and Dana Olsen, *Ph* Adam Greenberg, *Pro Des* Michael White and Leslie Dilley, *Ed* Thom Noble and Alan Cody, *M* John Debney; songs performed by Bentley Rhythm Ace, Smash Mouth, X, and Youngstown, *Costumes* Mary Vogt, *Animatronic effects* Stan Winston, *Visual effects* Richard Hoover.

Walt Disney Pictures/Caravan Pictures-Buena Vista International.
78 mins. USA. 1999. Rel: 17 December 1999. Cert U.

Instinct ★★

Theo Caulder is a young and hungry psychiatric resident making a name for himself at the University of Miami. When a psychiatric evaluation is needed of a deranged primatologist back from a killing spree in Rwanda, Caulder sees it as a career-making opportunity. But the homicidal professor is refusing to speak and no amount of ambition can unleash his inner demons without some major sacrifices ... Taking the essence of Daniel Quinn's novel *Ishmael* – that civilisation has become the downfall of the human soul – Jon Turteltaub's slick drama hammers home its message with the subtlety of a sledgehammer. Drawing on his characteristic intellect and physical powers, Anthony Hopkins is a natural for the role of the demented doctor (think Hannibal Lecter), but Cuba Gooding Jr is too lightweight to match him as his younger alter ego. The other actors deliver their dialogue in italics, while Danny Elfman's maniacal music thinks its accompanying a Stallone movie. This is one film that has anything but instinct on its side.

● *Ethan Powell* Anthony Hopkins, *Theo Caulder* Cuba Gooding Jr, *Ben Hillard* Donald Sutherland, *Lyn Powell* Maura Tierney, *Dr John Murray* George Dzundza, *Paul Dacks* John Ashton, *Warden Keefer* John Aylward, *Annie Bilden* Tracey Ellis, Thomas Q. Morris, Doug Spinuzza, Paul Bates, Rex Linn, Kim Ingram, Paul Collins, Marc Macaulay, Jim Grimshaw, Gary Bristow, Pat McNamara, Kevin McNally.
● *Dir* Jon Turteltaub, *Pro* Michael Taylor and Barbara Boyle, *Ex Pro* Wolfgang Petersen and Gail Katz, *Co-Pro* Richard Lerner, Brian Doubleday and Christina Steinberg, *Screenplay* Gerald DiPego, *Ph* Philippe Rousselot, *Pro Des* Garreth Stover, *Ed* Richard Francis-Bruce, *M* Danny Elfman, *Costumes* Jill Ohanneson, *Special Character Effects* Stan Winston.

Touchstone Pictures/Spyglass Entertainment-Buena Vista.
124 mins. USA. 1999. Rel: 17 September 1999. Cert 15.

An Intimate Affair
See Une Liaison Pornographique.

The Iron Giant ★★★★½
Rockwell, Maine; October 1957. Following a local fisherman's sighting of a 50-foot robot from outer space, a nine-year-old boy stumbles across the metal-eating giant in nearby woods. Saving the robot's life, the boy strikes up a friendship with him, resolving to protect the machine – a compassionate innocent armed with a lethal defence arsenal – from the destructive interference of the

Above: *Tripping the light fantastic –* Matthew Broderick in David Kellogg's *insulting* Inspector Gadget *(from Buena Vista)*

US army ... The surprising thing about *The Iron Giant* is that it doesn't behave like a children's cartoon. There are no wise-cracking, furry animals; no gushing end-of-title song; no characters who resemble the famous voice that gives them vocal life. Furthermore, the villain of the piece uses language that might startle your grandmother and there are disconcerting scenes of military destruction. Yet this is not an off-shoot of *South Park*, but an accomplished and moving animated version of Ted Hughes' 1968 children's story *The Iron Man*, which is now on the syllabus of British schools. Avoiding the cuteness of Disney, the film addresses significant moral issues by speaking to kids in their own language, making for fresh, appealing and, above all, accessible and relevant entertainment. FYI: The film is executive produced by The Who's Pete Townshend, who previously explored the story in his 1989 rock opera *The Iron Man*.

● Voices: *Annie Hughes* Jennifer Aniston, *Dean McCoppen* Harry Connick Jr., *The Iron Giant* Vin Diesel, *Marve Loach/Floyd Tubeaux* James Gammon, *Mrs Tensedge* Cloris Leachman, *Kent Mansley* Christopher McDonald, *General Shannon Rogard* John Mahoney, *Hogarth Hughes* Eli Marienthal, *Earl Stutz* M. Emmet Walsh, Mary Kay Bergman, Phil Proctor.
● *Dir* Brad Bird, *Pro* Allison Abbate and Des McAnuff, *Ex Pro* Pete Townshend, *Assoc Pro* John Walker, *Screenplay* Tim McCanlies, from a screen story by Brad Bird, *Pro Des* Mark Whiting, *Ed* Darren T. Holmes, *M* Michael Kamen, songs performed by Jimmie Rodgers, Mel Tormé, Ray Charles, The Coasters, etc, *Sound* Randy Thom.

Warner-Warner.
86 mins. USA. 1999. Rel: 17 December 1999. Cert U.

Isn't She Great ★¹/₂
Great she wasn't, but thanks to the tireless and extravagant marketing of herself as a commodity, Jacqueline Susann made her first novel, *Valley of the Dolls*, the top-selling title of all time. However, behind all the glitz and glamour, the celebrity bore more than her share of tragedy ... Screen biographies are notoriously difficult to pull off. Milos Forman succeeded with his profile of Andy Kaufman, *Man On the Moon*, precisely because he ignored the guidelines of the genre, instead creating a film that captured the *essence* of his subject. One could say the same for *Isn't She Great*, which recreates the trashy, sitcom milieu of its brazen protagonist. But where Kaufman was made out to be an inherently fascinating individual, Bette Midler's one-dimensional, cartoon caricature of Susann is nothing short of a dreadfully misconceived stand-up routine. Whether strutting round Manhattan in unbelievable frocks or screaming to the Gods (literally, as it happens), Midler's tragic heroine is a self-centred irritant. And the fact that Susann's sole ambition was to attain global fame hardly makes her a subject worthy of our patience. FYI: Susann was previously played by Michele Lee in the 1998

TV movie *Scandalous Me: The Jacqueline Susann Story*.

● *Jacqueline Susann* Bette Midler, *Irving Mansfield* Nathan Lane, *Florence Maybelle* Stockard Channing, *Michael Hastings* David Hyde Pierce, *Debbie* Amanda Peet, *Henry Marcus* John Cleese, *Maury Manning* John Larroquette, *Bambi Madison* Dina Spybey, *Lissy Hastings* Le Clanché du Rand, *Mimsy Hastings* Elizabeth Lawrence, *Aristotle Onassis* Frank Vincent, *Steve Lawrence* David Lawrence, *Eydie Gorme* Debbie Gravitte, Terrence Ross, Christopher McDonald, Paul Benedict, Pauline Little, Larry Block, Helen Stenborg, John Cunningham.
● *Dir* Andrew Bergman, *Pro* Mike Lobell, *Ex Pro* Ted Kurdyla, Gary Levinsohn and Mark Gordon, *Screenplay* Paul Rudnick, from the article *Wasn't She Great* by Michael Korda, *Ph* Karl Walter Lindenlaub, *Pro Des* Stuart Wurtzel, *Ed* Barry Malkin, *M* Burt Bacharach; Schubert; songs performed by Dionne Warwick, Vanessa Williams, Henri Rene, Deep Purple, James Brown, etc, *Costumes* Julie Weiss.

Universal/Mutual Film-UIP.
100 mins. USA. 1999. Rel: 23 June 2000. Cert 15.

It All Starts Today ... Ca Commence Aujourd'Hui ★★★¹/₂
Daniel Lefebvre is the director of a small nursery school in a depressed, rural area of Northern France. Strangled by bureaucracy and parental indifference, Daniel is finding it increasingly hard to access the passion and commitment he needs to get the job done. If it weren't for the children themselves, he would have given up hope a long time ago ... If Bertrand Tavernier's seemingly spontaneous and fiercely unsentimental film smacks of truth, it's because it is drawn from the experiences of the director's son-in-law, with whom he and his daughter collaborated on the screenplay. Empowered by a focused, credible performance from Philippe Torreton as the luckless principal and an urgent, fluid directorial style, the film grips the attention from the word go. Edgy, passionate, compassionate and immediate, it is everything a social document should be, even though it does lose steam near the end.

● *Daniel Lefebvre* Philippe Torreton, *Valeria* Maria Pitarresi, *Samia Damouni* Nadia Kaci, *Mme Delacourt* Francoise Bette, *Cathy* Nathalie Becue, Christine Citti, Emmanuelle Bercot, Veronique Ataly, Christina Crevillen, Sylviane Goudal.
● *Dir* Bertrand Tavernier, *Pro* Alain Sarde and Frederic Bourboulon, *Screenplay* Dominique Sampiero, Tiffany Tavernier and Bertrand Tavernier, *Ph* Alain Choquart, *Pro Des* Thierry Francois, *Ed* Sophie Brunet, *M* Louise Sclavis, *Costumes* Marpessa Dijan.

Les Films Alain Sarde/Little Bear/TF1 Films/Canal Plus, etc-Artificial Eye.
118 mins. France. 1999. Rel: 23 July 1999. Cert 12.

Jakob the Liar ★½

J Somewhere in Poland; 1944. The Jewish residents of a squalid ghetto have become prisoners in their own homes. Cut off from the outside world, they live in cramped quarters on meagre food rations and have all but given up hope. Then local cafe owner Jakob Heym overhears a Nazi news bulletin revealing that the Russians are but 400 kilometres away. Pretending that he has a secret radio, Jakob feeds his comrades fabricated snippets of good news and becomes a reluctant Messiah ... All the best intentions in the world cannot make a great movie and *Jakob the Liar* is dull, hackneyed and laboured. The sad thing is that the essence (adapted from the novel by Jurek Becker) is extremely promising, but Hungarian director Peter Kassovitz pours cliché onto cliché (a rubber-lipped, bespectacled Nazi anyone?) and then exacerbates it with sluggish, uninspired pacing. Filmed in Hungary. FYI: So eager was Robin Williams to see this film off the ground that he waived his usual $17.5 million fee in lieu of a percentage of the gross. Bad move.

● *Jakob Heym* Robin Williams, *Frankfurter* Alan Arkin, *Kowalsky* Bob Balaban, *Avron* Michael Jeter, *Kirschbaum* Armin Mueller-Stahl, *Mischa* Liev Schreiber, *Lina* Hannah Taylor Gordon, *Rosa* Nina Siemaszko, *Herschel* Mathieu Kassovitz, *Fajngold* Mark Margolis, Gregg Bello, Jan Becker, Grazyna Barszczewska, Agi Margitai.
● *Dir* Peter Kassovitz, *Pro* Marsha Garces Williams and Steven Haft, *Ex Pro* Robin Williams, *Screenplay* Peter Kassovitz and Didier Decoin, *Ph* Elemér Ragályi, *Pro Des* Luciana Arrighi, *Ed* Claire Simpson, *M* Edward Shearmur; Berlioz, *Costumes* Wieslawa Starska.

Columbia Pictures/Blue Wolf Prods/Kasso Inc.-Columbia TriStar.
119 mins. USA. 1999. Rel: 5 November 1999. Cert 12.

Janice Beard: 45 WPM ★★

Scotland/London; now. Since the birth of her daughter and the simultaneous death of her husband, Mimi Beard has suffered from agoraphobia. Now that Mimi's daughter, Janice, is 23, the latter travels to London to try and make enough money to pay for a miracle cure for her mother's malady. There, Janice lands a position as a temp at Kendon Cars and falls for the post boy, who happens to be an industrial spy... They don't come much more ludicrous than this, but even such *Billy Liar* flights of fancy can work with enough wit and panache. Unfortunately, *Janice Beard* is in short supply of both and has a hard time gathering any head of

steam. This is a shame as Eileen Walsh gives a good account of herself in her first starring film role, displaying both some emotional scope and an agile comic demeanour. [*Charles Bacon*]

● *Sean* Rhys Ifans, *Julia* Patsy Kensit, *O'Brien* David O'Hara, *Janice Beard* Eileen Walsh, *Mimi Beard* Sandra Voe, *Violet* Frances Gray, *Jane* Zita Sattar, Amelia Curtis, Mossie Smith, Sarah McVicar, Perry Fenwick, Maynard Eziashi, *young Janice* Amy Lynch, *young Violet* Laura Lumley, Gawn Grainger, Clive Merrison, Paul Jones, Ken Drury, Anna Copley, Peter Copley.
● *Dir* Clare Kilner, *Pro* Judy Counihan, *Ex Pro* Jonathan Olsberg, *Line Pro* Miara Martell, *Co-Pro* Torsten Leschly, *Screenplay* Kilner and Ben Hopkins, *Ph* Richard Greatrex and Peter Thwaites, *Pro Des* Sophie Becher, *Ed* Mary Finlay, *M* Paul Carr; Mozart, Gluck; songs performed by Lynn Anderson, Divine Comedy, Texas, Gloria Gaynor, Victor Hugo La banda, Vic Goddard, etc, *Costumes* Michele Clapton.

Above: In search of miracles – Eileen Walsh fails to salvage Clare Kilner's ludicrous Janice Beard: 45 WPM (from UIP)

The Film Consortium/Arts Council of England/WAVE
Pictures/Channel Four/Dakota Film/Hungry Eye Films/
National Lottery-UIP.
81mins. UK. 1999. Rel: 5 May 2000. Cert 15.

Joan of Arc ★★★¹/₂

France; 1421-31. Intoxicated by the pleasures of the
countryside and her love of Jesus, young Joan under-
goes a dramatic change when her older sister is killed
– and then raped – by the marauding English.
Convinced that she hears sacred voices telling her to
lead the French into battle against their aggressors,
she succeeds in getting the Dauphin, rightful heir to
the Gallic throne, crowned Charles VII. She then
imbues the King's soldiers with the courage and faith
they lack and leads them to victory ... The story of
the illiterate peasant girl who routed the English
against impossible odds has, understandably, been a
popular cinematic staple. Indeed, in the last six years
the virgin warrior has been played on screen by
Sandrine Bonnaire, Leelee Sobieski and Mira
Sorvino. Here, Milla Jovovich, wife of Luc Besson
(now estranged), conveys the passion and confusion
of Joan with rousing conviction. And while this spectacular edition met a lukewarm response from the
critics, it's still a powerful story that, told in broad,
vivid strokes, brings history screaming to life. The
battle scenes alone are worth the price of admission
(realistically brutal without being sadistically gratuitous) and the period detail is enthralling. US title:
The Messenger: The Story of Joan Arc.

● *Joan of Arc* Milla Jovovich, *the Dauphin* John
Malkovich, *Yolande of Aragon* Faye Dunaway,
Joan's Conscience Dustin Hoffman, *the Duke of
Alençon* Pascal Greggory, *Gilles de Rais* Vincent
Cassel, *Dunois* Tcheky Karyo, *La Hire* Richard
Ridings, *Aulon* Desmond Harrington, *Cauchon*
Timothy West, *Talbot* Andrew Birkin, *Catherine*
Joanne Greenwood, *Joan, at eight* Jane Valentine,
Rab Affleck, Christian Barbier, Timothy Bateson,
Christian Bergner, Paul Brooke, Patrice
Cossoneau, Tonio Descanvelle, Philippe du
Janerand, Barbara Elbourn, Christian Erickson,
David Gant, Framboise Gommendy, Jean Pierre
Gos, Michael Jenn, Richard Leaf, Carl McCrystal,
Gina McKee, Phil McKee, John Merrick, Joseph
O'Conor, Quentin Ogier, Brian Pettifer, Olivier
Rabourdin, Vincent Regan, Eric Tonetto, Tat
Whalley, Peter Whitfield.
● *Dir* Luc Besson, *Pro* Patrice Ledoux, *Co-Pro*
Bernard Grenet, *Screenplay* Besson and Andrew
Birkin, *Ph* Thierry Arbogast, *Pro Des* Hugues
Tissandier, *Ed* Sylvie Landra, *M* Eric Serra, *Costumes*
Catherine Leterrier, *Sound* Vincent Tulli.

Columbia Pictures/Gaumont Pictures-Columbia TriStar.
148 mins. France. 1999. Rel: 10 March 2000. Cert 15.

John Carpenter's Vampires ★★

New Mexico; today. After his team of vampire slay-
ers have been slaughtered by the omnipotent, 600-
year-old Ion Valek, hunter of the undead Jack Crow
goes ballistic. All Valek needs now to become
impervious to daylight is the elusive Black Cross of
Berziers. So Valek gathers about him his faithful
accomplice Tony, a young priest supplied by the
Vatican and a prostitute whose mortal days are
numbered. It's not much of an army but Crow does-
n't have much time... Without James Woods' characteristically energetic presence, this derivative,
muddled vampire entry would be a dull ride. As it
is, Carpenter makes the most of his story's picturesque locale (think *From Dusk Till Dawn* courtesy of Sam Peckinpah) but injects little new into a
tired medium. The treatment of women as sexual
objects is also inexcusable and the villain sadly one-
dimensional. [*Ewen Brownrigg*]

● *Jack Crow* James Woods, *Antonio 'Tony'
Montoya* Daniel Baldwin, *Katrina* Sheryl Lee, *Ion
Valek* Thomas Ian Griffith, *Cardinal Alba*
Maximilian Schell, *Father Adam Guiteau* Tim
Guinee, *Father Giovanni* Gregory Sierra, *Catlin*
Mark Boone Junior, Cary-Hiroyuki Tagawa,
Tommy Rosales, Henri Kingi, Michael
Huddleston, Todd Anderson, Robert L. Bush, *man
with Buick* Frank Darabont.
● *Dir and M* John Carpenter, *Pro* Sandy King,
Ex Pro Barr Potter, *Co-Pro and Screenplay* Don
Jakoby, from the novel *Vampire$* by John
Steakley, *Ph* Gary B. Kibbe, *Pro Des* Thomas A.
Walsh, *Ed* Edward A. Warschilka, *Costumes*
Robin Michel Bush, *Sound* John Pospisil,
Make-up effects Robert Kurtzman, Gregory
Nicotero and Howard Berger.

Columbia/Largo Entertainment-Storm King Prods-
Columbia TriStar.
108 mins. USA. 1997. Rel: 29 October 1999. Cert 18.

Julian Po ★★¹/₂

Julian Po checks into a boarding house in a nondescript town to take his own life. However, his presence within the close-knit community causes something of a stir and Po finds himself strangely revi-
talised. But the locals are determined to hold him to
his word... A parable on the suffocating effects of
old-fashioned conformist values, Alan Wade's debut
feature lacks the spiritual stamina that its protagonist would seem to inspire. Yet there is a satisfying,
off-key charm to the proceedings that keeps one
glued in spite of clunky dialogue and a general air of
inertia. There are also some delightful cameos from
a colourful cast and a wonderful, Gershwin-esque
score. Previously known as *The Tears of Julian Po.*
[*Ewen Brownrigg*]

● *Julian Po* Christian Slater, *Sarah* Robin Tunney, *Vern* Michael Parks, *Lucy, the maid* Cherry Jones, *Sheriff Leon* Frankie R. Faison, *Henry Leech, the mayor* Harve Presnell, *Lilah Leech* Allison Janney, *Darlene* LaTanya Richardson, Dina Spybey, Bruce Bohne, Roy Cooper, Zeljko Ivanek, Erik Jensen.
● *Dir and Screenplay* Alan Wade, based on the novella *La Mort de Monsieur Golouga* by Branimir Scepanovic, *Pro* Joseph Pierson and Jon Glascoe, *Ex Pro* Allan Mindel and Denise Shaw, *Ph* Bernd Heinl, *Pro Des* Stephen McCabe, *Ed* Jeffrey Wolf, *M* Patrick Williams, *Costumes* Juliet Polcsa.

New Line/Fine Line Features/Cypress Films-Entertainment.
83 mins. USA. 1997. Rel: 28 January 2000. Cert 12.

Julie and the Cadillacs ★★

Liverpool/London; 1964. Julie Carr and her backing singers The Cadillacs get a call to London where they are signed up by a record company. However, their first single features a song by the company's executive, while their own number is dropped to the B-side. The

record is a flop and The Cadillacs return to Liverpool, leaving Julie in London by herself... An astonishingly earnest look at the early 1960s pop scene, this naïve, low-grade musical looks like it's bounced straight out of the era it depicts. Unfortunately, its hackneyed dialogue and quality of acting underlines the illusion, creating something surreally quaint. Still, director Izzard provides plenty of bounce and the music goes a long way in coating over the cracks. [*Charles Bacon*]

● *Barbara Gifford* Toyah Willcox, *Cyril Wise* Victor Spinetti, *Phil Green* Peter Polycarpou, *Julie's grandmother* Thora Hird, *Mr Watkins* James Grout, *Mac MacDonald* Mike Berry, *Julie Carr* Tina Russell, Ben Richards, Tim Wallers, Cameron Blakely, Alan Ruscoe, and, as *The Cadillacs*: Billy Boyd, David Habbin, Chris O'Neill, Matt Rayner.
● *Dir* Bryan Izzard, *Pro* John Dean and Sean O'Mahony, *Assoc Pro* Jo O'Mahony, *Screenplay, M and lyrics* John Dean, *Ph* Les Young, *Pro Des* Jeremy Bear, *Ed* James Thomas, *Costumes* Stephen Adnitt.

Parker Mead-Capricorn Communications.
106 mins. UK. 1997. Rel: 20 August 1999. Cert PG.

Above: *Killing me softly* – Christian Slater succumbs to Robin Tunney in Alan Wade's clunky but charming *Julian Po* (from Entertainment)

K

K

Right: Larger louts –
Kathy Burke and
Harry Enfield do
their fing in Ed Bye's
wretched Kevin &
Perry Go Large
(from Icon)

Kevin & Perry Go Large ★

After unwittingly foiling a bank robbery (by setting off the alarm with a spontaneous erection), surly teenager Kevin and his mate Perry are rewarded with a trip to Ibiza. There, the rebellious duo resolve to lose their virginity but are dogged at every turn by Kevin's parents ... Recalling the wretched era of British cinema that called on the small screen for commercial opportunity (think *On the Buses, George and Mildred* and *Rising Damp*), this large-screen spin-off from *The Harry Enfield Show* is cheap, offensive and predictable. Resembling a 30-second sketch stretched to breaking point (which it is), *Kevin & Perry Go Large* takes infantile delight in celebrating such socially taboo activities as vomiting, zit-popping, defecating in the sea and maintaining a constant hard-on. If you thought *American Pie* was objectionable, wait until you suffer through this *Spotted Dick*.

● *Kevin* Harry Enfield, *Perry* Kathy Burke, *Eye*

Ball Paul Rhys Ifans, *Mum* Louisa Rix, *Dad* James Fleet, *Candice* Laura Fraser, *Gemma* Tabitha Wady, *Anne Boleyn* Natasha Little, Sam Parks, Kenneth Cranham, Patsy Byrne, Christopher Ettridge, Rupert Vansittart, Steven O'Donnell, Paul Whitehouse, Shugs.
● *Dir* Ed Bye, *Pro* Peter Bennett-Jones, Jolyon Symonds and Harry Enfield, *Ex Pro* Bruce Davey, Ralph Kamp and Barnaby Thompson, *Co-Pro* Paul Tucker, *Line Pro* Waldo Roeg, *Ph* Alan Almond, *Pro Des* Tom Brown, *Ed* Mark Wybourn, *M* songs performed by The Precious Brats, Jay Kay, Jools Holland and His Rhythm and Blues Orchestra, Nightmares on Wax, Hybrid and Chrissie Hynde, The Clash, Fatboy Slim, Lange, Tosca, CRW, William Orbit, Ayla, James Last, Gladys Knight, Southside Spinners, etc, *Costumes* Denise Simmons.

Tiger Aspect Pictures/Icon Prods/Fragile Films-Icon. 82 mins. UK. 2000. Rel: 21 April 2000. Cert 15.

Kikujiro ★★½

Technically accomplished, this comic road movie is an entirely new departure for the noted Japanese director Takeshi Kitano. It concerns the travels of a somewhat gormless yakuza deputed to help a nine-year-old boy who is in quest of his mother. The assignment may be unwanted, but a bond of friendship develops between man and child. Back in 1974 Wim Wenders showed how this kind of scenario can work in *Alice in the Cities*, but Kitano's film is fatally inconsistent, moving from believable comedy to near slapstick and also including a disturbing scene about a paedophile. In addition it's episodic, occasionally sentimental and much too long. Kitano's charmless performance in the lead role is no help, Joe Hisaishi's appealing music score is. [*Mansel Stimpson*]

● *Kikujiro* Beat Takeshi, *Masao* Yusuke Sekiguchi, *Kikujiro's wife* Kayoko Kishimoto, *Masao's grand-mother* Kazuko Yoshiyuiki, *fat biker* Great Gidayu, *Masao's mother* Yuko Daike, Rakkyo Ide, Akaji Maro, Fumie Hosokawa, Daigaku Sekine.
● *Dir, Screenplay* and *Ed* Takeshi Kitano, *Pro* Masayuki Mori and Takio Yoshida, *Line Pro* Shinji Komiya, *Ph* Katsumi Yanagishima, *Pro Des* Norihiro Isoda, *M* Joe Hisaishi, *Costumes* Fumio Iwasaki.

Bandai Visual/Tokyo FM/Nippon Herald/Office Kitano-Pathé.
122 mins. Japan. 1998. Rel: 30 June 2000. Cert 12.

A Kind of Hush ★★★★

King's Cross, London; today. Stu is torn between establishing a future with his girlfriend and acting out a strategy of revenge with his friends, all of whom share a history of sexual abuse. Randomly picking on men cruising for rent boys, the gang are ruthless in meting out their justice… Based on the autobiographical novel *Getting Even* by the child abuse counsellor Richard Johnson, *A Kind of Hush* exudes an authenticity that is at once touching and appalling. And it is this reality – stoked by vivid performances from a cast encouraged to improvise – that makes the film such an essential document. It challenges the viewer to think, is uncompromising in its portrayal of wayward youth, yet is not without compassion. [*Ewen Brownrigg*]

● *Stu* Harley Smith, *Kathleen* Marcella Plunkett, *Simon* Ben Roberts, *Mick* Paul Williams, *Tony* Nathan Constance, *Wivva* Peter Saunders, *Fish* Mike Fibbens, *Chef* Roy Hudd, *Jen* Hayley Danbury, *Peter Trewin* Paul Hayley, Jeanie Drynan, Tim Barlow, Tony Tang, Phil Nice.
● *Dir* and *Screenplay* Brian Stirner, *Pro* Roger Randall-Cutler, *Line Pro* Paul Cowan, *Ph* Jacek Petrycki, *Pro Des* Mark Stevenson, *Ed* David Martin, *M* Arvo Pärt; songs performed by

Radiator, *Costumes* Verity Hawkes.

First Film Company/British Screen/Arts Council of England/Tim White Film Prods/National Lottery-Metrodome.
95 mins. UK. 1998. Rel: 10 September 1999. Cert 15.

The King of Paris ★★

Paris; the 1930s. Exulting in his status as the premier stage actor of his day, Victor Derval leads a life of ostentatious luxury and, with a scathing wit, delights in keeping his various attendants in their place. However, when he takes on a wide-eyed admirer as his assistant, he begins to see himself for what he is – an egotistical clown who has become unable to distinguish the theatre from real life … While superficially a perfect role for the robust talents of Philippe Noiret, Derval is too grotesque a figure to be anything but an incurable bore. And Veronika Varga, while sweet and pretty enough, lacks the fiery spirit that would have us believe that she could transform so many lives. Dominique Maillet's turgid pacing and Lutric's unremarkable photography add to the malaise.

● *Victor Derval* Philippe Noiret, *Lisa Lanska* Veronika Varga, *Romain Coste* Jacques Roman, *Paul Derval* Manuel Blanc, *Marquis de Castellac* Michel Aumont, *Betty Favart* Corinne Clery, Paulette Dubost, Ronny Coutteure, Franco Interlenghi, Baetan Wenders.
● *Dir* Dominique Maillet, *Pro* Jean Gontier, *Ex Pro* Nicolas Daguet and Yann Gilbert, *Screenplay* Maillet, Jacques Fieschi, Jerome Tonnerre and Bernard Minoret, *Ph* Bernard Lutic, *Pro Des* Jacques Rouxel, *Ed* Marie Castro, *M* Quentin Damamme, *Costumes* Christian Gasc.

Pierre Grise Dist/RIO/TCA/Adventure Pictures/European Coproduction Script Fund/Canal Plus/Sofinergie/Cofimage/CNC-Gala.
98 mins. France/UK. 1993. Rel: 2 June 2000. Cert 12.

Above: *All the world's a stage … Philippe Noiret calls the shots in Dominique Maillet's turgid* The King of Paris *(from Gala)*

Above: Crocodile dandies – Bill Pullman, Bridget Fonda and Brendan Gleeson swap bon mots and sarcasm in Steve Miner's trim and witty thriller Lake Placid *(from Fox)*

Lake Placid ★★★¹/₂

Maine, New England; the present. During a routine excursion onto the still waters of Black Lake, Sheriff Hank Keough loses two thirds of his deputy to some underwater menace. Joined by Jack Wells, an easygoing Fish and Game Warden, Kelly Scott, an uptight palaeontologist from New York City, and Hector Cyr, an overbearing mythology professor, Keough sets out to discover the identity of the sub-aqueous killer. The evidence points to a crocodile but, as everybody knows, not even alligators travel this far north. Yet the killing continues ... Few thrillers come as trim and witty as this. But then few thrillers are penned by a writer of the calibre of David E. Kelly, the creative mind behind TV's *Picket Fences*, *Chicago Hope* and *Ally McBeal* (and, incidentally, the husband of Michelle Pfeiffer). While adhering closely to the conventions of the mutant-monster-run-amok scenario established by *Jaws*, the film spins a situation comedy around the four characters searching for the mythical beast. Bridget Fonda and Brendan Gleeson are particularly rewarding in richly comic roles, where a sarcastic remark can go a long way. The effects are good, too, supplying some dramatic ballast.

● *Jack Wells* Bill Pullman, *Kelly Scott* Bridget Fonda, *Hector Cyr* Oliver Platt, *Sheriff Hank Keough* Brendan Gleeson, *Mrs Delores Bickerman* Betty White, *Walt Lawson* David Lewis, *Stephen Daniels* Tim Dixon, *Janine* Natassia Malthe, *Myra Okubo*
Mariska Hargitay, *Deputy Sharon Gare* Meredith Salenger, Jed Rees, Richard Leacock, Jake T. Roberts.
● *Dir* Steve Miner, *Pro* David E. Kelley and Michael Pressman, *Ex Pro* Peter Bogart, *Screenplay* Kelley, *Ph* Daryn Okada, *Pro Des* John Willett, *Ed* Marshall Harvey and Paul Hirsch, *M* John Ottman; *Costumes* Jori Woodman, *Creature effects* Stan Winston.

Fox 2000 Pictures/Phoenix Pictures/Rocking Chair Prods-Fox. 82 mins. USA. 1999. Rel: 31 March 2000. Cert 15.

The Last Days ★★★¹/₂

Winner of the 1998 Oscar for best documentary feature, this is a harrowing account of how five Hungarian Jews survived the horrors of Auschwitz. Intercutting interviews with the above with rare newsreel footage and photographs, the film re-lives the inconceivable inhumanity of the Holocaust through the recollection of these survivors, who were teenagers at the time. One woman recalls how she held onto her mother's diamonds by systematically swallowing them and retrieving them from the latrine the next day; another remembers how the Nazis tore children in half by their legs. While the words are powerful enough, the footage of emaciated, starving prisoners are extremely distressing. Filmed in the US, Hungary, Germany, the Ukraine and Poland. Steven Spielberg executive produced.

● With Congressman Tom Lantos, Alice Lok

Cahana, Renée Firestone, Bill Basch, Irene Zisblatt. ● *Dir and Ed* James Moll, *Pro* June Beallor and Ken Lipper, *Ex Pro* Steven Spielberg, *Assoc Pro* Elyse Katz and Aaron Zarrow, *Ph* Harris Done, *M* Hans Zimmer, *Sound* Claude Letessier.

Survivors of the Shoah Visual History Foundation-Downtown Pictures.
87 mins. USA. 1998. Rel: 8 October 1999. Cert PG.

Last Night ★★¹/₂

At the stroke of midnight, Toronto time, the world is going to end. It is 6 p.m. and the natives are going crazy, the radio is playing the top 500 songs of all time and a gas company executive is methodically ringing his customers to thank them for their service. Craig wants to fulfil all his sexual fantasies, Lily would be happy with an orgasm and Sandra wants to find her husband so that they can kill each other. Patrick just wants to be by himself, but he's finding the prospect of a solitary end becoming increasingly unlikely ... Possibly the very first apocalyptic comedy, Don McKellar's directorial debut won glowing reviews in its native Canada. It is certainly a brave film, if not a downright foolhardy one, as genuine laughs are hard enough to come by, let alone when extracted from the mouth of ultimate tragedy. And so the prospect of human extinction looms over the proceedings like a damp blanket, suffocating the very oxygen of its humour. Not surprisingly, then, the film works best in its bittersweet moments, in its unexpected observations and revelations and the odd inconsequential detail that suddenly seems so important. Indeed, with so much at stake we can but focus on the details that make up the sum of our lives ... Made as part of a series of ten international films concentrating on the Millennium.

● *Patrick Wheeler* Don McKellar, *Sandra* Sandra Oh, *Craig Zwiller* Callum Keith Rennie, *Jennifer Wheeler* Sarah Polley, *Duncan* David Cronenberg, *Donna* Tracy Wright, *Mrs Carlton* Genevieve Bujold, *Mrs Wheeler* Roberta Maxwell, *Mr Wheeler* Robin Gammell, *Alex* Trent McMullen, *Lily* Karen Glave, Charmion King, Jessica Booker, Arsinee Khanjian, Chandra Muszka, Francois Girard, Michael McMurty, Pierre Elrick, Bob Martin, Michael Barry, Tom McCamus, *the runner* Jackie Burroughs.
● *Dir and Screenplay* Don McKellar, *Pro* Niv Fichman and Daniel Iron, *Ex Pro* Caroline Benjo and Carole Scotta, *Co-Pro* Joseph Boccia, *Ph* Douglas Koch, *Pro Des* John Dondertman, *Ed* Reginald Harkema, *M* Alexina Louie and Alex Pauk; songs performed by The 5th Dimension, Looking Glass, Parliament, Pete Seeger, etc, *Costumes* Lea Carlson.

Rhombus Media/TeleFilm Canada/La Septe ARTE, etc-Film Four.
94 mins. Canada/France. 1998. Rel: 2 July 1999. Cert 15.

The Last September ★★¹/₂

Cork, Ireland; 1920. An Anglo-Irish family and their guests uneasily frolic away the summer at their mansion while local insurgents attack and kill British army personnel stationed there to protect them ... Adapted from the Elisabeth Bowen novel, Deborah Warner's debut feature is beautifully designed and photographed and captures well the slow moving development of languid relationships at the decline of an Empire (recalling Joseph Losey's *The Go-Between*). However, Ms Warner fails to establish a fluid rhythm and cannot contain the more melodramatic tendencies of Maggie Smith and Michael Gambon. [*Peter Jaques*]

● *Lady Myra Naylor* Maggie Smith, *Sir Richard Naylor* Michael Gambon, *Lois Farquar* Keeley Hawes, *Marda Norton* Fiona Shaw, *Francie Montmorency* Jane Birkin, *Captain Gerald Colthurst* David Tennant, *Hugo Montmorency* Lambert Wilson, *Daventry* Richard Roxburgh, *Peter Connolly* Gary Lydon, *Laurence Carstairs* Jonathan Slinger, Tom Hickey, Emily Nagle, Catherine Walsh.
● *Dir* Deborah Warner, *Pro* Yvonne Thunder, *Ex Pro* Neil Jordan, Nik Powell, Stephen Woolley and Peter Fudakowski, *Co-Pro* Marina Gefter, *Co-Ex Pro* Geroges Benayoun, *Screenplay* John Banville, *Ph* Slawomir Idziak, *Pro Des* Caroline Amies, *Ed* Kate Evans, *M* Zbigniew Preisner, *Costumes* John Bright.

Matrix Films/Scala/Bord Scannán na hÉireann/BskyB/British Screen/IMA Films/Canal Plus/Irish Film Board-Metro Tartan.
103 mins. UK/Ireland/France. 1999. Rel: 5 May 2000. Cert 15.

The Last Yellow ★★

Overweight and out of work, Frank dupes himself into believing he's a vigilante for hire. In fact he's such a loser that even his mother's thrown him out. Then he meets Kenny, a lad half a sandwich short of a picnic, who employs him to settle a score concerning his older brother, who was beaten up in a pub in Leicester and is now in a wheelchair. Armed with a reconstituted handgun, this ill-formed pair head for London seeking revenge. *The Last Yellow* starts well as a black comedy but soon peters out, leaving the lovely Samantha Morton underused and overwhelmed. [*Marianne Gray*]

● *Frank* Mark Addy, *Kenny* Charlie Creed-Miles, *Jackie* Samantha Morton, *Keith* James Hooton, *Len* Kenneth Cranham, *Gragam* Steve Sweeney, *Donut* Alan Atherall, *Moose* Emil Marwa, June Watson, Glenn Cunningham, Nicola Stephenson.
● *Dir* Julian Farino, *Pro* Jolyon Symonds, *Ex Pro* Nik Powell, David M. Thompson and Sandra Schulberg, *Co-Pro* Jane Barclay and Sharon Harel, *Line Pro* Kathy Sykes, *Screenplay* Paul Tucker, from his own play, *Ph* David Odd, *Pro Des* John Paul

Kelly, *Ed* Pia Di Ciaula, *M* Adrian Johnston; songs performed by Engelbert Humperdinck, *Costumes* Anushia Nieradzik.

Scala Prods/Capitol Films/Hollywood Partners/Arts Council of England/BBC Films/National Lottery-Metrodome. 93 mins. UK/Germany. 1999. Rel: 10 December 1999. Cert 15.

Late August, Early September – Fin Aout, Debut Septembre ★★¹/₂

Paris; the present. In a period of just over 12 months, a group of people – an editor, novelist, fashion designer, schoolgirl, etc – are buffeted by the tides of love, friendship and imminent death ... Like a loosely bound album spilling a flutter of Polaroids, Olivier Assayas' eighth film casts off a spontaneity that is initially spellbinding. Thus, fragments of very real lives float into focus, creating a melange of moments, moods and memories. Luckily for Assayas he has some very fine actors to bring his snapshots alive, but only so much Gauloise-punctuated conversation can hold the concentration for so long. You can find as much real life in any Parisian cafe – and with as little plot.

● *Gabriel Deshayes* Mathieu Amalric, *Anne Rosenwald* Virginie Ledoyen, *Adrien Willer* Francois Cluzet, *Jenny* Jeanne Balibar, *Jeremie* Alex Descas, *Lucie* Arsinee Khanjian, *Vera* Mia Hansen-Love, *Naryelle Deshayes* Nathalie Richard, Eric Elmosino, Olivier Cruveiller, Jean-Baptiste Malartre, Catherine Mouchet, Elli Medeiros.
● *Dir and Screenplay* Olivier Assayas, *Pro* Georges Benayoun and Philippe Carcassonne, *Ex Pro* Francoise Guglielmi, *Ph* Denis Lenoir, *Pro Des* Francois-Renaud Labarthe, *Ed* Luc Barnier, *M* various, *Costumes* Francoise Clavel.

Dacia Films/Cinea/Canal Plus, etc-Artificial Eye. 111 mins. France. 1999. Rel: 20 August 1999. Cert 15.

Below: Song of the Ocean – Pruitt Taylor Vince and Tim Roth talk music in Giuseppe Tornatore's elegiac, passionate The Legend of 1900 (from Entertainment)

LA Without a Map ★★¹/₂

A 22-year-old undertaker with aspirations to write, Richard Tennant finds his world turned upside down one day in a cemetery in Bradford. It is there that he meets Barbara, a gorgeous American actress, with whom he instantly falls in love. Breaking off his engagement, he follows her out to Los Angeles where romance and filmmaking are not exactly what he expected... Based on Richard Rayner's autobiographical novel, this is an enjoyable satire on the L.A. scene that works well on a superficial level. However, in spite of an appealing and confident performance from Tennant as Tennant and some fine moments of observational comedy, the film falls apart whenever Vinessa Shaw is on screen. She just doesn't supply the substance that would make a bloke give up his fiancée and country, let alone any sense of being human. [*Charles Bacon*]

● *Richard Tennant* David Tennant, *Barbara* Vinessa Shaw, *Moss* Vincent Gallo, *Julie* Julie Delpy, *Takowsky* James Le Gros, *Patterson* Cameron Bancroft, *Sandra* Lisa Edelstein, *Michael* Joe Dallesandro, Matthew Faber, Joey Perillo, Saskia Reeves, Steve Huison, Amanda Plummer, Anouk Aimée, Jean-Pierre Kalfon, Malcolm Tierney, Margie Clarke, Monte Hellman, Joey Perillo, Jerzy Skolimowski, Robert Davi, Andy Bradford, and *uncredited* Johnny Depp.
● *Dir and Co-Pro* Mika Kaurismaki, *Pro* Julie Baines and Sarah Daniel, *Ex Pro* Deepak Nayar, *Screenplay* Kaurismaki and Richard Rayner, *Ph* Michel Amathieu, *Pro Des* Caroline Hanania, *Ed* Ewa J. Lind, *M* Sebastien Cortella and Leningrad Cowboys; songs performed by The Rascals, Houk, Vincent Gallo, Dubstar, Bandit Queen, Manfred Mann's Earth Band, Catatonia, Travis, Sleeper, etc, *Costumes* Magali Guidasci and Yasmine Abraham, *Sound* Paul Jyrälä.

Dan Films/Euro American Films/Marianna Films/Arts Council of England/European Co-Production Fund/ Yorkshire Media Production Agency-United Media. 107 mins. UK/France/Finland/Luxembourg. 1998. Rel: 17 September 1999. Cert 15.

The Legend of 1900 ★★★★¹/₂

Born on the first day of 1900, a baby is abandoned on the ocean liner The Virginian and is adopted by the ship's stoker. Named after the century he came in on, 1900 grows up on the ship, travelling back and forth across the Atlantic but never setting foot on land. Then, at the age of eight, he discovers a piano and releases from it a wonderful sound, music that comes straight out of his head. As he grows up, news of 1900's virtuosity travels further afield, but his extraordinary music remains at sea ... Occasionally a film comes along that is so unusual and so resolutely of its own creation that one is prepared to forgive it everything. Like the celluloid equivalent of an opera – complete with that genre's artificiality, corniness and overheated emotions – *The Legend of 1900* invites one to suspend one's disbelief and enter a world of enchantment and passion buoyed by the mysterious power of music. Recalling the later visual style of Sergio Leone, writer-director Giuseppe Tornatore (*Cinema Paradiso*) creates a mythic world of dashed hopes and endless opportunity swathed in a nostalgic, sepia glow, a canvas on which his dreamers can play out their acts of destiny. As the unlikely protagonist, Tim Roth is surprisingly good, an intense presence at once enigmatic, comical and pathetic, a perfect foil for such a bizarre story. And there's a wonderful cameo from Clarence Williams III as a flamboyant Jelly Roll Morton in just one of the film's many outstanding set pieces. Previously known as *The Legend of the Pianist On the Ocean*.

● *Nineteen Hundred* Tim Roth, *Max Tooney* Pruitt Taylor Vince, *the girl* Mélanie Thierry, *Danny Boodmann* Bill Nunn, *music shop owner* Peter Vaughan, *Plymouth harbour master* Niall O'Brien, *farmer* Gabriele Lavia, *Mexican stoker* Alberto Vazquez, *Jelly Roll Morton* Clarence Williams III, *four-year-old Nineteen Hundred* Easton Gage, *eight-year-old Nineteen Hundred* Harry Ditson, Norman Chancer, Heathcote Williams, Kevin McNally, Vernon Nurse, Bryan Pringle, and *uncredited* Wilson Du Bois.
● *Dir and Screenplay* Giuseppe Tornatore, based on the stage monoloque *Novecento* by Alessandro Baricco, *Pro* Francesco Tornatore, *Ex Pro* Laura Fattori, *Ph* Lajos Koltai, *Pro Des* Francesco Frigeri, *Ed* Massimo Quaglia, *M* Ennio Morricone; Jelly Roll Morton, Scott Joplin, *Costumes* Maurizio Millenotti, *Choreography* Leontine Snel.

Fine Line Features/Medusa/Sciarlò-Entertainment. 125 mins. Italy. 1998. Rel: 17 December 1999. Cert PG.

Une Liaison Pornographique – An Intimate Affair ★★

Paris; today. Answering a personals ad in an adult magazine, a man consents to act out a middle-aged woman's fantasy in a pre-booked hotel room. The exercise a success, the couple agree to meet every Thursday to carry out their unusual sexual liaison, whatever it may be. Then, one day, the man suggests to the woman that they go out on a date ... Inverting the normal romantic procedure of the standard love story, scenarist Blasband opens up a potentially fascinating scenario. But by superimposing a set of new narrative rules – a refusal to divulge the characters' names or their current or past lives – Blasband puts enormous pressure on the formula of the proceedings. For as engaging as Nathalie Baye and Sergi Lopez are within the confines of the conceit, there is little they can do to engage the viewer on anything but the most superficial level.

● *Her* Nathalie Baye, *Him* Sergi López, *M. Lignaux* Paul Pavel, Jacques Viala, Sylvie van den Elsen, Pierre Geranio.

● *Dir* Frédéric Fonteyne, *Pro* Patrick Quinet, *Screenplay* Philippe Blasband, *Ph* Virginie Saint-Martin, *Pro Des* Veronique Sacrez, *Ed* Chantal Hymans, *M* Jannot Sanavia, André Dziezukand Marc Mergen, *Costumes* Anne Schotte.

Artémis Prods/Les Productions Lazennec/ARP Sélection/ Samsa Film/Fama Film/Canal Plus, etc-Alliance Releasing. 89 mins. Belgium/France/Luxembourg/Switzerland. 1999. Rel: 16 June 2000. Cert 15.

Life ★½

As two convicts fill in the graves of a pair of lifers at the Mississippi State Prison, an old timer regales them of the deceased's life story. It transpires that, back in 1932, a pickpocket and a debtor are convicted of a murder they didn't commit and spend the next 67 years inside, squabbling ... This is one of those films that prompts the awkward and eternal question 'why'? Who on earth thought that the story of two men who hate each others' guts and are stuck in prison for life, could remotely support a comedy? Actually, it was Eddie Murphy's idea, so the blame rests with him. On the plus side, Murphy delivers an uncannily convincing turn as a man in the last stages of his life, aided by the remarkable make-up of Rick Baker. But it's a long, monotonous wait until this minor accomplishment.

● *Rayford Gibson* Eddie Murphy, *Claude Banks* Martin Lawrence, *Willie Long* Obba Babatunde, *Dexter Wilkins* Ned Beatty, *Jangle Leg* Bernie Mac, *Winston Hancock* Clarence Williams III, *Can't Get Right* Bokeem Woodbine, *Sylvia* Lisa Nicole Carson, *Mary Rose* Poppy Montgomery, *Sgt. Dillard* Nick Cassavetes, *Spanky Johnson* Rick James, *Stan Blocker* Noah Emmerich, Miguel A. Nunez Jr, Barry Shabaka Henley, Brent Jennings, Guy Torry, O'Neal Compton, Ned Vaughn, Michael 'Bear' Taliferro, R. Lee Ermey, Heavy D, Hildy Brooks, Armelia McQueen, Don Harvey, Jordan Lund.
● *Dir* Ted Demme, *Pro* Brian Grazer and Eddie Murphy, *Ex Pro* Karen Kehela and James D. Brubaker, *Assoc Pro* Tina L. Fortenberry, *Screenplay* Robert Ramsey and Matthew Stone, *Ph* Geoffrey Simpson, *Pro Des* Dan Bishop, *Ed* Jeffrey Wolf, *M* Wyclef Jean; songs performed by Bobby Pardlo, Buddy Johnson, Wyclef Jean, Destiny's Child, Maxwell, etc, *Costumes* Lucy Corrigan, *Make-up effects* Rick Baker.

Universal/Imagine-UIP. 108 mins. USA. 1999. Rel: 27 August 1999. Cert 15.

Limbo ★★★½

Writer-director John Sayles has built a number of his movies around people living on the fringes of the American dream – whether geographically or otherwise. For the first hour of *Limbo*, we are conducted through

Above: Killer instinct – Terence Stamp swings by the City of Angels in Steven Soderbergh's surprisingly cocky and stylish The Limey (from Film Four)

what seems to be typical Sayles territory. This time it's a quirky island community in Alaska, balanced on the cusp of major tourist development and personified by the likes of two feisty lesbians fed up with life in San Francisco. Meanwhile, Joe Gastineau – a fisherman with a guilty secret in his past – falls for itinerant singer Donna de Angelo. Donna's introverted teenage daughter Noelle has had enough of her mother's aimless lifestyle. And when Joe's half-brother Bobby returns to town and asks Joe for an unusual favour, the story veers off in an unexpected direction. Sayles' inventive plotting tests his central characters with challenges unforeseen at the outset, and cleverly involves the viewer in the outcome. This is high-class filmmaking, though perhaps a tad short of the director's very best work. [*Jeff Bench*]

● *Donna De Angelo* Mary Elizabeth Mastrantonio, *Joe Gastineau* David Strathairn, *Noelle De Angelo* Vanessa Martinez, *Smilin' Jack* Kris Kristofferson, *Bobby Gastineau* Casey Siemaszko, *Frankie* Kathryn Grody, *Lou* Rita Taggart, *Harmon King* Leo Burmester, Michael Laskin, Herminio Ramos, Dawn McInturff.
● *Dir, Screenplay* and *Ed* John Sayles, *Pro* Maggie Renzi, *Assoc Pro* Sarah Connors, *Ph* Haskell Wexler, *Pro Des* Gemma Jackson, *M* Mason Daring; songs performed by Mary Elizabeth Mastrantonio, *Costumes* Shay Cunliffe.

Screen Gems/Green/Renzi-Columbia TriStar.
127 mins. USA/Germany. 1999. Rel: 21 January 2000.
Cert 15.

The Limey ★★★¹/₂

Following a nine-year-stint in Parkhurst prison, armed robber 'Wilson' visits Los Angeles to find out how his beloved daughter was killed in a suspicious car accident. Thanks to an uncanny combination of luck and balls, Wilson quickly infiltrates the defences of a crooked music promoter and starts to stir up a major cross-section of LA's underground. But all Wilson wants is the truth and he doesn't care who he kills to get it ... If one had to trot out yet another one-man-army-on-the-rampage yarn one could not have done it a more interesting way. With Terence Stamp in his most comfortable film role in epochs – as a professional criminal dispensing Cockney rhyming slang and bullets in equal measure – this is a most satisfying homage to 1960s' chic. Also starring Peter Fonda (*Easy Rider*, 1969) as a refreshingly yellow-livered villain and Barry Newman (*Vanishing Point*, 1971) as his 'security advisor', the film basks in its pop cultural references. Only some pretentious time-jumping editing spoils what is otherwise a surprisingly cocky and stylish thriller.

● *Wilson* Terence Stamp, *Elaine* Lesley Ann Warren, *Ed* Luis Guzman, *Avery* Barry Newman, *Terry Valentine* Peter Fonda, *Uncle John* Joe Dallessandro, *Stacy* Nicky Katt, *Adhara* Amelia Heinle, *Jennifer 'Jenny' Wilson* Melissa George, William Lucking, Matthew Kimbrough, John Robotham, Steve Heinze, Allan Graf, and *uncredited* Bill Duke, George Clooney.
● *Dir* Steven Soderbergh, *Pro* John Hardy and Scott Kramer, *Screenplay* Lem Dobbs, *Ph* Ed Lachman, *Pro Des* Gary Frutkoff, *Ed* Sarah Flack, *M* Cliff Martinez; songs performed by The Who, The Hollies, Danny Saber, Boston, Steppenwolf, The Byrds, The Doobie Brothers, Terence Stamp, etc, *Costumes* Louise Frogley.

Artisan Entertainment-Film Four.
89 mins. USA. 1999. Rel: 10 December 1999. Cert 18.

Lola & Bilidikid ★★★¹/₂

A German film from a Turkish writer/director, this is a drama set in Berlin. Although a little slow to find its feet and rather too melodramatically plotted at the end, this is in the main a convincingly atmospheric piece built around the city's gay scene. Several leading characters are Turkish immigrants, but, despite the title picking out the transvestite performer Lola and his macho lover (who has named himself after Billy the Kid), the central character is a gay student named Murat. His coming to terms with his sexuality and his discovery of his family's hidden history makes for an involving tale, laced on occasion with witty observation while attacking the violence that stems from homophobia. [*Mansel Stimpson*]

● *Murat* Baki Davrak, *Lola* Gandi Mukli, *Bili* Erdal Yildiz, *Kalipso* Mesut Ffizdemir, *Sheherazade* Celal Perk, *Osman* Hasan Ali Mete, Michael Gerber, Inge Keller, Murat Yilmaz.
● *Dir and Screenplay* Kutlug Ataman, *Pro* Martin Hagemann, *Ex Pro* James Schamus, *Co-Pro* Martin Wiebel and Zeynep Özbatur, *Assoc Pro* Mary Jane Skalski, *Ph* Chris Squires, *Pro Des* John Di Manico, *Ed* Ewa J. Lind, *M* Arpad Bondy, *Costumes* Ulla Gothe, *Sound* Wolf Ingo Römer.

Zero Film/WDR/ARTE & Zeynep Özbatur, etc-Millivres Multimedia.
91 mins. Germany. 1998. Rel: 10 March 2000. Cert 18.

The Loss of Sexual Innocence ★★★¹/₂
A five-year-old boy stares on in wonder as a young black woman, dressed only in her underwear, reads falteringly in English to a very old man. A discontented American wife trapped in rain-swept Northumbria dreams of performing a provocative dance in a jazz club. A black man and a strawberry blonde woman emerge naked from a lake and gradually discover the contradiction of their bodies ... A deeply personal project which writer-director Mike Figgis has intermittently developed over a 16-year-period, this is a boldly original, almost wordless work born out of a series of short films. Here, Figgis has loosely tied them together, filtering them through the memories of a documentary filmmaker, while introducing connecting motifs that touch on everything from the death of Princess Diana to the comparison of brutal rites-of-passage in both Third World and Western civilisations. Ultimately, one's either going to go with this or reject it completely, but for those with a generous artistic disposition there is much to chew on, both intellectually and philosophically. Personally, I found myself entranced by the twists and turns of the narrative mosaic and thoroughly seduced by the visual and sonic feast laid before me. And, for better or worse, several of the film's sequences will be hard to forget.

● *Adult Nic* Julian Sands, *twins* Saffron Burrows, *Lucca* Stefano Dionisi, *Susan* Kelly Macdonald, *Susan's mum* Gina McKee, *Nic aged 15* Jonathan Rhys-Meyers, *Susan's father* Bernard Hill, *blind woman* Rossy De Palma, *Nic aged five* John Cowey, *Adam* Femi Ogumbanjo, *Eve* Hanne Klintoe, *Nic's wife* Johanna Torrel, *Nic aged 12* George Moktar, *first detective/man in dream* Mark Long, Nina McKay, Dickson Osa-Omorogbe, Jock Gibson Cowl, Justin Chadwick, Geraint Ellis, Red Mullet, Nick Figgis, Roderic Leigh, Rodney Charles, Phil Swinburne.
● *Dir and Screenplay* Mike Figgis, *Pro* Figgis and Annie Stewart, *Ex Pro* Patrick Wachsberger, *Co-Pro*

Barbey Reisz, *Ph* Benoît Delhomme, *Pro Des* Jessica Worrall, Mark Long and Giorgio Desideri, *Ed* Matthew Wood, *M* Figgis; Mozart, Schumann, Beethoven, Chopin, *Costumes* Florence Nicaise.

Summit Entertainment/Newmarket Capital/Red Mullet Prods-Columbia TriStar.
105 mins. USA/UK. 1998. Rel: 7 Janaury 2000. Cert 18.

Love, Honour & Obey ★★¹/₂
London; the present. Jonny is a courier who envies the glamorous lifestyle of his childhood mate Jude. Jude now works for his uncle, gangland boss Ray Kreed, wears designer togs and eats in the finest nosheries. Having convinced Jude that he's got what it takes to be a member of the criminal fraternity, Jonny is cautiously admitted into Kreed's inner circle. But Jonny is appalled by Kreed's laidback *modus operandi* and so sets about injecting a bit of his own rough justice ... Presenting a bizarre mix of black comedy, cruel violence and theatrical improvisation, *Love, Honour & Obey* sheds a refreshing if distempered light on the gangster genre. Ray Winstone is a delight as the genial Godfather (who's never happier than when indulging his love of karaoke) and the directors Burdis and Anciano

steal the show as Kreed's henchman, the former eternally preoccupied with his impotence. But the film's gratuitous taste for sadism does leave a nasty taste in the mouth.

● *Sadie* Sadie Frost, *Ray Kreed* Ray Winstone, *Jonny Lee* Jonny Lee Miller, *Jude* Jude Law, *Sean* Sean Pertwee, *Kathy* Kathy Burke, *Denise* Denise Van Outen, *Mathew* Rhys Ifans, *Dominic* Dominic Anciano, *Burdis* Ray Burdis, John Beckett, Trevor H. Laird, William Scully QGM, Perry Benson, Mark Burdis, Laila Morse, Damien Anciano, Sky Burdis, Enoch Frost.
● *Dir, Pro* and *Screenplay* Dominic Anciano and Ray Burdis, *Ex Pro* David M. Thompson, Jane Tranter and Jim Beach, *Line Pro* Mark Hudson, *Assoc Pro* Sadie Frost, *Ph* John Ward, *Pro Des* Nick Burnell, *Ed* Rachel Meyrick, *M* John Beckett; Grieg; songs performed by Jonny Lee Miller, Ray Winstone, Sean Pertwee, Kathy Burke & Ray Burdis, Sadie Frost, Noel Gallagher, Jamiroquai, Feelybooth, James Graydon, Thierry Lang and His Trio, and Richard Hawes, *Costumes* Ali Brown.

BBC Films/Fugitive-UIP.
98 mins. UK. 1998. Rel: 7 April 2000. Cert 18.

The Love Letter ★¹⁄₂

Loblolly By the Sea, Massachusetts; the present. Helen MacFarquhar is a businesslike single mother who runs a bookshop and has pretty much given up on romance. Then, one day, she stumbles across a passionate, unsigned love letter which opens the emotional floodgates of her heart. But who is the letter from? And, as the missive kick-starts an orgy of amour in the sleepy New England town, who is it really to? Even without the overkill of Luis Bacalov's saccharine score, this would have been manipulative Mills & Boon fluff. Set in an impossibly picturesque corner of Massachusetts and peopled with relics from TV (*Magnum P.I.*, *Ellen*, *Grace Under Fire*), *The Love Letter* is not only hard to believe in but suffers from a severe case of the cutes. Notwithstanding, *Ellen* fans may salvage a chuckle: the character played by Ellen DeGeneres not only works in a bookshop but gets to say: 'I can't believe your mother's in love with another woman.' Incidentally, the plot's device was previously utilised in the 1985 classic *Secret Admirer*.

● *Helen MacFarquhar* Kate Capshaw, *Lillian MacFarquhar* Blythe Danner, *Janet Hall* Ellen DeGeneres, *Mrs. Scattergoods* Geraldine McEwan, *Jennifer* Julianne Nicholson, *Johnny* Tom Everett Scott, *George Mathias* Tom Selleck, *Eleanor MacFarquhar* Gloria Stuart, *Officer Dan* Bill Buell, Alice Drummond, Erik Jensen, Patrick Donnelly, Margaret Ann Brady, Jessica Capshaw, Walter Covell, Lucas Hall, *girl with a sparkler* Sasha Spielberg.
● *Dir* Peter Ho-Sun Chan, *Pro* Sarah Pillsbury, Midge Sanford and Kate Capshaw, *Ex Pro* Beau Flynn and Stefan Simchowitz, *Co-Pro* Karen Koch, *Screenplay* Maria Maggenti, from the novel by Cathleen Schine,

Ph Tami Reiker, *Pro Des* Andrew Jackness, *Ed* Jacqueline Cambas, *M* Luis Bacalov; Puccini; songs performed by Louis Armstrong, Roy Orbison, The Clovers, and Chet Baker, *Costumes* Tracy Tynan.

DreamWorks-UIP.
87 mins. USA. 1999. Rel: 1 October 1999. Cert 15.

Lovers of the Arctic Circle – Los amantes del Circulo Polar ★★★

Ana was just eight the day her father died. But it was the day she met Otto, a boy her own age. And, imperceptibly, the children's lives begin to intersect, their future as preordained as fragments of their past would seem to be linked ... Recalling the romance of destiny so favoured by Claude Lelouch, *Lovers of the Arctic Circle* jettisons the sentiment of the French director in favour of a bleached-out, tragedy-tinged poetry. Told from both the viewpoint of Ana and Otto, the film unspools in a narrative zigzag across time as fate runs arctic circles around its protagonists. It's a terrific story, unfolded in surprising laps, but the leads lack an on-screen chemistry that would make us really care about what happens to them.

● *Ana* Najwa Nimri, *Otto* Fele Martínez, *Alvaro* Nancho Novo, *Olga* Maru Valdivielso, *Otto as a child* Peru Medem, *Ana as a child* Sara Valiente, *young Otto* Victor Hugo Oliveira, *young Ana* Kristel Diaz, *Javier* Pep Munne, *Alvaro Midelman* Jaroslaw Bielski, *Sofia* Rosa Morales, *Otto Midelman* Joost Siedhoff, Beate Jensen, Petri Heino.
● *Dir and Screenplay* Julio Medem, *Pro* Fernando Bovaira and Enrique López Lavigne, *Ex Pro* Txarli Llorente and Fernando de Garcillan, *Line Pro* Fernando Victoria de Lecea, *Ph* Kalo F. Berridi, *Pro Des* Satur Idarreta, *Ed* Ivan Aledo, *M* Alberto Iglesias, *Costumes* Estíbaliz Markiegi.

Alicia Produce/Bailando en la Luna/Canal Plus-Metro Tartan.
108 mins. Spain/France. 1998. Rel: 7 January 2000. Cert 15.

Love's Labour's Lost ★★★

Navarre, France; the 1930s. Entering into a public pact to renounce such hedonistic pursuits as a decent night's sleep, gluttony and women, the King of Navarre and three companions have their heads turned with the arrival of the Princess of France and three comely attendants ... Having stuck so slavishly to the text of *Hamlet*, Kenneth Branagh leaps the opposite way with this irreverent, frolicsome adaptation of Shakespeare's seldom performed 1594 romantic comedy. Jettisoning large chunks of the play in favour of ten classic songs from Hollywood's heyday, Branagh has created a bizarre cross between musical pastiche and Elizabethan farce. Bursting with visual gags, outrageous slapstick and some inventively staged dance sequences, the film pleases in parts but hardly

succeeds as a cohesive entertainment. Still, we must give thanks to Timothy Spall's inspired comic creation of Don Armado and to Branagh's miraculous segue from the line 'The voice of all the gods/Make Heaven drowsy with the harmony' to Irving Berlin's 'Cheek to Cheek' ('I'm in Heaven...').

● *Berowne* Kenneth Branagh, *Costard* Nathan Lane, *Dumaine* Adrian Lester, *Longaville* Matthew Lillard, *Rosaline* Natascha McElhone, *The King* Alessandro Nivola, *the Princess of France* Alicia Silverstone, *Don Armado* Timothy Spall, *Nathaniel* Richard Briers, *Boyet* Richard Clifford, *Maria* Carmen Ejogo, *Mercade* Daniel Hill, *Holofernia* Geraldine McEwan, *Katherine* Emily Mortimer, *Moth* Anthony O'Donnell, *Jaquenetta* Stefania Rocca, *Constable Dull* Jimmy Yuill, *Isabelle* Daisy Gough, *Jaques* Paul Moody, *Beatrice* Yvonne Reilly.
● *Dir* and *Screenplay* Kenneth Branagh, *Pro* Branagh and David Barron, *Ex Pro* Guy East, Nigel Sinclair, Alexis Lloyd, Harvey Weinstein and Bob Weinstein, *Ph* Alex Thomson, *Pro Des* Tim Harvey, *Ed* Neil Farrell and Dan Farrell, *M* Patrick Doyle; Irving Berlin, Desmond Carter, George Gershwin, Ira Gershwin, Jerome Kern and Cole Porter, *Costumes* Anna Buruma, *Choreography* Stuart Hopps.

Intermedia Films/Pathé/Arts Council of England/Canal Plus/Miramax/Shakespeare Film Company/National Lottery- Pathé. 93 mins. UK/France/USA. 1999. Rel: 31 March 2000. Cert U.

Lucia ★★★

Don Boyd's feature builds boldly on works by Carlos Saura which have blended famous music dramas with equally colourful backstage intrigue. Updating Scott's novel *The Bride of Lammermoor* and using highlights from the operatic treatment of it, *Lucia Di Lammermoor*, Boyd tells of a singer forced by her brother into a marriage for money. Nevertheless, her true love is a fellow singer, her co-star in a private staging of Donizetti's opera in celebration of the nuptials. Boyd's daughter, Amanda, plays the lead, but her singing voice is hardly distinguished enough. Add that this is stylised avant-garde cinema experimenting with video tape images transferred to 33mm, and it's clear that the film's appeal is very specialised indeed. The enterprise is whole-hearted but not infrequently misguided. [*Mansel Stimpson*]

● *Kate Ashton* Amanda Boyd, *Sam Ravenswood* Richard Coxon, *Hamish Ashton* Mark Holland, *Oliver Hickox* John Osborn, *Alice* Ann Taylor, Andrew Greenan, John Daszak, Jimmy Logan, Bill Boyd.
● *Dir and Screenplay* Don Boyd, *Pro* Stephanie Mills and Alison Kerr, *Ex Pro* Henry Herbert, *Ph* Dewald Aukema, *Pro Des* Robert Innes Hopkins, *Ed* Adam Ross, *M* Kiran Shiva Akal, *Costumes* Clare Mitchell, *Choreography* Jonathan Lunn.

Lexington Films-Telescope Pictures. 102 mins. UK. 1998. Rel: 1 October 1999. Cert 15.

Above: They're in Heaven – Kenneth Branagh and Natascha McElhone lead the love parade in Branagh's odd but pleasing Love's Labour's Lost (from Pathé)

Above: Wet Nurse – Joanna Lumley does her thing in Sara Sugarman's tedious Mad Cows (from Entertainment)

Mad Cows ★

Maddy is a single mother who can't persuade the father of her child, Alex, to accept his responsibilities. Circumstances cause her to end up in prison with Gillian (Joanna Lumley, playing a character remarkably like Patsy in *AbFab*), having to look after the infant… In ten years of reviewing, I have only walked out of two movies. One was an obscure Asian subtitled film, the other *Mad Cows*. Not one moment of this hideously tedious film rings true. The jokes, away from Kathy Lette's pages, all fall flat, you can't believe in any of the relationships, and the plot, or what passes for one, would be thrown out as unacceptable in a *Carry On* film. Ludicrous and staggeringly boring, *Mad Cows* is one to avoid at all costs – cameos from Mohamed Al Fayed and Meg Matthews notwithstanding. [*Simon Rose*]

● *Maddy* Anna Friel, *Gillian* Joanna Lumley, *Dwina Phelps* Anna Massey, *Lady Drake* Phyllida Law, *Alex* Greg Wise, *Johnny Vaguelawn* John Standing, *Detective Slynne* Nicholas Woodeson, *Maddy's mother* Judy Cornwall, *Dr Minny Stinkler* Prunella Scales, Geoffrey Robertson QC, David Ryall, *Harrods doorman* Mohamed Al Fayed, *Harrods shopper* Meg Matthews, Rustie Lee, Neil Stuke, Hermione Norris, Eddie Marson, Jodie Kidd, Sophie Dahl, Elizabeth Berrington, *browser in Mothercare* Kathy Lette, Sophie Okonedo, Rohan McCullough, Howard Jones, Tara Palmer-Tompkinson, Neville Phillips, John Wood.
● *Dir* Sara Sugarman, *Pro* Aaron Simpson and Frank Mannion, *Ex Pro* Sharon Harel, Jane Barclay, Chris J. Ball and William Tyrer, *Co-Pro* Liz Bunton, *Screenplay* Sugarman and Sasha Hails, from the novel by Kathy Lette, *Ph* Pierre Aïm, *Pro Des* Joseph Nemec III, *Ed* John Jympson, *M* Mark Thomas; songs performed by Billy Swan, The Corrs, Jane Birkin and Serge Gainsbourg, Blair, Robbie Williams, The Chi-Lites, Edwyn Collins, Sister Sledge, Gay Dad, Tom Jones, Space, Chic, Propellerheads, Dusty Springfield, Rod Stewart, Natalie Imbruglia, The Cardigans, Ultra, etc, *Costumes* Trisha Biggar.

Flashlight/Newmarket Capitol/Capitol Films/Entertainment-Entertainment.
90 mins. UK. 1999. Rel: 29 October 1999.

Magnolia ★★★★

Nr. Magnolia Boulevard, The San Fernando Valley, Los Angeles; the present. A bed-ridden TV tycoon lies stricken with cancer. His dying wish is to be reconciled with his son, a self-help guru who has come rich off his seminars promoting female seduction. The tycoon's wife, ravaged by pharmaceutical dependency, finds out too late that she loves the man she once married for money. A game show host who, too, is dying of cancer, is haunted by indiscretions he committed in his past. A well-meaning cop, with a low tolerance for strong language, finds himself falling for the presenter's daughter, a woman on the verge of a nervous breakdown … Strutting in front of an audience of eager would-be seducers, the narcissistic Frank Mackey declares, `the most useless thing in the world is that which is behind you.' Donnie Smith, a washed-up former child prodigy, shouts, `the book says we are through with the past, but the past is not through with us!' The past, and its overwhelming grip on our lives, is just one of the themes that runs through this operatic mosaic of contemporary alienation. Coincidence, redemption and the need to be loved also loom large as the lives of twelve characters intersect on one spectacular day in Los Angeles. Substantiating the talent he exhibited with his first two films, *Hard Eight* and *Boogie Nights*, the 29-year-old Paul Thomas Anderson unleashes an extraordinary film that washes over one with the power of a tsunami. At times a little over-produced and too self-indulgent for its own good, *Magnolia* is nonetheless a mesmerising, magical, bruising, brilliant, inspiring, unexpected, painful, hilarious and stunning experience.

● *Stanley Spector* Jeremy Blackman, *Frank T.J. Mackey* Tom Cruise, *Rose Gator* Melinda Dillon, *Jimmy Gator* Philip Baker Hall, *Phil Parma* Philip Seymour Hoffman, *Burt Ramsey* Ricky Jay, *Quiz Kid Donnie Smith* William H. Macy, *Solomon Solomon* Alfred Molina, *Linda Partridge* Julianne Moore, *Jim Kurring* John C. Reilly, *Earl Partridge* Jason Robards, *Claudia Wilson Gator* Melora Walters, *Gwenovier* April Grace, *Luis* Luis Guzman, *Worm* Orlando Jones, *Alan Kligman* Michael Murphy, *Rick Spector* Michael Bowen, *Thurston Howell* Henry Gibson, *Cynthia* Felicity Huffman, *Dixon* Emmanuel I. Johnson, *Dr Landon* Don McManus, *Mary* Eileen Ryan, *Dick Jennings* Danny Wells, *Marcie* Cleo King, *Brad, the bartender* Craig Kvinsland, *Julia* Natalie Marston, *Richard* Bobby Brewer, Thomas Jane, Veronica Hart, Miguel Perez, Patricia Forte, Patrick Warren, Pat Healy, Art Frankel, Bob Downey Snr, William Mapother, Dale Gibson.
● *Dir and Screenplay* Paul Thomas Anderson, *Pro* Joanne Sellar, *Ex Pro* Michael De Luca and Lynn Harris, *Co-Pro* Daniel Lupi, *Ph* Robert Elswit, *Pro Des* William Arnold and Mark Bridges, *Ed* Dylan Tichenor, *M* Jon Brion; songs performed by Aimee Mann; Supertramp, *Costumes* Mark Bridges.

New Line Cinema/Ghoulardi Film Co.-Entertainment. 185 mins. USA. 1999. Rel: 17 March 2000. Cert 18.

Mal – Evil ★¹/₂

Lisbon, Portugal; today. A desperate old man hovers at a railway station brandishing a photograph of his missing granddaughter. A middle-aged Irish woman clings to what remains of the love she has for her philandering husband. A teenage drug addict, in his increasing sociopathy, resorts to vandalism and theft. A hen-pecked jeweller decides to take a drastic path to his redemption ... Described by its director as an 'exercise in discontinuity,' this contemporary mosaic promises to be a Portuguese *Short Cuts*. Yet unlike Robert Altman's sprawling masterpiece, Santos' horrid little film sustains just one note: emotional cruelty. It is, I suppose, to the director's credit that his characters are credible enough that their ultimate humiliation is abhorrent to the viewer. But what exactly is the point? It's hard to imagine a film as mean-spirited as this being made in the English language, harder still that a British company should deign to distribute it.

● *Cathy Coelho* Pauline Cadell, *Pedro Coelho* Rui Morrisson, *Daniel* Alexandre Pinto, *Marta* Maria Santos, *Emilia* Lia Gama, *Assunçao* Zita Duarte, *Sean* Don Baker, Alicia Gomes Da Costa, Luis Lima Barreto, Luis Esparteiro, Helena Flór.
● *Dir* and *Screenplay* Alberto Seixas Santos, *Pro* Amândio Coroado, *Ph* Acácio de Almeida, *Pro Des* Maria José Branco, *Ed* Catarina Ruivo, *M* various; songs performed by Pat Boone, John McCormack, Don Baker, etc, *Costumes* Silvia Grabowski.

Rosa Filmes/Radiotelevisão Portuguesa/Metropolitan Films/ Camelot Pélis/Quimera Filmes/ICASM/Euroimages Fund/ SDA-Artificial Eye.
85 mins. Portugal/Ireland/Spain/Brazil. 1999. Rel: 2 June 2000. Cert 18.

Man is a Woman ★★★

This French tragi-comedy tells of a gay man named Simon who, to secure an inheritance from his uncle, is persuaded to marry. Since the chosen bride is a Yiddish singer and Simon himself plays Klezmer music on his clarinet, this proves to be a film rich in Jewish atmosphere, as it moves from Paris to New York and back. The film has other advantages, too, since it is good-looking and offers charming performances in the lead roles from Antoine de Caunes and Elsa Zylberstein. The drawback is that the comic aspect proves rather slight, while the dramatic elements lack the depth to make the tale moving rather than just sad. Gilles Taurand who wrote it with the director is more usually associated with Téchiné (*Alice et Martin*) and Ruiz (*Time Regained*). [*Mansel Stimpson*]

● *Simon* Antoine de Caunes, *Rosalie* Elsa Zylberstein, *David* Gad Elmaleh, *Uncle Salomon* Michel Aumont, *Rosalie's father* Maurice Benichou, *Simon's mother* Judith Magre, Catherine Hiegel, Stephane Metzger, Edwin Gerard.
● *Dir* Jean-Jacques Zilbermann, *Pro* Régine Konckier and Jean-Luc Ormières, *Line Pro* Robin O'Hara and Michael Johnson, *Screenplay* Zilbermann and Gilles Taurand, from an idea by Zilbermann and Joele Van Effenterre, *Ph* Pierre Aim, *Pro Des* Valérie Grall, *Ed* Monica Coleman, *M* Eric Michon; various, *Costumes* Edith Vesperini.

Les Films Balenciaga & M6 Films/Sofica Sofygram/Canal Plus, etc-Millivres Multimedia.
99 mins. France. 1997. Rel: 26 May 2000. Cert 15.

Man On the Moon ★★★¹/₂

Andy Kaufman always wanted to be a song-and-dance man. However, his unusual stage act was going nowhere until theatrical agent George Shapiro took him under his wing. Suspecting Kaufman of being insane but maybe also brilliant, Shapiro lands his client a regular spot on the hit TV sitcom *Taxi*. From there on Kaufman's career takes off, but it's a bumpy, unpredictable ride ... Taking its title from the song by REM, this is a mighty strange production about an even stranger man. Think about it. REM, Milos Forman and Jim Carrey working on the same picture? Well, you get what you deserve: a bizarre, sporadically very funny, provocative and accomplished film unlike any biography you will see this year (or many to come). Transforming embarrassment to an art form, Andy Kaufman was a true original, a character who tried to redefine the notions of entertainment and comedy. Carrey does him remarkable justice and Forman (who

Above: The People
Vs. Andy Kaufman –
Jim Carrey in his
Golden Globe-
winning performance
in Man On the
Moon *(from UIP)*

previously chronicled such mavericks as Mozart and Larry Flynt) ties everything together in the most unexpected of ways. Occupying its own space and time frame, the film sheds the straitjacket of most film biographies, presenting the spirit of Kaufman without the narrative junk (on-screen captions, ageing make-up). You'll either love it or hate it.

● *Andy Kaufman* Jim Carrey, *George Shapiro* Danny DeVito, *Lynn Margulies* Courtney Love, *Bob Zmuda* Paul Giamatti, *Tony Clifton* Tony Clifton, *Stanley Kaufman* Gerry Becker, *Janice Kaufman* Leslie Lyles, *little Andy Kaufman* Bobby Boriello, *Mr Besserman* George Shapiro, *Maynard Smith* Vincent Schiavelli, *Merv Griffin* Michael Villani, *Foxy Jackson* Tamara Bossett, Tom Dreesen, Pamela Abdy, Wendy Polland, Melanie Vesey, Michael Kelly, Miles Chapin, Howard West, Maureen Mueller, Brent Briscoe, Conrad Roberts, Marilyn Sokol, Reiko Aylesworth, Bob Zmuda, Tracey Walter, Doris Eaton Travis, Sydney Lassick, Melissa Carrey, and, *as themselves* Budd Friedman, Richard Belzer, Randall Carver, Howdy Doody, and Jerry Lawler, and (*uncredited*) Judd Hirsch, Marilu Henner, Carol Kane, Christopher Lloyd, Norm MacDonald.
● *Dir* Milos Forman, *Pro* Danny DeVito, Michael Shamberg and Stacey Sher, *Ex Pro* George Shapiro and Howard West and Michael Hausman, *Co-Ex Pro* Bob Zmuda, *Screenplay* Scott Alexander and Larry Karaszewski, *Ph* Anastas Michos, *Pro Des* Patrizia Von Brandenstein, *Ed* Christopher Tellefsen and Lynzee Klingman, *M* REM; Handel, Richard Strauss; songs performed by REM, Bob James, Bill Conti, Exile, The Bobs, The Sandpipers, Andy Kaufman, The Hues Corporation, etc, *Costumes* Jeffrey Kurland.

Mutual Film Company/Universal/Jersey Films/Cinehaus/ Shapiro/West Prods-UIP.
119 mins. USA. 1999. Rel: 5 May 2000. Cert 15.

Mansfield Park ★★

The eldest child of an impecunious naval officer, Fanny Price is taken in by her mother's wealthy sister, Lady Bertram, at the magisterial Mansfield Park in Northamptonshire. There, she is patronised by Lady Bertram's daughters, bullied by her mother's sister Mrs Norris and befriended by her cousin, Edmund Bertram. Reaching the full bloom of womanhood, she catches the eye of the dashing Henry Crawford but rejects his proposal of marriage because she doesn't trust him ... Following her lesbian-themed *I've Heard the Mermaids Singing* and *When Night is Falling*, the Canadian filmmaker Patricia Rozema has introduced a 'modern' and autobiographical note into Jane Austen's most successful novel. Published in 1814, *Mansfield Park* has long been considered the author's most personal work and Rozema has blended parts of Austen herself into the character of Fanny Price, even passing off some of Austen's own writings as her heroine's. Academically this is extremely revealing, but it puts little flesh on what, in cinematic terms, is an extremely tenuous story. Far from appearing a woman of admirable character, Fanny comes off as a wilful, stubborn bore, understandably forcing the noble and long-suffering Henry Crawford into an unfaithful act of hormonal release. And with such little narrative propulsion the film is sorely lacking in humour and empathetic detail. FYI: Kirby Hall in Northamptonshire served as the exteriors for Mansfield Park.

● *Mary Crawford* Embeth Davidtz, *Edmund Bertram* Jonny Lee Miller, *Henry Crawford* Alessandro Nivola, *Fanny Price* Frances O'Connor, *Sir Thomas Bertram* Harold Pinter, *Mrs Price/Lady Bertram* Lindsay Duncan, *Mrs Norris* Sheila Gish, *Tom Bertram* James Purefoy, *Maria Bertram* Victoria Hamilton, *Julia Bertram* Justine Waddell, *Mr Rushworth* Hugh Bonneville, *young Fanny Price* Hannah Taylor Gordon, *young Susan Price* Talya Gordon, *young Edmund Bertram* Philip Sarson, *Susan Price* Sophia Myles, *Mr Price* Hilton McRae, Elizabeth Eaton, Elizabeth Earl, Charles Edwards.
● *Dir* and *Screenplay* Patricia Rozema, *Pro* Sarah Curtis, *Ex Pro* Trea Hoving, David Aukin, Colin Leventhal, Harvey Weinstein, David M. Thompson and Bob Weinstein, *Line Pro* Cathy Lord, *Ph* Michael Coulter, *Pro Des* Christopher Hobbs, *Ed* Martin Walsh, *M* Lesley Barber, *Costumes* Andrea Galer.

Miramax/BBC Films/Arts Council of England/HAL Films-Buena Vista.
99 mins. USA/UK. 1999. Rel: 31 March 2000. Cert 15.

The Match ★★

Wullie Smith, a young milkman in the rural village of Inverdoune, is a football fanatic. Yet even though he has instant recall of the most obscure facts of football trivia, he cannot play the game himself. A gammy leg will do that to a fellow. However, his immediate circle of drinking buddies are not much better on the pitch. Which is a shame as their beloved local – Benny's Bar – is about to be turned into a car park. Unless, that is, they can trounce a rival team that they've failed to beat in the last one 99 years ... For all its heart and fine craftsmanship, *The Match* cannot escape the fact that it is the year's most predictable movie. Following in the tread marks of every 'losing side' fable from *The Mighty Ducks* to *Up 'n' Under*, it is almost obsequious in the way it obeys the rules of how to underestimate an audience. This fatality aside, the film is distinguished by an appealing turn from Max Beesley (a young Ewan McGregor if ever there was one) and attractive location work in Ayrshire.

● *Wullie Smith* Max Beesley, *Sheila Bailey* Isla Blair, *Billy Bailey* James Cosmo, *Rosemary Bailey* Laura Fraser, *Gorgeous Gus* Richard E. Grant, *Scrapper* David Hayman, *Big Tam* Ian Holm, *Mr 'piss off'* Doris Neil Morrissey, *Mechanic* David O'Hara, *Tommy Van Driver* Bill Paterson, *Danny Van Boy* Iain Robertson, *Buffalo* Tom Sizemore, *Dead-Eye McCormack* Gary Lewis, *Dingus* Michael Nardone,

Anna Smith Hope Ross, Russell Barr, Ron Donachie, Paul Doonan, Samantha Fox, Andy Gray, Sally Howitt, Gary McCormack, Edward McQuillan, Alan Sharer, *John McGhee* Pierce Brosnan.
● *Dir and Screenplay* Mick Davis, *Pro* Allan Scott and Guymon Casady, *Ex Pro* Steve Golin, Pierce Brosnan, Beau St Clair and Robert Kosberg, *Co-Pro* Chris Symes, *Ph* Witold Stok, *Pro Des* John Frankish, *Ed* Kate Williams, *M* Harry Gregson-Williams; songs performed by T. Rex, The Shadows, Bryan Ferry, Desmond Dekker, Manfred Mann, Kool and the Gang, Bachman-Turner Overdrive, Sutherland Brothers, The Troggs, Roxy Music, Gary Glitter, Spencer Davis Group, etc, *Costumes* Pam Downe.

Propaganda Films/Irish Dreamtime-Universal Pictures.
96 mins. UK/USA/Ireland. 1999. Rel: 6 August 1999. Cert 15.

Maybe Baby ★★★★

London; today. Sam Bell is a commissioning editor for the BBC. His wife, Lucy, is a theatrical agent. With a loving relationship, a nice flat and a compassionate basset hound they would seem to lead an idyllic life. But Lucy is desperate for a baby and Sam is desperate to find an idea for his first screenplay. Then he hits on the hunch of writing a comedy about his and Lucy's ill-fated attempts to conceive. All he needs is an ending ... Marking the directorial debut of all-round comic genius Ben Elton (playwright, novelist, stand-up comic, actor, joke meister) *Maybe Baby* is a very funny romantic comedy with a delicious premise. It's also got a strong footing in reality, drawing its wide range of comic flavours from often painfully recognisable situations. As a romantic leading man, Hugh Laurie is a revelation (move over Hugh Grant), while the supporting cast invariably hits its marks with comic aplomb. Favourite exchange: Matthew Macfadyen, screaming at Hugh Laurie: 'You wanker!' Laurie, incredulously: 'How did you know?' FYI: Laurie

Below: Inconceivable? Hugh Laurie and Joely Richardson cuddle up in Ben Elton's very funny Maybe Baby (from Redbus)

Right: For one wedding, many funerals – Hugh Grant and Jeanne Tripplehorn complicate matters in Kelly Makin's silly and uninspired Mickey Blue Eyes (from PolyGram)

and Joely Richardson previously appeared together (in very different roles) in *101 Dalmatians*.

● *Sam Bell* Hugh Laurie, *Lucy Bell* Joely Richardson, *George* Adrian Lester, *Carl Phipps* James Purefoy, *Ewan Proclaimer* Tom Hollander, *Sheila* Joanna Lumley, *Mr James* Rowan Atkinson, *Charlene* Dawn French, *Druscilla* Emma Thompson, *Nigel* Matthew Macfadyen, *Jan* Lisa Palfrey, Yasmin Bannerman, John Brenner, Serena Evans, John Fortune, Kelly Reilly, Stephen Simms, Rachael Stirling, Dave Thompson, Paul Tripp, Elizabeth Woodcock, *William the dog* Bill & Ben.
● *Dir* and *Screenplay* Ben Elton, *Pro* Phil McIntyre, *Ex Pro* Ernst Goldschmidt and David M. Thompson, *Assoc Pro* Lucy Ansbro, *Line Pro* Mary Richards, *Ph* Roger Lanser, *Pro Des* Jim Clay, *Ed* Peter Hollywood, *M* Colin Towns; songs performed by Paul McCartney, Lene Marlin, Air, Shack, Atomic Kitten, Roxy Music, Elvis Costello & The Attractions, George Michael, Westlife, Gold 'N' Delicious, Quivver, and Tin Tin Out, *Costumes* Anna Sheppard.

Pandora/BBC Films-Redbus.
100 mins. UK. 2000. Rel: 2 June 2000. Cert 15.

Mickey Blue Eyes ★★

New York City; the present. English auctioneer Michael Felgate has been dating New York schoolteacher Gina Vitale for three months when he pops her the question. However, her hysterical rebuttal is far from the response he expected. It turns out that her father is a key member of the Mob and she fears for Michael's safety should he marry into the Mafia. Michael, however, reckons that

true love can circumnavigate such familial complications ... The idea of Hugh Grant's bumbling Englishman caught up with the Mafia is an irresistible one, but after a promising start the film quickly descends into arch silliness. Part of the problem is that there is no chemistry between Grant and Tripplehorn, so it's hard to care what happens to either of them. One deftly written scene, a look or exchange of distinctive intimacy, would have made all the difference. The uninspired soundtrack of hackneyed Italian songs is another minus.

● *Michael Felgate* Hugh Grant, *Frank Vitale* James Caan, *Gina Vitale* Jeanne Tripplehorn, *Vito Graziosi* Burt Young, *Philip Cromwell* James Fox, *Vinnie* Joe Viterelli, *Ritchie Vitale* Paul Lazar, *Johnny Graziosi* John Ventimiglia, *Helen* Margaret Devine, *Mrs Horton* Beatrice Winde, *Gene Morganson* Mark Margolis, Gerry Becker, Maddie Corman, Tony Darrow, Vincent Pastore, Frank Pellegrino, Scott Thompson, Helen Lloyd Breed, Sybil Lines, Joseph R. Gannascoli, Frank Senger, Lori Tan Chinn, Aida Turturro.
● *Dir* Kelly Makin, *Pro* Elizabeth Hurley and Charles Mulvehill, *Assoc Pro* Karin Smith, *Screenplay* Mark Lawrence, Adam Scheinman and Robert Kuhn, *Ph* Donald E. Thorin, *Pro Des* Gregory P. Keen, *Ed* David Freeman, *M* Basil Poledouris and Wolfgang Hammerschmid; Nino Rota; songs performed by Clarence 'Frogman' Henry, Dean Martin, Percy Faith and His Orchestra, Sister Sledge, Nelson Riddle, Frank Sinatra, Louis Prima, James Caan, Paolo Conte, Al Green, Rosemary Clooney, Bryan Ferry, and Queen, *Costumes* Ellen Mirojnick.

Castle Rock/Simian Films-PolyGram.
102 mins. USA/UK. 1999. Rel: 20 August 1999. Cert 15.

A Midsummer Night's Dream
See William Shakespeare's A Midsummer Night's Dream.

Mifune ★¹/₂
More oddball than endearing, this Danish film is the third feature to reach us waving the banner of Dogme 95. But adopting the handheld cameras and other requirements of that method is less central to the film's character than its story, conceived by the director, Søren Kragh-Jacobsen. Following the death of a father whose existence he has denied, a newly married man becomes embroiled in the affairs of a half-wit brother and of the housekeeper, actually a prostitute, whom he hires to look after his sibling. An agreeable cast, not least Iben Hjejle as the prostitute, is hampered by a tone which switches distractingly from undeveloped drama into unengaging comedy, and by a plot which becomes increasingly contrived and ultimately unbelievable. Decidedly disappointing. [*Mansel Stimpson*]

● *Kresten Jensen* Anders W. Berthelsen, *Liva Psilander* Iben Hjejle, *Rud Jensen* Jesper Asholt, *Claire Hostrup-Jensen* Sofie Gråbøl, *Bjarke Psilander* Emil Tarding, *Gerner Mikkelsen* Anders Hove, Paprika Steen, Mette Bratlann, Susanne Storm.
● *Dir* Søren Kragh-Jacobsen, *Pro* Birgitte Hald and Morten Kaufmann, *Screenplay* Kragh-Jacobsen and Anders Thomas Jensen, *Ph* Anthony Dod Mantle, *Ed* Valdis Oskardottir, *M* Thor Backhausen, Karl Bille and Christian Sievert; Chopin, *Sound* Morten Degnbol and Hans Møller.

Nimbus Film/Zentropa Entertainments/DRTV/SVT Drama/ Nordisk Film og TV Fond and Det Danske Filminstitut-Alliance Atlantis.
101 mins. Denmark/Sweden. 1998. Rel: 1 October 1999. Cert 15.

The Million Dollar Hotel ★¹/₂
At the Million Dollar Hotel, California, Tom Tom works as a butler for the lost souls of the ghetto. There, he falls for Eloise, a delicate creature who believes she is a work of fiction. Dixie, a neighbour, is under the illusion that he is a member of The Beatles, and Joseph, another tenant, paints canvases of tar and thinks he is the Apache warrior Geronimo. Then there's the hunchback FBI agent Skinner, a cop from the future, investigating the suspicious suicide of Tom Tom's friend Izzy ... The brain child of U2 singer Bono, *The Million Dollar Hotel* is weirder than it sounds. Inspired by a real-life lodging (now the Frontier Hotel) used in the U2 video 'Where The Streets Have No Name', the film purports to be a poetic and paradoxical love story. The first five minutes certainly promise much lyricism, but thereafter the venture gets bogged down in its own inanity. But what does one expect from a collaboration between Bono, Wim Wenders and Mel Gibson? What next? Werner Herzog directing Clint Eastwood in a Spice Girls project?

● *Thomas 'Tom Tom' T. Barrow* Jeremy Davies, *Eloise* Milla Jovovich, *Det. Skinner* Mel Gibson, *Joseph* aka *Geronimo* Jimmy Smits, *Dixie* Peter Stormare, *Vivien* Amanda Plummer, *Jessica* Gloria Stuart, *Shorty* Bud Cort, *Stanley Goldkiss* Harris Yulin, *Jean Swift* Charlayne Woodard, *Joe* Richard Edson, Tom Bower, Donal Logue, Julian Sands, Conrad Roberts, Ellen Cleghorne, Tito Larriva, Jon Hassell, and (uncredited) *Izzy Goldkiss* Tim Roth.
● *Dir* Wim Wenders, *Pro* Wenders, Deepak Nayar, Bono, Nicholas Klein and Bruce Davey, *Ex Pro* Uli Felsberg, *Screenplay* Klein, from a story by Bono and Klein, *Ph* Phedon Papamichael, *Pro Des* Robert D. Freed and Arabella A. Serrell, *Ed* Tatiana S. Riegel, *M* Jon Hassell, Bono, Daniel Lanois and Brian Eno; songs performed by U2, Hal Willner, Bono and Daniel Lanois, MDH Band, Tito Larriva, etc, *Costumes* Nancy Steiner, *Sound* Elmo Weber.

Road Movie Prods/Icon Prods/Kintop Pictures-Icon. 122 mins. Germany/USA. 1999. Rel: 28 April 2000. Cert 15.

The Miracle Maker ★★
Judea; the 90th year of the Roman Occupation. The incurably ill daughter of an eminent Pharisee, Tamar observes from afar the teachings and miracles of a man dubbed the Magician of Nazareth. Believing that this miracle worker can relieve her own sickness, Tamar is prevented from seeking his help because of her father's strict grounding in the established church. Meanwhile, both the celebrity and notoriety of the so-called 'King of the Jews' continues to flourish ... There is so much to commend this distillation of Luke's Gospel that it seems churlish to point out its faults. But the fact remains that the sheer narrative ambition of the project defeats its emotional impact. Whether a story is animated or propelled by actors, it needs time to build characters. And *The Miracle Maker* is so determined to cram in as many miraculous events as possible that there's little opportunity to care about Tamar, Jesus or anybody else. Still, the animation – featuring 30cm-high models made of metal, foam and latex – is breathtaking, creating a unique three-dimensional world. FYI: A team of 250 Russians worked for over a year utilising 260 figures on six separate sets.

● Voices: *Jesus* Ralph Fiennes, *voice of God/the doctor* Michael Bryant, *Rachel* Julie Christie, *Tamar* Rebecca Callard, *Thomas* James Frain, *John the Baptist* Richard E. Grant, *Pilate* Ian Holm, *Jairus* William Hurt, *Herod* Anton Lesser, *Cleopas* Daniel Massey, *Barabbas* Tim McInnerny, *Simon the Pharisee* Alfred Molina, *Joseph of Arimathea* Bob Peck, *Mary Magdalene* Miranda Richardson, *Ben Azra* Antony Sher, *Andrew* Ewan Stewart, *Simon Peter* Ken Stott, *Judas* David Thewlis, Vass Anderson, Tony Armatrading, Robert Duncan, William Hootkins, Geraldine O'Rawe, David Schofield, Emily Mortimer, Phoebe Nicholls, Geraint Owen, Dougray Scott.

● *Dir* Stanislav Sokolov and Derek Hayes, *Pro* Naomi Jones, *Ex Pro* Christopher Grace, *Co-Ex Pro* Elizabeth Babakhina, *Screenplay* Murray Watts, *Ed* William Oswald and John Richards, *Art Design* Helena Livanova, *M* Anne Dudley, *Costumes* Anna Baibakova and Eugenia Bogolyubova, *Sound* Ian 'Spike' Banks, *dialogue direction* Joan Washington.

Ffilmiau S4C Films/British Screen/Icon Entertainment/BBC Cymru/Wales/Cartwn Cymru/Christmas Films-Icon. 91 mins. UK/Russia. 1999. Rel: 31 March 2000. Cert U.

Mission To Mars ★★★★

Mars; 2020-22. Shortly after the first manned touchdown on Mars, contact is lost with the astronauts. All that is left is an enigmatic video message. It will take six months for another ship to reach the red planet, but the mystery surrounding what happened to the original crew is too intriguing to ignore ... Films that explore new worlds invariably come in for flak just for trying something different. Yet where Tim Burton's sadistic *Mars Attacks!* is applauded for its audacity, a serious contemplation like *Contact* is ridiculed for being pretentious and/or far-fetched. The fact remains that we live in a mysterious universe and history has repeatedly proved that we cannot judge the cosmos by our own laws of physics – or logic. *Mission To Mars* is special in that it introduces fleshed-out characters on a remarkable objective to push forward the frontiers of human knowledge and, unlike in *Apollo 13*, we don't know how things are going to pan out – *because it hasn't happened yet*. Furthermore, Brian De Palma, a director not against trying out a new camera move, has created some astonishing sequences. The recreational scene on board the Mars Recovery ship is every bit as awe-inspiring as the parallel sequence in *2001*, while for pure singularity the zero-gravity dance between Tim Robbins and Connie Nielsen goes down in cinema history alongside anything Fred Astaire cooked up. *Mission To Mars* is not perfect but its combination of state-of-the-art sets, jaw-dropping effects and consummate production values make it superior escapism.

Below: Shallow space – Tim Hill's Muppets From Space (from Columbia TriStar)

● *Jim McConnell* Gary Sinise, *Luke Graham* Don Cheadle, *Terri Fisher* Connie Nielsen, *Phil Ohlmyer*

Jerry O'Connell, *Woody Blake* Tim Robbins, *Sergei Kirov* Peter Outerbridge, *Nicholas Willis* Kavan Smith, *Maggie McConnell* Kim Delaney, Jill Teed, Elise Neal, Robert Bailey Jr., Jody Thompson, Pamela Diaz, Story Musgrave, McCanna Anthony Sinise, and (*uncredited*) Armin Mueller-Stahl.
● *Dir* Brian De Palma, *Pro* Tom Jacobson, *Ex Pro* Sam Mercer, *Co-Pro* David Goyer, Justis Greene and Jim Wedaa, *Assoc Pro* Ted Tally, *Screenplay* Jim Thomas & John Thomas and Graham Yost, from a story by Lowell Cannon and Jim Thomas & John Thomas, *Ph* Stephen H. Burum, *Pro Des* Ed Verreaux, *Ed* Paul Hirsch, *M* Ennio Morricone; songs performed by Buckwheat Zydeco, and Van Halen, *Costumes* Sanja Milkovic Hays, *Visual effects* Hoyt Yeatman and John Knoll.

Touchstone Pictures/Jacobson Company-Buena Vista. 116 mins. USA. 2000. Rel: 14 April 2000.

A Monkey's Tale ★

Many centuries ago a cataclysmic flood separated a community of monkeys into two groups, those who took to the trees and those who stayed on the ground. Now divided by suspicion and fear, the two colonies are united by the curiosity of the rebellious Kom... While claiming to be 'the most ambitious animated feature produced outside of the Hollywood studios' (yeah, right), *A Monkey's Tale* is a low-point in a classic year for animation. Poorly drawn, clumsily constructed and voiced with surprising inertia by a stellar cast, this makes a monkey out of all of us. [*Charles Bacon*]

● Voices: *Chancellor Sebastian* John Hurt, *King* Michael York, *Gerard* Rik Mayall, *Master Martin* Michael Gambon, *Governess* Shirley Anne Field, *Gina* Sally-Anne Marsh, *Princess Ida* Diana Quick, *Kom* Matt Hill, *Korkonak* French Tickner, William Vanderpuye, Paul Dobson, Janyse Jaud.
● *Dir* Jean-Francois Laguionie, *Pro* Steve Walsh, Patrick Moine and Gerd Hecker, *Screenplay* Norman Hudis, *Art* Zoltán Szilágyi Varga, *Ed* Soizic Veillon and Ludovic Cassou, *M* Alexandre Desplat, 'We Are One' sung by Westlife, *Sound* Nigel Holland, *Animation Dir* Ginger Gibbons.

Miracle Communications/Les Films du Triangle/Cologne Cartoon/France 3 Cinéma/British Screen/European Co-Production Fund/BskyB/Canal Plus, etc-Miracle Communications. 76 mins. France/UK/Germany/Hungary. 1999. Rel: 26 May 2000. Cert PG.

Muppets From Space ★¹/₂

Following a startling encounter with his breakfast cereal, Gonzo realises that he may not be one of a kind after all. It seems that an extraterrestrial race is trying to make contact with him. Now, if only Gonzo could warn them

Left: Greek comedy – A bemused Andie MacDowell in Albert Brooks' bittersweet The Muse *(from Entertainment)*

before the dastardly government agency C.O.V.N.E.T. sabotage their landing ... After a promising start in which the Muppets are introduced during their morning ablutions, this sixth edition in the Muppet screen franchise gets very tiresome very soon. A fleet of guest stars are wasted in embarrassing cameos (except for Ray Liotta and Andie MacDowell in nifty turns), while the plot itself is propelled by a tired bag of gags and movie references. Good soundtrack, though (see credits).

● *K. Edgar Singer* Jeffrey Tambor, *Noah* F. Murray Abraham, *TV producer* Rob Schneider, *Agent Barker* Josh Charles, *gate guard* Ray Liotta, *Dr Tucker* David Arquette, *Shelley Snipes* Andie MacDowell, *female armed guard* Kathy Griffin, *General Luft* Pat Hingle, Hollywood (Hulk) Hogan, Veronica Alicino, David Lenthall, and *as themselves*: Gonzo, Kermit the Frog, Pepe the Prawn, Robin, Dr Phil Van Neuter, Clifford, Miss Piggy, Bunsen Honeydew, Waldorf, The Birdman, Rizzo the Rat, Beaker, Bobo As Rentro, Bubba the Rat, Statler, Sal Minella, Fozzie Bear, Animal, Sam Eagle, etc. Muppet performers: Dave Goelz, Steve Whitmire, Bill Barretta, Frank Oz, Jerry Nelson, Brian Henson, Kevin Clash, Rickey Boyd, Tim Parati, etc.
● *Dir* Tim Hill, *Pro* Brian Henson and Martin G. Baker, *Ex Pro* Kristine Belson and Stephanie Allain, *Co-Pro* Timothy M. Bourne and Alex Rockwell, *Screenplay* Jerry Juhl, Joseph Mazzarino and Ken Kaufman, *Ph* Alan Caso, *Pro Des* Stephen Marsh, *Ed* Michael A. Stevenson and Richard Pearson, *M* Jamshied Sharifi; songs performed by The Commodores, George Clinton and Pepe, James Brown, The Isley Brothers, Billy Preston, Earth Wind & Fire, Dust Brothers, The O'Jays, etc, *Costumes* Polly Smith, *Visual effects* Thomas G. Smith, *Choreography* Toni Basil.

Jim Henson Pictures/Columbia-Columbia TriStar. 88 mins. UK/USA. 1999. Rel: 26 December 1999. Cert U.

The Muse ★★★

In spite of having just been honoured for a Humanitarian Lifetime Achievement Award, screenwriter Steven Phillips finds his contract with Paramount terminated. He has lost his edge apparently, or so everybody keeps telling him. So, as a favour, his good friend Jack puts him in contact with a Muse, one of the nine daughters of Zeus. And in return for inspiration the latter demands that Steven install her in a $1,700-a-night suite at The Four Seasons and meets all her special dietary needs. And that's just the beginning of her demands ... Albert Brooks' films have always been limited in their appeal and in spite of the major stars he has corralled for this (his sixth picture as director), his aim has narrowed even further. A bittersweet love note to those in the know in Hollywood, *The Muse* is full of very funny in-jokes (with a roster of game cameos from top directors and stars), but there is also plenty of gentle humour that should be appreciated by the rest of the world.

● *Steven Phillips* Albert Brooks, *Sarah* Sharon Stone, *Laura Phillips* Andie MacDowell, *Jack Warrick* Jeff Bridges, *Josh Martin* Mark Feuerstein, *Hal* Bradley Whitford, *Stan Spielberg* Steven Wright, Cybill Shepherd, Monica Mikala, Jamie Alexis, Catherine MacNeal, Lorenzo Lamas, Jennifer Tilly, Skip O'Brien, Aude Charles, Ange Billman, Gannon Daniels, Bobby Ender, Stacy Travis, Michele Crosby Jones, Rob Reiner, Wolfgang Puck, James Cameron, Martin Scorsese, Dakin Matthews, Concetta Tomei.
● *Dir* Albert Brooks, *Pro* Herb Nanas, *Ex Pro* Barry Berg, *Screenplay* Brooks and Monica Johnson, *Ph* Thomas Ackerman, *Pro Des* Dina Lipton, *Ed* Peter Teschner, *M* Elton John; songs performed by Rick James, Jimmy Cliff, and Elton John, *Costumes* Betsy Cox.

October Films-Entertainment. 96 mins. USA. 1999. Rel: 10 December 1999. Cert PG.

The Music Freelancers – Les Cachetonneurs ★★★

Writer-director Denis Dercourt is also a musician, and he's had the engaging idea of making a comedy about six French instrumentalists giving a New Year's Eve concert in a rich man's country house. This ad hoc group – young, enthusiastic but somewhat out of their depth – are placed effectively at the film's centre, and we sit back to root for them, enjoying the humour and the music along the way (Johann Strauss being the composer most favoured). But, sadly, Dercourt seems uncertain how to carry the plot forward, and the lack of inspiration in the pedestrian second half makes even this short feature seem flimsy. Nevertheless, musicians especially are likely to warm to it, and to forgive the flaws. A special word for Henri Garcin who brings authority to the role of the conductor. [*Mansel Stimpson*]

● *Roberto* Pierre Lacan, *Lionel* Marc Citti, *Martial* Serge Renko, *Thérèse Marie* Marie-Christine Laurent, *the clarinetist* Wilfred Benaïche, *Diana* Clémentine Benoit, *the aristocrat* Philippe Clay, *Mr Svarowski* Henri Garcin, Ivry Gitlis, Sonia Mankaï, Baba Meyong Bekate.
● *Dir* Denis Dercourt, *Pro* Tom Dercourt, *Ph* Jérôme Peyrebrune, *Ed* Yann Coquart, *Costumes* Suen Mounicq.

Les films à un dollar-Winstone.
88 mins. France. 1998. Rel: 26 December 1999. Cert PG.

Music of the Heart ★★★★

When Roberta Guaspari's husband leaves her for another woman, she has no choice but to find a job to support her two young sons. Convincing the principal of an East Harlem school to take her on as a violin teacher (after an impromptu concert by her sons), Roberta struggles to motivate her students and to show that 'dead white men's music' has a vital place in contemporary society ... Disregarding the schmaltzy package that this remarkable story arrives in – the banal title, a gushing opening song from Aaliyah and an overactive score from Mason Daring – Wes Craven's first non-horror outing has much to commend it: a terrific performance from Meryl Streep, a host of photogenic children, some marvellous music, a priceless cameo from Isaac Stern and the laudable message that commitment, sacrifice and enterprise *can* win the day. Yes, the film is sentimental, but there's sentimental and there's Robin Williams. This, thankfully, has enough edge and genuine sincerity to nudge it into the former – and more palatable – category. Original title: *50 Violins*.

● *Roberta Guaspari* Meryl Streep, *Brian Turner* Aidan Quinn, *Isabel Vasquez* Gloria Estefan, *Janet Williams* Angela Bassett, *Dorothea von Haeften* Jane

Leeves, *Assunta Guaspari* Cloris Leachman, *Lexi at 15* Kieran Culkin, *Nick at 17* Charlie Hofheimer, *Dan* Jay O. Sanders, *Dennis Rausch* Josh Pais, *DeSean at 11* Jade Yorker, *Naeem at 9* Justin Spalding, Henry Dinhofer, Michael Angarano, Victoria Gomez, Zoe Sternbach-Taubman, Rosalyn Coleman, Betsy Aidem, Cole Hawkins, Arthur French, Dominic Walters, Jean Luke Figueroa, Eva Loomis, Olga Merediz, Adam LeFevre and, *as themselves*: Arnold Steinhardt, Isaac Stern, Mark O'Connor, Karen Biggs, Itzhak Perelman, Joshua Bell.
● *Dir* Wes Craven, *Pro* Marianne Maddalena, Walter Scheuer, Alan Miller and Susan Kaplan, *Ex Pro* Harvey Weinstein, Bob Weinstein and Amy Slotnick, *Co-Pro* Stuart Besser, *Screenplay* Pamela Gray, *Ph* Peter Deming, *Pro Des* Bruce Miller, *Ed* Patrick Lussier, *M* Mason Daring; Johann Sebastian Bach, Haydn; songs performed by Aaliyah, Cubanismo!, Julio Iglesias Jr., Kool G. Rap and Big Daddy Kane, Jennifer Lopez, Gloria Estefan, etc, *Costumes* Susan Lyall.

Miramax/Craven/Maddalena Films-Buena Vista.
124 mins. USA. 1999. Rel: 21 January 2000. Cert PG.

My Life So Far ★★

Kiloran House, Argyll, Scotland; the 1920s. Fraser Pettigrew, 10, is enjoying an idyllic childhood on his family's rambling rural estate. His father, 'an inventor and genius,' and mother, a former singer, are devoted to each other, the gardens are alive with the sound of children playing and there's plenty to explore in the surrounding woods. Then, one day, Uncle Morris turns up with his beautiful new fiancée ... A childhood drama set in the heart of Scotland, this is the cinematic equivalent of a tin Highland cowbell you'd find in a tourist shop – it just doesn't ring true. Beside the varying accents from an Anglo-American cast, the Pettigrews own a Scottish terrier, the 33-year-old Irene Jacob plays a 24-year-old and Beethoven fanatic Edward Pettigrew can't seem to get past Beethoven's Fifth. The sound is also poorly edited, Howard Blake's boisterous score works overtime and in a period when the word 'swimming trunks' was considered improper it's startling to see the costumes revealing Kelly Macdonald's nipples and Ms Jacob's panty-line. In all, the film is about as authentic as a pair of tartan underpants. Having said that, there are some humorous moments (Edward's insistence on speaking in Scottish clichés to the yokels) and Rosemary Harris turns in a sterling performance as Fraser's indomitable but kindhearted grandmother. But that's thin pickings from the director and producer of *Chariots of Fire*.

● *Edward Pettigrew* Colin Firth, *Gamma Macintosh* Rosemary Harris, *Heloise* Irène Jacob, *Gabriel Chenoux* Tcheky Karyo, *Moira Pettigrew* Mary Elizabeth Mastrantonio, *Uncle Morris Macintosh*

Malcolm McDowell, *Elspeth Pettigrew* Kelly Macdonald, *Fraser Pettigrew* Robert Norman, *Rollo* Roddy McDonald, *Andrew Burns* Sean Scanlan, *Uncle Crawford* John Bett, *Tom Skelly* Jimmy Logan, *Jim Menzies* Brendan Gleeson, *Reverend Finlayson* Freddie Jones, Daniel Baird, Jennifer Fergie, Kirsten Smith, Anne Lacey, Clive Russell, Paul Young.
● *Dir* Hugh Hudson, *Pro* David Puttnam and Steve Norris, *Ex Pro* Bob Weinstein, Harvey Weinstein and Paul Webster, *Co-Pro* Nigel Goldsack, *Screenplay* Simon Donald, based on the book *Son of Adam* by Sir Denis Forman, *Ph* Bernard Lutic, *Pro Des* Andy Harris, *Ed* Scott Thomas, *M* Howard Blake; Beethoven, *Costumes* Emma Porteous.

Miramax/Scottish Arts Council Lottery Fund/Enigma Prods/Scottish Screen-Buena Vista.
98 mins. USA/UK. 1998. Rel: 12 May 2000. Cert 12.

Mystery Men ★★¹/₂

They are superheroes of sorts, but the fork-throwing Blue Raja, spade-wielding The Shoveller and belligerent The Furious are no match for the athletic, square-jawed Captain Amazing. However, when all the super-villains of Champion City are bested, Amazing is in danger of losing his sponsors (Pepsi have already withdrawn their backing), so he conspires to have the evil Casanova Frankenstein released from his containment. Immediately betraying and imprisoning his liberator, 'Frankenstein' plots to destroy the city, leaving only our motley, ineffectual trio to stand in his way ... Based on the Dark Horse Comic Book series, *Mystery Men* starts with a promising premise but takes far too many wrong turns before reaching its overblown conclusion. There are some wonderful characters and running gags and even a few good jokes, but there are just as many awful ones, with Hank Azaria's embarrassing Blue Raja reaching a new low in comic fatuity ('may the fork be with you' indeed). A nice idea, but one baked to desperation.

● *Jeffrey/The Blue Raja* Hank Azaria, *Monica* Claire Forlani, *The Bowler* Janeane Garofalo, *Tony P* Eddie Izzard, *Captain Amazing/Lance* Greg Kinnear, *Eddie/The Shoveler* William H. Macy, *Invisible Boy* Kel Mitchell, *Dr Annabel Leek* Lena Olin, *The Spleen* Paul Reubens, *Casanova Frankenstein* Geoffrey Rush, *Roy/The Furious* Ben Stiller, *The Sphinx* Wes Studi, *Dr Heller* Tom Waits, *Tony C* Prakazrel Michel, *Violet* Louise Lasser, *Lucille* Jenifer Lewis, Ernie Lee Banks, Gerry Becker, Ned Bellamy, Ricky Jay, Monet Mazur, Stacey Travis, Joann Richter, Dane Cook.
● *Dir* Kinka Usher, *Pro* Lawrence Gordon, Mike Richardson and Lloyd Levin, *Ex Pro* Robert Engelman, *Co-Pro* Steven Gilder, *Screenplay* Neil Cuthbert and Brent Forrester, from the creation of Bob Burden, *Ph* Stephen H. Burum, *Pro Des* Kirk M. Petruccelli, *Ed* Conrad Buff, *M* Stephen Warbeck; songs performed by Mark Mothersbaugh, The Trammps, A Taste of Honey, Bee Gees, Chic, Wild Cherry, Freak Power, Dub Pistols, Violent Femmes, Jill Sobule, Spy, KC & The Sunshine Band, Smash Mouth, Petula Clark, The B-52's, etc, *Costumes* Marilyn Vance, *Visual effects* Lori Nelson.

Universal/Golar/Lloyd Levin/Dark Horse-UIP.
122 mins. USA. 1999. Rel: 26 December 1999. Cert PG.

Never Been Kissed ★'/2

At high school Jessie Geller was a dork. Now that she's 25 and a copy editor at *The Chicago Sun-Times* she's become a prim and proper stuffed shirt. Yet she still dreams of falling in love and being on the receiving end of the perfect kiss – something, incidentally, she's never experienced. Then she's assigned to go undercover at South Glen South to expose the lifestyle of high school days, a mission Jessie finds herself singularly unqualified for ... Drew Barrymore is still only 24 yet she has re-invented herself so many times, from cute child star to alcoholic to drug addict to *Scream* queen to Cinderella to movie mogul and now, tragically, to pantomime dame. Made up to look like Susan Sarandon in *Dead Man Walking*, young Barrymore has become a ham before her time, reduced to falling over and over-acting embarrassingly for easy laughs. The story itself is risible, the script retarded and the whole conceit flesh-crawling. It's enough to put the high school genre back to the dark ages pre-*Heathers*.

● *Josie Geller* Drew Barrymore, *Rob Geller* David Arquette, *Sam Coulson* Michael Vartan, *Anita* Molly Shannon, *Gus* John C. Reilly, *Rigfort* Garry Marshall, *Merkin* Sean Whalen, *George* Cress Williams, *Aldys* Leelee Sobieski, *Guy Perkins* Jeremy Jordan, Octavia L. Spencer, Sarah DeVincentis, Rock Reiser, Kathleen Marshall, Jessica Alba, Marley Shelton, Jordan Ladd, Katie Lansdale, Branden Williams, James Edward Franco, Gregory Sporleder, Denny Kirkwood.
● *Dir* Raja Gosnell, *Pro* Sandy Isaac and Nancy Juvonen, *Ex Pro* Drew Barrymore, *Co-Pro* Jeffrey Downer, *Screenplay* Abby John and Marc Silverstein, *Ph* Alex Nepomniaschy, *Pro Des* Steven Jordan, *Ed* Debra Chiate and Marcelo Sansevieri, *M* David Newman; *songs performed by* Block, John Lennon, Cyndi Lauper, Jimmy Eat World, Cutting Crew, Grandmaster Slice, Jeremy Jordan, Mister Jones, Pat Benatar, The New Seekers, Ozomatli, Madonna, Hole, BTK, Semisonic, REM, Swirl 360, The Cardigans, The Smiths, Radford, The Beach Boys, Sonichrome, The Moffatts, etc, *Costumes* Mona May.

Fox 2000/Flower Films/Bushwood Pictures-Fox.
107 mins. USA. 1999. Rel: 27 August 1999. Cert 12.

The New Eve – La Nouvelle Eve ★'/2

Camille, thirtysomething and single, is bored by the lifestyle of her peers and recoils from the thought of commitment and children. Prone to drinking too much and throwing up in the worst places, Camille samples S&M and free-love parties but seems to get little from it. Then, on the street, she meets Alexis, a bald Socialist with a devoted wife and two daughters, and decides that he is the man for her ... It could be the English translation, but this bleak black comedy just isn't funny with subtitles. Although competently acted and occasionally surprising, the film is scuttled by a character beyond the point of irritation. An unfocused, unprincipled, spiteful,

clumsy, irrational, neurotic and unstable drunk, Camille is no joke and makes for excruciating company.

● *Camille* Karen Viard, *Alexis* Pierre-Loup Rajot, *Isabelle* Catherine Frot, *Ben* Sergi López, *Louise* Mireille Roussel, *Solveig* Nozha Khouadra, *Emile* Laurent Lucas, *Sophie* Valentine Vidal, François Caron, Frédéric Gelard, Jean-Francois Galotte.
● *Dir* Catherine Corsini, *Pro* Paulo Branco, *Ex Pro* Philippe Saal and Philippe Rey, *Screenplay* Corsini and Marc Syrigas, *Ph* Agnès Godard, *Pro Des* Solange Zeitoun, *Ed* Sabine Mamou, *M* various, *Costumes* Anne Schotte.

Gemini Films/Arte France Cinéma/Canal Plus/Sofica Sofinergie 4/Madragoa Films-Gala.
94 mins. France. 1998. Rel: 14 April 2000. Cert 18.

The Next Best Thing ★★'/2

Los Angeles; the present. Besides being swept off his feet by a compassionate and handsome Adonis, the next best thing for homosexual English gardener Robert Whitaker would be to become a father courtesy of his best friend, yoga instructor Abbie. And, sure enough, after a night of carousing and cocktails, Robert gets Abbie pregnant. So they move in together and become a family, albeit a highly unconventional one ... Few high-concept packages come with such legitimate credentials. Pairing Madonna with her real best friend Rupert Everett, who happens to be gay, and hiring fellow homosexual John Schlesinger to direct the proceedings, is nothing short of a boon to Thomas Ropelewski's sharp and insightful screenplay. Yet in spite of some snappy dialogue and a few good performances (Madonna, Everett, Lynn Redgrave), what should have been a thought-provoking and hilarious comedy falls rather flat. For while kicking up some interesting questions concerning the legal position on parenting, the film fails to break free from its glossy packaging. Ultimately, then, it is neither very moving nor particularly funny.

● *Abbie* Madonna, *Robert Whitaker* Rupert Everett, *Ben* Benjamin Bratt, *Kevin* Michael Vartan, *Richard Whitaker* Josef Sommer, *Sam* Malcolm Stumpf, *David* Neil Patrick Harris, *Helen Whitaker* Lynn Redgrave, *Elizabeth Ryder* Illeana Douglas, *Ashby* William Mesnik, Mark Valley, Suzanne Krull, Stacy Edwards, John Carroll Lynch, Fran Bennett, Ricki Lopez, Ramiro Fabian, Joan Axelrod, George Axelrod, Jack Betts, Linda Larkin, Kimberly Davies.
● *Dir* John Schlesinger, *Pro* Tom Rosenberg, Leslie Dixon and Linne Radmin, *Ex Pro* Gary Lucchesi, Lewis Manilow and Ted Tannebaum, *Co-Pro* Marcus Viscidi and Richard S.Wright, *Screenplay* Thomas Ropelewski, *Ph* Elliot Davis, *Pro Des* Howard Cummings, *Ed* Peter Honess, *M* Gabriel Yared; *songs performed by* Metisse, Ethel Merman and Bruce Yarnell, Stan Watson, Don

Left: *Mike Epps and Ice-Cube swear allegiance to mediocrity in Steve Carr's moronic* Next Friday *(from Entertainment)*

McLean, Olive, Fred Astaire, Mandalay, Christina Aguilera, Moby, Solar Twins, Judy Garland, Groove Armada, Beth Orton, Andrew Dorfman, Madonna, etc, *Costumes* Ruth Myers.

Lakeshore Entertainment-Buena Vista.
109 mins. USA. 2000. Rel: 23 June 2000. Cert 12.

Next Friday ★¹/₂

Four years after Craig Jones helped put the neighbourhood bully, Debo, behind bars, he is still living with his parents in South Central Los Angeles looking for gainful employment. Then, when Debo breaks out of prison, Craig is sent to live with his eccentric Uncle Elroy and cousin Day-Day in the supposed 'safe' environment of the suburbs. So, will the 'burbs ever be the same again, bro'? Inviting comparisons to the Will Smith sitcom *Fresh Prince of Bel Air*, this sequel to the 1995 hit *Friday* is, astonishingly, even worse than its predecessor. Limp dialogue, grating caricatures and dumb slapstick all add to the misery. [*Charles Bacon*]

● *Craig Jones* Ice Cube, *Day-Day* Mike Epps, *Roach* Justin Pierce, *Mr Jones* John Witherspoon, *Uncle Elroy* Don 'DC' Curry, *Joker* Jacob Vargas, *D'Wana* Tamala Jones, *Pinky* Clifton Powell, *Debo* Tommy 'Tiny' Lister Jr, Kirk Jones, Kym E. Whitley, Lobo Sebastian, Ronn Riser-Muhammad, Amy Hill, Robyn Allen, Lisa Rodriguez, Sticky Fingaz.
● *Dir* Steve Carr, *Pro* and *Screenplay* Ice Cube, based on characters created by Ice Cube and DJ Pooh, *Ex Pro* Michael Gruber and Claire Rudnick-Polstein, *Co-Pro* Douglas Curtis and Matt Alvarez, *Ph* Christopher J. Baffa, *Pro Des* Dina Lipton, *Ed* Elena Maganini, *M*

Terence Blanchard; songs performed by Ice Cube, Mack 10 and Ms Toi, Con Funk Shun, The Gap Band, Harold Melvin & the Blue Notes, Lil' Zane, Big Tymers, Rufus and Chaka Kahn, Mtume, Eminem, Cameo, Tyrone Davis, Faze-O, Macy Gray, NWA, Vita, Wyclef Jean, David Bowie, Bizzy Bone, Dazz Band, Ohio Players, Chakachas, Aaliyah, The Isley Brothers, Wu-Tang Clan, etc, *Costumes* Jacki Roach.

New Line Cinema/Cubevision-Entertainment.
98 mins. USA. 2000. Rel: 10 March 2000. Cert 15.

The Ninth Gate ★★¹/₂

New York/Portugal/Paris; today. Dean Corso is an unscrupulous dealer in rare books. However, he knows his stuff and it is his expertise that prompts the obscenely rich Boris Balkan to hire him for a unique

Below: *Johnny Depp (yes, really) is brought to book in Roman Polanski's stylish, old-fashioned* The Ninth Gate *(from UIP)*

Right: A literary affair. Susan Lynch and Ewan McGregor try to remember their favourite scene from Finnegan's Wake – in Pat Murphy's underwhelming Nora (from Alliance Atlantis)

undertaking. Balkan has just acquired a copy of the 1666 volume *Novem Portis* – aka *The Nine Gates of the Kingdom of the Shadows* – which is just one of three surviving editions. The other two are in Portugal and Paris and Balkan wants Corso to verify their authenticity. For, it is said, Satan himself collaborated on the text ... Returning to the demonic oeuvre he explored to such success in the late 1960s, Roman Polanski injects some style and wit into his old-fashioned adaptation of Arturo Peréz-Reverte's novel *The Club Dumas*. But he's hamstrung by the story's predictable outcome, which a certain stiltedness in the telling hardly helps. Still, the journey is half the fun and Johnny Depp is on good form (aged with the help of a whimsical beard, wire-rimmed spectacles and streaks of grey hair). There's also a refreshing restraint in the pyrotechnics and a slew of choice cameos (the film's production manager José López Rodero excels in not one but *four* priceless appearances).

● *Dean Corso* Johnny Depp, *Boris Balkan* Frank Langella, *Liana Telfer* Lena Olin, *The Girl* Emmanuelle Seigner, *Baroness Kessler* Barbara Jefford, *Victor Fargas* Jack Taylor, *Bernie* James Russo, *Pablo* and *Pedro Ceniza* José López Rodero, *Witkin* Allen Garfield, Tony Amoni.
● *Dir* and *Pro* Roman Polanski, *Ex Pro* Wolfgang Glattes and Michel Cheyko, *Screenplay* Polanski, Enrique Urbizu and John Brownjohn, *Ph* Darius Khondji, *Pro Des* Dean Tavoularis, *Ed* Hervé de Luze, *M* Wojciech Kilar, *Costumes* Anthony Powell.

Orly Prods//R.P. Prods-UIP.
130 mins. France/Spain. 1999. Rel: 2 June 2000. Cert 15.

Nora ★¹/₂

Dublin/Trieste; 1904-1908. As James Joyce is portrayed here as a frightened, paranoid, jealous, self-centred and drunken individual, it is lucky for us that the film is not devoted to him. It is in fact about the singular relationship he had with Nora Barnacle, the simple girl from Galway who bore him two children and was the inspiration for his writing. With her hard-staring eyes, noble nose and generous mouth, Susan Lynch is a compulsive presence as Nora but is given little dramatic traction on which to build her performance. Indeed, the film is barely more than a series of domestic confrontations between Joyce and Nora, touching little on Joyce's work and just skimming over the emotional glue that held these two extraordinary people together. And Ewan McGregor, who also serves as co-producer, is hardly convincing as the tortured genius, resembling more a younger version of Michael Palin in a Monty Python sketch.

● *James Joyce* Ewan McGregor, *Nora Barnacle* Susan Lynch, *Stanislas Joyce* Peter McDonald, *Eva Joyce* Aedín Moloney, *Cosgrave* Darragh Kelly, *Gogarty* Alan Devine, *Roberto Prezioso* Roberto Citran, *Michael Bodkin* Andrew Scott, Vincent McCabe, Veronica Duffy, Franco Trevisi, Ignazio Oliva, Stefania Montorsi, Pauline McLynn, Neilí Conroy, Paul Hickey, Kate O'Toole.
● *Dir* Pat Murphy, *Pro* Bradley Adams, Damon Bryant and Tracey Seaward, *Ex Pro* Guy Collins, *Co-Pro* Ewan McGregor, James Flynn, Ulrich Felsberg and Gherardo Pagliel, *Screenplay* Murphy and Gerard Stembridge, based on the biography by Brenda Maddox, *Ph* Jean Francois Robin, *Pro Des* Alan MacDonald, *Ed* Pia di Ciaula, *M* Stanislas

Left: To Ma'am, With Love – Wei Minzhi in Zhang Yimou's heart-breaking Not One Less (from Columbia TriStar)

Syrewicz; vocals performed by Ewan McGregor, Susan Lynch, Karl Scully, and Ignazio Oliva, *Costumes* Consolata Boyle.

Natural Nylon/IAC Holdings/Volta Films/Road Movies Vierte/Gam Film/Metropolitan Films/Bord Scannán na hÉireann, etc-Alliance Atlantis.
106 mins. UK/Ireland/Germany/Italy. 1999. Rel: 19 May 2000. Cert 15.

Not One Less – Yi Ge Dou Bu Neng Shao ★★★★¹/₂

Zhenningbao, Chicheng County, Hebei Province, China; the present. Desperately short on funds, the mayor of a small rural community is forced to take on a 13-year-old substitute teacher for his village school. Promising the latter 50 yuan (about £5) on the condition that all the students are still accounted for within a month's time, the mayor lets the inexperienced Wei Minzhi get on with her business. So, when the class troublemaker disappears to the city, Minzhi desperately forms a plan to get him back ... Fitting his cast of non-professionals into the story so as to more or less play themselves, Zhang Yimou has realised a startlingly authentic tale that has all the immediacy of a documentary. A shaggy dog story that celebrates the smallest detail of its unfolding tale (adapted from the novel by Shi Xiangsheng), *Not One Less* gains considerable dramatic traction from its determination to avoid grabbing onto any obvious emotional handles. And, as the hopeless, unworldly 'teacher' who muddles by on an unshakeable optimism fuelled by ignorance, Wei Minzhi (a mere schoolgirl in real life) is a model of heart-breaking guilelessness.

● *Wei Minzhi* Wei Minzhi, *Zhang Huike* Zhang Huike, *Mayor Tian* Tian Zhenda, *Teacher Gao* Gao Enman, *Sun Zhimei* Sun Zhimei, *TV station receptionist* Feng Yuying, *TV host* Li Fanfan, Zhang Yichang, Xu Zhanqing, Liu Hanzhi, Wu Wanlu, Ming Xinhong.
● *Dir* Zhang Yimou, *Pro* Zhao Yu, *Ex Pro* Zhang Weiping, *Screenplay* Shi Xiangsheng, *Ph* Hou Yong, *Pro Des* Cao Jiuping, *Ed* Zhai Ru, *M* San Bao, *Costumes* Dong Huamiao.

Columbia Pictures Film Production Asia/Guangxi Film Studios/Beijing New Pictures-Columbia TriStar.
106 mins. People's Republic of China. 1998. Rel: 23 June 2000. Cert U.

La Nouvelle Eve

See The New Eve.

October Sky ★★★¹/₂

Coalwood, West Virginia; 1957. The world changed when, on 4 October 1957, the Russians launched the first satellite into space. Inspired by the possibilities of a new future, 17-year-old Homer Hickam turns his sights from working in his father's coal mine – or the slim prospect of winning a football scholarship – and opts to build a rocket. Initially discouraged by his narrow-minded father and ridiculed by his classmates, Homer perseveres with his dream, shrugging off impossible odds, increasing derision and repeated failure ... Bearing in mind that this is directed by the man who brought us *Honey I Shrunk the Kids*, *The Rocketeer* and *Jumanji*, *October Sky* is really rather good. The emotional buttons are nudged a little too conspicuously and the song list sounds like it's been lifted straight from *American Graffiti*, but the film is beautifully crafted and there are some wonderful sequences. Of the latter, Homer's failed attempts to launch his rocket (set to Fats Domino's 'Ain't That a Shame') and where Homer and his friends steal a track of railroad (as a train appears out of nowhere) are particularly effective. Based on a true story.

● *Homer Hickam* Jake Gyllenhaal, *John Hickam* Chris Cooper, *Roy Lee Cook* William Lee Scott, *Quentin Wilson* Chris Owen, *Sherman O'Dell* Chad Lindberg, *Elsie Hickam* Natalie Canerday, *Freida Riley* Laura Dern, *Jim Hickam* Scott Miles, *Leon Bolden* Randy Stripling, *Principal Turner* Chris Ellis, *Dorothy Platt* Courtney Fendley, Elya Baskin, David Dwyer, Terry Loughlin, Kaili Hollister.
● *Dir* Joe Johnston, *Pro* Charles Gordon and Larry Franco, *Ex Pro* Marc Sternberg and Peter Cramer, *Screenplay* Lewis Colick, from the book *Rocket Boys* by Homer H. Hickam Jr, *Ph* Fred Murphy, *Pro Des* Barry Robison, *Ed* Robert Dalva, *M* Mark Isham; songs perfromed by The Monroe Brothers, The Platters, Elvis Presley, Buddy Holly & The Crickets, The Coasters, Fats Domino, The Cadillacs, Frankie Lymon & The Teenagers, Tommy Edwards, etc, *Costumes* Betsy Cox.

Universal-UIP.
107 mins. USA. 1999. Rel: 10 December 1999. Cert PG.

Of Freaks and Men ★¹/₂

In St Petersburg at the beginning of the last century the proliferation of photography – both inanimate and cinematic – is taking a sinister turn. As snapshots of naked women in humiliating poses flood the black market, homicidal pornographer Johann and his sidekick Vicktor move in on two respectable households. Soon, and with little resistance, Johann and Vicktor have recruited the co-operation of two more subjects for their underground films...

Inevitably, with the relaxation of the censorship laws in Russia, a new generation of filmmakers have taken full advantage of the fact. Here, Alexei Balabanov sends up rotten the bourgeois values of 19th century St Petersburg and, in the process, spotlights a number of shapely Russian rumps. Yet with his wilfully studied pacing and heavy-handed symbolism he has produced a turgid, self-indulgent and pretentious curio which unfolds like a dislocated erotic dream that never reaches its climax.

● *Johann* Sergei Makovetsky, *Lisa* Dinara Drukarova, *Ekaterina Krillovna* Lika Nevolina, *Viktor Ivanovich* Victor Sukhorukov, *Kolya* Alyesha De, *Tolya* Chingiz Tsydendabayev, *Pytilov* Vadim Prokhorov, *Dr Stasov* Alexandr Mezentsev, *Grunya* Darya Lesnikova, Igor Shibanov, Tatyana Polonskaya, Olga Straumit, Richard Bogutskii, Valerii Krishtapenko.
● *Dir* and *Screenplay* Alexei Balabanov, *Pro* Sergei Selyanov and Oleg Botogov, *Ex Pro* Maksim Volodin, *Ph* Sergei Astakhov, *Pro Des* Vera Zelinskaya, *Ed* Marina Lipartia, *M* Grieg, Musorgsky, Prokofiev, Tchaikovsky, Michael Glinka, etc, *Costumes* Nadya Vasilyeva.

STV Film/Soiuzkino Producers' Group-Metrodome.
93 mins. Russia. 1998. Rel: 14 April 2000. Cert 18.

One Day in September ★★★★

The 1972 Munich Olympics were memorable for many reasons. Mark Spitz broke seven world records, the Americans lost their very first basketball tournament (to the Russians, no less) and Olga Korbut became an international star. It was also the first Games held in Germany since Hitler turned the 1936 Berlin Olympics into a shameful propaganda exercise. This time, 27 years after the war, the Germans were determined to get it right. So, with no police in sight and only an unarmed company of security guards at their disposal, the Munich Olympics became host to the most calculating and cold-blooded act of terrorism in the history of sport ... The producer John Battsek was so appalled by how little he knew about the full horror of the Munich Olympics that he decided to make a film about it. Enlisting the aid of director Kevin Macdonald (brother of *Trainspotting* producer Andrew Macdonald), he has created a documentary that intrigues, disturbs and ultimately leaves the jaw dangling in astonishment. While benefiting from a dramatic score and extensive film footage, the movie's greatest coup is an interview with Jamal Al Gashey, one of the Palestinian terrorists whose training for the Olympics had nothing to do with sport. Winner of the Oscar for best documentary feature.

● With Ankie Spitzer (widow of André Spitzer), Palestinian terrorist Jamal Al Gashey, ITN News reporter Gerald Seymour, Israeli wrestler Gad Zabari, Olympic runner Esther Roth, Mayor of Munich Hans Jochen Vogel, etc. *Narrator* Michael Douglas.
● *Dir* Kevin Macdonald, *Pro* John Battsek and Arthur Cohn, *Ex Pro* Lillian Birnbaum, *Ph* Alwin Küchler and Neve Cunningham, *Ed* Justine Wright, *M* Alex Heffes and Craig Armstrong; songs performed by Led Zeppelin, Deep Purple, Beta Band, Apollo 100, Craig Armstrong, Philip Glass, David Holmes, Moby, etc.

Passion Pictures-Redbus.
92 mins. UK. 1999. Rel: 19 May 2000. Cert 15.

Onegin ★★★¹/₂

Evgeny Onegin is a cynical, arrogant, smug, sarcastic and outspoken man with little interest in the company of others. However, when he is left a magnificent estate in the country by his late uncle, he befriends a neighbouring poet, the idealistic Vladimir Lensky. Spending more and more time with his new friend, Onegin comes into the company of Tatyana – the sister of Lensky's fiancée – who professes her undying love for him. Onegin is touched by her directness, but casts her aside with his characteristic civility ... It is easy to see what attracted Ralph Fiennes to what is arguably the greatest novel of the Russian language (and written

in verse, no less). Onegin is a fascinating character, a product of his time and a victim of destiny, yet not without fibre or wit. While affecting an unfortunate stoop (at times he resembles a Dickensian undertaker), Fiennes brings a well-judged majesty to the role, although his romantic counterpart, Liv Tyler, lacks the substance and ethereal grace that her part demands. Still, the look and feel of the film is extraordinary, a persuasive mix of the painterly and the authentic. For once, this is a Russian adaptation in which one can believe the characters really live there. Filmed in St Petersburg and at Shepperton Studios.

● *Evgeny Onegin* Ralph Fiennes, *Tatyana Larin* Liv Tyler, *Prince Nikitin* Martin Donovan, *Vladimir Lensky* Toby Stephens, *Olga Larin* Lena Headey, *Guillot* Jason Watkins, *Zaretsky* Alun Armstrong, *Princess Alina* Irene Worth, *Madame Larina* Harriet Walter, *Triquet* Simon McBurney, *Katiusha* Francesca Annis, Gwenllian Davies, Geoff McGivern, Margery Withers, Tim McMullan, Tim Potter, Elizabeth Berrington, Tom Eastwood.
● *Dir* Martha Fiennes, *Pro* Ileen Maisel and Simon Bosanquet, *Ex Pro* Ralph Fiennes, *Screenplay* Michael Ignatieff and Peter Ettedgui, from the 1833 novel by Alexander Pushkin, *Ph* Remi Adefarasin, *Pro Des* Jim Clay, *Ed* Jim Clark, *M* Magnus Fiennes, *Costumes* Chloe Obolensky and John Bright, *Choreography* Eleanor Fazan, *Russian etiquette advisor* Natasha Franklin.

Above: *An Olympic hurdle – A scene from Kevin Macdonald's Oscar-winning* One Day in September *(from Redbus)*

Right: Victim of destiny – Ralph Fiennes in his sister's painterly Onegin (from Entertainment)

Seven Arts International/Baby Productions/Protagonist Film-Entertainment.
106 mins. UK/USA. 1998. Rel: 19 November 1999. Cert 12.

One More Kiss ★★★★

Berwick-Upon-Tweed, the Scottish Borders; the present. Returning to her native Scotland after seven years in America, Sarah Hopson is a changed woman. At least, superficially. Diagnosed as suffering from an incurable brain tumour, she seeks to tie up a few loose ends, visiting first her old boyfriend and then her widowed father. Sarah is determined to make the most of her last days – and doesn't care who she inconveniences to do so… Exploring the old theme of discovering life within the shadow of death, Suzie Halewood's uplifting script neatly side-steps the pitfalls of the genre. With a gutsy performance from Valerie Edmond as the belligerent yet vulnerable Sarah and some glorious camerawork (utilising natural light), *One More Kiss* is a genuine inspiration. [*Charles Bacon*]

● *Sarah Hopson* Valerie Edmond, *Frank Hopson* James Cosmo, *Sam Murray* Gerard Butler, *Charlotte Murray* Valerie Gogan, *Jude* Danny Nussbaum, *Barry* Carl Proctor, *Mary* Dylis Miller, Ron Guthrie, Andrew Townley, Colette King, Nigel Pegram.
● *Dir* Vadim Jean, *Pro* Jean and Paul Brooks, *Ex Pro* Sara Giles and Derek Roy, *Co-Pro* Jane Walmsley and Michael Braham, *Line Pro* Ian Sharples, *Screenplay* Suzie Halewood, *Ph* Mike Fox, *Pro Des*

Simon Hicks, *Ed* Joe McNally, *M* John Murphy and David A. Hughes, *Costumes* Linda Brooker.

Mob Films/Jam Pictures/Freewheel International/Metrodome/European Script Fund-Metrodome.
102 mins. UK. 1999. Rel: 21 January 2000. Cert 12.

Open Your Eyes – Abre los ojos ★★★

Starting his day like any other, César finds the streets of Madrid completely deserted. Waking up again, it is the day of his 25th birthday and he is hosting his own party. There, he meets Sofia, a beautiful actress and his best friend's date for the evening. Eluding the attentions of the last woman he bedded, César moves in on Sofia and spends the night at her apartment. Sofia quickly becomes an obsession, but where does she fit into César's incarceration in a psychiatric penitentiary? Like a psychological onion, *Open Your Eyes* sheds layers of narrative as its central intensity increases. As compelling as it is irritating, the film stays a hair's breadth – or onion skin – away from total aggravation as writer-director Alejandro Amenábar keeps a tight rein on his story's loops of logic and credibility. Sweeping into the realms of solipsistic confusion already explored by *The Game* and *The Matrix*, its effectiveness stands or falls by the willing patience of the viewer. A stylish and intriguing exercise, nonetheless.

● *César* Eduardo Noriega, *Sofia* Penelope Cruz, *Antonio* Chete Lera, *Pelayo* Fele Martínez, *Nuria* Najwa Nimri, *Serge Duvernois* Gerard Barray, *department head* Jorge de Juan.
● *Dir* Alejandro Amenábar, *Pro* José Luis Cuerda, *Ex Pro* Cuerda and Fernando Bovaira, *Line Pro* Emiliano Otegui, *Screenplay* Amenábar and Mateo Gil, *Ph* Hans Burmann, *Pro Des* Wolfgang Burmann, *Ed* María Elena S. de Rozas, *M* Alejando Amenábar and Mariano Marin, *Costumes* Concha Solera.

Sogetel/Las Producciones del Escorpion/Les Films Alain Sarde/Lucky Red/Canal Plus/Eurimages-Redbus Films.
119 mins. Spain/France/Italy. 1997. Rel: 25 February 2000. Cert 15.

Ordinary Decent Criminal ★★★

Dublin; the present. Michael Lynch is not your run-of-the-mill crook. Jumping between the beds of his wife and sister-in-law, he is an ardent teetotaller, a fierce opponent of both the police and the IRA and an enterprising thief. Surrounded by loyal co-conspirators, Lynch is proud of his honour and fairness – and in thrall of his own mythology ... Described as a work of fiction, *Ordinary Decent Criminal* shares so many characteristics and plot devices with John Boorman's *The General* that it often feels like a remake. Partly based on the extraordinary criminal career of Martin

Cahill (played by Brendan Gleeson in *The General* and by Ken Stott on TV), Thaddeus O'Sullivan's glossy Irish thriller is certainly as entertaining – if not nearly as poetic or gritty – as the earlier film. However, it's hard to believe Kevin Spacey and Linda Fiorentino as an Oirish couple, but then Peter Mullan, Stephen Dillane, Helen Baxendale and David Hayman are no more Irish either. A plus is Damon Albarn's lively score and an ingenious story – and, of course, the remarkable career of Cahill himself.

● *Michael Lynch* Kevin Spacey, *Christine Lynch* Linda Fiorentino, *Stevie* Peter Mullen, *Noel Quigley* Stephen Dillane, *Lisa* Helen Baxendale, *Tony Brady* David Hayman, *Commissioner Daly* Patrick Malahide, *Friar Grogan* David Kelly, *Billy Lynch* Paul Ronan, *Shay Kirby* Vincent Regan, *Jerome Higgins* Tim Loane, Gerard McSorley, Gary Lydon, Colin Farrel, Christoph Waltz, Bill Murphy, Anthony Brophy, Alan Devlin, Ann O'Neill, Eva Barrett, Michael Hayes, Sarah Pilkington.
● *Dir* Thaddeus O'Sullivan, *Pro* Jonathan Cavendish, *Ex Pro* James Mitchell and Christine Ruppert, *Co-Pro* Martha O'Neill, *Screenplay* Gerry Stembridge, *Ph* Andrew Dunn, *Pro Des* Tony Burrough, *Ed* William Anderson, *M* Damon Albarn, *Costumes* Jane Robinson.

Icon Entertainment/Little Bird Prods/Tatfilm/Trigger Street-Icon.
93 mins. USA. 1999. Rel: 17 March 2000. Cert 15.

The Other Sister ★★★¹/₂
After several years in a 'special' school, Carla Tate, 24, is ready to make her own way in the real world. However, her over-protective mother is terrified of the consequences. But for Carla to discover her identity, and perhaps more importantly her dignity, she has to learn from her own mistakes ... As Lars Von Trier's controversial *The Idiots* so potently illuminates, there's something very disconcerting about normal people playing 'retards'. Here, we have two very visible, obviously intelligent young actors – Juliette Lewis and Giovanni Ribisi – portraying a pair of mentally challenged people for over two hours. Complete unknowns might have helped in such a difficult scenario, but Lewis and Ribisi are quite extraordinary, as are Keaton and Skerritt as Carla's tortured parents. Indeed, it is the acting which ultimately cuts through the sugar-coating of Rachel Portman's pushy music and the obvious manipulation of the story. Against my better judgement, I found a lump in my throat.

● *Carla Tate* Juliette Lewis, *Elizabeth Tate* Diane Keaton, *Radley Tate* Tom Skerritt, *Danny McMahon* Giovanni Ribisi, *Caroline Tate* Poppy Montgomery, *Heather Tate* Sarah Paulson, *Winnie* Juliet Mills, *Dr Johnson* Harvey Miller, *Ernie* Hector Elizondo, Linda Thorson, Joe Flanigan, Tracy Reiner, Hope Alexander-Willis, Shannon Wilcox, Frank Campenella, Richard Stahl, Jason Cottle, Jennifer Leigh Warren.
● *Dir* Garry Marshall, *Pro* Mario Iscovich and Alexandra Rose, *Ex Pro* David Hoberman, *Co-Pro* Ellen H. Schwartz, *Assoc Pro* Karen Stirgwolt, *Screenplay* Marshall & Bob Brunner, from a story by Rose and Blair Richwood, *Ph* Dante Spinotti, *Pro Des* Stephen J. Lineweaver, *Ed* Bruce Green, *M* Rachel Portman; Richard Wagner, Vivaldi, Mendelssohn; songs performed by Fine Young Cannibals, Fastball, Savage Garden, Carole King, Patsy Cline, Paula Cole, Alison Krause, Soup Dragons, Dave Grusin, Jewel, The Pretenders, The Lemonheads, New Order, Hector Elizondo, Joan Osborne, Juliette Lewis, etc, *Costumes* Gary Jones.

Touchstone Pictures-Buena Vista.
131 mins. USA. 1999. Rel: 19 November 1999. Cert 12.

The Out-of-Towners ★¹/₂
When their last child leaves home, Ohio couple Henry and Nancy Clark find that they have the rest of their lives to do exactly what they like. Nancy wants to 'suck the marrow out of life,' Henry would like to catch up on his reading. Somehow, between the children and encroaching late middle-age, Henry and Nancy have grown apart. Then they're thrown together again on a nightmarish trip to New York ... *The New York Times* suggested that the original, directed by Arthur Hiller in 1970, may 'rank as technically the sloppiest as well as the most wittlessly uncomfortable movie for some time.' Leonard Maltin called it 'excruciating.' So, here we have the remake, with Steve Martin, at 54, still doing his silly walk and Goldie Hawn screaming, shrieking and knocking things over. The only reprieve from this farcical contrivance is the promotion of John Cleese's Basil Fawlty to manager of an exclusive Manhattan hotel – but then they have to go and put him in drag. Deeply depressing.

● *Henry Clark* Steve Martin, *Nancy Clark* Goldie Hawn, *Mr Mersault* John Cleese, *Greg* Mark McKinney, *Alan Clark* Oliver Hudson, *Andrew Lloyd Webber* Tom Riis Farrell, Valerie Perri, William Duell, J.P. Bumstead, Anne Haney, Christopher Durang, Mo Gaffney, Monica Birt, Josh Mostel, Gregory Jbara, Amy Ziff, Cynthia Nixon, French Napier, Joseph Maher, Constance McCashin, Ernie Sabella, Rudolph Giuliani, Chris McKinney, Joe Grifasi, Jack McGee.
● *Dir* Sam Weisman, *Pro* Robert Evans, Teri Schwartz, Robert Cort and David Madden, *Ex Pro* Christine Forsythe-Peters and Philip E. Thomas, *Co-Pro* Andrew La Marca, *Screenplay* Marc Lawrence, *Ph* John Bailey, *Pro Des* Ken Adam, *Ed* Kent Beyda, *M* Marc Shaiman; songs performed by John Lennon, Mervyn Warren, Betty, Louis Prima, Donna Summer, etc, *Costumes* Ann Roth.

Paramount/Cherry Alley Prods/Cort/Madden Co.-UIP.
92 mins. USA. 1999. Rel: 12 November 1999. Cert 12.

Above: The cat's whiskers – Ben Daniels and accomplice in Lavinia Currier's hypnotic and compelling Passion in the Desert *(from Entertainment)*

Paperback Hero ★½

Queensland, Australia; today. Jack Willis is a long-distance lorry-driver who is terrified that his mates will discover that he1s a top-selling romantic novelist. So, to cover his tracks, Jack borrows the name of his spirited, tomboyish crop-dusting pilot chum Ruby Vale. But when his publisher turns up wanting to meet the great author, things get kinda complicated ... This is a great concept but writer-director Antony J. Bowman's pleasant but sedate treatment fritters it away. In this film, absolutely nothing is unexpected from the close of the opening credits. [*Simon Rose*]

● *Ruby Vale* Claudia Karvan, *Jack Willis* Hugh Jackman, *Ziggy Keane* Angie Milliken, *Hamish* Andrew S. Gilbert, *Suzie* Jeanie Drynan, *Artie* Bruce Venables, *Mack* Tony Barry, Ritchie Singer, Charlie Little, Barry Lee.
● *Dir and Screenplay* Anthony J. Bowman, *Pro* Lance W. Reynolds and John Winter, *Co-Pro* Dani Rogers, *Ph* David Burr, *Pro Des* John Dowding, *Ed* Veronika Jenet, *M* Berkhard Dallwitz; songs performed by Roy Orbison, Hugh Jackman and Claudia Karvan, Sue Thompson, Frank Ifield, Lighthouse Family, Human Nature, etc, *Costumes* Louise Wakefield.

Australian Film Finance Corp/Paperback Films/Archer Films Entertainment/Pacific Film & Television Commission-PolyGram.
96 mins. Australia. 1998. Rel: 3 September 1999. Cert 15.

Passion in the Desert ★★★★

Egypt; 1798. During Napoleon's ill-fated campaign in Egypt, a young captain, Augustin Robert, is entrusted to oversee an eminent artist as he records the exotic landscapes and monuments for posterity. But when a sandstorm descends on the regiment, Augustin and his ward find themselves separated from the other men and, worse, the water supply. Then, going in search of an oasis, the captain strikes up an unusual synergy with a female leopard ... Opening with a man having his arm hacked off, this commanding adaptation of the Honore de Balzac novel exercises a primal power. A story of man's vacillating relationship with nature, the film makes the most of its rugged locations (Jordan and Utah standing in for Egypt) and the photography is its trump card. Even so, the landscape fuels the story rather than overwhelms it, allowing Ben Daniels and his feline companion the space they need to bring their story alive. Hypnotic, compelling and chilling cinema. FYI: The African leopard that plays Mowgli was actually trained from birth for the role.

● *Augustin Robert* Ben Daniels, *Jean-Michel Venture de Paradis* Michel Piccoli, *Grognard* Paul Meston, Kenneth Collard, Nadi Odeh, *Simoon* Mowgli.
● *Dir and Pro* Lavinia Currier, *Ex Pro* Joel McCleary and Stephen Dembitzer, *Screenplay* Currier and Martin Edmunds, *Ph* Alexei Rodionov, *Pro Des* Amanda McArthur, *Ed* Nicolas Gaster, *M* Jose Nieto, *Costumes* Shuna Harwood, *Sound* Michael Stearns, *Leopards* Jungle Bookings.

Roland Films-Entertainment.
93 mins. France. 1997. Rel: 20 August 1999. Cert 12.

Pippi Longstocking – Pippi Langstrumpf ★★

By her seventh birthday, Pippi Delicatessa Windowshade Mackrelmint Longstocking – the daughter of a seafaring captain – had sailed the seven seas seven times. Now that she's nine, she has an insatiable appetite for life and is the strongest girl in the world. However, when her father is washed overboard and she returns home to await his return, her presence attracts the interference of the nosy Mrs Prysselius and Pippi's bounty the interest of two bungling burglars ... Bearing in mind that this is co-produced by the people who brought us *The Care Bears Movie* and *Babar: The Movie*, one's expectations shouldn't be too high. And, sure enough, the animation is basic and the plotting even more so. However, the spirited personality of Pippi herself and the subversive stance on discipline should delight children between the ages of four and five.

● Voices: *Mrs Prysselius* Catherine O'Hara, *Thunder-Karlsson* Dave Thomas, *Captain Efraim Longstocking* Gordon Pinsent, *Bloom* Wayne Robson, *Pippi Longstocking* Melissa Altro, *Tommy Settergren* Noah Reid, *Annika Settergren* Olivia Garratt, *Annika's vocals* Judy Tate, Carole Pope, Richard Binsley, Rick Jones, Chris Wiggins, Philip Williams.
● *Dir* Clive Smith, *Pro* Waldemar Bergendahl, Hasmi Giakoumis, Merle-Anne Ridley and Michael Schaak, *Ex Pro* Michael Hirsh, Patrick Loubert, Clive Smith and Lennart Wiklund, *Screenplay* Catharine Stackelber, from the books by Astrid Lindgren, *Design* Noda Tsamardos, *M* Anders Berglund.

A AB Svenk Filmindustri/Iduna Produktiongesellschaft/Telefilm Canada/Teletoon-Optimum Releasing.
77 mins. Sweden/Germany/Canada. 1997. Rel: 14 April 2000. Cert U.

Place Vendome ★★

In the exalted setting of Place Vendome, in the centre of Paris, Vincent Maliver, a reputable jeweller, is facing financial ruin. And, as his wife haunts a series of up-market rehab clinics, he entrusts much of his business to his lovely assistant, Nathalie. But what does Nathalie have in common with Mme Maliver and can the latter pull out of her alcoholic stupor in time to save the company? *Place Vendome* is one classy act. Yet for all its elegant veneer, enigmatic subtext and hushed tones, it remains a cold, detached experience, a dream-like sortie into a remote world of fine surfaces under which lurk just more surfaces. Still, Catherine Deneuve, recalling the unhinged manicurist she played in Roman Polanski's *Repulsion* all of 34 years ago, is marvellous as the older incarnation of the beautiful Nathalie, played by Emmanuelle Seigner, Polanski's wife. Deservedly, Deneuve won the best actress award for her performance at Cannes '98.

● *Marianne Maliver* Catherine Deneuve, *Jean-Pierre* Jean-Pierre Bacri, *Nathalie* Emmanuelle Seigner, *Vincent Maliver* Bernard Fresson, *Battistelli* Jacques Dutronc, *Eric Maliver* Francois Berleand, *Philippe Terence* Eric Ruf, Philippe Clevenot, Laszlo Szabo, Dragan Nikolic, Larry Lamb, Julian Fellowes, Michael Culkin, Coralie Seyrig.
● *Dir* Nicole Garcia, *Pro* Alain Sarde, *Ex Pro* Christine Gozlan, *Assoc Pro* Christine Gozlan, *Screenplay* Garcia and Jacques Fieschi, *Ph* Laurent Dailland, *Pro Des* Thierry Flamand, *Ed* Luc Barnier, Francoise Bonnot and Jean-Francois Naudon, *M* Richard Robbins, *Costumes* Nathalie Du Roscoat and Elisabeth Tavernier.

Les Films Alain Sarde/TF1 Films/Angel's Company/Canal Plus-Artificial Eye.
118 mins. France/Belgium/UK. 1998. Rel: 6 August 1999. Cert 15.

Playing by Heart ★★★½

A jazz musician once told Joan, an aspiring actress, that 'talking about music' is like 'dancing about architecture.' Joan feels the same way about love, yet after the acrimonious break-up of a five-month marriage she is determined to make fresh verbal sense of her romantic destiny ... In a top-heavy cast of star names, Angelina Jolie, as Joan, stole the lion's share of critical plaudits bestowed upon this ensemble mosaic of love in all its many guises (including an adulterous liaison, a tentative first date, a mother's belated breakthrough with her dying son, an aged-in-the-wood meltdown, etc). Like a series of one-act plays masterfully woven together, *Playing by Heart* is strong on theatrical mechanics but weak on real drama. Yet its tapestry of blunted, seeking and eloquent lovers, and their access to the right words at the right time ('don't look at me with that tone of voice,' 'you are the tenant of my heart – sometimes behind with the rent, but impossible to evict'), makes this a class act. Of course, people in real life don't talk like this (ask Mike Leigh), but this doesn't make the film any less seductive. Previously known as *Dancing About Architecture*.

Below: A symphony for lovers – Angelina Jolie, Sean Connery and Gena Rowlands in Willard Carroll's seductive Playing by Heart (from Buena Vista)

● *Meredith* Gillian Anderson, *Mildred* Ellen Burstyn, *Paul* Sean Connery, *Roger* Anthony Edwards, *Joan* Angelina Jolie, *Mark* Jay Mohr, *Keenan* Ryan Phillippe, *Hugh* Dennis Quaid, *Hannah* Gena Rowlands, *Trent* Jon Stewart, *Gracie* Madeleine Stowe, *Allison* Patricia Clarkson, *Melanie* Nastassja Kinski, April Grace, Alec Mapa, Jeremy Sisto, Matt Malloy, Christian Mills, David Clennon, Amanda Peet, Hal Landon Jr.
● *Dir and Screenplay* Willard Carroll, *Pro* Carroll, Meg Liberman and Tom Wilhite, *Ex Pro* Paul Feldsher, Bob Weinstein, Harvey Weinstein and Guy East, *Ph* Vilmos Zsigmond, *Pro Des* Missy Stewart, *Ed* Pietro Scalia, *M* John Barry; songs performed by Bran Van 3000, P.J. Harvey, Cracker, Gomez, Chet Baker, Morcheeba, Moby, Ben Lee, Soul II Soul, Bonnie Raitt, The Mavericks, Edward Kowalczyk and Neneh Cherry, etc, *Costumes* April Ferry.

Miramax/Intermedia Films/Morpheus/Hyperion-Buena Vista. 121 mins. USA. 1998. Rel: 6 August 1999. Cert 15.

Pokémon – The First Movie ★ ¹/₂

Pokémon, a race of bizarre creatures controlled by their human owners, are by nature friendly and prefer co-operation to confrontation. However, the rules are changed when the genetically engineered Mewtwo, designed to be the most powerful Pokémon of all, turns against his creators and opts to dominate the world. But first he must lure the best of the rest to his secret island to steal their genetic make-up for his own private army ... Starting out in 1996 as a humble hand-held video game, the Pokémon phenomenon spread like wildfire. The brainchild of the Japanese games giant Nintendo, Pokémon – the name being a condensation of 'Pocket Monsters' – rapidly became an international franchise, incorporating everything from trading cards to a top-rated TV series. Of course, one's appreciation of this rudimentarily animated film – a sort of moral *Mortal Kombat* for kids – largely depends on one's addiction to the craze. Can you name all 151 species of the Pokémon? Then forget it. As a movie, the phenomenon sucks.

● *Voices: Ash Ketchum* Veronica Taylor, *Mewtwo* Philip Bartlett, *Misty Williams, etc* Rachael Lillis, Eric Stuart, Addie Blaustein, Ikue Otani, Ed Paul, Jimmy Zoppi, Michael Haigney.
● *Dir* Kunihiko Yuyama, *English Adaptation Dir* Michael Haigney, *Pro* Norman J. Grossfeld, Choji Yoshikawa, Tomoyuki Igarashi and Takemoto Mori, *Ex Pro* Alfred R. Rahn, Masakazu Kubo and Takashi Kawaguchi, *Assoc Pro* Kathy Borland, *Screenplay* Takeshi Shudo, *English Adaptation* Haigney, Grossfeld and John Touhey, *Ph* Hisao Shirai, *Ed* Toshio Henmi, *Art* Katsuyoshi Kanemura, *M* John Siegler, John Loeffler, John Lissauer and Manny Corallo; songs performed by Billy Crawford, Angela, Vitamin C, Christina Aguilera, Emma Bunton aka

Baby Spice, Midnight Sons, Blessed Union of Souls, and M2M, *Chief Animator* Sayuri Ichiishi.

4Kids Entertainment/Warner-Warner. 75 mins. Japan/USA. 1999. Rel: 14 April 2000. Cert PG.

Pola X ★★¹/₂

Pierre Valombreuse is a cult novelist who lives with his mother on a magnificent estate in the countryside. Engaged to the beautiful Lucie de Boisieux, he would seem to have his life laid out on a plate. Then he meets a mysterious vagrant girl who tells him that she is his illegitimate sister. Overnight, Pierre decides to discard the shackles of his comfortable, bourgeoisie life ... Only the French can get away with making so many morose and self-indulgent films yet still enjoy a flourishing industry. Here, Léos Carax, who last directed the spellbinding and surreal *Les Amants du Pont-Neuf* eight years ago, has updated and transposed Herman Melville's 1852 novel *Pierre, or, The Ambiguities* to contemporary Normandy. The novel itself was a grim affair (written during a period of self-confessed madness) and one that ended on an even more pessimistic note than the movie does. Carax, who has expressed little interest in making another film, has created a pictorially arresting document, complete with a few scenes of startling sexual frankness (a naked Catherine Deneuve in the bath, a graphic episode of oral sex and 69), but the film remains disjointed and detached, like a dream one eagerly wants to wake from. Incidentally, the title is an acronym of the French translation of Melville's novel, the X standing for the tenth draft of the screenplay.

● *Pierre Valombreuse* Guillaume Depardieu, *Isabelle* Katerina Golubeva, *Marie Valombreuse* Catherine Deneuve, *Lucie de Boisieux* Delphine Chuillot, *Thibault Valombreuse* Laurent Lucas, Patruta Catana, Mihaella Silaghi, Patachou, Sharunas Bartas.
● *Dir* Léos Carax, *Pro* Bruno Pesery, *Ex Pro* Albert Prevost and Raimond Goebel, *Assoc Pro* Karl Baumgartner, Kenzo Horikoshi and Ruth Waldburger, *Screenplay* Carax, Lauren Sedofsky and Jean-Pol Fargeau, *Ph* Eric Gautier, *Pro Des* Laurent Allaire, *Ed* Nelly Quettier, *M* Scott Walker, *Costumes* Esther Walz.

Arena Films/Pola Prods/Théo Films/Pandora Filmproduktion/ Euro Space/Vega Film/Canal Plus/TV Tokyo, etc- Artificial Eye. 134 mins. France/Germany/Japan/Switzerland. 1999. Rel: 12 May 2000. Cert 18.

The Polish Bride – De poolse bruid ★★★¹/₂

Henk Woldring is a brusque, reclusive farmer in the Groningen 'highlands' of The Netherlands. Then, one day, a young woman collapses at his feet wearing nothing but a bloodied raincoat. He takes her in, showers her and lets her recuperate in his spare bedroom. Realising

Left: Romantic crosswinds – John Cusack (right) looks on as his rival (Billy Bob Thornton) takes the mike in Mike Newell's sharply observed Pushing Tin (from Fox). Anjelina Jolie simpers between them

that she does not speak Dutch, he buys her a Polish-Dutch dictionary. Gradually, she learns his language and takes over the domestic duties of his house. He doesn't know anything about her – and she knows little about him – but they get by, day by day ... A triumph of brevity over melodrama, this atmospheric, intimate romantic mystery revels in the everyday detail that binds its almost wordless protagonists. And by the very act of withholding irrelevant information, first-time writer-director Karim Traidia (who left Algeria for The Netherlands 18 years ago) sucks the viewer into the conspiratorial enigma of his awkward outsiders. Beautifully lit and underplayed, *The Polish Bride* expels a breath of fresh air that recalls the minimalist art of van Ruisdael and Hobbema.

● *Henk Woldring* Jaap Spijkers, *Anna Krzyzanowska* Monic Hendrickk, Rudi Falkenhagen, Roef Ragas, Hakim Traidia, Soraya Traidia.
● *Dir and Screenplay* Karim Traidia, *Pro* Joroen Beker and Frans Van Gestel, *Ph* Jacques Laurey, *Pro Des* Anne Winterink, *Ed* Chris Teerink, *M* Fons Merkies; 'Het Hogeland' sung by Ede Staal, *Costumes* Danielle van Eck and Monica Petit.

Motel Films/Ijswater Films/VPRO/Stichting Nederlands-Artificial Eye.
89 mins. The Netherlands. 1998. Rel: 16 July 1999. Cert 15.

Pushing Tin ★★★¹/₂

According to a spokesman for the Federal Aviation Administration, the current air traffic control system is 99.4% reliable. The fact remains that the men and women who guide the 10,000 planes a day that push their way through the congested air space above New York are only human. However, the trouble with Nick Falzone, the leading light of air traffic control, is that he is so obsessed by his job that he has lost sight of his humanity. And when an Irish-Indian controller from Arizona walks into Falzone's work space, he can only see the outsider as a threat ... The joy of Glen and Les Charles' multi-layered, sharply observed script is that it not only lifts the lid off a fascinating milieu but that it presents such intriguing, complex and contrasting characters. And with a dream quartet of actors supplying such depth and colour the film really comes alive in a refreshingly intelligent and quirky way. Displaying a fast, dark yet heart-felt rhythm all its own, *Pushing Tin* is the sort of film Barry Levinson used to make in his prime.

● *Nick Falzone* John Cusack, *Russell Bell* Billy Bob Thornton, *Connie Falzone* Cate Blanchett, *Mary Bell* Angelina Jolie, *Barry Plotkin* Jake Weber, *Ed Clabes* Kurt Fuller, *Tina Leary* Vicki Lewis, Matt Ross, Jerry Grayson, Michael Willis, Philip Akin, Mike O'Malley, Shaun Majumder, Dwight McFee, Rob Smith, Catherine Lloyd Burns, Molly Price.
● *Dir* Mike Newell, *Pro* Art Linson, *Ex Pro* Alan Greenspan and Michael Flynn, *Screenplay* Glen Charles and Les Charles, from the article *Something's Got To Give*, *Ph* Gale Tattersall, *Pro Des* Bruno Rubeo, *Ed* Jon Gregory, *M* Anne Dudley; Puccini; songs performed by Adam Hamilton, Billy Idol, Golden Earring, Marc Ferrari and Paul Taylor, Sly & The Family Stone, Bachman-Turner Overdrive, Patsy Cline, Dean Martin, Tom Jones, John Mellencamp, etc, *Costumes* Marie-Sylvie Deveau.

Fox 2000/Regency Enterprises/Linson Films-Fox.
123 mins. USA. 1999. Rel: 29 October 1999. Cert 15.

Above: Gun ho, ho – Joseph Fiennes in Ed Thomas's tiresome Rancid Aluminium (from Entertainment)

Rancid Aluminium ★'/₂

Following the death of his father, perennial teenager Pete Thompson, 33, discovers that his business owes a fortune to the tax man. Facing financial ruin and a romantic breakdown, Pete finds his life has all the taste of rancid aluminium (his term). Just then help arrives in the unlikely form of the Russian Mafia ... One can see the attraction of adapting James Hawes' novel to the screen. It's modern, sexy, articulate and in tune with a whole new world: free market economics. But in spite of an attractive cast and a few effective sequences, the film is a tiresome shambles. One-dimensional characters, comic-book Russians and a resonance more Rik Mayall than John Le Carré reduces the proceedings to pap.

● *Deeny* Joseph Fiennes, *Pete Thompson* Rhys Ifans, *Masha* Tara Fitzgerald, *Sarah* Sadie Frost, *Mr Kant* Steven Berkoff, *Dr Jones* Keith Allen, *Charlie* Dani Behr, *Trevor* Andrew Howard, *Harry* Nick Moran, Olegario Fedoro, Barry Foster, Brian Hibbard.
● *Dir* Ed Thomas, *Pro* Mike Parker and Mark Thomas, *Ex Pro* Nigel Green, *Co-Pro* and *Screenplay* James Hawes, *Ph* Tony Imi, *Pro Des* Hayden Pearce, *Ed* Chris Lawrence, *M* John Hardy; songs performed by The Bluetones, away TEAM, Ultrasound, Supergrass, Red Snapper, Philly, Robin Williams, Gay Dad, Elastica, David Bowie, etc, , *Costumes* Jany Temime.

Entertainment/Fiction Factory-Entertainment.
91 mins. UK. 2000. Rel: 21 January 2000. Cert 18.

Random Hearts ★★'/₂

Washington DC/Miami; the present. Dutch Van Den Broeck is a sergeant in Internal Affairs bent on exposing a vicious drug-dealing cop. Kay Spencer-Chandler is a Republican Congresswoman running for re-election against an extremely well-heeled opponent. Dutch and Kay come from vastly different worlds but find their paths inexorably linked when their respective spouses are killed in a horrific plane crash ... Let's get one thing straight: this is a terrific concept for a movie. And, sure enough, Sydney Pollack's elegant adaptation of Warren Adler's 1984 novel gets off to a cracking start. But by the time Harrison Ford and Kristin Scott Thomas meet up for their first rendezvous (90 minutes in) the movie is idling in first gear. In a performance of comatose dimensions, Ford looks consistently rumpled and constipated, offering his glamorous leading lady little reason to swap a *bon mot*, let alone anything wetter. Yet the script is not without intelligence; it's just that the whole thing runs out of steam at the precise moment it should catch fire.

● *Sgt. Dutch Van Den Broeck* Harrison Ford, *Kay Spencer-Chandler* Kristin Scott Thomas, *Alcee* Charles S. Dutton, *Wendy Judd* Bonnie Hunt, *Det. George Beaufort* Dennis Haysbert, *Carl Broman* Sydney Pollack, *Truman Trainor* Richard Jenkins, *Peyton Van Den Broeck* Susannah Thompson, *Cullen Chandler* Peter Coyote, *Molly Roll* Susan Floyd, *Jessica Chandler* Kate Mara, *Shyla Mumford* Ariana Thomas, Paul

Guilfoyle, Dylan Baker, Lynne Thigpen, Bill Cobbs, Nelson Landrieu, Brooke Smith, Christina Chang, Michelle Hurd, Reiko Aylesworth, Ray Anthony Thomas, Edie Falco, Jack Gilpin, Molly Price, and (*uncredited*) M. Emmet Walsh.
● *Dir* Sydney Pollack, *Pro* Marykay Powell, *Ex Pro* Ronald L. Schwary and Warren Adler, *Screenplay* Kurt Luedtke and Darryl Ponicsan, *Ph* Philippe Rousselot, *Pro Des* Barbara Ling, *Ed* William Steinkamp, *M* Dave Grusin; songs performed by Sunny Hilden, The Mills Brothers, Diana Krall, Patty Larkin, etc, *Costumes* Bernie Pollack and Ann Roth.

Columbia/Rastar/Mirage Enterprises-Columbia TriStar. 132 mins. USA. 1999. Rel: 19 November 1999. Cert 15.

Ratcatcher ★★★¹/₂

Glasgow; the mid-1970s. As mountains of rubbish accumulate during a dustbin strike, James Gillespie, 12, struggles to come to terms with his guilt over the accidental drowning of a friend in the nearby canal. Increasingly alienated from his family – in particular from his drunk of a father – James finds brief solace in the friendship of a 14-year-old girl and from the discovery of a half-built house on the outskirts of town … Uncompromisingly unsentimental and unremittingly bleak, *Ratcatcher* is a grim family album of moments that will be hard to erase from the memory. From the sight of James scratching his brand new sandals with a piece of broken glass to a mouse suspended from a helium balloon, the film is rich in imagery and builds to a powerful and atmospheric catalogue of misery, punctuated by brief flashes of lyricism. Yet, for all its meticulous craftsmanship and human credibility, it's hard to know who to recommend it to.

● *Da Gillespie* Tommy Flanagan, *Ma Gillespie* Mandy Matthews, *James Gillespie* William Eadie, *Ellen Gillespie* Michelle Stewart, *Anne Marie Gillespie* Lynn Ramsay Jr, *Margaret Anne* Leanne Mullen, *Kenny* John Miller, *Mrs Quinn* Jackie Quinn, *Matt Monroe* Craig Bonar, James Ramsay, Anne McLean, Andrew McKenna, Thomas McTaggart, John Comerford, Anne Marie Lafferty.
● *Dir and Screenplay* Lynne Ramsay, *Pro* Gavin Emerson, *Ex Pro* Andrea Calderwood, Barbara McKissack and Sarah Radclyffe, *Co-Pro* Bertrand Faivre, *Ph* Alwin Kuchler, *Pro Des* Jane Morton, *Ed* Lucia Zucchetti, *M* Rachel Portman; songs performed by The Chordettes, Eddie Cochran, Tom Jones, Frank and Nancy Sinatra, and Nick Drake, *Costumes* Gill Horn.

Pathé Pictures/BBC Films/Arts Council of England/Canal Plus/Holy Cow Films/National Lottery/BBC Scotland, etc-Pathé. 93 mins. UK/France. 1999. Rel: 12 November 1999. Cert 15.

Ravenous ★★★¹/₂

In the aftermath of the 1847 Mexican-American war, a shell-shocked soldier is 'decorated for cowardice' and sent to a remote military outpost in the Sierra Nevada mountains of California. There, he comes across an emotionally deranged Scotsman, Mr Colqhoun, who introduces his hosts to a terrible tale of cannibalism … Seldom does a film so proudly launch itself into the 'hate it or love it' camp. Yet, regardless of one's carnivorous or vegetarian inclinations, one cannot deny the raw originality of this bizarre and beautifully crafted black comedy. With Michael Nyman and Damon Albarn's delightfully idiosyncratic score setting the tone from the first drop of blood, *Ravenous* gnaws its way straight to the funny bone – or, if you like, the gall bladder. Hannibal Lecter would approve of Antonia Bird's full-blooded approach. FYI: Bird, who previously directed Robert Carlyle in *Priest*, *Safe* and *Face*, took over the directorial reins when the original helmer, the Macedonia-born Milcho Manchevski (*Before the Rain*), clashed with the studio, Fox 2000.

● *Captain John Boyd* Guy Pearce, *Mr Colqhoun/Colonel Ives* Robert Carlyle, *Cleaves* David Arquette, *Toffler* Jeremy Davies, *Colonel Hart* Jeffrey Jones, *General Slauson* John Spencer, *Major Knox* Stephen Spinella, *Reich* Neal McDonough, *George* Joseph Running Fox, *Martha* Sheila Tousey, Bill Brochtrup, David Heyman.
● *Dir* Antonia Bird, *Pro* Adam Fields and David Heyman, *Ex Pro* Tim Van Rellim, *Screenplay* Ted Griffin, *Ph* Anthony B. Richmond, *Pro Des* Bryce Perrin, *Ed* Neil Farrell, *M* Michael Nyman and Damon Albarn, *Costumes* Sheena Napier.

Fox 200-Fox. 101 mins. USA/UK. 1999. Rel: 10 September 1999. Cert 18.

Below: Gloom with a view – William Eadie and Leanne Mullen in Lynne Ramsay's meticulously crafted and uncompromisingly unsentimental Ratcatcher (from Pathé)

Richard Nichols, Lauren Stocks, Charles Edwards.
● *Dir* Eric Styles, *Pro* Chris Milburn, *Ex Pro* Steven Christian and Chris Harris, *Co-Ex Pro* Francesca Barra, Maud Nadler and Alex Swan, *Assoc Pro* and *Screenplay* Paul Rattigan and Michael Walker, *Ph* Jimmy Dibling, *Pro Des* Humphrey Jaeger, *Ed* Caroline Limmer and Ian Seymour, *M* John Debney, *Costumes* Nicolas Ede.

Midsummer Films/Overseas Film Group/Isle of Man Film Commission/Hallelujah Prods-Alliance Releasing.
89 mins. UK/USA. 2000. Rel: 23 June 2000. Cert PG.

Return To Me ★★¹/₂

Chicago; the present. At a glitzy fund raiser, committed zoologist Elizabeth Rueland solicits help to finance an extension to the gorilla compound at Lincoln Park Zoo. Touched by her dedication, her infatuated husband, architect Bob Rueland, promises to build the annex himself and, furthermore, to fulfil her dream of going to Italy. Meanwhile, in a nearby hospital, a young waitress lies in a critical condition awaiting a vital heart transplant ... The year's most predictable movie, *Return To Me* is corny, contrived and floating in a bog of schmaltz. It's also extremely badly directed (courtesy of actress Bonnie Hunt), sloppily edited and awkwardly constructed, missing a host of dramatic opportunities. And yet, in spite of such crippling setbacks, the film does have its charms. David Duchovny has never been more appealing and scores a number of points in a few difficult scenes (such as when he's landed with a date from hell). In addition, there are some marvellous little touches (Minnie Driver landing Duchovny an inadvertent uppercut). But the emotional tsunami one so desperately waits for just doesn't arrive. The 1997 British release *Heart* handled the same subject far more effectively.

● *Bob Rueland* David Duchovny, *Grace Briggs* Minnie Driver, *Marty O'Reilly* Carroll O'Connor, *Angelo Pardipillo* Robert Loggia, *Dr Charlie Johnson* David Alan Grier, *Megan Dayton* Bonnie Hunt, *Elizabeth Rueland* Joely Richardson, *Joe Dayton* James Belushi, *Emmet McFadden* Eddie Jones, *Wally Jayczaski* William Bronder, *Sophie* Marianne Muellerleile, *Marsha* Holly Wortell, Mike Brian Howe, Chris Barnes, Adam Tanguay, Karson Pound, Tyler Spitzer, Laura Larsen, Austin Samuel Hibbs, Dick Cusack, Joey Gian, Kevin Hunt, Carol Hunt, Patrick Hunt, Alice Hunt, Tom Hunt.
● *Dir* Bonnie Hunt, *Pro* Jennie Lew Tugend, *Ex Pro* C.O. 'Doc' Erickson and Melanie Greene, *Screenplay* Hunt and Don Lake, from a story by Hunt, Lake, Andrew Stern and Samantha Goodman, *Ph* Laszlo Kovacs, *Pro Des* Brent Thomas, *Ed* Garth Craven, *M* Nicholas Pike; songs performed by Dean Martin, Joey Gian, and Smokey Robinson and The Miracles, *Costumes* Lis Bothwell.

MGM/JLT Prods-UIP.
116 mins. USA. 2000. Rel: 9 June 2000. Cert PG.

Above: Heart of the matter – Minnie Driver and David Duchovny in Bonnie Hunt's corny and sentimental Return To Me *(from UIP)*

Reindeer Games
See Deception.

Relative Values ★★¹/₂

Marshwood House, Kent; 1954. It's not done for the English aristocracy to marry into the American glitterati, but Nigel, the Earl of Marshwood, has fallen desperately for Miranda Frayle, a Hollywood star. While preparing to receive her future daughter-in-law, the Countess of Marshwood discovers that her imminent guest is in fact the sister of Moxie, her personal maid of 19 years ... For Noël Coward's social burlesque to work on screen, it is essential that the outrageous conceits of the plot be disguised within the reality of the characters. Because if anybody was a master of understatement, Coward was. Unfortunately, director Styles seems to be under the illusion that he is orchestrating a Brian Rix farce and encourages everybody to overact outlandishly. Notwithstanding, the wit of The Master does shine through and Colin Firth seems particularly at ease with the writer's linguistic frippery.

● *Felicity, the Countess of Marshwood* Julie Andrews, *Miranda Frayle* Jeanne Tripplehorn, *Don Lucas* William Baldwin, *Peter* Colin Firth, *Crestwell* Stephen Fry, *Nigel, the Earl of Marshwood* Edward Atterton, *Moxie* Sophie Thompson, *Alice* Anwen Carlisle, Gaye Brown, Michael Culkin, Stephanie Beacham, Kathryn Dimery,

Left: Losing the plot – the wonderful Fabrice Luchini in Pascal Bonitzer's unpredictable and quirky Rien Sur Robert (from Millennium Film)

Ride With the Devil ★★★★

The Kansas/Missouri border; 1861-1865. As 'the Yankee aggressors' march into the Confederate states, two child-hood friends – Jake, the son of poor German immigrants, and Jack Bull, heir to a wealthy plantation, join up with The Bushwhackers, a pro-Southern guerrilla outfit that ambushes the enemy by somewhat casual rules of conduct ... It's extraordinary that such an insightful, nuanced and intelligent take on the American Civil War should be directed by a Taiwanese. But then maybe not. After all, it was Ang Lee who explored the polar worlds of Jane Austen and 1970s' American suburbia in his perceptive *Sense and Sensibility* and *The Ice Storm*. Here, as American kills American, neighbour fights neighbour and even family members betray each other, Lee brings a fresh perspective to the chaotic conflict of the so-called 'War Between the States,' as Jake sums it up at the end of the movie, 'it ain't right and it ain't wrong. It just is.' Presenting a relatively intimate canvas on which to paint such a national struggle, *Ride With the Devil* – adapted from the novel *Woe To Live On* by Daniel Woodrell – represents the human side of America's bloodiest hour. And while the film lacks the emotional punch of, say, the Civil War-themed *Glory* and *Gettysburg*, its individual scenes exhibit enormous resonance.

● *Jack Bull Chiles* Skeet Ulrich, *Jake 'Dutch' Roedel* Tobey Maguire, *Sue Lee Shelley* Jewel, *Daniel Holt* Jeffrey Wright, *George Clyde* Simon Baker, *Pitt Mackeson* Jonathan Rhys Meyers, *Black John* James Caviezel, *Cave Wyatt* Jonathan Brandis, *Wilma Brown* Margo Martindale, *Orton Brown* Tom Wilkinson, *William Quantrill* John Ales, Kathleen Warfel, David Darlow, John Judd, Matthew Faber, Thomas Guiry, Celia Weston, Mark Ruffalo, Stephen Mailer, Zach Grenier, Donna Thomason, James Urbaniak.
● *Dir* Ang Lee, *Pro* Ted Hope, Robert F. Colesberry and James Schamus, *Ex Pro* David Linde, *Assoc Pro* Anne Carey, *Screenplay* James Schamus, *Ph* Frederick Elmes, *Pro Des* Mark Friedberg, *Ed* Tim Squyres, *M* Mychael Danna, *Costumes* Marit Allen.

Universal Pictures/Good Machine Prods-Entertainment. 138 mins. USA. 1999. Rel: 5 November 1999. Cert 15.

Rien Sur Robert ★★★

Paris; the present. Didier Temple is a self-effacing journalist who's just written a brilliant thesis on a film he hasn't seen. Plagued by self-doubt, he thinks the whole world is conspiring against him and that a handsome stranger is stalking him. Then his girlfriend, the prickly Juliette, starts sleeping with another man ... For a start, there's nothing here about Robert. And the film, like its title, is equally cheeky. Anything can happen, and quite often does. In an engaging sequence of events, our bemused hero inadvertently gate-crashes a dinner party he hasn't been invited to, where he finds the guests have been arguing about his merits as a writer. Shortly afterwards, he's flashed by the host's step-daughter, just as the host walks in on them. And so it goes, with Didier becoming increasingly enmeshed in a plot he cannot understand. Thanks to Fabrice Luchini's restrained bewilderment – and the underplaying of the rest of the cast – the film's unpredictable quirkiness works wonders until, in the absence of a satisfactory narrative arc, the proceedings eventually loose steam. If only there'd been somebody to root for, this could have been comic nirvana. P.S. While quintessentially French in tone, the film could just as easily have been made by Hal Hartley in New Jersey.

● *Didier Temple* Fabrice Luchini, *Juliette Sauvage* Sandrine Kiberlain, *Jérôme Sauveur* Laurent Lucas, *Aurélie Coquille* Valentina Cervi, *Ariel Chatwick-West* Michel Piccoli, *Martin* Denis Podalydes, *Madame Sauvage* Bernadette Lafont, *Alain de Xantras* Edouard Baer, Valérie Boutefeu, Micheline Boudet, Violeta Sanchez, Alexis Nitzer, Dimitri Rataud.
● *Dir and Screenplay* Pascal Bonitzer, *Pro* Jean-Michel Rey and Philippe Liègeois, *Ex Pro* Catherine Chouridis, *Ph* Christophe Pollock, *Pro Des* Emmanuel de Chauvigny, *Ed* Suzanne Koch, *M* various, *Costumes* Khadija Zeggai.

Rezo Films/Assise Prods/France 2 Cinéma/Canal Plus, etc-Millennium Film Dist.
106 mins. France. 1998. Rel: 17 March 2000. Cert 18.

Romance ★★

Paris; today. Marie, a beautiful young teacher, is feeling increasingly abandoned and unfulfilled by her impotent boyfriend, Paul, a handsome model. Marie loves Paul but, for her, love and sex are inseparable, so in order to keep her love alive she embarks on a promiscuous sexual odyssey behind his back ... A superficially feminist spin on *Emmanuelle*, *Romance* is a negative, pessimistic and depressing meditation on female sexuality and one of the least romantic films ever made. Notwithstanding, 22-year-old newcomer Caroline Ducey makes an engaging heroine, a pretty, physically delicate creature unlike one you'd expect to find in such a sexually explicit enterprise. Talking of which, the film was passed completely uncut by the British censor in spite of scenes of genuine penetration and ejaculation.

● *Marie* Caroline Ducey, *Paul* Sagamore Stévenin, *Robert* François Berleand, *Paolo* Rocco Siffredi, Reza Habouhssein, Fabien De Jomaron, Emma Colberti, Ashley Wanninger.
● *Dir* Catherine Breillat, *Pro* Jean-François Lepetit, *Ex Pro* Catherine Jacques, *Screenplay* Severine Siaut, *Ph* Yorgos Arvanitis, *Pro Des* Frédérique Belvaux, *Ed* Agnès Guillemot, *M* D.J. Valentin and Rachael Tidas, *Costumes* Anne Dunsford Varenne.

Flach Film/CB Films et Arte France Cinema/Centre National de la Cinématographie/Canal Plus- Bluelight.
99 mins. France. 1998. Rel: 8 October 1999. Cert 18.

A Room for Romeo Brass ★★★★

Britain's young hopeful Shane Meadows gets better and better. Here he revisits his own childhood in Nottingham and finds both humour and pathos in this study of friendship between two twelve-year-olds. They are admirably played by Andrew Shim and Ben Marshall, and there's a lack of sentimentality in both the writing and the acting which adds considerably to the impact. But what makes the film so surprising is the unexpected yet totally convincing development of a third character, that of the initially comic young man whose influence comes to threaten the bond between the boys. Paddy Considine is superb in this role, and he's a creation of whom Mike Leigh would have been proud. A small film, perhaps, and unadventurous in technique, but a substantial achievement all the same. [*Mansel Stimpson*]

● *Romeo Brass* Andrew Shim, *Gavin 'Knocks' Woolley* Ben Marshall, *Morell* Paddy Considine, *Joseph Brass, Romeo's dad* Frank Harper, *Sandra Woolley, Knock's mum* Julia Ford, *Bill Woolley, Knock's dad* James Higgins, *Ladine Brass* Vicky McClure, *Carol Brass, Romeo's mum* Ladene Hall, *Steven Laws* Bob Hoskins, *Dennis Wardrobe* Martin Arrowsmith, Darren Campbell, Justin Brady, Anthony Clarke, Karl Collins, Johann Myers, *fish and chip man* Shane Meadows, Johann Myers, Tanya Myers, Arthur Meadows (Shane's dad).
● *Dir* Shane Meadows, *Pro* George Faber and Charles Pattinson, *Ex Pro* Andras Hamori and David M. Thompson, *Line Pro* Ronaldo Vasconcellos, *Screenplay* Shane Meadows and Paul Fraser, *Ph* Ashley Rowe, *Pro Des* Crispian Sallis, *Ed* Paul Tothill, *M* Nick Hemming; songs performed by The Specials, Beck, Ian Brown, Nick Hemming, Edwin Starr, Hank Williams, Beth Orton, Fairport Convention, P.P. Arnold, Christy Moore, Steps, Donovan, Sunhouse, Stone Roses, Billy Bragg, J.J. Cale, etc, *Costumes* Robin Fraser Paye.

Alliance Atlantis/BBC Films/Arts Council of England/ Company Pictures/Big Arty/National Lottery-Alliance Releasing.
90 mins. UK/Canada. 1999. Rel: 4 February 2000. Cert 15.

Rosetta ★¹/₂

Rosetta is 18 and lives with her alcoholic mother in a trailer park on the outskirts of a nondescript Belgian town. Desperate to belong to a world just beyond her fingertips, Rosetta strives to find work, keep her mother off the bottle and, well, be normal ... Maybe this depressing, virtually unwatchable film won the Palme d'Or at Cannes for its sheer originality. Certainly the fact that the camera barely leaves the face of its heroine – thus obscuring any sense of place and saving a fortune on production design – is a unique way to make a movie. But the restless hand-held camerawork and unremitting gloom of the subject is both an insult to the art of cinema and to the human spirit. Rosetta herself is little more than an animal, living off her basic instincts, while those around her show no redeeming qualities. Notwithstanding, Emilie Dequenne – in her first professional role – shows commendable stamina.

● *Rosetta* Emilie Dequenne, *Riquet* Fabrizio Rongione, *Rosetta's mother* Anne Yernaux, *the manager* Olivier Gourmet, Bernard Marbaix, Frederic Bodson, Florian Delain.

Left: Bridal fear – Julia Roberts squares up to Richard Gere in Garry Marshall's charmless Runaway Bride (from Buena Vista)

● *Dir and Screenplay* Luc and Jean-Pierre Dardenne, *Pro* Luc and Jean-Pierre Dardenne and Michèle and Laurent Pétin, *Assoc Pro* Arlette Zylberberg, *Ph* Alain Marcoen, *Ed* Marie-Hélène Dozo, *M* Jean-Pierre Cocco, *Costumes* Monic Parelle.

Les Films du Fleuve/ARP/RTBF/Canal Plus, etc-Artificial Eye. 94 mins. Belgium/France. 1999. Rel: 25 February 2000. Cert 15.

Runaway Bride ★★

Strapped for an idea for his next article, *USA Today* columnist Ike Graham hears of a multiple bride, Maggie Carpenter, who has left seven men standing at the altar. Making her the subject of his next column, he quickly lives to regret it, as his source turns out to be unreliable. Ike loses his job and sets off to see Maggie for himself, who is in the throes of preparing for her fourth wedding ... In its eagerness to replicate the magic of *Pretty Woman*, this high concept romantic comedy tries too hard to be all things and fails to generate any of its own charm. Julia Roberts and Richard Gere strive gamely to invest their parts with their customary magnetism, but are constantly scuttled by the ludicrous demands of the plot. And with James Newton Howard's score working overtime and all the other emotional buttons polished to desperation, what's left is an exercise in manipulative mediocrity.

● *Maggie Carpenter* Julia Roberts, *Ike Graham* Richard Gere, *Peggy* Joan Cusack, *Fisher* Hector Elizondo, *Ellie* Rita Wilson, *Walter* Paul Dooley, *Coach Bob* Christopher Meloni, *George Swilling* Reg Rogers, *Father Brian Norris* Donal Logue, *Gill Chavez* Yul Vazquez, *Grandma Julia* Jean Schertler,

Mrs Pressman Jane Morris, *Betty Trout* Laurie Metcalf, Kevin Murray, Douglas S. Ramer, James Richardson, Kathleen Marshall, Tom Hines, Garrett Wright, Larry Miller, Sela Ward, Sandra Taylor.
● *Dir* Garry Marshall, *Pro* Ted Field and Tom Rosenberg, Scott Kroopf and Robert Cort, *Ex Pro* Ted Tannebaum, David Madden and Gary Lucchesi, *Co-Pro* Karen Stirgwolt, Richard Wright and Ellen Schwartz, *Screenplay* Josann McGibbon and Sara Parriott, *Ph* Stuart Dryburgh, *Pro Des* Mark Friedberg, *Ed* Bruce Green, *M* James Newton Howard; Pachelbel, Mozart, J.S. Bach, Richard Wagner, Mendelssohn, Handel; songs performed by U2, Dangerman, Allure, Dixie Chicks, Daryl Hall and John Oates, Juggling Suns, Grateful Dead, Miles Davis, Roxette, Shawn Colvin, Martina McBride, Eric Clapton, Billy Joel, Coco Lee, etc, *Costumes* Albert Wolsky.

Touchstone Pictures/Paramount/Interscope Communications/Lakeshore Entertainment-Buena Vista. 116 mins. USA. 1999. Rel: 8 October 1999. Cert PG.

Run Lola Run – Lola rennt ★★★½

The most successful German film since *Das Boot* in 1981, *Run Lola Run* juggles stylistic motifs and temporal conceits like a Clio-winning TV commercial for transcendental transportation. Visually assertive and conceptually audacious, the film spins its frenetic magic off a very simple premise: girl dashes across Berlin to find DM 100,000 to save her boyfriend's life. Then, as a conspiracy of random accidents effects the heroine's race against the clock, the 20-minute endeavour is repeated two more times. While this exercise promises to be somewhat repetitive, writer-

Right: *Fast Forward – Franka Potente hot-foots it in Tom Tykwer's fun and inventive* Run Lola Run *(from Columbia TriStar)*

director Tom Tykwer introduces a number of brilliant distractions by providing passers-by – via a rush of Polaroids – with an encapsulated future history. Thus, *Run Lola Run* is fun because it redefines the language of cinema. It also presents a new star in the striking form of Franka Potente, who became the director's girlfriend six months after completion of the film.

● *Lola* Franka Potente, *Manni* Moritz Bleibtreu, *Lola's father* Herbert Knaup, *Mr Schuster* Armin Rohde, *the tramp* Joachim Krol, *Jutta Hanson* Nina Petri, Ludger Pistor, Suzanne von Borsody, Sebastian Schipper.
● *Dir and Screenplay* Tom Tykwer, *Pro* Stefan Arndt, *Ex Pro* Maria Köpf, *Ph* Frank Griebe, *Pro Des* Alexander Manasse, *Ed* Mathilde Bonnefoy, *M* Tykwer, Johnny Klimek and Reinhold Heil; songs performed by Franka Potente, Johnny Klimek, Dinah Washington, and Susie Van Der Meer, *Costumes* Monika Jacobs, *Sound* Dirk Jacob, *Lola's hair* Christa Krista.

X Filme Creative Pool-Columbia Tri Star.
80 mins. Germany. 1998. Rel: 22 October 1999. Cert 15.

Rushmore ★★★¹/₂

Max Fischer would like to think of himself as a high achiever. Sure, he's a prolific playwright, editor of the school newspaper and yearbook, captain of the fencing and debate teams and president of the French, German, chess and astronomy clubs – not to mention other extracurricular activities – but unless he hikes up his grade level *pronto* he's facing expulsion from his beloved Rushmore Academy. However, rather than spend more time in mere study, Max decides to operate a few devious administrative strings and pursue his love of the first-grade teacher Miss Cross ... *Rushmore* is a very strange film. And that is both its strength and its downfall. Featuring one of the most bizarre characters in recent screen memory and exuding an air of displaced reality, this is the sort of fable that could haunt your dreams for weeks. Equally, it so squarely occupies its own universe that it fails to engage on any emotional level whatsoever. It's also not as funny as it thinks it is but it does generate a fresh argument about what cinema is all about in the first place. Incidentally, for his contribution, Bill Murray was voted best supporting actor by the Los Angeles Film Critics' Association, the National Society of Film Critics and the New York Film Critics' Circle.

● *Max Fischer* Jason Schwartzman, *Rosemary Cross* Olivia Williams, *Herman Blume* Bill Murray, *Dr Guggenheim* Brian Cox, *Bert Fischer* Seymour Cassel, *Dirk Calloway* Mason Gamble, *Margaret Yang* Sara Tanaka, *Magnus Buchan* Stephen McCole, *Dr Peter Flynn* Luke Wilson, Deepak Pallana, Andrew Wilson, Marietta Marich, Ronnie McCawley, Keith McCawley, Connie Nielsen, Paul Schiff.
● *Dir* Wes Anderson, *Pro* Barry Mendel and Paul Schiff, *Ex Pro and Screenplay* Anderson and Owen Wilson, *Co-Pro* John Cameron, *Ph* Robert Yeoman, *Pro Des* David Wasco, *Ed* David Moritz, *M* Mark Mothersbaugh; songs performed by Creation, The Kinks, Cat Stevens, Donovan Leitch, The Who, The Rolling Stones, Mark Mothersbaugh, Yves Montand, John Lennon, Django Reinhardt, The Faces, etc, *Costumes* Karen Patch.

Touchstone Pictures/American Empirical Pictures-Buena Vista.
93 mins. USA. 1998. Rel: 20 August 1999. Cert 15.

Saving Grace ★★★

Grace Trevethan is a quiet mouse of a woman who lives in her own sheltered world of tea parties and orchid cultivation. Then, when her old man dies, her life is turned upside down as she discovers the true extent of her husband's debts and the crippling £500-per-week mortgage on her comfortable manor house. In the sleepy Cornish community where she lives, it seems that she is the last person to know of her plight. So how can she keep secret her plan to harvest a particularly lucrative crop of marijuana plants? Drawing on the stereotypes of bucolic English life and turning them inside out, *Saving Grace* is a delightful piece of whimsy that repeatedly hits its comic stride. From Martin Clunes's hard-drinking, spliff-smoking doctor to John Fortune's gay bank manager, this is a film that whips the Ealing comedy into the next Millennium. It's a shame, then, that the film descends into inane farce at the eleventh hour.

● *Grace Trevethan* Brenda Blethyn, *Matthew* Craig Ferguson, *Dr Bamford* Martin Clunes, *Jacques* Tcheky Karyo, *China McFarlane* Jamie Foreman, *Nicky* Valerie Edmond, *Harvey Sloggit* Tristan Sturrock, *Vicar* Leslie Phillips, *Honey* Diana Quick, *Margaret* Phyllida Law, *Diana* Linda Kerr Scott, *Charlie* Paul Brooke, *Sgt Alfred* Ken Campbell, Bill Bailey, Clive Merrison, Denise Coffey, John Fortune, Philip Wright, Bill Hallet.
● *Dir* Nigel Cole, *Pro* Mark Crowdy, *Ex Pro* Cat Villiers and Xavier Marchand, *Line Pro* Steve Clark-

Hall, *Co-Pro* Craig Ferguson and Torsten Leschley, *Screenplay* Ferguson and Crowdy, *Ph* John de Borman, *Pro Des* Eve Stewart, *Ed* Alan Strachan, *M* Mark Russell; songs performed by Filter, Steve Harley & Cockney Rebel, Norman Greenbaum, Koot, Pretenders, Robert Palmer, Sherena Dugani, A.F.T., and Plenty, *Costumes* Annie Symons.

Fox/Sky Pictures/Portman Entertainment/Wave Pictures/Homerun-Fox.
92 mins. UK. 1999. Rel: 19 May 2000. Cert 15.

Scream 3 ★½

So successful were *Stab* and *Stab 2* – the slasher films based on the Woodsboro killings – that a third production is now in the works in Hollywood. Meanwhile, Sidney Prescott, the beleaguered daughter of the first Woodsboro victim, has retreated to Northern California to keep out of harm's way. However, a new psycho has popped out of the woodwork to act out the murders depicted in the fictionalised *Stab 3 – Return to Woodsboro*. But with three different versions of the script – written 'to keep the ending off the Internet' – which one is he/she following? Hey, here's an idea. Having successfully sent up the concept of the horror sequel with *Scream 2* (international box-office gross: $170.1 million), how about a trilogy spoof? With predictable allusions to *Return of the Jedi* and *The Godfather Part III*, this 'final chapter'

Above: Third time yucky – Courteney Cox Arquette and Parker Posey in Wes Craven's gimmicky and predictable *Scream 3* (from Buena Vista) (don't hold your breath) quickly falls victim to its own gimmicky formula. And, to keep up the ante, there are even more in-jokes, cameo appearances and trick U-turns. But how can one respect a horror film that repeatedly uses characters bumping into each other as a scare tactic?

● *Dewey Riley* David Arquette, *Sidney Prescott* Neve Campbell, *Gale Weathers* Courteney Cox Arquette, *Det. Kincaide* Patrick Dempsey, *Sarah Darling* Jenny McCarthy, *Jennifer Jolie* Parker Posey, *Tyson Fox* Dean Richmond, *Roman Bridger* Scott Foley, *John Milton* Lance Henriksen, *Tom Prinze* Matt Keeslar, *Angelina Tyler* Emily Mortimer, *Steven Stone* Patrick Warburton, *Cotton Weary* Liev Schreiber, *Christine* Kelly Rutherford, *Detective Wallace* Josh Pais, *Randy Meeks* Jamie Kennedy, *Mr Loomis* C.W. Morgan, Beth Toussaint, Richmond Arquette, Lynn McRee, Nancy O'Dell, Roger Corman, John Embry, Lawrence Hecht, Kevin Smith, Jason Mewes, Heather Matarazzo.
● *Dir* Wes Craven, *Pro* Cathy Konrad, Kevin Williamson and Marianne Maddalena, *Screenplay* Ehren Kruger, *Ex Pro* Bob Weinstein, Harvey Weinstein, Cary Granat and Andrew Rona, *Co-Pro* Dixie J. Capp and Julie Plec, *Co-Ex Pro* Stuart M. Besser, *Ph* Peter Deming, *Pro Des* Bruce Alan Miller, *Ed* Patrick Lussier, *M* Marco Beltrami; songs performed by Creed, Nick Cave and The Bad Seeds, Static-X, System of a Down, Fuel, Ear2000, Finger Eleven, and American Pearl, *Costumes* Abigail Murray.

Miramax/Dimension/Konrad Pictures/Craven/Maddalena Films-Buena Vista.
116 mins. USA. 2000. Rel: 28 April 2000. Cert 18.

The Secret Laughter of Women ★★★

Raising her eight-year-old son by herself in a coastal town in southern France, Nimi is the subject of much gossip and speculation within the tightly knit Nigerian community where she lives. When a good-looking priest shows interest in her as a prospective wife, the match is actively encouraged by Nimi's mother and her friends. But Nimi's son, Sammy, thinks the local creator of a successful comic strip would make a far more eligible suitor, even if he is English and white ... There is an undeniable freshness and charm to this unusual little film, even when it teeters on the edge of cuteness. Thankfully, though, Colin Firth introduces a stabilising breeze of cynicism as the archetypal rumpled Englishman, even though he lacks the requisite passion for the film's later scenes. And Nia Long is good, too, as the dignified Nigerian who, for the most part, keeps her secret laughter in check, while there's a glorious Greek chorus of Anglo-African actresses adding a frisky commentary on all things sexual.

● *Matthew Field* Colin Firth, *Nimi da Silva* Nia Long, *Nene* Joke Jacobs, *Sammy da Silva* Fissy Roberts, *Madame Rosa* Bella Enahoro, *Talking Drum* Rakie Ayola, *Bitter Leaf* Ellen Thomas, *Jenny Field* Caroline Goodall, *Reverend Fola Kayode* Ariyon Bakare, *Mama Fola* Joy Elias-Rilwan, *Papa Fola* Thomas Baptiste, *John* Dan Lett, Willie Jonah, Ho Yi Wong, Hakim Kae Kazim, Christopher Bowen.
● *Dir* Peter Schwabach, *Pro* O.O. Sagay and Jon Slan, *Ex Pro* Gareth Jones, *Line Pro* Michael MacDonald and Michael Dreyer, *Assoc Pro* Janet E. Cuddy, *Screenplay* Sagay, *Ph* Martin Fuhrer, *Pro Des* Christopher J. Bradshaw, *Ed* Michael Christopher Pacek, *M* Yves Laferrière, *Costumes* Louise St Jernsward.

ELBA Films/Paragon Entertainment/HandMade Films/ European Co-production Fund/BskyB/Arts Council of England-Optimum Releasing.
99 mins. UK/Canada. 1998. Rel: 26 November 1999. Cert 12.

Sex: The Annabel Chong Story ★★

For almost a year Annabel Chong (née Grace Quek) held the world record for the most number of sexual encounters in a day – 251 men in a ten hour stretch. A dermally challenged, snaggle-toothed former convent girl, Chong cheerfully reveals that her reasons for becoming the focal point of 'the world's biggest gangbang' was to shake up the stereotypical view of the woman as passive sex object. But Chong's perpetual giggle is loaded with neurosis, at times sounding more like a sob than a laugh. As the camera mercilessly intrudes on the most intimate moments of her life (waking up in the morning, going to the loo), the layers of the confident porn star and USC student are stripped away to reveal a confused, frightened victim of a stifled upbringing. Back in Singapore (post-gangbang) we discover that modern music and dancing are a definite no-no, so that when Chong's mother discovers the nature of her daughter's Western notoriety the effect is thoroughly discomfiting. Gough Lewis's rough and ready documentary is not so much guilty of sexual voyeurism as of the exploitation of its subject's humiliation and misery.

● With Annabel Chong (aka Grace Quek), John Bowen, Ed Powers, Dick James (President of the Annabel Chong Fan Club), Al Goldstein, Ron Jeremy, Mr and Mrs Quek, Seymore Butts, Ona Zee, Chi Chi LaRue, Michael J. Coxx (star of *Oral Majority*), Donna Warner, Jack Hammer, Jasmin St Claire, Dick Nasty, etc.
● *Dir* Gough Lewis, *Pro* Lewis, Hugh F. Curry and David Whitten, *Ex Pro* Kathleen Curry and Suzanne Bowers Whitten, *Assoc Pro* Brad Brough and Gloria Pryor, *Ph* Jim Michaels, *Ed* Kelly Morris, *M* Peter Mundinger, and Paul Lopez.

Omni International/Greycat Releasing/Coffee House Films-Metrodome.
87 mins. USA/Canada. 1998. Rel: 21 April 2000. Cert 18.

Shergar ★★¹/₂

Ireland; 1983. Winner of both the English and Irish derby, Shergar is the world's most famous racehorse when he's kidnapped by a splinter group of the IRA, led by the fanatical Gavin O'Rourke. Ransomed for £2 million, Shergar is secreted away to a remote farm where he is befriended by the stable boy, Kevin, a runaway teenager. When the ransom isn't paid, O'Rourke orders the decapitation of the horse, but Kevin has other plans... A fanciful interpretation of a real-life mystery, *Shergar* is aimed squarely at the family market and makes the most of its picturesque locale (the Isle of Man doubling for Southern Ireland), abetted by a sweeping score from John Scott. And there are excellent turns from Ian Holm and Laura Murphy as a sympathetic tinker and his granddaughter. However, while kids should enjoy the adventure, grown-ups may find the whimsy laid on a little too thick. [*Ewen Brownrigg*]

● *Joe Maguire* Ian Holm, *Eamonn Garritty* David Warner, *Gavin O'Rourke* Mickey Rourke, *Kevin Doherty* Tom Walsh, *Kate Maguire* Laura Murphy, *Dermot Concannon* Andrew Connolly, *Mrs Garritty* Virginia Cole, Conor Mullen, Phelim Drew, Stephen Brennan, Billy Boyle, Jimmy Keogh.
● *Dir* and *Screenplay* Denis C. Lewiston, *Pro* Brian Agnew, Jeff Geoffray and Walter Josten, *Ex Pro* Agnew, *Ph* David Lewis, *Pro Des* Brian Ackland-Snow, *Ed* Alan Strachan, *M* John Scott, *Costumes* Louise Stjernsward, *Horsemaster* Roy Street.

Blue Rider Pictures/Morlaw Films/Isle of Man Film Commission-Sun Chariot Films.
95 mins. UK/USA. 1998. Rel: 2 June 2000. Cert PG.

Show Me Love – Fucking Åmål ★★★¹/₂

Åmål, south of Karlstad, Sweden; the present. In spite of living in Åmål for over a year, Agnes Ahlberg has made no friends. Now it's her 16th birthday and it's unlikely anybody will turn up for her party. But then, in a cruel twist of fate, Elin arrives with her sister Jessica, but only to poke fun. Cruel, for Agnes is besotted with Elin ... At first glance *Show Me Love* is a rejection of its Swedish film heritage. Gone are the measured tableaux of Bergman and the pristine precision of his successors. Instead, there is the hand-held, grainy, fidgety look one has come to associate with the cinema of urban America, complete with the latter's pop cultural allusions (there are pictures of Leonardo DiCaprio everywhere). But beneath this there is a freshness and generosity of spirit lacking in the oeuvre of Spike Lee, Kevin Smith and Richard Linklater. At once enchanting yet very real, sweet yet daring, timeless yet spontaneous, tender yet uncompromising, *Show Me Love* is a celebration of the immediacy of its art and is a humanist document at that. A huge hit on its home turf (helped, no doubt, by its provocative title), the film serves as a neat female counterpoint to Britain's own undervalued *Get Real* (in which a 16-year-old schoolboy falls for a popular jock).

● *Elin* Alexandra Dahlstr, *Agnes Ahlberg* Rebecca Liljeberg, *Jessica* Erica Carlson, *Johan Hult* Mathias Rust, *Markus* Stefan Hörberg, *Olof, Agnes's father* Ralph Carlsson, *Karin, Agnes's mother* Maria Hedborg, *Brigitta, Elin's mother* Jill Ung, *Camilla* Lisa Skagerstam, Josefin Nyberg, Axel Widegren, Nils Björkman.
● *Dir and Screenplay* Lukas Moodysson, *Pro* Lars Jönsson, *Co-Pro* Peter Aalbæk Jensen, *Assoc Pro* Anna Anthony, *Ph* Ulf Brantås, *Pro Des* Lina Strand and Heidi Saikkonen, *Ed* Michal Leszczylowski and Bernahard Winkler, *M* songs performed by Yvonne, Broder Daniel, Betty 'n' Boop, Evelyn, Foreigner, Robyn, etc, *Costumes* Maria Swenson.

Memfis Film/Zentropa Prods/Film i Väst, etc-Alliance Releasing.
89 mins. Sweden/Denmark. 1998. Rel: 3 March 2000. Cert 15.

Simon Magus ★¹/₂

Silesia, Prussia; the late 19th century. With the arrival of the steam train, a rural Jewish village finds its community dramatically dissipated. And with its adult male population reduced to nine, even a proper prayer meeting is now out of the question. However, there is Simon, an outcast allegedly imbued with magic powers – but even he is torn between his loyalty to the devil, a local gentile landlord and the prospect of Christianity ... Striving to be an amalgam of mysticism and fable, *Simon Magus* fails to generate enough magic to locate its own centre of gravity. An intrusive, soporific score and a general heaviness of tone drag what is potentially an interesting idea into the depths of multi-national discombobulation. Still, it's hard to ignore a film in which Ian Holm plays a mushroom.

● *Simon* Noah Taylor, *Leah* Embeth Davidtz, *Dovid* Stuart Townsend, *Hase* Sean McGinley, *Bratislav* Terence Rigby, *Sarah* Amanda Ryan, *Sirius/Boris* Ian Holm, *Squire* Rutger Hauer, *Rabbi* David De Keyser, Toby Jones, Jim Dunk, Ursula Jones, Cyril Shaps, Ken Dury, Tom Fisher, Walter Sparrow, Jean Anderson, Katharine Schlesinger, Maggie Steed, Barry Davis.
● *Dir* and *Screenplay* Ben Hopkins, *Pro* Robert Jones, *Line Pro* Anita Overland, *Ph* Nic Knowland, *Pro Des* Angela Davies, *Ed* Alan Levy, *M* Deborah Mollison, *Costumes* Michelle Clapton.

Film Four/Lucky Red/ARP/Hollywood Partners/Arts Council of England-Film Four.
106 mins. UK. 1998. Rel: 26 May 2000. Cert PG.

Simpatico ★

Lexington, Kentucky/Cucamonga, California; 1999/many years ago. Simpatico is the name of a thoroughbred stallion belonging to wealthy Kentucky breeder Lyle Carter. But, just as Lyle is about to reap the rewards of a lucrative sale, he is contacted by an old friend in dire straits. Begging Lyle to come to his rescue in California, Vinnie Webb kick-starts a scheme that is to bring the ghosts of the past rattling back to life ... What starts off as an intriguing game of deceit, betrayal and role reversal gradually descends into contrivance and melodrama. In spite of committed acting from a top-flight cast and stylish theatrics from Yorkshire-born stage director Warchus, *Simpatico* spends far too long shielding what turns out to be a rudimentary hand of jacks. Ultimately, then, these tragic figures appear no more than pawns in Sam Shepard's circuitous drama, having little to do with the viewer. Nonetheless, Sharon Stone turns in a particularly selfless performance, recalling Faye Dunaway shortly after her sell-by date had expired.

● *Vincent 'Vinnie' T. Webb* Nick Nolte, *Lyle Carter* Jeff Bridges, *Rosie/Mrs Carter* Sharon Stone, *Cecilia Ponz* Catherine Keener, *Darryl P. Simms aka Ryan Ames* Albert Finney, *young Vinnie* Shawn Hatosy, *young Rosie* Kimberly Williams, *young Carter* Liam Waite, *Charlie* Ken Struck, Whit Crawford, Bob Harter, Ashley Guthrie.
● *Dir* Matthew Warchus, *Pro* Dan Lupovitz, Jean-Francois Fonlupt and Timm Oberwelland, *Ex Pro* Sue Baden-Powell, Joel Lubin and Greg Shapiro, *Assoc Pro* Leon Melas, *Screenplay* Warchus and Davis Nicholls, *Ph* John Toll, *Pro Des* Amy Ancona, *Ed* Pasquale Buba, *M* Stewart Copeland; Haydn, Mozart; songs performed by Copeland and Stan Ridgway, Petula Clark, Felice Taylor, Dyke and The Blazers, etc, *Costumes* Karen Patch.

Below: 'I see dead people' – Haley Joel Osment sees through Bruce Willis in M. Night Shyamalan's hugely successful The Sixth Sense (from Buena Vista)

Emotion Pictures/Canal Plus/Kingsgate-Alliance Atlantis. 106 mins. USA/France. 1999. Rel: 28 January 2000. Cert 15.

Simply Irresistible ★

Amanda Shelton is a lousy cook at the 70-year-old Southern Cross eatery, which is about to close. Tom Bartlett is a slick, womanising executive about to open an exclusive five-star restaurant in a department store uptown. Amanda and Tom couldn't be more disparate, but a fairy godfather can do wonders with a magic crab ... Think *You've Got M@il* without the charm and you're halfway there. When one starts anticipating the punch line to a movie's one-liners, you know it's in trouble. In fact, the only irresistible thing about this leaden contrivance is the temptation not to see it.

● *Amanda Shelton* Sarah Michelle Gellar, *Tom Bartlett* Sean Patrick Flanery, *Lois McNally* Patricia Clarkson, *Jonathan Bendel* Dylan Baker, *Gene O'Reilly* Christopher Durang, *Nolan Traynor* Larry Gilliard Jr, *Aunt Stella* Betty Buckley, Amanda Peet, Olek Krupa, Andrew Seear, Meg Gibson, Alex Draper, Bill Raymond, Margaret Sophie Stein.
● *Dir* Mark Tarlov, *Pro* John Fielder, Jon Amiel and Joe Caracciolo Jr, *Ex Pro* Arnon Milchan and Elisabeth Robinson, *Co-Pro* Brian Maas, *Screenplay* Judith Roberts, *Ph* Robert Stevens, *Pro Des* John Kasarda and William Barclay, *Ed* Paul Karasick, *M* Gil Goldstein; songs performed by The Hollowbodies, Marcy Playground, Donna Lewis, Shawn Colvin, Semisonic, Katalina, Jennifer Paige, etc, *Costumes* Katherine Jane Bryant, *Choreography* Jerry Mitchell.

Regency Enterprises/Polar Prods/Taurus Film-Fox. 95 mins. USA/Germany. 1999. Rel: 22 October 1999. Cert PG.

The Sixth Sense ★★½

A child psychologist honoured by the mayor of Philadelphia, Dr Malcolm Crowe is not so sure of his powers to heal. And when he takes on a deeply disturbed eight-year-old boy, he really begins to feel out of his depth. Is the child hallucinatory, schizophrenic or paranoid? Or are the shocking things he sees and hears the real thing? A monumental hit at the US box-office, this low-key chiller proves that you don't need extravagant effects to win an audience over. Unfortunately, though, it's a one-gimmick film that treads water for much of its running time. It's also downright unconvincing, due in part to a somnambulant performance from Bruce Willis and to the lack of background given his own character and his deteriorating marriage. Far more effective, though, is Toni Collette as the boy's confused mother and the eleven-year-old Haley Joel Osment (who played Forrest Gump as a boy), who acts Willis off the screen. And there are a few nice effects supplied by the Stan Winston Studio.

● *Malcolm Crowe* Bruce Willis, *Lynn Sear* Toni Collette, *Anna Crowe* Olivia Williams, *Cole Sear* Haley Joel Osment, *Vincent Gray* Donnie Wahlberg, Trevor Morgan, Peter Tambakis, Jeffrey Zubernis, Bruce Norris,

Above: '*I spy with…*' – *Johnny Depp investigates the scene of the crime in Tim Burton's visually stunning* Sleepy Hollow *(from Pathé)*

Glenn Fitzgerald, Greg Wood, Mischa Barton, Angelica Torn, Samia Shoaib, *Dr Hill* M. Night Shyamalan.
● *Dir and Screenplay* M. Night Shyamalan, *Pro* Frank Marshall, Kathleen Kennedy and Barry Mendel, *Ex Pro* Sam Mercer, *Ph* Tak Fujimoto, *Pro Des* Larry Fulton, *Ed* Andrew Mondshein, *M* James Newton Howard; Schubert; songs performed by Chet Baker, The Supremes, Tin Star, Second Coming, etc, *Costumes* Joanna Johnston, *Sound* Michael Kirchberger.

Hollywood Pictures/Spyglass Entertainment-Buena Vista. 107 mins. USA. 1999. Rel: 5 November 1999. Cert 15.

SLC Punk! ★½
Salt Lake City, Utah; 1985. Stevo's mother and father are desperate to see him go to Harvard but Stevo just wants to rebel. However, with his friends beginning to sell out to the Establishment, Stevo is wondering how long he can go on rejecting the values that his divorced parents hold dear… A surprisingly formulaic and derivative examination of a period of American anarchy, *SLC Punk!* is a soft look at a hard subject. Thematically muddled and visually bland, the film has little new to say and does so with considerable effort. Furthermore, Matthew Lillard gives Stevo little credibility or depth, although Annabeth Gish and Summer Phoenix more than rise above their limited material. [*Ewen Brownrigg*]

● *Stevo* Matthew Lillard, *Bob* Michael Goorjian, *Trish* Annabeth Gish, *Sandy* Jennifer Lien, *Father* Christopher McDonald, *Sean* Devon Sawa, *Eddie* Adam Pascal, *Mike* Jason Segel, *Brandy* Summer Phoenix, *John 'The Mod'* James Duval, *Mark* Til Schweiger, Chiara Barzini, Kevin Breznahan, Christina Karras, Christopher Ogden, Francis Capra, Scott Brady, Don Walsh, Adam Lawson.
● *Dir* and *Screenplay* James Merendino, *Pro* Sam Maydew and Peter Ward, *Ex Pro* Jan De Bont, Michael Peyser and Andrea Kreuzhage, *Co-Pro* Tam Halling, *Ph* Greg Littlewood, *Pro Des* Charlotte Malmloff, *Ed* Esther P.Russel, *M* Melanie Miller; songs performed by The Suicide Machines, Blondie, Exploited, Generation X, Fear, The Velvet Underground, Adam and the Ants, Moondog, The Stooges, Fifi, The Specials, Adolescents, The Ramones, and Dead Kennedys, *Costumes* Fiora.

Beyond Films/Blue Tulip-Columbia TriStar. 97 mins. USA/Australia. 1998. Rel: 31 March 2000. Cert 15.

Sleepy Hollow ★★★
Sleepy Hollow, the Hudson Valley; 1799. Banished to the northern reaches of New York State for his unfashionable views on justice, constable Ichabod Crane is faced with his most daunting case yet. For here the locals are being decapitated on a regular basis, apparently by a sword-wielding, headless horseman … Nobody could summon up the otherworldly atmosphere of Washington Irving's whimsical 1820 short story better than Tim Burton, the grand master of Gothic cinema. And with the help of magnificent sets,

digital technology and lots of fog, Burton has created a creepy, bewitching and mud-slapped world where anything could happen. Deeply influenced by the Hammer horror films and laced with a self-mocking humour, the film manages to be both unsettling and engaging – but on the most superficial of levels. A major flaw is the casting of Christina Ricci, a chubby American adolescent at sea amongst a raft of wonderfully Rabelaisian character actors, and so the film lacks the emotional ballast that made Burton's *Edward Scissorhands* so affecting. Still, the gory effects will delight the less romantically inclined. In fact, it does for decapitation what *The Exorcist* did for vomiting. FYI: Johnny Depp apparently modelled his performance on Angela Lansbury.

● *Ichabod Crane* Johnny Depp, *Katrina Van Tassel* Christina Ricci, *Lady Van Tassel/crone* Miranda Richardson, *Baltus Van Tassel* Michael Gambon, *Brom Van Brunt* Casper Van Dien, *Reverend Steenwyck* Jeffrey Jones, *Magistrate Philipse* Richard Griffiths, *Doctor Lancaster* Ian McDiarmid, *Notary Hardenbrook* Michael Gough, *Hessian Horseman* Christopher Walken, *young Masbath* Marc Pickering, *Lady Crane* Lisa Marie, *Burgomaster* Christopher Lee, Steven Waddington, Claire Skinner, Alun Armstrong, Mark Spalding, Jessica Oyelowo, Peter Guinness, Gabrielle Lloyd, Michael Feast, Jamie Foreman, Philip Martin Brown, and (*uncredited*) Martin Landau.
● *Dir* Tim Burton, *Pro* Scott Rudin and Adam Schroeder, *Ex Pro* Francis Ford Coppola and Larry Franco, *Co-Pro* Kevin Yagher, *Screenplay* Andrew Kevin Walker and (*uncredited*) Tom Stoppard, from a 'screen' story by Walker and Yagher, *Ph* Emmanuel Lubezki, *Pro Des* Rick Heinrichs, *Ed* Chris Lebenzon, *M* Danny Elfman, *Costumes* Colleen Atwood, *Special effects* Joss Williams, *Visual effects* Jim Mitchell, *Creature effects* Yagher.

Paramount/Mandalay/American Zoetrope/Dieter Geissler/Karol Film-Pathé.
105 mins. USA/Germany. 1999. Rel: 7 January 2000. Cert 15.

Small Time Obsession ★★★

Following a bungled break-in of their local Polish club, events quickly escalate as Chris, a South London chancer, pushes his partners-in-crime into increasing danger. Now his friend Michael is faced with the dilemma of whether to go along with Chris or save his own skin. And matters are further complicated by an infatuation with Chris's long-standing girlfriend, Ali … Writer/director Piotr Szkopiak's debut feature is for the most part an engrossing, well acted and ultimately quite moving story of a close-knit group of friends facing life-changing decisions. Set amidst the Polish community of South London, it's also a fascinating, gripping and realistic urban gangster story

revealing a London rarely seen on film. If *Lock, Stock* is the fantasy, this is the reality. [*Barbra Michaels*]

● *Michael* Alex King, *Ali* Juliette Caton, *Chris* Jason Merrells, *Steve* Oliver Young, *John* Richard Banks, *Jackie* Kirsten Parker, *Geordie* Geoff Lawson, *Pope* Giles Ward, *Mr Page* Andrew Tiernan, Jurek Jarosz, Teresa Nowakowska, Leoanrd Trusty, Daniel Peacock, Simon Merrells, Mark Sloper, Julian Boote.
● *Dir, Pro* and *Screenplay* Piotr Szkopiak, *Ex Pro* David Nicholas Wilkinson, *Co-Pro* Ian David Diaz and Julian Boote, *Assoc Pro* Geoff Lawson, Kevin Nelson and Mark Sloper, *Ph* Niels Reedtz Johansen, *Pro Des* Vince Raj, *Ed* Piotr Szkopiak, *M* Martin Bell; songs performed by Dexy's Midnight Runners, Astrid, Nugget, The Famous Five, Hackney Five0, etc, *Costumes* Anabel Campbell and Silvano Sacco.

Guerilla Films/Solo Films/Seventh Twelfth Collective-Guerilla Films.
119 mins. UK. 2000. Rel: 16 June 2000. Cert 15.

Snow Day ★★

When an unexpected snowfall engulfs a small-town community outside Syracuse, New York, schools are closed for the day. And so the next 12 hours are host to no end of possibilities as the local kids attempt to capitalise on their various aspirations. Because, on a snow day, anything can happen … Drawing on every cliché in nivenclature (snow culture, to you) – tobogganing, snowmen, ice sculptures, skating, state-of-the-art snowballs, you name it – this amiable comedy jumps along the dotted line with varying degrees of success. At times extremely bad and at others less so, the film should entertain the young at heart. For if a hamburger's function is to stave off hunger, then this innocuous entertainment achieves its directive.

● *Snowplowman* Chris Elliott, *Hal Brandston* Mark Webber, *Laura Brandston* Jean Smart, *Tom Brandston* Chevy Chase, *Lane Leonard* Schuyler Fisk, *Mr Zellweger* Iggy Pop, *Tina* Pam Grier, *Chad Symmonz* John Schneider, *Natalie Brandston* Zena Grey, *Wayne Alworth* Josh Peck, *Principal Weaver* Damian Young, *Randy Brandston* Connor Matheus, *Claire Bonner* Emmanuelle Chriqui, *Chuck Wheeler* David Paetkau, Jade Yorker, J. Adam Brown, 'Chilli'.
● *Dir* Chris Koch, *Pro* Albie Hecht and Julia Pistor, *Ex Pro* Raymond Wagner, *Screenplay* Will McRobb and Chris Viscardi, *Ph* Robbie Greenberg, *Pro Des* Leslie McDonald, *Ed* David Finfer, *M* Steve Bartek; songs performed by Cal Tjader and Carmen McRae, Smash Mouth, Foreigner, The Mighty Mighty Bosstones, The Wiseguys (UK), LFO, Sixpence None the Richer, Schuyler Fisk, Al Martino, The Hippos, Boyzone, Jordan Knight, Dina Carroll, 98º, Hoku, etc, *Costumes* Wendy Partridge.

Paramount/Nickleodeon Movies-UIP.
89 mins. USA. 2000. Rel: 21 April 2000. Cert PG.

Snow Falling On Cedars ★★'/₂

San Piedro Island, Puget Sound, North-West Washington; 1950. Following the death of a local fisherman, the deceased's childhood friend, a first-generation American of Japanese descent, is put on trial for his murder. With anti-Japanese sentiment still running high since the bombing of Pearl Harbor, can Kazuo Miyamoto hope to expect justice? Attempting to create a film about `the process of revealing' (his words), director/co-writer Scott Hicks has fashioned a stunning testament to self-indulgence. With every painstakingly crafted sequence screaming with self-importance, the film is not only protracted and overblown but its very revelation is barely a surprise. A faithful adaptation of David Guterson's wildly acclaimed novel (which took the author ten years to write), the film is rife with good intentions and period accuracy (which may delight many), but its story's impact is lessened by such a self-consciously arty approach. Still, one cannot help but admire the haunting, Oscar-nominated cinematography and a delicious turn from Max Von Sydow as Kazuo's crusty old lawyer.

● *Ishmael Chambers* Ethan Hawke, *Judge Fielding* James Cromwell, *Sheriff Art Moran* Richard Jenkins, *Hatsue Miyamoto* Youki Kudoh, *Alvin Hooks* James Rebhorn, *Arthur Chambers* Sam Shepard, *Kazuo Miyamoto* Rick Yune, *Nels Gudmundsson* Max Von Sydow, *young Ishmael Chambers* Reeve Carney, *young Hatsue Miyamoto* Anne Suzuki, *Susan Marie Heine* Arija Bareikis, *Carl Heine Jr* Eric Thal, *Etta Heine* Celia Weston, *Carl Heine Snr* Daniel Von Bargen, *Zenhichi Miyamoto* Cary-Hiroyuki Tagawa, *Horace Whaley* Max Wright, *Helen Chambers* Caroline Kava, Akira Takayama, Ako, Zak Orth, Jan Rube_, Sheila Moore, Zeljko Ivanek, Seiji Inouye.
● *Dir* Scott Hicks, *Pro* Harry J. Ufland, Ron Bass, Kathleen Kennedy and Frank Marshall, *Ex Pro* Carol Baum and Lloyd A. Silverman, *Co-Pro* Richard Vane and David Guterson, *Screenplay* Bass and Hicks, *Ph* Robert Richardson, *Pro Des* Jeannine Oppewall, *Ed* James Newton Howard, *Costumes* Renee Erlich Kalfus.

Universal-UIP.
127 mins. USA. 1999. Rel: 12 May 2000. Cert 15.

South Park: Bigger, Longer & Uncut ★★'/₂

South Park, a redneck community in Colorado; the present. When Cartman, Kyle, Stan and Kenny sneak into an NC-17-rated Canadian comedy (*Asses of Fire*), their language takes a decided turn for the worse. Outraged by their children's behaviour, the kids' parents take the issue all the way to the White House and war is declared on Canada ... As TV extensions go, this cult cartoon certainly makes the most of its opportunities, both employ-

ing fruitier language and themes, while opening out the story to embrace World War III and Armageddon. And that takes *chutzpah*. Yet the infantile tone remains and the preponderance of the 'f' word and clitoris just seems to underline the humour's limitations. However, compared to the tired shenanigans of *American Pie*, at least this adolescent smutfest has some inventiveness and novelty value. And the numerous musical songs are a scream. P.S. Satan, Bill Clinton, Saddam Hussein, Winona Ryder and the Baldwin and Arquette families appear without their consent.

● *Voices: Stan Marsh, Eric Cartman, Mr Garrison, Mr Hat, Officer Barbrady, etc* Trey Parker, *Kyle Broflovski, Kenny McCormick, Pip, Jesus, Jimbo, etc* Matt Stone, *Mrs Cartman, Sheila Broflovski, Sharon Manson, Mrs McCormick, Wendy Testaburger, Principal Victoria, etc* Mary Kay Bergman, *Chef* Isaac Hayes, *Dr Gouache* George Clooney, *Conan O'Brien* Brent Spiner, *Brooke Shields* Minnie Driver, *Alec, Daniel, Stephen and William Baldwin* Dave Foley, *Dr Vosknocker* Eric Idle, Jesse Howell, Bruce Howell, Jennifer Howell, Stewart Copeland, Mike Judge.
● *Dir* Trey Parker, *Pro* Parker and Matt Stone, *Screenplay* Parker, Stone and Pam Brady, *Ex Pro* Scott Rudin and Adam Schroeder, *Co-Pro* Anne Garefino and Debborah Liebling, *Line Pro* Gina Shay, *Ed* John H. Venzon, *Art* J.C. Wegman, *M* Marc Shaiman; *songs* Parker, *Sound* Bruce Howell, *Animation* Eric Stough.

Paramount/Warner/Comedy Central-Warner.
81 mins. USA. 1999. Rel: 27 August 1999. Cert 15.

Star Wars: Episode I The Phantom Menace ★★★★

In a galaxy far, far away, the Trade Federation plans to invade Naboo, a peaceful planet ruled by a teenage queen. But as the evil Senator Palpatine masses his forces, the Jedi knight Qui-Gon Jinn and his spunky apprentice Obi-Wan Kenobi rescue her highness and take off to the desert planet of Tatooine. There they encounter a nine-year-old boy called Anakin Skywalker ... Conceived, written, financed, directed and controlled by George Lucas, *The Phantom Menace* is an extraordinary vision from just one man. Playfully laying the narrative roots for what is to come in the original *Star Wars* trilogy (with the introduction of R2-D2, the discovery of C-3PO, the apprenticeship of Obi-Wan Kenobi, etc), the initial prequel establishes the foundations of what has become the cinema's greatest mythology. And with an actor of Liam Neeson's nobility and presence as the first character to utter the immortal words 'may the force be with you', the film is in good hands. Yet with its catalogue of characters, creatures and contraptions, *Episode 1* is ultimately too complicated and confusing a concoction to be anything more than a visually exhilarating experience. In his eagerness to cram the screen with detail, Lucas has embodied the maxim that more can most definitely be less.

Right: *Liam Neeson and Ewan McGregor cross lightsabres with Ray Park in George Lucas's hype-impaired* Star Wars: Episode I The Phantom Menace *(from Fox)*

● *Qui-Gon Jinn* Liam Neeson, *Obi-Wan Kenobi* Ewan McGregor, *Padmé Naberrie Amidala* Natalie Portman, *Anakin Skywalker* Jake Lloyd, *Shmi Skywalker* Pernilla August, *Jedi Master Yoda* Frank Oz, *Senator Palpatine* Ian McDiarmid, *Sio Bibble* Oliver Ford Davies, *Captain Panaka* Hugh Quarshie, *Jar Jar Binks* Ahmed Best, *C-3PO* Anthony Daniels, *R2-D2* Kenny Baker, *Chancellor Valorum* Terence Stamp, *Boss Nass* Brian Blessed, *Watto* Andrew Secombe, *Darth Maul* Ray Park, *Sebulba* Lewis MacLeod, *Wald* Warwick Davis, *Captain Tarpals* Steven Speirs, *Nute Gunray* Silas Carson, *Rune Haako* Jerome Blake, *Daltay Dofine* Alan Ruscoe, *Ric Olié* Ralph Brown, *Mace Windu* Samuel L. Jackson, Celia Imrie, Benedict Taylor, Clarence Smith, Dominic West, Cristina da Silva, Friday (Liz) Wilson, Candice Orwell, Sofia Coppola, Kiera Knightley, Bronagh Gallagher, Gregg Proops, *voice of TC-14* Lindsay Duncan.
● *Dir, Ex Pro and Screenplay* George Lucas, *Pro* Rick McCallum, *Ph* David Tattersall, *Pro Des* Gavin Bocquet, *Ed* Paul Martin Smith and Ben Burtt, *M* John Williams, *Costumes* Trisha Biggar, *Sound* Ben Burtt, *Visual effects* John Knoll, Dennis Muren and Scott Squires, *Animation* Rob Coleman.

Lucasfilm-Fox.
132 mins. USA. 1999. Rel: 15 July 1999. Cert U.

Stigmata ★★¹/₂

Father Andrew Kiernan is a globe-trotting agent for the Vatican whose job is to expose ersatz miracles.

However, when he discovers warm human blood pouring from the eyes of a statue in a small town in Brazil, he is taken off the case. Instead, he is assigned to investigate the inexplicable wounds appearing on the wrists and back of an atheist Pittsburgh hairdresser. Strangely, she seems to be expecting him ... Taking its premise from the historically anomalous Gospel of St Thomas renounced by the Vatican, *Stigmata* is a theologically intriguing and visually arresting thriller. However, in spite of the story's grounding in religious specifics, the film so resembles a Dubonnet commercial in style that it's hard to take any of its characters or situations seriously. Notwithstanding, some spectacular scenes of possession (levitation, spontaneous conflagrations and the speaking of forgotten tongues) make for diverting entertainment. Previously known as *Toby's Story.*

● *Frankie Paige* Patricia Arquette, *Father Andrew Kiernan* Gabriel Byrne, *Cardinal Daniel Houseman* Jonathan Pryce, *Donna Chadway* Nia Long, *Marion Petrocelli* Rade Sherbedgia, *Father Durning* Thomas Kopache, *Jennifer Kelliho* Portia de Rossi, *Steven* Patrick Muldoon, *Father Paulo Alameida* Jack Donner, Enrico Colantoni, Dick Latessa, Ann Cusack, Frankie Thorn, Mariah Nunn.
● *Dir* Rupert Wainwright, *Pro* Frank Mancuso Jr., *Line Pro* Vikki Williams, *Screenplay* Tom Lazarus and Rick Ramage, *Ph* Jeffrey L. Kimball, *Pro Des* Waldemar Kalinowski, *Ed* Michael R. Miller and Michael J. Duthie, *M* Billy Corgan, Elia Cmiral and Mike Garson; songs performed by Chumbawamba, Bjork, David Bowie, Sinéad O'Connor, Massive Attack, Natalie Imbruglia, etc, *Costumes* Louise

Frogley, *Make-up effects* Ve Neill, *Titles* Diane Van Ussel, Monkeyshine.

MGM/FGM Entertainment-UIP.
102 mins. USA. 1999. Rel: 21 January 2000. Cert 18.

Stir of Echoes ★★★¹/₂

Chicago; the present. Tom and Maggie's five-year-old son is acting strangely, speaking to imaginary beings and talking in tongues. But that's nothing compared to what Tom goes through after he's hypnotised by his sister-in-law. Suddenly Tom is plagued by disturbing hallucinations and gains a power to see beyond the merely tangible. And what he sees isn't pretty ... Following a bumper crop of spectral thrillers (*The Sixth Sense*, *The Haunting*, *House On Haunted Hill*), *Stir of Echoes* supplies so much more by delivering less. With a simple premise – derived from Richard Matheson's novel of 1958 – the film jumps straight into the action aided by sharply drawn characters placed in a realistic setting. And with the intrusion of urban noise adding to the unease (the rumble of the subway, the roar of overhead aircraft), director Koepp summons up gooseflesh with the simplest of devices. Of course, a good story always goes a long way, particularly one that's not reliant on a solitary gimmick.

● *Tom Witzky* Kevin Bacon, *Maggie Witzky* Kathryn Erbe, *Jake Witzky* Zachary David Cope, *Lisa* Illeana Douglas, *Frank McCarthy* Kevin Dunn, *Harry Damon* Conor O'Farrell, *Debbie Kozac* Liza Weil, *Samantha Kozak* Jennifer Morrison, *Kurt* Steve Rifkin, *Adam Kozak* Chalon Williams, *Neil, the cop* Eddie Bo Smith Jr., Lusia Strus, Stephen Eugene Walker, Mary Kay Cook, Lisa Lewis.
● *Dir* and *Screenplay* David Koepp, *Pro* Gavin Polone and Judy Hofflund, *Ex Pro* Michele Weisler, *Ph* Fred Murphy, *Pro Des* Nelson Coates, *Ed* Jill Savvitt, *M* James Newton Howard; songs performed by Steve Wynn, Moist, Wild Strawberries, Dishwalla, SuperSkank, Gob, Beth Orton, Poe, etc, *Costumes* Leesa Evans, *Sound* Martin Maryska.

Artisan Entertainment-Fox.
99 mins. USA. 1999. Rel: 26 May 2000. Cert 15.

The Story of Us ★★★¹/₂

Los Angeles/Venice; 1982-1999. There comes a point in many marriages – *most* marriages – when the magic dries up and the silences become unbreakable. Ben Jordan, a TV scriptwriter, and Katie Jordan, a crossword compiler, have been married 15 years and can no longer stand each other. The smallest thing sets them off and if it weren't for their two children they would have divorced years ago ... An unusual film in that it deals with the convolutions of hanging on to a disintegrating marriage, *The Story of Us* hits enough real notes to make for compelling viewing. And, once one has got over the shock of Bruce Willis

and Michelle Pfeiffer playing a married couple, there is substantial emotional meat to chew over. The problem is that Willis seems out of his depth here – even while playing the more sympathetic spouse – but on the other hand, Pfeiffer, in a difficult, under-written role, ends the film on a sensational note of sustained emotion.

● *Ben Jordan* Bruce Willis, *Katie Jordan* Michelle Pfeiffer, *Marty* Tim Matheson, *Stan* Rob Reiner, *Rachel* Rita Wilson, *Dave* Paul Reiser, *Liza* Julie Hagerty, *Erin at 10* Colleen Rennison, *Josh at 12* Jake Sandvig, *Dot* Jayne Meadows, *Andy Kirby* Bill Kirchenbauer, *Joanie Kirby* Lucy Webb, Tom Poston, Betty White, Red Buttons, Adam Zweibel, Alan Zweibel, Jessie Nelson, Jordan Lund, Art Evans.
● *Dir* Rob Reiner, *Pro* Reiner, Jessie Nelson and Alan Zweibel, *Ex Pro* Jeffrey Stott and Frank Capra III, *Assoc Pro* Tammy Glover, *Screenplay* Nelson and Alan Zweibel, *Ph* Michael Chapman, *Pro Des* Lilly Kilvert, *Ed* Robert Leighton and Alan Edward Bell, *M* Eric Clapton and Marc Shaiman, *Costumes* Shay Cunliffe.

Warner/Castle Rock-Warner.
96 mins. USA. 1999. Rel: 21 April 2000. Cert 15.

The Straight Story ★★★★★

Laurens, Iowa/Mount Zion, Wisconsin; 1994. Alvin Straight is a stubborn 73-year-old widower suffering from failing eyesight and the onset of emphysema. Living alone with his idiot savant daughter, he learns that his older brother – who lives 300 miles away – has had a stroke. So, determined to make amends for a falling out ten years previously, Alvin sets off to visit him on his lawnmower ... One extraordinary thing about *The Straight Story* is that a film this tender, meditative and character-driven could come out of America (albeit financed by French sources). Another extraordinary thing is that such a human, compassionate and *straightforward* film could come from David Lynch, Hollywood's resident weirdo and director of such off-the-wall projects as *Eraserhead*, *Blue Velvet* and *Twin Peaks*. But, most extraordinary of all, is Richard Farnsworth's performance, an object lesson in understatement in which his expressive eyes speak more in a single look than most actors can convey in a 12-page soliloquy. But then everybody in this outstanding film is first-rate, from Sissy Spacek as Straight's emotionally damaged daughter to the hysterical motorist who's killed 13 deer in seven weeks. In short, this is an authentic masterpiece of humanist cinema that ought to be required viewing for repeat offenders. Based on a true story.

● *Alvin Straight* Richard Farnsworth, *Rose Straight* Sissy Spacek, *Lyle Straight* Harry Dean Stanton, *Tom, the John Deere dealer* Everett McGill, *Thorvald Olsen* John Farley, *Harald Olsen* Kevin Farley, *Dorothy* Jane Galloway Heitz, *Bud* Joseph A. Carpenter, *Brenda* Jennifer Edwards-Hughes, Donald Wiegert, Tracey Maloney, Dan Flannery, Jack Walsh, Anastasia Webb, *deer woman*

Springfield, Faithless, Nusrat Fateh Ali Khan, etc, *Costumes* Emily Seresin, *Sound* Craig Carter.

Australian Film Finance Corp/Premium Movie Partnership/ Showtime Australia & the New South Wales Film & TV Office-Redbus.
96 mins. Australia. 1999. Rel: 21 January 2000. Cert 15.

Such a Long Journey ★★★★

Bombay; 1971. Sooni Taraporevala, who wrote *Salaam Bombay!*, has adapted Rohinton Mistry's tragi-comic novel for an Indian cast performing in English. With a humble bank clerk (Seth) at the centre, the film studies not only relationships within a family where the son feels at odds with his father but a wide social and political spectrum. The latter is linked to an old friend of the father's who seeks his help when working on behalf of freedom fighters in Bangladesh. By the end, government corruption has become a major theme, but no less important is the way in which events cause the father to grow in understanding and humanity. The blend of absurdity and pathos is more familiar in literature, but this atmospheric film carries you with it. [*Mansel Stimpson*]

● *Gustad Noble* Roshan Seth, *Dilnavaz Noble* Soni Razdan, *Ghulam* Om Puri, *Major Jimmy Bilimoria* Naseeruddin Shah, *the pavement artist* Ranjit Chowdhry, *Dinshawji* Sam Dastor, Kurush Deboo, Vrajesh Hirjee, Pearl Padamsee, Shazneen Damania, Kurush Dastur.
● *Dir* Sturla Gunnarsson, *Pro* Paul Stephens and Simon MacCorkindale, *Ex Pro* Victor Solnicki, *Screenplay* Sooni Taraporevala, from the novel by Rohinton Mistry, *Ph* Jan Kiesser, *Pro Des* Nitin Desai, *Ed* Jeff Warren, *M* Jonathan Goldsmith; songs performed by Lata Mangeshkar, *Costumes* Lovleen Bains.

Film Works/Amy International/Telefilm Canada/British Screen/BskyB, etc-Optimum Releasing.
113 mins. Canada/UK. 1998. Rel: 15 October 1999. Cert 15.

Summer of Sam ★★

The summer of 1977; New York City. In an Italian-American neighbourhood of the Big Apple, a group of friends – an adulterous hairdresser, his meek waitress wife, a punk rocker with a mysterious secret life – start to crack under the uncommon heat. But more unsettling still is the media-fuelled hysteria surrounding the random killings of an unknown gunman calling himself the Son of Sam. As the bodycount rises, so does the prejudiced suspicion of the locals ... Echoing the introductory words of the real Jimmy Breslin, *Summer of Sam* is a love-hate valentine to New York. Focusing on one of the most dramatic periods in the city's history – a summer that saw a record-breaking heat wave, a legendary blackout, devastating riots and, of course, the reign of terror perpetrated by David Berkowitz – director Spike Lee has created another

Above: Propping up the bar in the disappointing Strange Planet *(from Redbus)*

Barbara Robertson, Sally Wingert, *priest* John Lordan.
● *Dir and Sound* David Lynch, *Pro* Alain Sarde, Mary Sweeney and Neal Edelstein, *Assoc Pro* Pierre Edelman and Michael Polaire, *Screenplay* John Roach and Mary Sweeney, *Ph* Freddie Francis, *Pro Des* Jack Fisk, *Ed* Mary Sweeney, *M* Angelo Badalamenti, *Costumes* Patricia Norris.

Alain Sarde/Canal Plus/Film Four/Picture Factory-Film Four.
111 mins. USA/France/UK. 1999. Rel: 3 December 1999. Cert U.

Strange Planet ★★

With her debut feature *Love and Other Catastrophes* Australia's Emma-Kate Croghan brought energy and freshness to a comedy-drama about adolescent students. She captured too that elusive balance between material designed to get laughs and realism sufficient to make you care about the characters. This second outing retains some of the vitality, but only initially: this tale of three Sydney girls and their boyfriends takes on all the bland forgettability of TV fodder, and does so long before we reach the end of the year in their lives traced by the movie. The pleasing young actresses outshine the young actors, but can't really do much with this material (some of the plot details are downright silly). As for Hugo Weaving, he is totally wasted as a womanising TV producer. Disappointing. [*Mansel Stimpson*]

● *Judy Robinson* Claudia Karvan, *Alice* Naomi Watts, *Sally* Alice Garner, *Ewan* Tom Long, *Joel* Aaron Jeffrey, *Neil* Felix Williamson, *Steven Schumacher* Hugo Weaving, Rebecca Frith, Marshall Napier, Leone Carmen.
● *Dir* Emma-Kate Croghan, *Pro* Stavros Kazantzidis and Anastasia Sideris, *Ex Pro* Bruno Charlesworth, *Line Pro* Maggie Lake, *Screenplay* Kazantzidis and Croghan, *Ph* Justin Brickle, *Pro Des* Annie Beauchamp, *Ed* Ken Sallows, *M* songs performed by Future Funk, Waldo Fabian, Swirl, Dusty

vivid, atmospheric and colourful cinematic document. It is also overlong, heavy-handed, abrasive and ugly and something of an endurance test, in spite of fine performances from the three leads – Leguizamo, Brody and Sorvino.

● *Vinny* John Leguizamo, *Ritchie* Adrien Brody, *Dionna* Mira Sorvino, *Ruby* Jennifer Esposito, *Detective Lou Petrocelli* Anthony LaPaglia, *Joey T* Michael Rispoli, *Gloria* Bebe Neuwirth, *Helen* Patti LuPone, *Eddie* Mike Starr, *Luigi* Ben Gazzara, *Jimmy Breslin* Jimmy Breslin, *David Berkowitz* Michael Badalucco, *John Jeffries* Spike Lee, *Midnight* Michael Imperioli, *voice of Harvey the Black Dog* John Turturro, Saverio Guerra, Brian Tarantino, Al Palagonia, Ken Garito, Roger Guenveur Smith, Joe Lisi, James Reno, John Savage, Peter Maloney, Reggie Jackson, Bill Raymond, Michael Sorvino, Joie Lee, Susan Batson, Evander Holyfield.
● *Dir* Spike Lee, *Pro* Spike Lee and Jon Kilik, *Ex Pro* Michael Imperioli and Jeri Carroll-Colicchio, *Screenplay* Spike Lee, Victor Colicchio and Michael Imperioli, *Ph* Ellen Kuras, *Pro Des* Thérèse DePrez, *Ed* Barry Alexander Brown, *M* Terence Blanchard; songs performed by The Who, ABBA, Heatwave, Machine, First Choice, Elvin Bishop, Roy Ayers, Mike Starr, Talking Heads, War, Chic, Elton John and Kiki Dee, The Emotions, Adrien Brody and Jennifer Esposito, Grace Jones, Marvin Gaye, Barry White, Peter Brown, Thelma Houston, Frank Sinatra, etc, *Costumes* Ruith E. Carter, *Sound* Blake Leyh.

Touchstone Pictures/Forty Acres and a Mule Filmworks-Downtown.
142 mins. USA. 1999. Rel: 14 January 2000. Cert 18.

Sunshine ★★★★
Visually ravishing and of epic proportions (it lasts three hours), István Szabó's take on Hungarian history since the 1860s is not subtitled art house fare like the distinguished 'Diary' films of Márta Mészáros. Instead, while fully confronting historical events (the First World War, the Holocaust, the anti-Communist rising of 1956), his film plays like a foreign *Forsyte Saga* as the story of three generations of a Jewish family, made in English for an audience who will appreciate Ralph Fiennes portraying three characters, one in each generation. Central to the film's concern for individual freedom is the family name of Sonnenschein (Sunshine), dropped under pressure in the earlier part of the story but proudly re-adopted at the close. The novelettish treatment of the love affairs supplied for each role taken by Fiennes is a mistake. But it's still an absorbing tale, aided by distinguished performances from such players as Rosemary Harris, David De Keyser and John Neville. [Mansel Stimpson]

● *Ignatz Sonnenschein/Adam Sors/Ivan Sors* Ralph Fiennes, *older Valerie Sors* Rosemary Harris, *Greta Sors* Rachel Weisz, *young Valerie Sors* Jennifer Ehle, *Hannah Wippler* Molly Parker, *Major Carola Kovacs* Debrah Kara Unger, *young Gustave Sors* James Frain, *older Gustave Sors* John Neville, *Andor Knorr* William Hurt, *Rose Sonnenschein* Miriam Margolyes, *Emmanuel Sonnenschein* David De Keyser, *Istvan Sors* Mark Strong, *General Jakofalvy* Rüdiger Vogler, Bill Paterson, Trevor Peacock, Hanns Zischler, Frederick Treves, Gábor Mádi Szábó, Israel Horovitz.
● *Dir* István Szabó, *Pro* Robert Lantos and András Hamori, *Ex Pro* Rainer Kölmel and Jonathan Debin, *Co-Pro* Danny Krausz and Lajos Óvári, *Screenplay* Szabo and Israel Horovitz, *Ph* Lajos Koltai, *Ed* Michel Arcand and Dominique Fortin, *Pro Des* Attila F. Kovács, *M* Maurice Jarre, *Costumes* Györgyi Szakács.

Alliance Atlantis/Serendipity Point Films/Kinowelt/Film Four/Bavarian Film /Eurimages/Telefilm Canada, etc-Alliance Atlantis.
180 mins. Hungary/Germany/Canada/Austria/UK. 1999. Rel: 28 April 2000. Cert 15.

Supernova ★★★
In the early part of the 22nd century the crew of the medical spaceship Nightingale 229 are called out on a routine rescue mission. But no sooner have they pulled out of their dimensional spin than they find themselves in the path of an active supernova. With their fuel supply reduced by 82 percent, they have the added problem of coping with an ominous stranger and a multi-dimensional artefact that may just be an alien toy or something entirely more sinister ... Bearing the scars of post-production meddling, *Supernova* has lost its emotional meat but is still a gripping sci-fi thriller with a number of neat twists on an old genre. Flushed with sexy jargon and concepts (dig those dimensional stabilisation chambers), the film makes up in thrills what it lacks in character development. FYI: Director Walter Hill was so appalled by MGM's interference that he removed his name from the credits (allegedly, Francis Ford Coppola was called in to trim the material to a lean 90 minutes).

● *Nick Vanzant* James Spader, *Kaela Evers* Angela Bassett, *A.J. Marley* Robert Forster, *Yerzy Penalosa* Lou Diamond Phillips, *Karl Larson* Peter Facinelli, *Danika Lund* Robin Tunney, *Benj Sotomejor* Wilson Cruz, *voice of Sweetie* Vanessa Marshall.
● *Dir* Thomas Lee (aka Walter Hill), *Pro* Ash R. Shah, Daniel Chuba and Jamie Dixon, *Ex Pro* Ralph S. Singleton, *Screenplay* David Campbell Wilson, from a story by William Malone and Daniel Chuba, *Ph* Lloyd Ahern, *Pro Des* Marek Dobrowolski, *Ed* Michael Schweitzer and Melissa Kent, *M* David Williams, *Costumes* Bob Ringwood, *Visual effects* Mark Steson.

MGM/Screenland Pictures/Hammerhead-UIP.
90 mins. USA. 1999. Rel: 16 June 2000. Cert 15.

Above: Sean Penn (right) as Emmet Ray, in a performance that secured him an Oscar nomination – in Woody Allen's sweet and funny Sweet and Lowdown *(from Columbia TriStar)*

Cephas Jones, Carolyn Saxon, Molly Price, Denis O'Hare, Katie Hamill, Kaili Vernoff, William Addy, Jerome Richardson, Brad Garrett, and (*as themselves*): Woody Allen, Ben Duncan, Nat Hentoff, Douglas McGrath.
● *Dir* and *Screenplay* Woody Allen, *Pro* Jean Doumanian, *Ex Pro* J.E. Beaucaire, *Co-Pro* Richard Brick, *Co-Ex Pro* Jack Rollins, Charles H. Joffe and Letty Aronson, *Ph* Zhao Fei, *Pro Des* Santo Loquasto, *Ed* Alisa Lepselter, *M* Dick Hyman; guitar played by Howard Alden, *Costumes* Laura Cunningham Bauer.

Sony Pictures Classics/Sweetalnd Films-Columbia TriStar. 95 mins. USA. 1999. Rel: 9 June 2000. Cert PG.

Sweet and Lowdown ★★★

New York/Chicago/Hollywood; the 1930s. Much like *The Blair Witch Project*, Woody Allen's affectionate trifle if a *faux* docudrama, a step up from the over-exploited genre of the mockumentary. Here, Woody and other jazz experts proffer anecdotes on the legendary American guitarist Emmet Ray, a sort of amalgam of all the greats – which says a lot for legendary jazz guitarists. Emmet – played with a fixed weaselly grin by Sean Penn – certainly believes that he is the best (except, as he repeatedly confesses, for Django Reinhardt, 'that gypsy in France'). He is also a pimp, gambler, alcoholic, kleptomaniac and womaniser, although his habit of taking his dates trainspotting scores him few points. The result is a sweet and funny – if slight – film, perked up by a poignant performance from Samantha Morton as a melancholy mute and, needless to say, some splendid guitar music. A highlight is three conflicting stories recounting Emmet's discovery of his wife's adultery, an event that sees him a) abducted by highwaymen, b) nervously confronting the adulterous couple with a gun and c) taking off in his rival's car and crashing headlong into Django Reinhardt.

● *Al Torrio* Anthony LaPaglia, *Ellie* Gretchen Mol, *Hattie* Samantha Morton, *Emmet Ray* Sean Penn, *Blanche* Uma Thurman, *Harry* James Urbaniak, *Bill Shields* Brian Markinson, *Mr Haynes* John Waters, *Sid Bishop* Vincent Guastaferro, Tony Darrow, Constance Shulman, Kellie Overbey, Darryl Alan Reed, Marc Damon Johnson, Ron

Sweet Angel Mine ★★

Bombing round Nova Scotia on his motorbike to locate his long-lost father, London welfare worker Paul rests up at a remote stretch of coastline. There, he encounters a timid girl in the woods and is immediately drawn by her reticent, maidenly manner. It transpires that she lives alone with her mother, a striking woman in early middle-age with a major attitude problem. For the arrogantly self-assured stranger, the pair of them prove too much of a challenge to resist ... Borrowing liberally from the original *Psycho* and any number of backwoods chillers, this chilling psychological thriller offers fertile dramatic material. The premise itself – based on Tim Willocks' screenplay *Love's Executioner* – is an intriguing one, but first-time director Curtis Radclyffe cannot breath real life into it. For all the photographic richness of the setting, the actors appear to be reading their lines and sleepwalking through the motions of a sick nightmare. Odd, too, that Anna Massey (who is awful, by the way) should take an identical role to the one she played in the surprisingly similar *Driftwood* made the same year.

● *Paul Davis* Oliver Milburn, *Rauchine* Margaret Langrick, *Mother* Anna Massey, *Megan* Alberta Watson, *Billy Lee Davis* John Dunsworth, *Sergeant Taylor* Mike Crimp, Joel Sapp, John Fulton, Marguerite MacNeil.
● *Dir* Curtis Radclyffe, *Pro* Sam Taylor and Christopher Zimmer, *Ex Pro* Gareth Jones, *Assoc Pro* David Redman and Gilles Belanger, *Screenplay* Sue Maheu and Tim Willocks, *Ph* Witold Stok, *Pro Des* Maria Djurkovic, *Ed* Anne Sopel, *M* John McCarthy and Daniel Lanois, *Costumes* Ann Taylor, *Sound* Jim Rillie.

HandMade Films/British Screen/Telefilm Canada/Nova Scotia Development Corporation/State Screen Prods/Picture Palace, etc-Optimum Releasing. 88 mins. UK/Canada. 1996. Rel: 17 September 1999. Cert 18.

The Talented Mr Ripley ★★¹/₂

New York/Italy; 1959. In Tom Ripley's mind it is better to be a fake somebody than a real nobody. So when he is mistaken for a graduate of Princeton, the talented impersonator and forger accepts the $1,000 offered him by the shipping magnate Herbert Greenleaf. The latter asks Ripley to go to Italy to find his son Dickie and bring him back. But after Ripley samples the lifestyle of Greenleaf's dilettante heir, he decides to become Dickie himself ... A sumptuous production if ever there was one, with glorious shots of Venice, Naples, Rome and Jude Law's bronzed torso, Anthony Minghella's first film since *The English Patient* is a classic case of style overwhelming content. Displaying little variation in dramatic tone, the film glides from one instant to the next, coating – and embalming – its protagonists in an admiring gloss. Even at the half-way mark, when Ripley finally reveals his true colours, Gabriel Yared's gushing score makes no concessions to the fact. And why did Gwyneth Paltrow and Cate Blanchett take such thankless parts? Previously filmed in 1960 as *Plein Soleil* (at a more appetising running time of 119 minutes).

● *Tom Ripley* Matt Damon, *Marge Sherwood* Gwyneth Paltrow, *Dickie Greenleaf* Jude Law, *Meredith Logue* Cate Blanchett, *Freddie Miles* Philip Seymour Hoffman, *Peter Smith-Kingsley* Jack Davenport, *Herbert Greenleaf* James Rebhorn, *Inspector Roverini* Sergio Rubini, *Alvin MacCarron* Philip Baker Hall, *Aunt Joan* Celia Weston, *Silvana* Stefania Rocca, Rosario Fiorello, Ivano Marescotti, Anna Longhi, Lisa Eichhorn, Larry Kaplan, Roberto Valentini.

● *Dir and Screenplay* Anthony Minghella, from the novel by Patricia Highsmith, *Pro* William Horberg and Tom Sternberg, *Ex Pro* Sydney Pollack, *Co-Pro* Paul Zaentz, *Ph* John Seale, *Pro Des* Roy Walker, *Ed* Walter Murch, *M* Gabriel Yared; Beethoven, J.S. Bach, Tchaikovsky, Vivaldi; songs performed by Sinead O'Connor, Dizzy Gillespie, Charlie Parker, Matt Damon, Chet Baker, Jude Law, Miles Davis, Sonny Rollins, Bing Crosby, The Guy Barker International Quintet, The Mancuso Brothers, John Martyn, etc, *Costumes* Ann Roth and Gary Jones.

Paramount/Miramax/Mirage Enterprises/Timnick Films-Buena Vista.
139 mins. USA. 1999. Rel: 25 February 2000. Cert 15.

Tango ★★★★

Spurned by his wife, a film director attempts to overcome his grief by making a film about tango. He casts the young mistress of the film's main investor in the lead and finds himself dancing to another tune as the film starts to dangerously reflect his own life. With original music by Lalo Schifrin and directed breathtakingly close to the edge by Carlos Saura, this visually intoxicating musical with its slim plot and exciting characters is rich and sensual. A Spanish-Argentinian co-production that was Oscar nominated as Best Foreign Film in 1998, it moves far beyond the dance movie genre. [*Marianne Gray*]

● *Mario Suárez* Miguel Angel Solá, *Elena Flores* Mia Maestro, *Laura Fuentes* Cecilia Narova,

Above: The slow burn – Gwyneth Paltrow and Jude Law take some sun in Anthony Minghella's glossy and monotonous The Talented Mr Ripley (from Buena Vista)

Norberto Nebbia Juan Carlos Copes, *Ernesto Landi* Carlos Rivarola, Julio Bocca, Juan Luis Gagliardo, Enrique Pinti.
● *Dir and Screenplay* Carlos Saura, *Pro* Luis A. Scalella, Carlos A. Mentasti and Juan C. Codazzi, *Ex Pro* Carlos Rizzuti, *Co-Pro* José M. Calleja and Alejandro Bellaba, *Ph* Vittorio Storaro, *Pro Des* Emilio Basaldúa, *Ed* Julia Juaniz, *M* Lalo Schifrin, *Costumes* Beatriz Di Benedetto, *Choreographers* Juan Carlos Copes, Ana Mario Steckleman and Carlos Rivarola.

Pandora Cinema/Argentina Sono Film/Alma Ata International/Hollywood Partners, etc- Metrodome.
115 mins. Spain/Argentina/France/Germany. 1998. Rel: 9 July 1999. Cert 12.

Tarzan ★★★★

Old stories don't die, they just get animated by Disney. Here, the loin-clothed ape man of Edgar Rice Burroughs' classic 1914 novel is reinvented for the 1990s, given a whole new set of muscles (and a chin shaped like a spatula) and a heroine who steals the show. With spectacular use made of an other-worldly rainforest (like the set for some fantastic rollercoaster ride), five songs from Phil Collins and a colourful menagerie of talking animals (recalling *The Jungle Book*), this is entertainment writ large. Funny, touching and breathtaking, the film hits its marks with dynamism. Yet it's the little things one remembers: a butterfly perched on the young Tarzan's nose (its spotted wings replicating the boy's wide eyes), Jane's scream as the adult Tarzan explores the unfamiliarity of her body and a gaggle of elephants discussing the geographic location of piranhas. P.S. After Sherlock Holmes, Frankenstein's Creature and Count Dracula, Tarzan is the most frequently filmed character from literary fiction.

● Voices: *Tarzan* Tony Goldwyn, *Kala* Glenn Close, *Jane* Minnie Driver, *Terk* Rosie O'Donnell, *Professor Porter* Nigel Hawthorne, *Clayton* Brian Blessed, *Kerchak* Lance Henriksen, *Tantor* Wayne Knight, *young Tarzan* Alex D. Linz, *young Tantor* Taylor Dempsey.
● *Dir* Kevin Lima and Chris Buck, *Pro* Bonnie Arnold, *Assoc Pro* Christopher Chase, *Screenplay* Tab Murphy and Bob Tzudiker & Noni White, *Art* Daniel St Pierre, *Ed* Gregory Perler, *M* Mark Mancina; songs by Phil Collins, *Computer graphics* Eric Daniels.

Walt Disney-Buena Vista.
88 mins. USA. 1999. Rel: 8 October 1999. Cert U.

Taxi ★★¹/₂

Marseilles, France; today. Pulled in by the police for speeding, rookie taxi driver Daniel Morales is cut a deal: he can retain his driving licence if he helps the cops track down a gang of speeding bank robbers…

First and foremost Luc Besson is an entertainer. So, should his name be attached to a modest slice of escapism like this, the more fashionable critics will flaunt his participation like a banner. But, dare he mess with history – à la *Joan of Arc* (qv) – he is branded a crass, insensitive philistine (as if nobody had ever fine-tuned the dramatic potential of real events). Be that as it may, *Taxi* – which Besson merely scripted – is a rip-roaring, slapstick vehicular trip that is admirable for its unpretentious sense of pretension (don't miss those opening credits to see what I mean). This is snap, crackle and pop entertainment writ large, the cinematic equivalent of a TV dinner. But, like Chinese take-away, while it seduces the taste buds, it leaves one begging for more. Incidentally, there were no less than 110 vehicles used for the film's chase scenes, while director Pirès' previous credits include a stint as a racing driver. [*Charles Bacon*]

● *Daniel Morales* Samy Nacéri, *Emilien Coutan Kermadec* Frédéric Diefenthal, *Lilly* Marion Cotillard, *Petra* Emma Sjöberg, *Camille* Manuela Gourary, *Chief Inspector Gibert* Bernard Farcy, Edouard Montoute, Dan Herzberg, Grégory Knop.
● *Dir* Gérard Pirès, *Pro* Michèle & Laurent Pétin, *Screenplay* Luc Besson, *Ph* Jean-Pierre Sauvaire, *Pro Des* Jean-Jacques Gernolle, *Ed* Véronique Lange, *M* IAM, *Costumes* Chattoune.

Luc Besson/TF1 Films/Canal Plus/Cofimage 9 & Studio Images 4-Metrodome.
90 mins. France. 1998. Rel: 26 November 1999. Cert 15.

10 Things I Hate About You ★★★

Seattle; the present. Panicked by his daughters' burgeoning sexuality, obstetrician and single parent Walter Stratford bans his younger child, Bianca, from dating until her older sister is asked out first. As the latter, Katarina, is a prima donna with an ugly attitude, Bianca is destined for a life of solitude. So, in order to woo the former's sister, Joey Donner bribes the school troublemaker to win over Katarina … Fair or not, most high school comedies these days are probably judged by the standard set by *Clueless*. And where that film took its inspiration from Jane Austen's *Emma*, so *10 Things …* takes it cue from *The Taming of the Shrew*. Of course, times have changed dramatically since Shakespeare wrote his farce of the sexes back in 1593 and, wisely, the writers here have circumvented the sexist nature of the original. And so, as in *Clueless*, the heroine is a spunky outsider at odds with her own emotions and sexuality. The film is blessed by a sexy, subtly comic turn from Julia Stiles as the shrewish, rebellious Katarina, but no less by an enthusiastic and creditable supporting cast. Larry Miller, as Katarina's discombobulated father, gains considerable comic mileage, as does Allison Janney as an oversexed school psychologist. The story does get a

bit cheesy by the end, but some sharp dialogue and the mandatory quota of rock music camouflage any real weaknesses.

● *Patrick Verona* Heath Ledger, *Katarina Stratford* Julia Stiles, *Cameron James* Joseph-Gordon Levitt, *Bianca Stratford* Larisa Oleynik, *Michael Eckman* David Krumholtz, *Joey Donner* Andrew Keegan, *Mandella* Susan May Pratt, *Chastity* Gabrielle Union, *Walter Stratford* Larry Miller, *Mr Morgan* Daryl 'Chill' Mitchell, *Ms Perky* Allison Janney, *Mr Chapin* David Leisure, Greg Jackson, Kyle Cease, Terence Heuston.
● *Dir* Gil Junger, *Pro* Andrew Lazar, *Ex Pro* Jeffrey Chernov and Seth Jaret, *Co-Pro* Jody Hedien, *Screenplay* Karen McCullah Lutz and Kirsten Smith, *Ph* Mark Irwin, *Pro Des* Carol Winstead Wood, *Ed* O. Nicholas Brown, *M* Richard Gibbs; Chopin; songs performed by Barenaked Ladies, Joan Jett, Air, Ralph Sall, Brick, Cameo, Leroy, Letters To Cleo, George Clinton, Salt 'N' Pepa, The SOS Band, The Notorious B.I.G., The Thompson Twins, The Cardigans, Madness, Joan Armatrading, Semisonic, Sister Hazel, Save Ferris, Jessica Riddle, etc, *Costumes* Kimberly A. Tillman.

Touchstone/Mad Chance/Jaret Entertainment-Buena Vista. 98 mins. USA. 1999. Rel: 9 July 1999. Cert 12.

The Theory Of Flight ★★¹/₂

After jumping off a City building wearing wings (which he had constructed himself), Richard, an artist, is compelled to do community service. Renting a barn, he builds a biplane he hopes to fly and becomes helper to Jane, a sarcastic motor neurone sufferer. After initial problems, Jane and Richard become friends but as her condition deteriorates, she makes a difficult demand. Before it's too late, she wants to know what it is like to have sex… Although this could have been terribly sentimental, a constant vein of humour keeps the syrup at bay so that, although occasionally sad and touching, there are also plenty of laughs. The metaphors about flight are a bit heavy-handed at times but this is a very sweet, albeit modest, film. It may sit more happily on TV than on the big screen, but you should try to catch it at some time. [*Simon Rose*]

● *Jane Hatchard* Helena Bonham Carter, *Richard* Kenneth Branagh, *Anne* Gemma Jones, *Julie* Holly Aird, *gigolo* Ray Stevenson, *Catherine* Sue Jones Davies, Gwenyth Petty, Robert Blythe, Aneirin Hughes.
● *Dir* Paul Greengrass, *Pro* David M. Thompson, Ruth Caleb, Anant Singh and Helena Spring, *Line Pro* Shân Davies, *Screenplay* Richard Hawkins, *Ph* Ivan Strasburg, *Pro Des* Melanie Allen, *Ed* Mark Day, *M* Rolfe Kent; Chopin; songs performed by Archive, Van Morrison, Clarence Carter, John Hiatt, Booker T and the MGs, The Specials, etc, *Costumes* Dinah Collin, *Sound* Nicky De Beer.

Distant Horizon/BBC Films-Buena Vista. 100 mins. South Africa/UK. 1998. Rel: 24 September 1999. Cert 15.

Above: Wings of their love – Kenneth Branagh and Helena Bonham Carter in Paul Greengrass's funny, sad and touching The Theory of Flight (from Buena Vista)

Third World Cop ★★½

Kingston, Jamaica; today. Friends since childhood, Capone and Ratty are reunited when the former is transferred to his old hunting ground as a cop. However, Ratty has taken to a life of crime, so the friends' loyalty comes in for a bit of turbulence… Emulating the weighty shoot-up quotient of John Woo's Hong Kong crime thrillers, *Third World Cop* is neither frightfully original nor very polished. But thanks to a surplus of energy and a rocking reggae and dancehall soundtrack from Sly & Robbie – not to mention its exotic setting – the film gets by as a relatively diverting slice of slam-bang entertainment. Indeed, it broke box-office records in its native Jamaica. [*Ewen Brownrigg*]

● *Capone* Paul Campbell, *Ratty* Mark Danvers, *One Hand* Carl Bradshaw, *Rita* Audrey Reid, *Floyd* Winston Bell, *Not Nice* Lenford Salmon, Desmond Ballentine aka Ninja Man, O'Neil 'Elephant Man' Bryan, Winsome Wilson, Natalie Thompson, Clive Anderson, Robbie Shakespeare, Buccaneer.
● *Dir* Chris Browne, *Pro* Carolyn Pfeiffer Bradshaw, *Ex Pro* Chris Blackwell and Dan Genetti, *Line Pro* Natalie Thompson, *Screenplay* Suzanne Fenn, Chris Browne and Chris Salewicz, *Ph* and *Pro Des* Richard Lannaman, *Ed* Suzanne Fenn, *M* Wally Badarou and Sly & Robbie; songs performed by Sly & Robbie, Beenie Man, Red Dragon, Innocent Crew, Luciano, Lady G, Buccaneer, etc, *Costumes* Michelle Haynes.

Palm Pictures/Hawk's Nest Prods-Optimum Releasing. 98 mins. Jamaica. 1999. Rel: 24 March 2000. Cert 15.

The 13th Warrior ★★½

The North lands; AD 922. Banished from his homeland, Arab emissary Ahmad Ibn Fadlan falls in with a ragbag of warrior Vikings. Worse, he is selected to join twelve of their finest to help protect a township besieged by an army of bear-like, cannibalistic creatures … With the directorial skill of John McTiernan (*Die Hard*, *The Hunt for Red October*), the imagination of Michael Crichton (*Westworld*, *Jurassic Park*) and a reputed budget of $140 million, this was an opportunity to realise the ultimate Norse adventure. But from the bungled opening (in which reams of extraneous exposition is lost in the credits) to the uninspired fight choreography, this sombre, plodding epic is a resounding disappointment. This could have and should have been a rousing blend of *Seven Samurai* and *Braveheart* with a dash of *Conan the Barbarian*. Instead we have *Ravenous* without the glint in its eye. Pillage alone is not enough. A good Norse epic needs romance and a villain to kill for. *The 13th Warrior* has neither.

● *Ahmad Ibn Fadlan* Antonio Banderas, *Queen Weilew* Diane Venora, *Melchisidek* Omar Sharif, *Herger*

the Joyous Dennis Storhoi, *Buliwyf* Vladimir Kulich, *Wigliff, King Hrothgar's son* Anders T. Andersen, *Skeld the Superstitious* Richard Bremmer, *Weath the Musician* Tony Curran, *Rethel the Archer* Mischa Hausserman, *Roneth the Horseman* Neil Maffin, *Halga the Wise* Asbjorn Riis, *Helfdane the Large* Clive Russell, *King Hrothgar* Sven Wollter, *Olga* Maria Bonnevie, Daniel Southern, Oliver Sveinall, Albie Woodington, John DeSantis, Suzanne Bertish, Sven-Ole Thorsen.
● *Dir and Screenplay* John McTiernan, *Pro* McTiernan, Michael Crichton and Ned Dowd, *Ex Pro* Andrew G. Vajna and Ethan Dubrow, *Co-Pro* Lou Arkoff, *Screenplay* William Wisher and Warren Lewis, *Ph* Peter Menzies, *Pro Des* Wolf Kroeger, *Ed* John Wright, *M* Jerry Goldsmith, *Costumes* Kate Harrington, *Sound* Chris Boyes, *Visual effects* John Sullivan.

Touchstone Pictures-Buena Vista. 103 mins. USA. 1999. Rel: 3 September 1999. Cert 15.

The Thomas Crown Affair ★★★½

New York City; the present. Educated at Oxford and blessed with a razor-sharp mind and dashing good looks, top financier and womaniser Thomas Crown is a man who has found life all too easy. And so, risking both his reputation as a benefactor and his considerable fortune, he plots the audacious robbery of Monet's seminal, $100 million painting *San Giorgio Maggiore at Twilight* – just for the hell of it. But no sooner has he pulled off the theft (without a hitch) than insurance investigator Catherine Banning moves in for the kill. Sharing Crown's highly developed intellect and his passion for high stakes, she may be the first woman to put Crown in his place … A slick remake of the classic 1968 crime caper which starred Steve McQueen and Faye Dunaway, this is escapism with a pedigree. With Alan R. Trustman's original story refined and updated for the 1990s, the plot's irresistible recipe of like minds locked in intellectuial and sexual combat still carries a terrific punch. And while Brosnan and Russo may not pull off the cool chemistry of McQueen and Dunaway, they certainly look the part. P.S. Perhaps wisely, director McTiernan (who first worked with Brosnan on the 1986 film *Nomads*) elects not to reproduce the first film's legendary chess-as-foreplay sequence.

● *Thomas Crown* Pierce Brosnan, *Catherine Banning* Rene Russo, *Det. Michael McCann* Denis Leary, *Andrew Wallace* Ben Gazzara, *Det. Paretti* Frankie R. Faison, *John Reynolds* Fritz Weaver, *psychiatrist* Faye Dunaway, *Golchan* Charles Keating, *Anna Knutzhorn* Esther Canadas, Mark Margolis, Michael Lombard, James Saito.
● *Dir* John McTiernan, *Pro* Pierce Brosnan and Beau St Clair, *Ex Pro* Michael Tadross, *Co-Pro* Roger Paradiso, *Screenplay* Leslie Dixon and Kurt Wimmer, from a story by Alan R. Trustman, *Ph* Tom Priestley,

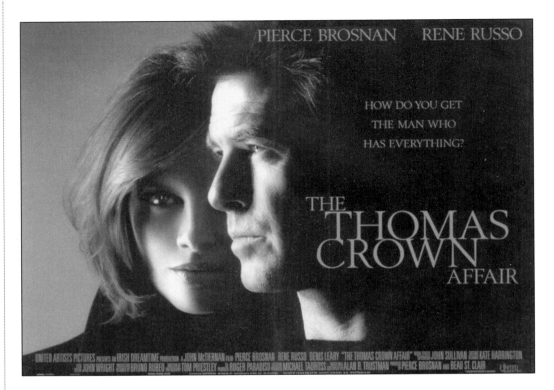

Pro Des Bruno Rubeo, *Ed* John Wright, *M* Bill Conti; songs performed by Nina Simone, Jamshied Sharifi, Kali, Wasis Diop, Sting ('The Windmills of Your Mind'), etc, *Costumes* Kate Harrington.

MGM/Irish Dreamtime-UIP.
120 mins. USA. 1999. Rel: 20 August 1999. Cert 15.

Three Kings ★★★★

Iraq; March 1991. Just as the war has ended, a mysterious map is discovered secreted in the backside of an Iraqi prisoner. Realising that the chart points to the location of gold bullion, Special Forces Captain Gates suggests that he and three others go and find the bounty for themselves. However, no sooner have they arrived at their destination than their plans are complicated by the intervention of Saddam's soldiers and Iraqi rebels ... Starting out like a Desert Sabre edition of *M*A*S*H*, then switching into *Dirty Dozen* territory, *Three Kings* ends up as a Gulf War *Deer Hunter*. Scripted by director David O. Russell (*Spanking the Monkey*, *Flirting With Disaster*) from a story by John Ridley, the film generates an extraordinary energy as the plot whips around like a liberated hose pipe. Utilising grainy, bleached-out photography (with Arizona doubling for Iraq) and featuring graphic shots of bullets penetrating human innards (filmed from *within* the body), the film is anything if not original. And its uneasy mix of black humour and brutal, sudden outbursts of violence makes for an enthralling combination of all-out action and moral excavation of America's role in foreign policy.

● *Special Forces Captain Archie Gates* George Clooney, *Sergeant Troy Barlow* Mark Wahlberg, *Chief Elgin* Ice Cube, *Conrad Vig* Spike Jonze, *Adriana Cruz* Nora Dunn, *Walter Wogaman* Jamie Kennedy, *Colonel Horn* Mykelti Williamson, *Amir Abdulah* Cliff Curtis, *Captain Said* Saïd Taghmaoui, *Captain Van Meter* Holt McCallany, *Cathy Daitch* Judy Greer, Christopher Lohr, Jon Sklaroff, Liz Stauber, Marsha Horan, Alia Shawkat, Brian Bosworth.
● *Dir and Screenplay* David O. Russell, *Pro* Charles Roven, Paul Junger Witt and Edward L. McDonnell, *Ex Pro* Kelley Smith-Wait, Gregory Goodman and Bruce Berman, *Co-Pro* Douglas Segal and Kim Roth, *Ph* Newton Thomas Sigel, *Pro Des* Catherine Hardwicke, *Ed* Robert K. Lambert, *M* Carter Burwell; J.S. Bach; songs performed by Rare Earth, The Beach Boys, Public Enemy, Chicago, Eddie Murphy, Snap, U2, etc, *Costumes* Kym Barrett.

Warner/Village Roadshow/Village -A.M. Film Partnership/ Coast Ridge Films/Atlas Entertainment-Warner.
115 mins. USA/Australia. 1999. Rel: 3 March 2000. Cert 15.

Three Seasons – Ba Mua ★★★★★

A sumptuous and elegant valentine to post-war Ho Chi Minh City, *Three Seasons* highlights the striking contrasts of this beautiful and thriving metropolis by following the lives of six of its inhabitants. Kien An is a young woman hired by a reclusive 'teacher' to pick and sell his lotus blossoms. Hai is a cyclo driver who falls for a beautiful but haughty prostitute, following her from rendezvous to rendezvous. Woody is a young street urchin who sells lighters and watches from a suitcase strapped around his neck and falls foul of his master when the case is stolen. And James Hager, a former G.I., searches doggedly for the daughter he never knew he had. Each character, in their own way, is on a quest and each finds a kind of enlightenment with the connection to another. Graceful, poignant, beautifully photographed and terribly, terribly touching, this first film from the 26-year-old Saigon-born, California-raised director Tony Bui is a masterpiece in every sense of the word. FYI: *Three Seasons* is the first feature shot in Vietnam since the war.

● *Hai* Don Duong, *Kien An* Nguyen Ngoc Hiep, *Teacher Dao* Tran Manh Cuong, *James Hager* Harvey Keitel, *Lan* Zoë Bui, *Woody* Nguyen Huu Duoc, *little girl* Thach Thi Kim Trang, Hoang Phat Trieu, Diem Kieu, Duong Tan Dung.
● *Dir and Screenplay* Tony Bui, *Pro* Jason Kliot, Joana Vicente and Tony Bui, *Ex Pro* Harvey Keitel, *Co-Ex Pro* Charles Rosen, *Co-Pro* Timothy Linh Bui, *Line Pro* Trish Hofmann, *Ph* Lisa Rinzler, *Pro Des* Wing Lee, *Ed* Keith Reamer, *M* Richard Horowitz; *Vietnamese songs* Vy Nhat Tao, *Costumes* Ghia Ci Fam.

October Films/Open City/Goatsingers/Giai Phong Film/Sundance Institute-Pathé.
108 mins. USA/Vietnam. 1998. Rel: 14 January 2000. Cert 12.

Three To Tango ★★
Oscar Novak is an architect who is pitching a multi-million dollar project to slimy businessman Charles (a sadly wasted Dylan McDermott). Charles thinks that Oscar is gay and wants him to keep an eye on his perky mistress, Amy. However, Oscar isn't gay and falls for Amy, who also thinks he's gay. The only person who is gay is Oscar's partner, Peter. But then everyone else thinks Peter is straight. Confused? You will be, if you have the energy to endure this rather queasy little comedy. Even the obvious charm of its leads fails to save it, and I am a big Neve Campbell fan. Eventually, she started to remind me of the Andrex puppy, all crinkly smiles and warm melting brown eyes. However, the film does have one thing going for it. It does for projectile vomiting what *Last Tango In Paris* did for butter. [*Barbie Wilde*]

● *Oscar Novak* Matthew Perry, *Amy Post* Neve Campbell, *Charles Newman* Dylan McDermott, *Peter Steinberg* Oliver Platt, *Kevin Cartwright* Cylk Cozart, *Strauss* John C. McGinley, *Decker* Bob Balaban, *Lenore* Deborah Rush, Kelly Rowan, Rick Gomez, Patrick Van Horn, Kent Staines.
● *Dir* Damon Santostefano, *Pro* Bobby Newmyer, Jeffrey Silver and Bettina Sofia Viviano, *Ex Pro* Lawrence B. Abramson and Bruce Berman, *Co-Pro* John M. Eckert and Keri Selig, *Screenplay* Rodney Vaccaro and Aline Brosh McKenna, *Ph* Walt Lloyd,

Pro Des David Nichols, *Ed* Stephen Semel, *M* Graeme Revell, *Costumes* Vicki Graef.

Warner Bros/Village Roadshow/Village-Hoyts Film Partnership/Outlaw Prods-Warner.
99 mins. USA. 1999. Rel: 30 June 2000. Cert 12.

The Tichborne Claimant ★★★¹⁄₂
In 1866 Sir Roger Tichborne, heir to one of England's greatest fortunes, vanished while sailing round the world. When, ten years later, reports surfaced of his whereabouts in Australia, Sir Roger's mother sent her youngest son and a manservant, Old Bogle, to find him. However, the former promptly drank himself to death and it was up to Bogle, with the help of a missing persons agency, to locate the truant heir. But on Sir Roger's return to England, his family denounced him as an impostor ... Like the similarly-themed *Sommersby* and *Anastasia*, *The Tichborne Claimant* is based on real events. But, unlike the former two, this wry and eloquent drama sticks closely to the known facts. The result is a fascinating document that slyly jockeys the viewer's expectations as it basks in the extraordinary ambiguities of its story. There are also marvellous performances, particularly from the great South African actor John Kani as the dignified Bogle, a suitably robust turn from Robert Pugh as the possible impostor and a roster of splendid cameos from the likes of Stephen Fry, John Gielgud and Paola Dionisotti. Filmed on location in Liverpool and on the Isle of Man.

● *Andrew Bogle* John Kani, *Sir Roger Charles Doughty Tichborne/Thomas Castro/Arthur Orton* Robert Pugh, *Henry Hawkins* Stephen Fry, *Lord Rivers* Robert Hardy, *Cockburn* John Gielgud, *Mary-Anne* Rachael Dowling, *Lord Arundell* Charles Gray, *Seymour* James Villiers, *Onslow* Dudley Sutton, *Gibbes* Christopher Benjamin, *Cubitt* Roger Hammond, *The Dowager* Paola Dionisotti, *Dr Kenealy* Tom McCabe, *Lady Doughty* Ursula Howells, John Challis, Chas Bryer, Anita Dobson, Roger May, Matt Wilkinson, Jenifer Henessy, Tom Harrison, Iain Cuthbertson, Fiona Carnegie, Sean Tudor-Owen, Ralph Nossek, Vladimir Vega, Clare McCabe, Max McCabe, Myles McCabe, Sara Sutcliffe.
● *Dir* David Yates, *Pro* Tom McCabe, *Assoc Pro* Christopher Payne, *Line Pro* Annie Harrison Baxter, *Screenplay* Joe Fisher, *Ph* Peter Thwaites, *Pro Des* Brian Sykes, *Ed* James Trevill, *M* Nicholas Hooper, *Costumes* Pam Downe, *Sound* Paul Davies.

Bigger Picture Company/Swiftcall International Telephone Co/The Isle of Man Film Commission-Redbus Film Dist.
98 mins. UK. 1999. Rel: 12 November 1999. Cert PG.

The Tigger Movie ★¹⁄₂
Although Tigger is very fond of his friends, they just don't share his enthusiasm – or his skill – for bouncing.

So he sets off in search of other tiggers ... Forget the fact that the folks at Disney have desecrated the memory of A.A. Milne, they have produced a charmless, uninspired and dull cartoon. Dull, that is, when the most irritating occupant of the Three Acre Wood – Tigger – isn't demolishing his friends' homes while jumping aimlessly about looking for more of the same. As Tigger would put it, 'the wonderful thing about tiggers is I'm the only one'. So let's hope that this is his only film.

● Voices: *Tigger* and *Winnie the Pooh* Jim Cummings, *Roo* Nikita Hopkins, *Rabbit* Ken Sansom, *Piglet* John Fielder, *Eeyore* Peter Cullen, *Owl* André Stojka, *Kanga* Kath Soucie, *Christopher Robin* Tom Attenborough, *Narrator* John Hurt.
● *Dir* and *Screenplay* Jun Falkenstein, from a story by Eddie Guzelian, based on characters created by A.A. Milne, *Pro* Cheryl Abood, *Assoc Pro* Jennifer Blohm, *Art* Toby Bluth, *Ed* Robert Fisher Jr., *M* Harry Gregson-Williams; *songs by* Richard M. Sherman & Robert B. Sherman, *Dir of Animation* Takamitsu Kawamura.

Walt Disney Pictures/Walt Disney Televison Animation-Buena Vista.
77 mins. USA. 2000. Rel: 14 April 2000. Cert U.

Time Regained ★★★¹/₂

As the great French writer Marcel Proust lies on his deathbed, he sifts through old photographs and lapses into a distorted remembrance of things past. So vivid were the characters that populated his life's work, he can no longer separate them from the real friends and family that he once knew ... A difficult one, this. But then if you are tackling such a Proustian work as *Remembrance of Things Past* (aka *In Search of Lost Time*), then you are going to encounter some damn tricky problems. A montage of recollections of characters, observations and dialogues – some real, some invented and others merely imagined – *Time Regained*, Proust's final instalment of his life's work, is as good as unfilmable. Yet the Chilean filmmaker (and former playwright) Raoul Ruiz has conjured up a cinematic kaleidoscope of image and anecdote that goes some way in bringing the book to life. A supremely elegant homage to a quintessentially literary work, Ruiz' film draws on the possibilities of its own parallel medium, providing superimposed, distorted and reflected images as an extension of Proust's fevered imagination. But without a cohesive narrative, the film's 155 minutes do pile up. Of course, scholars of Proust may well get a thrill out of all this, but for the rest of us it is something of an endurance test.

● *Odette de Crecy* Catherine Deneuve, *Gilberte* Emmanuelle Beart, *Charlie Morel* Vincent Perez, *Baron de Charles aka 'Palamède'* John Malkovich, *Robert de Saint Loup* Pascal Greggory, *Marcel Proust, the narrator* Marcello Mazzarella, *Madame Simone Verdurin* Marie-France Pisier, *Madame de Farcy*

Arielle Dombasle, *Albertine* Chiara Mastroianni, *Oriane de Guermantes* Edith Scob, *Rachel* Elsa Zylberstein, *Albert Bloch* Christian Vadim, *Marcel* Andre Engel, *young Marcel* Georges Du Fresne, *the voice of Marcel Proust* Patrice Chereau, Dominique Labourier, Philippe Morier-Genoud, Melvil Poupaud, Mathilde Seigner, Jacques Pieiller, Hélène Surgère, Alain Robbe-Grillet, Ingrid Caven.
● *Dir* Raoul Ruiz, *Pro* Paulo Branco, *Line Pro* Philippe Saal, *Assoc Pro* Leo Pescarolo and Massimo Ferrero, *Screenplay* Gilles Taurand and Raoul Ruiz, *Ph* Ricardo Aronovich, *Pro Des* Bruno Beaugé, *Ed* Denise De Casabianca, *M* Jorge Arriagada; 'Time Regained' sung by Natalie Dessay, *Costumes* Gabriella Pescucci and Caroline De Vivaise.

Gemini Films/France 2 Cinéma/Blu Cinematografica/Madragoa Filmes/Canal Plus, etc-Artificial Eye.
162 mins. France/Italy/Portugal. 1999. Rel: 7 January 2000. Cert 18.

Topsy-Turvy ★★★★¹/₂

London; 1884-85. Following the critical disappointment of *Princess Ida* – and a falling out with his composer Arthur Sullivan – the librettist W.S. Gilbert finds fresh inspiration in a visiting Japanese exhibition. And so *The Mikado* begins to take shape ... In a year that saw David Lynch, David Mamet and Wes Craven take such dramatic U-turns – and to such enormous critical dividends – it may not seem so surprising that Mike Leigh should follow suit. Yet this remarkably rich and engaging period saga works so well because so many of Leigh's intrinsic attributes are still in evidence: his attention to eccentric detail, his larger-than-life characters and a general rejec-

Above: Taking the Mikado – Timothy Spall excels in Mike Leigh's remarkably rich and engaging Topsy-Turvy (from Pathé)

tion of conventional cinematic form. It's as if he's jump-started the manicured excellence of Merchant Ivory with the attendant warts and colour of real life, resulting in a funny, exuberant and totally fresh experience. For not only has Leigh brought the world of Gilbert and Sullivan resoundingly to life, but he has made the time that they lived in feel totally modern (Sullivan, surveying a pen that contains its own ink: 'Whatever will they think of next?'). And it goes without saying that the acting, production design, music, *et al*, are all top hole.

● *William Schwenck Gilbert* Jim Broadbent, *Arthur Sullivan* Allan Corduner, *Richard Temple* Timothy Spall, *Lucy 'Kitty' Gilbert* Lesley Manville, *Richard D'Oyly Carte* Ron Cook, *Helen Lenoir* Wendy Nottingham, *Durward Lely* Kevin McKidd, *Leonora Braham* Shirley Henderson, *Jessie Bond* Dorothy Atkinson, *George Grossmith* Martin Savage, *Fanny Ronalds* Eleanor David, *Richard Barker* Sam Kelly, *Gilbert's father* Charles Simon, *Mr Seymour* Nicholas Woodeson, *John D'Auban* Andy Serkis, Dexter Fletcher, Sukie Smith, Stefan Bednarczyk, Geoffrey Hutchings, Francis Lee, Kate Doherty, Kenneth Hadley, Gary Yershon, Katrin Cartlidge, Julia Rayner, Jenny Pickering, David Neville, Matthew Mills, Theresa Watson, Lavinia Bertram, Eve Pearce, Vincent Franklin, Michael Simkins, *Madame Leon* Alison Steadman, Angela Curran, Jonathan Aris, Louise Gold, Bríd Brennan, Mark Benton, Simon Butteriss.
● *Dir and Screenplay* Mike Leigh, *Pro* Simon Channing Williams, *Assoc Pro* Georgina Lowe, *Ph* Dick Pope, *Pro Des* Eve Stewart, *Ed* Robin Sales, *M* Carl Davis; Arthur Sullivan, *Costumes* Lindy Hemming, *Choreography* Francesca Jaynes, *make-up/hair design* Christine Blundell.

October Films/Thin Man Films/Greenlight Fund/Newmarket Capital Group-Pathé.
160 mins. UK. 1999. Rel: 18 February 2000. Cert 12.

To Walk With Lions ★★
Kenya; the late 1980s. Two decades after the release of *Born Free*, the conservationist George Adamson has retreated to his private reservation of Kora. But times have changed dramatically, with George's wife Joy long gone, poachers making a fortune from their illegal kills and an unstable political climate threatening the very future of George's lions. Into this unstable environment arrives Tony Fitzjohn, a hard-drinking womaniser who reluctantly takes on the position of George's assistant ... This is not so much a sequel to *Born Free*, the enchanting family film about Elsa the lion cub, as a cancerous outgrowth. Offering a dorky romance, murder, sex in the grassland and the upsetting slaughter of animals, the film will appal fans of the original and send children screaming for the exits. It's also a dire piece of filmmaking, with poorly executed action sequences, animatronic lions and another wooden performance from John Michie (from *Monk Dawson*). Yet in spite of such woeful shortcomings, the film still exerts a hold, due largely to the glorious setting, an emotive score and the powerful subject matter.

● *George Adamson* Richard Harris, *Tony Fitzjohn* John Michie, *Lucy Jackson* Kerry Fox, *Terence Adamson* Ian Bannen, *Maxwell* Hugh Quarshie, *Joy Adamson* Honor Blackman, *Victoria Andrecelli* Geraldine Chaplin, David Mulwa, Steenie Njoroge, Tirus Gathwe.
● *Dir* Carl Schultz, *Pro* Piter Kroonenburg and Julie Allan, *Ex Pro* John Buchanan, *Co-Pro* Jamie Brown, *Line Pro* Helene Boulay, *Screenplay* Keith Ross Leckie, *Ph* Jean Lepine, *Pro Des* Michael Devine, *Ed* Angelo Corrao, *M* Alan Reeves, *Costumes* Suzy Belcher and Nicole Pelletier.

Kingsborough Greenlight Pictures/IAC Holdings-Optimum Releasing.
105 mins. Canada/UK/Kenya. 1999. Rel: 26 May 2000. Cert 12.

Toy Story 2 ★★★★¹/₂
Just before Andy departs for summer camp, his favourite toy, Woody, suffers a debilitating tear on the right shoulder and is left behind. Then, in Andy's absence, Wheezy the penguin is dumped in a yard sale, Woody goes to rescue him and is stolen by a toy merchant. It turns out that Woody is something of a collector's item and is now set to end up in a Japanese museum ... Drawing on the magical components of the first film, this outstanding sequel adds some wonderful new elements, including a rival Buzz Lightyear, a spirited romantic interest for Woody and even a homily on the importance of being a toy. Again, the animation is so good that one almost forgets the entire film is realised by computers, and the story is even better developed than in the original. In addition, there are some choice allusions to other films (*The Wizard of Oz*, *Jurassic Park*, *The Empire Strikes Back*) and Slinky Dog really comes into his own. Best scene: where the toys cross a busy road disguised as traffic cones.

● Voices: *Woody* Tom Hanks, *Buzz Lightyear* Tim Allen, *Mr Potato Head* Don Rickles, *Slinky Dog* Jim Varney, *Rex* Wallace Shawn, *Hamm* John Ratzenberger, *Aliens* Jeff Pidgeon, *Bo Peep* Annie Potts, *Andy* John Morris, *Andy's Mom* Laurie Metcalf, *Sarge* R. Lee Ermey, *Jessie* Joan Cusack, *Prospector* Kelsey Grammer, *Mrs Potato Head*® Estelle Harris, *Barbie* Jodi Benson, *Wheezy* Joe Ranft, *Emperor Zurg* Andrew Stanton, *Al McWhiggin* Wayne Knight.
● *Dir* John Lasseter, *Co-Dir* Lee Unkrich and Ash Brannon, *Pro* Helene Plotkin and Karen Robert Jackson, *Ex Pro* Sarah McArthur, *Screenplay* Andrew Stanton, Rita Hsiao, Doug Chamberlin and Chris Webb, from a story by Lasseter, Pete Docter, Brannon and Stanton, *Ph* Sharon Calahan, *Pro Des* William Cone and Jim Pearson, *Ed* Edie Bleiman, David Ian Salter and Lee Unkrich, *M* Randy Newman; Strauss; songs per-

Left: Trenchant warfare – A scene from William Boyd's powerfully atmospheric The Trench *(from Entertainment)*

formed by Riders in the Sky, Sarah McLachlan, Randy Newman, and Robert Goulet, *Sound* Gary Rydstrom, *Supervising animation* Glenn McQueen.

Walt Disney Pictures/Pixar-Buena Vista. 95 mins. USA. 1999. Rel: 4 February 2000. Cert U.

The Trench ★★★★

Northern France; 29 June-1 July, 1916. Set entirely in a trench 36 hours prior to the Battle of the Somme, this is almost inevitably the stuff of great drama. However, the claustrophobic format does lend itself more to the theatre than the big screen. Having said that, first-time director William Boyd, working from his own screenplay, has built up a tremendous atmosphere, helped by consummate sound design. He has also hewn some remarkable performances from his unknown cast, a difficult feat for a first-timer even with more experienced actors. But the film's real power rests with its attention to detail, the sort more readily found in a good novel. But then, as one of Britain's most highly acclaimed novelists (*Stars and Bars*, *A Good Man in Africa*, *Armadillo*), Boyd would know that.

● *Billy Mcfarlane* Paul Nicholls, *Sgt. Telford Winter* Daniel Craig, *Ellis Harte* Julian Rhind-Tutt, *Victor Dell* Danny Dyer, *Colin Daventry* James D'Arcy, *Eddie Mcfarlane* Tam Williams, *Horace Beckwith* Anthony Strachan, *Charlie Ambrose* Ciarán McMenamin, Michael Moreland, Adrian Lukis, Cillian Murphy, John Higgins, Ben Whishaw, Danny Nutt.
● *Dir and Screenplay* William Boyd, *Pro* Steve Clark-Hall, *Ex Pro* Xavier Marchand, *Co-Pro* Jacques Perrin

and Christophe Barratier, *Ph* Tony Pierce-Roberts, *Pro Des* Jim Clay, *Ed* Jim Clark and Laurence Méry-Clerk, *M* Evelyn Glennie and Greg Malcangi, *Costumes* Lindy Hemming and David Crossman.

Blue PM/Skyline Films/Galatée Films/British Screen/Arts Council of England/Bonaparte Films/Canal Plus/National Lottery/European Co-Production Fund-Entertainment. 98 mins. UK/France. 1999. Rel: 17 September 1999. Cert 15.

trick ★★★

New York City; today. An aspiring writer of musicals, Gabriel is a sweet, diffident homosexual who shares a small apartment with a voracious heterosexual. When he meets a hunky go-go dancer – Mark – in the subway, he brings him home but is thrown by the unexpected presence of his friend Katherine, who has let herself in to use Gabriel's printer. As the evening wears on, Gabriel and Mark strive to consummate their 'one night stand' but are constantly hindered by unforeseen interruptions… The story of two homosexuals spending the night trying to find somewhere to score doesn't sound like the stuff of romantic comedy. Yet the sheer delight of *trick* – the first film from theatre director Jim Fall – is its ability to turn preconceptions on their head. Economically plotted and studded with prize cameos (enthusiastically played by an unknown cast), *trick* is, like its leading protagonist, cute, lightweight and kind of innocent. P.S. Christian Campbell is the brother of actress Neve Campbell.

● *Gabriel* Christian Campbell, *Mark Miranda* John Paul Pitoc, *Katherine Lambert* Tori Spelling, *Judy*

Lorri Bagley, *Rich* Brad Beyer, *Perry* Steve Hayes, *Miss Coco Peru* Clinton Leupp, Kevin Chamberlin, Jamie Gustis, Helen Hanft, Lacey Kohl, Missi Pile, Bobby Peaco, and *Trixie* Camilla.
● *Dir* Jim Fall, *Pro* Fall, Eric d'Arbeloff and Ross Katz, *Ex Pro* Anthony Bregman and Mary Jane Skalski, *Co-Pro* Robert Hawk, *Co-Ex Pro* Mark Beigelman, *Screenplay* Jason Schafer, from a story by David Friedman, *Ph* Terry Stacey, *Pro Des* Jody Asnes, *Ed* Brian A. Kates, *M* Tracy McKnight; Beethoven; songs performed by Tori Spelling, Christian Campbell, Erin Hamilton, Steve Hayes, David Friedman, The Candyskins, Valerie Pinkston, etc, *Costumes* Mary Gasser, *Choreography* Robin Carrigan.

Good Machine/Roadside Attractions-Millivres Multimedia. 90 mins. USA. 1999. Rel: 5 May 2000. Cert 15.

Tumbleweeds ★★★★
West Virginia/Missouri/San Diego, California; the present. Prone to marrying the men she dates and moving states after her divorce, Mary Jo Walker sets off on the road again after she breaks up with her fourth husband. Accompanied by her 12-year-old daughter, Ava, Mary Jo sets her sights on San Diego, where, for a while, it looks like she and Ava may have found a new life ... Bearing uncanny comparisons to *Anywhere But Here* (qv), *Tumbleweeds* is an object lesson in how the former film went wrong. Eschewing snappy one-liners and schematic set pieces, *Tumbleweeds* focuses on the mercurial relationship between mother and daughter with unblinking honesty. And thanks to sensationally authentic performances from Janet McTeer and Kimberly J. Brown, the film solicits the audience's sympathy – not through manipulation or sentimentality – but through the sheer force of realism. The fact that Ms McTeer is actually the Yorkshire daughter of a British Rail employee makes her transition into a down-to-earth Southern Belle all the more extraordinary. FYI: The film is inspired by the itinerant upbringing of co-scenarist Angela Shelton, who wrote the script with her partner Gavin O'Connor, the latter also directing, producing and co-starring.

● *Mary Jo Walker* Janet McTeer, *Dan Miller* Jay O. Sanders, *Ava Walker* Kimberly J. Brown, *Jack Ranson* Gavin O'Connor, *Mr Cummings* Michael J. Pollard, *Laurie Pendleton* Laurel Holloman, *Ginger* Lois Smith, *Zoe Broussard* Ashley Buccille, *Adam Riley* Cody McMains, Linda Porter, Brian Tahash, Josh Carmichael, Lisa Persky, and (*uncredited*) *Vertis Dewey* Noah Emmerich.
● *Dir* Gavin O'Connor, *Pro* Gregory O'Connor, *Ex Pro* Ted Demme, Joel Stillerman, Thomas J. Mangan, Gavin O'Connor and Gregory O'Connor, *Co-Pro* Lisa Bruce *Screenplay* Gavin O'Connor and Angela Shelton, *Ph* Dan Stoloff, *Ed* John Gilroy, *Pro*

Des Bruce Eric Holtshousen, *M* David Mansfield; songs performed by Big Sandy and His Fly-Rite Boys, Buck Owens, Lyle Lovett, Emmylou Harris, Shawn Jones Band, Johnny Cash, Lucinda Williams, Blue Mountain, Robert Bradley's Blackwater Surprise, etc, *Costumes* Mimi Maxmen.

Spanky Pictures/Solaris/River One Films-Entertainment. 102 mins. USA. 1999. Rel: 3 March 2000. Cert 12.

28 Days ★★★¹/₂
New York/North Carolina; the present. Gwen Cummings is a successful writer whose fun-loving lifestyle is getting out of hand. Goaded on by her hard-drinking English boyfriend, she is constantly late, often drunk and suffers frequent bouts of memory loss. Then, after ruining her sister's wedding, she crashes a limousine and is ordered to spend 28 days in rehab ... A mainstream picture about an alcoholic in rehab, *28 Days* could have taken a number of routes. It could have sent the whole thing up. It could have made Gwen into a monster. It could have made Gwen into a victim. It could even, God forbid, have made Gwen into a fallen angel. As it is, the film manages to address the issues that have made Gwen what she is and neither judges nor forgives her. Neither does it make a saint of her sister, a woman who has worked hard to carve out a sensible, conventional life. With humour, insight and some deftly drawn characters (and the odd caricature), *28 Days* constantly sidesteps the predictable outcome. There are also some surprising casting choices that actually work in the film's favour. Where one would expect Steve Buscemi to be perfect as a recovering addict of any description, he actually plays the rehab's counsellor (having conquered his addiction). And Sandra Bullock – as the party animal who 'makes it impossible for anybody to love her' – gives the best performance of her career.

● *Gwen Cummings* Sandra Bullock, *Eddie Boone* Viggo Mortensen, *Jasper* Dominic West, *Bobbie Jean* Diane Ladd, *Lily* Elizabeth Perkins, *Cornell* Steve Buscemi, *Gerhardt* Alan Tudyk, *Oliver* Michael O'Malley, *Andrea* Azura Skye, *Daniel* Reni Santoni, *Roshanda* Marianne Jean-Baptiste, *Betty* Margo Martindale, Susan Krebs, Loudon Wainwright III, Corinne Reilly, Jim Moody.
● *Dir* Betty Thomas, *Pro* Jenno Topping, *Co-Pro* Celia Costas, *Screenplay* Susannah Grant, *Ph* Declan Quinn, *Pro Des* Marcia Hinds-Johnson, *Ed* Peter Teschner, *M* Richard Gibbs; songs performed by The Clash, Fantastic Plastic Machine, NRBQ, David Crosby, Loudon Wainwright III, Otis Redding, Three Dog Night, Mitch Miller, Ray Stevens, and Tom Jones, *Costumes* Ellen Lutter.

Columbia Pictures/Tall Trees-Columbia TriStar. 104 mins. USA. 2000. Rel: 16 June 2000. Cert 15.

Left: Sub-history — Matthew McConaughey and Harvey Keitel in Jonathan Mostow's confusing, one-dimensional but still incredibly gripping U-571 (from Entertainment)

U-571 ★★★

North Atlantic; Spring, 1942. With Nazi U-boats having sunk over 1,000 Allied ships, the US Navy is determined to break the enemy's stronghold on the North Atlantic. So, when the German U-571 is crippled by an English destroyer, the Yanks rush in to capture its top secret coding device ('Enigma') before it can be rescued by the home team. However, no sooner have the largely inexperienced American crew boarded the enemy craft, than their own sub is sunk by a direct hit ... With his first film, *Breakdown*, writer-director Jonathan Mostow demonstrated a talent for producing toe-curling suspense. But here, working on a much bigger canvas with a large number of characters, he has come somewhat adrift. Thus, the film's first half takes an age to kick into gear, sabotaged by confused plotting and unintelligible dialogue. Only in the second hour does Mostow successfully pull together the tried and tested formulae of the submarine thriller: the claustrophobia, the leaking beams, the ominous sound of creaking and the deathly silent anticipation of the next depth charge. At times the suspense is almost unbearable, even though the characters who meet such a frightful end are strictly one-dimensional. FYI: *U-571* marks the 600th film from producer Dino De Laurentiis. The movie has been criticised for its distortion of historical fact (it was the British who captured that damn sub!).

● *Lt. Andrew Tyler* Matthew McConaughey, *Lt. Commander Mike Dahlgren* Bill Paxton, *Chief Klough* Harvey Keitel, *Lt. Pete Emmett* Jon Bon Jovi, *Lt. Hirsch* Jake Weber, *Marine Major Coonan* David Keith, *Ensign Larson* Matthew Settle, *Kapitanlieutenant Wassner* Thomas Kretschmann, *Wentz* Jack Noseworthy, *Trigger* Thomas Guiry, *Rabbit* Will Estes, *Eddie* T.C. Carson, *Mazzola* Erik Palladino, Dave Power, Derk Cheetwood, Rebecca Tilney, Carolyna De Laurentiis, Dina De Laurentiis, *British seaman* Robin Askwith.

● *Dir* Jonathan Mostow, *Pro* Dino De Laurentiis and Martha De Laurentiis, *Ex Pro* Hal Lieberman, *Line Pro* Lucio Trentini, *Screenplay* Mostow, Sam Montgomery and David Ayer, *Ph* Oliver Wood, *Pro Des* William Ladd Skinner and Götz Weidner, *Ed* Wayne Wahrman, *M* Richard Marvin, *Costumes* April Ferry, *Visual effects* Peter Donen.

Studio Canal/Universal-Entertainment.
116 mins. USA. 2000. Rel: 2 June 2000. Cert 12.

Universal Soldier – The Return ★¹/₂

Former cadaver and human robot Luc Deveraux is now a caring father and widower. He is also technical advisor for a special government project developing an even stronger and more indestructible breed of soldier. Then the project's master robot SETH (i.e. the Self-Evolving Thought Helix) develops a counter-productive agenda all its own ... They don't come much dumber or cheesier than this. It's like the Muscles from Brussels has fallen into a time warp, doffing his cap to a period when slam-bang action movies were by definition mindless and gratuitous. Here, innovation is forfeited in favour of good old basic action, just like when the titans of the screen used to pummel each other with, er, their fists. And we wonder why the diminutive Jackie Chan is a bigger star than Jean-Claude? [*Charles Bacon*]

● *Luc Deveraux* Jean-Claude Van Damme, *SETH* Michael Jai White, *Erin* Heidi Schanz, *Maggie* Kiana Tom, *General Radford* Daniel Von Bargen, *Dylan Cotner* Xander Berkeley, *Romeo* Bill Goldberg, Justin Lazard, James Black, Karis Paige Bryant.
● *Dir* Mic Rodgers, *Pro* Craig Baumgarten, Allen Shapiro and Jean-Claude Van Damme, *Ex Pro* Michael Rachmil, *Co-Pro* Richard G. Murphy, Adam

Merims and Bennett R. Specter, *Screenplay* William Malone and John Fasano, *Ph* Michael A. Benson, *Pro Des* David Chapman, *Ed* Peck Prior, *M* Don Davis, *Costumes* Jennifer L. Bryan, *Stunts* Michael Runyard.

TriStar Pictures/Baumgarten Prophet Entertainment/Indie Prods/Long Road prods.-Columbia TriStar.
84 mins. USA. 1999. Rel: 17 September 1999. Cert 18.

Up at the Villa ★★

Florence; 1938. An impoverished aristocratic widow 'with nothing but the jewels she stands up in,' Mary Panton is proposed to by the wealthy and dependable Sir Edgar Swift. While given two days to consider his offer, Mary is thrown into the company of Rowley Flint, a married American playboy. Rebuffing the latter's sexual overtures, Mary turns instead to an Austrian refugee she feels sorry for, a move that holds disastrous consequences ... A story of passion and intrigue, *Up at the Villa* is neither passionate nor intriguing. Part of the problem is in the casting. While Kristin Scott Thomas is perfect as the glacial, brittle widow tripped into a night of indiscretion, Sean Penn lacks the charismatic swagger and good looks to make his night in shining white linen sparkle. In fact, it's hard to imagine Ms Scott Thomas and Penn in the same movie, let alone a romance. Be that as it may, the locations are glorious and there's fine thespian support from James Fox, Jeremy Davies and Derek Jacobi.

● *Mary Panton* Kristin Scott Thomas, *Rowley Flint* Sean Penn, *Princess San Ferdinando* Anne Bancroft, *Sir Edgar Swift* James Fox, *Karl Richter* Jeremy Davies, *Lucky Leadbetter* Derek Jacobi, *Beppino Leopardi* Massimo Ghini, *Harold Atkinson* Dudley Sutton, *Nina* Lorenza Indovina, Roger Hammond, Clive Merrison, Linda Spurrier, Ben Aris, Anne Ridler, Anne Bell, Barbara Hicks.
● *Dir* Philip Haas, *Pro* Geoff Stier, *Screenplay* and *Ed* Belinda Haas, *Ex Pro* Sydney Pollack, Arnon Milchan and Stanley Buchthal, *Co-Pro* David Brown, *Co Ex-Pro* Guy East and Nigel Sinclair, *Assoc Pro* Davien Littlefield and Guido Cerasuolo, *Ph* Maurizio Calvesi, *Pro Des* and *Costumes* Paul Brown, *M* Pino Donaggio.

Intermedia Films/October Films/Mirage-UIP.
116 mins. USA/UK. 1999. Rel: 14 April 2000. Cert 12.

Varsity Blues ★★¹/₂

West Canaan, Texas; the present. Football is important. It teaches you team spirit, it's great for a cardiovascular workout and it can get you an academic scholarship. However, Jonathan Moxon is not so into the whole sports thing and, once he's out of college (and away from the football-mad town he's grown up in), he aims to concentrate on worthier matters. Then, when his high school's number one quarterback pulls a tendon, Jonathan finds himself the new star of the season ... With its recipe of adolescent hi-jinks, soft-core sex, gridiron stunts and rock songs, it's easy to see why *Varsity Blues* was a box-office hit in the States. At the very least it's prime Saturday night entertainment for teenage devotees of American football. It also boasts an array of decent performances from a promising cast (my money is on James Van Der Beek and Amy Smart for future stardom), a scenery-chewing earful from the new head of ham, Jon Voight, and a vigorous rejection of all things original.

● *Jonathan Moxon* James Van Der Beek, *Coach Bud Kilmer* Jon Voight, *Lance Harbor* Paul Walker, *Billy Bob* Ron Lester, *Tweeder* Scott Caan, *Joe Harbor* Richard Lineback, *Collette Harbor* Tiffany C. Love, *Julie Harbor* Amy Smart, *Wendell* Eliel Swinton, *Darcy* Ali Larter, Thomas Duffy, Jill Parker Jones.
● *Dir* Brian Robbins, *Pro* Tova Laiter, Mike Tollin and Robbins, *Ex Pro* David Gale and Van Toffler, *Assoc Pro* Elysa Koplovitz, *Screenplay* W. Peter Iliff, *Ph* Charles Cohen, *Pro Des* Jaymes Hinkle, *Ed* Ned Bastille, *M* Mark Isham; songs performed by Shawn Camp, The Iguanas, Southern Culture On the Skids, Stevie Ray Vaughan, Tex Ritter, Saffron Henderson, Aaliyah, AC/DC, Offspring, Loudmouth, Green Day, Foo Fighters, Collective Soul, Fastball, Third Eye Blind, Janus Stark, Van Halen, etc, *Costumes* Wendy Chuck.

Paramount/MTV Films/Marquee Tollin/Tova Laiter Prods-UIP.
105 mins. USA. 1998. Rel: 10 September 1999. Cert 15.

The Virgin Suicides ★★

Michigan; 1974. Following the attempted suicide of Cecilia Lisbon, it is suggested that the Lisbon girls – Cecilia, 13, Lux, 14, Bonnie, 15, Mary, 16, and Therese, 17 – be allowed to interact more within the community. A coven of loveliness, the girls quickly attract the attention of the local boys, but their lustre seems destined to be short lived ... If ever a subject matter demanded a strong sense of style this is it. Whether it be the confrontational satire of Neil LaBute, the social caricature of Mike

Right: Tuscan dreams – Derek Jacobi gives Kristin Scott Thomas the guided tour in Philip Haas's misconceived Up at the Villa *(from UIP)*

Leigh, the naturalism of Ken Loach, or even the tasteless irony of John Waters, Jeffrey Eugenides' novel screamed out for a decisive cinematic approach. As it is, the film washes over one with a dream-like inconsequence, while the sisters themselves are supplied with little individuality (other than a group personality). Lacking wit, vitality and credibility, *The Virgin Suicides* seems a pointless exercise. FYI: Helmer Sofia Coppola is the daughter of legendary filmmaker Francis Ford Coppola and the wife of acclaimed director Spike Jonze (of *Being John Malkovich* fame).

● *Ronald A. Lisbon* James Woods, *Mrs Lisbon* Kathleen Turner, *Lux Lisbon* Kirsten Dunst, *Trip Fontaine* Josh Hartnett, *Father Moody* Scott Glenn, *Trip Fontaine '97* Michael Paré, *Dr Hornicker* Danny DeVito, *Mary Lisbon* A.J. Cook, *Cecilia Lisbon* Hanna Hall, *Bonnie Lisbon* Chelse Swain, *Therese Lisbon* Leslie Hayman, *Chase Buell* Anthony DeSimone, *David Barker* Lee Kagan, *Paul Baldino* Robert Schwartzman, Noah Shebib, Jonathan Tucker, Joe Roncetti, Hayden Christensen, Chris Hale, Jonathan Whittaker, Dustin Ladd, Melody Johnson, Tim Adams, *narrator* Giovanni Ribisi.
● *Dir* and *Screenplay* Sofia Coppola, *Pro* Julie Costanzo, Chris Hanley, Dan Halsted and Francis Ford Coppola, *Ex Pro* Fred Fuchs and Willi Baer, *Co-Pro* Fred Roos and Gary Marcus, *Line Pro* Suzanne Colvin, *Ph* Edward Lachman, *Pro Des* Jasna Stefanovic, *Ed* James Lyons and Melissa Kent, *M* Air; songs performed by Sloan, The Hollies, ELO, Styx, Gilbert O'Sullivan, Carole King, Todd Rundgren, Air, Al Green, 10CC, and The Bee Gees, *Costumes* Nancy Steiner, *Sound* Richard Beggs.

American Zoetrope/Muse/Eternity Pictures-Pathé. 97 mins. USA. 1999. Rel: 19 May 2000. Cert 15.

Virtual Sexuality ★★★¹/₂

London; the present. When fussy virgin Justine visits a virtual reality exhibit, a freak explosion traps her in the body of a computer-generated Adonis of her own making. Now, armed with her very own male equipment, Justine discovers what it means to be a man ... Fresh, inventive, energetic, innovative and fun, this cinematic equivalent of a girls' teen magazine will probably generate a string of pale imitations. With its unique blend of computer graphics, on-screen captions (complete with bar codes!) and made-up patois, *Virtual Sexuality* boasts some interesting ideas, while the lively performances from a largely unknown and attractive cast supply considerable human ballast. Incidentally, the parallels to *Clueless* are extraordinary – the virginal heroine, the black best friend, the unappreciated platonic

boyfriend, the creative jargon – but, hey, even Shakespeare borrowed stuff.

● *Justine* Laura Fraser, *Jake* Rupert Penry-Jones, *Chas* Luke de Lacey, *Alex* Kieran O'Brien, *Fran* Marcelle Duprey, *Isabella aka 'Hoover'* Natasha Bell, *Monica* Laura Macaulay, *Jason* Steve John Shepherd, *Frank* Roger Frost, *Jackie* Ruth Sheen, Laura Aikman, Ram John Holder, Amanda Holden, Stewart Harwood, Melinda Messenger.
● *Dir* Nick Hurran, *Pro* Christopher Figg, *Ex Pro* Kevin Loader and Jonathan Darby, *Screenplay* Nick Fisher, *Ph* Brian Tufano, *Pro Des* Chris Edwards, *Ed* John Richards, *M* Rupert Gregson-Williams; Mozart; songs performed by Imani Coppola, Mandalay, Destiny's Child, Touch and Go, All Saints, K7, Basement Jaxx, Imogen Heap, Poe, etc, *Costumes* Joanna Freedman.

The Bridge/Noel Gay Motion Picture Company-Columbia TriStar. 92 mins. UK. 1998. Rel: 2 July 1999. Cert 15.

Above: *Chill-leader – Kirsten Dunst casts her spell in Sofia Coppola's pointless* The Virgin Suicides *(from Pathé)*

Right: Tim Roth's emotionally numbing, mind-churning *The War Zone* (from Film Four)

A Walk On the Moon ★★★¹/₂

Setting off for their traditional holiday at a lakeside campsite in the Catskills ('the same stupid thing every summer'), Marty and Pearl Kantrowitz, their 14-year-old daughter Alison, younger son Daniel and Marty's psychic mother are about to encounter some major transitions in their lives. As Alison experiences her first period and Marty is called back to work, Pearl faces the unrelieved oppression of approaching middle-age. Thus, with the dual excitement of Woodstock and the moon landing in the air, Pearl finds herself succumbing to the sexual overtures of a travelling garment salesman ... In spite of ploughing such familiar territory – rites of passage during a time of major social transition – first-time director Tony Goldwyn (better known as an actor in *Ghost* and as the voice of Disney's *Tarzan*) invests his material with such subtle emotional nuances and splendid acting that one forgives the film its more predictable flourishes. The philanderer, as played with slick ease by Viggo Mortensen (who stole Gwyneth Paltrow from Michael Douglas in *A Perfect Murder*) is given short moral thrift and no motive and the ending doesn't ring true. However, so much of Pamela Gray's screenplay is steeped in recognisable pain and frustration and is so well illuminated by a wonderful cast (Anna Paquin turns in another revelatory performance as the hormonally dazed Alison) that it's hard not to be totally involved and deeply moved.

● *Pear Kantrowitz* Diane Lane, *Walker Jerome* Viggo Mortensen, *Marty Kantrowitz* Liev Schreiber, *Alison Kantrowitz* Anna Paquin, *Lilian 'Bubbie' Kantrowitz* Tovah Feldshuh, *Daniel Kantrowitz* Bobby Boriello, *Myra Naidell* Lisa Jakub, Stewart Bick, Jess Platt, Mahee Paiment, Ellen David, and (*uncredited*) the voice of Julie Kavner.
● *Dir* Tony Goldwyn, *Pro* Neil Koemgsberg, Lee Gottsegen and Murray Schisgal, and Dustin Hoffman, Tony Goldwyn and Jay Cohen, *Ex Pro* Graham Burke and Greg Coote, *Co-Pro* Josette Perotta, *Screenplay* Pamela Gray, *Ph* Anthony Richmond, *Pro Des* Dan Leigh, *Ed* Dana Congdon, *M* Mason Daring; songs performed by Bobby Darin, Wayne Newton, Dusty Springfield, Grateful Dead, The Youngbloods, Tom Jones, Jefferson Airplane, Joni Mitchell, Judy Collins, Richie Havens, Country Joe McDonald, Bob Dylan, Dean Martin, etc, *Costumes* Jess Goldstein.

First Independent/Punch Prods/Village Roadshow/Groucho Film Partnership-First Independent.
107 mins. USA. 1999. Rel: 19 November 1999. Cert 15.

The War Zone ★★★★

Devon; today. In a featureless house in a featureless landscape a featureless family awaits the birth of a child. Dad has something to do with buying and selling fireplaces, Mum is the earth mother type who attends to her husband's every whim and Jessie and Tom are well into their teens and are miserable about it. So it's odd that Mum should be pregnant again. But without a home computer or even a TV, this is no ordinary family. Something is very wrong ... Like his occasional co-star Gary Oldman, Tim Roth has chosen an extremely sensitive subject for his directorial debut. And, as in Oldman's blistering *Nil By Mouth*, Ray Winstone plays an abusive father. But here the theme is not wife abuse and alcoholism but incest. And unlike Oldman's kinetic, frenzied filmmaking style, Roth opts for a starker, more measured approach, letting the horror of his domestic nightmare sink in via a series of oppressive waves. With a formidable command of sound and imagery, Roth has created a work of astonishing reality, forcing the viewer to take on the role of voyeur. The effect is emotionally numbing and intellectually mind-churning. FYI: *Nil By Mouth* ends with the words 'in memory of my father,' *The War Zone* with the legend 'for my father.' With fathers like these...

● *Dad* Ray Winstone, *Jessie* Lara Belmont, *Tom* Freddie Cunliffe, *Mum* Tilda Swinton, *Lucy* Kate Ashfield, *Nick* Colin J. Farrell, *Carol* Aisling O'Sullivan, Annabelle Apsion, Kim Wall.
● *Dir* Tim Roth, *Pro* Sarah Radclyffe and Dixie Linder, *Ex Pro* Eric Abraham, *Screenplay* Alexander Stuart, from his novel, *Ph* Seamus McGarvey, *Pro Des* Michael Carlin, *Ed* Trevor Waite, *M* Simon Boswell, *Costumes* Mary Jane Reyner.

Film Four/Portobello Pictures/Fandango/Mikado/European Script Fund-Film Four.
99 mins. UK/Italy. 1998. Rel: 3 September 1999. Cert 18.

West Beirut – West Beyrouth ★★★

Beirut, Lebanon; 1975-83. Something of a rebel at school, Tarek Noueiri is delighted when the outbreak of civil war prevents him from attending his classes. So, accompanied by his best friend, Omar, and a Christian neighbour, May, Tarek roams the streets in search of adventure while recording the escalation of hostilities with a Super 8 camera ... It's hard to believe that first-time director Ziad Doueiri started out working for Quentin Tarantino (on all four of his films, no less), as the uneven pace of this autobiographical drama is one of its major drawbacks. Still, there are wonderful moments and Doueiri's alter ego, played by the gangly, cocky Rami Doueir (the director's brother), has a real screen presence. Yet it is the boy's parents, beautifully created by Joseph Bou Nassar and Carmen Lebbos, who really crystallise the anguish and frustrations of the futility of war.

● *Tarek Noueiri* Rami Doueir, *Omar* Mohamad Chamas, *May* Rola Al Amin, *Hala Noueiri* Carmen Lebbos, *Reeyad Noueiri* Joseph Bou Nassar, *Madam Oum Walid* Leila Karam, *Hassan, the baker* Mahmoud Mabsout.
● *Dir and Screenplay* Ziad Doueiri, *Pro* Rachid Bouchareb and Jean Brehat, *Ph* Ricardo Jacques Gale, *Pro Des* Hamze Nasrallah, *Ed* Dominique Marcombe, *M* Stewart Copeland, *Costumes* Pierre Matard.

La Sept ARTE, etc-Metrodome.
110 mins. France/Lebanon/Belgium/Norway. 1998. Rel: 23 July 1999. Cert 15.

Whatever Happened To Harold Smith? ★★★¹/₂

Sheffield, Yorkshire; 1977. Harold Smith, like his name, is a bit of a cliché. A pipe-smoking, slipper-wearing father of two, Harold is never happier than when nestled in his favourite armchair watching the box. But there's more to the old duffer than meets the eye, such as an ability to move objects at will and to read other people's minds. And, just as Harold's 18-year-old son Vince is coming to terms with his own sexual and musical orientations (is punk better than disco?), Harold becomes a national celebrity ... One of Britain's greatest acting institutions, Tom Courtenay has graced the cinema all too rarely of late. Here, he's on terrific form as usual, in a part that seems as natural an extension of the man as any he's played. The film itself is delightfully idiosyncratic, playful and original which, in spite of its freshness and novelty, oozes an old-fashioned sweetness. And the scene in which a naked Stephen Fry teaches his nine-year-old daughter the facts of life is a classic.

● *Harold Smith* Tom Courtenay, *Peter Robinson* Stephen Fry, *Vince Smith* Michael Legge, *Joanna Robinson* Laura Fraser, *Irene Smith* Lulu, *Keith Nesbitt* David Thewlis, *Roland Thornton* Mark Williams, *Lucy Robinson* Charlotte Roberts, *Margaret Robinson* Amanda Root, *Daz* Charlie Hunnam, *Ray Smith* Matthew Rhys, *Walter Bennett* James Corden, Rosemary Leach, Charles Simon, John Higgins, Keith Chegwin, Jeremy Child, Patrick Monckton, Janus Stark, Angela Rippon, John Craven, Alan Whicker, Jan Leeming.
● *Dir* Pete Hewitt, *Pro* Ruth Jackson and David Brown, *Ex Pro* Guy East and Nigel Sinclair, *Screenplay* Ben Steiner, *Ph* David Tattersall, *Pro Des* Gemma Jackson, *Ed* Martin Walsh, *M* Harry Gregson-Williams; songs performed by The Buzzcocks, The Bee Gees, The Members, Lulu, Roy Wood and Wizzard, Maxine Nightingale, Tina Charles, Heatwave, The Real Thing, John Higgins, The Sex Pistols, The Clash, Charlie Hunnam, Crap Attack, The Stranglers, Janus Stark, and Michael Legge, *Costumes* Marie France.

Intermedia Films/October Films/Arts Council of England/West Eleven Films/Yorkshire Media/European Regional Development Fund-UIP.
96 mins. UK. 1999. Rel: 10 March 2000. Cert 15.

When the Sky Falls ★★★

Dublin; 1996. Above the doorway of a police station in Dublin, a Latin slogan reads: `Let justice be done or the sky falls.' However, as Detective Sergeant Mackey and crusading journalist Sinead Hamilton see it, justice is having a hard day: current legislation seems to be protecting the very criminals feeding off the system. Yet, in spite of repeated threats, Hamilton is determined to expose the drug barons corrupting the youth of Ireland ... Veronica Guerin, the thinly veiled subject of this film, was herself

Right: Gulp fiction – Bruce Willis and Matthew Perry in Jonathan Lynn's breezy and engaging The Whole Nine Yards *(from Warner)*

involved with an early version of the script when, in June of 1996, she was shot dead in her car. Her murder simultaneously altered the course of the plot and raised the profile of the production. The result, though, is a mixed bag. Directed by John MacKenzie (he of *The Long Good Friday* fame), the film is predictably slick and hard-hitting but is too rooted in the gangster genre to ring really true. Guerin's home life is touched on, but the scenes of domestic *frisson* seem forced. Patrick Bergin's brutish cop is a charismatic dramatic foil, but is too one-dimensional. And the villains, be they skinhead, IRA dignitary or drug tsar, never rise about docudrama stereotyping. Ken Loach's *Hidden Agenda* (also starring an American actress) remains a far more resonant and credible take on Irish corruption.

● *Sinead Hamilton* Joan Allen, *Mackey* Patrick Bergin, *John Cosgrave, The Runner* Liam Cunningham, *Martin Shaughnessy* Pete Postlethwaite, *Mickey O'Fagan* Jimmy Smallhorne, *Tom Hamilton* Kevin McNally, *Dempsey* Jason Barry, *Dave Hackett* Gerard Flynn, *Jimmy Keaveney* Des McAleer, *John O'Connor* Owen Roe, *Jamie Thornton* Ruaidhri Conroy, Fearghal Geraghty, Gavin Kelty, Mark Dunne, Jeff O'Toole, Ian Cregg, Vincent Walsh, Sarah Pilkington.
● *Dir* John MacKenzie, *Pro* Nigel Warren-Green and Michael Wearing, *Ex Pro* Kevin Menton, Peter Newman and Marie Louise Queally, *Co-Pro* David McLoghlin, *Co-Ex Pro* Bruce Davey, Ralph Kamp and Rod Stoneman, *Line Pro* John McDonnell, *Screenplay* Michael Sheridan, Ronan Gallagher and Colum McCann, *Ph* Seamus Deasy, *Pro Des* Mark Geraghty, *Ed* Graham Walker, *M* Pól Brennan, *Costumes* Lorna Marie Mugan.

Sky Pictures/Irish Screen/Bord Scannán na hÉireann/Irish Film Board/Redeemable Features-Fox.
107 mins. Ireland/USA. 1999. Rel: 16 June 2000. Cert 18.

The Whole Nine Yards ★★★¹/₂

Montreal/Chicago; the present. Nicholas 'Oz' Oseransky is a mild-mannered dentist stuck in a dead-end marriage and saddled with a massive debt courtesy of his late father-in-law. Then his life gets really complicated when a notorious contract killer moves next door and his wife forces him to leak the latter's whereabouts to the Mob. But, once in Chicago, Oseransky falls passionately in love with the hitman's estranged missus ... A lightweight black comedy, *The Whole Nine Yards* suffers from one pratfall too many but is redeemed by an ingenious plot that keeps one guessing up until the satisfying finale. Add a cast of colourful, likeable characters (even though they all seem to one want somebody dead) and you have a surprisingly breezy and engaging confection. Perry handles the slapstick surprisingly well, Amanda Peet is delightful as his bloodthirsty assistant and Bruce Willis rounds things off with a nice line in sustained menace. But what gives the film that little extra are the incidental moments, the funny things that *don't* usually happen in comedies but do in real life.

● *Jimmy 'The Tulip' Tudeski* Bruce Willis, *Nicholas 'Oz' Oseransky* Matthew Perry, *Sophie Oseransky* Rosanna Arquette, *Frankie Figs* Michael Clarke Duncan, *Cynthia Tudeski* Natasha Henstridge, *Jill* Amanda Peet, *Janni Gogolak* Kevin Pollak, *Agent Hanson* Harland Williams, *Sophie's mom* Carmen Ferlan, *Mr Boulez* Serge Christiaenssens, Howard Bilerman, Stephanie Biddle, Charles Biddle, Robert Burns, France Arbour, Sean Devine, Richard Jutras.
● *Dir* Jonathan Lynn, *Pro* David Willis and Allan Kaufman, *Ex Pro* Elie Samaha and Andrew Stevens, *Co-Pro* Don Carmody, James Holt and Tracee Stanley, *Line Pro* Mike Drake, *Screenplay* Mitchell Kapner, *Ph* David Franco, *Pro Des* David L. Snyder, *Ed* Tom Lewis, *M* Randy Edelman, Mozart; songs

Left: Future past –
Kevin Kline and
Will Smith in
Barry Sonnenfeld's
innovative and
spectacular Wild
Wild West
(from Warner)

performed by Mose Allison, Bruce Willis, The Charlie Biddle Trio, Charles Mingus, The Up Top Orchestra, etc, *Costumes* Edi Giguere.

Morgan Creek/Franchise Pictures/Rational Packaging/ Lansdown Films-Warner.
99 mins. USA. 2000. Rel: 19 May 2000. Cert 15.

Wild Wild West ★★★¹/₂

Louisiana/West Virginia/Utah; 1869. James West is a smooth-talking, hard-punching, fast-drawing federal agent. Artemus Gordon is a master of disguise and inventor of fantastic gadgetry. When on assignment, they both prefer to work on their own. But then the President himself orders them to join forces to track down Dr Arliss Loveless, a legless, evil genius bent on overtaking the United States ... The original *Wild, Wild West* TV series (1965-69) was perceived as a cross between *Maverick* and *The Man from U.N.C.L.E.* This spectacular film version (with a starting budget of $102 million) is more like *Blazing Saddles* reinvented by Jules Verne and H.G. Wells, being an innovative, futuristic vision of the West as it could have been. With Will Smith's effortless charm supplying some human ballast, the film is a rip-roaring, darkly comic odyssey in which two scientific geniuses (Kline and Branagh) pit their wits in a technological showdown. Exhibiting his customary flair for the picturesque, director Sonnenfield (*The Addams Family, Men in Black*), creates a unique cinematic universe that takes the breath away. Packed with visual invention and witty badinage, the film falls down on comic chemistry (Smith and Kline are no Smith and Jones), but makes up for it with an endless series of inspired sight gags.

● *James West* Will Smith, *Artemus Gordon/President Ulysses S. Grant* Kevin Kline, *Dr Arliss Loveless*

Kenneth Branagh, *Rita Escobar* Salma Hayek, *'Bloodbath' McGrath* Ted Levine, *Coleman* M. Emmet Walsh, *Miss East* Bai Ling, *girl in water tower* Garcelle Beauvais, *George Washington* Jerry Potter, Frederique van der Wal, Musetta Vander, Sofia Eng, Rodney A. Grant, E.J. Callahan, Ian Abercrombie.
● *Dir* Barry Sonnenfeld, *Pro* Sonnenfeld and Jon Peters, *Ex Pro* Bill Todman Jr, Joel Simon, Kim LeMasters, Tracy Glaser and Barry Josephson, *Co-Pro* Graham Place, *Screenplay* S.S. Wilson, Brent Maddock, Jeffrey Price and Peter S. Seaman, from a story by Jim Thomas and John Thomas, *Ph* Michael Ballhaus, *Pro Des* Bo Welch, *Ed* Jim Miller, *M* Elmer Bernstein; 'Wild Wild West' performed by Will Smith, *Costumes* Deborah L. Scott, *Visual effects* Eric Brevig.

Warner/Peters Entertainment/Sonnenfeld-Josephson/ Todman, Simon, LeMasters Prods-Warner.
106 mins. USA. 1999. Rel: 13 August 1999. Cert 12.

Wild Side ★★¹/₂

Long Beach, California; the present. Bruno Buckingham is the 'Leonardo Da Vinci of dirty money,' a loose cannon who uses his wealth as a weapon to subjugate others. Alex Lee is a bank employee who moonlights as a hooker and gets caught up in Bruno's sticky web. Tony is an undercover cop posing as Bruno's right-hand man, a thug who uses physical force to get what he wants. And Virginia is Bruno's wife, a Hong Kong beauty who applies her sexuality to ensnare all around her. But maybe Alex's basic cunning is the most effective tactic of all ... Between 1970 and 1995, the Edinburgh-born Donald Cammell made four films, the first of which, *Performance*, he co-directed with Nicolas Roeg. His last, *Wild Side*, was completely re-edited – against his wishes – and reduced to a piece of bland exploitation, shortly after which he committed suicide. Since then Cammell's long-standing editor, Frank Mazzola, has reassembled the film using the director's original storyboard and notes and has attempted to recreate what Cammell had envisaged, which the latter had co-scripted with his wife, China Kong. The result recalls the idiosyncrasy of *Performance* and features an extraordinary performance from Christopher Walken. But, sadly, *Wild Side* is more a work of interesting moments than an engrossing experience in its own right.

● *Bruno Buckingham* Christopher Walken, *Virginia Chow* Joan Chen, *Tony* Steven Bauer, *Alex Lee* Anne Heche, *Dan Rackman* Allen Garfield, *Lyle Litvak* Adam Novack, *Hiro Sakamoto* Zion, Richard Palmer, Michael Rose, Lewis Arquette.
● *Dir* Donald Cammell, *Pro* Elie Cohn and John Langley, and (in 2000) Hamish McAlpine, Nick Jones and Frank Mazzola, *Ex Pro* Avi Lerner, Danny Dimbort and Trevor Short, *Co-Pro* Boaz Davidson, and (in 2000) China Kong and Roger Trilling, *Screenplay* China Kong and Donald Cammell, *Ph* Sead Mutarevic, *Pro Des* Claire Bowin, *Ed* Frank Mazzola, *M* Jon Hassell, and (in 2000) Ryuichi Sakamoto; Mozart, *Costumes* Alison Hirsch.

Nu Image-Metro Tartan.
115 mins. USA. 1995/2000. Rel: 30 June 2000. Cert 18.

Winter Sleepers – Winterschlafer ★★¹/₂

Below: Love potion run-around – Kevin Kline and Michelle Pfeiffer in Michael Hoffman's sumptuous, robustly funny William Shakespeare's A Midsummer Night's Dream

Four young people – a translator, her skiing instructor boyfriend, an amnesiac cinema projectionist and the owner of a remote mountain villa – find their lives irrevocably changed following a near-fatal car crash… Prior to making his phenomenally successful *Run Lola Run*, Tom Tykwer trained his camera on the Bavarian Alps to set up this extremely visual tale of today's rootless thirtysomething generation. But after an intriguing start, the film fumbles about in a somewhat superfluous fashion until culminating in a melodramatic finale. A bit of pace and focus would have reaped dividends. [*Charles Bacon*]

● *Rebecca* Floriane Daniel, *Marco* Heino Ferch, *Rene* Ulrich Matthes, *Laura* Marie-Lou Sellem, *Nina* Laura Tonke, *Otto* Sebastian Schipper, Agathe Taffertshofer, Sofia Dirscherl, Robert Meyer.
● *Dir* Tom Tykwer, *Pro* Stefan Arndt, *Line Pro* Milanka Comfort, *Screenplay* Tykwer and Françoise Pyszora, *Ph* Frank Griebe, *Pro Des* Alexander Manasse, *Ed* Katja Dringenberg, *M* Tykwer, Johnny Klimek and Reinhold Heil, *Costumes* Aphrodite Kondos, *Sound* Matthias Lempert and Dirk Jacob.

X Filme Creative Pool/Filmstiftung NRW/BMI, etc-City Screen.
123 mins. Germany/France. 1997. Rel: 2 July 1999. Cert 15.

William Shakespeare's A Midsummer Night's Dream ★★★¹/₂

Monte Athena, Tuscany, Italy; the late 1800s. As Hermia and her forbidden lover Lysander flee to the woods, they are pursued by Demetrius, who loves Hermia, and Helena, who dotes on Demetrius. Then the romantic apple cart is really upturned when the mischievous wood nymph Puck switches the mismatched lovers' desires … Sharpening the original text to a comic foil, this sumptuous, visually rich adaptation of Shakespeare's 1595 play puts the accent on comedy and pulls off a robustly funny romp, bolstered by a terrific cast. Stand-outs include Michelle Pfeiffer as a seductive Titania, Calista Flockhart as a peevish Helena, Stanley Tucci a wry Puck and, best of all, Kevin Kline as a priceless Nick Bottom, a rakish ham emphatically rhyming 'blood' with 'good.' Director Michael Hoffman also draws considerable humour from a series of incredulous reaction shots and shores the whole thing up with a score of opera's greatest hits.

● *Oberon* Rupert Everett, *Helena* Calista Flockhart, *Nick Bottom* Kevin Kline, *Titania* Michelle Pfeiffer, *Puck* aka *Robin Goodfellow* Stanley Tucci, *Hermia* Anna Friel, *Demetrius* Christian Bale, *Lysander* Dominic West, *Theseus* David Strathairn, *Hippolyta* Sophie Marceau, *Peter Quince* Roger Rees, *Robin Starveling* Max Wright, *Snug the Joiner/Lion* Gregory Jbara, *Tom Snout/Moon* Bill Irwin, *Francis Flute* Sam Rockwell, *Egeus* Bernard Hill, *Philostrate* John Sessions, Deirdre A. Harrison, Heather Elizabeth Parisi, Annalisa Cordone, Paola Pessot.
● *Dir and Screenplay* Michael Hoffman, *Pro* Hoffman and Leslie Urdang, *Ex Pro* Arnon Milchan, *Co-Pro* Ann Wingate, *Ph* Oliver Stapleton, *Pro Des* Luciana Arrighi, *Ed* Garth Craven, *M* Simon Boswell; Mendelssohn, Verdi, Bellini, Rossini, Roberto Alagna, *Costumes* Gabriella Pescucci.

Fox Searchlight/Regency Enterprises/Taurus Film-Fox.
120 mins. USA/Germany. 1999. Rel: 24 September 1999. Cert PG.

The Winslow Boy ★★★★★

London, 1909-10. An exacting but fair-minded man, retired bank official Arthur Winslow is devastated when his 14-year-old son is expelled from Naval College for stealing a five-shilling postal order. Convinced of his son's innocence, Winslow embarks on an extensive and financially crippling campaign to clear the Winslow name. It's not so much a case of seeing justice served as the upholding of what is right ... Empowered by understatement, *The Winslow Boy* has more emotion in its little pinkie than most films have in a month of climaxes. Superbly underplayed (in the tradition of *Brief Encounter*), the film is an extraordinary achievement for Mamet, an American writer best known for his scabrous, kinetic and profane works set in urban Chicago. But here nuance is everything, where an eyebrow halted in mid-elevation can destroy a chap's afternoon tea. Communicating these subtleties is a cast to the manor born, although Jeremy Northam is a particular (and happy) surprise as the righteous, cut-glass barrister (played by Robert Donat in the 1948 film). Based on a true story.

● *Arthur Winslow* Nigel Hawthorne, *Sir Robert Morton* Jeremy Northam, *Catherine Winslow* Rebecca Pidgeon, *Grace Winslow* Gemma Jones, *Ronnie Winslow* Guy Edwards, *Dickie Winslow* Matthew Pidgeon, *Desmond Curry* Colin Stinton, *John Watherstone* Aden Gillett, *Violet, the maid* Sarah Flind, Neil North, Sara Stewart, Perry Fenwick, Alan Polanski, Eve Bland.
● *Dir and Screenplay* David Mamet, from the 1946 play by Terrence Rattigan, *Pro* Sarah Green, *Line Pro* Sally French, *Ph* Benoit Delhomme, *Pro Des* Gemma Jackson, *Ed* Barbara Tulliver, *M* Alaric Jans, *Costumes* Consolata Boyle.

Sony Pictures Classics-Columbia TriStar.
104 mins. USA. 1998. Rel: 29 October 1999. Cert U.

Without Limits ★★★

Oregon/Finland/Munich; 1969-1975. Against the advice of his coach, university track star Steve Prefontaine always started ahead of the pack. If he was going to win, he argued, he wanted to win from the word go. And so Prefontaine was to become America's most popular athlete of the early 1970s, even though he was dogged by bad luck. For while he broke a new record during the Munich Olympics of 1972, he was prevented from winning by being trapped on all sides by other runners. Then, shortly after turning down $200,000 in order to compete at Montreal, he met an untimely end ... Robert Towne, who previous directed the Olympic-set *Personal Best* (1982), has crafted a handsome film to furnish the amazing story of the athlete who, in his brief lifetime, broke every American record in the 2,000 to 10,000 metre range.

Above: Upholding what is right – Gemma Jones, Rebecca Pidgeon and Nigel Hawthorne in David Mamet's superbly underplayed The Winslow Boy (from Columbia TriStar)

Yet while Billy Crudup meets the physical requirements of the role, he fails to let us share the demons that drove Prefontaine to such success. Which leaves the acting honours to Donald Sutherland, who supplies his best performance in aeons as Bill Bowerman, the whimsical coach who befriended and wrestled with Prefontaine in the name of athletic greatness. Incidentally, Bowerman went on to co-found the sports outfit Nike. FYI: The athlete's life was previously explored in the 1996 *Prefontaine* featuring Jared Leto in the title role.

● *Steve Prefontaine* Billy Crudup, *Bill Bowerman* Donald Sutherland, *Mary Marckx* Monica Potter, *Frank Shorter* Jeremy Sisto, *Kenny Moore* Billy Burke, *Bill Dellinger* Dean Norris, *Don Kardong* Gabe Olds, *Barbara Bowerman* Judith Ivey, *Roscoe Devine* Matthew Lillard, *Mac Wilkins* Adam Setliff, *Bob Peters* William Mapother, Amy Jo Johnson, Lisa Banes, Frank Shorter, Charlie Jones, William Friedkin, David Coleman, Jamie Schwering.
● *Dir* Robert Towne, *Pro* Tom Cruise and Paula Wagner, *Ex Pro* Jonathan Sanger and Kenny Moore, *Screenplay* Towne and Moore, *Ph* Conrad L. Hall, *Pro Des* William Creber, *Ed* Claire Simpson, Robert K. Lambert and Charles Ireland, *M* Randy Miller; songs performed by The Boston Pops Orchestra, Joe Walsh, David Crosby, Lou Reed, Barry White, Jefferson Airplane, Blind Faith, Cream, David Bowie, Elton John, etc, *Costumes* Grania Preston.

Warner/Cruise/Wagner-Warner.
118 mins. USA. 1998. Rel: 2 July 1999. Cert 12.

Wonderland ★★★¹/₂

Shot on the lam with a hand-held camera, *Wonderland* presents a kaleidoscopic slice-of-life portrait of six members of a family living in London. Utilising natural light and a somewhat jagged structure in order to convey a documentary realism, director Winterbottom (*Jude, Welcome to Sarajevo*) has elicited some remarkable performances from a wonderful cast. And with Michael Nyman's powerfully poignant score, the film gathers considerable emotional power. Funny, desperately sad and above all startlingly true-to-life (a birth sequence is stunning in its naturalism), *Wonderland* is a hard film to ignore. It also presents a unique perspective of London, which here looks more like a Third World city than the cultural capital it is.

● *Dan* Ian Hart, *Debbie Phillips* Shirley Henderson, *Eileen* Kika Markham, *Nadia* Gina McKee, *Molly* Molly Parker, *Bill* Jack Shepherd, *Eddie* John Simm, *Tim* Stuart Townsend, *Darren* Enzo Cilenti, *Melanie* Sarah-Jane Potts, *Franklyn* David Fahm, *Donna* Ellen Thomas, *Jack* Peter Marfleet, Nathan Constance, Anton Saunders.

● *Dir* Michael Winterbottom, *Pro* Michele Camarda and Andrew Eaton, *Ex Pro* Stewart Till and David Thompson, *Co-Pro* Gina Carter, *Line Pro* Anita Overland, *Screenplay* Laurence Coriat, *Ph* Sean Bobbit, *Pro Des* Mark Tildesley, *Ed* Trevor Waite, *M* Michael Nyman; songs performed by Pulp, James, Faithless, The Jam, Dusty Springfield, Massive Attack, and Ali, *Costumes* Natalie Ward.

Universal Pictures/BBC Films/Kismet Film Company/ Revolution Films/British Screen Finance/PolyGram-UIP. 108 mins. UK. 1999. Rel: 14 January 2000. Cert 15.

The Wood ★★★

Inglewood ('The Wood'), Los Angeles; 1986/1999. On his wedding day, a nervous Roland gets drunk and decides to abandon his nuptials. However, his childhood friends Mike and Slim take him on a tour of their old haunts and try to convince him that, although their friendship will never be the same again, Roland has to do the right thing… In contrast to most urban Afro-American films, *The Wood* is a warm-hearted tale of middle-class values. With its catalogue of 1980s' black culture – jheri curls, K-Swiss trainers, hip-hop soundtrack – it puts nostalgia and charm before social commentary or human insight. It's a tribute, then, to the acting skills of the three stars – Diggs, Epps and Jones – that they bring their characters so resoundingly alive. [*Ewen Brownrigg*]

● *Roland* Taye Diggs, *Mike* Omar Epps, *Slim* Richard T. Jones, *young Mike* Sean Nelson, *young Roland* Trent Cameron, *young Slim* Duane Finley, *young Alicia* Malinda Williams, *Stacey* De'Aundre Bonds, *Alicia* Sanaa Lathan, *the bride* LisaRaye, *Tanya* Tamala Jones, Elayn Taylor, Patricia Belcher, Jascha Washington, Todd Boyd.
● *Dir* and *Screenplay* Rick Famuyiwa, from a story by Famuyiwa and Todd Boyd, *Pro* Albert Berger, Ron Yerxa and David Gale, *Ex Pro* Van Toffler, *Co-Pro* Douglas Curtis, *Ph* Steven Bernstein, *Pro Des* Roger Fortune and Maxine Shepard, *Ed* John Carter, *M* Pilar McCurry; songs performed by Joe, Marc Dorsey, Whodini, Biz Markie, Ahmad, and Luther Vandross and Cheryl Lynn, *Costumes* Darryle Johnson.

Paramount/MTV Films/Bona Fide Prods/Sundance Institute-Nubian Tales. 106 mins. USA. 1999. Rel: 28 January 2000. Cert 15.

The World is Not Enough ★★★¹/₂

Spain/London/Scotland/Azerbaijan/France/Kazakhstan /Turkey; the present. With a bullet lodged in his brain, international terrorist Renard feels no pain and is growing stronger every day. Dedicated to the propagation of total chaos, Renard assassinates an English businessman – within the very confines of M16's headquarters – in a move to sabotage Britain's involvement in a lucrative oil reserve under the Caspian Sea. Time, then, for top secret agent James Bond to step in ... The one-liners are marginally above average (Bond's *double* double-entendre to Christmas Jones: 'I always wanted to have a Christmas in Turkey'), the cast agreeably eclectic and the pre-credit sequence – a speedboat chase down The Thames culminating in a collision with the Millennium Dome – is a classic. Bond is back and, now in his eighties, looks amazing as he runs, jumps and seduces his way through his 19th (official) cinematic adventure. While the film remains locked within the Bond formula and there are a few too many double agents, traitors and villains, the thing holds up because of the fresh ingredients added to the stew: John Cleese's bumbling gadget geek, M's unexpected involvement in the plot and, of course, some nifty devices, such as an inflatable, avalanche-proof jacket and a giant, air-borne chain of saw wheels. And is this the first Bond film to see 007 show signs of embarrassment and compunction?

● *James Bond* Pierce Brosnan, *Elektra King* Sophie Marceau, *Renard* Robert Carlyle, *Christmas Jones* Denise Richards, *Valentin Zukovsky* Robbie Coltrane, *M* Judi Dench, *Q* Desmond Llewelyn, *R* John Cleese, *Gigar girl* Maria Grazia Cucinotta, *Moneypenny* Samantha Bond, *Tanner* Michael Kitchen, *Charles Robinson* Colin Salmon, *The Bull* Goldie, *Dr Molly Warmflash* Serena Scott Thomas, Ulrich Thomsen, John Seru, Claude-Oliver Rudolph, Patrick Malahide, Jeff Nutall, Justus Von Dohnanyi, Martyn Lewis, Daisy Beaumont, David Calder.
● *Dir* Michael Apted, *Pro* Michael G. Wilson and Barbara Broccoli, *Line Pro* Anthony Waye, *Screenplay* Neal Purvis & Robert Wade, and Bruce Feirstein, from a story by Purvis & Wade, *Ph* Adrian Biddle, *Pro Des* Peter Lamont, *Ed* Jim Clark, *M* David Arnold; title song performed by Garbage, *Costumes* Lindy Hemming, *visual effects* Mara Bryan, *main title design* Daniel Kleinman.

Eon Prods/MGM-UIP.
128 mins. UK/USA. Rel: 26 November 1999. Cert 12.

You're Dead ★★'/2

Following an extended siege of the formidable Richardson Bank, the bodies of its prospective robbers are discovered in a sepulchral heap. The sole survivor of the debacle, a young undercover police officer, is interrogated by the head of the enigmatic government agency Cyclops and forced to give her own account of events ... Displaying the cheekiness of *The Italian Job*, the flash style of *Lock, Stock and Two Smoking Barrels* and all the subtle ingenuity of a Rik Mayall retrospective, *You're Dead* tries too hard to be all things to all boys. Littered with buffoons and caricatures and redundant dialogue – and boasting John Hurt's worst performance for thirty years – the film's main problem is its awkward structure. The whole story is told through flashback – intersected by more flashbacks – which rather takes the steam out of things. There are, however, a few wonderful visual flourishes and a nice turn from Rhys Ifans as a demented bank robber.

● *Michael Maitland* John Hurt, *Eddie* Rhys Ifans, *Jo Simpson* Claire Skinner, *Professor Corner* Barbara Flynn, *Ian* David Schneider, *Inspector Richard Badger* John Benfield, *D.I. Guffin* Patrick Field, *bank manager Cliff Swinton* Roger Ashton-Griffiths, *Dr Chandra* Badi Uzzaman, *Versuvius* Jane Peachey, George Osman, Tony Osman, Rayner Bourton, Simon Paul, Felicity Dean.
● *Dir and Screenplay* Andy Hurst, *Pro* Marco Weber, *Ex Pro* Rolf Engelhart, *Ph* Wedigo von Schultzendorff, *Pro Des* Frank Bollinger, *Ed* Andrew Starke, *M* Robert Folk, *Costumes* Jany Temme.

Concorde Filmverleih/Atlantic Streamline-Entertainment.
93 mins. UK/Germany. 1999. Rel: 1 October 1999. Cert 15.

Above: Your money or his life – John Hurt in Andy Hurst's over-ambitious You're Dead (from Entertainment)

Left: Denise Richards as rocket scientist Christmas Jones with Pierce Brosnan as James Bond in Michael Apted's entertaining The World is Not Enough (from UIP)

Video Releases

from July 1999 through to June 2000

Compiled by Howard Maxford

Against the Law

In this variation on *The Quick and the Dead*, a modern day gunfighter goes about challenging all comers to a series of televised duels so as to earn the reputation of being the fastest gunslinger alive. Unfortunately, the double threat of star Richard Grieco and director Jim Wynorski is the only deadly thing on display here. At just 81 minutes, at least it's done and dusted quickly.

● With Richard Grieco, Nancy Allen, Nick Mancuso, Steven Ford.

Warner. March 2000. Cert 15.

Alien Cargo

This routine sci-fi shocker sees two space hauliers transformed into psychotic killers having been infected by a mysterious virus. As you'd expect from such fare, there's lots of running up and down corridors.

● With Missy Crider, Jason London.

CIC. August 1999. Cert 15.

Angel's Dance

Quite intriguing comedy-thriller about a novice hitman who is told to pick a name at random from the phone book so as to assassinate that person. As you'd expect, things don't quite go according to plan. Not too bad for a High Fliers release.

● With James Belushi, Sheryl Lee, Kyle Chandler.

High Fliers. January 2000. Cert 15.

The Audrey Hepburn Story

Standard made for television biopic about the *Breakfast at Tiffany's* star.

● With Jennifer Love Hewitt, Keir Dullea, Frances Fisher.

Odyssey. April 2000. Cert 15.

BASEketball ★★

Too lazy to dash about a basketball court – but nonetheless expert shooters – social outcasts Joe Cooper and Doug Remer invent their own amalgam of baseball and basketball. The game takes off and Joe and Doug become national icons, but can their friendship withstand the pressures of fame and glory? In an attempt to spice up the skewered comic vision of director David Zucker (who made his name with *Kentucky Fried Movie* and *Airplane!*) rising stars Trey Parker and Matt Stone – the creators of TV's cult cartoon *South Park* – bring their own darker, smuttier humour to this outrageous parody of American sport. The result, however, is mixed, as the frenetic spoofery that proved so fresh and surprising in 1980 has now become extremely tired (for every one good chuckle there are nine or ten groans here) while the moronic duo have already been well represented by Wayne & Garth and Beavis & Butthead. Furthermore, much of the film's topical humour will be lost on audiences outside of the States – who, for instance, won't appreciate that much of the commercial lunacy in the film actually takes place (such as stadiums changing their names to comply with their sponsor) or, indeed, understand why basketball star Shaquille O'Neal made more money in college. [JC-W]

● Also with Yasmine Bleeth, Jenny McCarthy, Robert Vaughn, Ernest Borgnine, Dian Bachar, Robert Stack, Reggie Jackson, Kareem Abdul-Jabbar, Jill Gascoine, Charlotte Zucker, Danielle Zucker. M James Ira Newborn.

Universal. December 1999. Cert 15.

B Monkey

A strait-laced teacher is seduced by a young woman who subsequently introduces him to the seamier side of London in this fitfully intriguing thriller from director Michael Radford.

● With Asia Argento, Jared Harris, Rupert Everett, Jonathan Rhys-Meyers, Ian Hart.

Buena Vista. April 2000. Cert 18.

Brave New World

Predictable futuristic drama, based on the novel by Aldous Huxley, about two people who find their lives transformed in a society in which human emotions are forbidden (yep, that old chestnut). On the whole, Ira Levin's novel *This Perfect Day* tackled the same theme with more flair.

● With Peter Gallagher, Leonard Nimoy.

Universal. February 2000. Cert 12.

Breach of Trust

A distaff variation on the equally wet but bigger budgeted *Random Hearts*. Here a woman discovers that her husband, who's just survived a plane crash, has been having an affair with the lady – killed in the accident – who was travelling in the seat next to him.

● With Roma Downey, William Russ, Kristina Malota.

Odyssey. January 2000. Cert PG.

Candyman: Day of the Dead

The law of diminishing returns sets in with this second sequel to *Candyman*, in which the hook-handed killer returns to claim his only living relative, his artist granddaughter. The expected shocks and gore may well satisfy fans of the previous two entries in the series, but otherwise this is an exhausted effort.

● With Tony Todd, Donna D'Errico.

Mosaic. March 2000. Cert 18.

Chameleon

A ruthless female assassin with chameleon-like abilities suffers a change of heart when a boy awakens her maternal instincts. So-so sci-fi.

● With Bobbie Phillips, Eric Lloyd, Jerome Ehlers.

Paramount. August 1999. Cert 18.

Club Wildside

A soft core sex film in which a married couple play the field only to realise that

monogamy's best. As you'd expect, though, much flesh is revealed on the way to this revelation.
● With Sage Kirkpatrick, Benjamin Sheffer.
Eros. January 2000. Cert 18.

Complicity
Violent low budget thriller about a journalist on the trail of a serial killer.
● With Jonny Lee Miller, Brian Cox, Bill Paterson. *Dir* Gavin Millar.
Entertainment in Video. June 2000. Cert 18.

A Cooler Climate
Straightforward romantic drama about opposites attracting. Has a good cast, though.
● With Sally Field, Judy Davis, Winston Rekert, Jerry Wasserman.
Paramount. May 200. Cert 15.

The Day Lincoln Was Shot
A plot synopsis isn't necessary in this straightforward historical drama which fails to beg the old question, 'Apart from that, Mrs Lincoln, how did you enjoy the show?'
● With Lance Henriksen, Rob Morrow, Donna Murphy.
Warner. August 1999. Cert 15.

Denial
See *Something About Sex*

The Disciples
A made for television pilot, this features the adventures of a *Mission: Impossible* team for hire. Silly, but quite fun at times. Directed by the ubiquitous Alan Smithee.
● With Ice T, Erin Daniels, Eva Mendez.
Paramount. July 1999. Cert 15.

Dream House
Originally made for television, this low rent shocker sees a family terrorised by the computer controlling all the gadgets and gizmos in their house. Catch *The Amityville Horror* on the late show instead.
● With Timothy Busfield.
Paramount. October 1999. Cert 12.

The Eternal
Standard spooky house thriller involving the embalmed body of a druid princess which has the ability to wreak havoc from beyond the grave. As you'd expect,

there's lots of wandering around in dark places, with things unexpectedly jumping out of the shadows. If that sort of thing appeals to you, then this will provide a satisfying jolt or two.
● With Alison Elliott, Christopher Walken, Jared Harris.
High Fliers. April 2000. Cert 15.

The Extreme Adventures of Super Dave
Desperate comedy about a retired stunt man who returns for one last gig, to help raise money for charity. Dire.
● With Bob Einstein, Dan Hedaya, Don Lake.
Warner. April 2000. Cert PG.

A Face to Kill For
A facially scarred woman dumped on big time by her husband seeks plastic surgery and then revenge in this absurd thriller.
● With Crystal Bernard, Doug Savant.
Paramount. October 1999. Cert 15.

Forget Me Never
A well acted but otherwise overly worthy drama about a businesswoman who develops Alzheimer's' disease. By the way, did I tell you this is a well acted but otherwise overly worthy drama about a businesswoman who develops Alzheimer's disease?
● With Mia Farrow, Martin Sheen, Diane McGowin.
Alliance Atlantis. April 2000. Cert PG.

Fury Within
Slightly better than average horror flick in which a family, the adults of which are having marital problems, suffers a series of seemingly unexplainable phenomena.
● With Ally Sheedy, Jodie Dry, Vincent Berry, Costas Mandylor.
Paramount. July 1999. Cert 12.

Gang Law
A black teenager finds himself drawn into gang culture, despite his better judgement. Expect the usual clichés.
● With Gary Busey, C. Thomas Howell.
Mosaic. May 2000. Cert 18.

Glory and Honor
An account of Robert Peary's trip to the Pole, as seen through the experiences of his black valet, Matthew Henson, who accompanied him there.

● With Delroy Lindo, Henry Czerny, Bronwen Booth.
Warner. August 1999. Cert PG.

Houdini
Better than you'd expect biopic of the celebrated escapologist. The 1953 version starring Tony Curtis is still preferable, though.
● With Johnathon Schaech, Stacy Edwards, Rhea Perlman, David Warner.
Warner. July 1999. Cert PG.

The Hunley
Set in 1864, this tells the absorbing story of the submarine CSS Hunley, the first man-powered sub to destroy an enemy ship in battle.
● With Donald Sutherland, Armand Assante, Alex Jennings.
Warner. April 2000. Cert 12.

I Married a Monster
Tolerable *Stepford Wives/Invasion of the Body Snatchers/I Married a Monster from Outer Space* hybrid in which the men in a small town suddenly start to become attentive to their wives. Can they have been taken over by aliens? You betcha!
● With Susan Walters, Tim Ryan, Richard Burgi.
Paramount. July 1999. Cert 15.

Inferno
The expected group of disparate types pull together when a flaming cloud descends upon Washington. Given it was originally made for television, a fairly tolerable disaster drama.
● With James Remar, Anthony Starke, Daniel Von Bargen.
Paramount. August 1999. Cert 12.

The Invisible Child
Oddball drama about a nanny who turns up to look after a young girl, only to find her a figment of her so-called mother's imagination.
● With Rita Wilson, Victor Garber.
Odyssey. August 1999. Cert PG.

Jerry and Tom
Fairly effective black comedy about a couple of used car salesmen who also sideline as assassins. Helped immeasurably by the performances of its two stars, plus some slick handling by actor-turned-director Saul Rubinek.

● With Joe Mantegna, Sam Rockwell, William H. Macy, Ted Danson.
High Fliers. August 1999. Cert 15.

Joan of Arc

Made for television version of the story of the Maid of Orleans' last campaign. Rent the Luc Besson version instead.
● With Leelee Sobieski, Jacqueline Bisset, Powers Boothe, Maury Chaykin, Olympia Dukakis, Jonathan Hyde, Robert Loggia, Peter O'Toole, Maximilian Schell, Peter Strauss, Shirley MacLaine. Dir: Christian Duguay.
Odyssey. March 2000. Cert 15.

Kidnapped in Paradise

The Island meets *Dead Calm* in this tolerable action drama about two estranged sisters who re-unite on a Caribbean island only to find themselves kidnapped and at the mercy of a bunch of murderous modern day pirates.
● With Joely Fisher, Charlotte Ross.
Universal. February 2000. Cert 12.

Killers in the House

A family's first night in their new home turns into something of a nightmare when they are besieged by a gang of murderous bank robbers in this tolerable variation on the twice-filmed *Desperate Hours*.
● With Mario Van Peebles, Andrew Robinson.
Universal. February 2000. Cert 15.

King Cobra

With a title like this, you know you're in for little more than a variation on *Anaconda*. This time the beastie in question is a thirty-foot King Cobra-Eastern Diamondback Rattlesnake hybrid which has escaped the biological lab at which it was created following an explosion. Naturally, it slithers towards the nearest town, which just happens to be having its annual beer fest, so there are plenty of pot-bellied yokels for the serpent to get its fangs into. Despite the hackneyed premise, a fair amount of fun is provided, with Erik Estrada in particular enjoying his non-PC turn as the town's camp mayor.
● With Scott Brandon, Kasey Fallo, Pat Morita, Erik Estrada.
High Fliers. March 2000. Cert 15.

K9 II

If you though the 1988 comedy *K9*, about a cop and his slobbering sidekick

dog, was bad, then you should avoid this belated but unwanted sequel like dog dirt on the pavement. Pooper scooper anyone?
● With James Belushi, Christine Tucci.
Universal. April 2000. Cert 12.

Laserhawk

Two teenagers, who turn out to be aliens, fight off an attack by deadly spider-like aliens bent on destroying mankind (aren't they always?). Run of the mill stuff.
● With Jason James Richter.
Alliance Atlantis. August 1999. Cert 15.

Last Bus Home

An effective drama set in Dublin in 1979, this follows the attempts of a punk band to make it in the music business. More surprisingly, it also has several interesting points to make about the Catholic church's stance on sexuality.
● With John Cronin, Annie Ryan, Anthony Brophy.
High Fliers. September 1999. Cert 18.

Life of a Gigolo

A journalist goes undercover to investigate the work of a gigolo. Cue lots of soft core bumping and grinding.
● With Lauren Hays, Gwen Somers, Brad Bartram.
Eros. September 1999. Cert 18.

Loop

Dismal comedy-drama about failed relationships in a countryside setting.
● With Emer McCourt, Andy Serkis, Susannah York (who deserved better than this).
Showcase. August 1999. Cert 15.

Lost and Found

A romantic comedy with aspirations to *There's Something About Mary*, this follows the attempts by a restaurateur to attract the attention of his new neighbour, a beautiful French cellist, which he does by kidnapping her beloved terrier. A fair degree of comic mayhem follows, involving a missing anniversary ring, Neil Diamond (don't ask!) and surly loan officers. A bit desperate at times, there are nevertheless some amusingly screwy moments along the way.
● With David Spade, Sophie Marceau, Patrick Bruel, Frankie Muniz.
Warner Bros. February 2000. Cert 12.

Major League: Back to the Minors

Enough already with the *Major League* sequels. Charlie Sheen and Tom Berenger wisely gave this one a miss.
● With Scott Bakula, Corbin Bernsen, Dennis Haysbert.
Warner. August 1999. Cert 12.

Max Q

Though co-produced by Jerry Bruckheimer, this variation on themes from *Apollo 13* was originally made for television. Here it's the crew of a space shuttle sent to launch a satellite that finds itself in trouble.
● With Bill Campbell, Paget Brewster.
Touchstone. October 1999. Cert 12.

Mistaken Identity

Standard true life tele-drama about a couple who discover that their child was mistakenly switched at birth. You want to care, but it's all oh-so earnest.
● With Rosanna Arquette, Melissa Gilbert, James McCaffrey, David Andrews.
Odyssey Platinum. March 2000. Cert 15.

Netforce

Needlessly complex thriller involving control of the Internet. At 154 minutes, it's much too long to sustain interest.
● With Scott Bakula, Joanna Going, Brian Dennehy, Kris Kristofferson, Judge Reinhold.
High Fliers. July 1999. Cert 15.

New World Disorder

Likeable 1980s teen lead Andrew McCarthy here turns tough and plays a software thief pursued by cops. Otherwise unremarkable, though.
● With Rutger Hauer, Andrew McCarthy, Tara Fitzgerald.
Mosaic. October 1999. Cert 18.

No Looking Back

An almost wholly predictable small town romantic drama, this follows the tedious plight of a young woman who is given the opportunity to escape from her confining surroundings when an old flame turns up on the scene. `You can't relive your past,' runs the tag line, so don't waste any of your life watching this unimaginative slosh.
● With Ed Burns, Lauren Holly, Jon Bon Jovi, Blythe Danner. *Dir* and

Screenplay Ed Burns.
Fox Pathé. March 2000. Cert 15.

Office Space

Beavis and Butt-head creator Mike Judge goes live with this gag-strewn comedy based on an original short he made back in 1990, since when he has featured the central character, Milton, in a series of shorts. Here the character is played by Stephen Root (one of the voices on the Judge-created cartoon *King of the Hill*), with Judge calling the shots from behind the camera. Neither the first nor the last office comedy, but with Judge in control, the chuckles come at fairly regular intervals.
● With Stephen Root, Gary Cole.
Fox. January 2000. Cert 15.

Office Killer

First a comedy, now a stalk and slash thriller, in which workers in a busy magazine office literally find themselves being down-sized. A better cast than usual for this sort of thing helps to make the scenes between the gore and the thrills more tolerable.
● With Carol Kane, Jeanne Tripplehorn, Molly Ringwald, Barbara Sukowa, David Thornton, Michael Imperioli.
Buena Vista. December 1999. Cert 15.

Old New Borrowed Blue

See *With or Without You*.

Phantasm IV: Oblivion

One for fans of the *Phantasm* series only. An increasingly tired variation on all the old themes.
● With A Michael Baldwin, Angus Scrimm, Reggie Bannister.
Mosaic. August 1999. Cert 15.

Polish Wedding

What do Polish men give their wives that's long and hard on their wedding day? A new surname! A Polish-American family gathers for a wedding with the expected confrontations.
● With Claire Danes, Lena Olin, Gabriel Byrne, Mili Avital.
Dir Theresa Connelly.
Fox. August 1999. Cert 15.

Prague Duet

Though based on a true story, this is just another routine romancer, this time involving an American woman's love affair with a celebrated Czech writer whilst visiting Prague. As expected, though, the path to true love is a troubled one. At least the backgrounds are eye-catching.
● With Gina Gershon, Rade Sherbedgia.
Warner Bros. February 2000. Cert 15.

Raw Nerve

Foolish thriller about a cop attempting to clear his name. Yep, they're still reworking that old chestnut.
● With Mario Van Peebles, Nicollette Sheridan.
High Fliers. April 2000. Cert 18.

Sabrina Goes to Rome

Mild feature-length comedy derived from the popular sitcom, this sees the teenage witch travel to the eternal city to discover the secret of a magic locket.
● With Melissa Joan Hart.
CIC. September 1999. Cert 18 (Just kidding, actually it's a U)

Shattered Image

Foolish thriller in which a woman with amnesia has memory flashes to her past as an assassin. A dumb *La Femme Nikita-The Long Kiss Goodnight* hybrid.
● With Anne Parillaud, William Baldwin, Graham Greene, Bulle Ogier. *Dir* Raul Ruiz.
Metrodome. March 2000. Cert 18.

Shiloh 2: Shiloh Season

If you warmed to the 1996 family film *Shiloh*, which told the story a young boy and the runaway beagle he takes care of, then this floppy-eared sequel, in which the dog's original owner, a drunken ex-hunter, demands the creature back, should appeal in equal measure.
● With Zachary Brown, Rod Steiger, Scott Wilson.
Warner Bros. February 2000. Cert U.

Shriek

Dull horror hokum involving kids being bumped off by a dimension-hopping killer in a deserted hospital, this could and should have been more fun that it actually is.
● With Parry Allen, Tanya Dempsey, Jamie Gammon.
High Fliers. September 1999. Cert 15.

Soldier

Expensive but unimaginative sci-fi piece in which dwellers living on a garbage planet are helped in their fight by a soldier with a Terminator-like personality. Director Paul Anderson helmed the equally disappointing *Event Horizon*.
● With Kurt Russell, Jason Scott Lee, Gary Busey, Sean Pertwee, Jason Isaacs, Connie Nielsen.
Warner. July 1999. Cert 18.

Something About Sex

Originally titled *Denial*, this hit and miss comedy examines three couple's views on fidelity, most of which prove to be hypocritical.
● With Jonathan Silverman, Christine Taylor, Amy Yasbeck, Patrick Dempsey, Jason Alexander.
Dir Adam Rifkin.
High Fliers. October 1999. Cert 18.

Storm Trooper

Another *Terminator* rip-off from director Jim Wynorski, with a dash of *Judge Dredd* thrown in for good measure, this unambitious sci-fi thriller follows the military's attempts to destroy a top secret cyborg – the ultimate cop – which has escaped in a murderous rage from the Tannis Corporation's labs before being perfected. The plot and action are strictly by the numbers, but if accompanied by a pizza and six-pack it passes its brief 83 minute running time relatively painlessly.
● With John Laughlin, Corey Feldman, Zach Galligan.
Warner Bros. March 2000. Cert 18.

Strike!

1963, and the pupils at a single-sex girls school strike at the prospect of going co-ed. Quite amusing, thanks to the energetic performance of its young cast.
● With Kirsten Dunsten, Rachael Leigh Cook, Gaby Hoffmann, Lynn Redgrave, Tom Guiry, Heather Matarazzo.
M Graeme Revell.
Alliance Atlantis. July 1999. Cert 15.

Strong Language

Surprisingly well-knitted collection of low-life stories, triggered by a further story being told by the film's narrator. Worth a look.
● With Paul Tonkinson, Stuart Laing, David Groves.
Third Millennium. March 2000. Cert 18.

The Substitute: Winner Takes All

Amazingly, this is the second sequel to the 1996 action thriller about a mercenary turned substitute teacher. You may want to sit at the back and play with raffia rather than take this particular lesson.
● With Treat Williams, James Black, Claudia Christian.
Mosaic. June 2000. Cert 18.

Susan's Plan

This disastrous black comedy about a murder-plot-gone-awry sees *American Werewolf* director John Landis bury his once-flourishing career even further into the ground. That said, it's not quite as awful as *The Stupids* (but it runs a close second).
● With Nastassja Kinski, Dan Aykroyd, Michael Biehn, Billy Zane, Rob Schneider, Lara Flynn Boyle, Joey Travolta, Thomas Haden Church, Sheree North.
High Fliers. September 1999. Cert 18.

Taxman

The taxman cometh in this low rent thriller in which the man from the Inland Revenue attempts to uncover a tax fraud being perpetrated by the Russian Mafia. Doesn't add up to an entertaining movie.
● With Joe Pantoliano, Elizabeth Berkley.
High Fliers. June 2000. Cert 15.

Testing the Limits

Soft core tut in which a young couple become involved in the sexual antics of a group of models during a fashion shoot at a ranch.
● With Scott Carson, Brandy Davis, Lorissa McComas.
Eros. August 1999. Cert 18.

Thick as Thieves

A surprisingly slick and action-packed thriller, this follows the exploits of Mackin, a crack thief who is hired by the Mob to steal $250 000 in food stamps, only to find himself ambushed by two crooked cops having successfully pulled off the heist. Out to avenge himself against the traitor who shopped him, a middle man named Pointy, things quickly build to explosive proportions, much to the Mob's consternation. Given the star talent involved, this

is a surprise candidate for a video premiere, but action fans will find it well worth checking out.
● With Alec Baldwin, Rebecca De Mornay, Michael Jai White, Andre Braugher, Bruce Greenwood, Richard Edson. *Dir* Scott Sanders.
Alliance Atlantic. March 2000. Cert 18.

Tom Clancy's Netforce

See *Netforce*.

Two for Texas

Passable Western adventure in which two escaped cons find themselves involved in the fight for the freedom of Texas.
● With Kris Kristofferson, Scott Bairstow, Peter Coyote.
Warner. July 1999. Cert 15.

200 Cigarettes

On New Year's Eve in 1981 New York, a group of self-seeking trendies look for a lay before the clock strikes twelve. With this wonderful cast it's a shame the characters they are asked to play are so damned unlikeable, although Ben Affleck, Christina Ricci and Courtney Love are exceptionally good value. [CB]
● Also with Casey Affleck, Jay Mohr, Dave Chappelle, Gaby Hoffmann, Paul Rudd, Catherine Kellner, Martha Plimpton, Janeane Garofalo, Guillermo Diaz, Angela Featherstone, Nicole Parker, Kate Hudson, Elvis Costello. Dir Risa Bramon Garcia.
CIC. October 1999. Cert 15.

Underground

Ultra tough thriller following a drug pusher's attempts to escape the wrath of a rave organiser out for revenge.
● With Billy Smith, Nick Sutton, Zoe Smale.
Showcase. October 1999. Cert 18.

Universal Soldier II: Brothers in Arms

The first of two unofficial made for television sequels to the 1992 Dolph Lundgren/Jean-Claude Van Damme hit, with the Swedish meatball and the Muscles from Brussels replaced by Jeff Wincott and Matt Battaglia.
● With Jeff Wincott, Matt Battaglia, Gary Busey.
Paramount. August 1999. Cert 18.

The Van Boys

A gang makes a living by stealing pavement slabs. Yes, that's the plot! Not exactly what you'd call thrilling, but the performances are real enough.
● With Scot Williams, Paul Usher.
Metrodome. June 2000. Cert 15.

The Vivero Letter

Poor action thriller centring on the search for treasure in the Mayan jungles.
● With Fred Ward, Robert Patrick.
High Fliers. April 2000. Cert 18.

Water Damage

Water-clogged thriller about a marriage-gone-wrong following the death of a young boy. For Daniel Baldwin fans only. Hope you both enjoy it.
● With Daniel Baldwin, Dean Stockwell.
Mosaic. May 2000. Cert 18.

Welcome to Woop Woop

Fitfully amusing comedy about an Aussie conman who finds himself trapped in a small outback township. Writer-director Stephan Elliott, who gave us *Priscilla, Queen of the Desert*, ensures a few chuckles along the way.
● With Rod Taylor, Susie Porter, Johnathon Schaech, Dee Smart, Richard Moir, Rachel Griffiths, Barry Humphries. *M* Stewart Copeland.
MGM. September 1999. Cert 18.

Why Do Fools Fall In Love

Engaging biography of the 1950's teen idol Frankie Lymon, the Harlem-born do-wop swinger who had a propensity for heroin and collecting wives. The girls are terrific although we learn little about what drove this charismatic sensation to self-destruction. [CB]
● With Larenz Tate, Halle Berry, Lela Rochon, Vivica A. Fox, Paul Mazursky, Pamela Reed, Little Richard, Ben Vereen, Lane Smith. *Dir* Gregory Nava.
Warner. September 1999. Cert 15.

Wing Commander

Disappointing big screen transfer of the popular video game. But then again *Super Mario Bros, Mortal Kombat* and *Double Dragon* weren't exactly great, either.
● With Freddie Prinze Jr., Saffron Burrows, David Warner, Jürgen Prochnow, Matthew Lillard,

Tcheky Karyo, David Suchet. *Dir* Chris Roberts.
Fox. January 2000. Cert PG.

With or Without You

Belfast; today. Vincent and Rosie Boyd have been happily married for five years and now want a baby. But, while resorting to platefuls of spinach and administering ice cubes to his testicles, Vincent just cannot seem to get his wife pregnant. Then an old French boyfriend of Rosie's turns up out of the blue and moves in with them ... If Michael Winterbottom, director of such dark, edgy and stylised films as *Butterfly Kiss*, *Welcome to Sarajevo* and *I Want You*, was to make a romantic comedy, this is what it would be like. So, no surprises there. Of course, one could do without the split screen effects and the quaint `iris fades' (in which images recede in a circle). Mr Winterbottom should trust more in the strength of his own story and his actors. Here, his trio of stars give fresh impressions of themselves, while Belfast makes an unusual and refreshingly neutral backdrop to the domestic drama (and is happily free of any of the `Troubles'). So, technical pretensions aside, this is a funny, warm, emotionally bruising and unexpected film that really gets under the skin. Previously known as *Old New Borrowed Blue* [JC-W]
● With Christopher Eccleston, Dervla Kirwan, Yvan Attal, Julie Graham, Alun Armstrong, Lloyd Hutchinson, Fionnula Flanagan, Michael Liebmann, Doon MacKichan. *M* Adrian Johnston.
Film Four. March 2000. Cert 18.

Witness Protection

Accused of fixing the Mafia's books, an accountant takes his family into the witness protection scheme after his life is threatened. This is an offer you will want to refuse.
● With Tom Sizemore, Mary Elizabeth Mastrantonio, Forest Whitaker.
High Fliers. June 2000. Cert 15.

Wrongfully Accused

The latest Leslie Nielsen movie spoof sees the star in a lukewarm take-off of *The Fugitive*. Never less than obvious, this makes *Dracula, Dead and Loving It* look like a classic.
● With Leslie Nielsen, Kelly LeBrock, Michael York, Sandra Bernhard.
Warner. August 1999. Cert PG.

Y2K

Not at all bad actioner in which the military has to deactivate a missile silo which has been wrongfully activated by the millennium bug. Unfortunately, they have to overcome a series of deadly protection devices to do so.
● With Louis Gossett Jr, Malcolm McDowell, Ed O'Ross, Jaimz Woolvett.
Entertainment. August 1999. Cert 18.

You Know My Name

A 20s-set Western drama, this centres on retired lawman Bill Tilghman, who has turned to the movies to chronicle his former exploits. However, on the eve of his silent movie debut, he gets the chance for one last stab at glory when he's asked to clean up the troubled town of Cromwell, where drinking, gambling and whoring are a way of life. A curious amalgam of motifs familiar from *The Magnificent Seven*, *A Fistful of Dollars* and *Sunset*, this nevertheless passes the time amiably enough, thanks to the presence of its moustachioed star.
● With Sam Elliott, Arliss Howard, Carolyn McCormick.
Warner Bros. February 2000. Cert 15.

OTHER VIDEO RELEASES

Armstrong

Bog standard action fare about an ex-CIA operative who helps his old mentor track down his kidnapped wife. It's directed by Menahem Golan, which should be warning enough. With Frank Zargarino, Joe Lara, Charles Napier, Kimberley Kates. Nu Image. January 2000. Cert 18.

Black and Blue

Familiar story of a family's breakdown owing to the violence meted out by dad, who just happens to be a high ranking cop. With Mary Stuart Masterson, Anthony Lapaglia. Odyssey. February 2000. Cert 15.

The Brass Ring

Reasonably intriguing if somewhat complex political thriller apparently based on an unproduced screenplay by Orson Welles. With William Hurt, Nigel Hawthorne, Irene Jacob, Miranda Richardson, Jim Metzler. *Dir* George Hickenlooper. Nu Image. January 2000. Cert 18.

Breeders

Low budget British horror flick about an evil alien on the loose at a (supposedly American) college campus. And yes, Janus does get her kit off. With Samantha Janus, Oliver Tobias. Digital Entertainment. November 1999. Cert 15.

Clear Target

Also known as *Operation Delta Force III*, this routine actioner follows the US military as they take on the might of the Colombian drug barons. Cue lots of gunfire and macho attitudinising. With Greg Collins, Bryan Genesse, Darcy La Pier. Nu Image. November 1999. Cert 18.

A Cool Dry Place

Dumped by his wife, a lawyer attempts to cope with his five-year-old son whilst at the same time trying to get his love life back on track. With Vince Vaughn, Joey Lauren Adams, Monica Potter, Devon Sawa. *Dir* John N. Smith. Fox Pathé. February 2000. Cert 15.

Dying to Live

A so-what variation of TV's *Highway to Heaven*, this has *Star Trek*'s Jonathan Frakes as a ghost who helps a depressed schoolteacher get over the loss of his girlfriend. Paramount. April 2000. Cert 15.

From Dusk Till Dawn 2 – Texas Blood Money

Lively made-for-video sequel to the 1995 Quentin Tarantino/Robert Rodriguez vampire comedy. Not quite in the same league, but with enough going on to satisfy the late night crowd. With Robert Patrick, Bruce Campbell, Bo Hopkins, Tiffani-Amber Thiessen. Buena Vista. January 2000. Cert 18.

Golfballs

If you've seen the two *Caddyshack* comedies, then you'll have seen most of the gags featured in this cheap but not particularly cheerful breast-obsessed rip-off. With Amy Lynn Baxter. Marquee. November 1999. Cert 15.

Happy Face Murders

Based on a true story, this otherwise routine thriller about a serial killer at least has a value for money cast. With Ann-Margret, Henry Thomas, Marg Helgenberger. Paramount. February 2000. Cert 18.

Kolobos

An early *Blair Witch* wannabe, this involves the mysterious goings on in an isolated house where six strangers have been invited to take part in a social inter-action study, only to find themselves being bumped off in front of the video cameras. A load of Kolobos. With Amy Weber, Donny Terranova, Leanna Quigley. Metrodome. January 2000. Cert 18.

Last Line of Defence

Dismal low budget variation on *Men in Black*. Brad Dourif's in it. What else do you need to know? Also with Olivier Gruner, Brad Dourif, Ernie Hudson, Glenn Plummer. Planet. February 2000. Cert 18.

Life in a Day

Sci-fi thriller about a wonder drug called Accelerate which regenerates cells. Naturally, the wrong sort of people want to get hold of it for the wrong sort of rea-sons. With Michael Goorjian, Chandra West. Paramount. April 2000. Cert PG.

Lost in the Bermuda Triangle

Standard mysterious goings-on in the leg-endary stretch of ocean. With Graham Beckel, Ron Canada. Paramount. February 2000. Cert PG.

The Naked Man

Wrestling ring comedy about a chiroprac-tor by day-turned champion wrestler by night. Should please WWF fans. With Michael Rapaport, Rachael Leigh Cook. EV. December 1999. Cert 15.

No Fear

In Florida, two working class teens attempt to overcome their social restrictions. With Jeremy Sisto, Jaime Pressly, Eric Michael Cole, Grace Zabriskie, Veronica Cartwright. Xscapade. March 2000. Cert 18.

The Only Thrill

Talkative romantic weepie helped along by the performances of its stars. Otherwise, not what you'd call a barrel of laughs. With Diane Keaton, Sam Shepherd, Tate Donovan, Diane Lane, Robert Patrick, Stacey Travis. *Dir* Peter Masterson. Alliance. January 2000. Cert 15.

Operation Delta Force III

See *Clear Target*

Our Guys

A mentally challenged teenager has to stand up for her rights after being sexually assaulted by members of a football squad. A reasonably involving 'issue' drama with echoes of *The Accused*. With Ally Sheedy, Eric Stoltz, Heather Matarazzo. Odyssey. November 1999. Cert 15.

Perpetrators of the Crime

Like *A Simple Plan* and *Fargo* before it, this is another snowbound thriller, this time involving three broke college bud-dies who decide to kidnap the daughter of a local millionaire and hold her to ransom for a quick $1m. Of course, things don't quite go according to plan (do they ever?). With Tori Spelling, William B. Davis, Danny Strong, Mark Burgess. Xscapade. January 2000. Cert 15.

Pirates of Silicon Valley

The true life battle between computer geeks Steve Jobs and Bill Gates, the cre-ators of Apple and Microsoft. With Noah Wyle, Anthony Michael Hall. Warner Bros. January 2000. Cert 12.

Singapore Sling

Low grade crime thriller with plenty of opportunities for Shannon Tweed to get her kit off. Also with James Hong, Rena Riffel. Xscapade. December 1999. Cert 18.

Sword of Vengeance

Stylish medieval Shogun actioner in the style of an Italian spaghetti western. Subtitled, but with gore galore to com-pensate. With Tomisaburo Wakayama, Kayo Matsuo. Warrior. November 1999. Cert 18.

Twenty Dates

A movie wannabe decides to make a low budget film about his love life. Quite amusing in spots. With Myles Berkowitz, Tia Carrere. Fox Pathé. February 2000. Cert 15.

Understanding Jane

Lively youth comedy which should please fans of *The Lakes* star John Simm. Also with Kevin McKidd, Amelia Curtis, Louisa Millwood Haigh. Metrodome. February 2000. Cert 15.

Universal Soldier III: Unfinished Business

The second of two unofficial sequels to the 1992 Dolph Lundgren/Jean-Claude Van Damme hit, this one offers the usual blend of undiscerning action and violence for fans of that kind of stuff (you know who you are). With Matt Battaglia, Burt Reynolds, Chandra West, Jeff Wincott. CIC. December 1999. Cert 18.

Warlock III: The End of Innocence

You know the name, you know the game, though even Julian Sands had the sense to bail out of this one. With Bruce Payne, Ashley Lawrence. High Fliers. February 2000. Cert 18.

Wishmaster 2

The original *Wishmaster* was bad enough. For sado-masochists only. Mosaic. January 2000. Cert 18.

The Yakuza Way

The familiar story of drugs, murder and betrayal onto which is hung a handful of spectacular fights and action sequences. Nothing new, but quite slickly done. With George Cheung, Riki Takeuchi. Film 2000. January 2000. Cert 18.

Faces of the Year

Vin Diesel

Born: 18 July 1967 in New York City
Real name: Vincent Diesel
Education: Dropped out of Hunter College, New York (where he was an English major)
Previous occupation: Bouncer in a Manhattan night-club (for eight years, no less)
Film debut: *Strays* (1997)
The other films: *Saving Private Ryan* (as Private Adrian Caparzo); *The Iron Giant* (voice only, as the eponymous robot); *Boiler Room*; *Pitch Black*
Next up: *Knockaround Guys*, a crime drama with Barry Pepper, John Malkovich and Dennis Hopper, followed by the street-racing actioner *Red Line* for director Rob Cohen, and then *Doormen* which he is directing from his own screenplay
Strengths: Charisma, presence, geniality, danger, muscle power
Infamy: He was fired by John Frankenheimer from *Reindeer Games*. He not only refused to wear a sleeveless T-shirt but demanded re-writes to boost the size of his role. Good for him
Also: Wrote, financed, produced, directed and starred in *Multi-Facial*, a short film that so impressed Steven Spielberg,

the director cast Diesel in *Saving Private Ryan*. Diesel then went on to write, produce, direct and star in the feature *Strays*, which competed in the 1997 Sundance Film Festival
He said it: 'He [Steven Spielberg] talked to me about lenses, he talked to me about camera angles. So he gave me a 35mm camera to operate. And there are actually shots in the final film [*Saving Private Ryan*] that *I* shot, which is bizarre'

Aaron Eckart

Born: 1968 in Northern California
Education: Brigham Young University, Utah (where he befriended filmmaker Neil LaBute)
Film debut: *Slaughter of the Innocents* (1994)
The other films: *In the Company of Men*, *Your Friends & Neighbors*, *Thursday*, *Molly*, *Any Given Sunday*, *Nurse Betty*, *Erin Brockovich*
Next up: Sean Penn's *The Pledge*, also starring Jack Nicholson, Robin Wright Penn, Vanessa Redgrave and Mickey Rourke
Strengths: Dedication, flexibility, extraordinary versatility, innate charisma, hunk appeal
Significant other: Engaged to actress Emily Cline, split up in 1998
Awards: For his performance as the brutal male chauvinist in *In the Company of Men*, he won the Golden Satellite for Outstanding New Talent and the Independent Spirit Award for Best Debut Performance
Infamy: He piled on forty pounds of junk food-fuelled flab to play the egotistical Barry in Neil LaBute's morally excoriating *Your Friends & Neighbors*
Also: Four years of his childhood were spent in Walton-on-Thames in Surrey, England
Role model: Robert De Niro
A bit like: A handsome Jeff Daniels

Iben Hjejle

Born: 22 March 1971 in Copenhagen, Denmark
Pronunciation: Ibin Haler
Education: State Theatre School of Denmark
Current occupation: Actress, wife, mother
Film debut: *Portland*
The other films: *Mifune*; *Besat*; *High Fidelity*
Next up: *The Emperor's New Clothes*
Strengths: Talent, beauty, great bone structure, excellent American accent
Awards: Voted best young actress at the 49th Berlin International Film Festival (for her role in *Mifune*)
Also: She speaks fluent Danish, Swedish and English
Role model: Max Von Sydow
A bit like: Robin Wright Penn

Samantha Morton

Born: 1977 in Nottingham, England
Education: Central Junior Television Workshop, Nottingham
Current occupation: Actress, mother
Strengths: Naturalness, spontaneity, passion, extraordinary talent
Significant others: Actor Hans Matheson (1995-97); actor Charlie

Creed-Miles (the father of her daughter)
Offspring: Esme, born 5 February 2000
Awards: For her role in *Under the Skin* – as a girl who turns to promiscuity in order to overcome the trauma of her mother's death – she was voted best actress by The Boston Society of Film Critics; for *Dreaming of Joseph Lees* she was named best actress by the London *Evening Standard*; and for her role as the simple, mute laundress Hattie in *Sweet and Lowdown* she was nominated for an Oscar as best supporting actress
Film debut: May in *The Future Lasts a Long Time* (1996)
The other films: *Under the Skin, This is the Sea, Dreaming of Joseph Lees, The Last Yellow, Pandemonium, Sweet and Lowdown, Jesus' Son*
TV: *Boon, Soldier Soldier, Cracker, Band of Gold, Jane Eyre* (title role), *Tom Jones* (as Sophia), *Jane Austen's Emma* (as Harriet Smith)
Also: She is one of eight children and from the age of three grew up in and out of foster care on a council housing estate
On her new celebrity: 'I just want to sit here with [my daughter] Esme and shut the rest of the world off'

Frances O'Connor

Born: 1970 in Oxford, Oxfordshire (she moved to Australia at two)
Previous occupations: model, English teacher, rock singer
Film debut: Emma-Kate Croghan's award-winning *Love and Other*

Catastrophes, in which she played Mia, a lesbian afraid of commitment
The other films: *Kiss or Kill, Thank God He Met Lizzie* (with Cate Blanchett), *A Little Bit of Soul* (with Geoffrey Rush), *Mansfield Park, Bedazzled, About Adam*
TV: *Blue Heelers, Shark Bay* (as Dr Jane), the BBC's *Madame Bovary* (as Emma Bovary)
Next up: The female lead in Steven Spielberg's *AI*, the long-awaited sci-fi project originally to have been directed by Stanley Kubrick
Strengths: Intelligence, adaptability, a wicked smile and a ski-slope nose
Awards: Voted best actress at the 1997 Montreal International Film Festival for her portrayal as a con artist in Bill Bennett's *Kiss or Kill.*
Also: Her parents moved to Australia when she was two-years-old
She said it: 'I really like people and why we do what we do, and acting is a great way of exploring that'

Haley Joel Osment

Born: 10 April 1988 in Los Angeles
Previous occupation: Schoolboy
Film debut: Forrest Gump Jr in *Forrest Gump*
The other films: *Mixed Nuts, For Better or Worse, Bogus, Last Stand at Saber River* (for TV), *Beauty and the Beast: The Enchanted Christmas* (voice only), *The Lake* (TV movie), *The Ransom of Red Chief* (TV), *Cab to Canada* (TV), *I'll Remember April, The Sixth Sense, Sebastian's Love, Pay It Forward*
TV: *Murphy Brown, Walker, Texas Ranger, The Pretender, Ally McBeal*
Next up: The Polish-set drama *Edges of the Lord*, with Willem Dafoe, and then Steven Spielberg's sci-fi blockbuster *AI* also starring Jude Law and Frances O'Connor
Strengths: Eye-catch good looks, credibility, eloquence, confidence, professionalism, modesty, maturity, great at crying
Awards: An Oscar nomination for playing Cole Sear, a boy who can see the dead, in *The Sixth Sense*
Don't tell anyone: He was named after his mother, Haley

Also: He has a large collection of pets, including Amazon tree frogs, geckos and rats
A bit like: A short adult
He said it: 'I try to make sure I'm not over-confident, but putting yourself down is not the way to a balanced ego. I just think, this [celebrity] is great but it's not about me, it's about acting'

Amanda Peet

Born: 11 January 1972 in New York City
Education: Columbia University (graduated in 1994)
Film debut: *Grind*, New Jersey drama starring Billy Crudup
The other films: *Animal Room, She's the One, One Fine Day, Touch Me, Ellen Foster* (for TV), *Origin of the Species, 1999, Southie, Playing by Heart, Whipped, Two Ninjas, Takedown, Jump, Simply Irresistible, Body Shots, The Whole Nine Yards, Isn't She Great*
TV: Robyn Gainer in *Central Park West, Law & Order, Spin City, Seinfeld, Partners*, Jacqueline 'Jack' Barrett in WBTV's romantic comedy series *Jack & Jill* (1999)
Next Up: *Saving Silverman*, a comedy with Jack Black, Jason Biggs and Steve Zahn, and then *Whipped*
Significant other: actor Brian Van Holt
Strengths: Natural bonhomie, personality, loveable mouth, heart-locking eyes
Role model: Meryl Streep
A bit like: Julia Roberts

Dougray Scott

Born: 25 November 1965 in Fife, Scotland
Real name: Stephen Scott
Education: Welsh College of Music and Drama (1986-1989)
Film debut: *Black Beauty* (1994), in which he played a street vendor
The other films: *Princess Caraboo, Regeneration* (as Robert Graves), *Twin Town, Another 9½ Weeks* (aka *Love in Paris*), *Deep Impact, Ever After, This Year's Love, Gregory's Two Girls, The Miracle Maker* (voice only), *Mission: Impossible 2*
TV: *Taggart, Lovejoy, The Harry Enfield Show, Stay Lucky, Kavanagh Q.C., Soldier Soldier; Highlander, The Crow Road, Arabian Nights*
Next up: The lead in *Enigma*, in which he plays Tom Jericho, a brilliant but tormented code-breaker. Kate Winslet and Jeremy Northam co-star
Strengths: Dedication, versatility, smouldering good looks, a grounding in reality
Wife: Casting director Sarah Trevis
Offspring: Gabriel and Eden, a twin boy and girl
Infamy: Determined to keep up with co-star Tom Cruise in *Mission: Impossible 2*, Scott insisted on doing his own motorcycle stunts, resulting in a six-week stay in hospital (and a substantial delay in shooting)
Awards: Named Most Promising Student at drama college
Role Model: Alec Guinness
He said it: 'When I see myself on screen I see a character. When I look in my own mirror I see my life. People say I'm a good-looking guy, and I think, what does that mean? It's vacuous, because it's what's behind the eyes, what's inside someone's heart and soul that counts'

Philip Seymour Hoffman

Born: 23 July 1967 in Fairport, New York
Education: NYU's Tisch School of Drama
Previous occupations: Waiter (but of course), lifeguard
Film debut: *Triple Bogey on a Par 5 Hole* (1991)
The other films: *My New Gun, Scent of a Woman, Leap of Faith, My Boyfriend's Back, Money for Nothing, Joey Breaker, Nobody's Fool, When a Man Loves a Woman, The Getaway,* Paul Thomas Anderson's *Sydney* (aka *Hard Eight*), *Twister,* Paul Thomas Anderson's *Boogie Nights, Montana, Next Stop Wonderland, The Big Lebowski, Happiness, Patch Adams, Culture, The Talented Mr Ripley, Flawless,* Paul Thomas Anderson's *Magnolia, State and Main*
TV: *Law & Order, The Yearling*
Next up: Cameron Crowe's *Almost Famous*, an ensemble romantic drama with Frances McDormand, Billy Crudup, Fairuza Balk and Anna Paquin
Strengths: Willingness to go where other actors fear to tread, enormous physical presence, surprising tenderness, powerhouse talent
Awards: Voted best supporting actor by the National Board of Review for his work in *Magnolia* and *The Talented Mr Ripley*
Also: Directed the off-Broadway production *In Arabia, We'd All Be Kings*
Role models: Al Pacino and Paul Scofield
They said it: 'Philip is not vain. He'll go where you take him. He'll go as ugly as it gets. He's not worried about whether anyone will like him. He'll say the unsayable, do the unthinkable, and take the consequences' – Joel Schumacher, director of *Flawless*

Hilary Swank

Born: 30 July 1974 in Lincoln, Nebraska
Real name: Hilary Swank
Education: South Pasadena High School

('the worst')
Previous occupation: Swimmer, competing in the Junior Olympics and Washington state championships; also in Washington, she ranked fifth in all-around gymnastics
Film debut: *Buffy the Vampire Slayer* (as Kimberly, Buffy's best friend)
The other films: *The Next Karate Kid* (as the next Karate Kid, Julie Pierce), Sam Raimi's romantic thriller *The Gift*, starring Cate Blanchett, Keanu Reeves and Giovanni Ribisi
TV: *Beverly Hills 90210* (as Carly Reynolds)
Next up: The lead in *The Affair of the Necklace*, an 18th-century drama co-starring Adrien Brody and Christopher Walken
Strengths: Athleticism, smarts, dedication, courage, terrific bone structure, real talent
Husband: Actor Chad Lowe (married 2 October, 1997)
Famous relative: Brother-in-law Rob Lowe (since 2 October, 1997)
Awards: For her role as true-life cross-dresser Teena Brandon in *Boys Don't Cry* she won the Oscar, Golden Globe and Golden Satellite and was voted best actress by The Los Angeles Film Critics Association, The New York Film Critics' Circle, The Boston Society of Film Critics, The Broadcast Film Critics Association, The Dallas-Fort Worth Film Critics' Association and The Toronto Film Critics Association; voted Female Star of Tomorrow at ShoWest
Infamy: Forgot to mention her husband's name in her Oscar acceptance speech
Also: In her spare time, Ms Swank river rafts, skis and sky-dives

Film World Diary
July 1999 – June 2000

JULY 1999

Tarzan grosses $100 million at the US box-office ● *Notting Hill* becomes the first British film to gross more than $100m at the US box-office ● *Big Daddy* grosses $100m in the US ● In court in Beverly Hills, **Oliver Stone** denies charges of possessing drugs and driving while under the influence of alcohol ● **Helen Hunt**, 36, and **Hank Azaria**, 35, tie the knot at a private ceremony in their Los Angeles home. A top secret affair,

the wedding is even a surprise to the 100 or so guests (including **Mike Myers**, **Matthew Perry** and **Anthony Edwards**) who were expecting a party ● **Rosie Perez** (Oscar nominee for *Fearless*) and her boyfriend of six years, film-maker/playwright **Seth Zvi Rosenfeld**, make it legal in Brooklyn ● *Star Wars: Episode I The Phantom Menace* shatters box-office records in the UK ● **Martin Scorsese** marries book

editor Helen Morris in New York ● **Keanu Reeves** and his girlfriend Jennifer Syme are expecting their first child in the new year ● **Robert De Niro** files for divorce from his second wife, Grace Hightower. The couple were secretly married in June 1997 and have produced one son, Elliot ● **Richard Gere** and girlfriend **Carey Lowell** are also expecting a new bundle of joy around the turn of the next century.

AUGUST 1999

Below: Kevin Kline and Will Smith in the critically slated but hugely popular Wild Wild West

Robert Downey Jr is sentenced to a three year prison term for violating his probation by continuing to indulge his drug habit ● **Geena Davis** makes it through to being

one of the 32 finalists to compete in the United States women's Olympic archery team ● **William Shatner** finds his wife, former model Nerine, dead in their swimming pool. The couple had married in November 1997 ● *Wild Wild West* grosses $100m in the US ● *Star Wars: Episode One – The Phantom Menace* grosses $400m in the US ● **Martin Sheen** is arrested during an anti-nuclear protest to commemorate the 54th anniversary of the bombing of Nagasaki. The actor is apprehended outside the Los Alamos National Laboratory where plutonium pits are constructed ● **Ben Affleck** is stopped for speeding by Massachusetts police. He is later ordered to pay

$135 in fines for driving with a suspended licence ● Amid a blaze of publicity, **Warren Beatty** confirms that he is 'interested' in running for president. To compete as a Democratic candidate, he has till November to make up his mind ● *The Blair Witch Project*, which was made for a mere $22,000, grosses $100m in the US ● *Austin Powers: The Spy Who Shagged Me* grosses $200m in the US ● *The General's Daughter* grosses $100m in the US ● **Mike Myers** is the latest star to land a $20 million payday, for his next comedy, *Sprockets* ● *The Sixth Sense* grosses $100m in the US ● **Judi Dench**'s actor husband, **Michael Williams**, reveals that he has cancer.

SEPTEMBER 1999

As it grosses $34.2 million in one week, *The Sixth Sense* sets a new Labour Day holiday record – in its sixth week on release ● **Juliette Lewis** marries professional skateboarder Steve Berra in an outdoor ceremony near the ocean cliffs of Big Sur, California ● It's official: After five years together, **Kenneth Branagh** and **Helena Bonham Carter** are no longer a couple ● *American Pie* grosses $100 million in the US ● *The Sixth Sense* grosses $200 million in the US – in 45 days ● **Ryan Phillippe** and **Reese Witherspoon** are the proud parents of a bouncing daughter, Ava Elizabeth ● **Jenny McCarthy** (*Diamonds*, *Scream 3*) marries director **John Asher** (*Diamonds*) at the Beverly Hills Hotel. **Paula Abdul** and **Brooke Shields** look on ● **Dudley Moore** reveals that he is suffering from a rare degenerative brain disease called Progressive Supranuclear Palsy. Apparently, one person in 100,000 suffers from the ailment, a figure not lost on the star. 'There are 100,000 members of the Screen Actors Guild who are working every day,' he notes. 'I think, therefore, it is in some way considerate of me that I have taken on the disease for myself, thus protecting the remaining 99,999 members from this fate.' ● **Jean-Claude Van Damme** is apprehended on Sunset Boulevard and charged with drunk driving ● **Vanessa Williams** marries **Rick Fox** – forward for the Los Angeles Lakers – at the Church of the Holy Trinity in Manhattan. The couple had been dating for over a year, following an introduction by supermodel **Tyra Banks**, Fox's former girlfriend.

OCTOBER 1999

The Mummy grosses $400 million worldwide ● **Michael Douglas**, 55, and **Catherine Zeta-Jones**, 30, announce their engagement ● *The Matrix* sells one million DVDs, making it the most profitable title in the format's history ● **Charlie Sheen**'s request to end his probation for drug abuse and spousal battery is thrown out of court ● **Giancarlo Parretti**, erstwhile owner of MGM, is arrested in Orvieto, Italy. Convicted of mismanagement, perjury and witness tampering by a Delaware court in 1997, Parretti had fled to Italy. Then, in April of this year, he was found guilty of fraud by a French court and sentenced, in absentia, to four years in prison. In the US, the fugitive tycoon faces up to 10 years imprisonment and a $1.5 billion fine ● A naked **Matthew McConaughey** is arrested at his home after neighbours complain that he is playing his music too loud. He is fined $50 for 'disturbing the peace' ● BBC Worldwide announces its commitment to invest $67 million into feature film production over the next five years ● Planet Hollywood, the movie-themed restaurant that was launched in 1991 by **Arnold Schwarzenegger**, **Sylvester Stallone** and **Bruce Willis**, files for 'bankruptcy reorganisation' ● **Farrah Fawcett** reveals that she is planning to retire from acting.

Below: Fight Club
(with Brad Pitt) is cut
by the British censor

NOVEMBER 1999

Ian Bannen, 71, is killed in a car crash off the coast of Loch Ness ● *Double Jeopardy* grosses $100m in the US ● It's official: *Notting Hill* is now the highest grossing British film of all time, accumulating $350 million across the world ● The British censor insists on cuts before giving *Fight Club* an 18 certificate ● **Richard Widmark**, 84, marries Susan Blanchard, former wife of **Henry Fonda** ● **Gina Lollobrigida** is appointed goodwill ambassador by the United Nations' Food and Agricultural Organisation ● Child star **Jena Malone** (*Contact*, *Stepmom*, *The Dangerous Lives of Altar Boys*) sues her own mother for living off her earnings ● **Martin Sheen** is arrested during a protest at an army training centre in Fort Benning, Georgia. The demonstration, which is an annual affair, is in protest of the murder of six Jesuit priests in El Salvador ten years ago. The actor had daubed himself in fake blood to add colour to the occasion.

DECEMBER 1999

After 28 years, *A Clockwork Orange* is to be released in Britain with an 18 certificate – and with no cuts ● **Jennifer Lopez** insures her body for $1 billion. According to an insider, 'we believe it is the highest insurance ever taken out by a female star' ● **Julie Walters** becomes the first showbusiness personality to attend a televised investiture at Buckingham Palace. She is awarded an OBE for services to drama and admits, 'I had been practising curtsying since four o'clock this morning' ● **Greg Wise** and **Emma Thompson** are the proud parents of a bouncing 7_lb girl, tentatively dubbed 'jane.com' ● *Toy Story 2* grosses $100 million in the US – in just over two weeks ● **Ashley Judd** is engaged in secret to the Indy racing car driver **Dario Franchitti** ● *The World is Not Enough* grosses $100 million in the US ● **Jennifer**

Lopez and rapper boyfriend **Puff Daddy** are arrested after leaving the Manhattan nightclub Club N.Y. where three people where shot. 'Daddy' – aka Sean Combs – is found with a stolen gun in his car ● **Ben Stiller** and actress **Christine Taylor** (*The Brady Bunch Movie*, *The Wedding Singer*) announce their engagement ● **Eddie Murphy** is the proud farther of a seven pound, 13-ounce baby girl, Zola Ivy, born on Christmas Eve ● Also on Christmas Eve, **Keanu Reeves** and girlfriend Jennifer Syme's baby arrives stillborn ● Having denounced the rumours that she would not resurrect her role as Clarice Sterling in *Hannibal*, the sequel to *The Silence of the Lambs*, **Jodie Foster** announces that she will pass on the film after all in order to direct *Flora Plum*, a period romance with a circus setting.

JANUARY 2000

Julie Andrews and **Elizabeth Taylor** are made dames in the New Year's Honours and **Sean Connery** a knight ● *Toy Story 2* grosses $200 million in the US ● **Rosie Perez** is arrested during her protest against the US Navy's presence in Puerto Rico ● **Michael Douglas**, 55, and **Catherine Zeta-Jones**, 30, 'officially' announce their engagement ● **Jane Fonda** and CNN chief **Ted Turner** announce their separation ● *Stuart Little* grosses $100 million in the US ● *The*

Green Mile grosses $100 million in the US ● The Internet giant America Online and the entertainment group Time Warner combine forces in a $350 billion merger ● **Joe Roth**, chairman of Walt Disney Pictures, announces his resignation. The executive, who previously headed Twentieth Century Fox, announces plans to start up a new film company that will involve the services of **Bruce Willis**, **Julia Roberts** and **Adam Sandler**, i.e. the world's most pow-

erful actor, actress and comic. **Peter Schneider** takes over as new chief at Disney ● **Michael J. Fox** quits his TV sitcom *Spin City* to focus on his fight with Parkinson's disease ● The four-storey Kensington home of **Anthony Hopkins** is badly damaged by fire. However, Sir Anthony's Oscar for *The Silence of the Lambs* is rescued by firemen ● **Christian Bale** reveals that he and his girlfriend – film producer **Sandra 'Sibi' Blasic** – have tied the knot.

FEBRUARY 2000

After being rescued by fire fighters from a disabled lift in Berlin, **Sadie Frost** is jailed for eight hours without food, water or toilet facilities. According to police the actress 'was under the influence of alco-

hol' and 'for her own safety' was put into a drying-out cell. Ms Frost complained that she was manhandled, bruised and subjected to a humiliating ordeal where she was reduced to urinating on

the floor ● At the ripe old age of 50, **Richard Gere** becomes a dad for the first time. The mother of his son, Homer James Jigme, is actress **Carey Lowell** (*Licence to Kill*, *Leaving Las Vegas*) ●

Following the discovery of an 'irregularity', **Steven Spielberg** has a kidney removed ● Hammer Film Productions are to be resurrected after being bought by a private consortium. A spokesman for the company revealed that the outfit would be marketing the Hammer brand name to licence horror films, a TV series, magazines, books, computer games and, possibly, its own digital television channel ● **Samantha Morton**, 22, gives birth to her first child, Esme. The day after she is voted best actress at the *Evening Standard* awards for her role in *Dreaming of Joseph Lees*. Nine days later she is nominated for an Oscar for her role in *Sweet and Lowdown* ● In the words of the tabloids, **Rachel Weisz** 'dumps' boyfriend **Neil Morrissey** ● **Nicolas Cage** files for divorce from his wife of five years, **Patricia Arquette** ● **Christian Slater** marries Ryan Haddon, his girlfriend of two years (and mother

of their son Jaden Christopher). **Mike Myers** and **Rob Lowe** look on ● *Toy Story 2* smashes records at the UK box-office, grossing a phenomenal £14.2 million in just three days. In fact, it takes over twice as much as its predecessor which, back in 1996, opened to the tune of £3.3 million ● **Michael Grade**, former chief executive of Channel 4, sets up an investment corporation to buy Pinewood Studios for £62 million ● **Sylvester Stallone** and Universal Pictures end their five-year collaboration which, to date, has only produced one movie, *Detox* ● **Halle Berry** faces a maximum sentence of three years in a state prison following a felony hit-and-run. Apparently, the actress ran her rented Chevy Blazer through a red light on Sunset Boulevard, slammed into a Pontiac Sunbird and left the driver trapped in the wreckage as she speeded off. The victim suffered neck and back

injuries while Berry required 20 stitches to her forehead ● *The Sixth Sense* grosses $600 million worldwide ● **Harrison Ford** backs out of Steven Soderbergh's *Traffic*, leaving pregnant co-star **Catherine Zeta-Jones** high and dry.

Above: Michael Grade eyes Pinewood Studios

MARCH 2000

The stepbrother of **Leonardo DiCaprio**, Adam Farrar, is arrested on suspicion of attempted murder and for making a terrorist threat against his girlfriend. DiCaprio, who credits Farrar for inspiring him to act, refused to comment ● Citing 'irreconcilable differences', **Kiefer Sutherland** files for divorce from his wife Kelly Winn ● *American Beauty* grosses $100m in the US ● **Michael Douglas** takes over the role of the judge-cum-drug trafficker in *Traffic*, so that he can be by the side of his pregnant fiancee, co-star **Catherine Zeta-Jones** ● **Madonna** is pregnant again, this time with the help of her British boyfriend, director **Guy Ritchie** (*Lock, Stock...*, *Snatch*) ● One year after the seminal 'video nasty' *The Driller Killer* is given a rating by the British Board of Film Classification, it is to end up on television. A spokesman for Channel Four, the company

unspooling the 1979 film, declares, 'what was once considered unsuitable can now be viewed in a different light. We're keen for viewers to judge for themselves' ● Patriotic Welshman **Anthony Hopkins** angers his countrymen by becoming an American. **Steven Spielberg** and **John Travolta** witness the actor's pledge of allegiance to the United States ● Details of the 25 September wedding of **Michael Douglas** and **Catherine Zeta-Jones** at Skibo Castle in Scotland are leaked by the press. Because of the disclosure, the venue may now be changed. Meanwhile, Douglas lobbies **Tony Blair** – Britain's Prime Minister – to push for more progress on nuclear disarmament ● **William Baldwin**, president of the Creative Coalition, urges American Congress to jack up the National Endowment for the Arts budget by $50 million ● **Woody Harrelson** is ordered to stand trial

for 'misdemeanour marijuana possession' ● **Liam Neeson** turns down the honour of the Freedom of the Borough, offered to him by his hometown of Ballymena, Northern Ireland ● In a statement on behalf of the EarthAction environmental campaign network, **Leonardo DiCaprio** attacks the state of world pollution ● **Nicolas Cage** offers his estranged wife **Patricia Arquette** $5 million as a 'peace offering'. According to a friend, 'Nic realised within hours of filing for divorce that he had made a mistake. But while most women get a bunch of roses or jewellry, he gave her cash' ● **Charlie Sheen**'s three-year probation for 'misdemeanour battery' against his then-girlfriend, Brittany Ashland, is called off 71 days early ● Following his disassociation with Sweetland Films, **Woody Allen** signs a three-picture deal with DreamWorks.

APRIL 2000

Above: Erin Brockovich *(with Julia Roberts and Aaron Eckhart) becomes the first film of the new century to gross over $100 million*

Sleepy Hollow grosses $100 million in the US ● **Pierce Brosnan**, 47, announces his engagement to girl-friend Keely Shaye-Smith, 31 ● **Dana Giacchetto**, a 37-year-old New York financier well known as an investment advisor to the stars (**DiCaprio**, **Ben Affleck**, **Winona Ryder**), is charged with securities fraud in a federal criminal complaint. It is alleged that he misappropriated at least $6 million in client funds ● **Billy Bob Thornton** and **Laura Dern** announce the conclusion to their three-year romance ● It's official: **Billy Bob Thornton** and **Angelina Jolie** are a couple ● Following his separation from **Jane Fonda**, CNN mogul **Ted Turner** is now stepping out with sometime actress **Bo Derek** ● *Erin Brockovich* grosses $100m in the US, the first 2000 release to break the century mark ● **Leonardo DiCaprio** goes public with his passion for Brazilian supermodel **Gisele Bündchen**. At New York's Saci nightclub, Leo openly snogs 'The Boobs from Brazil' in front of such onlookers as **Sean 'Puffy' Combs**, **Carmen Electra** and **Tommy Hilfiger**.

MAY 2000

In a quickie Las Vegas ceremony, Oscar-winner **Billy Bob Thornton**, 44, and Oscar-winner **Angelina Jolie**, 24, make it legal ● What's this? **Elizabeth Hurley** is seen cozying up to Wall Street billionaire **Teddy Forstmann** while **Hugh Grant** is in Europe working on *Bridget Jones's Diary*. Forstmann, who sold his Gulfstream jet company for $2 billion last year, is 24 years Ms Hurley's senior ● **Noah Wyle**, 28, John Carter in TV's *ER*, weds makeup artist Tracy Warbin, 32, in Santa Barbara, California ● Near her home in Maida Vale, London, the actress **Jenny Seagrove** (*Don't Go Breaking My Heart*) is punched in the face as she assists a police officer by holding two teenage vandals hostage in a telephone box ● *Gladiator* grosses $100m in the US ● It's official: After almost 13 years as a couple, **Hugh Grant** and **Elizabeth Hurley** split up ● **Dana Carvey** (*Wayne's World*) sues San Francisco surgeon Elias Hanna for operating on the wrong artery during the comedian's double bypass in 1998. In his defence, the surgeon argues that Carvey has an 'unusual anatomy' and that his blood vessels were in atypical positions ● **Patsy Kensit** is admitted to hospital for depression.

JUNE 2000

Below: Mission: Impossible 2 *(with Tom Cruise) starts its climb towards becoming the top-grossing film of 2000*

Mission: Impossible 2 grosses over $100 million in the US – in just over a week ● After two years as one of Hollywood's coolest couples, actor-director **Ed Burns** and actress-siren **Heather Graham** call it a day ● *Dinosaur* grosses $100m in the US ● **Jack Nicholson**, **Salma Hayek** and 'dozens' of Hollywood agents and producers are trapped for two-and-a-half hours inside the Staples Center arena in Los Angeles. As more than 10,000 basketball fans gather to celebrate the win of the Los Angeles Lakers, violence erupts, resulting in the looting of shops and burning of police cars. **Shaquille O'Neal**, the Lakers' star player, is attacked inside his limousine as he tries to leave the centre ● **Keanu Reeves** and **Amanda DeCadenet** are back together again – four years after their official engagement and Keanu's flings with **Carrie-Anne Moss** and Jennifer Syme ● Following the commercial disappointment of *Fight Club*, *Anna and the King* and *Titan A.E.*, Bill Mechanic, president and chairman of Twentieth Century Fox, tenders his resignation ● Following a series of miscarriages, **Sharon Stone** adopts a baby boy from Texas ● Following a flirtatious dalliance with **Russell Crowe**, her co-star in *Proof of Life*, **Meg Ryan** announces the end of her nine-year marriage to **Dennis Quaid**.

Movie Quotations of the Year

‘My name is Lester Burnham. This is my neighbourhood. This is my street. This ... is my life. I'm 42-years-old. In less than a year I'll be dead. Of course, I don't know that yet.’ Kevin Spacey's opening words on the soundtrack of *American Beauty*

‘Men are like parking spaces – all the good ones are taken, all the available ones are handicapped.’ Clea DuVall in *The Astronaut's Wife*

‘She had the personality of a zip code in Kansas’. Steve Martin in *Bowfinger*

Babs, after being sized up by the ruthless Mrs Tweedy: ‘All my life flashed before my eyes. It was really boring.’ Jane Horrocks in *Chicken Run*

Rocky to Ginger: ‘I've met some hard-boiled eggs in my time – but you're 20 minutes.’ Mel Gibson in *Chicken Run*

Bethany Sloane to Rufus, the 13th apostle: ‘You knew Christ?’ Rufus: ‘Knew him? The nigga owes me 12 bucks!’ Linda Fiorentino and Chris Rock in *Dogma*

‘You Catholics don't celebrate your faith, you mourn it.’ Salma Hayek in *Dogma*

‘I measured my love by the extent of my jealousy.’ Ralph Fiennes in *The End of the Affair*

‘In pain, we're all drably individual.’ Ralph Fiennes in *The End of the Affair*

‘I hate you, God. I hate you as if you existed.’ Ralph Fiennes in *The End of the Affair*

‘You are a good hater.’ Catholic priest Jason Isaccs to Ralph Fiennes, in *The End of the Affair*

George, to his new neighbour Erin Brockovich: ‘Come on. Gimme your number, I'll call you up proper and ask you out and everything.’ Erin: ‘You want my number? How 'bout *this* for a number: Six is the age of my daughter.

Eight is the age of my son. Two is the number of times I've been divorced. Sixteen is the number of dollars in my bank account.’ Aaron Eckhart and Julia Roberts in *Erin Brockovich*

Sports commentator Vin Scully setting the scene for Kevin Costner's latest game (while stressing the significance of America's all-consuming pastime, baseball): ‘After 19 years in the big leagues, 40-year-old Billy Chapel has trudged to the mound for over 4000 innings. But tonight he's pitching against time, he's pitching against the future, against age, against ending. Tonight, he will make the fateful walk to the loneliest spot in the world, the pitching mound at Yankee Stadium, to push the sun back into the sky and give us one more day of summer.’ From *For Love of the Game*

Rob Gordon, record shop owner, to employee (and friend) Barry: ‘What did you tell her about the shop for?’ Barry: ‘I didn't know it was classified information. I mean, I know we don't have any customers, but I thought that was a bad thing, not, like, a business strategy.’ John Cusack and Jack Black in *High Fidelity*

‘Eddie, can I ask you something? I wanna ask you something. You don't mind? I'm just very curious about the nature of certain patterns of bullshit by which people pull the wool over their own eyes.’ Garry Shandling in *hurlyburly*

‘I cannot stand this semantic insanity any more! I'm finished! I cannot be so specific about my feelings. I can't!’ Robin Wright Penn in *hurlyburly*

‘Fame has a 15 minute lifespan; infamy lasts a little longer.’ Christopher Plummer in *The Insider*

‘Life is too short to spend it breaking new people in.’ Dan Aykroyd, on why he has no new friends – in *The House of Mirth*

‘I work harder than God. If He'd hired me, He would've made the world by Thursday.’ A

workaholic Jenna Elfman, in *Keeping the Faith*

‘God was showing off when he made you.’ A smitten Ben Stiller to Jenna Elfman, in *Keeping the Faith*

‘For goodness sake, stop looking like an Oxfam poster and come and have an ice cream.’ Colin Firth to his eight-year-old black friend Fissy Roberts in *The Secret Laughter of Women*

Angry murder suspect to NYPD cop John Shaft: ‘Do you know who my father is?’ Shaft, dismissive: ‘No. Do you?’ Christian Bale and Samuel L. Jackson, in *Shaft*

‘It's my duty to please that booty.’ Samuel L. to his flavoursome woman, in *Shaft*

‘I like you, Lois. You think like a man – you think with your nuts.’ Dylan Baker to Patricia Clarkson in *Simply Irresistible*

Judge Fielding, to elderly lawyer Nels Gudmundsson: ‘Try to act your age!’ Gudmundsson: ‘If I did that, your Honour, I would be dead.’ James Cromwell and Max Von Sydow, in *Snow Falling On Cedars*

‘Accidents rule every corner of the universe – except, maybe, the chambers of the human heart.’ Max Von Sydow, in *Snow Falling On Cedars*

‘It is virtually impossible to French kiss a person who leaves the new roll of toilet paper resting on top of the empty cardboard roll.’ Rita Wilson, in *The Story of Us*

‘When is that moment in a marriage when a spoon just becomes a spoon?’ Michelle Pfeiffer, in *The Story of Us*

‘Fear and guilt are the only two emotions that keep society humming.’ Rob Reiner, in *The Story of Us*

'Love is just lust in disguise.' Rob Reiner, in *The Story of Us*

'The only real sin is regret.' A philosophical Peter Facinelli in *Supernova*

'Only a fool would speculate about the life of a woman.' Cameron Diaz in *Things You Can Tell Just By Looking at Her*

Buzz Lightyear, to the evil Emperor Zurg: 'You killed my father!' Zurg: 'No Buzz, I am your father.' From *Toy Story 2*

'If you wish to write a grand opera about a prostitute dying of consumption in a garret, I suggest you contact Mr Ibsen in Oslo. I'm sure he will be able to furnish you with something suitably dull.' W.S. Gilbert (Jim Broadbent) to Arthur Sullivan (Allan Corduner) in *Topsy-Turvy*

'It's not important that I've killed 17 people. What's important is how I get along with the people that are still alive.' Contract killer Bruce Willis to mild-mannered neighbour Matthew Perry – in *The Whole Nine Yards*

Gay literary editor Terry Crabtree, admiring aspiring writer James Leer: 'I see myself in him.' Grady Tripp: 'I'm sure you do.' Robert Downey Jr and Michael Douglas in *Wonder Boys*

Quotes, off-screen
(that is, notable lines not scripted)

'To watch updates of your relationships on CNN is bizarre in a way I cannot explain. You think, isn't there something happening in Bosnia, by God?' Ben Affleck

'Why would you give up being Warren Beatty to be president? Every president wants to be Warren Beatty.' Alec Baldwin on Beatty's alleged interest in the White House

'Throw a stick anywhere in the Western world and you'll hit a dozen people who find him arse-paralysingly boring, meaningless and tedious.' Kenneth Branagh on the appeal of Shakespeare

'Marriages are like tornadoes. There's all this blowing and sucking at the beginning; and at the end you lose your house.' James Caan

'Tom, if you'd have won this, your pot price would have gone down so fast. Have you

any idea what supporting actors get paid? And we only get one motor home. A small one.' Michael Caine, addressing fellow nominee Tom Cruise, after receiving the Oscar for best supporting actor

'If we get to the point where I look like a basset hound, I'll just play basset hounds.' Clint Eastwood on his maturation as a senior citizen

'I know these moments don't last forever. I'll probably be caught with my pants down at the George Michael memorial toilet in Beverly Hills one of these days.' Rupert Everett, on his current celebrity

'Let's face it: I'm just a sex machine to both genders. It's all very exhausting. I need a lot of sleep.' Rupert Everett on his current attraction

'To me, the story is more like *The Graduate* than anything else. You know, Tyler is Mrs Robinson – the catalyst that allows you to see your own destiny.' David Fincher, describing his film *Fight Club*

'You never have the perspective to truly assess what it is you've done until it's too late.' David Fincher

'What happened to me happened to Monica Lewinsky and Linda Tripp. All people have talked about is the way they look. It's a cheap way to take away women's power.' Calista Flockhart, on the media's attention to her weight loss

'I saw myself in a huge white pullover, pushing logs into a wood burner, smoking an oddly shaped pipe and writing the odd bit of melancholy poetry. A kind of Max Von Sydow, only plumper.' Stephen Fry on his proposed retirement, after he walked out of the West End production of Simon Gray's *Cell Mates*

'I enjoy watching lesbians. Who doesn't want to see good-looking girls make out?' Janeane Garofalo

'Of course, what I'm best known for of late is the doctoring job I did on *Good Will Hunting*. The truth? I did not just doctor it. I wrote the whole thing from scratch. Miramax got the flick, cast them [Matt Damon and Ben Affleck] in the leads, and decided I would kill the commercial value of the flick if the truth were known. Harvey Weinstein gave me a lot of money for my silence, plus 20 per cent of the gross. Which is why I'm writing this from

the Riviera.' William Goldman, writing in *Premiere*, on his contribution to the Oscar that Messrs Damon and Affleck won for 'their' Best Original Screenplay

'She's terrifying, terrifying. She'd be all right in an Iranian jail. She'd end up running it.' Hugh Grant on his fearful girlfriend Elizabeth Hurley

'One guy at a gas station in New York said to me, "Hey, you look like Hugh Grant. No offence".' Hugh Grant

'Let's face it: the teeth are getting more and more British every day. I look in the mirror and see Austin Powers staring back at me.' Hugh Grant

'I get away with less because my wife is incredibly intelligent. She's insightful and well versed in the pathology of men. She's not dumb, which is a drag.' Ethan Hawke on his missus, Uma Thurman

'She's Mother Teresa, Princess Diana, the Queen of England and Wendy.' Michael Jackson on Elizabeth Taylor

'The golf course is the only place I can go dressed as a pimp with lime green pants and alligator shoes and fit in perfectly.' Samuel L. Jackson

'In movies, it doesn't really matter if you're good. It matters if the audience likes you.' John Malkovich

'When you are with your girlfriends, and you try on this pretty pink dress, you think it's so great. Now when I look at a picture of me in that dress, I am just *so* over it.' Gwyneth Paltrow on her Oscar night apparel

'He called me and left a message on my answering machine: "Hey, Matthew, it's Bruce Willis. Call me back or I'll burn your house down".' Matthew Perry on his new friend and co-star in *The Whole Nine Yards*

'He cast me in the part of a completely angelic, sweet and naive young thing. I thought, "Wow, he must not have seen any of my other movies".' Christina Ricci, on being given the female lead in Tim Burton's *Sleepy Hollow*

'I've never had to pretend to be having sex with somebody. I'm, like, the queen of the foreplay dissolve.' Chaste bunny Julia Roberts

Film Soundtracks

Perusing the Billboard music charts one would be forgiven for thinking that film soundtracks were made up almost entirely of rap, hip hop and heavy metal. Indeed, this was often – and depressingly – the case. Even a mainstream endeavour like *The Hurricane*, set in the years 1949 to 1985, suffered from a preponderance of rap – at least, that which ended up on the CD. However, there was still a lot of good old-fashioned film music around, if not necessarily to be found in the racks of WH Smith. Such titles as the Chinese *The Emperor and the Assassin* and *Xiu Xiu: The Sent-down Girl*, the Pakistani *Earth* and the Nepalese *Himalaya* (the latter winning the Cesar for best music) all had outstanding scores. But where to find them?

In the UK, film buffs had to content themselves with the usual fare from the giants of the industry, **Hans Zimmer** (*Gladiator, Mission: Impossible 2*), **James Horner** (*The Perfect Storm*) and **John Williams** (*The Phantom Menace, Angela's Ashes,*

The Patriot). While it's true that great films often produce great music (think *The Third Man, Lawrence of Arabia, Schindler's List*), it's not always the case. True, the year's most applauded movie, *American Beauty*, brought us a decent enough album. But even this was made up of a jumble of incongruous tracks (fancy a combo of The Who, Bobby Darin and Eels?), while **Thomas Newman**'s music was reduced to two tracks. Worse, Newman virtually recycled the same theme for *Erin Brockovich*. As for the film music singled out by the American Academy, two of the scores – Rachel Portman's *The Cider House Rules* and Gabriel Yared's *The Talented Mr Ripley* – left me cold. In fact, I found that the latter's monotonous lush tones seriously compromised the dramatic impact of Anthony Minghella's movie.

Still, with 300 or so movies opening in the UK, there were a number of fine soundtracks, both compilations and straight scores. Here are my favourites.

SOUNDTRACKS OF THE YEAR

American Beauty
The year's 'best' film just had to have a decent soundtrack and it doesn't disappoint. Here is a marvellous array of tracks that run the gamut from Eels' head-spinning 'Cancer For the Cure' to Bobby Darin's glitzy 'Don't Rain On My Parade' via Elliott Smith's haunting cover of Lennon & McCartney's 'Because.' Plus there's Folk Implosion, Free, Bill Withers, The Who, Gomez and of course **Thomas Newman**'s unsettling and subtly repetitive theme ('Dead Already') on xylophone.

Angela's Ashes
Emotive, elegiac score from **John Williams** that takes the damp out of Limerick poverty and replaces it with real feeling. The composer's best work since, er, *Saving Private Ryan*.

Anywhere But Here
A splendid collection of songs

of the 'Lilith Fair' variety, including sterling numbers from Carly Simon and her daughter Sally Taylor, k.d. lang, Sarah McLachlan, Marie Wilson, Poe, Sinéad Lohan, Bif Naked and up-and-comer Lili Haydn. The chick flick soundtrack of the year.

Austin Powers: The Spy Who Shagged Me
A mega-seller thanks in large part to the Madonna song 'Beautiful Stranger', this does boast a splendid line-up: The Who, REM, Lenny Kravitz, Melanie G and even that mushy duet between Burt Bacharach and Elvis Costello. But best of all is Dr Evil's rapadelic 'Just the Two Of Us': 'I know that Scott would look up to me/Run the business of the fam-ily/Be *evil*, but have my feelings too/Change my life with Oprah and Maya Ange-lou...' (apologies to Will Smith).

The Barber of Siberia
Running at over one hour and

six minutes, this robust, romantic and exceptionally varied work from **Edward Nicolay Artemyev** is one of the most satisfying and competent pieces of classical scoring of the year. Another case of a flawed movie producing a memorable sound.

The Beach
A typically consumer-friendly (and top-selling) compilation from the *Trainspotting* triumvirate, including ear-catching cuts from All Saints, Moby, Dario G, Underworld, Blur, Faithless and Barry Adamson.

The Blair Witch Project
For aficionados of the movie, this is a marvellous memento: an atmospheric mix of dialogue, sound effects, background noise and the sort of Gothic rock that the 'late' Joshua Leonard would've listened to on his Walkman. So, not so much a soundtrack as a canny celebration of the spirit of the film.

Above left to right:
High Fidelity,
The Patriot *and*
Topsy-Turvy

Buena Vista Social Club
The album that launched a major documentary, this laid-back, accomplished recording is the last word on Cuban funk. Featuring the belated legends singer-composer Ibrahim Ferrer, pianist Ruben Gonzales and singer-guitarist Compay Segundo, this is a collector's item – nay, a musical event – that demands a place in every discerning CD rack.

Chicken Run
A delicious homage to the music of *The Great Escape* and any number of recognisable classics (*Where Eagles Dare*, *The Dam Busters*), **John Powell** and **Harry Gregson-Williams**' score is funny because it doesn't try to be. Surprisingly versatile in its scope, it runs the gamut from military pomp to swingin' jazz. If every comedy benefited from such an accomplished, po-faced score, the world would be a better place.

The Closer You Get
Pick through the familiar silky cues of **Rachel Portman** and you'll find some real delights here: a soul-soaring version of the traditional 'At the Dance', The Proclaimers' joyous 'I'm Gonna Be (500 Miles)', Ricky Valance's heart-wrenching 1960 hit 'Tell Laura I Love Her' and more.

Down To You
Of the cling-wrapped, oven-ready pop packages of the year, this actually had a surprisingly high standard, with lovely tracks from

such fresh acts as Billie Myers, Ginger Mackenzie, Deanna Kirk and Miranda Lee Richards (although such old hands as David Bowie, Everything But the Girl, Barry White and Al Green – all heard in the film – were noticeably absent).

The End of the Affair
Yet another powerful, mesmerising score from **Michael Nyman** that just seeps into the subconscious and takes over the soul. This man really knows how to mix music with film to create a unique emotional experience.

Eyes Wide Shut
Mesmerising smorgasbord of distinctive tracks that could only have come from Stanley Kubrick's haunting, extraordinary film – from Shostakovitch's sweeping, catchy *Waltz 2* to Jocelyn Pook's chillingly sparse piano chords.

Fantasia/2000
A curious one, this, being the musical equivalent of a one-hour tour through the history of art, cramming Michelangelo up against Picasso. So, while it's good to hear Respighi, Shostakovich and Stravinsky, Beethoven's Fifth, Gershwin's 'Rhapsody in Blue' and Elgar's 'Pomp and Circumstance' are a bit old hat and make for extremely odd bed-fellows.

Gladiator
A thrusting, percussive and rousing score, this collaboration between **Hans Zimmer** and **Lisa Gerrard** really does hit its marks. With Zimmer supplying the

movie's epic voice and Gerrard adding some haunting Celtic vocals (as she does in that other wonderful Russell Crowe vehicle *The Insider*), *Gladiator* is a classic of its genre.

High Fidelity
In keeping with the mentality of the film's protagonist, the music here is suitably eclectic, ranging in style from the slow come-on of Barry White to the heartbreak of Bob Dylan via the hypnotic cheek of The Stereophonics. It makes you proud to have ears.

The Insider
An exotic and haunting score from **Lisa Gerrard** and **Pieter Bourke** that really creates a mood of seductive menace, chilling one to the bone even as it ravishes the eardrums. **Graeme Revell** adds a few tracks of his own which aren't half bad either.

The Legend of 1900
A gut-achingly beautiful soundtrack from **Ennio Morricone**, the Italian maestro creating a world of jazz and classical magic that skims off the fingertips of music wunderkind Tim Roth.

Magnolia
Considering that these songs by **Aimee Mann** were the inspiration for Paul Thomas Anderson's remarkable film, it's no surprise that this is a remarkable album. Profound, pensive and moody, it creates an atmosphere ripe for major brooding.

Maybe Baby
Very much in the *Four*

Weddings/Notting Hill school of feel-good slush, this is a genuine winner, with class acts from Lene Marlin, Melanie C, Westlife, Atomic Kitten, George Michael and the usual suspects. The title track by Paul McCartney is a bit much, though.

Millennium Movies

An ambitious conceit if ever there was one, this 43-track, two-hour, 34-minute double CD attempts to be a musical companion to the Millennium poll conducted by SKY Premier (dreamed up to determine the British public's top hundred favourite films). While containing songs and themes from ten films that didn't even make the list (including, perversely, *Sliver* and *The Saint*), it is nonetheless a welcome valentine to the cinema's first century. Inevitably, there are painful omissions (no zither from *The Third Man*, no *Gone With the Wind*), but there's enough here to lubricate the cogs of nostalgia well into the next decade.

Mission To Mars

An uncharacteristic score from **Ennio Morricone**, but one that serves its material well, providing an eerie, epic and hypnotic timbre that totally sucks one into its otherworldly universe. Listen and be seduced – and be disturbed.

Ordinary Decent Criminal

A deliciously eccentric collection of tracks (from Yma Sumac's absurd 'Gopher Mambo' to Shack's REM-ish 'I Want You') this is one of those rare occasions that a soundtrack really defines a film. And **Damon Albarn**'s throbbing, frenetic score is really quite addictive.

The Patriot

Not vintage **John Williams**, but an accomplished score nonetheless, with enough period flavour,

military bombast and jingoistic fever to sweep along the film's 167 minutes.

Ravenous

One of the year's most original scores, this bizarre mix from **Michael Nyman** and **Damon Albarn** perfectly captures the tone of Antonio Bird's misconstrued black comedy. With Nyman's characteristically seductive drone punctuated by the monotonous plucking of a banjo and with the atmospheric addition of a brass, string and banjo ensemble, this is a soundtrack that gets under the skin.

Ride With the Devil

A sweeping, dramatic and lyrical evocation of the period of the American Civil War, this is yet another towering achievement from **Mychael Danna**, still the unsung hero of contemporary movie music.

Sweet and Lowdown

As in keeping with so many of Woody Allen's films, the music here is light and breezy, but its gentle *bonhomie* is a real tonic to the soul. **Howard Alden** plays the guitar pieces (mimed to by Sean Penn in the film) and the Dick Hyman Group provides the jazzy interludes.

The Thomas Crown Affair

If only all soundtracks were this good. Neatly divided between a piano-driven score from **Bill Conti** and three outstanding numbers, this is a musical gem in a sea of paste. Producing a playful, jazzy work, Conti is on particularly fine form, while the hand-picked 'songs' are distinctively haunting, from the exotic seduction of Wasis Diop and the uplifting, Caribbean-flavoured sound of Georges Fordant to a spectacular display from Nina Simone. Oh yeah, and there's even Sting crooning his version of 'Windmills of Your Mind' (in his characteristically anaemic way).

To Infinity and Beyond!

If you buy one *Toy Story* album this year, make sure it's this one – the best of both cartoons. There's also some fun extras, such as The Aliens' 'The Claw' and Bill Henry and The Green Machine's 'Cadence 2' ('we are little plastic men, doing just the best we can...'). However, *four* versions of 'You've Got a Friend In Me' (Randy Newman, Lyle Lovett, Robert Goulet and an instrumental) might be too much for more sensitive listeners.

Topsy-Turvy

Regardless of what Gilbert & Sullivan purists make of this album, its combination of **Carl Davis**'s lively score and songs from *The Mikado*, *Princess Ida*, *The Sorcerer* and *Yeomen of the Guard* should make G&S fans of us all. A richly pleasurable experience.

Toy Story 2

See *To Infinity and Beyond!*

Tumbleweeds

Here are some good ol' Country tunes from the likes of Lyle Lovett, Emmylou Harris, Johnny Cash, Lucinda Williams and Blue Mountain. And, with four tracks from **David Mansfield**'s touchingly meditative and invigorating score, notch this up as a most agreeable compliment to a wonderful film.

William Shakespeare's A Midsummer Night's Dream

A cornucopia of classical and operatic highlights – intermingled with a blithely flamboyant score from **Simon Boswell** – this is a marvellous keepsake of a woefully undervalued film.

Wonder Boys

Fabulous collection of meditative, mellow and grown-up tracks from Bob Dylan, Leonard Cohen, Buffalo Springfield, Neil Young, Van Morrison, John Lennon, and others. Puts one in a euphoric trance.

Bookshelf

Compiled by Howard Maxford

A round-up of the year's best film books

The Year's Top Ten...

● Beyond Terror – The Films of Lucio Fulci

For fans of Italian horror movies, this lavishly illustrated tribute to the maestro of mayhem will be required reading. Fulci's films, which include such cult favourites as *Zombie Flesh Eaters* and *House by the Cemetary*, may be an acquired taste, but author Stephen Thrower is keen to spread the word, which he does with great enthusiasm (though thankfully he's also enough of a realist to admit that not all of the director's films are of the high quality of his 1981 hit *The Beyond*). FAB Press, £29.99 h/b or £19.99 p/b.

● Carry On Uncensored

If you're a devoted Carry On fan, then this collection of previously unpublished stills showing the stars of the series at work and play will be a must. The book also contains script extracts of scenes cut by the censor for being too saucy, as well as scenes cut by the makers for the sake of length, among them a sequence from *Carry On at Your Convenience*, which saw series regular Terry Scott end up on the cutting room floor! Compiled by Carry On devotees Robert Ross and Morris Bright, this has something to surprise on practically every page. Boxtree, £14.99 h/b.

● Come Play with Me – The Life and Films of Mary Millington

The true story of 1970s porn queen Mary Millington, this fascinating biography-cum-filmography explores an avenue of British cinema that has mostly been ignored. Author Simon Sheridan at last not only recognises Millington's star status, but also examines her many films, among them *The Playbirds*, *Queen of the Blues* and *Come Play with Me*, all of which proved incredibly popular at a time when the British film industry was going through one of its worst slumps (in fact *Come Play with Me* ran at one London cinema for an incredible 201 weeks, raking in an aston-ishing £550,000 at that venue alone). The story ends with Millington's suicide. Although hers is a sometimes seedy tale, Sheridan treats his subject with dignity throughout. FAB, £14.99 p/b.

● English Gothic: A Century of Horror Cinema

The British horror film, be it the Eastmancolored shockers from Hammer or the rough and ready exploitation items by Pete Walker and Norman J. Warren, has been written about many times in the past, but never with such authority as by Jonathan Rigby, who here offers the ultimate chronology of the genre from the British angle. A major achievement, the book examines all the major titles, and manages to exhume quite a few obscurities too, all of which will make this irresistable for aficionados. Lavishly illustrated throughout with many rare stills, this is quite easily the book of the year. With a foreword by producer Richard Gordon and an after-word by screenwriter David McGillivray. Reynolds & Hearn, £17.95 p/b.

● The Essential Monster Movie Guide

A bumper guide to every monster movie, cartoon and television show ever made, this epic A-Z not only contains entries on such mainstream favourites as Dracula, Frankenstein and The Mummy, but also delights in tracking down the offbeat, such as the sex spoof *The Maddams Family*. By turns informative and entertaining, the book also contains mini biogs of noted actors, writers and directors, along with a plethora of stills. If some of the material looks familiar, then that's because the book has been compiled from author Stephen Jones' previous *Illustrated Vampire*, *Frankenstein*, *Werewolf* and *Dinosaur Guides*, though there's enough new material included here to make this volume well worth a look if you already own those. Titan, £16.99 p/b.

● Hitchcock's Secret Notebooks

A Hitchcock book with a difference, this fascinating tome by Dan Auiler is the first to freely draw upon the legendary director's private papers, among them first draft screenplays, telegrams, office memos and conference minutes, all of which help to build a picture of the great man at work. The most notable section deals with Hitchcock's unfilmed pet project, *Kaleidoscope*, elements of which later re-emerged in *Frenzy*. Bloomsbury, £20 h/b.

● John Carradine: The Films

Not only does this exhaustive study of the actor's career include a substantial biography by Gregory William Mank, it also has a film-by-film chronology of Carradine's lengthy film career, compiled by Tom Weaver, which began in 1930 with *Tol'able David* and went on to include such classics as *Stagecoach*, *The Grapes of Wrath* and *House of Frankenstein*, though the entries on the star's lesser films, such as the best forgotten *Vampire Hookers*, are given equally substantial coverage. McFarland, £67.50 h/b.

● Life's a Scream

This engrossing autobiography by glamorous scream queen Ingrid Pitt not only chronicles her experiences in such genre favourites as *The Vampire Lovers* and *Countess Dracula*, it also recalls in unflinching detail her childhood years in a Nazi concentration camp, her daring escape from East Germany and her later adventures in Argentina just prior to the military coup. By turns harrowing and amusing, this would be hard to swallow if it was fiction, yet it's all happened to Pitt, who writes about her experiences with refreshing candour. Heinemann, £17.99 h/b.

● Monkey Business

The definitive biography of the five Marx Brothers (Groucho, Chico, Harpo, Zeppo and the little mentioned Gummo), this classic study of their stage and film work is easily up to the high standards set by author Simon Louvish with his previous book on W.C. Fields, *Man on the Flying Trapeze*. The chapters on the Brothers' early stage appearances are quite outstanding, and frequently leave one marvelling at the amount of research that must have gone into them, though the Brothers' time in Hollywood is no less studiously covered. A brilliant piece of work. Faber, £16.99 p/b.

● The Peter Cushing Companion
The life and career of beloved genre star Peter Cushing, 'the gentleman of horror', is paid tribute to in this astonishingly thorough look at his stage, screen, radio and television work, which naturally highlights all his Hammer appearances, as well as his performance as Grand Moff Tarkin in *Stars Wars*. However, though crammed with facts, trivia and credit data, not to mention some eye-catching stills, author David Miller makes sure that Cushing the man shines through, particularly when dealing with the actor's relationship with his wife Helen, whom he loved beyond all measure. With a foreword by Cushing's co-star Veronica Carlson. Reynolds & Hearn, £15.95 p/b.

Best of the Rest...

● About John Ford
A welcome reprint of Lindsay Anderson's fascinating examination of the career of director John Ford, this takes in such classics as *Stagecoach*, *The Grapes of Wrath* and *The Searchers*, and also contains interview extracts between Anderson and Ford. Plexus, £12.99 p/b.

● The Art of Stars Wars
Featuring the work of concept artist Doug Chiang, this visually arresting look at the design work for *The Phantom Menace* includes pencil sketches, computer generated images and lavish paintings, all of which have been beautifully reproduced on top quality paper. Accompanied by an informative text by Jonathan Bresman. Ebury, £25 h/b.

● Bloomsbury Movie Guide No 5: Jaws
A solid entry in Bloomsbury's somewhat variable Movie Guide series, this comprehensive 'making of' by Nigel Andrews chronicles the filming and marketing of the Spielberg-directed box office phenomenon. A real page turner, and with more trivia than you can shake a stick at.

Bloomsbury, £10.99 p/b.

● British Cinema of the 90s
Editor Robert Murphy has here compiled an excellent collection of essays examining the state of the British film industry in the 1990s, when such hits as *Four Weddings*, *The Full Monty* and *Trainspotting* helped to put Britain on the movie map again, though the most fascinating chapters deal with such lesser known titles as *Love is the Devil*, *Gallivant* and *Stella Does Tricks*. BFI, £14.99.

● British Crime Cinema
A thoughtful and thorough examination of the British crime film, a genre which authors Steve Chibnall and Robert Murphy claim to have rescued from critical parole. Among the films under discussion are *No Orchids for Miss Blandish*, *Villain* and *Get Carter*. Routledge, £14.99.

● British Science Fiction Cinema
British sci-fi might not be in the same league as Hollywood's in terms of effects and budgets, yet this informed study proves that imaginative scripts and taut direction do count for something, citing *The Quatermas Xperiment* and *Village of the Damned* as examples of Brit sci-fi at its best. Edited by I.Q. Hunter. Routledge, £14.99 p/b.

● Chicken Run – Hatching the Movie
This colourfully designed and illustrated 'making of' by Brian Sibley goes behind the scenes of the hit animated feature by Nick Park and Peter Lord, tracing the project from script to screen. With a foreword by Mel Gibson. Boxtree, £20.

● Claude Rains
A superior portrait by John T. Soister and JoAnna Wioskowski of the debonair actor's stage and film career, taking in such notable productions as *The Invisible Man*, *Casablanca*, *King's Row* and *Lawrence of Arabia*. McFarland, £33.75 h/b.

● The Confessions of Robin Askwith
Despite some glaring spelling and punctuation gaffes, this entertaining and often self-deprecatingly humorous autobiography naturally highlights Askwith's work on the Confessions films, as well as the likes of *Carry On Girls*, *Horror Hospital* and Passolini's *Canterbury Tales*. With a foreword by Windsor Davies. Ebury, £14.99 h/b.

● Conversations with Wilder
Writer-director Cameron Crowe talks extensively to legendary writer-director

Billy Wilder about his classic films, among them *Double Indemnity*, *Some Like it Hot* and *The Apartment*. Faber, £20 h/b.

● Count Dracula Goes to the Movies
An excellent guide to the vampire king's many movie outings, this highlights such films as *Nosferatu* (the 1922 and 1979 versions) and *Dracula* (1931, 1958, 1979 and 1992) as well as such deviations as *Nadja*, *Count Yorga* and *The Brides of Dracula*. Written by Lyndon W. Joslin, this is a scholarly but highly approachable work. McFarland, £33 h/b.

● The Director's Cut
In this fascinating autobiography, top British director Roy Ward Baker recalls his career, which takes in such classics as *Morning Departure*, *A Night to Remember* and *Quatermass and the Pit*, as well as such popular television fare as *The Avengers*, *The Saint* and *The Flame Trees of Thika*. With a foreword by Roger Moore and an afterword by Samuel Goldwyn Jr. Reynolds & Hearn, £19.95 h/b.

● Disney – The First 100 Years
From the birth of Walt Disney in 1901 through to the projected opening of the company's latest hotel, The Animal Kingdom Lodge, in 2001, this glossy chronology by David Smith and Steven Clark charts every single development of note in the company's history, from the early cartoon shorts through to the building of the theme parks. Hyperion, £27.50.

● The Encyclopaedia of Indian Cinema
A year-by-year A-Z of Indian films, from *Pundalik* in 1912 through to *Kadhal Desam* in 1995, this monumental guide also contains a thorough chronology of Indian film, beginning in 1896 with the first screening of a film in a Bombay hotel room. As compiled by Ashis Rajadhyaksha and Paul Willemen, this one-stop reference source is clearly a labour of love. BFI, £19.99.

● Fantasia 2000 – A Vision of Hope
This glossy behind-the-scenes look at the making of the new *Fantasia* project contains an informative text by John Culhane, though as you'd expect, it's the deluxe stills that are the real focus of attention here. Hyperion, £50.

● Greasepaint and Gore
A lavishly illustrated tribute to Hammer's chief monster maker, make-up artist Roy Ashton, including fragments from his unpublished autobiography. By Bruce Sachs and Russell Wall.

With a prologue by Peter Cushing. Tomahawk, £24.95 p/b.

● **Hitchcock Poster Art**

This top quality coffee table item contains posters and lobby cards from each of Hitchcock's movies, from *The Pleasure Garden* to *Family Plot*. A real feast for the eyes. By Tony Nourmand and Mark H. Wolff. Aurum, £14.95.

● **Halliwell's Film & Video Guide 2000**

With an incredible 23 000 entries, this perennial favourite remains the King Kong of film guides in a jungle of Mighty Joe Youngs. If you own only one film book, this has to be it. Edited by John Walker. Harper-Collins, £19.99 p/b.

● **Halliwell's Who's Who in the Movies**

The ultimate A-Z of actors, producers, directors, writers and composers. As indispensible as ever. Edited by John Walker. Harper-Collins, £16.99 p/b.

● **Inside the Wicker Man**

This fascinating book by Allan Brown follows the making of this rightly revered shocker from inception through to distribution, which proved to be a bumpy journey indeed, with the film losing eighteen minutes of valuable footage along the way. Featuring interviews with the cast and crew (among them Anthony Shaffer, Robin Hardy, Christopher Lee and Edward Woodward), this is the ultimate word on the cult classic. With a foreword by Edward Woodward. Sidgwick & Jackson, £14.99 p/b.

● **Making Mischief – The Cult Films of Pete Walker**

A well informed if sometimes slightly hyperbolic examination of the films of cult director Pete Walker, which include *Frightmare*, *House of Whipcord* and *The Four Dimensions of Greta*. Written with enthusiasm by Steve Chibnall, with contributions by Walker himself. FAB, £12.95.

● **Marilyn Monroe – Cover to Cover**

Thankfully, not another tedious Marilyn biography raking over the old coals, but an eye-catching collection of all the magazine covers the star adorned during her life, all of which have been stunningly reproduced. Compiled by Clark Kidder and with a foreword by Mamie Van Doren. Gazelle, £18.99 p/b.

● **Marlon Brando – A Life in Our Times**

Another top biography by Richard Schickel, this one details the life of the Oscar-winning legend from his heyday in the likes of *On the Waterfront* and *The Godfather* through to such recent drek *The Island of Dr Moreau*. Pavilion, £19.99 h/b.

● **Mighty Movies**

As compiled by Lawrence Bassoff, this is a ravishing collection of epic film posters, featuring examples from such classics as *Lawrence of Arabia*, *El Cid* and *Cleopatra*, all of them beautifully reproduced in full colour and on suitably widescreen pages. Gazelle, £28.50 p/b.

● **Movie Locations**

If you're into hunting down famous movie locations, this guide by Mark Adams will prove indispensible, be it the blue door in *Notting Hill* or the train station in *Brief Encounter* you're trying to tace. Happy hunting! Boxtree, £12.99 p/b.

● **North by Northwest**

One of the greatest original screenplays ever written, Ernest Lehman's devilishly witty script astonishingly lost the Oscar to *Pillow Talk*. Packed with witty dialogue and sophisticated sexual innuendo, it makes for delightful reading. Faber, £8.99 p/b.

● **Paper Dreams**

A fascinating look by John Canemaker behind the scenes of the Disney cartoons, this examines the contributions of the overlooked storyboard artists, from the black and white days of Mickey Mouse through to *Kingdom of the Sun*. Needless to say, the accompanying illustrations are an eyeful. Hyperion, £40 h/b.

● **Science Fiction Serials**

One of several recent books dedicated to serials, this particular volume by Roy Kinnard homes in on such favourites as *Flash Gordon*, *Buck Rogers* and *King of the Rocket Men*. Shelwing/McFarland, £35.95.

● **Sergio Leone: Something to Do with Death**

Satisfyingly thorough biography by Christopher Frayling of the celebrated spaghetti western director Sergio Leone, whose work includes *Fistful of Dollars* and *The Good, the Bad and the Ugly*. Best enjoyed with a side order of garlic bread. Faber, £20 p/b.

● **Silent Films**

A critical guide to over 600 silent films, this extremely informative and approachable catalogue by Robert K. Klepper takes in the likes of *The Kiss*, *A Trip to the Moon*, *Queen Elizabeth* and *Birth of a Nation*, as well as the most recent silent film, *The Taxi Dancer*, made in 1996. Shelwing/McFarland, £76.50.

● **Still Memories**

An 'autobiography in photography', this sumptuous album of stills taken by screen legend Sir John Mills is practically a pictorial chronology of the British film industry in the 20th century, with the composition in some of the pictures revealing a real artist's eye. Hutchinson, £20 h/b.

● **3-D Movies**

Cracking history of the 3-D process, taking in such titles as *House of Wax*, *The Creature from the Black Lagoon* and, er, *Emanuelle IV* (don't ask!). McFarland, £27 p/b.

● **The Virgin Film Guide**

Next to Halliwell's, this is the one to have. It may not contain as many entries, but the reviews are longer and the credit information, which includes character names for each actor, is more comprehensive. Virgin, £16.99 p/b.

● **What Lie Did I Tell?**

Oscar-winning screenwriter William Goldman returns to regail us with *More Adventures in the Screen Trade*, this time recalling his experiences on *The Princess Bride*, *Absolute Power* and *Maverick*. Delicious. Bloomsbury, £16.99 h/b.

● **The World is Not Enough – A Companion**

An access all areas account of the making of the latest Bond by Iain Johnstone, this also contains interviews with Pierce Brosnan, Judi Dench, Sophie Marceau, Robert Carlyle and director Michael Apted. Boxtree, £14.99 h/b.

And the Year's Worst?

● **Cult Movies**

A scrappy, dust dry A-Z of cult titles, this consists primarily of deadly dull plot synopses and fourth-hand facts. Among the inevitable titles discussed are *Pink Flamingos*, *The Rocky Horror Picture Show* and *The Producers*, yet *Halloween*, *Repulsion*, *Chelsea Girls* and Hammer's *Dracula* have been overlooked entirely by the authors in lieu of several arthouse titles most cult fans wouldn't be bothered about. Compiled by Karl and Philip French, who should have known better, this is a poor book indeed. Pavilion, £14.99 p/b.

Internet

by Josephine Botting

The creators of *The Blair Witch Project* would be the first to admit that the film's phenomenal success cannot be entirely attributed to its qualities as a horror film; its triumph at the box office was largely due to the hype which swamped the media before the film hit the screen. The innovative publicity exercise was centred largely on the Internet but rejected its usual, rather prosaic employment as just another information source about a new film. The website (www.blairwitch.com) was a key device in the propagation of an urban legend, creating an audience eager for the shocking 'documentary' they were soon to see.

Directors Eduardo Sanchez and Daniel Myrick came up with the idea of using the net to develop the pretence that the film used genuine footage of three researchers who disappeared in the woods while investigating a local tale of witchcraft. To this end, a site was set up presenting the case as pure fact and displaying photos of the missing persons and their vehicle. The filmmakers received a lot of positive feedback from it and began to build up a fanbase long before the film saw the light of day.

When the rights to *Blair Witch* were bought by Artisan, they took over the website as well, elaborating upon the information already there and including a history of Burkittsville, a real town in Maryland and the only factual reference in the tale. According to the site, it was built on the foundations of a deserted town called Blair where, in 1785, a terrible history of sorcery and murder began. In that year, local inhabitant Elly Kedward was banished, having been accused of luring children into her house and draining their blood. By the following year, all those who had persecuted her had disappeared and the town was abandoned by those who remained. Photographs of a book published about the case in 1809, *The Blair Witch Cult*, were reproduced on the website.

Nearly forty years later, Burkittsville was founded and, within a year, children again begin to vanish. A party of men sent out to hunt for one missing child was discovered horribly mutilated. The story resumes in 1941, when a local man, Rustin Parr, turned himself in to the police, who found the disembowelled corpses of seven children in the cellar of his remote dwelling. Parr claimed to have heard voices that instructed him to commit the crimes. His execution was described in an 'extract' from the *Washington Post*.

The next event in the Blair Witch chronology is the arrival of three intrepid researchers who, deter-

mined to investigate the myth for a college project, set out into the woods near Burkittsville in October 1994 armed with two cameras and a large dose of bravado. When they failed to return, a ten-day search was launched but no trace of them was found until a year later when their film and video equipment was discovered in a bag also containing Heather Donahue's journal.

Extracts from her increasingly frantic scribblings appeared on the website, allegedly with the permission of Heather's mother Angie, who granted the compilers an interview. Also interviewed were the police who had taken part in the search, and a private investigator, 'Bucky' Buchanan.

The Blair Witch website was incredibly popular, achieving two million hits a day in the United States. 'Word of mouse' spread fast and in the week before the film's release, 75 million people logged on. Spin-off sites began to appear, heightening the air of excitement surrounding the film, although industry executives have suggested that these were set up by friends of Sánchez and Myrick. The film's UK distributors, Pathé, set up their own site, attracting 300,000 visitors in its first two days.

This was the first time that the Internet had been used so effectively to create advance publicity, sustaining the film's conceit across the media and immersing visitors to the site in an alternative world. The originality and attention to detail in the story of the Blair Witch made it a highly effective back story, taking it beyond the realms of mere film to become a multimedia marvel. A range of merchandising appeared to

Above: Eduardo Sanchez and Daniel Myrick used the Internet to create the impression that the events in their film The Blair Witch Project *were based on truth*

Opposite page: The last video and testament of Heather (Heather Donahue) in The Blair Witch Project

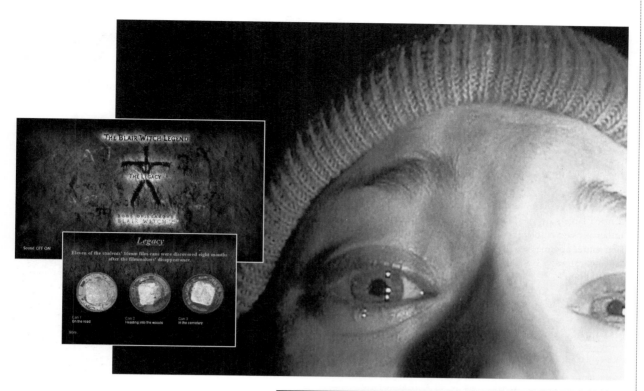

rival the summer's big budget release, *Star Wars*: Episode I *The Phantom Menace*. There were books recounting the legend, hats (to keep your head warm during nights running around in the woods), T-shirts, torches and even a CD soundtrack, despite the fact the film contains no music.

As well as the mirror sites, countless parodies began to spring up on the web, copying the style, layout and distinctive twig-arrangement logo of the original. Among these were The Bell Witch Project (three rednecks go out drinking and never return; a year later their throwaway Fujimatic camera and beer cooler is found), The Blair Warner Project (a student disappears after being accused of practising beauty techniques without a licence and locals die horrible deaths by manicure and waxing), The Blair Kitsch Project (an evil spirit is invented by parents to deter kids from requesting expensive brand-name clothes) and The Bare Witch Project (a group of girls lost in the woods with no map, no compass … and no clothes.)

Despite the clever attempts at artifice, it is doubtful that anyone but the most out-of-touch audience member fell for the film's supposed documentary nature. Allegedly, though, one New York private detective did offer his services to track down the missing students and the Internet Movie Database was conned into listing the actors in the film as 'missing believed dead.'

The Blair Witch Project's Internet-driven publicity campaign was a triumph for the low-budget filmmaker, who cannot afford the huge amounts the majors pour into pushing their product. Haxan

STUDIO SITES

BUENA VISTA
www.movies.go.com

DIMENSION FILMS
www.dimensionfilms.com

DREAMWORKS SKG
www.dreamworks.com

MGM
www.mgm.com

MIRAMAX
www.miramax.com

NEW LINE CINEMA
www.newline.com

PARAMOUNT
www.paramount.com

**SONY PICTURES
ENTERTAINMENT**
www.sonypictures.com

20TH CENTURY FOX
www.foxmovies.com

**UNITED INTERNATIONAL
PICTURES**
www.uip.com

UNIVERSAL PICTURES
www.universalpictures.com

WALT DISNEY PICTURES
www.disney.go.com/
disneypictures/

WARNER BROS
www.warnerbros.com

showed that with a bit of imagination and innovative spirit the net can be exploited as an effective way to reach a global audience. With this freely available access to a huge public, combined with the availability of cheaper and better quality digital video equipment, small producers can take on the big guys and win.

Awards and Festivals

The 72nd American Academy of Motion Picture Arts and Sciences Awards ('The Oscars') and Nominations for 1999, Los Angeles, 26 March 2000

● **Best Film:** *American Beauty*. **Nominations:** *The Cider House Rules*; *The Green Mile*; *The Insider*; *The Sixth Sense*.

● **Best Director:** Sam Mendes, for *American Beauty*. **Nominations:** Spike Jonze, for *Being John Malkovich*; Neil Jordan, for *The End of the Affair*; Michael Mann, for *The Insider*; Anthony Minghella, for *The Talented Mr. Ripley*.

● **Best Actor:** Kevin Spacey, for *American Beauty*. **Nominations:** Russell Crowe, for *The Insider*; Richard Farnsworth, for *The Straight Story*; Sean Penn, for *Sweet and Lowdown*; Denzel Washington, for *The Hurricane*.

● **Best Actress:** Hilary Swank, for *Boys Don't Cry*. **Nominations:** Annette Bening, for *American Beauty*; Janet Mcteer, for *Tumbleweeds*; Julianne Moore, for *The End of the Affair*; Meryl Streep, for *Music of the Heart*.

● **Best Supporting Actor:** Michael Caine, for *The Cider House Rules*. **Nominations:** Tom Cruise, for *Magnolia*; Michael Clarke Duncan, for *The Green Miles*; Jude Law, for *The Talented Mr Ripley*; Haley Joel Osment, for *The Sixth Sense*.

● **Best Supporting Actress:** Angelina Jolie, for *Girl, Interrupted*. **Nominations:** Toni Collette, for *The Sixth Sense*; Catherine Keener, for *Being John Malkovich*; Samantha Morton, for *Sweet and Lowdown*; Chloë Sevigny, for *Boys Don't Cry*.

● **Best Original Screenplay:** Alan Ball, for *American Beauty*. **Nominations:** Paul Thomas Anderson, for *Magnolia*; Charlie Kaufman, for *Being John Malkovich*; Mike Leigh, for *Topsy-Turvy*; M. Night Shyamalan, for *The Sixth Sense*.

● **Best Screenplay Adaptation:** John Irving, for *The Cider House Rules*. **Nominations:** Alexander Payne, for *Election*; Frank Darabont, for *The Green Mile*; Eric Roth and Michael Mann, for *The Insider*; Anthony Minghella, for *The Talented Mr Ripley*.

● **Best Cinematography:** Conrad L. Hall, for *American Beauty*. **Nominations:** Roger Pratt, for *The End of the Affair*; Dante Spinotti, for *The Insider*; Emmanuel Lubezki, for *Sleepy Hollow*; Robert Richardson, for *Snow Falling on Cedars*.

● **Best Editing:** Zach Staenberg, for *The Matrix*. **Nominations:** Tariq Anwar and Chris Greenbury, for *American Beauty*; Lisa Zeno Churgin, for *The Cider House Rules*; William Goldenberg and Paul Rubell, for *The Insider*; Andrew Monshein, for *The Sixth Sense*.

● **Best Original Score:** John Corigliano, for *The Red Violin*. **Nominations:** Thomas Newman, for *American Beauty*; Rachel Portman, for *The Cider House Rules*; John Williams, for *Angela's Ashes*; Gabriel Yared, for *The Talented Mr. Ripley*.

● **Best Original Song:** 'You'll Be in My Heart' from *Tarzan*. **Nominations:** 'Blame Canada,' from *South Park: Bigger, Longer and Uncut*; 'Music of My Heart' from *Music of the Heart*; 'Save Me' from *Magnolia*; 'When She Loved Me' from *Toy Story 2*.

● **Best Art Direction:** Rick Heinrichs (art direction) and Peter Young (set direction), for *Sleepy Hollow*. **Nominations:** Luciana Arrighi (art) and Ian Whittaker (set), for *Anna and the King*; David Gropman (art) and Beth Rubino (set), for *The Cider House Rules*; Roy Walker (art) and Bruno Cesari (set), for *The Talented Mr. Ripley*; Eve Stewart (art) and John Bush (set), for *Topsy-Turvy*.

● **Best Costume Design:** Lindy Hemming, for *Topsy-Turvy*. **Nominations:** Jenny Beavan, for *Anna and the King*; Colleen Atwood, for *Sleepy Hollow*; Ann Roth and Gary Jones, for *The Talented Mr Ripley*; Milena Canonero, for *Titus*.

● **Best Sound:** John Reitz, Gregg Rudloff, David Campbell and David Lee, for *The Matrix*. **Nominations:** Robert J. Litt, Elliot Tyson, Michael Herbick and Willie D. Burton, for *The Green Mile*; Andy Nelson, Doug Hemphill and Lee Orloff, for *The Insider*; Leslie Shatz, Chris Carpenter, Rick Kline and Chris Munro, for *The Mummy*; Gary Rydstrom, Tom Johnson, Shawn Murphy and John Midgley, for *Star Wars: Episode I The Phantom Menace*.

● **Best Sound Effects Editing:** Dane A. Davis, for *The Matrix*. **Nominations:** Ren Klyce and Richard Hymns, for *Fight Club*; Ben Burtt and Tom Bellfort, for *Star Wars: Episode I The Phantom Menace*.

● **Best Make-Up:** Christine Blundell and Trefor Proud, for *Topsy-Turvy*. **Nominations:** Michele Burke and Mike Smithson, for *Austin Powers: The Spy Who Shagged Me*; Greg Cannom, for *Bicentennial Man*; Rick Baker, for *Life*.

● **Best Visual Effects:** John Gaeta, Janet Sirrs, Steve Courtley and Jon Thum, for *The Matrix*. **Nominations:** John Knoll, Dennis Muren, Scott Squires and Rob Coleman, for *Star Wars: Episode One – The Phantom Menace*; John Dykstra, Jerome Chen, Henry F. Anderson III and Eric Allard, for *Stuart Little*.

● **Best Animated Short Film:** *The Old Man of the Sea*. **Nominations:** *Humdrum*; *My Grandmother Ironed the King's Shirts*; *3 Misses*; *When the Day Breaks*.

● **Best Live Action Short Film:** *My Mother Dreams of Satan's Disciples in New York*. **Nominations:** *Bror, Min Bror*; *Killing Joe*; *Kleingeld*; *Major and Minor Miracles*.

● **Best Documentary Feature:** *One Day in September*, by Kevin Macdonald. **Nominations:** *Buena Vista Social Club*; *Genghis Blues*; *On the Ropes*; *Speaking in Strings*.

● **Best Documentary Short:** *King Gimp*. **Nominations:** *Eyewitness*; *The Wildest Show in the South: The Angola Prison Rodeo*.

● **Best Foreign-Language Film:** *All About My Mother* (Spain). **Nominations:** *Caravan* – aka *Himalaya* (Nepal); *East-West* (France/ Russia/Spain/Bulgaria); *Solomon and Gaenor* (United Kingdom); *Under the Sun* (Sweden).

● **Irving G. Thalberg Award:**
Warren Beatty.
● **Honorary Award:** Andrzej Wajda.

The 41st Australian Film Institute Awards, 13 November 1999

● **Best Film:** *Two Hands.*
● **Best Actor:** Russell Dykstra, for *Soft Fruit.*
● **Best Actress:** Sacha Horler, for *Praise.*
● **Best Supporting Actor:** Bryan Brown, for *Two Hands.*
● **Best Supporting Actress:** Sacha Horler, for *Soft Fruit.*
● **Best Director:** Gregor Jordan, for *Two Hands.*
● **Best Original Screenplay:** Gregor Jordan, for *Two Hands.*
● **Best Screenplay Adaptation:** Andrew McGahan, for *Praise.*
● **Best Cinematography:** Martin McGrath, for *Passion.*
● **Best Production Design:** Murray Picknett, for *Passion.*
● **Best Editing:** Lee Smith, for *Two Hands.*
● **Best Music:** David Bridie, for *In a Savage Land.*
● **Best Costumes:** Terry Ryan, for *Passion.*
● **Best Sound:** *In a Savage Land.*
● **Best Foreign Film:** *Life is Beautiful,* by Roberto Benigni (Italy).
● **The Byron Kennedy Award (for pursuit of excellence):** director Baz Luhrmann and designer Catherine Martin.
● **The Raymond Longford Award (for services to the industry):** programmer and consultant John Politzer.

Presenters: Nicole Kidman, Cate Blanchett, Geoffrey Rush, etc.

The 1999 British Academy of Film and Television Arts Awards ('BAFTAs'), 9 April 2000

● **Best Film:** *American Beauty.*
● **David Lean Award for Best Direction:** Pedro Almodóvar, for *All About My Mother.*
● **Best Original Screenplay:** Charlie Kaufman, for *Being John Malkovich.*
● **Best Adapted Screenplay:** Neil Jordan, for *The End of the Game.*

● **Best Actor:** Kevin Spacey, for *American Beauty.*
● **Best Actress:** Annette Bening, for *American Beauty.*
● **Best Supporting Actor:** Jude Law, for *The Talented Mr Ripley.*
● **Best Supporting Actress:** Maggie Smith, for *Tea With Mussolini.*
● **Best Cinematography:** Conrad L. Hall, for *American Beauty.*
● **Best Production Design:** Rick Heinrichs, for *Sleepy Hollow.*
● **Best Editing:** Tariq Anwar and Christopher Greenbury, for *American Beauty.*
● **The Anthony Asquith Award for Best Music:** Thomas Newman, for *American Beauty.*
● **Best Costumes:** Colleen Atwood, for *Sleepy Hollow.*
● **Best Sound:** John Reitz, Gregg Rudloff, David Campbell and David Lee, for *The Matrix.*
● **Best Special Visual Effects:** John Gaeta, Janek Sirrs, Steve Courtley and Jon Thum, for *The Matrix.*
● **Best Make-up/hair:** Christine Blundell, for *Topsy-Turvy.*
● **Alexander Korda Award for Best British Film:** *East is East.*
● **Best Foreign Language Film:** *All About My Mother* (Spain).
● **Best Short Film:** *Who's My Favourite Girl?*
● **Best Animated Short:** *The Man With Beautiful Eyes.*
● **Carl Foreman Award for British Newcomer:** Lynne Ramsay, writer-director of *Ratcatcher.*
● **Michael Balcon Award for Outstanding British Contribution to the Cinema:** Joyce Herlihy.
● **BAFTA Fellowships:** Michael Caine and Stanley Kubrick.
● **The Orange Audience Award:** *Notting Hill.*

The 20th Canadian Film Awards ('Genies'), Toronto, Ontario, 30 January 2000

● **Best Film:** *Sunshine.*
● **Best Director:** Jeremy Podeswa, for *The Five Senses.*
● **Best Actor:** Bob Hoskins, for *Felicia's Journey.*
● **Best Actress:** Sylvie Moreau, for *Post Mortem.*

● **Best Supporting Actor:** Mark McKinney, for *Dog Park.*
● **Best Supporting Actress:** Catherine O'Hara, for *The Life Before This.*
● **Best Original Screenplay:** Louis Bélanger, for *Post Mortem.*
● **Best Adapted Screenplay:** Atom Egoyan, for *Felicia's Journey.*
● **Best Cinematography:** Paul Sarossy, for *Felicia's Journey.*
● **Best Editing:** Ronald Sanders, for *eXistenZ.*
● **Best Art Direction:** François Séguin, for *Souvenirs intimes.*
● **Best Music:** Mychael Danna, for *Felicia's Journey.*
● **Best Original Song:** Tim Burns, for 'It's a Treat To Be a Creep,' from *Jacob Two Two Meets the Hooded Fang.*
● **Best Costumes:** Renée April, for *Grey Owl.*
● **Best Sound Editing:** Jane Tattersall, Fred Brennan, Dina Eaton, Andy Malcolm and David McCallum, for *Sunshine.*
● **Best Overall Sound:** Daniel Pellerin, Keith Elliott, Glen Gauthier and Peter Kelly, for *Sunshine.*
● **Claude Jutra Award for Best First Feature:** *Post Mortem.*
● **Best Feature-length Documentary:** *Just Watch Me: Trudeau and the 70s Generation,* by Gerry Flahive, Catherine Annau and Yves Bisaillon.
● **Best Short Documentary:** *Hemingway: A Portrait,* by Bernard Lajoie, Eric Canuel and Tatsuo Shimamura.
● **Best Animated Short:** *When the Day Breaks,* by David Verrall, Amanda Forbis and Wendy Tilby.
● **Best Live-Action Short:** *Moving Day,* by Tina Goldlist and Chris Deacon.
● **The Golden Reel Award for Box-Office Performance:** *Les Boys II.*

The 53rd Cannes Film Festival Awards, 22 May 2000

● **Palme d'Or for Best Film:** *Dancer in the Dark* (Denmark/Sweden/France), by Lars von Trier .
● **Grand Prix du Jury:** *Devils On the Doorstep* (China), by Jiang Wen.
● **Jury Prize:** *Blackboards,* by Samira Makhmalbaf (Iran); and *Songs From the Second Floor,* by Roy Andersson (Sweden).

Below: Catherine Deneuve in Dancer
in the Dark, *the controversial winner
of the Palme d'Or at Cannes*

● **Best Actor:** Tony Leung, for *In the
Mood For Love* (Hong Kong).
● **Best Actress:** Bjork, for *Dancer
in the Dark.*
● **Best Director:** Edward Yang, for *Yi Yi*
(*A One and a Two*), (Taiwan).
● **Best Screenplay:** John Richards and
James Flamberg, for *Nurse Betty* (USA).
● **Palme d'Or for Best Short:** *Anino*, by
Raymond Red (Philippines).
● **Fipresci International Critics' Award:**
Eureka (Japan), by Shinji Aoyama.
● **Ecumenical Prize:** *Eureka.*

*Jury: Luc Besson (president);
Jonathan Demme, Nicole Garcia,
Jeremy Irons, Mario Martone, Patrick
Modiano, Arundhati Roy, Aitana
Sanchez-Gijon, Kristin Scott Thomas
and Barbara Sukowa*

The 25th Deauville Festival of American Cinema, 12 September 1999

● **Grand Prix for Best Film:** *Being John
Malkovich*, by Spike Jonze.
● **Jury Prize:** *Twin Falls Idaho*, by
Michael Polish; and *Guinevere*, by
Audrey Wells.
● **International Critics' Grand Prix:**
Being John Malkovich.
● **Fun Radio Trophy:** *Twin Falls Idaho.*
CinéLive Award: *Twin Falls Idaho.*
● **Best short:** *Protest*, by S.D. Katz.

Jury: Régis Wargnier (head of jury)

(France); *Marie Gillain (France);
Marie-France Pisier (Indochina/
France); Elsa Zylberstein (France);
Jean-Hugues Anglade (France);
Humbert Balsan (France); Richard
Berry (France); Gabriel Byrne (Ireland);
Jean-Pierre Dionnet (France); Michel
Houellebecq (France)*

The 12th European Film Awards ('The Felixes'), Schiller Theatre, Berlin, Germany, 4 December 1999

● **Best European Film:** *All About My
Mother*, produced by Agustín
Almodóvar.
Best Actor: Ralph Fiennes, for *Sunshine.*
● **Best Actress:** Cecilia Roth, for *All
About My Mother*
● **Best Screenplay:** István Szabo and
Israel Horovitz, for *Sunshine.*
● **Best Cinematography:** Lajos Koltai,
for *The Legend of 1900* and *Sunshine.*
● **Best Short Film:** *Benvenuto a San
Salvario*, by Enrico Verra.
● **Discovery of the Year (Fassbinder
Award):** Tim Roth, director of *The
War Zone.*
● **Best Documentary (Prix Arte):** *Buena
Vista Social Club*, by Wim Wenders.
● **Best Documentary (Special
Mention):** *Mobutu, roi du Zaire*, by
Thierry Michel.
● **People's Awards:**
Best Actor: Sean Connery,
for *Entrapment.*
Best Actress: Catherine Zeta-Jones,
for *Entrapment.*
Best Director: Pedro Almodóvar,
for *All About My Mother.*
● **Best Non-European Film (Five
Continents Award):** *The Straight Story*
(USA), by David Lynch
● **Achievement in World Cinema:**
Antonio Banderas, director of
Crazy in Alabama; and Roman
Polanski, for *The Ninth Gate* and
his body of work.
● **FIPRESCI Award:** Otar Ioseliani,
for *Adieu, plancher des vaches!*
● **Lifetime Achievement Award:**
Ennio Morricone.

The 25th French Academy ('Cesar') Awards, 19 February 2000

● **Best Film:** *Venus Beauty.*
● **Best Director:** Tonie Marshall,
for *Venus Beauty.*
● **Best Actor:** Daniel Auteuil, for
The Girl On the Bridge.
● **Best Actress:** Karin Viard, for
Haut les Coeurs.
● **Best Supporting Actor:** Francois
Berleand, for *My Little Business.*
● **Best Supporting Actress:**
Charlotte Gainsbourg, for *La Buche.*
● **Most Promising Young Actor:**
Eric Caravaca, for *What is Life?*
● **Most Promising Young Actress:**
Audrey Tautou, for *Venus Beauty.*
● **Best First Film:** *Voyages*, by
Emmanuel Finkiel.
● **Best Screenplay:** Tonie Marshall,
for *Venus Beauty.*
● **Best Photography:** Eric Guichard,
for *Himalaya.*
● **Best Production Design:**
Philippe Chiffre, for *Rembrandt.*
● **Best Editing:** Emmanuelle Castro,
for *Voyages.*
● **Best Music:** Bruno Coulais,
for *Himalaya.*
● **Best Costumes:** Catherine Leterrier,
for *Joan of Arc.*
● **Best Sound:** Vincent Tulli,
Francois Groult and Bruno Tarriere,
for *Joan of Arc.*
● **Best Short:** *Salle Battars*, by
Delphine Gleize.
● **Best Foreign Film:** *All About My
Mother*, by Pedro Almodóvar (Spain).
● **Honorary Cesars:** Martin Scorsese.

Host: Alain Delon

Golden Raspberries ('The Razzies'), 25 March 2000

● **Worst Film:** *Wild Wild West.*
● **Worst Actor:** Adam Sandler, for
Big Daddy.
● **Worst Actress:** Heather Donahue, for
The Blair Witch Project.
● **Worst Screen Couple:** Will Smith and
Kevin Kline, for *Wild Wild West.*
● **Worst Supporting Actress:**
Denise Richards, for *The World is
Not Enough.*
● **Worst Supporting Actor:** Jar-Jar Binks

(voice by Ahmed Best), for *Star Wars: Episode I The Phantom Menace.*
● **Worst Director:** Barry Sonnenfeld, for *Wild Wild West.*
● **Worst Screenplay:** Jim Thomas & John Thomas, S.S. Wilson & Brent Maddock and Jeffrey Price & Peter S. Seaman, for *Wild Wild West.*
● **Worst 'Original' Song:** 'Wild Wild West,' from *Wild Wild West,* by Stevie Wonder, Kool Mo Dee and Will Smith.
● **Worst Actor of the Century:** Sylvester Stallone.
● **Worst Actress of the Century:** Madonna.
● **Worst Picture of the Decade:** *Showgirls.*
● **Worst New Star of the Decade:** Pauly Shore.

The 57th Hollywood Foreign Press Association ('Golden Globes') Awards, 23 January 2000

● **Best Picture – Drama:** *American Beauty.*
● **Best Picture – Musical or Comedy:** *Toy Story 2.*
● **Best Actor – Drama:** Denzel Washington, for *The Hurricane.*
● **Best Actress – Drama:** Hilary Swank, for *Boys Don't Cry.*
● **Best Actor – Musical or Comedy:** Jim Carrey, for *Man on the Moon.*
● **Best Actress – Musical or Comedy:** Janet McTeer, for *Tumbleweeds.*
● **Best Supporting Actress:** Angelina Jolie, for *Girl, Interrupted.*
● **Best Supporting Actor:** Tom Cruise, for *Magnolia.*
● **Best Director:** Sam Mendes, for *American Beauty.*
● **Best Screenplay:** Alan Ball, for *American Beauty.*
● **Best Original Score:** Ennio Morricone, for *The Legend of 1900.*
● **Best Original Song:** 'You'll be in My Heart' from *Tarzan,* by Phil Collins.
● **Best Foreign Language Film:** *All About My Mother* (Spain), by Pedro Almodóvar.
● **Best TV Film or miniseries:** *RKO 281.*
● **Cecil B. De Mille Award for Lifetime Achievement:** Barbra Streisand.

The 20th London Film Critics' Awards ('The Alfs'), The Dorchester, London, 2 March 2000

● **Best Film:** *American Beauty.*
● **Best Actor:** Kevin Spacey, for *American Beauty.*
● **Best Actress:** Annette Bening, for *American Beauty.*
● **Best Director:** Sam Mendes, for *American Beauty.*
● **Best Screenwriter:** Alan Ball, for *American Beauty.*
● **Best British Film:** *East is East.*
● **Best British Producer:** Leslee Udwin, for *East is East.*
● **Best British Director:** Lynne Ramsay, for *Ratcatcher.*
● **Best British Screenwriter:** Ayub Khan Din, for *East is East.*
● **Best British Actor:** Jeremy Northam, for *Happy Texas, An Ideal Husband* and *The Winslow Boy.*
● **Best British Actress:** Emily Watson, for *Angela's Ashes* and *Hilary & Jackie.*
● **Best British Supporting Actor:** Michael Caine, for *Little Voice.*
● **Best British Supporting Actress:** Lynn Redgrave, for *Gods and Monsters.*
● **Best British Newcomer:** Martha Fiennes, director of *Onegin.*
● **Best Foreign Language Film:** *All About My Mother* (Spain).
● **Dilys Powell Award:** Mike Leigh.

Presenters: John Marriott, Mariella Frostrup, James Cameron-Wilson, Paul Gambaccini, Marianne Gray, Karen Krizanovich, Wendy Lloyd, Simon Rose

The Los Angeles Film Critics' Association Awards, 11 December 1999

● **Best Picture:** *The Insider.*
● **Best Actor:** Russell Crowe, for *The Insider*
● **Best Actress:** Hilary Swank, for *Boys Don't Cry*
● **Best Supporting Actor:** Christopher Plummer, for *The Insider.*
● **Best Supporting Actress:** Chloë Sevigny, for *Boys Don't Cry.*
● **Best Director:** Sam Mendes, for *American Beauty.*
● **Best Screenplay:** Charlie Kaufman, for *Being John Malkovich.*

● **Best Cinematography:** Dante Spinotti, for *The Insider.*
● **Best Production Design:** Rich Heinrichs, for *Sleepy Hollow.*
● **Best Music:** Trey Parker and Marc Shaiman, for *South Park: Bigger, Longer and Uncut.*
● **Best Animated Feature:** *The Iron Giant.*
● **Best Documentary:** *Buena Vista Social Club.*
● **New Generation Award:** Alexander Payne and Jim Taylor, for their screenplays *Citizen Ruth* and *Election.*
● **Best Foreign-Language Film:** *All About My Mother* (Spain).
● **Special Citation:** Rick Schmidlin (Turner Classic Movies) and Roger Mayer (Turner Classic Movies) for their work on the recreation and presentation of Erich Von Stroheim's *Greed* (1925).
● **Independent/Experimental Film or Video Award:** Owen Land, for his body of work.

The 91st National Board of Review of Motion Picture Awards, New York, 18 January 2000

● **Best Film:** *American Beauty.*
● **Best Actor:** Russell Crowe, for *The Insider.*
● **Best Actress:** Janet McTeer, for *Tumbleweeds.*
● **Best Supporting Actor:** Philip Seymour Hoffman, for *Magnolia* and *The Talented Mr Ripley.*
● **Best Supporting Actress:** Julianne Moore, for *Cookie's Fortune, An Ideal Husband, Magnolia* and *A Map of the World.*
● **Best Director:** Anthony Minghella, for *The Talented Mr Ripley.*
● **Best Screenplay:** John Irving, for *The Cider House Rules.*
● **Best Directorial Debut:** Kimberly Peirce, for *Boys Don't Cry.*
● **Best Ensemble Cast:** *Magnolia.*
● **Best Documentary:** *Buena Vista Social Club.*
● **Best Foreign Films:** *All About My Mother* (Spain), *Run Lola Run* (Germany), *East-West* (France/Russia/Spain/Bulgaria), *The Emperor and the Assassin* (Japan/China/France) and *Cabaret*

Balkan (France).

● **Breakthrough Performance:** Hilary Swank, for *Boys Don't Cry*; and Wes Bentley, for *American Beauty*.

● **Special Achievement in Filmmaking Award:** Tim Robbins, for writing and directing *Cradle Will Rock*.

The 34th National Society of Film Critics' Awards, Algonquin Hotel, New York, 8 January 2000

● **Best Film:** *Being John Malkovich* and *Topsy-Turvy* (tie).

● **Best Actor:** Russell Crowe, for *The Insider*.

● **Best Actress:** Reese Witherspoon, for *Election*.

● **Best Director:** Mike Leigh, for *Topsy-Turvy*.

● **Best Supporting Actor:** Christopher Plummer, for *The Insider*.

● **Best Supporting Actress:** Chloë Sevigny, for *Boys Don't Cry*.

● **Best Screenplay:** Charlie Kaufman, for *Being John Malkovich*.

● **Best Cinematography:** Conrad L. Hall, for *American Beauty*.

● **Best Foreign Film:** *An Autumn Tale* (France), by Eric Rohmer.

● **Best Documentary:** *Buena Vista Social Club*.

The 65th New York Film Critics' Circle Awards, 9 January 2000

● **Best Film:** *Topsy-Turvy*.

● **Best Actor:** Richard Farnsworth, for *The Straight Story*.

● **Best Actress:** Hilary Swank, for *Boys Don't Cry*.

● **Best Supporting Actor:** John Malkovich, for *Being John Malkovich*.

● **Best Supporting Actress:** Catherine Keener, for *Being John Malkovich*.

● **Best Director:** Mike Leigh, for *Topsy-Turvy*.

● **Best Screenplay:** Alexander Payne and Jim Taylor, for *Election*.

● **Best Cinematography:** Freddie Francis, for *The Straight Story*.

● **Best Foreign Film:** *All About My Mother* (Spain).

● **Best Non-Fiction Film:** *Buena Vista Social Club*.

● **Best First Film:** *Being John Malkovich* (USA), by Spike Jonze.

● **Best Animated Film:** *South Park: Bigger, Longer & Uncut*.

The 16th Sundance Film Festival, Park City, Utah, 30 January 2000

● **The Grand Jury Prize (best feature):** *Girlfight*, by Karyn Kusama; and *You Can Count On Me*, by Ken Lonergan.

● **The Grand Jury Prize (best documentary):** *Long Night's Journey Into Day*, by Frances Reid and Deborah Hoffmann.

● **Best Performance:** Donal Logue, for *The Tao of Steve*.

● **Best Ensemble Performance:** Janet McTeer, Aidan Quinn, Pat Carroll, Jane Adams, Gregory Cook and Iris DeMent, for *Songcatcher*.

● **Best Direction:** Karyn Kusama, for *Girlfight*.

● **Best Direction (documentary):** Robert Epstein and Jeffrey Friedman, for *Paragraph 175*.

● **Best Cinematography:** Tom Krueger, for *Committed*.

● **Best Cinematography (documentary):** Andrew Young, for *Americanos: Latino Life in the United States*.

● **Audience Award (best feature):** *Two Family House*, by Raymond De Felitta.

● **Audience Award (best documentary):** *Dark Days*, by Marc Singer.

● **Audience Award (world cinema):** *Saving Grace*, by Nigel Cole.

● **Short Filmmaking Award:** *Five Feet High and Rising*, by Peter Sollett.

● **Waldo Salt Screenwriting Award:** Ken Lonergan, for *You Can Count On Me*.

● **Freedom of Expression Award:** *Dark Days*.

● **Special Jury Award (documentary):** *The Ballad of Ramblin' Jack*, by Aiyana Elliott.

● **Latin American Cinema Award:** *El Coronel no tiene quien le escriba*, by Arturo Ripstein; and *La Ley de Herodes*, by Luis Estrada.

The 56th Venice International Film Festival Awards, 11 September 1999

● **Golden Lion for Best Film:** *Not One Less*, by Zhang Yimou (China).

● **Special Jury Grand Prix:** *The Wind Will Carry Us*, by Abbas Kiarostami (France/Iran).

● **Best Actor:** Jim Broadbent, for *Topsy-Turvy* (UK).

● **Best Actress:** Nathalie Baye, for *A Pornographic Affair* (Belgium/France).

● **Marcello Mastroianni Award for Emerging Actor:** Nina Proll, for *Northern Skirts* (aka *Nordrand*) (Austria/Germany/Switzerland).

● **Best Short:** *Portrait of a Young Man drowning*, by Teboho Mahlatsi (South Africa).

● **Gold Medal (for a film which emphasises civil progress and human solidarity):**

● **Fipresci International Critics' Award:** *The Wind Will Carry Us*.

● **Venezia Opera Prima Luigi De Laurentiis Award for Best First Feature:** *This is the Garden*, by Davide Maderna (Italy).

● **Fipresci Award (out of competition):** *Being John Malkovich*, by Spike Jonze (USA).

● **Special Prize For Direction:** Zhang Yuan, for *Seventeen Years* (China/Italy).

● **Gold Medal of the Italian Senate:** *Empty Days* (France), by Marion Vernoux.

Jury: Emir Kusturica (president), director Marco Bellocchio, actress Maggie Cheung, writer Jonathan Coe, critic Jean Douchet, producer Shozo Ichiyama, director Arturo Ripstein and artist Cindy Sherman

In Memoriam

by Howard Maxford

LEWIS ALLEN

Born: 25 December 1905, Shropshire, England. **Died**: 3 May 2000.

● Though born in Britain, director Allen spent most of his career in Hollywood. Following experience as a stage actor and director at home, he moved to America, where he was signed to an apprenticeship with Paramount, making his directorial debut for the studio with the classic ghost story *The Uninvited* in 1944, the success of which provoked the similarly-*themed The Unseen* in 1945. His other credits include *Our Hearts Were Young and Gay* (1944), *Those Endearing Young Charms* (1946) and *Another Time, Another Place* (1958). He returned to Britain to make *Whirlpool* in 1959. His last film was *Decision at Midnight* in 1963.

IAN BANNEN

Born: June 29 1928 in Airdrie, Scotland. **Died**: 3 November 1999 in a car crash off the coast of Loch Ness, Scotland.

● A respected actor on stage, screen and television, Bannen provided reliable support in over fifty films, making his debut in *Private's Progress* for the Boulting Brothers in 1956. Following further small roles in the likes of *The Long Arm* (1956) and *Carlton-Browne of the FO* (1959, again for the Boultings), he found himself increasingly in demand in the 1960s by some of the world's top directors, among them Ronald Neame for *Mister Moses* (1965), Sidney Lumet for *The Hill* (1965) and Robert Aldrich for *The Flight of the Phoenix* (1965), which earned him a best supporting actor Oscar nomination. Perhaps Bannen's best screen performance came in 1972 in *The Offence*, again for Sidney Lumet, in which he more than held his ground as a suspected child molester being interrogated by Sean Connery's tough, rule-breaking copper. His other films include *The Mackintosh Man* (1973), *Bite the Bullet* (1975), *Hope and Glory* (1987) and *Waking Ned* (1999), whilst on television the 1990s saw him in the likes of *Doctor Finlay* and *The Politician's Wife*.

PAUL BARTEL

Born: 6 August 1938 in New York. **Died**: 13 May 2000 in his sleep, in his New York apartment.

● Perhaps best remembered for directing the savagely satirical *Death Race 2000* in 1975, actor-writer-director Paul Bartel made his directorial debut in 1972 with the equally black *Private Parts*, which contained an eccentric blend of sex, comedy and murder in the John Waters manner. Prior to this, Bartel had studied at UCLA, where he specialised in animation and documentary shorts, after which he went to Rome to study direction. In the late 60s he worked as an assistant director on army training films, and made Spanish-language newsreels for the US Information Agency. Having had a hit with *Death Race 2000*, Bartel remained in the car race genre for his next outing, *Cannonball* (1976, aka *Carquake*). Though a success, Bartel didn't direct again for six years, returning in 1982 with the acclaimed cannibal comedy *Eating Raoul*, which he also starred in opposite Mary Woronov, his close friend and most frequent screen partner. His other films as a director are *Not for Publication* (1984), *Lust in the Dust* (1985), *The Longshot* (1986) and *Scenes from the Class Struggle in Beverly Hills* (1989). As a performer he can be spotted in such diverse fare as *Hollywood Boulevard* (1977), *Piranha* (1978), *White Dog* (1982), *Chopping Mall* (1986), *Gremlins 2* (1990), *The Usual Suspects* (1995) and Michael Almereyda's *Hamlet* (2000).

JEFFREY BOAM

Born: November 30, 1949 in Rochester, New York. **Died**: 26 January 2000 of a rare lung disease.

● A screenwriter with a penchant for block-busting action subjects, Jeffrey Boam made his film debut with the Dustin Hoffman vehicle *Straight Time* in 1978, which he co-wrote with Alvin Sargent and Edward Bunker (he also doubled as the film's assistant director). His breakthrough came in 1983 with an adaptation of Stephen King's *The Dead Zone* for director David Cronenberg, which also earned him an associate producer credit. Sticking with fantasy, Boam turned out *Innerspace* (in which he also briefly appears) and *The Lost Boys* (both 1987), after which he hitched to the successful *Lethal Weapon* series, penning episodes 2 (1989) and 3 (1992). 1989 also saw him join the Indiana Jones franchise with *Indiana Jones and the Last Crusade*, which led to his scripting the unfilmed *Indiana Jones and the Lost City of Atlantis*.

CHILLI BOUCHIER

Born: 12 September 1909, London. **Died**: 9 September 1999.

● Though she made over fifty films, the career of British leading lady Chili Bouchier (real name Dorothy Irene Bouchier) is often overlooked today, even by buffs. A major stage star, she made her film debut in 1927 in *A Woman in Pawn*, which she followed with a further five films in 1928 alone, among them *Shooting Stars* and *You Know What Sailors Are*. Hollywood beckoned, but she found herself *persona non grata* when she walked out on a contract, and so returned to Britain, where she churned out countless films in the 30s, among the more memorable being *The Blue Danube* (1932), *The Ghost Goes West* (1936) and *Gypsy* (1936). Her other films include *The Case of Charles Peace* (1948), *Old Mother Riley's New Venture* (1949) and *Dead Lucky* (1960). Bouchier continued to perform on stage well into her eighties, and occasionally popped up on television in the likes of *The Vision* and *Catch a Fallen Star* (both 1987). She also penned two volumes of autobiography: *For Dogs and Angels* (1968) and *Shooting Star* (1995).

MARGUERITE CHAPMAN

Born: 9 March 1920 in Chatham, New York.
Died: 31 August 1999 in Burbank, California.

● A mainstay of Columbia's B unit in the 1940s, Marguerite Chapman brought a touch of glamour to such standard World War Two action fare as *Submarine Raider* (1942), *Destroyer* (1943) and *Counter Attack* (1945). Her other films include *Flight to Mars* (1951) and *The Seven Year Itch* (1955), whilst in the 1950s and 60s she became a well known face on American television. In the 1960s she semi-retired to Hawaii, though subsequently popped up in several episodes of *Hawaii Five-O*. She was formerly married to British film producer Anthony Havelock-Allan.

NICHOLAS CLAY

Born: 18 September 1946, Streatham, London. **Died**: 25 May 2000, from cancer of the liver at his home in London.

● This handsome British leading man made his screen debut in 1971 as a murderous handyman in *The Night Digger* which, despite a Roald Dahl script, a cast that included Dahl's wife Patricia Neal, and a Bernard Herrmann score, was barely released. In the 1970s Clay appeared in three more interesting failures: *The Darwin Adventure* (1975), *Tristan and Isolde* (1976) and *Zulu Dawn* (1978). In 1979 Clay came close to winning the role of Perseus in *Clash of the Titans*, but lost out to Harry Hamlin who, ironically, he'd beaten for the role of Tristan in *Tristan and Isolde*. However, Clay did finally gain some attention as Lancelot in *Excalibur* (1981), a brief nude scene in which led to his being cast as the gardener in *Lady Chatterley's Lover* (1981) opposite Sylvia Kristel. Clay's best role came as the murderous Patrick Redfern in the deliciously camp Agatha Christie thriller *Evil Under the Sun* (1982). Unfortunately, the film's lacklustre box office failed to give the actor's career that extra push it needed to take him to the front rank.

CHARLES CRICHTON

Born: 6 August 1910, in Wallsay, England. **Died**: 14 September 1999.

● Like David Lean and Clive Donner, director Charles Crichton began his career as an editor, working on a variety of films for producer Alexander Korda at Denham Studios, among them *Things to Come* (1936) and *The Thief of Bagdad* (1940). In 1941 he directed a short, *The Young*

Veterans, though it was another three years before he directed his first feature, the semi-documentary air-sea rescue drama *For Those in Peril*, which he made for Ealing. Crichton remained at Ealing until 1956, where he made such imperishable comedies as *Hue and Cry* (1947), *The Lavender Hill Mob* (1951) and *The Titfield Thunderbolt* (1953). Once he left Ealing, his career became more uncertain, though he continued to mine the same vein of comedy with *Law and Disorder* (1958) and *The Battle of the Sexes* (1960). In 1962 he abandoned work on his first American film, *The Birdman of Alcatraz* (which was taken over by John Frankenheimer) and returned to Britain, but his resultant dramas, *The Third Secret* (1964) and *He Who Rides a Tiger* (1965), were disappointments. Consequently, Crichton turned increasingly to television, where he brought a touch of cinematic style to such series as *The Avengers* and *Danger Man*. Crichton made a triumphant return to the big screen at the age of 78 in 1988 with *A Fish Called Wanda*, which he also co-wrote with the film's star, John Cleese.

EDWARD DMYTRYK

Born: 4 September 1908 in Grand Forks, British Columbia. **Died**: 1 July 1999.

● Better known today as one of the Hollywood 10 – those filmmakers who refused to cooperate with the House UnAmerican Activities Committee – than for his films, Dmytryk was nonetheless a highly respected director. The son of Ukrainian immigrants, he graduated from messenger boy to being an exemplary editor at Paramount and made his directorial debut on the $5,000 independent Western *Trail of the Hawk* (1935). At Columbia and RKO he honed his directorial skills on a series of B-movies before gaining recognition for the Philip Marlowe classic *Murder,*

My Sweet (1944) and the controversial *Crossfire* (1947), the latter gaining him his only Oscar nomination. His other notable films include *Till the End of Time* (1946), *Broken Lance* and *The Caine Mutiny* (both 1954) and *Mirage* (1965). Called to testify before the HUAC in 1947, Dmytryk refused to name names and was blacklisted, fired by RKO and jailed for six months. However, after serving half of his sentence, he opted to recant and divulged the names of more than 20 Hollywood members of the Communist Party, a betrayal that caused considerable acrimony among his peers. In 1979 he penned his autobiography, *It's a Hell of a Life, but Not a Bad Living* and ended up teaching film studies at the University of Texas. [JC-W]

GEORGE DUNING

Born: 25 February 1928 in Richmond, Indiana. **Died**: 27 February 2000 in San Diego, California of cardio-vascular disease.

● This busy composer began his career in 1939 as an arranger, having studied music at the Cincinnati Conservatory of Music, where he specialised in the trumpet. Following work for the popular band leader Kay Kyser, as well as wartime experience in the Navy, Duning was contracted to Columbia in 1944 as an arranger and orchestrator, in which capacity he contributed to such scores as *Down to Earth* (1947, composed by Heinz Roemheld) and *The Guilt of Janet Ames* (1947, by Morris Stoloff). His first solo effort was for *Johnny O'Clock* (1947). Some 250 scores followed, among them *Jolson Sings Again* (1949), *No Sad Songs for Me* (1950), *From Here to Eternity* (1953), *Picnic* (1955) and *The Eddy Duchin Story* (1956), all of which earned him Oscar nominations. His other films include *The Man from Laramie* (1955), *The Notorious Landlady* (1962) and *Hotel* (1967), whilst for television he contributed episode scores *to The Big Valley*, *Star Trek* and *The Partridge Family*.

DOUGLAS FAIRBANKS JR

Born: 9 December 1909 in New York. **Died**: 7 May 2000 in Manhattan, New York.

● Given that his father was the swashbuckling legend Douglas Fairbanks, Fairbanks Jr had a lot to live up to, yet after a hesitant start he appeared in a number of equally popular slices of derring-do, among them *The Prisoner of Zenda* (1937, as the devious Rupert Hentzau), *Gunga Din* (1939), *The Corsican Brothers* (1941, in dual duelling

roles), *Sinbad the Sailor* (1947), *The Exile* (1948, which he also wrote) and *The Fighting O'Flynn* (1948, which he co-wrote). At the age of nine, Fairbanks Jr's parents divorced, and the young Douglas was raised solely by his mother. It wasn't until he was in his twenties that Jr became close again with Sr, who was now married to 'America's Sweetheart' Mary Pickford. By this time Jr had already made several movies, making his debut in *Stephen Steps Out* (1923) when he was just 13. Appearances in *Stella Dallas* (1925), *Man Bait* (1927) and *A Woman of Affairs* (1928, with Greta Garbo) followed. First rank stardom was slow in coming though, but following his marriage to Joan Crawford in 1928, Fairbanks' career began to soar with *The Dawn Patrol* (1930), *Little Caesar* (1931) and *Morning Glory* (1933). Following his divorce from Crawford in 1933, Fairbanks made his first film in England, *Catherine the Great* (1934, as Grand Duke Peter to Elisabeth Bergner's Catherine). This began a long association with Britain, where Fairbanks went on to make, among others, *The Amateur Gentleman* (1936), *State Secret* (1950) and *Mr Drake's Duck* (1950), as well as the long-running television series *Douglas Fairbanks Presents* (1955-59), which he also produced. Following a long absence from the big screen, he returned for one last hurrah in *Ghost Story* (1981), in which he starred with Fred Astaire, John Houseman and Melvyn Douglas. He also occasionally popped up on television, guesting on the likes of *The Love Boat* and *B. L. Stryker*. He wrote about his life in three volumes of autobiography: *The Fairbanks Album* (1975), *Salad Days* (1988) and *A Hell of a War* (1993), the latter recalling his experiences in World War Two, during which he was a lieutenant commander in the US Navy.

VITTORIO GASSMAN

Born: 1 September 1922 in Genoa. **Died**: 30 June 2000 in Rome from a heart attack.
● Long before Al Pacino won an Oscar for the 1992 remake of *Scent of a Woman*, Vittorio Gassman won the best actor prize at Cannes for the original Italian version in 1975. By this point in his career, he was considered one of the great leading men of Italian cinema, thanks to performances in *Bitter Rice* (1948) and *Anna* (1951). However, prior to graduating from Rome's National Academy of Dramatic Art, Gassman could very well have had a career in sport (he was a star basketball player at school) or in law (he studied to be a lawyer). Instead he turned to the theatre, notching up some forty productions before the movies finally beckoned in 1946 with *Shamed*. His international status was slower in arriving, despite a short-lived marriage to Shelley Winters in 1952. Nevertheless he made welcome appearances in such English-speaking films as *Rhapsody* (1954), *War and Peace* (1956) and *The Miracle* (1959), although it was at home on stage that he earned his greatest acclaim, notably in Luchino Visconti's production of *Tobacco Road*. His other films included *Woman Times Seven* (1967), *A Wedding* (1978), *Sharky's Machine* (1981) and *Sleepers* (1996). His son, Alessandro Gassman, is also an actor, having appeared in *A Month By the Lake* (1994).

JOHN GIELGUD

Born: 14 April 1904, in London.
Died: 21 May 2000 in his sleep at his home in Buckinghamshire, England.
● On stage from 1921, following training at RADA where he was tutored by Claude Rains, John Gielgud (real name Arthur John Gielgud) came to be regarded as his generation's most eminent exponent of Shakespeare. His performance in *Hamlet* at the Old Vic in 1930 was the first of many triumphs in the role, which also included a celebrated Broadway run in 1936. He made his film debut in *Who is the Man?* in 1924, and though he appeared in a couple of key 1930s movies – *The Good Companions* (1933) and Hitchcock's *Secret Agent* (1937) – film work was sporadic until the 1950s, when he became increasingly involved in higher brow productions, among them *Julius Caesar* (1953, as Cassius), *Richard III* (1955, as Clarence) and *Saint Joan* (1957, as Warwick). In 1953 he was knighted for services to theatre. In 1964 he earned a best

supporting actor Oscar nomination for his performance as Louis VII in *Becket*, after which he provided excellent character support in *The Loved One* (1965), *The Charge of the Light Brigade* (1968, as Lord Raglan), *Oh! What a Lovely War* (1969), *11 Harrowhouse* (1974), *Murder on the Orient Express* (1974), *Providence* (1977), *The Elephant Man* (1980) and *Arthur* (1981), winning an Oscar for his foul-mouthed butler, Hobson. There followed several misjudgements, among them *Scandalous* (1984, in which he played punk pensioner Uncle Willie), *Invitation to the Wedding* (1984, in which he made an unconvincing American evangelist) and the dismal *Arthur 2: On the Rocks* (1988). When the opportunity arose, however, Gielgud continued to provide delicious support in the likes of *Plenty* (1985), *Shine* (1996) and *Hamlet* (1996, as Priam), whilst he had another personal triumph when he took the leading role in Peter Greenaway's *Prospero's Books* (1991). On television, meanwhile, Gielgud was equally memorable in *Brideshead Revisited* (1981) and *War and Remembrance* (1988). His various books include *Early Stages* (1939) and *An Actor and His Times* (1979).

CHARLES GRAY

Born: 29 August 1928, in Bournemouth, England. **Died**: 7 March 2000 in London.
● One of Britain's great character stars, Charles Gray (real name Donald Marshall Gray) will be best remembered for his silky voice, which could be sinister and sarcastic in equal measure. To most film fans he was known for playing Blofeld in the James Bond epic *Diamonds Are Forever* (1971), though this wasn't his first brush with the series; he'd also appeared as Dikko Henderson, Bond's contact in Japan, in *You Only Live Twice* (1967). His best role, how-

ever, was as the Satanist Mocata in Hammer's *The Devil Rides Out* (1968). Gray also taught us how to do the Time Warp in *The Rocky Horror Picture Show* (1975) and was an excellent Mycroft Holmes in *The Seven Per Cent Solution* (1976), a role he returned to for television's *The Adventures of Sherlock Holmes* (1984). His other film work includes *Cromwell* (1970), *The Legacy* (1978) and *The Tichborne Claimant* (1999), plus a cameo in TV's *An Englishman Abroad* (1983). He also dubbed Jack Hawkins from 1966 onwards, after the star lost his voice following surgery for throat cancer.

BRION JAMES

Born: 20 February 1945.
Died: 7 August 1999.
● A former stand-up comedian, Brion James is chiefly known for the number of rat-faced psychos he played, an image he hilariously parodied in Sam Raimi's underrated *Crimewave* (1985). Busy in both film and television, his appearances include *Blade Runner* (1982), *Silverado* (1985) and *Radioland Murders* (1994), plus several for director Walter Hill: *Southern Comfort* (1981), *48 HRS* (1982), *Red Heat* (1988), *Another 48 HRS* (1990).

PETER JONES

Born: 12 June 1920 in Wem Shropshire.
Died: 10 April 2000.
● A television sitcom favourite, Peter Jones was best known for his harassed factory boss Mr Fenner in the various incarnations of *The Rag Trade*. He also co-wrote and appeared in both *Mr Big* and *I Thought You'd Gone*, whilst on radio he co-wrote and performed in *In All Directions* with Peter Ustinov in the 1950s. More recently he was a frequent panellist on *Just a Minute*. His film work was mostly confined to cameo appearances in a variety of comedies, among them *Private's Progress* (1955), *Blue Murder at St Trinian's* (1957), *Smashing Time* (1967, memorable as a tacky quiz show host), *Carry On Doctor* (1967), *Hot Millions* (1968), *Return of the Pink Panther* (1974), *Confessions of a Pop Performer* (1975) and *Whoops Apocalypse!* (1986).

MADELINE KAHN

Born: 29 September 1942 in Boston, Massachusetts. **Died**: 3 December 1999 of ovarian cancer in New York.
● Quirky character comedienne Madeline Kahn brought a touch of barely contained vivacity to a number of key comedies in the

1970s, notably *What's Up, Doc?* (1972) and *Paper Moon* (1973), both for director Peter Bogdanovich, the latter earning her a best supporting actress Oscar nomination. She then became a regular fixture in the Mel Brooks repertory company with *Blazing Saddles* (1974), which earned her another supporting nomination for her Dietrich-like Lily von Shtupp, *Young Frankenstein* (1974) and *High Anxiety* (1977). Her other films included *At Long Last Love* (1974, for Bogdanovich), *The Cheap Detective* (1978), *History of the World, Part 1* (1981, for Brooks) and *Betsy's Wedding* (1990). She also starred in two TV sit-coms, *Oh, Madeline!* (1983) and *Mr President* (1989). She actually trained to be an opera singer, and appeared in several Broadway musicals, making her debut in the chorus of *Kiss Me, Kate* in the 1965 revival.

LILA KEDROVA

Born: 9 October 1918, Leningrad.
Died: 16 February 2000.
● Though born in Russia, Lila Kedrova lived in Paris from the age of ten, and later used the city as a base from which to appear in a number of European films, making her debut in the German *Weg ohne Umkehr* in 1953. Her other European ventures include *Le Defroque* (1954, France), *Calle Mayor* (1956, Spain) and *La Femme et la Pantin* (1959, Italy). Following her best supporting actress Oscar for *Zorba the Greek* (1964), in which she played ageing prostitute Mme Hortense, Kedrova found herself in demand as a support in a number of American films, notably Hitchcock's *Torn Curtain* (1966), Arthur Hiller's *Penelope* (1966) and John Huston's *The Kremlin Letter* (1970), after which her work was again based mostly in Europe, where she made Roman Polanski's *The Tenant* (1976) and *Claire de Femme* (1979). Her most recent films include *Some Girls* (1993) and *Getting Away With Murder* (1996).

HEDY LAMARR

Born: 9 November 1913, in Vienna, Austria. **Died**: 19 January 2000 of 'natural causes' in Orlando, Florida.
● One of the screen's great beauties, though not one of its great actresses, Hedy Lamarr (real name Hedwig Eva Maria Kiesler) made her film debut in the German short *Geld auf der Strasse* in 1930, prior to which she'd worked as a script girl and occasional walk-on. She made several more films in Germany, though it was her

appearance in the Czech-made *Ecstasy* (1933), in which she appeared nude, that brought her to world attention, leading to a career in Hollywood, beginning in 1938 with *Algiers*. Her other films include *Boom Town* (1940), *Comrade X* (1940), *Ziegfeld Girl* (1941) and *Experiment Perilous* (1944), though perhaps her most famous role was as Delilah in Cecil B. de Mille's lavish *Samson and Delilah* (1949). Her career declined in the 50s, during which she made such variable films as *Copper Canyon* (1950) and *The Story of Mankind* (1957, as Joan of Arc). Following *The Fame Animal* in 1958, she didn't appear on the big screen again until 1990, when she popped up in the instantly forgettable *Instant Karma*. Married six times, her husbands included munitions magnate Fritz Mandl (who'd tried to buy up all the copies of *Ecstasy*), screenwriter Gene Markey and actor John Loder. She wrote about her life in *Ecstasy and Me* (1966).

DESMOND LLEWELYN

Born: 12 September 1914. **Died**: 19 December 1999 in a car crash.
● The much-loved Desmond Llewelyn will forever be remembered for his turn as Major Boothroyd – better known as Q – in the official series of James Bond films, of which he appeared in seventeen, missing only *Dr No* (in which Boothroyd was played by Peter Burton) and *Live and Let Die*. His best Bond appearances were in *Goldfinger* (1964), in which he first uttered what came to be his catchphrase, 'Now pay attention, 007,' and *Licence to Kill* (1989), in which he joined Bond in the field. Ironically, in his last appearance as Q in *The World is Not Enough* (1999), his parting line is a piece of advice for Bond: 'Never let them see you bleed... and always have an escape plan,' after which he

descends into the floor. His other films included *Ask a Policeman* (1938), *The Lavender Hill Mob* (1951), *A Night to Remember* (1958), *The Curse of the Werewolf* (1961) and *Chitty Chitty Bang Bang* (1968).

VICTOR MATURE

Born: 29 January 1915, in Louisville, Kentucky. **Died**: 4 August 1999 in Rancho Santa Fe, California following a three year struggle with cancer.

● The embodiment of the term 'beefcake,' action star Victor Mature began his acting career on stage at the Pasadena Playhouse, following which he was signed to a contract with producer Hal Roach, making his screen debut in the comedy *The Housekeeper's Daughter* (1939). However, it was his second film for Roach, *One Million BC* (1940), that better displayed his physical attributes. A further Roach comedy, *Captain Caution* (1940), followed, after which Mature appeared in a wide variety of films, among them musicals and westerns. It was, however, his performance as Samson in Cecil B. de Mille's spectacular *Samson and Delilah* (1949) that firmly pinned him as a muscle-bound hero and earned him the publicity tag a 'beautiful hunk of man.' He lived up to this image in the likes of *Androcles and the Lion* (1953), *The Robe* (1953), *The Egyptian* (1954) and *The Sharkfighters* (1956). Nevertheless, he was happy to send up his beefcake image in the comedy *After the Fox* (1966), in which he played the vain but insecure Hollywood star Tony Powell. His later films included *Head* (1968), *Every Little Crook and Nanny* (1972) and *Firepower* (1979). Although a much better actor than the critics would have him be, he himself claimed that, 'Hell, I'm no actor, and I've got 28 pictures to prove it!'

NANCY MARCHAND

Born: 19 June 1928 in Buffalo, New York. **Died**: 18 June 2000 of lung cancer.

● Cherished by television audiences as the publisher Mrs Pynchon in *Lou Grant* (for which she won four consecutive Emmys), and more recently as the scheming matriarch in *The Sopranos*, actress Nancy Marchand spent much of her career on the small rather than the large screen. Indeed, following stage work from the age of eighteen, she broke into television in 1950 in a live broadcast of *Little Women*. She also appeared in the original 1953 broadcast of Paddy Chayefsky's *Marty* with Rod Steiger, but was overlooked for the film version. She finally made her film debut in 1957 in *The Bachelor Party* which was based on another Chayefsky tele-play. Other screen appearances include *Me, Natalie* (1969), *Tell Me That You Love Me, Junie Moon* (1970), *The Hospital* (1970), *The Bostonians* (1984), *The Naked Gun* (1988) and *Sabrina* (1995). Always dependable, Marchand brought a touch of wit and class to everything she appeared in, and though the characters she played were often haughty, she always gave them a touch of fallibility.

ABRAHAM POLONSKY

Born: 5 December 1910 in New York City. **Died**: 26 October 1999 of alleged heart failure in Beverly Hills, California.

● Writer-director Abraham Polonsky came to film following experience as a lawyer, teacher, novelist and radio scriptwriter, earning his first credit for Mitchell Leisen's *The Golden Earrings* in 1947, though much of his dialogue was re-worked. He earned an Oscar nomination for his second script, the boxing drama *Body and Soul* (1947), which led to his directing that film's star, John Garfield, in *Force of Evil* (1948), which he also co-wrote. However, just as Polonsky's career was gaining momentum, a run-in with the House Un-American Activities Committee in April 1951 saw him blacklisted, which forced him to write TV scripts and doctor film scripts under a variety of assumed names. He 'officially' returned to the screen in 1968 with his script for Don Siegel's *Madigan*, which he co-wrote with Henri Simoun. He directed just two more films: *Tell Them Willie Boy is Here* (1970, which he also wrote) and *Romance of the Horse Thief* (1971).

STEVE REEVES

Born: 21 January 1926 in Glasgow, Montana. **Died**: 1 May 2000 of lymphoma in hospital in San Diego, California.

● The Arnold Schwarzenegger of his day, Steve Reeves came to fame as Hercules and a variety of other muscle-bound heroes whom he played in a number of Italian 'sword and sandal' epics from the late 1950s to the late 1960s. A former Mr Universe, Mr World and Mr America, he made his screen debut in the MGM musical *Athena* in 1954, which he followed with *The Hidden Face* and *Jailbait* (both 1954) after which he moved to Italy in 1957 when contracted to play Hercules in *Fatiche di Ercole* (aka *Hercules/The Labours of Hercules*). He played the role again in *Hercules Unchained* (1958, aka *Hercules and the Queen of Sheba*), after which he flexed his pecs in the likes of *Goliath and the Barbarians* (1959), *The Thief of Baghdad* (1960), *Son of Spartacus* (1962) and *Sandokan the Great* (1963). Following *Vivo per la Tua Morte* (1968, aka *A Long Ride from Hell*), a spaghetti western which he also scripted, Reeves returned permanently to America to run a fruit plantation.

RUTH ROMAN

Born: 22 December 1922 in Boston. **Died**: 9 September 1999.

● Following stage experience and a brief appearance in *Stage Door Canteen* (1943), Ruth Roman all but crawled to stardom during the 40s, appearing in some twenty productions, including *Since You Went Away* (1944), the 13-part serial *Jungle Queen* (1945), *Gilda* (1946) and *Good Sam* (1948) before getting showier parts in *The Window* (1949), *Champion* (1949) and Hitchcock's *Strangers on a Train* (1951). Her time at the top in the 50s was comparatively brief, and few of her films – among them *Tanganyika* (1954), *Joe Macbeth* (1955) and *Bitter Victory* (1958) – could be considered classics. Her later films include *The Old Man Who Cried Wolf* (1970, TV), *The Baby* (1972), *Punch and Jody* (1974, TV), *Day of the Animals* (1979) and *When in Rome* (1991). She also appeared in the TV series *The Long Hot Summer* (1965) and *Knots Landing* (1986).

GEORGE C. SCOTT

Born: 18 October 1926, in Wise, Virginia. **Died**: 22 September 1999.
● One of the most dynamic screen actors of his generation, George Campbell Scott turned to acting following a stint in the Marines, gaining experience first in stock and then on Broadway. He made his film debut in the western *The Hanging Tree* in 1959, which he followed with the career-establishing role of prosecutor Claude Dancer in *Anatomy of a Murder* (also 1959), earning himself a best supporting actor Oscar nomination in the process. *The Hustler* came in 1962 (which earned him another Oscar nomination), which was itself followed by *The List of Adrian Messenger* (1963) and *Dr Strangelove* (1963, as General 'Buck' Turgidson), whilst on television Scott earned plaudits for the drama series *East Side, West Side* (1963). Scott's film career tripped slightly in the mid-60s, though in 1970 he recovered with *Patton*, which won him an Oscar. However, having previously described the Oscar race as a meaningless meat parade, he became the first actor to turn the award down, though this didn't prevent the Academy from nominating him again for his performance in *The Hospital* (1972). Scott's other films include

Day of the Dolphin (1973), *The Hindenberg* (1975), *Hardcore* (1979) and *The Exorcist III* (1990), whilst his TV movies included *Jane Eyre* (1972, as Rochester), *Oliver Twist* (1982, as Fagin), *A Christmas Carol* (1984, as Scrooge), *Mussolini: The Untold Story* (1985) and *The Last Days of Patton* (1985). He also directed two movies: *Rage* (1973) and *The Savage is Loose* (1974). His four wives, all actresses, were Carolyn Hughes, Patricia Reed, Colleen Dewhurst (whom he married twice) and Trish Van Devere (with whom he appeared in the underrated ghost story *The Changeling* in 1979). He is also the father of the actor Campbell Scott.

RICHARD B. SHULL

Born: 24 February 1929 in Evanston, Illinois. **Died**: 13 October 1999 of a heart attack in New York.
● Former stage manager and director Richard B. Shull came to acting comparatively late in life, becoming a professional performer in 1971 at the age of 42, making his film debut the same year in Sidney Lumet's *The Anderson Tapes*. Most at home playing lugubrious characters and, later, cheerful old duffers, he can be seen in *Klute* (1972), *The Big Bus* (1976), *Splash* (1984), *Trapped in Paradise* (1994) and *Private Parts* (1997). His best role was in *House Sitter* (1992) in which he and Laurel Cronin played drunken tramps hired to impersonate Goldie Hawn's (sober) parents.

SYLVIA SIDNEY

Born: 8 August 1910 in The Bronx, New York. **Died**: 1 July 1999.
● On stage from the age of sixteen, Sylvia Sidney (real name Sophia Kosow) was a Broadway star before she turned twenty, by which time she'd appeared in a couple of films: *Broadway Nights* (1927) and *Thru Different Eyes* (1929). By the time she made her third film, *City Streets* (1931), not only was she under contract to Paramount and working with one of their top directors, Rouben Mamoulian, she was also receiving top billing with her co-star Gary Cooper. Throughout the 1930s, Sidney worked with many more top directors, notably Josef von Sternberg on *An American Tragedy* (1931), King Vidor on *Street Scene* (1931), Dorothy Arzner on *Merrily We Go to Hell* (1932), Alfred Hitchcock on *Sabotage* (1936), Fritz Lang on both *Fury* (1936) and *You Only Live Once* (1937) and William Wyler on *Dead End* (1937).

Meanwhile, with her leading role in the non-musical version of *Madame Butterfly* (1932) she became a big star in Japan, where her likeness was used to advertise a brand of condoms which came to be known as Sylvia Sidneys. By the 40s, however, she had become dissatisfied with her screen career (she made only five films during that decade), and so again began to concentrate on the theatre. Indeed, the 50s saw her appear in just three films, after which she forsook the cinema for almost twenty years, returning to the screen in 1973 with *Summer Wishes, Winter Dreams*, which earned her a best supporting actress Oscar nomination. In her occasional films since, she supplied able support in the likes of *Damien: Omen II* (1978), *Hammett* (1982), *Beetlejuice* (1988), *Used People* (1992) and *Mars Attacks!* (1996).

NORA SWINBURNE

Born: 24 July 1902, in Bath England. 1902. **Died**: 1 May 2000.
● On stage from the age of ten as a dancer and performer, Nora Swinburne (real name Elinore Johnson) became a popular fixture in British silents in the 20s, beginning with *Branded* in 1920, which she followed with the likes of *Autumn Pride* (1921), *Hornet's Nest* (1923) and *A Girl of London* (1925), whilst in 1923 she went to America to appear in *Red Trail*. Her early talkies included *Alf's Button* (1930) and *Potiphar's Wife* (1931), whilst in the 40s she played character parts in such popular fare as *The Man in Grey* (1943), *Jassy* (1947) and *Quartet* (1948). In 1951 she went to India to make *The River* for director Jean Renoir, after which she returned to America to appear as Pomponia in the humongus *Quo Vadis?* (1951). Her remaining films include *Helen of Troy* (1956, as Hecuba), *Interlude* (1968), *Anne of the Thousand Days* (1969) and, finally, *Up the Chastity Belt* (1971). Her third husband was actor Esmond Knight, with whom she worked on *The River*, *Helen of Troy* and *Anne of the Thousand Days*.

DAVID TOMLINSON

Born: 17 May 1917 in Henley-on-Thames, England. **Died**: 24 June 2000.
● Character comedian David Tomlinson, who specialised in amiable upper class types, began his acting career in rep as an assistant stage manager and player of small parts in 1936. He made his film debut in the short *Name, Rank and Number* in

1940, which he followed with *Garrison Follies* the same year. However, it was whilst in a stage production of *A Quiet Wedding* that he was spotted by director Anthony Asquith, who cast him in the subsequent film version (1941). However, following a further two films – *My Wife's Family* and *Pimpernel Smith* (both 1941) – Tomlinson's burgeoning film career was interrupted by war service in the RAF. Tomlinson returned to the screen in 1945 with *The Way to the Stars* (again for Anthony Asquith), after which he gradually perfected his silly ass character in such films as *School for Secrets* (1946), *Sleeping Car to Trieste* (1948), *Miranda* (1948), *The Chiltern Hundreds* (1949) and *All for Mary* (1955). In 1964 he made the first of three highly successful films for Walt Disney, appearing as the stuffy Mr Banks in *Mary Poppins*, which he followed with *The Love Bug* (1968, as the villainous Peter Thorndyke) and *Bedknobs and Broomsticks* (1971). Tomlinson's other films include *Up the Creek* (1958), *The Liquidator* (1965) and, er, *Wombling Free* (1977). His last film was the disastrous Peter Sellers comedy *The Fiendish Plot of Dr Fu Manchu* (1980).

CLAIRE TREVOR

Born: 8 March 1909 in New York City.
Died: 8 April 2000 in Newport Beach, California.
● Actress Claire Trevor (real name Claire Wemlinger) will always be remembered for her Oscar-winning performance as Edward G. Robinson's alcoholic moll Gaye Dawn in *Key Largo* (1948). This was by no means her only moll, though. Indeed, her career was peppered with floozies and good-time girl types, notably as Humphrey Bogart's moll Francie in *Dead End* (1937), which earned her an Oscar nomination, Dallas the prostitute in *Stagecoach* (1939), the literally duplicitous Velma in *Farewell, My Lovely* (1945) and the jaded May Hoist in *The High and the Mighty* (1954), which earned her yet another Oscar nomination. On stage from the late 20s, Trevor was a Broadway star by 1932, during which period she made several Vitaphone shorts in New York. She made her feature debut in 1933 with *Life in the Raw*. Her other films include *Dante's Inferno* (1935), *Career Woman* (1936), *The Babe Ruth Story* (1948) and *Two Weeks in Another Town* (1962). On television she won an Emmy in 1956 for her performance in *Dodsworth*. Her last theatrical feature was *Kiss Me Goodbye*

(1982), which was the US remake of *Dona Flor and Her Two Husbands*.

ROGER VADIM

Born: 26 January 1928, in Paris.
Died: 11 February 2000 of cancer in Paris.
● Though writer-director Roger Vadim (real name Roger Vadim Plemiannikov) made twenty-five films in almost as many years, he is primarily remembered for his debut, *And God Created Woman* (1956), which starred his then wife Brigitte Bardot. In fact the film hung over the rest of his career to such a degree that he remade it in 1987 with Rebecca De Mornay, though lightning failed to strike twice. A variable talent at best, Vadim's other key films include *Les Liaisons Dangereuses* (1959), *Blood and Roses* (1960), *Pretty Maids All in a Row* (1971) and *Night Games* (1980). His second wife was actress Annette Stroyberg, and his third Jane Fonda, whom he directed in *La Ronde* (1964), *Barbarella* (1968) and *Histoires Extraordinaires* (1968, the *Metzengerstein* episode only). He also had a lengthy relationship with Catherine Deneuve. His most recent film was *Amour Fou* (1994, aka *Mad Love*). Vadim also appeared as an actor in, among others, *The Testament of Orpheus* (1959) and *Into the Night* (1985). In 1986 he wrote his autobiography, *Bardot, Deneuve and Fonda: My Life with the Three Most Beautiful Women in the World*.

JIM VARNEY

Born: 15 June, Lexington, Kentucky.
Died: 10 February 2000 of lung cancer in White House, Tennessee.
● Highly resistible comedy star who nevertheless proved popular with younger audiences in the dim-witted *Ernest* films, which number *Ernest Goes to Camp* (1987), *Ernest Saves Christmas* (1988), *Ernest Goes to Jail*

(1990), *Ernest Scared Stupid* (1991), *Ernest Rides Again* (1993) and *Ernest Goes to School* (1994). Varney brought a similarly leaden touch to *Wilder Napalm* (1993) and the dismal big screen version of *The Beverly Hillbillies* (1993) in which he played Jed Clampett. He also provided the voice for Slinky Dog in *Toy Story* (1995).

JACK WATLING

Born: 15 May 1921 in London.
Died: 4 August 1999.
● Though he played many gruff sergeant-major types, Jack Watling got his first break as a stooge to his father, musical hall comedian Nosmo King (geddit?). Watson followed his father's career path for some fifteen years, working as a comic monologist, occasionally appearing in the odd film, making his debut in the short *Pathe Radio Music Hall* in 1945, which highlighted his stage act. He followed this with brief roles in *The Small Back Room* (1948, the first of three films for director Michael Powell), *Captain Horatio Hornblower RN* (1953) and *A Cry from the Streets* (1958). His other films include *This Sporting Life* (1963), *The Hill* (1965) and *Grand Prix* (1965). He was also frequently cast in the films of director Andrew V. McLaglen, among them *The Devil's Brigade* (1968), *The Wild Geese* (1977, his best sergeant-major role), *North Sea Hijack* (1979) and *The Sea Wolves* (1980). His last film was *Tangier* (1983). He was also familiar to television audiences via a number of series, including *The Plane Makers*, *The Power Game*, *The Pathfinder* and *Bergerac*. He is the father of actress Deborah Watling and the step-father of actress Dylis Watling.

Also sadly missed:

● Country singer and actor **Hoyt Axton**: 25 March 1938 – 26 October 1999. *The Black Stallion* (1979), *Gremlins* (1984), *Season of Change* (1994)

● New York-born director **John Berry**: 1917 – 29 November 1999. *From This Day Forward* (1946), *Casbah* (1948), *The Bad News Bears Go to Japan* (1978).

● American comedy actor **Billy Benedict**, formerly 'Whitey' of the Bowery Boys: 16 April 1917 – 25 November 1999. *Captain January* (1936), *Bowery Champs* (1944), *Funny Girls* (1968), plus literally hundreds of others.

● American screenwriter **Jim Cash**: 1941 – 24 March 2000. *Top Gun* (1986), *Legal Eagles* (1986), *The Flintstones in Viva Rock Vegas* (2000).

● American actress **Margueritte Churchill**: 25 December 1909 – 9 January 2000. *The Valiant* (1929), *Dracula's Daughter* (1936), *Bunco Squad* (1956).

● French star **Pierre Clementi**: 28 September 1942 – 27 December 1999. *The Leopard* (1963), *Belle de Jour* (1967), *Benjamin* (1968), *The Conformist* (1971), *Steppenwolf* (1974), *Hideous Kinky* (1999).

● Canadian character actor **John Colicos**: 10 December 1928 – 6 March 2000. *Anne of the Thousand Days* (1969), *The Changeling* (1979), *The Postman Always Rings Twice* (1981). Also television's *Battlestar Galactica* (1978, as Count Baltar).

● English actor, writer and gay icon **Quentin Crisp** (real name Denis Pratt): 1909 – 21 November 1999. *The Naked Civil Servant* (1975, TV), *The Bride* (1985), *Orlando* (1993, as Elizabeth I), *Desolation Angels* (1995).

● American composer **Frank de Vol**: 1925 – 27 October 1999. *The Big Knife* (1955), *Whatever Happened to Baby Jane?* (1962), *Guess Who's Coming to Dinner* (1967).

● Academy Award-winning British art director **Carmen Dillon**: 25 October 1908 – 12 April 2000. *Henry V* (1944), *Hamlet* (1948, AA), *Carry On Cruising* (1962), *Julia* (1977).

● Singer and actor **Ian Dury**: 12 May 1942 – 27 March 2000. *Radio On* (1979), *Pirates* (1986), *The Cook, The Thief, His Wife and Her Lover* (1989), *Different For Girls* (1996).

● British actor and MP **Andrew Faulds**: 1 March 1923 – 31 May 2000. *The Card* (1952), *Jason and the Argonauts* (1963), *The Devils* (1970), *Mahler* (1974).

● British actress **Meriel Forbes** (real name Meriel Forbes-Robertson), long married to Sir Ralph Richardson: 13 September 1913 – 7 April 2000. *Borrow a Million* (1935), *Home at Seven* (1952), *Oh! What a Lovely War* (1969).

● American actress **Nancy Guild**: 11 October 1925 – 24 August 1999. *Give My Regards to Broadway* (1949), *Abbott and Costello Meet the Invisible Man* (1951), *Such Good Friends* (1971).

● English comedy actor and washboard player extraordinaire **Deryck Guyler**: 29 April 1914 – 7 October 1999. *The Fast Lady* (1962), *A Hard Day's Night* (1964), *Please, Sir!* (1971). Also much television, including *Sykes* (1960 – 1979, as Corky) and *Please, Sir!* (1968 – 1972).

● Oslo-born actress **Greta Gynt** (real name Margarethe Woxholt): 15 November 1916 – 2 April 2000. *Sangen till Henne* (1936, Sweden), *It Happened in Paris* (1935), *Soldiers Three* (1951). Sister of cinematographer Egil Woxholt.

● Czech actor **Francis Lederer** (real name Frantisek Lederer): 6 November 1906 – 25 May 2000. *Pandora's Box* (1929), *Atlantic* (1929), *Confessions of a Nazi Spy* (1939), *The Return of Dracula* (1958).

● Irish character actor **Donal McCann**: 6 April 1943 – 18 July 1999. *The Fighting Prince of Donegal* (1966), *Cal* (1984), *The Dead* (1987), *December Bride* (1990), *Stealing Beauty* (1995), *Illuminata* (1998).

● English comedy actor **Bill Owen** (real name Bill Rowbotham): 14 March 1914 – 12 July 1999. *The Way to the Stars* (1945), *Carry On Sergeant* (1958), *Georgy Girl* (1966). Also television's long-running sit-com *Last of the Summer Wine* (1974 – 2000, as Compo).

● American novelist and Academy Award-winning screenwriter **Mario Puzo**: 15 October 1920 – 2 July 1999. *The Godfather* (1972, AA), *The Godfather Part II* (1974), *Earthquake* (1974), *Superman* (1978), *Christopher Columbus: The Discovery* (1992).

● American stage and screen actor **Lee Richardson**: 11 December 1926 – 2 October 1999. *Prizzi's Honor* (1985), *The Fly II* (1989), *The Cemetery Club* (1992), *A Stranger Among Us* (1992, aka *Close to Eden*).

● British character actor **Michael Ripper**, known for his appearances in Hammer horror films and the late seventies sit-com

Butterflies: 22 May 1913 – 28 June 2000. *The Mummy* (1959), *The Reptile* (1966), *Dracula Has Risen From the Grave* (1968), *Scars of Dracula* (1970).

● Former MGM chairman **Frank Rothman**: 1927 – 25 April 2000.

● British singer and dancer **Frankie Vaughan** (real name Frank Abelsohn): 3 February 1928 – 17 September 1999. *Ramsbottom Rides Again* (1956), *Let's Make Love* (1960), *It's All Over Town* (1964).

● Texan actress **Helen Vinson** (real name Helen Rulfs): 17 September 1907 – 7 October 1999. *I Am a Fugitive from a Chain Gang* (1932), *Broadway Bill* (1934), *The Thin Man Goes Home* (1945).

● Editor **Ernest Walter** 28 November 1919 – 14 December 1999. *The Inn of the Sixth Happiness* (1958), *The Private Life of Sherlock Holmes* (1970), *Nicholas and Alexandra* (1971).

● American screenwriter **Norman Wexler**: 6 August 1926 – 23 August 1999. *Joe* (1970, Oscar nomination), *Serpico* (1973, Oscar nomination), *Saturday Night Fever* (1977), *Staying Alive* (1983).

● British Academy Award-winning special effects technician **Albert Whitlock**: 1915 – 26 October 1999. *The Birds* (1963), *Earthquake* (1974), *The Hindenberg* (1975), *Dracula* (1979), *Dune* (1984).

● Swiss film director (and actor) **Bernhard Wicki**: 28 October 1919 – 5 January 2000. *The Bridge* (1959), *The Longest Day* (1962), *The Visit* (1964), *Morituri* (1965), *The Spider's Web* (1989), *Success* (1990).

Index

Names of films and videos appear in the index in *italics*. Page references for illustrations appear in **BOLD**. The last separate word of an individual's name is used as the index entry. Thus Max Von Sydow appears under 'S' as Sydow, Max Von. Where the position of an entry on a page with three columns may not be obvious the references will include an a, b or c (as: 164a) to indicate the reference will be found in the first, second or third column.

À la Place de Coeur 11-12
Aaliyah 95
Abbate, Allison 73
Abdou, Hacen 18
Abood, Cheryl 134
About John Ford (book) 170
Abrahams, F Murray 94
Abre los ojos see *Open Your Eyes*
actresses who have played actresses 12
Adami, Messaouda 18
Adams, Bradley 99
Adams, Joey Lauren 25
Aday, Meat Loaf 54
Addy, Mark 80
Adler, Gilbert 68
Adventures of Elmo in Grouchland, The 10-11
Affleck, Ben 39, 43, 165a
After Life 11
Against the Law 149
Agnes Browne **10**, 11
Agnew, Brian 118
Aird, Holly 130
Aitken, Isabella 26
Alarmist, The 12
Albarn, Damon 110
Alfs 2000 177
Algar, James 53
Alice et Martin 12
Alien Cargo 149
All About My Mother 12-13, **13**
All the Little Animals 13
Allan, Julie 135
Allen, Joan 143
Allen, Kevin 26
Allen, Lewis 179
Allen, Tim 58, 135
Allen, Woody 127
Alley, Kirstie 45
Almodóvar, Agustín 13
Almodovar, Pedro 13
Altman, Robert 36
Altro, Melissa 106
Amalric, Mathieu 81
Amantes del Circulo Polar, Los see *Lovers of the Arctic Circle*
Amenábar, Alejandro 103
American Academy of Motion Picture Arts and Sciences Awards 1999 174-175
American Beauty, 13-14, 164a, 166
American Pie 8, 14
American Psycho 14, **15**
Amiel, Jon 50, 119
Amin, Rola Al 142
Analyze This 14-15
Anciano, Dominic 54, 85
Anderson, Gillian 107
Anderson, Miles 53
Anderson, Paul Thomas 88
Anderson, Wes 115
Andersson, Rikke Louise 27
Andrews, Giuseppe 40
Andrews, Julie 111
Angel's Dance 149
Angela's Ashes 15-16, 166
Aniston, Jennifer 73
Anna and the King 16, **16**
Another Day in Paradise 16-17
Any Given Sunday 17
Anywhere But Here 17-18, 166
Aouffen, Myriam 18
Apo Tin Akri Tis Polis see *From the Edge of the City*

Appleton, Natalie 68
Appleton, Nicole 68
Apted, Michael 148
Arata 11
Arche du desert, L' 18
Arditi, Pierre 33
Arendt, Stefan 145
Arkin, Alan 74
Armstrong 154
Arndt, Stefan 115
Arnold, Bonnie 129
Arnold, Keri 39
Arnold, Susan 65
Arquette, Courtney Cox 117
Arquette, David 12, 94, 97, 110, 117
Arquette, Patricia 30, 63, 66, 123
Arquette, Richmond 117
Arquette, Rosanna 143
Art of Star Wars, The (book) 170
Ascaride, Ariane 11
Ashkenazy, Vladimir 34
Asholt, Jesper 92
Asimov, Isaac 24
Askew, Desmond 62
Assayas, Olivier 81
Astaire, Fred 98
Asterix & Obelix Contre Caesar see *Asterix & Obelix Take On Caesar*
Asterix & Obelix Take On Caesar 18
Astronaut's Wife, The 18-19, 164a
Ataman, Kutlug 84
Atkinson, Rowan 91
Audrey Hepburn Story, The 149
Aumont, Michel 88
Austin Powers: The Spy Who Shagged Me 19, **19**, 166
Australian Film Institute Awards 1999 175
Auteuil, Daniel 61
Autin Powers: The Spy Who Shagged Me 8, **8**
Axton, Hoyt 185
Aykroyd, Dan 164b
Ayres, Rosalind 22
Azaria, Hank 37, 96

B Monkey 149
Ba Mua see *Three Seasons*
Babatunde, Obba 82
Baby's Hollywood Screen Kiss 26
Bachelor, The 20
Bacon, Kevin 124
Bacri, Jean-Pierre 106
Baeyens, Dominique 33
BAFTAs 1999 175
Bagley, Lorri 137
Baines, Julie 81
Baker, Dylan 164c
Baker, Martin G 94
Baker, Rick 82
Baker, Simon 112
Balaban, Bob 74
Balabanov, Alexei 32, 101
Baldwin, Alec 165a
Baldwin, Daniel 75
Baldwin, William 111
Bale, Christian 13, 14, 164c
Bamborough, Karin 56
Bancroft, Anne 139
Banderas, Antonio 131
Bankole, Isaach de 59
Bannen, Ian 23, 135, 179, **179**
Baranski, Christine 29
Barber of Siberia, The 20, 166

Bareikis, Arija 41
Barkin, Ellen 45
Barnathan, Michael 24
Barron, David 86
Barrymore, Drew 97
Bartel, Paul 179
Bartlett, Philip 107
Basch, Bill 80
BASEketball 149
Bass, Ron 122
Basset, Linda 46
Bassett, Angela 95, 126
Bates, Alan 34
Bats 21
Battlefield Earth 21
Battsek, John 102
Bauer, Steven 145
Baumgarten, Craig 138
Baxendale, Helen 104
Baye, Nathalie 56, 82
Beach, The 8, **20**, 21-22, 166
Beallor, June 80
Bean, Orson 22
Beart, Emmanuelle 134
Beaufoy, Simon 39
Beautiful People 22
Becker, Jean 34
Beckett, John 54
Beckinsale, Kate 31
Bedelia, Bonnie 18
Beek, James Van Der 139
Beesley, Max 90
Being John Malkovich **21**, 22
Beker, Joroen 108
Bell, Ross Grayson 54
Belly 22-23
Belmont, Lara 142
Benayoun, Georges 81
Bender, Lawrence 16
Benedict, Billy 185
Benedict, Claire 53
Benigni, Roberto 18
Bening, Annette 13
Bennett-Jones, Peter 77
Bensalah, Djamel 30
Bentley, Wes 14
Benzali, Daniel 13
Beresford, Bruce 43
Bergen, Patrick 51
Bergendahl, Waldemar 106
Berger, Albert 48, 147
Bergin, Patrick 143
Bergman, Andrew 73
Bergman, Mary Kay 122
Berleand, François 113
Berlin, Irving 86
Berling, Charles 49
Bernardi, Barry 41
Bernstein, Armyan 42, 49, 56, 69
Berry, John 185
Berthelsen, Anders W 92
Best 23
Best Man, The 23-24
Best, George 23
Bettany, Paul 59
Bette, Francoise 73
Bevan, Tim 66
Beyond Terror – The Films of Lucio Fulci (book) 169
Beyond the Mat 24
Bicentennial Man 24
Big Daddy 24-25, **25**
Big Momma's House 25-26
Big Tease, The 26

Biggins, Christopher 36
Biggs, Jason 14
Binoche, Juliette 12
Birch, Thora 13
Bird, Antonia 110
Bird, Brad 73
Birnbaum, Roger 71
Bisson, Chris 46
Black and Blue 154
Black, Jack 164b
Blackman, Jeremy 88
Blades, Ruben 37
Blair Witch Project, The 8, 26-27, **27**, 166, 172-173, **172-173**
Blair, Isla 90
Blair, Selma 44, 60
Blake, Howard 96
Blanchett, Cate 108, 128
Blaney, Mark 39
Blasband, Philippe 82
Blatt, Melanie 68
Blaustein, Barry W 24
Bleeder 27
Bleibtreu, Moritz 115
Blessed, Brian 129
Blethyn, Brenda 116
Bloom, Barry 24
Bloomsbury Movie Guide No 5: Jaws (book) 170
Blue Streak 27-28, **28**
Blyth, Stuart Sinclair 67
Boam, Jeffrey 179
Bodnia, Kim 27
Bodrov, Sergei 32
Body Shots 28
Boiler Room 28-29
Bolam, James 49
Bolz, Elvira 23
Bone Collector, The 29
Bonitzer, Pascal 113
Bono 92
Bont, Jan De 65
Borden, Bill 49
Borg, Laurie 52
Boriello, Bobby 141
Bosanquet, Simon 102
Botogov, Oleg 101
Bouchareb, Rachid 142
Bouchier, Chilli 179
Boudet, Jacques 11
Bouquet, Carole 70
Bourboulon, Frederic 73
Bovaira, Cuerda 103
Bovaira, Fernando 85, 103
Bowen, John 117
Bowfinger 29, **29**, 164a
Bowman, Anthony J 105
Boyd, Amanda 86
Boyd, Don 86
Boyd, William 136
Boyle, Barbara 72
Boyle, Danny 21
Boys Don't Cry 30
Boys On the Beach 30
Bradsell, Dick 56
Bradshaw, Carl 131
Bradshaw, Carolyn Pfeiffer 131
Branagh, Kenneth 86, 130, 144, 165a
Branco, Paulo 49, 97, 134
Brannon, Ash 135
Brass Ring, The 154
Brat see *Brother*
Bratt, Benjamin 97
Braugher, Andre 57

Brave New World 149
Breach of Trust 149
Breeders 154
Bregman, Martin 29
Brehat, Jean 142
Breillat, Catherine 113
Brennan, Brid 53
Brett, Justin 32
Bridges, Jeff 94, 119
Bringing Out the Dead 30-31
British Academy of Film and Television Arts Awards 1999 175
British Cinema of the 90s (book) 170
British Crime Cinema (book) 170
British Science Fiction Cinema (book) 170
Brizzi, Gaëtan 53
Brizzi, Paul 53
Broadbent, Jim 135, 165a
Broccoli, Barbara 148
Broderick, Matthew 48, 71
Brody, Adrien 126
Brokedown Palace 31
Broken Vessels 31-32
Brooks, Albert 94
Brooks, Jean 103
Brooks, Paul 103
Brosnan, Pierce 9, **9**, 131, 148
Brother 32
Brown, David 16, 142
Brown, Kimberly J 137
Browne, Chris 131
Brugge, Pieter Jan 71
Bryant, Damon 99
Bryant, Michael 92
Buck, Chris 129
Buena Vista Social Club 32, 167
Bui, Tony 133
Bui, Zoë 133
Bullock, Sandra 137
Burdis, Ray 54, 85
Burrows, Saffron 40, 59, 84
Burstyn, Ellen 107
Burton, Tim 121
Buscemi, Steve 137
Bussières, Pascale 55
Butler, Gerard 103
Butoy, Hendel 53
Bye, Ed 77
Byrne, Gabriel 49, 123

Ca Commence Aujourd'hui see *It All Starts Today*
Caan, James 91, 165a
Cachetonneurs, Les see *The Music Freelancers*
Cacoyannis, Michael 34
Cadell, Pauline 88
Cage, Nicolas 30
Cahana, Alice Lok 79-80
Caine, Michael 35, 165b
Caleb, Ruth 130
Callard, Rebecca 92
Camarata, Anita 54
Camarda, Michele 147
Cammell, Donald 145
Campbell, Christian 136
Campbell, David 43
Campbell, Neve 117, 133
Campbell, Paul 131
Campion, Jane 67
Canadian Film Awards 2000 175
Candyman: Day of the Dead 149
Canet, Guillaume 70

Cannes Film Festival Awards 2000 175-176
Cantona, Eric 34
Capshaw, Kate 12, 85
Capsis, Paul 66
Caracciolo, Joe Jr 119
Carax, Léos 107
Carcassonne, Philippe 81
Cardinale, Rebecca 32
Carlson, Erica 118
Carlyle, Robert 9, 15, 110, 148
Carpenter, John 75
Carr, Steve 98
Carraro, Bill 24, 57
Carré, Isabelle 34
Carrey, Jim 89
Carriers Are Waiting, The 33
Carroll, Willard 107
Carry On Uncensored (book) 169
Carter, Helen Bonham 54, 130
Cartlidge, Katrin 34
Casady, Guymon 90
Cash, Jim 186
Cassel, Seymour 115
Cassel, Vincent 64
Cassidy, Elaine 53
Caton, Juliette 121
Caunes, Antoine de 88
Cavendish, Jonathan 59, 104
Caviezel, Jim 57
Cervi, Valentina 113
Cesar Awards 2000 176
Chaffin, Cean 54
Chamas, Mohamed 142
Chameleon 149
Chan, Peter Ho-Sun 85
Chance or Coincidence 33, **33**
Channing, Stockard 73
Chapman, Jan 67
Chapman, Marguerite 180
Chappelle, Dave 27
Charles, Glen 108
Charles, Josh 94
Charles, Les 108
Chartomatsidis, Panagiotis 57
Chase, Chevy 121
Chaykin, Maury 50
Cheadle, Don 93
Chen, Joan 145
Cherry Orchard, The 34
Chestnut, Morris 24
Chevrier, Arno 11
Chicken Run 34, 164a, 167
Chicken Run – Hatching the Movie (book) 170
Children of the Marshland, The 34
Chill Factor 35
Chin, Stephen 17
Chiullot, Delphine 107
Chokling, Neten 38
Chong, Annabel 117
Chouikh, Mohammed 18
Chowdhry, Ranjit 125
Christian, Roger 21
Christie, Julie 92
Chuba, Daniel 126
Churchill, Marguerite 186
Cider House Rules, The **35**, 35-36
Ciel, les oiseaux...et ta mere!, Le see *Boys On the Beach*
Circus 36
Citti, Marc 95
Clair, Beau St 131
Clandestine Marriage, The 36
Clark, Larry 17
Clark-Hall, Steve 136
Clarkson, Patricia 119
Claude Rains (book) 170
Clavier, Christian 18
Clay, Nicholas 180
Clear Target 154
Cleese, John 104, 148
Clementi, Pierre 186
Clermont, Nicolas 51
Cloke, Kristen 55
Clooney, George 9, 132
Close, Glenn 36, 129
Closer You Get, The 167
Club Wildside 149-150
Clunes, Martin 116

Cluzet, Francois 81
Coates, Anne V 50
Codazzi, Juan C 129
Cohen, Bruce 14
Cohen, Jay 141
Cohn, Arthur 102
Cohn, Elie 145
Cole, Nigel 116
Coleman, Charlotte 22
Colesberry, Robert F 112
Colicos, John 186
Collard, Kenneth 105
Collette, Toni 119
Collins, Joan 36
Collins, Phil 129
Colomby, Harry 28
Coltrane, Robbie 148
Columbus, Chris 24
Come Play With Me – The Life and Films of Mary Millington (book) 169
Complicity 150
Confessions of Robin Askwith, The (book) 170
Conley, Brian 36
Connelly, Joe 30
Connery, Sean 9, 50, 107
Connick, Harry Jr 73
Considine, Paddy 113
Constance, Nathan 78
Conversations with Wilder (bok) 170
Convoyeurs Attendant, Les see *The Carriers Are Waiting*
Cooder, Joachim 32
Cooder, Ry 32
Cook, Douglas S 43
Cook, Paul 54
Cook, Ron 135
Cookie's Fortune 36, **37**
Cool Dry Place, A 154
Cool J, LL 17, 40
Cooler Climate, A 150
Cooper, Chris 101
Cope, Zachary Davd 124
Copes, Juan Carlos 129
Coppola, Francis Ford 140
Coppola, Sofia 140
Corduner, Allan 135
Corfixen, Liv 27
Coroado, Amândio 88
Corsini, Catherine 97
Cort, Robert 104, 114
Cosmo, James 90, 103
Costanzo, Julie 140
Costner, Kevin 56
Cotillard, Marion 129
Cotsianidis, Costas 57
Cotton Mary 37
Counihan, Judy 74
Count Dracula Goes to the Movies (book) 170
Courteney, Tom 142
Covert, Allen 25
Cowie, Robin 27
Cox, Brian 115
Cox, Veanne 50
Coxon, Richard 86
Cradle Will Rock 37-38, **38**
Craig, Daniel 136
Cranshaw, Patrick 32
Craven, Wes 95, 117
Creed-Miles, Charlie 80
Creste, Didier 30
Crichton, Charles 180, **180**
Crichton, Michael 131
Crisp, Quentin 186
Cristofer, Michael 28
Crogham, Emma-Kate 125
Cromwell, James 59, 122, 164c
Crouse, Lindsay 71
Crowdy, Mark 116
Crowe, Russell 7, 62, 70
Crudup, Billy 66, 147
Cruise, Tom 9, 51, 88, 147
Cruz, Penelope 103
Cruz, Penelope 12, 103
Crystal, Billy 15
Cuerda, José Luis 103
Cult Movies (book) 171

Cummings, Tim 134
Cunliffe, Freddie 142
Cunnigham, Liam 143
Cuong, Tran Manh 133
Cup, The 38
Currier, Lavinia 105
Curry, Hugh F 117
Curtis, Sarah 90
Cusack, John 22, 37, 108, 114, 164b

d'Arbeloff, Eric 137
D'Arcy, James 136
Dafoe, Willem 14
Dahlstr, Alexandra 118
Dairy Queens see *Drop Dead Gorgeous*
Damme, Jean-Claude Van 138
Damon, Matt 43, 128
Dancer in the Dark 167
Dancing About Architecture see *Playing By Heart*
Danes, Claire 31
Daniel, Chris 63
Daniel, Floriane 145
Daniel, Sarah 81
Daniels, Anthony 123
Daniels, Ben 52, 105
Daniels, Phil 34
Danna, Mychael 53
Danner, Blythe 85
Danstrup, Henrik 27
Danvers, Mark 131
Dardenne, Jean-Pierre 114
Dardenne, Luc 114
Daring, Mason 95
Darkest Light, The 39
Darkness Falls 39
Darroussin, Jean-Pierre 11
Das, Nandita 46
Dastor, Sam 125
Davey, Bruce 53, 92
Davidtz, Embeth 24, 90, 118
Davies, Jeremy 92, 110, 139
Davis, Mick 90
Davis, Phil 67
Davrak, Baki 84
Day Lincoln Was Shot, The 150
Dean, John 76
Deauville Festival of American Cinema 1999 176
Debbouze, Jamel 30
DeBello, James 40
Deception 39
Deep Blue Sea 8, 39-40, **40**
DeGeneres, Ellen 47, 63, 85,
Delamere, Matthew 47
Delpy, Julie 81
Demme, Ted 82
Dench, Judi 148
Deneuve, Catherine 106, 107, 134, **176**
Denial see *Something About Sex*
Depardieu, Gerard 18
Depardieu, Guillaume 107
Depp, Johnny 9, 19, 99, 121
Dequenne, Emilie 113
Dercourt, Denis 95
Dercourt, Tom 95
Detroit Rock City 40-41, **41**
Deuce Bigalow: Male Gigolo 41
DeVito, Danny 51, 89, 140
Diaz, Cameron 17, 22, 165a
DiCaprio, Leonardo 9, 9, 21
Diefenthal, Frédéric 129
Dien, Casper Van 16
Diesel, Vin 28, 73, 156, **156**
Diggs, Taye 24, 62, 68, 147
Dillane, Stephen 39, 104
Dillon, Carmen 186
Dillon, Melinda 88
Dimitriades, Alex 66
Diner de Cons, Le 41-42, **42**
Dinner Game, The see *Le Diner de Cons*
Dionisi, Stefano 84
Dionisotti, Paola 133
Director's Cut, The (book) 170
Disciples, The 150
Disney – The First 100 Years

(book) 170
Disney, Roy Edward 53
Disturbing Behaviour 42
Dixon, Jamie 126
Dixon, Leslie 97
Dizdar, Jasmin 22
DMX 22
Dmytryk, Edward 180
Dogma 43, 164a
Dombasle, Arielle 49
Donahue, Heather 27, 172-173, **173**
Donner, Lauren Shuler 17
Donovan, Martin 102
Double Jeopardy 43
Doueir, Rami 142
Doueiri, Ziad 142
Doug's 1st Movie 43-44
Douglas, Illeana 65, 124
Douglas, Michael 165a
Doumanian, Jean 127
Dowd, Ned 131
Down To You 44, **44**, 167
Downey, Robert jr 165a
Drazan, Anthony 69
Dream House 150
Dreaming of Joseph Lees 44
Drive Me Crazy 44-45
Driver, Minnie 111, 129
Drop Dead Gorgeous 45, **45**
Drukarova, Dinara 101
Ducey, Caroline 113
Duchovny, David 111
Dugan, Dennis 25
Dunaway, Faye 75, 131
Duncan, Michael Clarke 63, 143
Duning, George 180
Dunkerton, Julian 32
Dunkerton, Martin 32
Dunn, Kevin 124
Dunsky, Evan 12
Dunst, Kirsten 45, 140
Duoc, Nguyen Huu 133
Duong, Don 133
Dury, Ian 186
Dussollier, André 34
Dutton, Charles S 36, 109
Dutton, Tim 39
DuVall, Clea 19, 164a
Duvall, Clea 61
Dyer, Danny 136
Dying to Live 154
Dzandzanovic, Edin 22

Eadie, William 110
Earth 46
East is East 8, 46, 46-47
Eastwood, Clint 165b
Eaton, Andrew 147
Eckhart, Aaron 50, 156, 164b
Edelstein, Lisa 25
Edmond, Valerie 103
Edmondson, Adrian 64
EDtv 47, **47**
Edwards, Anthony 107
Edwards, Guy 146
Eginton, Madison 51
Egoyan, Atom 53
Ehle, Jennifer 126
8½ Women 47-48
Ejiofor, Chiwetel 63
Elbert, Ed 16
Election 48
Elfman, Danny 72
Elfman, Jenna 47, 164c
Elizondo, Hector 114
Elliott, Chris 121
Elliott, Stephen 51
Elmaleh, Gad 88
Elton, Ben 91
Eltringham, Bille 39
Emerson, Gavin 110
Emmerich, Noah 57
Emmerich, Toby 57
En plein coeur see *In All Innocence*
Encyclopaedia of Indian Cinema, The (book) 170
End of Days 48, 48-49
End of the Affair, The 49, 164a, 167

Enfants du Maris, Les see *The Children of the Marshland*
Enfield, Harry 9, 77
English Gothic: A Century of Horror Cinema (book) 169
Enman, Gao 100
Ennui, L' 49
Entrapment 49-50
Ephron, Delia 65
Ephron, Nora 65
Epps, Mike 98
Epps, Omar 147
Erbe, Kathryn 124
Erin Brockovich **50**, 50-51, **163**, 164b
Ernst, Donald W 53
Esposito, Jennifer 126
Essentila Monster Movie Guide, The (book) 169
Estefan, Gloria 95
Eternal, The 150
European Film Awards 1999 176
Evans, Robert 104
Everett, Rupert 71, 97, 145, 165b
Evil see *Mal*
Extreme Adventures of Super Dave, The 150
Eye of the Beholder 51
Eyes Wide Shut 51, **51**, 167

Faber, George 113
Face to Kill For, A 150
Facinelli, Peter 68, 165a
Fairbanks, Douglas jr 180-181, **181**
Falck, Thomas 27
Falkenhagen, Rudi 108
Falkenstein, Jun 134
Fall, Jim 137
Famuyiwa, Rick 147
Fanny & Elvis 52
Fantasia 2000 – A Vision of Hope (book) 170
Fantasia/2000 52-53, 167
Farina, Dennis 39
Farino, Julian 80
Farley, John 125
Farley, Kevin 125
Farnsworth, Richard 125
Fast Food 53
Faulds, Andrew 186
Faulkner, James 13
Fayed, Mohamed Al 87
Fechner, Christian 34, 61
Fehr, Oder 41
Feldshuh, Tovah 141
Felicia's Journey 53, **52**
Felixes 1999 176
Fellner, Eric 66
Felsberg, Ulrich 32
Felton, Tom 16
Fenn, Sherilyn 39
Ferch, Heino 145
Ferguson, Craig 26, 116
Ferguson, Lynn 34
Ferrer, Ibrahim 32
Feuerstein, Mark 94
Ffizdemir, Mesut 84
Fichman, Niv 80
Fichtner, William 62
Field, Ted 114
Field, Todd 32, 51
Fielder, John 119
Fielding, Fenella 64
Fields, Adam 31, 110
Fiennes, Joseph 109
Fiennes, Martha 102
Fiennes, Ralph 49, 92, 102, 126, 164a
50 Violins see *Music of the Heart*
Figg, Christopher 140
Figgis, Mike 84
Fight Club 53-54, **54**, **160**
Fille sur le pont, La see *The Girl on the Bridge*
Filth and the Fury, The 54, **55**
Fin Aout, Debut Septembre see *Late August, Early September*
Fina, Barbara De 31, 66
Final Cut 54

Final Destination 54-55
Fincher, David 54, 165b
Finlay, Frank 44
Finney, Albert 50, 119
Fiorentino, Linda 43, 104, 164a
Firestone, Renée 80
Firth, Colin 95, 111, 117, 164c
Firth, Peter 35
Fisher, Frances 26
Fisher, Joely 71
Fitzgerald, Tara 109
Five Senses, The 55-56
Flanagan, Tommy 110
Flanery, Sean Patrick 28, 119
Fletcher, Brendan 55
Flockhart, Calista 145, 165b
Flynn, Barbara 148
Flynn, Jerome 23
Foley, Mick 'Mankind' 24
Following 56
Fonda, Bridget 79
Fonda, Peter 83
Fonteyne, Frédéric 82
Food of Love 56
For Love of the Game 56, 57, 164d
Forbes, Meriel 186
Ford, Harrison 109
Ford, Julia 113
Forget Me Never 150
Forlani, Claire 96
Forman, Milos 89
Forster, Robert 126
Forsyth, Bill 64
Forsythe, William 41
Fortune, John 116
Foster, Jodie 16
Fox, James 139
Fox, Kerry 39, 52, 135
Foxx, Jamie 17
Frain, James 92
Franco, Larry 101
Frankenheimer, John 39, 59
Franzoni, David 62
Fraser, Brendan 9, 9
Fraser, Laura 90, 140, 142
Frears, Stephen 66
Fredenburgh, Daniel 32
Freeman, J E 62
Freeman, Matt 62
French Academy Awards 2000 176
French, Dawn 91
Frequency 56-57
Fresson, Bernard 106
Frieberg, Camelia 55
Friel, Anna 87
Friendly, David T 25
From Dusk to Dawn 2 – Texas Blood Money 154
From the Edge of the City 57
Frost, Sadie 54, 85, 109
Frot, Catherine 42, 97
Fry, Stephen 23, 111, 133, 142, 165b
Fucking Amål see *Show Me Love*
Fuller, Kurt 108
Funk, Terry 24
Furlong, Edward 40
Fury Within 150

Galaxy Quest 58, **58**
Gale, David 48, 147
Gallo, Vincent 81
Galloway, Jane 125
Gamblin, Jacques 34
Gambon, Michael 80, 93, 121
Gammon, James 73
Gang Law 150
Gangster No 1 58-59
Ganis, Sid 25, 41
Ganoung, Richard 26
Garcia, Nicole 106
Garcin, Henri 95
Garland, Judy 98
Garner, Alice 125
Garner, Julian 66
Garofalo, Janeane 96, 165b
Garvin, Joanna 32
Gashey, Jamal Al 102
Gassman, Vittorio 181
Gazzara, Ben 131

Gellar, Sarah Michelle 119
General's Daughter, The 59
Genies 2000 175
Geoffray, Jeff 118
Georgalas, Demetre 61
Gere, Richard 114
Gestel, Frans Van 108
Ghost Dog: The Way of the Samurai 59-60, **60**
Giakoumis, Hasmi 106
Giamatti, Paul 25, 89
Giannaris, Constantino 57
Giarraputo, Jack 25
Gibb, James 36
Gibson, Mel 34, 92, 164a
Gielgud, Sir John 133, 181
Gilbert, Yann 30
Girl 60
Girl on the Bridge, The 61, **61**
Girl, Interrupted 60-61
Gish, Annabeth 43, 120
Gladiator 7, 8, 62, **62**, 167
Gladstein, Richard N 35, 69
Glascoe, Jon 76
Gleeson, Brendan 79
Glory and Honor 150
Go 62
Gogan, Valerie 103
Goldberg, Eric 53
Goldberg, Leonard 43
Golden Globes 2000 177
Golden Raspberries 2000 176-177
Goldman, Alain 70
Goldman, William 165c
Goldsman, Akiva 40
Goldwyn, Tony 29, 141
Golfballs 154
Golin, Steve 22
Golubeva, Katerina 107
Gontier, Jean 78
González, Juan de Marcos 32
Goodbye Lover 62-63
Gooding, Cuba Jr 35, 72
Goodman, John 30
Goorjian, Michael 120
Gordon, Charles 101
Gordon, Dan 69
Gordon, Lawrence 96
Gordon-Sinclair, John 64
Gorman, Cliff 59
Gosnell, Raja 25, 97
Gottsegen, Lee 141
Gråbøl, Sofie 92
Grade, Michael **162**
Graham, Heather 19, 29
Grant, Hugh 9, **9**, 91, 165c
Grant, Richard E 56
Graves, Rupert 44
Gray, Charles 181, 181-182
Gray, Pamela 141
Grazer, Brian 24, 29, 47, 8229
Greasepaint and Gore (book) 170-171
Green Mile, The **6**, 63
Green, Michael 25
Green, Sarah 146
Greenaway, Peter 47
Greene, Peter 27
Greengrass, Paul 130
Greenwich Mean Time 63
Greenwood, Bruce 43
Greggory, Pascal 75
Gregory's Two Girls 64, **64**
Gregory, Eileen 68
Gregson-Williams, Harry 34
Grenier, Adrian 45
Grenier, Zach 54
Grey, Alice 49
Grier, Pam 67
Griffin, Eddie 41
Griffith, Melanie 17
Griffith, Thomas Ian 75
Grisanti, Melanie 43
Grossfield, Norman J 107
Guay, Richard 60
Guédiguian, Robert 11
Guest House Paradiso 64, **64**
Guild, Nancy 186
Guillemin, Sophie 49
Gunnarsson, Sturla 125

Gunner, Rod 36
Gunton, Bob 21
Gutteridge, Melanie 63
Guyler, Deryck 186
Guzman, Luis 83
Gyllenhaal, Jake 101
Gynt, Greta 186

Haas, Philip 139
Haase, Kathleen 41
Hackford, Taylor 63
Hafizka, Nayeem 37
Haft, Steven 74
Hagemann, Martin 84
Haigney, Michael 107
Hald, Brigitte 92
Hale, Gregg 27
Halewood, Suzie 103
Hall, Philip Baker 71, 88
Hall, Steve Clark 36
Halliwell's Film & Video Guide 2000 (book) 171
Halliwell's Who's Who in the Movies (book) 171
Hallström, Lasse 35
Halsted, Dan 17, 140
Halvorson, Gary 11
Hamburger, David S 69
Hamilton, Julie 67
Hamori, András 126
Hancock, Sheila 67
Hanging Up 65
Hanks, Tom **6**, 9, **9**, 63, 135
Hanley, Chris 14, 60, 140
Hannah, John 36, 69
Hannah, John 69
Happy Face Murders 154
Happy, Texas 65
Hardy, John 83
Hardy, Robert 133
Harlin, Renny 40
Harper, Frank 113
Harrelson, Woody 47, 66
Harris, Richard 20, 135
Harris, Rosemary 95, 126
Harron, Mary 14
Hart, Ian 23, 49, 147
Hart, John 30
Hart, Melissa Joan 45
Hasards ou coincidences see *Chance or Coincidence*
Haunting, The 65-66, **66**
Hauser, Cole 66
Haw, Alex 56
Hawes, Keeley 80
Hawke, Ethan 122, 165c
Hawking, Stephen 57
Hawley, Richard 37
Hawn, Goldie 104
Hawthorne, Nigel 36, 129, 146
Hayek, Salma 43, 144, 164a
Hayes, Derek 92
Hayes, Isaac 122
Hayes, Sean P 26
Haygarth, Tony 34
Hayman, David 104
Head On 66
Headey, Lena 102
Heche, Anne 145
Hecht, Albie 121
Hecker, Gerd 93
Helgenberger, Marg 50
Henderson, Shirley 147
Hendrickk, Monic 108
Henshall, Douglas 53
Henson, Brian 94
Henstridge, Natasha 143
Hertzberg, Michael 50
Hewitt, Pete 142
Heyman, David 110
Heyman, Norma 59
Heyward, Andy 71
Hi-Lo Country, The 66
Hibbin, Sally 44
Hicks, Scott 122
Hicks, Taral 22
Hiep, Nguyen Ngoc 133
Higgins, James 113
High Fidelity 164b, 167, **167**
Hilaire, Laurent 33

Hill, Tim 94
Hird, Thora 76
Hirokazu, Kore-eda 11
Hisaishi, Joe 78
Hitchcock Poster Art (book) 171
Hitchcock's Secret Notebooks (book) 169
Hjejle, Iben 92, 156, **156**
Hoblit, Gregory 57
Hofflund, Jody 45, 124
Hoffman, Dustin 75, 141
Hoffman, Michael 145
Hoffman, Philip Seymour 88, 158
Holbrook, Hal 20
Holland, Mark 86
Hollander, Tom 36, 91
Hollogne, Marc 33
Hollywood Foreign Press Association Awards 2000 177
Holm, Ian 118
Holmes, Katie 42, 62
Holy Smoke 67, **67**
Homeboys On the Beach see *Boys On the Beach*
Honest 68, **68**
Hooton, James 80
Hope, Ted 112
Hopkins, Anthony 72
Hopkins, Ben 118
Hopkins, Nikita 134
Horberg, William 128
Horrocks, Jane 164a
Hoskins, Bob 53
Houdini 150
House! 68-69
House of Mirth, The 164b
House on Haunted Hill 68
Howard, James Newton 114
Howard, Ron 24, 47
Howenstein, Bing 20
Hudson, Hugh 96
Hughes, Jason 69
Huike, Zhang 100
Hunley, The 150
Hunt, Bonnie 63, 109, 111
Hunt, Phil 53
Hunt, Pixote 53
Huntington, Sam 40-41
Hurley, Elizabeth 91
hurlyburly 69, 164b
Hurricane, The 69
Hurrran, Nick 140
Hurst, Andy 148
Hurt, John 13, 93, 148
Huster, Francis 42
Huston, Anjelica 11
Hutton, Timothy 59
Hyams, Peter 49

I Married a Monster 150
Ice Cube 98, 132
Ifans, Rhys 74, 77, 109, 148
Igarashi, Tomoyuki 107
Illsley, Mark 65
In All Innocence 70, **70**
Inferno 150
Inoh, Shizuka 47
Inside the Wicker Man (book) 171
Insider, The 70-71, **71**, 164b, 167
Inspector Gadget 71-72, **72**
Instinct 72
Intimate Affair, An see *Une Liaison Pornographique*
Invisible Child, The 150
Iron Giant, The 72-73
Iron, Daniel 80
Isaac, Sandy 97
Isaacs, Jason 49
Isacsson, Kris 44
Iscovich, Mario 104
Isn't She Great 73
It All Starts Today 73
Izzard, Bryan 79
Izzard, Eddie 96

Jackman, Hugh 105
Jackson, Michael 165c
Jackson, Ruth 142
Jackson, Samuel L 164c, 165c

Jacob, Irène 95
Jacobi, Derek 62, 139
Jacobs, Daren 32
Jacobs, Joke 117
Jacobson, Tom 93
Jaffe, Toby 28
Jaffrey, Madhur 37
Jaffrey, Sakina 37
Jakob the Liar 74
James, Brion 182
James, Dick 117
Jane, Thomas 40
Janice Beard: 45 WPM 74, 74-75
Jann, Michael Patrick 45
Janne, Dominique 33
Janney, Allison 130
Jannsen, Famke 36, 68
Jarmuscvh, Jim 59
Jay, Ricky 88
Je M'Appelle Crawford see *The Big Tease*
Jean, Vadim 103
Jenkel, Brad 21
Jenkins, Richard 122
Jerry and Tom 150-151
Jewel 112
Jewison, Norman 69
Jimkins, Jim 43
Jinks, Dan 14
Joan of Arc 75, 151
Joffé, Roland 63
John Carpenter's Vampires 75
John Carradine: The Films (book) 169
Johnson, Hugh 35
Johnson, Mark 58
Johnston, Joe 101
Jolie, Angelina 29, 61, 107, 108
Jolivet, Pierre 70
Jones, Cherry 50, 76
Jones, Freddie 69
Jones, Gemma 130, 146
Jones, James Earl 53
Jones, Nick 145
Jones, Peter 182
Jones, Quincy 53
Jones, Richard T 147
Jones, Robert 118
Jones, Steve 54
Jones, Terry 18
Jones, Tommy Lee 43
Jönsson, Lars 118
Jonze, Spike 22, 132
Jordan, Neil 49
Josten, Walter 118
Jovi, Jon Bon 138
Jovovich, Milla 75, 92
Joyce, Maurice 43
Judd, Ashley 43, 51
Julian Po 75-76, **76**
Julie and the Cadillacs 76
Junger, Gil 130
Juvonen, Nancy 97

K9 II 151
Kaci, Nadia 73
Kahn, Cédric 49
Kahn, Jonathan 60
Kahn, Madeline 182
Kalins, Marjorie 11
Kani, John 133
Kaplan, Jonathan 31
Kaplan, Susan 95
Kartheiser, Vincent 17
Karvan, Claudia 105, 125
Karyo, Tcheky 116
Kasander, Kees 48
Kassovitz, Peter 74
Katt, Nicky 28
Katz, Gail 24
Katz, Marty 39
Katz, Ross 137
Kaufman, Allan 143
Kaufman, Morten 92
Kaurismaki, Mika 81
Kay, Charles 22
Kazantzidis, Stavros 125
Keaton, Diana 65, 104
Kedrova, Lila 182
Keener, Catherine 22

Keeping the Faith 164c
Keitel, Harvey 67, 133, 138
Kelk, Michael 69
Kelley, David E 79
Kellogg, David 71
Kemp, Julian 69
Kennedy, Kathleen 120, 122
Kennedy, Maria Doyle 64
Kensit, Patsy 74
Keohane, Jennifer 28
Kerner, Jordan 71
Kerr, Alison 86
Ketcham, John 69
Kevin & Perry Go Large 8, 77, 77
Keyser, David De 126
Khan, Aamir 46
Khanna, Rahul 46
Kiberlain, Sandrine 113
Kidnapped in Paradise 151
Kikujiro 78
Killers in the House 151
Kilner, Clare 74
Kind of Hush, A 78
King Cobra 151
King of Paris, The 78, **78**
King, Alex 121
King, Sandy 75
Kishimoto, Kayoko 78
Kitano, Takeshi 'Beat' 78
Kitt, Sam 24
Klein, Chris 14, 48
Klein, Nicholas 92
Kline, Kevin 144, 145
Kliot, Jason 44, 133
Knaup, Herbert 115
Koch, Chris 121
Koch, Hawk 57
Koemgsberg, Neil 141
Koepp, David 124
Kokkinos, Ana 66
Kolobos 155
Kolodner, Eva 30
Konckier, Régine 88
Kong, China 145
Konrad, Cathy 61, 117
Kragh-Jacobsen, Søren 92
Kramer, Robert 49
Kramer, Scott 83
Krane, Jonathan D 21
Krikes, Peter 16
Kristofferson, Kris 83
Krol, Joachim 115
Kroonenburg, Piter 135
Kroopf, Scott 114
Kubrick, Stanley 51
Kudrow, Lisa 15, 65
Kurita, Toyomichi 36

LA Without a Map 81
Labbe, Patrick 33
Lacan, Pierre 95
Lacey, Luke de 140
Ladd, Diane 137
Laguionie, Jean-Francois 93
Laiter, Tova 139
Lake Placid 79, **79**
Lamarr, Hedy 182, **182**
Landay, Vincent 22
Lane, Diane 141
Lane, Nathan 73, 86
Langella, Frank 99
Langham, Chris 26
Langley, John 145
Langrick, Margaret 127
Lanners, Bouli 33
Lansbury, Angela 53
Lantos, Robert 126
Lantos, Tom 79
Lanvin, Gérard 70
LaPaglia, Anthony 127
Lappin, Arthur 11
Larter, Ali 55, 68
Lascault, Catherine 61
Laserhawk 151
Lasseter, John 135
Last Bus Home 151
Last Days, The 79-80
Last Line of Defence 155

Last Night 80
Last September, The 80
Last Yellow, The 80-81
Late August, Early September 81
Latham, Alan 36, 39
Latifah, Queen 29
Laurent, Marie-Christine 95
Laurentiis, Dino De 138
Laurentiis, Martha De 138
Laurie, Hugh 91
Lavigne, Enrique López 85
Law, Jude 54, 85, 128
Law, Phyllida 87
Lawrence, Martin 25, 27, 82
Lazar, Andrew 19, 130
Leachman, Cloris 73
Leary, Denis 131
Lebbos, Carmen 142
Leconte, Patrice 61
Lederer, Francis 186
Ledger, Heath 130
Ledoux, Patrice 75
Ledoyen, Virginie 21, 70, 81
Lee, Ang 112
Lee, Jason 43
Lee, Malcolm D 24
Lee, Sheryl 75
Lee, Spike 24, 126
Lee, Thomas 126
Leeves, Jane 95
Legend of 1900, The **81**, 81-82, 167
Legend of the Pianist on the Ocean, The see *The Legend of 1900*
Legge, Michael 142
Leguizamo, John 126
Leigh, Mike 135
Lelouch, Claude 33
Leon 21
Leonard, Joseph 27
Lepetit, Jean-François 113
Lera, Chete 103
Lester, Adrian 86, 91
Leto, Jared 14, 54
Levin, Lloyd 96
Levine, Barry 41
Levitt, Joseph-Gordon 130
Lewis, Gough 117
Lewis, Juliette 104
Lewiston, Denis C 118
Leydendecker, Joel 30
Lhermitte, Thierry 42
Liaison Pornographique, Une 82
Liberman, Meg 107
Liddell, Mickey 62
Liègeois, Philippe 113
Life 82
Life During Wartime see *The Alarmist*
Life in a Day 155
Life of a Gigolo 151
Life's a Scream (book) 169
Liljeberg, Rebecca 118
Lillard, Matthew 86, 120
Lima, Kevin 129
Liman, Doug 62
Limbo 82-83
Limey, The 83, **83**
Lindberg, Chad 101
Linder, Dixie 142
Lindo, Delroy 35
Ling, Bai 16
Linson, Art 54
Liotta, Ray 94
Lipper, Ken 80
Lively, Gerry 39
Llewelyn, Desmond 148, 182-183
Lloyd, Jake 123
Lobell, Mike 73
Lodro, Jamyang 38
Loggia, Robert 111
Lola & Bilidikid 83-84
Lola rennt see *Run Lola Run*
London Film Critics' Awards 2000 177
London, Jason 32
Long, Nia 24, 25, 28, 117, 123
Long, Tom 125
Loop 151
Lopez, Jennifer **161**
López, Sergi 82

Lord, Peter 34
Lord, Stephen 53
Loret, Alexis 12
Los Angeles Film Critics' Assocaition Awards 1999 177
Loss of Sexual Innocence, The 84
Lost and Found 151
Lost in the Bermuda Triangle 155
Love Letter, The 85
Love's Labour Lost 85-86, **86**
Love, Courtney 89
Love, Honour & Obey 84, 84-85
Lovers of the Arctic Circle 85
Lucas, George 123
Lucas, Laurent 113
Luchini, Fabrice 113
Lucia 86
Ludwig, Tony 40
Lulu 142
Lumley, Joanna 87, 91
Lupovitz, Dan 119
Lustig, Branko 62
Lutic, Bernard 78
Lynch, David 125
Lynch, John 23
Lynch, Susan 99
Lynn, Jonathan 143
Lynn, Meredith Scott 26
Lyonne, Natasha 14
Lyons, John 19

MacCorkindale, Simon 125
Macdonald, Andrew 21
Macdonald, Kelly 69, 84, 96
Macdonald, Kevin 102
MacDowell, Andie 94
Macfadyen, Matthew 91
MacKenzie, John 143
Macy, William H 65
Mad Cows 87, **87**
Maddalena, Marianne 95, 117
Madden, David 104
Madonna 97
Maestro, Mia 128
Magnolia 87-88, 167
Maguire, Tobey 35, 112
Maillet, Dominique 78
Maisel, Ileen 102
Major League: Back to the Minors 151
Makin, Kelly 91
Making Mischief – The Cult Films of Pete Walker (book) 171
Makovetsky, Sergei 101
Mal 88
Malkovich, John 22, 75, 134, 165c
Malone, Jena 56
Malone, William 68
Man is a Woman 88
Man on the Moon 88-89, **89**
Mancuso, Frank Jr 123
Mangold, James 61
Mann, Michael 71
Mannion, Frank 87
Mansfield Park 89-90
Manville, Lesley 135
Manzano, Sonia 10
Marceau, Sophie 148
Marchand, Nancy 183
Margolis, Mark 131
Margolyes, Miriam 44, 69
Mariage, Benoît 33
Marilyn Monroe – Cover to Cover (bbok) 171
Mark, Laurence 18, 24, 65
Markham, Kika 147
Marlon Brando – A Life in Our Times (book) 171
Marnet, David 146
Marsden, James 42
Marshall, Ben 113
Marshall, Frank 120, 122
Marshall, Garry 104, 114
Martin, Steve 29, 53, 104, 164a
Martines, Alessandra 33
Martínez, Fele 85, 103
Martinez, Vanessa 83
Marwa, Emil 46
Massey, Anna 87, 127
Masson, Anne 46

Mastrantonio, Mary Elizabeth 83
Match, The 90
Matheson, Tim 124
Mathis, Samantha 14
Matlock, Glen 54
Matrix, The 8
Matthau, Walter 65
Matthes, Ulrich 145
Matthews, Mandy 110
Matthews, Meg 87
Mature, Victor 183, **183**
Maura, Carmen 12
Max Q 151
Mayall, Rik 64, 93
Maybe Baby **90**, 90-91, 167-168
Maydew, Sam 120
Mayfield, Les 28
Mazzola, Frank 145
McAlpine, Hamish 145
McAnuff, Des 73
McCabe, Tom 133
McCallum, Rick 123
McCann, Donal 78
McConaughey, Matthew 47, 138
McDarrah, Patrick 63
McDermott, Dylan 133
McDonald, Christopher 73
McDonald, Peter 53, 99
McDonnell, Edward L 132
McDowell, Malcolm 59
McEwan, Geraldine 85
McGann, Joe 56
McGill, Everett 125
McGregor, Ewan 51, 99, 123
McGuckian, Mary 23
McGuigan, Paul 59
McHugh, Thomas 43
McIntyre, Phil 64, 91
McKee, Gina 147
McKellar, Don 80
McKenzie, Jacqueline 40
McKinney, Mark 104
McLeod, Eric 19
McQueen, Glenn 136
McTeer, Janet 137
McTiernan, John 131
Meadows, Shane 113
Medem, Julio 85
Meerson, Steve 16
Mehta, Deepa 46
Meistrich, Larry 22
Mellor, Kay 52
Mendel, Barry 115, 120
Mendes, Sam 14
Menshikov, Oleg 20
Mentasti, Carlos A 129
Merchant, Ismail 37
Merendino, James 120
Merrells, Jason 121
Messenger, The: The Story of Joan of Arc see *Joan of Arc*
Meston, Paul 105
Mewes, Jason 43
Meyer, Dina 21
Meylan, Gérard 11
Michie, John 135
Mickey Blue Eyes 91, **91**
Midler, Bette 53, 73
Mifune 92
Mighty Movies (book) 171
Mikhalkov, Nikita 20
Mikkelsen, Mads 27
Milburn, Chris 44, 111
Milburn, Oliver 127
Milchan, Alexandra 92
Miles, Christopher 36
Millennium Movies 168
Miller, Alan 59
Miller, Jonny Lee 85, 90
Miller, Larry 26, 130
Miller, Neal 24
Milliken, Angie 105
Million Dollar Hotel, The 92
Mills, Stephanie 86
Miner, Steve 79
Minghella, Anthony 128
Minzhi, Wei 100
Miracle Maker, The 92-93
Mirren, Simon 63
Mission Impossible 2 163

Mission to Mars 93, 168
Mistaken Identity 151
Mitchell, Daryl 58
Mitchell, Elizabeth 57
Mitchell, Mike 41
Moine, Patrick 93
Mol, Gretchen 127
Moll, James 80
Mongo, Stéphane Soo 30
Monkey Business (book) 169-170
Monkey's Tale, A 93
Montgomery, Rick 65
Moodysson, Lukas 118
Moore, Chris 14, 39
Moore, Demi 19
Moore, Julianne 36, 49
Moreau, Veronique 33
Morgan, Glen 55
Mori, Masayuki 78
Mori, Takemoto 107
Moriotz, Neal H 28
Morneau, Louis 21
Morrissey, Neil 90
Morrisson, Rui 88
Morse, David 63
Mortensen, Viggo 137, 141
Morton, Joe 19
Morton, Samantha 156-157, **157**
Mosier, Scott 43
Mosley, David 26
Most, Jeff 60
Mostow, Jonathan 138
Movie Locations (book) 171
movies about movies 29
Mowgli (leopard) 105
Mukli, Gandi 84
Mulan 8
Mullen, Peter 104
Mulroney, Dermot 63
Mulvehill, Charles 91
Mummy, The 8
Muppets From Space **93**, 93-94
Murphy, Brittany 61
Murphy, Eddie 19, 82
Murphy, Laura 118
Murphy, Pat 99
Murray, Bill 115
Muse, The 94, **94**
Music Freelancers, The 95
Music of the Heart 95
My Life So Far 95-96
Myers, Mike 9, **9**, 19
Myrick, Daniel 27, 172, **172**
Mystery Men 96, **96**

Nacéri, Samy 129
Naked Man, The 155
Nanas, Herb 94
Narova, Cecilia 128
Nas 22
Nassar, Joseph Bou 142
National Board of Review of Motion Picture Awards 2000 177-178
National Society of Film Critics' Awards 2000 178
Nayar, Deepak 32, 92
Neal, Patricia 36
Neeson, Liam **8**, 9, 65, 123
Neill, Sam 24
Nelson, Jessie 124
Nelson, Sean 147
Netforce 151
Neufeld, Mace 59
Never Been Kissed 97
Neville, John 126
Nevolina, Lika 101
New Eve, The 97
New World Disorder 151
New York Film Critics' Circle Awards 2000 178
Newell, Mike 108
Newirth, Charles 58
Newman, Alec 93
Newman, Barry 83
Newman, Fred 43
Newmyer, Bobby 133
Next Best Thing, The 97-98
Next Friday 98, **98**
Next To You see *Drive Me Crazy*

Nicholas, Thomas Ian 14
Nicholls, Paul 36, 136
Nielsen, Connie 62, 93
Nighy, Bill 64
Nikolakopoulos, Tony 66
Nimri, Najwa 85
Ninth Gate, The **98**, 98-99
Niro, Robert De 15
Nivola, Alessandro 90
No Fear 155
No Looking Back 151-152
Noiret, Philippe 78
Nolan, Christopher 56
Nolan, John 56
Nolte, Nick 119
Nora **99**, 99-100
Norbu, Khyentse 38
Noriega, Eduardo 103
Norris, Steve 96
North by Northwest (book) 171
Northam, Jeremy 65, 146
Norton, Edward 54
Not One Less **100**, 100
Notting Hill 8
Nottingham, Wendy 135
Nouvelle Eve, La see *The New Eve*
Novo, Nancho 85
Noyce, Philip 29
Nunn, Bill 82
Nussbaum, Danny 103
Nutter, David 42
Nyima, Kunzang 38
Nyman, Michael 110, 147

O'Brien, Kieran 140
O'Connell, Jerry 28, 93
O'Connor, Carroll 111
O'Connor, Frances 90, 157
O'Connor, Gavin 137
O'Connor, Gregory 137
O'Donnell, Chris 20, 36
O'Donnell, Damien 46
O'Donnell, Rosie 129
O'Dwyer, Marion 11
O'Hara, Catherine 106
O'Hara, David 74
O'Haver, Tommy 26
O'Mahony, Sean 76
O'Sullivan, Thaddeus 104
October Sky 101
Oda, Erika 11
Of Freaks and Men 101
Office Killer 152
Office Space 152
Ogou, Alexandre 11
Oh, Sandra 80
Old New Borrowed Blue see *With or Without You*
Oleynik, Larisa 130
Olin, Lena 99
One Day in September 101-102, **102**
One More Kiss 103
Onegin 102-103, **103**
Only Thrill, The 155
Open Your Eyes 103
Operation Delta Force III see *Clear Target*
Ordinary Decent Criminal 103-104, 168
Orman, Roscoe 10
Ormières, Jean-Luc 88
Ormond, Julia 20
Orth, Zak 44
Oscars 1999 174-175
Osment, Haley Joel 119, 157
Other Sister, The 104
Otis, James 17
Our Guys 155
Out-of-Towners, The 104
Owen, Bill 186
Owen, Chris 101
Owens, Ciaran 15
Oz, Frank 29

Pacino, Al 17, 70
Palma, Brian De 93
Palminteri, Chazz 69
Paltrow, Gwyneth 9, 128, 165c
Panjabi, Archie 46

Papadopoulus, Stathis 57
Paper Dreams (book) 171
Paperback Hero 105
Paquin, Anna 69, 141
Paradis, Vanessa 61
Pardes, Marisa 12
Parisot, Dean 58
Park, Nick 34
Parker, Alan 16
Parker, Mary-Louise 55, 63
Parker, Mike 109
Parker, Molly 55
Parker, Trey 122
Parks, Michael 76
Passion in the Desert 105, **105**
Patinkin, Mandy 10
Patriot, The **167**, 168
Pattinson, Charles 113
Patton, Will 50
Pavel, Paul 82
Paxton, Bill 138
Payne, Alexander 48
Pearce, Guy 110
Peet, Amanda 28, 143, 157, **157**
Peirce, Kimberly 30
Penn & Teller 53
Penn, Robert Wright 69
Penn, Robin Wright 164b
Penn, Sean 69, 139
Penry-Jones, Rupert 140
Pepper, Barry 21
Perelman, Itzhak 53, 95
Perez, Vincent 134
Perkins, Elizabeth 137
Perpetrators of the Crime 155
Perrineau, Harold 24
Perry, Craig 14, 55
Perry, Matthew 133, 143, 165c
Pesery, Bruno 107
Pesery, Bruno 107
Peter Cushing Companion, The (book) 170
Peters, Jon 144
Peterson, Wolfgang 24
Pétin, Laurent 114, 129
Pétin, Michèle 114
Petit-Jacques, Isabelle 61
Peyser, Michael 68
Pfeiffer, Michelle 124, 145, 164c
Pfulger, Frédéric 61
Phantasm IV: Oblivion 152
Phillips, Leslie 116
Phillips, Lou Diamond 21, 126
Phoenix, Joaquin 62
Phoenix, Summer 60, 120
Phörpa see *The Cup*
Piccoli, Michel 105
Pidgeon, Matthew 146
Pidgeon, Rebecca 146
Pierce, Justin 98
Pierson, Joseph 76
Pilcher, Lydia Dean 38
Pillsbury, Sarah 85
Pinsent, Gordon 106
Pinter, Harold 90
Pippi Langstrumpf see *Pippi Longstocking*
Pippi Longstocking 106
Pirates of Silicon Valley 155
Pirès, Gérard 129
Pismichenko, Svetlana 32
Pistor, Julia 121
Pitarresi, Maria 73
Pitoc, John Paul 136
Pitt, Brad 9, 54
Place Vendome 106
Platt, Oliver 24, 79, 133
Playing By Heart **106**, 106-107
Plummer, Christopher 70, 164b
Plunkett, Marcella 78
Podeswa, Jeremy 55
Poelvoorde, Benoît 33
Poire, Alain 42
Pokémon – The First Movie 8, 107
Pola X 107
Polanski, Roman 99
Poliakoff, Stephen 56
Polish Bride, The 107-108
Polish Wedding 152
Pollack, Sydney 51, 110
Pollak, Kevin 49

Pollard, Michael J 137
Polley, Sarah 80
Polone, Gavin 45, 124
Polonsky, Abraham 183
Polycarpou, Peter 76
Polychronidis, Anestis 57
Poolse bruid, De see *The Polish Bride*
Portman, Natalie 18, 123
Portman, Rachel 35, 104
Postlethwaite, Pete 143
Potente, Franka 115
Potter, Monica 147
Powell, John 34
Powell, Marykay 110
Powers, Ed 117
Prague Duet 152
Pressman, Edward R 14
Pressman, Michael 79
Preston, Kelly 56
Prevost, Daniel 42
Prinze, Freddie Jr 44
Pryce, Jonathan 123
Pugh, Robert 133
Pullman, Bill 79
Purefoy, James 91
Puri, Om 46, 125
Pushing Tin 108, **108**
Puttnam, David 96
Puzo, Mario 186

Quaid, Dennis 17, 57
Quinet, Patrick 82
Quinn, Aidan 95

Radcliffe, Mark 24
Radclyffe, Curtis 127
Radclyffe, Sarah 142
Radmin, Linne 97
Ragas, Roef 108
Raimi, Sam 56
Rajot, Piere-Loup 97
Ramis, Harold 15
Rampling, Charlotte 34
Ramsay, Lynn Jr 110
Ramsay, Lynne 110
Rancid Aluminium 109, **109**
Randall-Cutler, Roger 78
Random Hearts 109-110
Rapp, Anne 36
Rasche, David 26
Ratcatcher 110, **110**
Rauist, Laure 11
Ravenous 110, 168
Ravich, Rand 19
Raw Nerve 152
Razdan, Soni 125
Razzies 2000 176-177
Rea, Stephen 49
Redgrave, Lynn 97
Reed, Oliver 7, 62
Reeves, Keanu 9, **9**
Reeves, Phil 48
Reeves, Steve 183, **183**
Refn, Nicolas Winding 27
Reid, Audrey 131
Reid, Tara 14, 60
Reilly, John C 56
Reindeer Games see *Deception*
Reiner, Rob 124, 164c, 165a
Relative Values 111
REM 89
Renko, Serge 95
Rennie, Callum Keith 80
Renzi, Maggie 83
Return to Me 111, **111**
Rey, Jean-Michel 113
Reynolds, Lance W 105
Reynolds, Ryan 12
Rhames, Ving 50
Rhind-Tutt, Julian 136
Ribisi, Giovanni 104
Ricci, Christina 121, 165c
Richards, Denise 45, 148
Richardson, Joely 91
Richardson, Lee 186
Richardson, Marie 51
Richardson, Mike 96
Richardson, Miranda 121
Riche, Alan 40
Rickles, Don 135

Rickman, Alan 58
Ride With the Devil **112**, 112, 168
Ridley, Merle-Anne 106
Rien Sur Robert 112-113
Rifkin, Adam 41
Ripper, Michael 186, **186**
Rippon, Angela 142
Rivarola, Carlos 129
Rix, Louisa 77
Roach, Jay 19
Robbins, Brian 139
Robbins, Tim 38, 93
Roberts, Ben 78
Roberts, Fissy 117
Roberts, Jake 'The Snake' 24
Roberts, Julia 9, **9**, 50, 114, 164b, 165c
Robinson, Amy 45, 56
Robinson, James G 35
Robson, Wayne 106
Rock, Chris 164a
Rockwell, Alex 11
Rockwell, Sam 58, 63
Rodero, José López 99
Rodgers, Mic 138
Roff, Chris 23
Rohde, Armin 115
Roman, Jacques 78
Roman, Ruth 183-184
Romance 113
Rongione, Fabrizio 113
Roodman, Joel 63
Rooker, Michael 29
Room for Romeo Brass, A 113
Ropelewski, Thomas 97
Rose, Alexandra 104
Rose, Philip 26
Rosenberg, Michael 24
Rosenberg, Paul 62
Rosenberg, Tom 97, 114
Rosenthal, Jane 15
Rosetta 113-114
Rosner, Louise 21
Ross, Lee 44
Roth, Cecilia 12
Roth, Donna Arkoff 65
Roth, Tim 82, 142
Rothman, Frank 186
Rotholz, Ron 22
Rotten, Johnny 54
Rourke, Mickey 118
Routledge, Jordan 46
Roven, Charles 132
Rowe, Brad 26
Rozema, Patricia 90
Rudd, Paul 35
Rudin, Scott 16, 31, 121
Ruiz, Raoul 107
Run Lola Run 114-115, **115**
Runaway Bride 114, **114**
Rush, Geoffrey 68
Rushmore 115
Russell, David O 132
Russell, Lucy 56
Russell, Tina 76
Russo, Rene 131
Rust, Mathias 118
Ryan, Meg 65
Ryder, Winona 61

Sabrina Goes to Rome 152
Sadler, William 63
Sagay, O O 117
Saint-Jean, Michel 12
Salerno, Robert 22
Samaha, Elie 21
Samiotis, Dionysis 57
Samples, Keith 48
Sanchez, Eduardo 27, 172, **172**
Sanders, Jay O 137
Sandler, Adam 25
Sandoz, Gilles 11
Sands, Julian 84
Sanford, Midge 85
Santos, Alberto Seixas 88
Santostefano, Damon 133
Sarandon, Susan 18
Sarde, Alain 12, 73, 106, 125
Sarossy, Paul 53
Sarsgaard, Peter 30

Saura, Carlos 129
Saving Grace 116
Sawa, Devon 55
Sayles, John 83
Scacchi, Greta 37
Scalella, Luis A 129
Scales, Prunella 87
Schaak, Michael 106
Schamus, James 112
Schanz, Heidi 138
Schelsinger, John 97
Scheuer, Walter 95
Schiff, Paul 115
Schifrin, Lalo 129
Schisgal, Murray 141
Schneider, Rob 41, 94
Schreiber, Liev 69, 141
Schroeder, Adam 121
Schultz, Carl 135
Schultz, John 45
Schwabach, Peter 117
Schwartz, Teri 104
Schwartzman, Jason 115
Schwarzenegger, Arnold 49
Science Fiction Serials (book) 171
Scorsese, Martin 31
Scott, Allan 90
Scott, Dougray 64, 158, **158**
Scott, George C 184, **184**
Scott, Jane 66
Scott, John 118
Scott, Ridley 62
Scott, William Lee 101
Scream 3: **116**, 116-117
Scrosese, Martin 66
Scully, Vin 164b
Seaward, Tracey 99
Secret Laughter of Women, The 117, 164c
Segan, Lloyd 20
Seigner, Emmanuelle 106
Sekiguchi, Yusuke 78
Sellar, Joanne 88
Selyanov, Sergei 32, 101
Sergio Leone: Something to Do with Death (book) 171
Serrault, Michel 34
Seth, Roshan 125
Sevigny, Chloë 30
Sex Pistols, The 54
Sex: The Annabel Chong Story 117
Sexton, Brendan III 30
Seydoux, Michel 20
Seymour, Gerald 102
Shaft 164c
Shah, Ash R 126
Shah, Naseeruddin 125
Shalhoub, Tony 58
Shamberg, Michael 51, 89
Shandling, Garry 69, 164b
Shapiro, Allen 138
Sharif, Omar 131
Sharifi, Jamshied 94
Sharp, Jeffrey 30
Shattered Image 152
Shaw, Fiona 80
Shaw, Vinessa 81
Shelton, Angela 137
Shepherd, Steve John 63
Sher, Stacey 51, 89
Shergar 118
Sheridan, Jim 11
Shestack, Jon 42
Shiloh 2: Shiloh Season 152
Shim, Andrew 113
Show Me Love 118
Shriek 152
Shull, Richard B 184
Shulman, Constance 43
Shyamalan, M Night 120
Sideris, Anastasia 125
Sidney, Sylvia 184
Siffredi, Rocco 113
Silent Films (book) 171
Silva, Henry 59
Silver, Jeffrey 133
Silver, Joel 68
Simmons, Gene 41
Simon Magus 118
Simon, Morgane 33

Simpatico 119
Simply Irresistible 119, 164c
Simpson, Aaron 87
Singapore Sling 155
Singh, Anant 130
Sinise, Gary 39, 93
Sinyor, Gary 20
Sisto, Jeremy 147
Sixth Sense, The 8, **8**, **119**, 119-120
Skerritt, Tom 104
Skinner, Claire 148
Slan, Jon 117
Slater, Christian 76
SLC Punk! 120
Sleepy Hollow 8, **120**, 120-121
Sloman, Roger 22
Sly & Robbie 131
Small Time Obsession 121
Smart, Amy 139
Smart, Jean 121
Smith, Anjela Lauren 63
Smith, Clive 106
Smith, Greg 11
Smith, Harley 78
Smith, Kerr 55
Smith, Kevin 43
Smith, Maggie 80
Smith, Mossie 69
Smith, Tony 51
Smith, Will 9, 144
Smits, Jimmy 92
Snow Day 121-122
Snow Falling on Cedars 122, 164c
Soderbergh, Steven 51, 83
Sokolov, Stanislav 92
Solá, Miguel Angel 128
Soldier 152
Solomon, Christian Halsey 14
Something About Sex 152
Sonnenfeld, Barry 144
Sorvino, Mira 126
South Park: Bigger, Longer & Uncut 122
Spacek, Sissy 125
Spacey, Kevin 9, **9**, 13, 69, 104, 164a
Spader, James 126
Spall, Timothy 36, 86, 135
Spelling, Tori 136
Spijkers, Jaap 108
Spillum, Jack 43
Spinetti, Victor 76
Spitzer, Ankie 102
Spring, Helen 130
Sproxton, David 34
Stables, Johnathan B 36
Stahl, Nick 42
Stamp, Terence 83
Standing, John 47
Stanton, Harry Dean 125
Star Wars: Episode I The Phantom Menace 8, **8**, 122-123, **123**, 172
Steiger, Rod 49
Steiner, Raymond 38
Stephens, Paul 125
Stephens, Toby 102
Stern, Isaac 95
Stern, Sandy 22
Sternberg, Tom 128
Stévenin, Sagamore 113
Stewart, Annie 84
Stewart, David A 68
Stewart, Jon 25
Stewart, Michelle 110
Stier, Geoff 139
Stigmata 123-124, **124**
Stiles, Julia 44, 130
Still Memories (book) 171
Stiller, Ben 164c
Stipe, Michael 22
Stir of Echoes 124
Stirner, Brain 78
Stone, Dan 12
Stone, Ed 65
Stone, Matt 122
Stone, Oliver 17
Stone, Sharon 94, 119
Storhoi, Dennis 131
Storm Trooper 152
Stormare, Peter 36

Story of Us, The 124, 164c, 165a
Stowe, Madeleine 59
Straight Story, The 124-125
Strange Planet 125
Strathairn, David 83
Streep, Meryl 95
Strickland, John 63
Strike! 152
Stroh, Etchie 36
Stroller, Louis A 29
Strong Language 152
Styles, Eric 44, 111
Substitute, The: Winner Takes All 153
Such a Long Journey 125
Sugarman, Sara 87
Sugg, Stewart 53
Sukhorukov, Viktor 32
Summer of Sam 125-126
Sundance Film Festival 2000 178
Sungha, Kavita 39
Sunshine 126
Supernova 126, 165a
Susan's Plan 153
Sutherland, Donald 72, 147
Suvari, Mena 14
Swain, Dominique 60
Swank, Hilary 30, 158, **158**
Sweeney, Mary 125
Sweet and Lowdown 127, **127**, 168
Sweet Angel Mine 127
Swinburne, Nora 184
Swinton, Tilda 21, 142
Sword of Vengeance 155
Sydow, Max Von 122, 164c
Symonds, Jolyon 77, 80
Szabó, István 126
Szkopiak, Piotr 121

Taibouni, Nadjet 18
Talented Mr Ripley, The 128, 1288
Tambor, Jeffrey 94
Tango 128-129
Tarlov, Mark 119
Tarzan 8, 129
Taxi 129
Taxman 153
Taylor, Lili 65
Taylor, Michael 72
Taylor, Noah 118
Taylor, Sam 127
Taylor, Veronica 107
Tears of Julian Po, The see *Julian Po*
Téchiné, André 12
Temple, Amanda 54
Temple, Julien 54
10 Things I Hate About You 129-130
Tennant, Andy 16
Tennant, David 81
Terajima, Susumu 11
Testing the Limits 153
Theobald, Jeremy 56
Theory of Flight, The 130, **130**
Theron, Charlize 19, 35, 39
Thewlis, David 59
Thick as Thieves 153
Thierry, Mélanie 82
Things You Can Tell Just By Looking At Her 165a
Third World Cop 131
13th Warrior, The 131
Thomas Crown Affair, The 131-132, **132**, 168
Thomas, Betty 137
Thomas, Dave 106
Thomas, Ed 109
Thomas, Jeremy 13
Thomas, Kristin Scott 109, 139
Thomas, Mark 109
Thompson, David M 130
Thompson, Emma 91
Thornton, Billy Bob 108
Three Kings 132
Three Seasons 132-133
Three to Tango 133
3-D Movies (book) 171
Thunder, Yvonne 80
Tichborne Claimant, The 133
Tigger Movie, The 133-134

Time Regained 134
To Infinity and Beyond! 168
To Walk With Lions 135
Tobgyal, Orgyen 38
Tobias, Heather 22
Toby's Story see *Stigmata*
Todd, Jennifer 19, 28
Todd, Suzanne 19, 28
Todd, Tony 55
Todo sobre mi madre see *All About My Mother*
Tollefson, Rhonda 50
Tollin, Mike 139
Tom Clancy's Netforce see *Netforce*
Tomlinson, David 184-185
Topping, Jenno 137
Topsy-Turvy **134**, 134-135, 165a, **167**, 168
Tormey, John 59
Tornatore, Francesco 82
Tornatore, Giuseppe 82
Torreton, Philippe 73
Tour, Frances de la 34
Tovey, Clifford Haydn 39
Towne, Robert 147
Townsend, Clayton 17
Townsend, Stuart 118
Townshend, Pete 73
Trachtenberg, Michelle 71
Traidia, Karim 108
Trang, Thach Thi Kim 133
Travolta, John 21, 59
Tremarco, Christine 67
Trench, The 136, **136**
Trevor, Claire 185
trick 136-137
Tripplehorn, Jeanne 91, 111
Tucci, Stanley 12, 145
Tugend, Jennie Lew 111
Tumbleweeds 137, 168
Tunney, Robin 49, 76
Turner, Kathleen 140
Turteltaub, Jon 72
Twenty Dates 155
28 days 137
Two for Texas 153
200 Cigarettes 153
Tykwer, Tom 115, 145
Tyler, Liv 36, 102

U-571 138, **138**
Udwin, Leslee 46
Ufland, Harry J 122
Ulrich, Skeet 35, 112
Underground 153
Understanding Jane 155
Unger, Deborah Kara 69
Universal Soldier – The Return 138-139
Universal Soldier II: Brothers in Arms 153
Universal Soldier III: Unfinished Business 155
Unkrich, Lee 135
Up at the Villa 139, **139**
Urdang, Leslie 145
Usher, Kinka 96

Vachon, Christine 30
Vadim, Roger 185, **185**
Valdivielso, Maru 85
Van Boys, The 153
Vandernoot, Alexandra 42
Vannier, Nicolas 30
Varga, Veronika 78
Varney, Jim 135, 185
Varsity Blues 139
Vartan, Michael 97
Vasiliou, Anastasios 57
Vaughan, Frankie 186
Vaughan, Peter 82
Veber, Francis 42
Venice International Film Festival Awards 1999 178
Venora, Diane 71, 131
Vernet, Sandrine 18
Viard, Karen 97
Vicente, Joana 44, 133

Vicious, Sid 54
Villeret, Jacques 34, 42
Vince, Pruitt Taylor 82
Vinson, Helen 186
Viterelli, Joe 15
Vivero Letter, The 153
Viviano, Bettina Sofia 133
Voight, Jon 139
Vol, Frank de 186

Wade, Alan 76
Wagner, Natasha Gregson 17
Wagner, Paula 147
Wagner, Robert 19
Wahlberg, Mark 132
Wainwright, Rupert 123
Walk on the Moon, A 141
Walken, Christopher 145
Walker, Ally 65
Walker, Paul 139
Walker, Rob 36
Walsh, Eileen 74
Walsh, Steve 93
Walsh, Tom 118
Walter, Ernest 186
Wang, Wayne 18
War Zone, The **141**, 141-142
Warchus, Matthew 119
Ward, Peter 120
Warlock III: The End of Innocence 155
Warner, David 118
Warner, Deborah 80
Warren, Lesley Ann 83
Warren-Green, Nigel 143
Washington, Denzel 29, 69
Water Damage 153
Waters, Benjamin 63
Watling, Jack 185
Watson, Emily 15
Watson, Malcolm 38
Watts, Naomi 125
Wearing, Michael 143
Weaver, Sigourney 58
Weaving, Hugo 125
Webber, Mark 121
Weber, Jake 108
Weber, Marco 148
Weinstein, Bob 39
Weinstein, Paula 15
Weisberg, David 43
Weisman, Sam 104
Weisz, Rachel 126
Weitz, Chris 14
Weitz, Paul 14
Welcome to Woop Woop 153
Wenders, Wim 32, 92
West Beirut 142
West Beyrouth see *West Beirut*
West, Dominic 137
West, Simon 59
West, Timothy 75
Wexler, Norman 186
What Lie Did I Tell? (book) 171
Whatever Happened to Harold Smith? 142
When the Sky Falls 142-143
Whitaker, Forest 21, 59
White, Michael Jai 138
Whitford, Bradley 94
Whitlock, Albert 186
Whitten, David 117
Whole Nine Yards, The 143, **143**, 165a
Why Do Fools Fall in Love 153
Wick, Douglas 61, 62
Wicki, Bernhard 186
Wilby, James 37
Wild Side 144-145
Wild Wild West 144, **144**, **159**
Wilhite, Tom 107
Willcox, Toyah 76
William Shakespeare's A Midsummer Night's Dream 145, **145**, 168
Williams, Clarence III 59, 82
Williams, Hype 22

Williams, Marsha Garces 74
Williams, Michael 27
Williams, Olivia 115, 119
Williams, Paul 78
Williams, Robin 24, 74
Williams, Simon Channing 135
Williams, Vanessa 10
Williamson, Kevin 117
Willis, Bruce 9, **9**, 119, 124, 143, 165a
Wilson, Colin 65
Wilson, Luke 27
Wilson, Michael G 148
Wilson, Owen 65
Wilson, Rita 124, 164c
Wing Commander 153-154
Winkler, Henry 44
Winslett, Kate 67
Winslow Boy, The 146, **146**
Winstone, Ray 11, 39, 53, 54, 85, 142
Winter Sleepers 145
Winter, John 105
Winterbottom, Michael 147
Winterschlafer see *Winter Sleepers*
Wishmaster 2: 155
With or Without You 154
Witherspoon, Reese 48
Without Limits 146-147
Witness Protection 154
Witt, Paul Junger 132
Wonder Boys 165a, 168
Wonderland 147
Wong, James 55
Wood, The 147
Woods, James 17, 75, 140
Woof, Emily 53
Woolford, Ben 22
Woolley, Stephen 49
World is Not Enough, The 8, **8**, 147-148, **148**
World is Not Enough, The – A Companion (book) 171
Wright, Jeffrey 112
Wrongfully Accused 154
Wu, Vivian 47
Wyman, Brad 60

Y2K 154
Yakuza Way, The 155
Yared, Gabriel 128
Yates, David 133
Yernaux, Anne 113
Yerxa, Ron 48, 147
Yi Ge Dou Bu Neng Shao see *Not One Less*
Yildiz, Erdal 84
Yimou, Zhang 100
York, Michael 19, 93
Yoshida, Takio 78
Yoshikawa, Choji 107
Yoshiyuiki, Kazuko 78
You Know My Name 154
You're Dead 148, **148**
Young, Christopher 64
Young, Oliver 121
Younger, Ben 28
Yu, Zhao 100
Yun-Fat, Chow 16
Yune, Rick 122
Yuyama, Kunihiko 107

Zabari, Gad 102
Zahn, Steve 65
Zal, Roxana 32
Zellweger, Renée 20
Zemeckis, Robert 68
Zeta-Jones, Catherine 50, 65
Zhenda, Tian 100
Zhimei, Sun 100
Zhukova, Maria 32
Zide, Warren 14, 55
Zidi, Claude 18
Ziehl, Scott 32
Zilbermann, Jean-Jacques 88
Zimble, Lisa 12
Zimmer, Christopher 127
Zisblatt, Irene 80
Zweibel, Alan 124
Zylberstein, Elsa 88